COST AND FINANCIAL ANALYSIS

PROFESSOR JAWAHAR LAL
Department of Commerce
Delhi School of Economics, University of Delhi
DELHI - 110007

Himalaya Publishing House

MUMBAI • NEW DELHI • NAGPUR • BENGALURU • HYDERABAD • CHENNAI • PUNE • LUCKNOW • AHMEDABAD • ERNAKULAM • BHUBANESWAR • INDORE • KOLKATA • GUWAHATI

First Edition - 2007
Second Edition - 2010
Third Edition - 2011
Fourth Edition - 2012
Reprint - 2014

Published by : Mrs. Meena Pandey for **Himalaya Publishing House Pvt. Ltd.**, "Ramdoot", Dr. Bhalerao Marg, Girgaon, **Mumbai - 400 004.** Phone: 022-23860170/23863863, Fax: 022-23877178 **E-mail: himpub@vsnl.com; Website: www.himpub.com**

Branch Offices :

New Delhi : "Pooja Apartments", 4-B, Murari Lal Street, Ansari Road, Darya Ganj, New Delhi - 110 002. Phone: 011-23270392, 23278631; Fax: 011-23256286

Nagpur : Kundanlal Chandak Industrial Estate, Ghat Road, Nagpur - 440 018. Phone: 0712-2738731, 3296733; Telefax: 0712-2721215

Bengaluru : No. 16/1 (Old 12/1), 1st Floor, Next to Hotel Highlands, Madhava Nagar, Race Course Road, Bengaluru - 560 001. Phone: 080-32919385; Telefax: 080-22286611

Hyderabad : No. 3-4-184, Lingampally, Besides Raghavendra Swamy Matham, Kachiguda, Hyderabad - 500 027. Phone: 040-27560041, 27550139; Mobile: 09848130433

Chennai : No. 85/50, Bazullah Road, T. Nagar, Chennai - 600 017. Phone: 044-28144004/28144005

Pune : First Floor, "Laksha" Apartment, No. 527, Mehunpura, Shaniwarpeth (Near Prabhat Theatre), Pune - 411 030. Phone: 020-24496323/24496333

Lucknow : Jai Baba Bhavan, Church Road, Near Manas Complex and Dr. Awasthi Clinic, Aliganj, Lucknow - 226 024. Phone: 0522-2339329, 4068914; Mobile: 09305302158, 09415349385, 09389593752

Ahmedabad : 114, "SHAIL", 1st Floor, Opp. Madhu Sudan House, C.G. Road, Navrang Pura, Ahmedabad - 380 009. Phone: 079-26560126; Mobile: 09327324149, 09377088847

Ernakulam : 39/104 A, Lakshmi Apartment, Karikkamuri Cross Rd., Ernakulam, Cochin - 622011, Kerala. Phone: 0484-2378012, 2378016; Mobile: 09344199799

Bhubaneswar : 5 Station Square, Bhubaneswar - 751 001 (Odisha). Phone: 0674-2532129, Mobile: 09861046007

Indore : Kesardeep Avenue Extension, 73, Narayan Bagh, Flat No. 302, IIIrd Floor, Near Humpty Dumpty School, Indore - 452 007 (M.P.). Mobile: 09301386468

Kolkata : 108/4, Beliaghata Main Road, Near ID Hospital, Opp. SBI Bank, Kolkata - 700 010, Phone: 033-32449649; Mobile: 09910440956

Guwahati : House No. 15, Behind Pragjyotish College, Near Sharma Printing Press, P.O. Bharalumukh, Guwahati - 781009 (Assam). Mobile: 09883055590, 09883055536

Printed at : **Sri Manjunatha Printers - on behalf of Hph blr**

Preface

Accounting is a discipline which aims to provide information to managers, external users and stakeholders and others for accomplishing their varying objectives. Managers and others who participate in the management of an organization require information for use in planning, decision making, performance evaluation, control, management of costs, cost ascertainment and analysis, formulating strategies, to discharge managerial responsibilities and to achieve business objectives. External users and stakeholders are primarily concerned with assessing performance, profitability, financial position, earning capacity and sustainability and future prospects of an enterprise. The users of the information are also interested in knowing and judging the responsiveness and capability of an enterprise to meet emerging challenges, competition and opportunities in the business world. To accomplish their goals the users have to familiarize and develop understanding of accounting information, different tools and techniques available in accounting area and their strengths and weaknesses, and the uses to which these tools can be put to for satisfying their informational goals. Modern business is becoming complex, competitive, globalised, diversified and opportunities taker (or loser) day-by-day. The future managers now require to be more knowledgeable and capable of understanding the issues involved and deciding the strategies to achieve business mission. Developing knowledge is a regular process and those who are pursuing Bachelor Degrees can seize the opportunity and orient themselves to be well-versed in all the techniques essential to be a successful manager.

The textbook Cost and Financial Analysis has been written for BBM Course of Bangalore University which has introduced this programme to provide management education to the students. The book will be useful in other programmes also where cost and financial analysis paper is included.

The book contains nine chapters.

Chapter One, Accounting - Nature, Concepts and Principles, gives conceptual framework of accounting and discusses basic accounting concepts and principles.

Chapter Two, Understanding Financial Statements, provides an overview of financial statements and different types of analysis such as comparative statement, common size statement, trend analysis that can be made of financial statements.

Chapter Three, Ratio Analysis, describes different ratios of liquidity, profitability, capital structure, market strength, growth and stability.

Chapter Four, Statement of Changes in Financial Position (SCFP) explains the procedure of preparing funds flow statement based on working capital and cash basis.

Chapter Five, Marginal Costing, discusses cost-volume-profit analysis and its application in different managerial areas.

Chapter Six, Differential Cost Analysis for Managerial Decisions, provides discussion of different decision areas where differential analysis techniques can be used.

Chapter Seven, Standard Costing, explains the methods of computing different variances and the utility of variance analysis for managerial purpose.

Chapter Eight, Budgeting, discusses the concept and advantages of budgeting, budget formulation, preparation of different functional and financial budgets.

Chapter Nine, Accounting for Price-Level Changes, is devoted to focusing on preparing inflation - adjusted accounts and Current Purchasing Power Accounting and Current Cost Accounting.

The book has an Appendix, Skill Development, which provides published financial statements of Indian Companies meant for the students for making financial statement analysis and drawing conclusions about financial position, profitability, liquidity etc.

All the Chapters in the book contain adequate materials an concepts, techniques and gives examples on numerical problems, theory questions and practical problems.

The book has been written in a clear, and concise manner alongwith logical presentation. The book is student-friendly and aims to provide a comprehensive and updated coverage of the topics to help the students develop better understanding of the subject.

Comments and suggestions, if any, are invited to improve the book and to make it more useful to the students.

I have got continuous support from my family-wife Pratibha and children Sanjay, Seema and Rajnish - in my all-academic works and in completing this book as well I sincerely acknowledge and appreciate their valuable cooperation.

Prof. JAWAHAR LAL

ABOUT THE AUTHOR

Dr. Jawahar Lal is Professor in Department of Commerce. Earlier he has been Head, Department of Commerce, Delhi School of Economics, University of Delhi, Delhi and Dean, Faculty of Commerce & Business, Delhi School of Economics, University of Delhi. In the early stage of his teaching career, he has worked at Shri Ram College of Commerce, University of Delhi. He has Ph.D. Degree from Delhi School of Economics, University of Delhi. He possesses thirty five years of teaching and research experience. He has completed two advanced research projects funded by Indian Council of Social Science Research. More than 10 Ph.D. students and 20 M.Phil, students have completed their dissertations under his supervision. He has contributed fifty papers in reputed National and International journals. He has attended several national and international conferences and presented papers in such conferences. He has chaired technical session in many conferences. He has ten books to his credit - Corporate Annual Reports: Theory and Practice, Financial Reporting by Diversified Companies, Contemporary Accounting Issues Understanding Indian Investors, Accounting Theory, Managerial Accounting, Cost Accounting, Cost Management, Corporate Financial Reporting, Advanced Management Accounting, Text and Cases.

ABOUT THE BOOK

The book, Cost and Financial Analysis, has been primarily written for BBM course of Bangalore University. It will be useful to the students of other programmes also where Cost and Financial Analysis course has been included. The book covers discussion on accounting, financial statements, ratios analysis, statement of changes in financial position (SCFP), Variable costing, differential cost analysis, standard costing, budgeting, accounting for price-level changes.

Written in clear and concise manner alongwith logical presentation and updated and comprehensive coverage, the book is student-friendly and will prove very useful to students of Bangalore University pursuing BBM Course. The book will also be useful to other programmes / courses which are having Cost and Financial Analysis paper in their syllabi.

Contents

CHAPTER 1

Accounting — Nature, Concepts and Principles

DEFINITION OF ACCOUNTING

What is accounting? This basic question has never been answered precisely and many definitions of the term 'accounting' are available.

Back in 1941, The Committee on Terminology of the American Institute of Certified Public Accountants (AICPA) formulated the following definition, which was widely quoted for many years:

> "Accounting is the art of recording, classifying and summarising in a significant manner and in terms of money, transactions and events which are, in part at least, of a financial character, and interpreting the results thereof."

In 1966, The American Accounting Association (AAA), in order to emphasise the broader perspective of accounting, provided the following definition of accounting:

> "Accounting is the process of identifying, measuring and communicating economic information to permit informed judgements and decisions by users of the information."

More recently, in 1970, the AICPA of USA defined accounting with reference to the concept of information:

> "Accounting is a service activity. Its function is to provide quantitative information primarily financial in nature about economic activities that is intended to be useful in making economic decisions."

The term, 'quantitative information' used in the above definition is wider in scope than financial or economic information. Both the definitions, AAA (1966), and AICPA (1970) emphasise on using the information for the purposes of decision-making. The modem accounting, therefore, is not merely concerned with record keeping but also with a whole range of activities involving planning, control, decision-making, problem solving, performance measurement and evaluation, coordinating and directing, auditing, tax determination and planning, cost and management accounting.

Both, managers within an organisation and interested outside parties use accounting information in making decisions that affect the organisation. The today's accounting focuses on the ultimate needs of those, who use accounting information, whether these users are inside or outside the business itself.

Others have also given their definitions of accounting, but none has succeeded in clearly establishing the nature and scope of accounting. Of the several available definitions of accounting, the one developed by

American Accounting Association Committee is perhaps the best because of its focus on accounting as an aid to decision-making.

ACCOUNTING AS AN INFORMATION SYSTEM

The term 'system' may be defined a set of elements which operate together in order to attain a goal. A system does not consist of random sets of elements but elements which may be identified as belonging together because of a common goal. A system contains three activities: (i) input, (ii) processing of input, and (iii) output. A business organisation is regarded as an open system which has a dynamic interplay with its environment from which it draws resources and to which it consigns its product and services.

Accounting comprises a series of activities linked together among themselves. The accounting activities form a progression of steps, beginning with observing, then collecting, recording, analysing and finally communicating information to its users. In other words, accounting process involves the accumulation, analysis, measurement, interpretation, classification, and summarisation of the results of each of the many business transaction that affected the entity during the year. After this processing, accounting then transmits or projects messages to potential decision-makers. The messages are in the form of financial statements, and the decision-makers are the users. Accounting generally does not generate the basic information (raw financial data) rather the raw financial data result from the day-to-day transactions of the enterprise.

As an information system, accounting links an information source or transmitter (generally the accountant), a channel of communication (generally the financial statements) and a set of receivers (external users).

Figure 1.1 displays how accounting as an information system helps in business and economic decisions made by user-decision-makers. In this service activity, as shown in Fig. 1.1, accounting assumes a link between business activities and transactions and the decision-makers. First, accounting measures business activities and transactions through recording data. Second, the recorded data are processed and stored until needed. The processing can be done in such a manner or format as to become useful information. Alternatively, sometimes, the processed data are further processed or prepared to provide useful information to users. Thirdly, the processed and prepared information is communicated to users and decision-makers in the forms of financial statements, other statements, reports etc. In this accounting system, business transactions and activities are the input and statements and reports given to decision-makers are the output.

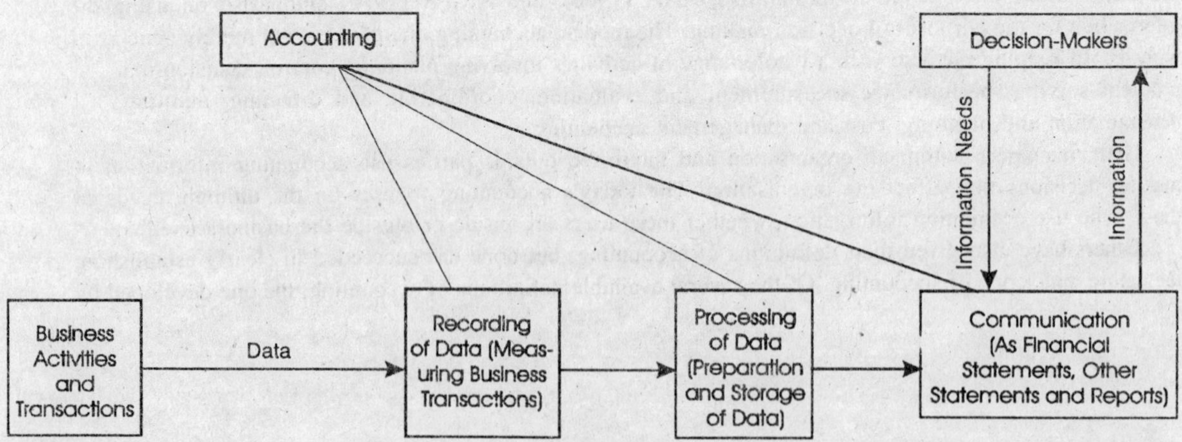

Fig. 1.1. Accounting as an Information System in Business and Economic Decisions

Thus, as an information system accounting has a basic goal, *i.e.,* to provide information. In order to accomplish this goal, the accounting system should be designed to classify financial information on a basis suitable for decision-making purposes and to process the tremendous quantities of data efficiently and accurately. Also, the information system must be designed to report the results periodically, in a realistic and concise format that is comprehensible to users who generally have only a limited accounting knowledge. Furthermore, the information system must be designed to accommodate the special and complex needs of internal management of the enterprise on a continuing basis. These internal needs extend primarily to the planning and control responsibilities of the managers of the enterprise. The information output is used by a group of decision-makers, and therefore, it is evident that a decision-oriented information system should produce information which meets the needs of its users.

ACCOUNTING AS A LANGUAGE

Accounting is often called the "language of business." It is one means of communicating information about a business. As a new language is to be learnt to converse and communicate, so the accounting is to be learnt and practiced to communicate events about a business. Many accounting writers and researchers, accounting profession have referred to accounting as language of business. For instance, Yuji Ijiri[1] observes:

> "As the language of business, accounting has many things in common with other languages. The various business activities of a firm are reported in accounting statements using accounting language, just as news events are reported in newspapers, in the English Language. To express an event in accounting or in English we must follow certain rules. Without following certain rules diligently, not only does one run the risk of being misunderstood but also risks a penalty for misrepresentation, lying or perjury. Comparability of statements is essential to the effective functioning of a language whether it is in English or in Accounting. At the same time, language has to be flexible to adopt to a changing environment.'

There are important similarities between a language and accounting. A language has broadly two components (i) Symbols and (ii) Rules, to make it purposeful. Symbols are the meaningful units or words identifiable in any language, known as linguistic objects and which are used to convey particular meaning or concepts. The arrangement of symbols in a systematic manner becomes a language. The rules which influence the usage and pattern of the symbols are known as grammar of language or grammatical rules.

In accounting too, there are two components (i) symbols and (ii) grammatical rules. In accounting, numerals and words and debits and credits are accepted as symbols which are unique to the accounting discipline." The grammatical rules in accounting refer to the general set of procedures followed to create all financial data for the business. Jain[2] draws the similarities between grammatical rules of a language and accounting rules in the following words:

> "The CPA (the expert in accounting) certifies the correctness of the application rules as does an accomplished speaker of a language for the grammatical correctness of the sentence. Accounting rules formalise the structure of accounting in the same way as grammar formalises the inherent structure of a natural language."

Anthony and Recce[3] also draw the following parallel between accounting and language:

1. Yuji Ijiri, Theory of Accounting Measurement, Accounting Research Study No. 10, AAA, 1975, p.4
2. Tribhowan N. Jain, "Alternative Methods of Accounting and Decision-making", The Accounting Review (January 1973), p. 101.
3. Robert N. Anthony and James S. Reece, Accounting Principles, Richard D. Irwin, 1991, p. 14.

"Accounting resembles a language in that some of its rules are definite whereas others are not. Accountants differ as to how a given event should be reported, just as grammarians differ as to many matters of sentence structure, punctuation and choice of words. Nevertheless, just as many practices are clearly poor English (language), many practices are definitely poor accounting. Languages evolve and change in response to the changing needs of society, and so does accounting."

NATURE OF FINANCIAL STATEMENTS

The end product of the financial accounting process is a set of reports that are called financial statements. The purpose of financial statements is to convey an understanding of some financial aspects of a business firm. It may depict a position at a moment in time, as in the case of a balancesheet or may reveal a series of activities during a particular period of time, as in the case of an income statement. These statement are used to convey to management and other interested outsiders the profitability and financial position of a business organisation. Financial statements essentially, are interim reports, presented annually and reflect a division of the life of an enterprise into more or less arbitrary accounting period—more frequently a year.

Financial statements are generally prepared on the basis of recorded facts. The recorded facts are those which can be expressed only in monetary terms. All the transactions are recorded in a chronological order throughout the year. Financial statements are prepared from the records which are based on historical costs. The financial statements are summarises of the items recorded in the business and these statements are prepared periodically, generally for the accounting period.

The American Institute of Certified Public Accountants States the nature of financial statements as "financial statements are prepared for the purpose of presenting a periodical review of report on progress by the management and deal with the states of investment in the business and the results achieved during the period under review. They reflect a combination of recorded facts, accounting principles and personal judgements". The American Accounting Association expresses, "Every corporate statement should be based on accounting principles which are sufficiently uniform objective and well understood to justify opinions as to the condition and progress of business enterprise. The purpose of periodic financial statements of a corporation is to furnish information that is necessary for the formation of dependable Judgements".

The following features explain the nature of financial statement :

(i) **Recorded faces :** The term recorded faces refers to the data which are taken out of the accounting records. The records are maintained on the basis of actual cost data. The historical cost is the basis of recording various transactions. The figures of various accounts such as cash in hand, cash at Bank, bills receivables, sundry debtors, land and building, furniture, are taken as per the figures recorded in the accounting books. As recorded facts are based on original cost, the financial statements do not show current value financial condition of the concern.

(ii) **Conventions :** Certain accounting conventions should be followed while preparing financial statements. The materiality convention is followed in dealing with small items like pencils, match box, postage stamps etc. These items are treated as expenditure in the year in which they are purchased even though they are assets in nature. Likewise, the stationery is valued at cost by not on the principle of cost or market-price which ever is less. The accounting conventions makes financial statements more simple and realistic.

(iii) **Postulates :** The accountant follows certain basic assumption while making accounting records. One of these assumption is the business entity concept. This means business and businessman are two separate persons. So if the businessman used any goods or cash from business, it will be treated as drawings. Another important assumption is that the concern is treated as a going concern. The other alternative to this assumption is that the concern is to be litigated. However, the assets are shown on a going concern basis. There assumptions are known as postulates.

(iv) **Personal Judgements :** Although during the preparation of financial statements certain accounting concepts, principles and conventions are followed, but still personal judgement of the accountant plays an important role. For example, in applying cost or market price whichever is lower to inventory valuation, the accountant will have to use his judgement in computing the cost in a particular case. There are a number of methods for valuing opening stock or closing stock, *viz* last in first out (LIFO), first in first out (FIFO). Highest in first out (HIFO), average cost method, Base stock method, weighted average method etc. The accountant will use one of these methods for valuing materials. The selection of depreciation method, period for writing off intangible assets are some of the examples where judgement of the accountant will play an important role in selecting the most appropriate course of action.

PARTIES INTERESTED IN FINANCIAL STATEMENTS

Financial statements are the means of communicating accounting information which is generated in the various accounting process to the external users. The external users include (i) Investors (ii) Employees (iii) Lenders (iv) Suppliers and other trade creditors (v) Customers (vi) Government and their agencies and (vii) The public at large. The information given in the financial statements is of much interest to a number of external parties. There include the following.

(i) **Shareholders.** Shareholders or proprietors or partners of the business are interested in the well-being of the business. They like to know the earning capacity of the business and its future prospects. Since they are not involved generally in the day-to-day working, they will be eager to know the result of operations and financial positions of the business. This is possible only through financial statements.

(ii) **Potential Investors and Lenders.** Like shareholders, potential investors like debenture holders, Bankers are also interested in knowing the earning capacity of the business and its prospects of future growth. Further, they will also be interested to know, how safe their investments will be. This can be only assessed through a proper financial statements.

(iii) **Suppliers and Trade Creditors.** The suppliers and other creditors are interested to know about the solvency of the business *i.e.* the ability of the company to meet the debts when they fall due. Trade creditors are likely to be interested in an interprise over a shorter period than lender unless they are dependent in the enterprise as a major lender.

(iv) **Employees and Trade unions.** Employees are entitled to bonus which depends on the profits earned, they are thus interested in knowing the profits earned or loss suffered by the business. Financial statements also help them is knowing the same. Financial statement also help the trade unions in negotiating the wages/salaries.

(v) **Costomers.** Customers have an interest in information about continuance of an enterprise. *e.g.* the enterprise may be the supplier of raw materials to many of its customers. Accordingly, the acitivities of its customers are largely linked with its ability to continue. In case it appears that the enterprise will not be able to continue in the long run, the customers have to explore alternative sources.

(vi) **Government and their agencies.** Government and their agencies need financial information to regulate the activities of the enterprise, determine taxation policy, compilation of national income statistics etc.

(vii) **Public.** Enterprise affect members of public in a variety of ways. *e.g.* the activities of an enterprise largely influence the local economy. So the public at large is interested to know the growth of enterprise which they may understand from financial statements.

(viii) **Taxation Authorities.** Income-tax Authorities are interested in knowing the profits of the business so that income-tax can be computed there on. Like wine, sales tax authorities are also interested in the sales and excise authorities in the production of goods. Financial statements help them a great deal in determining the taxes payable.

(ix) **Stock Exchange.** Stock exchange in an institution which facilitates dealings of sales and purchases of shares and debentures of companies. The stock exchanges provide information about companies to their members. The stock exchange members take interest in financial statements, beacause they give useful information about a company.

Thus, different parties have interest in financial statements for different purposes. Financial statements mect the common information needs of most of the users. They provide the financial effects of past events only and do not provide non-financial information. Accordingly, financial statements do not provide all the information which the external users may need for decision-makings.

OBJECTIVE OF FINANCIAL STATEMENTS

Financial statments are the main sources of information on the basis of which conclusion are drawn about the profitability and financial position of a concern. The primary aim of financial statements is to help in decision making. The Accounting Principles Board of USA (APB) describes the following as the objectives of financial statements.

- To provide reliable financial information about economic resources and obligations of a business firm.
- To provide other needed information about changes in such economic resources and obliqation.
- To provide reliable inormations about changes in net resources arising out of business activities.
- To provide financial information that assists in estimations the earning potentials of business.
- To disclose, other information related to the financial statments that is relevant to the needs of the users of there statements.

TYPES OF FINANCIAL STATEMENTS

Financial statements mainly comprise two basic statments (i) the position statement or the balance sheet and (ii) the income statement or the profit and loss account. However, Generally Accepted Principles (GAAP) specify that a complete set of financial statements should include the following statements (Fig. 1.2).

- A Balance Sheet
- An Income Statement
- A statement of changes in owners account
- A statement of changes in financial position.

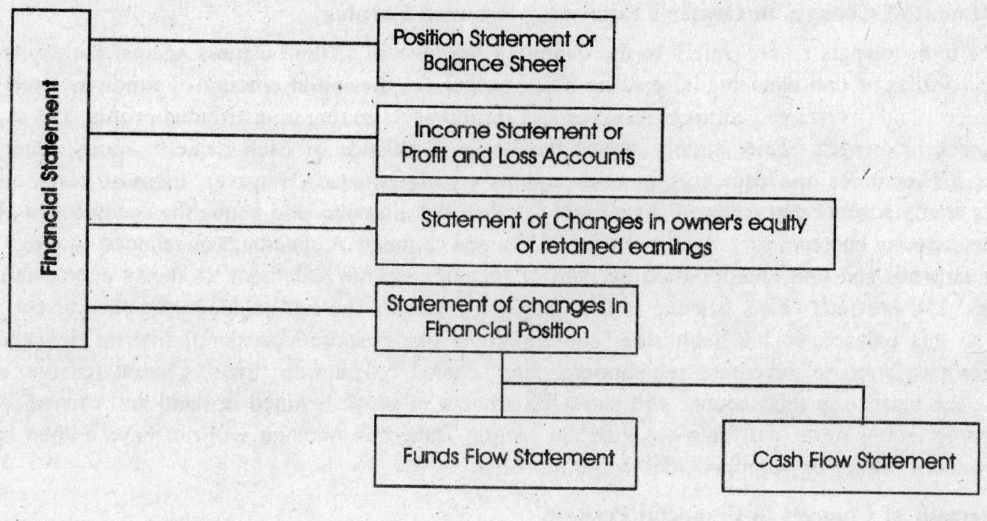

Fig. 1.2

Before we discuss the form and contents of there statements, Let us explain briefly the meaning and importance of each of there statements.

1. Balance Sheet

The American Institute of Certified Public Accountants defines balancesheet as, "A tabular statement of summary of balance (debits and credits) carried forward after an actual and constructive closing of books of account and kept according to principles of accounting". The main objective of the balance sheet is to show the resources that the company has *i.e.* the assets and from where there resources come from *i.e.* its liabilities and investments by owners and creditors. The balance sheet is one of the important statements which shows financial strength of the concern on a particular date. It depicts on one side the properties that it owns and in another side the sources of the properties. The balance sheet also shows all the assets owned by the concern and all the liablities and capital it owes to owners and outsiders. The balance sheet is prepared on a particular date. The right hand side shows all assets and the left hand side shows capital and all kinds of liabilities. The Companies Act 1956, has prescribed a particular form for showing assets and liabilties in the balance sheet for companies registered under their Act. These companies are also required to give figure for the previous year along with the current year figure.

2. Income Statment/ Profit and Loss A/c

Income statment is prepared to determine the operational position of a concern. It is a statement of income earned and the expenses incurred for earning that income. If there is excess of income ever expenditure, it will show a profit and if the expenditures are more than the income, there will be a loss. The income statement is generally prepared for a particular year i.e. current year. When income statement is prepared for a particular year, say for the year ending 31st December 2006, then all income and expenses falling due in that year will be taken into account irrespective of their receipt or payment. This statement can be prepared in the form of a manufacturing account find out the cost of goods,, in the form of a profit and loss Account to determine net profit or loss. A statement of Retained Earnings may also be prepared to show the distribution of profits.

3. Statement of Changes in Owner's Equity (or Retained Earning)

The term 'owners equity' refers to the claims of the owners of the business against the assets of the firm. It consists of two elements (i) paid-up share capital *i.e.* the initial amount of funds invested by the shareholders and (ii) retained earnings/reserves and surplus representing undistributed profits. The statement of changes in owner's equity simply shows the begining balance of each owner's equity account, the reasons for increases and decreases in each and its ending balance. However, in most cases, the only owner's equity account that changes significantly is Retained Earnings and hence the statement of changes in owner's equity becomes merely a statement of retained earnings. A statement of retained earnings is also known as profit and loss appropriation account or income disposal statement. It shows appropriations of earnings. The previous year's balance is first brought forward. The net profit during the current year is added to this balance on the debit side, appropriations like proposed dividend, Interim dividend paid, amounts transferred to debenture redemptions fund, capital redemption funds, general reserve, etc are shown. The balance in this account will show the amount of profit retained in hand and carried forward. The appropriations never will be more than the profits. Thus, this Account will not have a debit balance. Further, there cannot be appropriations without profits.

4. Statement of Changes in Financial Position

The basic financial statements *i.e.* the balance sheet and the profit and loss account or income statement of a business reveal the net effect of the various transactions on the operational and financial position of the company. The balance sheet gives a static view of the resources of a business and the uses to which these resources have been put at a point of time. The profit and loss account in a general way, indicates the resource provided by operations. But there are many transactions that do not operate through profit and loss account. Then, for a better understanding another statement called statement of changes in financial position has to be prepared to show the changes in assets and liabilities from the end of one period to the end of another point of time. The öbective of this statement is to show the movement of funds during a particular period. The statement of changes in financial position may take any of the following two forms.

(a) Funds Flow Statement : The funds flow statement is designed to analyse the changes in the financial condition of a business enterprise between two periods. This statement will show the sources from which the funds are received and the uses to which the have been put. This statement enables the management to have an idea about the sources of funds and their uses. This statement helps the management in policy formulation and performance apprecinal.

(b) Cash Flow Statement : A statement of changes in the financial position of a firm on cash basis is called cash flow statement. It summarises the causes of changes in cash position of a business enterprise between dates of two balance sheet. This statement is very much similar to the statement of changes in working capital *i.e.* fund flow statement. A cash flow statement focuses attention on cash changes only. It describes the sources of cash and its uses.

FORM AND CONTENTS OF BALANCE SHEET

There is no particular form for the preparation of Balance Sheet in the case of proprietory concerns and partnership firm. Generally, the balance sheet is divided into three parts *i.e.* assets, liabilities and capital. The balance sheet is very often prepared in a horizontal form by almost all the companies and other organisations. The assets are shown on the right hand side and capital and liabilities are shown on the left hand side. The order of assets and liabilities is either on liquidity basis or on permanency basis. When balance sheet is prepared on liquidity basis, then more liquid assets live cash in hand, cash at Bank, Investments are shown first and the non-liquid assets will be shown in the last. Likewise, on liabilities side, the liabilities to be paid in the short paid are shown first, long-term liabilities next and capital in the last. How ever, when balancesheet is prepared on permanency basis, on assets side fixed assets are shown first and liquid assets are shown at last. On liabilities side the capital is shown first, long-term liabilities next, short-term and current liabilities in the last.

The Companies Act, 1956 has prescribed a form for the preparation of Balance Sheet. This form is set out in part I of schedule VI. Further, Section 211(i) states that every Balance sheet of a company shall give a true and fair view of the state of affairs of the company at the end of the financial year and shall, subject to the provisions of the Sections, be in the form set out in part I of schedule VI or in such other forms as may be approved by the central government either generally or in particulars case; and in preparing the Balance sheet due regard shall be had, as far as may be to be general instructions for preparation of balance sheet under the heading "Notes" at the end of that part. Provided that nothing contained in this sub-section shall apply to any insurance or banking company or any company engaged in the generation or supply of electricity or to any other class of company for whom a form of balance sheet has been specified in or under the Act governing such classes of companies.

The balance sheet of a company may be either in (A) Horizontal Form or (B) Vertical Form. Both the farms are reproduced below.

Schedule VI

(See section 211)

[Part I Form of Balance Sheet]

[The balance sheet of a company shall be either in horizontal form or vertical form]

A. HORIZONTAL FORM

Balance sheet of .... [Here enter the name of the Company]

As at .... [Here enter the date as at which the balance sheet is made out.]

	LIABILITIES		ASSETS		
Instructions in accordance with which liabilities should be made out	*Figures for the previous year Rs. (b)*	*Figures for the current year Rs. (b)*	*Figures for the previous year Rs. (b)*	*Figures for the current year Rs. (b)*	*Instructions in accordance with which assets should be made out*
	*SHARE CAPITAL		*FIXED ASSETS		
*Terms of redemption or conversion (if any), of any redeemable preference capital to be stated, together with earliest date of redemption or conversion	Authorised .... shares of Rs. ... each + Issued (distinguishing between the various classes of capital and stating the particulars specified below. in respect of each class) ..... shares of Rs. ..... each.		Distinguishing as far as possible between expenditure upon (a) goodwill, (b) land, (c) buildings, (d) leaseholds, (e) railway sidings, (f) plant and machinery, (g) furniture fittings, (*h*) development of property. (*i*) patents, trade marks and designs. (*j*) live-stock and (*k*) vehicles, etc.		*Under each head the original cost, and the additions there to and deductions there from during the year, and the total depreciation written off or provided up to the end of the year to be stated.
+Particulars of any option on un-issued share capital to be specified.	+ Subscribed (distinguishing between the various classes of Capital and stating the particulars specified the				[1][Where the original cost aforesaid and additions and deductions thereto, relate to any fixed asset which has

Instructions in accordance with which liabilities should be made out	**LIABILITIES** *Figures for the previous year* *Rs.* (*b*)	*Figures for the current year* *Rs.* (*b*)	**ASSETS** *Figures for the previous year* *Rs.* (*b*)	*Figures for the current year* *Rs.* (*b*)	*Instructions in accordance with which assets should be made out*
+Particulars of the different classes of preference shares to be given.	particulars specified below in respect of each class). (c) ..... shares of Rs. .... each. Rs. ... . called up. of the above shares..... shares are allotted as fully paid-up pursuant to a contract without payments being received in cash.				been acquired from a country outside India, and in consequence of a change in the rate of exchange at any time after the acquisition of such asset, there has been an increase or reduction in the liability of the company, as expressed in Indian currency, for making payment towards
[Specify the source from which bonus shares are issued, *e.g.*, capitalisation of profits or Reserves or from Share Premium Account.]	[2][Of the above shares.... shares are allotted as fully paid up by way of bonus shares*] *Less*: Calls unpaid:				the whole or a part of the cost of the asset or for repayment of the whole or a part of moneys borrowed by the company from any person, directly or indirectly
	[3][(*i*) By managing agent or secretaries and treasurers and where the managing agent or secretaries and treasurers are a firm, by the partners thereof, and where the managing agent or secretaries and treasurers are a private company by the directors or members of that company. (*ii*) By directors. (*iii*) By others.				in any foreign currency specifically for the purpose of acquiring the asset (being in either case the liability existing immediately before the date on which the change in the rate of exchange takes effect), the amount by which the liability is so increased or reduced during the year, shall be added to, or, as the case may be deducted from the cost, and the amount arrived at after such addition or deduction shall be taken to be the cost of the fixed asset.
[1][+Any capital profit on reissue of forfeited shares should be transferred to Capital Reserve.	[2][+ Add: Forfeited shares (amount originally paid up)].				*Explanation* 1 : This paragraph shall apply in relation to all balance-sheets that may be made out as at the 6th day of June, 1966, or any day thereafter and where, at the date of issue of the notification of the Government of India, in the Ministry of Industrial Development and Company

Instructions in accordance with which liabilities should be made out	**LIABILITIES**		**ASSETS**		*Instructions in accordance with which assets should be made out*
	Figures for the previous year Rs. (*b*)	*Figures for the current year* Rs. (*b*)	*Figures for the previous year* Rs. (*b*)	*Figures for the current year* Rs. (*b*)	
					Affairs (Department of Company Affairs), G. S. R. No. 129, dated the 3rd day of January, 1968, any balance sheet, in relation, to which this paragraph applies, has already been made out and laid before the company in Annual General Meeting, the adjustment referred to in this paragraph may be made in the first balance-sheet made out after the issue of the said notification. *Explanation* 2.— In this paragraph unless the context otherwise requires, the expression "rate of exchange", "foreign currency" and "Indian currency" shall have the meaning respectively assigned to them under sub-section (I) of section 43A of the Income-tax Act, 1961 (43 of 1961), and *Explanation* 2 and *Explanations* 3 of the said sub-section shall, as far as may be, apply in relation to the said paragraph as they apply to the said sub-section (1). [1][In every case where the original cost cannot be ascertained, without unreasonable expense or delay, the valuation shown by the books shall be given. For the purpose of this paragraph, such valuation shall be the net amount at which an asset stood in the company's books at the commencement of this Act

	LIABILITIES		ASSETS		
Instructions in accordance with which liabilities should be made out	*Figures for the previous year Rs.* (*b*)	*Figures for the current year Rs.* (*b*)	*Figures for the previous year Rs.* (*b*)	*Figures for the current year Rs.* (*b*)	*Instructions in accordance with which assets should be made out*
					after deduction of the amounts previously provided or written off for depreciation or diminution in value, and where any such asset is sold, the amount of sale proceeds shall be shown as deduction.] Where sums have been written off on a reduction of capital or a revaluation of assets, every balance sheet, (after the first balance sheet) subsequent to the reduction or revelations shall show the reduced figures and with the date of the reduction in place of the original cost. Each balance sheet for the first five years subsequent to the date of the reduction, shall show also the amount of the reduction made. Similarly, where sums have been added by writing up the assets, every balance sheet subsequent to such writing up shall show the increased figures with the date of the increase in place of the original cost. Each balance sheet for the first five years subsequent to the date of writing up shall also show the amount of increase made. [1][*Explanation.*—Nothing contained in the preceding two paragraphs shall apply to any adjustment made in accordance with the second paragraph].

Instructions in accordance with which liabilities should be made out	**LIABILITIES** *Figures for the previous year* *Rs.* (*b*)	*Figures for the current year* *Rs.* (*b*)	**ASSETS** *Figures for the previous year* *Rs.* (*b*)	*Figures for the current year* *Rs.* (*b*)	*Instructions in accordance with which assets should be made out*
*Additions and deductions since last balance sheet to be shown under each of the specified heads. The word “fund” in relation to any “Reserve” should be used only where such Reserve is specifically represented by earmarked investments.	*RESERVES AND SURPLUS [2][(1) Capital Reserves. (2) Capital Redemption Reserve. (3) Share Premium Account (*cc*). (4) Other Reserves specifying the nature of each Reserve and the amount in respect thereof. *Less:* Debit balance in profit and loss account (if any) (*h*) (5) Surplus *i.e.*, balance in profit and loss account after providing for proposed allocations, namely:- Dividend, Bonus or Reserves. (6) Proposed additions to Reserves (7) Sinking funds.]		INVESTMENTS Showing nature of investments and mode of valuation, for example, cost or market value and distinguishing between *(1) Investments in government or Trust Securities. *(2) Investments in shares, debentures or bonds (showing separately shares fully paid-up and partly paid up and also distinguishing the different classes of shares and showing also in similar details investments in shares, debentures or bonds of subsidiary companies. (3) Immovable properties. [1][(4) Investments in the capital of partnership firms.] [2][(5) Balance of unutilised monies raised by issue.]		*Aggregate amount of company's quoted investment and also the market value thereof shall be shown. Aggregate amount of company's unquoted investment shall also be shown. [1][All unutilised monies out of the issue must be separately disclosed in the Balance Sheet of the company indicating the form in which such unutilised funds have been invested.]
[3][Loans from Directors, [4][***] Manager should be shown separately. Interest accrued and due on Secured Loans should be included under the appropriate sub-heads under the head “Secured Loans” *The nature of the security to be specified in each case. Where loans have been guaranteed by [1][* * *] managers and or directors, a	SECURED LOANS: *(1) Debentures+ *(2) Loans and Advances from Banks. *(3) Loans and Advances from subsidiries. *(4) Other Loans and Advances.		CURRENT ASSETS, LOANS AND ADVANCES : A. CURRENT ASSETS (1) Interest accrued on Investments ++(2) Stores and spare parts. [5][(3) Loose Tools.] ++(4) Stock-in-trade. **(5) Works-in-Progress. +(6) Sundry debtors— (*a*) Debts outstanding for a period exceeding six		++Mode of valuation of stock shall be stated and the amount in respect of raw material shall also be stated separately where practicable. **Mode of valuation of works-in-progress shall be stated.

Instructions in accordance with which liabilities should be made out	LIABILITIES Figures for the previous year Rs. (b)	Figures for the current year Rs. (b)	ASSETS Figures for the previous year Rs. (b)	Figures for the current year Rs. (b)	Instructions in accordance with which assets should be made out
mention thereof shall also be made and also the aggregate amount of such loans under each head. +Terms of redemption or conversion (if any) of debentures Issued to be stated together with earliest date of redemption or conversion.			months. (*b*) Other debts. [2][*Less*: Provision)		+In regard to Sundry Debtors particulars to be given separately of— (*a*) debts considered good and in respect of which the company is fully secured; and (b) debts considered good for which the company holds no security other than the debtor's personal security; and (c) debts considered doubtful or bad. Debts due by directors or other officers of the company or any of them either severally or jointly with any other person or debts due by firms or private companies respectively in which any director is a partner or a director or a member to be separately stated. [1][Debts due from other companies under the same management within the meaning of sub-section (1B) of section 370, to be disclosed with the names of the Companies. The maximum amount due by directors or other officers of the company at any time during the year to be shown by way of a note. The [1][Provisions to be shown under this head should not exceed the amount of debts stated to be considered doubtful or bad and any surplus of such [2][provision if already created, should be shown at every closing under [Reserves and Surplus" (in

Instructions in accordance with which liabilities should be made out	**LIABILITIES** *Figures for the previous year Rs.* (*b*) — *Figures for the current year Rs.* (*b*)	**ASSETS** *Figures for the previous year Rs.* (*b*) — *Figures for the current year Rs.* (*b*)	*Instructions in accordance with which assets should be made out*
			the liabilities side) under a separate sub-head "Reserve for Doubtful or Bad Debts".
		1[(7A) Cash balance on hand. *(7B) Bank balances— (*a*) with Scheduled Banks, and (*b*) with others.	4[*In regard to bank balances, particulars to be given separately of — (*a*) the balance lying with Scheduled Banks on Current accounts, call accounts and deposit account; (*b*) The names of the bankers other than Scheduled Banks and the balance lying with each such banker on current accounts, call accounts and deposit accounts and the maximum amount outstanding at any time during the year from each such banker; and (*c*) the nature of the interest, if any, of any director or his relative or the 1[* * *] in each of the bankers (other than Scheduled Banks) referred to in (*b*) above.] 2[All unutilised monies out of the issue must be separately disclosed in the Balance Sheet of the company indicating the form in which such unutilised funds have been invested.]
+1[Loans from directors, 2[* * *] manager should be shown separately. Interest accrued and due on Unsecured Loans should be included under the appropriate sub-heads under the head "Unsecured	UNSECURED LOANS : (1) Fixed Deposits. +(2) Loans and Advances from subsidiaries. +(3) Short Term Loans and Advances : (*a*) From Banks. (*b*) From others. (4) Other Loans and Advances :	B. LOANS AND ADVANCES (8)3(*a*) Advances and loans	*The above instructions regarding "Sundry Debtors"

Instructions in accordance with which liabilities should be made out	LIABILITIES Figures for the previous year Rs. (b)	 Figures for the current year Rs. (b)	ASSETS Figures for the previous year Rs. (b)	 Figures for the current year Rs. (b)	Instructions in accordance with which assets should be made out
Loans".] +Where loans have been guaranteed by [4][* * *] managers and/or directors, a mention thereof shall also be made and also the aggregate amount of such loans under each head. *See note (d) at foot of Form [2][The name(s) of small scale industrial under-taking(s) to whom the company owe any sum together with interest outstanding for more than thirty days, are to be disclosed.]	(a) From Banks. (b) From others. **CURRENT LIABILITIES AND PROVISIONS** A.CURRENT LIABILITIES [3][(1) Acceptances. (2) Sundry creditors. 1[(i) total outstanding dues to small scale industrial under-taking(s) : and (ii) Total outstanding dues of creditors other than small scale industrial undertaking (s).] (3) Subsidiary companies (4) Advance payments and unexpired discounts for the portion for which value has still to be given e.g., in the case of the following classes of companies: — Newspaper, Fire Insurance, Theatres, Clubs, Banking, Steamship Companies, etc. [2][(5) Investor Education and Protection Funds shall be amounts namely:— (a) Unapaid dividend; (b) Unpaid application money received by the companies for allotment of securities and due for refund; (c) Unpaid Matured Deposits: (d) unpaid Matured Debentures:		to subsidiaries [5][(b) Advances and loans to partnership firm in which the company or any of its subsidiaries is a partner.] (9) Bills of Exchange. (10) Advances recoverable in cash or in kind or for value to be received, e.g., Rates, Taxes, Insurance, etc. [1][(11) * * *] (12) Balances with Customs. Port Trust, etc. (where payable on demand).		apply to "Loans and Advances" also .

	LIABILITIES		ASSETS		
Instructions in accordance with which liabilities should be made out	*Figures for the previous year* *Rs.* (*b*)	*Figures for the current year* *Rs.* (*b*)	*Figures for the previous year* *Rs.* (*b*)	*Figures for the current year* *Rs.* (*b*)	*Instructions in accordance with which assets should be made out*
	(*e*) Interest accrued on (*a*) to (*d*) above. (6) Other Liabilities (if any), (7) Interest accrued but not due on loans.] B. PROVISIONS [1][(8) Provision for taxation. (9) Proposed dividends. (10) For contingencies. (11) For provident fund scheme. (12) For insurance, pension and similar staff benefit schemes. (13) Other provisions] A foot-note to the balance-sheet may be added to show separately: (1) Claims against the company not acknowledged as debts.				
The period for which the dividends are in arrear or if there is more than one class of shares, the dividends on each such class are in arrear, shall be stated.	(2) Uncalled liability on shares partly paid. [1](3) Arrears of fixed cumulative dividends.		**MISCELLANEOUS EXPENDITURE** (to the extent not written off [1][or adjusted]) : (1) Preliminary expenses. (2) Expenses including commission or brokerage on underwriting or subscription of shares or debentures.		
The amount shall be stated before deduction of income-tax, except that in the case of tax- free dividends the amount shall be shown free of income-tax and the fact that it is so shown shall be stated.	(4) Estimated amount of contracts remaining to be executed on capital account and not provided for. +(5) Other money for which the company is contingently liable.		(3) Discount allowed on the issue of shares or debenturs. (4) Interest paid out of capital during construction (also stating the rate of interest). (5) Development expenditure not adjusted. (6) Other Items (specifying nature)		
+The amount of any guarantees given by the company on behalf of Directors or other officers of the company shall be stated and where practicable, the general nature and amount of each such contingent liability, if material, shall also be specified.			[1][**PROFIT AND LOSS ACCOUNT**].		[2][+Show here the debit balance of profit and loss account carried forward after deduction of the uncommitted reserves, if any.]

Notes : General instructions for propartion of balance sheet.

(a) The information required to be given under any of the items or sub-items in this Form if it cannot be conveniently included in the balance sheet itself, shall be furnished in a separate Schedule or Schedules to be annexed to and to form part of the balance sheet. This is recommended when items are numerous.

(b) Naye Paise can also be given in addition to Rupees, if desired.

(c) In the case of '[subsidiary companies] the number of shares held by the holding company as well as by the ultimate holding company and its subsidiaries must be separately stated.

The auditor is not required to certify the correctness of such shareholdings as certified by the management.

[2][(cc) The item "Share Premium Account" shall include details of its utilisation in the manner provided in section 78 in the year of utilisation.]

(d) Short Term Loans will include those which are due for not more than one year as at the date of the balance sheet.

(e) Depreciation written off or provided shall be allocated under the different asset heads and deducted in arriving at the value of Fixed Assets.

(f) Dividends declared by subsidiary companies after the date of the balance sheet '[should not be included] unless they are in respect of period which closed on or before the date of the balance sheet.

(g) Any reference to benefits expected from contracts to the extent not executed shall not be made in the balance sheet but shall be made in the Board's report.

(h) The debit balance in the Profit and Loss Account shall be shown as a deduction from (he uncommitted reserves, if any.

(i) As regards Loans and Advances, [amounts due by the Managing Agents or Secretaries and Treasurers, either severally or jointly with any other persons to be separately staled:] [the amounts due from other companies under the same management within the meaning of sub-section (1B) of section 370 should also be given with the names of the companies] the maximum amount due from every one of these at any time during the year must be shown.

(j) Particulars of any redeemed debentures which the company has power to issue should be given.

(k) Where any of the company's debentures are held by a nominee or a trustee for the company, the nominal amount of the debentures and the amount at which they arc stated in the books of the company shall be stated.

[1][(l) A statement of investments (whether shown under "Investment" or under "Current Assets" as stock-in-trade) separately classifying trade investments and other investments should be annexed to the balance sheet, showing the names of the bodies corporate (indicating separately the names of the bodies corporate under the same management) in whose shares or debentures, investments have been made (including all investments whether existing or not, made subsequent to the date as at which the previous balance sheet was made out) and the nature and extent of the investment; so made in each such body corporate; provided that in the case of an investment company that is to say, a company whose principal business is the acquisition of shares, stock, debentures or other securities, it shall be sufficient if the statement shows only the investments existing on the date as at which the balance sheet has been made out. In regard to the investments in the capital of partnership firms, the names of the firms (With the names of all their partners total capital and the shares of each partner) shall be given in the statement.]

(m) If, in the opinion of the Board, any of the current assets, loans and advances have not a value on realisation in the ordinary course of business at least equal to the amount at which they are stated, the fact that the Board is of that opinion shall be stated.

(n) Except in the case of the first balance sheet laid before the company after the commencement of the Act, the corresponding amounts for the immediately preceding financial year for all items shown in the balance sheet shall be also given in the balance sheet. The requirement in this behalf shall, in the case of companies preparing quarterly or half-yearly accounts, etc., relate to the balance sheet f6r the corresponding date in the previous year.

(o) The amounts to be shown under Sundry Debtors shall include the amounts due in respect of goods sold or services rendered or in respect of other contractual obligations but shall not include the amounts which are in the nature of loans or advances.

[2][(p) Current accounts with directors, [* * *] and Manager, whether they are in credit or debit, shall be shown separately.]

[4][(q) A small scale industrial undertaking has the same meaning as assigned to it under clause *(j) of* section 3 of the Industries (Development and Regulation) Act, 1951.]

Companies Act, 1956 Part-II

[1][B. VERTICAL FORM

Name of the Company ....

Balance Sheet as at.........................

	Schedule No.	Figures as at the end of current financial year	Figures as at the end of previous financial year
I. Sources of funds:			
(1) *Shareholder's funds*			
(a) Capital			
(b) Reserves and Surplus			
(2) *Loan funds*			
(a) Secured loans			
(b) Unsecured loans			
TOTAL:			
II. Application of funds:			
(1) *Fixed assets*			
(a) Gross block			
(b) Less depreciation			
(c) Net block			
(d) Capital work-in-progress			
(2) *Investments*			
(3) *Current assets, loans, and advances:*			
(a) Inventories			
(b) Sundry debtors			
(c) Cash and bank balances			
(d) Other current assets			
(e) Loans and advances			
Less:			
Current liabilities and provisions:			
(a) Liabilities			
(b) Provisions			
Net current assets			
(4) (a) Miscellaneous expenditure to the extent not written off or adjusted			
(b) Profit and Loss account			
TOTAL:			

Notes. 1. Details under each of the above items shall be given in separate Schedules. The Schedules shall incorporate all the information required to be given under A—Horizontal Form read with notes containing general instructions for preparation of balance sheet.

2. The Schedules, referred to above, accounting policies and explanatory notes that may be attached shall form an integral part of the balance sheet.

[1][3. The figures in the balance sheet may be rounded off as under :

Where the turnover of the company in any financial year is:	Round off permissible:
(i) less than one hundred crore rupees thereof.	to the nearest hundreds, or thousands, or decimals thereof.
(ii) one hndred core rupees or more but less five hundred crore rupees.	to the nearest hundreds, thousands, lakhs or millions, or decimals thereof.
(iii) five hundred crore rupees or more.	to the nearest hundreds, thousands, lakhs, millions, or crores, or decimals thereof.]

4. A foot-note to the balance sheet may be added to show separately contingent liabilities.

PART II
Requirements as to Profit and Loss Account

1. The provisions of this Part shall apply to the income and expenditure count referred to in sub-section (2) of section 210 of the Act, in like manner as they apply to a profit and loss account, but subject to the modification of references as specified in that sub-section.

2. The profit and loss account :

(a) shall be so made out as clearly to disclose the result of the working of the company during the period covered by the account; and

(b) shall disclose every material feature, including credits or receipts and debits or expenses in respect of non-recurring transactions or transactions of an exceptional nature.

3. The profit and loss account shall set out the various items relating to the income and expenditure of the company arranged under the most convenient heads; and in particular, shall disclose the following information in respect of the period covered by the account

(i)[2][(a) The turnover, that is, the aggregate amount for which sales are effected by the company, giving the amount of sales in respect of each class of goods dealt with by the company, and indicating the quantities of such sales for each class separately.]

[3][(b) Commission paid to sole selling agents within the meaning of section 294 of the Act.

(c) Commission paid to other selling agents.

(d) Brokerage and discount on sales, other than the usual trade discount]

[4][(ii) (a) In the case of manufacturing companies,—

(1) The value of the raw materials consumed, giving item-wise break-up and indicating the quantities thereof. In this break-up, as far as possible, all important basic raw materials shall be shown as separate items. The intermediates or components procured from other manufacturers may, if their list is too large to be included in the break-up, be grouped under suitable headings without mentioning the quantities, provided all those items which in value individually account for 10 per cent or more of the total value of the raw material consumed shall be shown as separate and distinct items with quantities thereof in the break-up.

(2) The opening and closing stocks of goods produced, giving break-up in respect of each class of goods and indicating the quantities thereof.

(b) In the case of trading companies, the purchases made and the opening and closing stocks, giving break-up in respect of each class of goods traded in by the company and indicating the quantities thereof.

(c) In the case of companies rendering or supplying services, the gross income derived from services rendered or supplied.

(d) In the case of a company, which falls under more than one of the categories mentioned in (a). (b) and (c) above, it shall be sufficient compliance with the requirements herein if the total amounts are shown in respect of the opening and closing stocks, purchases, sales and consumption of raw material with value and quantitative break-up and the gross income from services rendered is shown.

(e) In the case of other companies, the gross income derived under different heads.

Note 1.—The quantities of raw materials purchases, stocks, and the turnover shall be expressed in quantitative denominations in which these are normally purchased or sold in the market.

Note 2.—For the purpose of items *(ii)(a), (ii)(b)* and *(ii)(d),* the items for which the company is holding separate industrial licences, shall be treated as separate classes of goods, but where a company has more than one industrial licence for production of the same item at different places or for expansion of the licensed capacity, the item covered by all such licences shall be treated as one class. In the case of trading companies, the imported items shall be classified in accordance with the classification adopted by the Chief Controller of Imports and Exports in granting the import licences.

Note 3.—In giving the break-up of purchases, stocks and turnover,. items like spare parts and accessories, the list of which is too large to be included in the break-up, may be grouped under suitable headings without quantities, provided all those items, which in value individually account for 10 percent or more of the total value of the purchases, stocks, or turnover, as the case may be. are shown as separate and distinct items with quantities thereof in the break-up.]

(iii) In the case of all concerns having works-in-progress, the amounts for which [1][such works have been completed] at the commencement and at the end of the accounting period.

(iv) The amount provided for depreciation, renewals or diminution in value of fixed assets.

If such provision is not made by means of a depreciation charge, the method adopted for making such provision.

If no provision is made for depreciation, the fact that no provision has been made shall be stated [1][and the quantum of arrears of depreciation computed in accordance with section 205(2) of the Act shall be disclosed by way of a note.]

(v) The amount of interest on the company's debentures and other Fixed loans, that is to say, loans for fixed periods, stating separately the amount of interest, if any, [2][paid or payable] to the managing director [3][* * *] and the manager, if any.

(vi) The amount of charge for Indian income-lax and other Indian taxation on profits, including, where practicable, with Indian income-tax any taxation imposed elsewhere to the extent of the relief, if any. from Indian income-tax and distinguishing, where practicable. between income-tax and other taxation.

(vii) The [4][amounts reserved for—]

(a) repayment of share capital; and

(b) repayment of loans.

(viii) (a) The aggregate, if material, of any amounts set aside or proposed to be set aside, to reserves, but not including provisions made to meet any specific liability, contingency or commitment known to exist at the date as at which the balance-sheet is made up.

(b) The aggregate, if material, of any amounts withdrawn from such reserves.

(ix) (a) The aggregate, if material, of the amounts to set aside to provisions made for meeting specific liabilities, contingencies or commitments.

(b) The aggregate, if material, of the amounts withdrawn from such provisions, as no longer required.

(x) Expenditure incurred on each of the following items, separately for each item:—

(a) Consumption of stores and spare parts

(b) Power and fuel.

(c) Rent.

(d) Repairs to buildings.

(e) Repairs to machinery.

(f) (1) Salaries, wages and bonus.

(2) Contribution to provident and other funds.

(3) Workmen and staff welfare expenses [5][to the extent not adjusted from any previous provision or reserve.

Note [1][1].—Information in respect of this item should also be given in the balance sheet under the relevant provision or reserve account.]

Note 2 —[2][* * *]

(g) Insurance.

(h) Rates and taxes, excluding taxes on income.

(i) Miscellaneous expenses:

[3][Provided that any item under which the expenses exceed one per cent of the total revenue of the company or Rs. 5,000 whichever is higher shall be shown as a separate and distinct item against an appropriate account head in the Profit and Loss Account and shall not be combined with any other item to be shown Under 'Miscellaneous expenses'.]

(xi) (a) The amount of income from investments, distinguishing between trade investments and other investments.

(b) Other income by way of interest, specifying the nature of the income.

(c) The amount of income-tax deducted if the gross income is stated under sub-paragraphs (a) and (b) above.

(xii) (a) Profits or losses on investments [4][showing distinctly the extent of the profits or losses earned or incurred on account of membership of a partnership firm] [5][to the extent not adjusted from any previous provision or reserve.

Note—Information in respect of this item should also be given in the balance sheet under the relevant provision or reserve account.]

(b) Profits or losses in respect of transactions of a kind, not usually undertaken by the company or undertaken in circumstances of an exceptional or non-recurring nature, if material in amount.

(c) Miscellaneous income.

(xiii) (a) Dividends from subsidiary companies.

(b) Provisions for losses of subsidiary companies.

(xiv) The aggregate amount of the dividends paid, and proposed, and stating whether such amounts are subject to deduction of income-tax or not.

(xv) Amount, if material, by which any items shown in the profit and loss account are affected by any change in the basis of accounting. [6][4. The profit and loss account shall also contain or give by way of a note detailed information, showing separately the following payments provided or made during the financial year to the directors (including managing directors). [7][* * *] or manager, if any, by the company, the subsidiaries of the company and any other person:

(i) managerial remuneration under section 198 of the Act paid or payable during — the financial year to the directors (including managing directors), [1][***] manager, if any;

(ii) [2][* * *];
(iii) [3][* * *];
(iv) [4][* * *];
(v) [5][* * *];
[6][(vi) other allowances and commission including guarantee commission (details to be given)];
(vii) any other perquisites or benefits in cash or in kind (stating approximate money value where practicable);
(viii) pensions, etc.,—
(a) pensions,
(b) gratuities,
(c) payments from provident funds, in excess of own subscriptions and interest thereon,
(d) compensation for loss of office,
(e) consideration in connection with retirement from office.]

4 A. The profit and loss account shall contain or give by way of a note a statement showing the computation of net profits in accordance with section 349 of the Act with relevant details of the calculation of the commissions payable by way of percentage of such profits, to the directors (including managing directors), [7][* * *] or manager (if any).

4B. The profit and loss account shall further contain or give by way of a note detailed information in regard to amounts paid to the auditor, [8](whether as fees, expenses or otherwise for services rendered—]
(a) as auditor, [9][* * *]
[10][(b) as adviser, or in any other capacity, in respect of :
(i) taxation matters;
(ii) company law matters;
(iii) management services; and
(c) in any other manner].]

[11][4C. In the case of manufacturing companies, the profit and loss account shall also contain, by way of a note in respect of each class of goods manufactured, detailed quantitative information in regard to the following, namely:
(a) the licensed capacity (where licence is in force);
(b) the installed capacity; and
(c) the actual production.

Note 1.—The licensed capacity and installed capacity of the company as on the last date of the year to which the profit and loss account relates, shall be mentioned against items (a) and (b) above, respectively.

Note 2.—Against item (c). the actual production in respect of the finished products meant for sale shall be mentioned. In cases where semi-processed products are also sold by the company, separate details thereof shall be given.

Note 3.—For the purposes of this paragraph, the items for which the company is holding separate industrial licences shall be treated as separate classes of goods but where a company has more than one industrial licence for production of the same item at different places or for expansion of the licensed capacity, the item covered by all such licences shall be treated as one class.

4D. The profit and loss account shall also contain by way of a note the following information, namely:
(a) value of imports calculated on C.I.F. basis by the company during ihe financial year in respect of :
(i) raw materials;
(ii) components and spare parts; and
(iii) capital goods;
(b) expenditure in foreign currency during the financial year on account of royalty, know-how, professional, consultation fees, interest, and other matters:

(c) value of all imported raw materials, spare parts and components consumed during the financial year and the value of all indigenous raw materials, spare parts and components similarly consumed and the percentage of each to the total consumption;

(d) the amount remitted during the year in foreign currencies on account of dividends, with a specific mention of the number of non-resident share-holders, the number of shares held by them on which the dividends were due and the year to which the dividends related:

(e) earnings in foreign exchange classified under the following heads. namely:— (i) export of goods calculated on F.O.B. basis;

(ii) royalty, know-how, professional and consultation fees;

(iii) interest and dividend;

(iv) other income, indicating the nature thereof.]

5. The Central Government may direct that a company shall not be obliged to show the amount set aside to provisions other than those relating to depreciation, renewal or diminution in value of assets, if the Central Government is satisfied that the information should not be disclosed in the public interest and would prejudice the company, but subject to the condition that in any heading stating an amount arrived at after taking into account the amount set aside as such, the provision shall be so framed or marked as to indicate, that fact.

6. (1) Except in the case of the first profit and loss account laid before the company after (he commencement of the Act, the corresponding amounts for the immediately preceding financial year for all items shown in the profit and loss account shall also be given in Ihe profit and loss account.

(2) The requirement in sub-clause (1) shall, in the case of companies preparing quarterly or half-yearly accounts, relate to the profit and loss account for the period which entered on the corresponding date of the previous year.

PART III

Interpretation

7. (1) For the purposes of Parts I and II of this Schedule, unless the context otherwise requires,

(a) the expression "provision" shall, subject to sub-clause (2) of this clause, mean any amount written off or retained by way of providing for depreciation, renewals or diminution in value of assets, or retained by way of providing for any known liability of which the amount cannot be determined with substantial accuracy;

(b) the expression "reserve" shall not, subject as aforesaid, include any amount written off or retained by way of providing for depreciation, renewals or diminution in value of assets or retained by way of providing for any known liability;

(c) the expression "capital reserve" shall not include any amount regarded as free for distribution through the profit and loss account; and the expression "revenue reserve" shall mean any reserve other than capital reserve:

and in this sub-clause the expression "liability" shall include all liabilities in respect of expenditure contracted for and all disputed or contingent liabilities.

(2) Where

(a) any amount written off or retained by way of providing for depreciation, renewals or diminution in value of assets, not being an amount written off in relation to fixed assets before the commencement of this Act; or

(b) any amount retained by way of providing for any known liability; is in excess of the amount which in the opinion of the directors is reasonably necessary for the purpose, the excess shall be treated for the purposes of this Schedule as a reserve and not as a provision.

8. For the purposes aforesaid, the expression "quoted investment" means an investment which has been granted a quotation or permission to deal on a recognised stock exchange, and the expression "unquoted investment" shall be construed accordingly.

[1][PART IV
Balance Sheet Abstract and Company's General Business Profile

I. Registration Details

Registration No. [ ] Slate Code [ ] (Refer Code List)

Balance Sheet Date [ ] Date [ ] Month [ ] Year

II. Capital raised during the year (Amount in Rs. Thousands)

Public Issue [ ] Rights Issue [ ]

Bonus Issue [ ] Private Placement [ ]

III. Position of Mobilisation and Deplovement of Funds (Amount in Rs. Thousands)

Total Liabilities [ ] Total Assets [ ]

Source of Funds

Paid-up Capital [ ] Reserves & Surplus [ ]

Secured Loans [ ] Unsecured Loans [ ]

Application of Funds

Net Fixed Assets [ ] Investments [ ]

Net Current Assets [ ] Misc. Expenditure [ ]

Accumulated Losses [ ]

IV. Performance of Company (Amount in Rs. Thousands)

Turnover [ ] Total Expenditure [ ]

+ – [ ] Profit/Loss Before Tax [ ] + – [ ] Profit/Loss After Tax [ ]

(Please tick appropriate box + for profit – for loss)

Earning Per Share in Rs. [ ] Divided rate % [ ]

V. Generic Names of Three Principle Products/Services of Company (as per monetary terms)

Item Code No.

(ITC Code)

Product Description

Item Code No.

(ITC Code)

Product Description

Item Code No.

(ITC Code)

Product Description

Note : for ITC Code of Products please refer to the publication Indian Trade Classification based on harmonized commodity description and coding system by Ministry of Commerce, Directorate General of Commercial Intelligence & Statistics, Calcutta-700 001.

Schedules

The details regarding various items are shown separately is Schedule. The schedule will incorporate all the information required under Part IA of Schedule VI. The schedules, accounting policies and other explanatory notes will form a part of the Balance sheet.

DESCRIPTION OF SOME BALANCE SHEET ITEMS

Liabilities side

Share capital. It is the first item on the liabilities side of the balance sheet. Authorised and issued capital is shown giving the number of shares and their amount. The number of shares for which public has applied *i.e.* subscribed capital are mentioned along with the type of capital *i.e.* preference share capital and equty share capital. The bonus share and share issued other than cash is also mentioned. Any unpaid calls are deducted from the called up capital. If forfeited shares are re-issued then this amount is added to the paid-up capital.

Reserves and Surplus. Under this heading all kinds of reserves which are created out of profits are shown. Reserves are classified as Capital reserve and revenue reserves. Capital reserves are those reserves which are not used for distribution as profits but revenue reserve can be used for distribution as profits. Various kinds of reserves are (i) capital reserve (ii) capital redemption reserve (iii) share premium account (iv) other reserves (v) surplus *i.e.* profit and loss account (vi) sinking-fund.

Secured Loans. The loans which are given against securities are shown. Debentures are also shown under the heading. Loans and advances from bank, subsidiary companies etc. shown separately.

Unsecured Loans. These are the loans and advances against which the company has not given any securities. It includes deposit, loans and advances from bank, subsidiary comapny and loans and advances from other sources. Short-term loans are also included in this category. Short-term loans include those which are due for not more than one year on the date of the Balance sheet.

Current Liabilities and Provisions. These are divided into (i) current liabilities (ii) provisions.

(i) Current liabilities includes
- — Acceptance
- — Sundry creditors
- — Subsidiary companies
- — Advance payment
- — Unclaimed dividends
- — Other liabilities item
- — Interest accrued

(ii) Provisions includes
- — Provision for taxation
- — Proposed dividends
- — Provision for contingencies
- — Provision for Provident-Fund Scheme
- — Provision for Insurance, Pension and Similar Staff Benefits Scheme
- — Other provisions

Assets side

1. Fixed Assets. Fixed assets are those which are purchased for use over a long period. These assets are meant to increase production capacity of the business. These assets should be shown in such away that balance sheet depicts true financial position of business. Examples of fixed assets are goodwill, land, building, lease-lands cost, Plant and machinery, furniture, patern, livestock, etc. These assess are shown at their original cost. The amount of depreciation upto the previous year and during the current year is separately deducted from the assets.

2. Investments. Investments are shown by giving their nature and mode of valuation. Investments under various sub-heads such as investments in government or private securities, in shares, debentures, bonds and immovable are given separately in the inner column of the balance sheet.

3. Current Assets. Current assets are such assets which in the ordinary and natural course of business move onward through the various process of production, distribution and payment of goods, until they become cash or its equivalent in which debts may be readily and immediately paid. Current assets are either cash in hand and at bank or shortly convertible into cash. Examples of current assets are stock, debtors, bills receivable, prepaid expenses.

4. Miscellaneous Expenditure. Under this heading deferred expenditure. There are the expenses which are not debited fully to the Profit and Loss account of the year in which they have been incurred. They are shown under the heading, deferred expenditure.

FORM AND CONTENTS OF INCOME STATEMENT

The Income Statement or Profit and Loss Account is prepared according to the nature of business. A trading concern will prepare trading and profit and loss account for finding gross profit and net profit respectively. A manufacturing concern will first prepare manufacturing account for finding the cost of production and then it will prepare trading and profit and loss account. In case of sole proprietors and partnership concerns there are no prescribed forms for income statement. In case of Joint Stock Company, the preparation of Income Statement according to section 211 of Companies Act is compulsory. However, a specific form for income statement is given for Banking company and Insurance Company as per their corresponding Acts. The manufacturing, trading and Profit and Loss Account are generally prepared in T-form.

The general froms are given below:

Manufacturing Account for Company X

for the year ending.....................

	Rs.		Rs.
To Opening Stock :	....	By Cost of finished	....
Raw materials	....	Goods transfered to Trading A/c	....
To Purchases : raw materials	....	By Closing Stock :	....
To Manufacturing wages	....	Raw Materials	....
To Carriage in ward	....		
To Factory rent	....		
To Depreciation:	....		
Factory building, machinery	....		
To Repair Plant	....		
To Loading	....		
To Salary of Managers	....		

Tradis and Profit and Loss Account

for the year ended.....................

	Rs.		Rs.
To Opening Stock of finished goods	....	By Sales	....
To Cost of finished goods transferred		By Closing Stock	....
from manufacturing Account	....	By Finished goods	....
To Gross Profit c/d	....	By Gross Loss c/d	
Total		Total	
To Gross Loss b/d	....		
To Salaries	....	By Gross Profit b/d	....
To Office Rent	....	By Discount Received	....
To Advertising	....	By Net Loss transferred to	
To Carriage outward	....	Capital Account	....
To Discount allowed			
To Provision for Bad and			
doubtful debts	....		
To Depreciation : Building			
Office Furniture	....		
To Net Profit transferred to	....		
Capital account	....		
Total		Total	

POSTULATES, CONCEPTS AND PRINCIPLES

Terms such as postulates, concepts, principles (and others like procedure, rule) are widely used, but with no general agreement as to their precise meaning. Often, what is referred to as 'postulates' by some writers, are called as 'concepts' or 'principles' by other writers and *vice versa.* To give a few examples of such conflicting opinions, the views of Belkaoui, Anthony and Reece, Financial Accounting Standards Board (USA) have been given below:

ACCOUNTING POSTULATES

1. Entity Postulate
2. Going Concern Postulate
3. Unit of Measure Postulate
4. Accounting Period Postulate

ACCOUNTING PRINCIPLES

1. Cost Principle
2. Revenue Principle
3. Matching Principle
4. Objectivity Principle
5. Consistency Principle
6. Full Disclosure Principle
7. Conservatism Principle
8. Materiality Principle
9. Uniformity and Comparability Principle

Source : Ahmed Riahi Belkaoui, Accounting Theory, Thomson Learning. 2000, pp. 161-192.

ACCOUNTING CONCEPTS

1. Money Measurement	2. Entity
3. Going Concern	4. Cost
5. Dual-Aspect	6. Accounting Period
7. Conservatism	8. Realisation
9. Matching	10. Consistency
11. Materiality	

Source: Robert N. Anthony and James S. Reece, *Accounting Principles*, Richard D. Irwin, 1991, p. 22.

FUNDAMENTAL CONCEPTS OF ACCOUNTING

A. Assumptions of Accounting	B. Principles of Accounting
1. Separate-entity assumption.	1. Cost Principle.
2. Continuity assumption.	2. Revenue Principle.
3. Unit-of-measure assumption.	3. Matching Principle.
4. Time-period assumption.	4. Full-disclosure Principle.

Source: Financial Accounting Standards Board, USA, Statement of Financial Accounting Concepts No. 6, Elements of Financial Statements, December 1985.

Note: Financial Accounting Standards Board (FASB) USA refers to assumptions and principles of accounting as 'concepts of accounting'.

Thus, it can be observed that finding a precise terminology has always been one of the most difficult task in accounting. Further, the lack of agreement about their precise meaning has affected, to some extent, the attempts made towards developing a theory for financial accounting.

The purpose here is not to engage the readers on a debate of suitable terminology but to explain something which are widely accepted as of greatest importance and universal applicability, whether as postulates, concepts or principles. But before this, an attempt has been made to define the terms postulates, concepts and principles.

Postulates

Accounting postulates are basic assumptions concerning the business environment. They are generally accepted as self-evident truths in accounting. Postulates are established or general truths which do not require any evidence to prove them. They are the propositions taken for granted. As basic assumptions postulates cannot be verified. They serve as a basis for inference and a foundation for a theoretical structure that consists of propositions derived from them. Postulates in accounting are few in numbers and stem from the-economic and political environments as well as from the customs and underlying viewpoints of the business community.

Belkaoui[4] defines accounting postulates:

> "as self-evident statements or axioms, generally accepted by virtue of their conformity to the objectives of financial statements, that portray the economic, political, sociological and legal environment in which accounting must operate."

American Institute of Certified Public Accountants (USA) observes:

> "Postulates are few in numbers and are the basic assumptions on which principles rest. They necessarily are derived, from the economic and political environment and from the modes of thought and customs of all segments of the business community. The profession, however, should make clear their understanding and interpretation of what they are, to provide a meaningful foundation for the formulation of principles and the development of rules or other guides for the application of principles in specific situations."

Concepts

Accounting concepts are also self-evident statements or truths. Accounting concepts are so basic that people accept them as valid without any questioning. Accounting concepts provide the conceptual guidelines for application in the financial accounting process, *i.e.*, for recording, measurement, analysis and communication of information about an organisation. These concepts provide help in resolving future accounting issues on a permanent or a longer basis, rather than trying to deal with each issue on an *ad hoc* basis. The concepts are important because they (a) help explain the "why" of the accounting (b) provide guidance when new accounting situations are encountered and (c) significantly reduce the need to memorise accounting procedures when learning about accounting.[6]

Principles

Accounting principles or concepts are not laws of nature. They are broad ideas developed as a way of describing current accounting practices and prescribing new and improved practices.

Accounting principles are general decision rules derived from the accounting concepts. According to AICPA (USA), principles means "a general law or rule adopted or professed as a guide to action; a settled

4. Ahmed Riahi Belkaoui, Accounting Theory, Thomson Learning, 2000, p. 163.
5. American Institute of Certified Public Accountants. The Basic Postulates of Accounting, Accounting Research Study No. 1, AICPA, 1961.
6. Glenn A. Wisch and Daniel G. Short, Fundamentals of Financial Accounting, Irwin, 1987 p. 144.

ground or basis of conduct or practice." Principles are general approaches used in the recognition and measurement of accounting events. Accounting principles are characterised as 'how to apply' concepts. Anthony and Reece[7] comment:

> "Accounting principles are man-made. Unlike the principles of physics, chemistry and other natural sciences, accounting principles were not deducted from basic axioms, nor can they be verified by observation and experiment. Instead, they have evolved. This evolutionary process is going on constantly; accounting principles are not eternal truths."

A principle is an explanation concisely framed in words to compress an important relationship among accounting ideas into a few words. Principles are concise explanations. Accounting principles do not suggest exactly as to how each transaction will be recorded. This is the reason that accounting practices differ from one enterprise to another. The differences in accounting practices is also due to the fact that GAAP (generally accepted accounting principles) provides flexibility about the recording and reporting of business transactions.

To explain the relationship among postulates, concepts and principles and accounting techniques, the example of cost principle is taken. Cost concept or principle emphasises historical cost which is based on going concern postulate and the going concern postulate says that there is no point in revaluing assets to reflect current values since the business is not going to sell its assets.

Accounting concepts or principles serve two purposes: First, they provide general descriptions of existing accounting practices. In doing this, they serve as guidelines in accounting. Thus, after learning how the concepts or principles are applied in a few situations, one can develop the ability to apply them in different situations. Second, these concepts or principles help accountants analyse unfamiliar situations and develop procedures to account for those situations.

Larsen and Miller[8] observe :

> "As business practices have evolved in recent years; however, these concepts have become less useful as guides for accountants to follow in dealing with new and different types of transactions. This problem has occurred because the concepts are intended to provide general descriptions of current accounting practices. In other words, they describe what accountants currently do; they do not necessarily describe what accountants should do. Also, since these concepts do not identify weaknesses in accounting practices, they do not lead to major changes or improvements in accounting practices."

ACCOUNTING POSTULATES

(1) *Entity Postulate.* The entity postulate assumes that the financial statements and other accounting information are for the specific business enterprise which is distinct from its owners. Attention in financial accounting is focused on the economic activities of individual business enterprises. Consequently, the analysis of business transactions involving costs and revenue is expressed in terms of the changes in the firm's financial conditions. Similarly, the assets and liabilities devoted to business activities are entity assets and liabilities. The transactions of the enterprise are to be reported rather than the transaction of the enterprise's owners. This concept, therefore, enables the accountant to distinguish between personal and business transactions. The concept applies to sole proprietorship, partnerships, companies, and small and large enterprises. It may also apply to a segment of a firm, such as division,. or several firms, such as when interrelated firms are consolidated.

The assumption of a business entity somewhat apart and distinct from the actual persons conducting its operations, is a conception which has been greatly deplored by some writers and staunchly defended by

7. Robert N. Anthony and James S. Reece, Accounting Principles, Irwin 1991, p. 15.
8. Kermit D. Larsen and Paul B.W. Miller, Financial Accounting, Irwin 1995, p. 602.

others. The distinction between the business entity and outside interests is a difficult one to make in practice in those business in which there is a close relationship between the business and the people who own it. In the case of small firms where the owners exert day-to-day control over the affairs of the business and personal and business assets are intermingled, the definition of the business activity is more difficult for financial as well as managerial accounting purposes.

However, in the case of a company, the distinction is often quite easily made. A company has a separate legal entity, separate from persons who own it. One possible reason for making distinction between the business entity and the outside world is the fact that an important purpose of financial accounting is to provide the basis for reporting on stewardship. Owners, creditors, banks and others entrust funds to management and management is expected to use these funds effectively. Financial accounting reports are one of the principal means to show how well this responsibility, or stewardship, has been discharged. Also, one entity may be a part of a larger entity. For example, a set of accounts may be prepared for different major activities within a large organisation, and still another set of accounts may be prepared for the organisation as a whole.

(2) *Going Concern Postulate.* An accounting entity is viewed as continuing in operation in the absence of evidence to the contrary.* Because of the relative permanence of enterprises, financial accounting is formulated assuming that the business will continue to operate for an indefinitely long period in the future. Past experience indicates that continuation of Operations is highly probable for most enterprises although continuation cannot be known with certainty. An enterprise is not viewed as a going concern, if liquidation appears imminent.

The going concern concept justifies the valuation of assets on a non-liquidation basis and it calls for the use of historical cost for many valuations. Also, the fixed assets and intangibles are amortised over their useful life rather than over a shorter period in expectation of early liquidation.

The significance of going concern concept can be indicated by contrasting it with a possible alternative, namely, that the business is about to be liquidated or sold. Under the later assumption, accounting would attempt to measure at all times what the business is currently worth to a buyer; but under the going concern concept, there is no need to do this, and it is in fact not done. Instead, a business is viewed as a mechanism for creating value, and its success is measured by the difference between the value of its outputs (*i.e.*, sales of goods and service) and the cost of resources used in creating those outputs.

The going concern concept leads to the proposition that individual financial statements are part of a continuous, interrelated series of statements. This further implies that data communicated are tentative and that current statements should disclose adjustments to past year statements revealed by more recent developments.

(3) *Money Measurement Postulate.* A unit of exchange and measurement is necessary to account for the transactions of business enterprises in a uniform manner. The common denominator chosen in accounting is the monetary unit. Money is the common denominator in terms of which the exchangeability of goods and services, including labour, natural resources, and capital, are measured. Money measurement concept holds that accounting is a measurement and communication process of the activities of the firm that are measurable in monetary terms. Obviously, financial statements should indicate the money used.

Money measurement concept implies two limitation of accounting. First, accounting is limited to the production of information expressed in terms of a monetary unit; it does not record and communicate other relevant but non-monetary information. Accounting does not record or communicate the state of chairman's health, the attitude of the employees, or the relative advantage of competitive products or the fact that the sales manager is not on speaking terms with the production manager. Accounting therefore does not give a complete account of the happenings in a business or an accurate picture of the condition of the business.

*A related proposition is that liquidation appears imminent, financial information may be prepared on the assumption that liquidation will take place.

Accounting information is perceived, as essentially monetary and quantified, while non-accounting information is non-monetary and non-quantified. Although accounting is a discipline concerned with measurement and communication of monetary activities, it has been expanding into areas previously viewed as qualitative in nature. In fact, a number of empirical studies refer to the relevance of non-accounting information compared with accounting information.

Secondly, the monetary unit concept concerns the limitations of the monetary unit itself as a unit of measure. The primary characteristics of the monetary unit - purchasing power, or the quantity of goods or services that money can acquire - is of concern. Traditionally, financial accounting has dealt with this problem by stating that this concept assumes either that the purchasing power of the monetary unit is stable over time or that the changes in prices are not significant. While still accepted for current financial reporting, the stable monetary unit concept is the object of continuous and persistent criticisms.

(4) *Time Period Postulate.* The financial accounting provides information about the economic activities of an enterprise for specified time periods that are shorter than the life of the enterprise. Normally the time periods are of equal length to facilitate comparisons. The time period is identified in the financial statements. The time periods are usually twelve months in length. Some companies also issue quarterly or half yearly statements to shareholders. They are considered to be interim, and essentially different from annual statements. For management use, statements covering shorter periods such as a month or week may be prepared.

ACCOUNTING CONCEPTS AND PRINCIPLES

(1) *Cost Principle.* The cost principle requires that assets be recorded at their exchange price, *i.e.*, acquisition cost, or historical cost. Historical cost is recognised as the appropriate valuations basis for recognition of the acquisition of all good and services, expenses, costs and equities. In other words, an item is valued a the exchange price at the date of acquisition and shown in the financial statements at that value or an amortised portion of it. For accounting purpose business transactions are normally measured in terms of the actual prices or costs at the time the transaction occurs. That is, financial accounting measurements are primarily based on exchange prices at which economic resource and obligations are exchanged. Thus, the amounts at which assets are listed in the accounts of a firm do not indicate what the assets could be sold for. However, some accountants argue that accounting would be more useful if estimates of current and future values were substituted for historical costs under certain conditions.

The historical cost concept implies that since the business is not going to sell its assets as such, there is little point in revaluing assets to reflect current values. In addition, for practical reasons, the accountant prefers the reporting of actual costs to market values which are difficult to verify. By using historical costs, the accountant's already difficult task is not further complicated by the need to keep additional records of changing market value. Thus, the cost concept provides greater objectivity and greater feasibility to the financial statements.

(2) *Dual-Aspect Principle.* This principle lies at the heart of the whole accounting process. The Accountant records events affecting the wealth of a particular entity. The question is — which aspect of this wealth are important? Since an accounting entity is an artificial creation, it is essential to know to whom its resources belong or what purpose they serve. It is also important to know what kind of resources it controls, *e.g.*, cash, buildings or land. Accounts recording systems have therefore, developed so as to show two main things (a) the source of wealth and (b) the form it takes.

Suppose Mr. X decides to establish a business and transfers Rs. 1,00,000 from his private bank account to a separate business account. He might record this event as follows:

Business entity records

Liabilities		*Assets*	
Source of wealth		Form of wealth	
X's capital	1,00,000	Cash at Bank	1,00,000

Clearly the source of wealth must be numerically equal to the form of wealth. Since they are simply different aspects of the same things, *i.e.*, in the form of an equation: S (sources) must equal F (forms).

Moreover, any transaction or event affecting the wealth of entity must have two aspects recorded in order to maintain the equality of both sides of the accounting equation. If business has acquired an asset, it must have resulted in one of the following:

(a) Some other asset has been given up.
(b) The obligation to pay for it has arisen.
(c) There has been a profit, leading to an increase in the amount that the business owes to the proprietor or
(d) The proprietor has contributed money for the acquisition of asset.

This does not mean that a transaction will affect both the source and form of wealth. There are four categories of events affecting the accounting equation:

(a) Both sources and forms of wealth increase by the same amount.
(b) Both sources and forms of wealth decrease by the same amount.
(c) Some forms of wealth increase while others decrease without any change in the source of wealth.
(d) Some sources of wealth increase while others decrease without any change in the form in which wealth is held.

The example given above illustrates category (a) since the commencing transaction for the entity results in the source of wealth and form of wealth, cash, both increasing from zero to Rs. 1,00,000. By contrast, X might decide to withdraw Rs. 20,000 cash from the business. Then financial positions of business entity would result:

Liabilities		*Assets*	
Source of Wealth		*Form of Wealth*	
X's capital	80,000	Cash	80,000

It is essential to appreciate why both sides of the equation decrease. By taking out cash, X automatically reduces his supply of private finance to the business and by the same amount.

Suppose now that Mr. X buys stocks of goods for Rs. 30,000 with the available cash. His supply of capital does not change, but the composition of the business assets does,

Source of Wealth		*Form of Wealth*	
X's capital	80,000	Stocks	30,000
		Cash	50.000
	80,000		80,000

The two aspects of this transaction are not in the same direction but compensatory, an increase in stocks offsetting a decrease in cash.

Similarly sources of wealth also may be affected by a transaction. Thus, if X gives his son Y, a Rs. 20,000 share in the business by transferring part of his own interest, the effect is as follows:

Source of wealth		*Forms of wealth*	
X's capital	60,000	Stocks	30,000
Y's capital	20.000	Cash	50,000
	80,000		80,000

If however, X gives Y Rs. 20,000 in cash privately and Y then puts it into the business, both sides of equation would be affected, Y's capital of Rs. 20,000 being balanced by an extra Rs. 20,000 in cash, X's capital remaining at Rs. 80,000.

(3) *Acctual Principle.* According to Financial Accounting Standards Board (USA) "accrual accounting attempts to record the financial effects on an enterprise of transactions and other events and circumstances

that have cash consequences for the enterprise in the periods in which those transactions, events and circumstances occur rather than only in the periods in which cash is received or paid by the enterprise. Accrual accounting is concerned with the process by which cash expended on resources and activities is returned as more (or perhaps less) cash to the enterprise, not just with the beginning and end of that process. It recognizes that the buying, producing, selling and other operations of an enterprise during a period, as well as other events that affect enterprise performance, often do not coincide with the cash receipts and payments of the periods."

A business enterprise's economic activity in a short period seldom follows the simple form of a cycle from money to productive resources to product to money. Instead, continuous production, extensive use of credit and long-lived resources, and over-lapping cycles of activity complicate the evaluation of periodic activities. As a result, non-cash resources and obligations change in time periods other than those in which money is received or paid. Recording these changes is necessary to determine periodic income and to measure financial position. This is the essence of accrual accounting.

Thus, accrual accounting is based not only on cash transactions but also on credit transactions, barter exchanges, changes in prices, changes in the form of assets or liabilities, and other transactions, events, and circumstances that have cash consequence for an enterprise but involve no concurrent cash movement. Although it does not ignore cash transactions, accrual accounting is primarily accounting for non-cash assets, liabilities, revenues, expenses, gains and losses.

(4) *Conservatism Principle.* This principle is often described as "anticipate no profit, and provide for all possible losses." This characterisation might be viewed as the reactive version of the minimix managerial philosophy, *i.e.*, minimise the chance of maximum losses. The concept of accounting conservatism suggests that when and where uncertainty and risk exposure so warrant, accounting takes a wary and watchful stance until the appearance of evidence to the contrary. Accounting conservatism does not mean to intentionally understate income and assets; it applies only to situations in which there are reasonable. doubts. For example, inventories are valued at the lower of cost, or current replacement value.

In its applications to the. income statement, conservatism encourages the recognition of all losses that have occurred or are likely to occur but does not acknowledge gains until actually realised. The procedure of reducing inventory values when market has declined below cost but the failure to countenance "writeups" under reverse conditions can be attributed to conservatism. The early amortisation of intangible assets and the restrictions against recording appreciation of assets have also, at least to some extent, been motivated by conservatism. Failure to recognise revenue until a sale has transferred is still another manifestation of conservatism.

(5) *Matching Principle.* The matching concept in financial accounting is the process of matching (relating) accomplishments or revenues (as measured by the selling prices of goods and services delivered) with efforts or expenses (as measured by the cost of goods, and services used) to a particular period for which the income is being determined. This concept emphasises which items of cost are expenses in a given accounting period. That is, costs are reported as expenses in the accounting period in which the revenue associated with those costs is reported. For example, when the sales value of some goods is reported as revenue in a year, the cost of that goods would be reported as an expense in the same year.

Matching concept needs to be fulfilled only after realisation (accrual) concept has been completed by the accountant; first revenues are measured in accordance with the realisation concept and then costs are associated with these revenues. Costs are matched with revenues, not the other way around. The matching process, therefore, requires cost allocation which is significant in historical cost accounting. Past (historical) costs are examined and, despite their historic nature, are subjected to a procedure whereby elements of cost regarded as having expired service potential are allocated or matched against relevant revenues. The remaining elements of costs which are regarded as continuing to have future service potential are carried forward in the historical balance sheet and are termed as assets. Thus the balance sheet is nothing more than a report of unallocated past costs waiting expiry of their estimated future service potential before being matched with suitable revenues.

(6) *Consistency Principle. This* principle requires that once an organisation has decided on one method, it should use the same method for all subsequent transactions and events of the same nature unless it has sound reason to change, methods. If accounting methods are frequently changed, comparison of its financial statements for one period with those of another period would be difficult. The consistent use of accounting methods and procedures over time will check the distortion of profit and loss account and balance sheet and the possible manipulation of these statements. Consistency is necessary to help external users in comparing financial statements of a given firm over time and in making their decisions.

(7) *Materiality Principle.* Materiality concept implies that the transactions and events that have immaterial or insignificant effects, should not be recorded and reported in the financial statements. It is argued that the recording of insignificant events cannot be justified in terms of its subsequent poor utility to users.

There is no agreement as to the meaning of materiality and what can be said to be material or immaterial events and transactions. It is for the preparer of accounts to interpret what is and what is not material. Probably the materiality of an event or transaction can be decided in terms of its impact on the financial position, results of operations, changes in the financial position of an organisation and on evaluations or decisions made by users.

(8) *Full-disclosure Principle.* The concept of full disclosure requires that a business enterprise should provide all relevant information to external users for the purpose of sound economic decisions. This concept implies that no information of substance or of interest to the average investors will be omitted or concealed from an entity's financial statements.

GENERALLY ACCEPTED ACCOUNTING PRINCIPLES

General purpose financial statements prepared by the business enterprises communicate the results of the business operations during the financial year and the state of financial affairs as at the end of the financial year. These financial statements are used by the investors, lenders and others in taking their economic and business decisions connected with the dealings with such enterprises. The users who use such information and rely on such data have a, right to be assured that the data are reliable and free from bias. In this task, GAAP plays a vital role and financial accounting information can be meaningful only when prepared according to some agreed-on principles and procedures i.e. Generally Accepted Accounting Principles.

The phrase "Generally Accepted Accounting Principles" (GAAP) is a technical accounting term that encompasses the conventions, rules and procedures necessary to define accepted accounting practices at a particular point in time. It includes not only broad guidelines of general application but also detailed practices and procedures. Those conventions, rules and procedures provide a standard by which to measure presentations in the financial statements. GAAP are the ground rules for financial reporting. These principles provide the general framework in determining what information is presented in the financial statements and how the information is to be presented. The phrase "GAAP" encompasses the basic objectives of financial reporting as well as numerous broad concepts and many detailed rules.

GAAP guide the accounting profession in the choice of accounting techniques and in the preparation of financial statements in a way considered to be good accounting practice. GAAP are simply guides to action and may change overtime. They are not immutable laws like those in the physical sciences. Sometimes specific principles must be altered or new principles must be formulated to fit changed economic circumstances or changes in business practices. In response to changing environments, values and information needs, GAAP are subject to constant examination and critical analysis. Changes in the principles occur mainly as a result of the various attempts to provide solutions to emerging accounting problems and to formulate a theoretical framework for the accounting discipline. Accounting principles originate from problems situations such as changes in the law, tax regulations, new business orignisational arrangements, or new financing or ownership techniques. In response to the effect such problems have on financial reports, certain accounting techniques or procedures are tried. Through comparative use and analysis, one or more of these techniques are judged most suitable, obtain substantial authoritative support and are then considered a generally accepted accounting principle.

In India, Organisations like Accounting Standard Board (ASB), Institute of Chartered Accountants of India, Department of Company Affairs (Government of India), Securities and Exchange Board of India (SEBI), Institute of Costs and Works Accountants of India, Institute of Company Secretaries, Stock Exchange, and the literature each publishes—are instrumental in the development of most accounting principles. In USA, Financial Accounting Standards Board (FASB), American Institute of Certified Public Accountants (AICPA), Securities and Exchanged Commission (SEC), Internal Revenue Service and the American Accounting Association are instrumental in the formulation of accounting principles.

SELECTION OF ACCOUNTING PRINCIPLES

Generally Accepted Accounting Principles are primarily relevant to financial accounting. In management accounting, the main objective of using GAAP is to help management in making decision, and in operating effectively and, therefore, in the area of management accounting it is frequently useful to depart from accounting principles used in financial accounting. On many occasions, financial accounting data are reassembled or altered to be most useful in solving internal business problems and in making decision. Similarly, different accounting principles may need to be used for financial reporting purposes and income-tax reporting purposes. That is. accounting principles useful for determining taxable income under the income-tax regulations may differ from the accounting principles used for determining income acceptable for financial reporting, business reporting purpose. The considerations which guide the selection of accounting principles fop financial reporting purposes are follows :[9]

(1) *Accurate Presentation.* One of the criteria for assessing the usefulness of accounting information is accuracy in presentation of the underlying events and transactions. This criterion may be used by the firm as a basis for selecting accounting principles and methods. For example, assets have been defined as resources having future service potential and expenses defined as a measurement of the cost of services consumed during the period. In applying the accuracy criterion, the firm would select the inventory cost flow assumption and depreciation method that most accurately measure the amount of services consumed during the period and the amount of services still available at the end of period. As a basis for selecting an accounting principle, this approach has at least one serious limitation. It is difficult to know accurately the services consumed and the service potential remaining. Without this information the accountant cannot ascertain which accounting principles lead to the most accurate presentation of the underlying events. This criterion can serve only as a normative criterion towards which the development and selection of accounting principles should be directed.

(2) *Conservatism.* In choosing among alternative generally acceptable principles, the firm may select the set that provides the most conservative measure of net income. Considering the uncertainties involved in measuring benefits received as revenue and services consumed as expenses, some have suggested that a conservative measure of earnings should be provided. Conservatism implies that methods should be chosen that minimize cumulative reported earnings. That is, expenses should be recognised as quickly as possible and the recognition of revenues should be postponed as long as possible. This reporting objective, for example, would lead to selecting an accelerated depreciation method, selecting the LIFO cost flow assumption if periods of rising prices are anticipated, expensing research development cost in the year incurred.

---

9. Sidney Davidson et al, Financial Accounting, The Dryden Press, 1984. pp. 629-631.

(3) *Profit Maximization. A* reporting objective having an effect opposite to conservatism may be employed in selecting among alternative generally accepted accounting principles. Somewhat loosely termed reported profit maximization, this criterion suggests, the selection of accounting principles that maximize cumulative reported earnings. That is revenue should be recognized as quickly as possible, and the recognition of expense should be postponed as long as possible. For example, the straight-line method of depreciation would be used, and when periods of rising prices were anticipated, the FIFO cost flow assumption would be selected. The use of profit maximization as a reporting objective is an extension of the notion that the firm is in business to generate profits, and it should present as favourable a report on performance as possible within currently acceptable accounting methods. Some firm's managers whose compensation depends in part on reported earnings, prefer larger reported earnings to smaller. Profit maximization is subject to a similar criticism as the use of conservatism as a reporting objective. Reporting income earlier under the profit maximization criterion must mean that smaller income will be reported in some later period.

(4) *Income Smoothing. A* final reporting objective that may be used in selecting accounting principles is income smoothing. This criterion suggests selecting accounting methods that result in the smoothest earnings trend over time. Advocates of income smoothing suggest that if a company can minimize fluctuations in earnings, the perceived risk of investing in shares of its stock will be reduced and, all else being equal, its stock price will be higher. It is significant to note that this reporting criterion suggests that net income, not revenues and expenses individually, is to be smoothed. As a result, the firm must consider the total pattern of its operations before selecting the appropriate accounting principles and methods. For example, the straight-line method of depreciation may provide the smoothest amount of depreciation expense on a machine over its life. If, however, the productivity of the machine declines with age so that revenues decrease in later years, net income using the straight-line method may not provide the smoothest net income stream.

Due to the flexibility permitted in selecting accounting principles, it is generally now required that business enterprises will disclose the accounting principle used in preparing financial statements, either in a separate statement or as a note to the principal statements.

Although a business firm can use different accounting principles for difference purposes, this does not necessarily mean that business enterprises may keep more than one set of records to satisfy the different requirements. In most cases, certain items taken for financial accounting purposes may have to be omitted and certain other items may have to be included for determining taxable income and tax liability. Even if an organisation maintains different sets of records and books, one for financial reporting purposes and the other for income-tax reporting purposes, this practice cannot be said to be illegal or unethical. In fact, there is nothing wrong or illegal about keeping separate records to fulfil separate needs, so long as all the records and books are open to examination by the appropriate parties. However, as stated earlier, business enterprises attempt to meet the different requirements of shareholders and investors (through financial reporting) and tax authorities (through tax reporting) using the same set of data.

AS1, DISCLOSURE OF ACCOUNTING POLICIES

The Institute of Chartered Accountants of India (ICAI) issued AS1 titled 'Disclosure of Accounting Policies' in November 1979. This standard is now mandatory and deals with the disclosure of significant accounting policies followed in preparing and presenting Financial Statements.

In general accounting policies are not at present regularly and fully disclosed in all financial statements. Many enterprises include in the Notes on the Accounts, description of some of the significant accounting policies.

Even among the few enterprises that presently include in their annual reports a separate statement of accounting policies, considerable variation exists. The statement of accounting policies forms part of the accounts in some cases while in others it is given as supplementary information.

The purpose of this statement is to promote better understanding of financial statements by establishing through an accounting standard the disclosure of significant accounting policies and the manner in which accounting policies are disclosed in the financial statements. Such disclosure would also facilitate a more meaningful comparison between financial statements of different enterprises.

AS 1 contains explanations on following points:

1. Fundamental Accounting Assumptions

Certain fundamental accounting assumptions underlie the preparation and presentation of financial statements. They are usually not specifically stated because their acceptance and use are assumed. Disclosure is necessary if they are not followed.

The following have been generally accepted as fundamental accounting assumptions :

(a) *Going Concern.* The enterprise is normally viewed as a going concern, that is, as continuing in operation for the foreseeable future. It is assumed that the enterprise has neither the intention nor the necessity of liquidation or of curtailing materially the scale of the operations.

(b) *Consistency* - It is assumed that accounting policies are consistent from one period to another.

(c) *Accrual.* Revenues and costs are accrued, that is, recognised as they are earned or incurred (and not as money is received or paid) and recorded in the financial statements of the periods to which they relate. (The considerations affecting the process — of matching costs with revenues under the accrual assumption are not dealt with in this Statement).

2. Nature of Accounting Policies

(i) The accounting policies refer to the specific accounting principles and the methods of applying those principles adopted by the enterprise in the preparation and presentation of financial statements.

(ii) There is no single list of accounting policies which are applicable to all circumstances. The differing circumstances in which enterprises operate in a situation of diverse and complex economic activity make alternative accounting principles and methods of applying those principles acceptable. The choice of the appropriate accounting principles and the methods of applying those principles in the specific circumstances of each enterprise calls for considerable judgement by the management of the enterprise.

(iii) The various statements of the Institute of Chartered Accountants of India combined with the efforts of government and other regularity agencies and progressive managements have reduced in recent years the number of acceptable alternatives particularly in the case of corporate enterprises. While continuing efforts in this regard in future are likely to reduce the number still further, the availability of alternative accounting principles and methods of applying those principles is not likely to be eliminated altogether in view of the differing circumstances faced by the enterprises.

3. Areas in which differing accounting policies are encountered

The following are examples of the areas in which different accounting policies may be adopted by different enterprises :

- Method of depreciation, depletion and amortisation
- Treatment of expenditure during construction
- Conversion of translation of foreign currency items
- Valuation of inventories
- Treatment of goodwill
- Valuation of investments
- Treatment of retirement benefits
- Recognition of profit on long-term contracts
- Valuation of fixed assets
- Treatment of contingent liabilities.

The above list of examples is not intended to be exhaustive.

4. Considerations in the Selection of Accounting Policies

The primary consideration in the selection of accounting policies by an enterprise is that the financial statements prepared and presented on the basis of such accounting policies should represent a true and fair view of the state of affairs of the enterprise as at the balance sheet date and of the profit or loss for the period ended on that date.

For this purpose, the major considerations governing the selection and application of accounting policies are :

(a) *Prudence.* In view of the uncertainty attached to future events, profits are not anticipated but recognised only when realised though not necessarily in cash. Provision is made for all known liabilities and losses even though the amount cannot be determined with certainty and represents only a best estimate in the light of available information.

(b) *Substance over Form.* The accounting treatment and presentation in financial statements of transactions and events should be governed by their substance and not merely by the legal form.

(c) *Materiality.* Financial statements should disclose all "material" items, *i.e.*, items the knowledge of which might influence the decisions of the user of the financial statements.

5. Disclosure of Accounting Policies

(i) To ensure proper understanding of financial statements, it is necessary that all significant accounting policies adopted in the preparation and presentation of financial statements should be disclosed.

(ii) Such disclosure should form part of the financial statements.

(iii) It would be helpful to the reader of financial statements if they are all disclosed as such in one place instead of being scattered over several statements, schedules and notes.

(iv) Examples of matters in respect of which disclosure of accounting policies adopted will be required are contained in point No. 3. This list of examples is not, however, intended to be exhaustive.

(v) Any change in an accounting policy which has a material effect should be disclosed. The amount by which any item in the financial statements is affected by such change should also be disclosed to the extent ascertainable. Where such amount is not ascertainable, wholly or in part, the fact should be indicated. If a change is made in the accounting policies which has no material effect on the financial statements for the current period but which is reasonably expected to have a material effect in later periods, the fact of such change should be appropriately disclosed in the period in which the change is adopted.

(vi) Disclosure of accounting policies or of changes therein cannot remedy a wrong or inappropriate treatment of the item in the accounts.

6. Accounting Standard in AS1

(i) All signficant accounting policies adopted in the preparation and presentation of financial statements should be disclosed.

(ii) The disclosure of the significant accounting policies as such should form part of the financial statements and the significant accounting policies should normally be disclosed in one place.

(iii) Any change in the accounting policies which has a material effect in the current period or which is reasonably expected to have a material effect in later periods should be disclosed. In the case of a change in accounting policies which has a material effect in the current period, the amount by which any item in the financial statements is affected by such change should also be disclosed to the extent ascertainable. Where such amount is not ascertainable, wholly or in part, the fact should be indicated.

(iv) If the fundamental accounting assumptions, *viz*. Going Concern, Consistency and accrual are followed in financial statements, specific disclosure is not required. If a fundamental accounting assumption is not followed, the fact should be disclosed.

THEORY QUESTIONS

1. Define accounting. What is its importance ?
2. Discuss the nature of financial statements. What is the subject matter of financial statements ?
3. Explain the users of financial statements and their informational requirements.
4. What are the objectives of financial statements ?
5. Discuss the nature and utility of diferent accounting and reporting statements covered under the term financial statements.
6. Explain fully the form and contents of balance sheet of a business enterprise.
7. What is Schedule VI on the balance sheet ?
8. What is the vertical and horizontal form of balance sheet ?
9. Explain the following items :
   (i) Reserve and surplus
   (ii) Current liabilities
   (iii) Provisions
   (iv) Investments
   (v) Current assets
10. Discuss the form and contents of Profit and Loss Account.
11. Explain the following terms :
    (i) Accounting Postulates
    (ii) Accounting concepts
    (iii) Accounting Principles
12. Explain the following accounting postulates :
    (i) Entity
    (ii) Going concern
    (iii) Money Measurement
    (iv) Time Period
13. Discuss the following accounting concepts and principles :
    (i) Cost principle
    (ii) Dual Aspect
    (iii) Accrual
    (iv) Conservatism
    (v) Matching
14. What is the meaning of Generally Accepted Accounting Principles ? What is their importance in preparing financial statements ?
15. What are the criteria in selection of accounting principles for preparing financial statements of a business concern ?
16. Discuss the contents and suggestions given in AS1 Disclosure of Accounting Policies.

CHAPTER 2

Understanding Financial Statements

Financial statements are prepared mainly for decision-making purposes. The information given in the financial statements is of immense use is making decisions through analysis and interpretation of financial statements. Financial analysis is the process of identifying the financial strengths and weaknesses of a firm by properly establishing relationship between the items of the balance sheet and profit and loss account. There are a number of methods or techniques which are generally used in analysis of financial statements such as comparative statements, trend analysis, common-size statements, schedule of changes in workers capital, funds flow analysis, cash-flow analysis, time-series analysis, cost-volume-profit analysis and ratio analysis.

CONCEPT OF FINANCIAL STATEMENT ANALYSIS

The term financial statement analysis refers to the process of determining financial strengths and weaknesses of the firm by establishing relationship between the items of the Balance Sheet and Profit and Loss account. It is also a process of the total examination of the financial information contained in the financial statements in order to understand and make decisions regarding the operations of the firm. The financial statements analysis is basically a study of the relationship among various financial facts and figures provided in the financial statements. The complex figure as given in the financial statements are brokenup or dissected into simple and valuable elements and significant relationships are established between the elements of the same statements or different financial statements. This process of dissection for establishing relationships and interepretatsis thereof to understand the working and financial position of a firm is called the Financial Statement Analysis.

Financial Statement Analysis is a process of evaluations of the relationship between components part of a financial statement to obtain a better understanding of a firm's position and performance. In this way, the main objectives of financial statement analysis is to analyse and evaluate the information contained in financial statements to judge the profitability, solvency and financial soundness of a firm. A financial analysts analyses the financial statements with various tools of analysis before commenting upon the financial health or weakness of an enterprise. The analysis and interpretation of financial statements is essential to bring out the mystery behind the figures in financial statements.

OBJECTIVES OF FINANCIAL STATEMENTS ANALYSIS

The basic objective of the analysis of financial statements is to understand the information contained in financial statements with a view to know the weaknesses and strengths of the firm and to make a forecast about the future prospects of the firm and thereby enabling the financial analyst to take different decisions regarding the operation of the firm. However, some of the specific objectives of the analysis of financial statements can be identified as

— To assen the current profitability position and operating efficiency of the firm and as well as of different departments.
— To find out the relative importance of different components of the financial position of the firm.
— To identify the reasons for change in the profitability position of the firm.
— To assess the short as well as long-term liquidity position of the firm.

The financial statements analysis includes both analysis and interpretation. A distinction should be made between the two terms. While the term analysis is used to mean the simplification of financial data by methodical classification of the data given in the financial statements, the interpretation means explaining the meaning and significance of the data. However, both the terms are interlinked and complementaries to each other. Any analysis is useless without proper interpretation and we that proper interpretation, it is very difficult to interpret the things. Sometimes the term analysis is used to cover both analysis and interpretation as the objective of analysis.

Financial Statement analysis may be (i) external analysis and (ii) internal analysis.

External analysis. External analysis is one which is conducted by an outsider without having any access to the basic accounting record of the firm. These include investors, potential investors, creditors, potential creditors, government agencies, credit agencies and the general public. For financial analysis these external parties depend almost entirely on the published financial statements. Thus, external analysis serves only a limited purpose. However, the recent changes in the government regulations requiring business firms to make available more detailed information to the public through audited published accounts have considerably improved the scope of the external analysis.

Internal analysis. The financial statement analysis is said to be internal when it is done by a person who has access to the books of the account and other related infomrations of the firm. This type of financial statement analysis is undertakes for measuring the operational and managerial efficiency at different hierarchy levels of the firms. This type of analysis is more comprehensive and retiable one. Such an analysis, therefore is performed by executives and employees of the organisation as well as government agencies which have statutory powers vested in them. Financial statement analysis for managerial purpose is the internal type of analysis that can be affected depending upon the purpose to be achieved.

According to the methodology in the analysis, financial analysis can be of two types (i) Horizontal Analysis, (ii) Vertical Analysis.

Horizontal Analysis. Horizontal analysis means the comparison of a company for several years. The figures for this type of analysis are shown horizontally over a number of columns. The figures of the various years are compared with standard year/leave year. A base/standard year is choosen at the beginning point. The analysis is based on the data from year to year rather than on data of any one year. This analysis makes it possible to focus attention on items that have changed significantly during the period. Comparison of an item over a several period with a base year may show that trend is developing. Generally, two tools are used in horizontal analysis *i.e.* comparative statement and trend percentage.

Vertical analysis. Vertical analysis refers the study of relationship of the various items in the financial statement of a year, compared with a standard or base year selected from the same year statement. It is also known as static analysis. The two important tools which are generally used in vertical analysis are common-size Financial Statements and financial ratio. Since vertical analysis considers data for one time period only it is not very conductive to a proper analysis of financial statement. However, it may be used along with horizontal analysis to make it more effective and meaningful.

Financial statement analysis helps in making following useful analysis for the managements as well as external users.

1. Inter-firm comparison. It is a technique of financial statements analysis which represents comparative financial features of an enterprise in comparison to another comparable enterprise. Under this method, some financial features of an enterprise are selected and then they are put in comparison to another similar enterprise. It lets the user of financial statement to make comparison of a firm's particular characteristics with some other firm. Various financial characteristics which may be selected for the purpose of comparison, may include profitability, liquidity, solvency and other such similar features. Say, 20 per cent profitability of a particular firm means nothing unless and until it is put in relation to the profitability of another similar firm.

2. Intra-firm comparison. It is also known as time series analysis. Under this technique financial features of an enterprise are depicted and shown over a long period of time. It is a reflection of movement of various financial parameters in the long-run. It forms a particular trend with the help of which the users of financial statements can assess the financial statements in a better manner.

3. Cross-sectional-cum-time series analysis. Under this technique, financial characteristics of two or more firms are compared for more than one financial accounting periods. This technique is considered more effective to analyse the financial statements because of the presence of both comparative financial features of two or more firms and for a sufficient long period of time. Since financial statements are the indicators of the performance of the firms, hence, better inter-firm comparison is possible.

(e) Financial Forecasts & Budgets. Analysis of financial statements also helps in making financial forecasts and budgets. Post financial statements as well as future projections help to prepare budgets and to make financial forecasts.

PROCEDURE OF FINANCIAL STATEMENT ANALYSIS

Generally, there are three steps, involved in the analysis of financial statements. They are : Selection, classification and interpretation. The first step involves selection of information/data relating to the purpose of analysis of financial statements. The second steps involves the methodical classification of the data and the last and third step includes drawing inferences and conclusions. Thus, the main elements which are used in the process of analysis and interpretation are as follows:

- Re-arrangement of financial statements : For analysis, it is necessary to reclassify the data contained in the financial statements into purposive classes so that minimum information from every data for analysis can be obtained. Reclassification and rearrangement of different data depend upon the purpose of analysis.
- *Comparison.* After the classification of data of financial statement into different categories, it is necessary to derive comparative data of the same enterprise of the past period if it is a time series analysis. In case of cross sectional analysis, it is necessary to derive comparative data of the same accounting period of the similar or comparable enterprise. For this, comparative study is very essential.
- *Analysis.* Comparative financial data are then analysed with references to financial characteristics such as profitability, solvency and liquidity.
- *Interpretation.* The concluding part of financial statement analysis is interpretation of financial information generated in the process of financial statement analysis. The interpretation should be precise and point towards the movement of various financial parameters. Finally it will be presented to the management in the form of reports.

METHODS OF FINANCIAL STATEMENT ANALYSIS

The analysis and interpretation of financial statements is used to determine the financial position and as well as, results of operation. A number of methods or devices are used to study the relationship between data and different statements. The following methods of analysis are generally used :

1. Comparative financial statements
2. Common size statements
3. Trend analysis
4. Funds flow analysis
5. Cash flow analysis
6. Cost volume profit analysis
7. Ratio analysis.

This chapter discusses the first three methods of analysis *i.e.* comparative statement, common size statement, trend analysis. Methods of analysis from point No. (iv) to (vii) above have been discussed in other chapters in this book.

1. Comparative financial statements

In comparative financial statements two or more Balance sheets and or the income statement of a firm are presented simultaneously in Columnar form. The financial data for two or more years are placed and presented in adjacent columns and thereby the financial data is provided a times perspective in order to facilitate periodic comparison. In comparative financial statements, the Balance sheet and the Income statements for a number of years are presented in condensed form for year to year comparison and to exhibt the magnitude and direction of changes.

The preparation of the comparative financial statements is based on the premise that a statement covering a period of a number of years is more meaningful and significant than for a single year only and that the financial statements for one period represent only one phase of the long and continuous history of the firm. At present, most of the published annual reports of the companies provide important statistical information about the company in condensed form for the last so many years. The presentation of such data enhances the usefulness of these reports and brings out more clearly the nature and trends of changes affecting the profitability and financial position of the firm. Thus, the comparative financial statements helps a financial analyst in horizontal analysis of the firm and in establishing operating and positional trend of the firm. The comparative financial statements may be prepared to show

— The absolute amount of different items in monetary terms.

— The amount of periodic changes in monetary terms.

— The percentage of periodic changes to reveal the propertionate changes. The comparative financial statement can be prepared for both the Balance sheet and the Income Statement. The analyst is able to draw useful conclusions when figures are given in a comparative position. The figures of sales for a quarter or half year or one year may tell only the present position of sales efforts. When sales figures of previous periods are given along with the figures of current periods then the analyst can use the information to draw more valid inferences.

Comparative Balance Sheet

The comparative balance sheet analysis is the study of the trend of the same items, group of items and computed items in two or more balance sheets of the same business enterprise on different dates. The changes in periodic balance sheet items reflect the conduct of a business. The changes can be observed by comparison of the balance sheet at the beginning of the year and at the end of the year. These changes will help in forming an opinion about the progress of an enterprise. The comparative balance sheet has two columns for the data of orginal balance sheets. A third columns is used to show increase in figures. The fourth and last column may be added for showing percentages of increases or decreases.

ASPECTS OF ANALYSIS AND INTERPRETATION

While analysing the comparative balance sheet the interpreter is expected to study at least the following aspects.

(i) Current financial position
(ii) Current liquidity position
(iii) Long-term financial position
(iv) Profitability of the concern

(i) For studying current financial position, the interpreter should see the working capital in both the years. The excess of current assets over current liabilities will show the figures of working capital. The increase in working capital indicates an improvement in the current financial position of the business. An increase in current assets accompanied by the increase in current liabilities of the same amount will not show any impowerment in the current/short-term financial position.

(ii) The second aspect that should be studied in the current financial position is the liquidity position of the concern. If liquid assets like cash in hand, cash at bank, bills receivables, debtors, marketable securities etc show an increase in the second year over the first year, this will be an indication of increase of liquidity of the concern.

(iii) The long-term financial position of the concern can be interpreted by examining the changes in fixed assets, long-term liabilities and capital. The proper financial policy of concern will be to finance fixed assets by the issue of either long-term securities such as debentures, bonds, loans from financial institutions or issue of fresh share capital. An increase is fixed assets should be compared to the increase in long-term loans and capital. If the increase in fixed assets is more than the increase in the long-term securities then part of fixed assets has been financed from the working capital. However, if the increase in long-term securities is more than the increase in fixed assets then fixed assets have not only been financed from long-term sourcess but part of working capital has also been financed from long-term sourcess. Thus, a wise policy will be to finance fixed assets by raising long-term funds. The nature of assets which have increased or decreased should also be studied to form an opinion about the future production possibilities. Thus, an opinion on the long-term financial position should be framed after considering above—mentioned aspects.

(iv) The next aspect to be studied by the interpreter in comparative balance sheet is the profitability of the concern. The study of increase or decrease is retained learnings various reserves and surpluses etc will enable the interpreter to see whether the profitability has improved or not. An increase in the balance of profit and loss account and other resources created from profits will mean an increase in profitability to the concern. The decrease in such accounts may mean payment of dividend, issue of bonus shames or decline in profitability of the concern.

After minimising various aspects of assets and liabilities an opinion should be formed about the financial position of the concern. One can not say if short-term financial position is good then long-term financial position will also be good or vice-versa. A concluding remarks about the overall financial position of the concern should be given at the end.

Example 1

The Following are the Balance Sheets of a concern for the years 2005 and 2006. Prepare a comparative Balance Sheet and study the financial position of the concern.

Balance Sheet
as on 31st December

Liabilities	*2005* *Rs.*	*2006* *Rs.*	*Assets*	*2005* *Rs.*	*2006* *Rs.*
Sundry Creditors	1,00,000	1,20,000	Prepaid Expenses	—	2,000
Bill Payables	50,000	45,000	Bills Receivables	1,50,000	90,000
Debentures	2,00,000	3,00,000	Furniture & Fixtures	20,000	25,000
Reserves and Surplus	3,30,000	2,22,000	Plant & Machinery	4,00,000	6,00,000
Capital (Equity Share)	6,00,000	8,00,000	Land & Building	3,70,000	2,70,000
Long-term Loans on Mortgage	1,50,000	2,00,000	Other Fixed Assets	25,000	30,000
Other Current Liability	5,000	10,000	Cash in hand & at Bank	20,000	80,000
			Sundry Debtors	2,00,000	2,50,000
			Stock	2,50,000	3,50,000
	14,35,000	16,97,000		14,35,000	16,97,000

Solution

Comparative Balance Sheet of a Company
for the year ending December 31, 2005 and 2006

	Year ending 31 December 2005	*2006*	*Increase/ Decrease (Amount)*	*Increase Decrease (Percentage)*
ASSETS	*Rs.*	*Rs.*	*Rs.*	
Current Assets :				
Cash in hand and at Bank	20,000	80,000	+60,000	+300
Sundry debtors	2,00,000	2,50,000	+50,000	+25
Stock	2,50,000	3,50,000	+1,00,000	+40
Bills Receivables	1,50,000	90,000	–60,000	–40
Prepaid Expenses	—	2,000	+2,000	—
Total Current Assets	6,20,000	7,72,000	+1,52,000	+24.52
Fixed Assets :				
Plant & Machinery	4,00,000	6,00,000	+2,00,000	+50.00
Furniture & Fixtures	20,000	25,000	+5,000	+25.00
Other fixed Assets	25,000	30,000	+5,000	+20.00
Land & Buildings	3,70,000	2,70,000	–1,00,000	–27.03
Total Fixed Assets	8,15,000	9,25,000	+1,10,000	+13.49
Total Assets	14,35,000	16,97,000	+2,62,000	+18.26
LIABILITIES & CAPITAL				
Current assets :				
Sundry creditors	1,00,000	1,20,000	+ 20,000	+ 20
Bills payables	50,000	45,000	– 5,000	– 10
Other current liabilities	5,000	10,000	+ 5,000	+ 100
Total current liabilities	1,55,000	1,75,000	+ 20,000	+ 12.9
Debentures	2,00,000	3,00,000	+ 1,00,000	+ 50
Long term loans on mortgage	1,50,000	2,00,000	+ 50,000	+ 33
Total liabilities	5,05,000	6,75,000	1,70,000	+ 33.66
Equity share capital	6,00,000	8,00,000	+ 2,00,000	+ 33
Reserves and surpluses	3,30,000	2,22,000	–1,08,000	–32.73
Total	14,35,000	16,97,000	+2,62,000	+18.26

Interpretation

The comparative balance sheet of the company shows that during the year 2006 there has been an increase in fixed assets Rs. 110,000 *i.e.* 13.49% long-term liabilities while have recently increased by Rs. 1,50,000 and equity hare capital his increased by Rs. 2,00,000. This fact indicates that the policy of the company is to purchase fixed assets from long-term sources of finance and it is nor affecting working capital.

Further, the current assess have increased by Rs. 1,52,000 *i.e.* around 24.52% and cash has increased by Rs. 60,000. There has been increase in inventories amounting to Rs. 1,00,000. However, the current liabilities have increased only by Rs. 2,00,000 *i.e.* 12.9%.

This confirms that the company has raised long-term finances even for the current assets resulting into an improvement in the liquidity position of the company. Reserves and Surplus have also decreased from Rs. 3,30,000 to Rs. 2,22,0000 *i.e.* 32.73% which shows that the company has utilised reserves and surpluses for the payment of dividends to shareholders either in cash or by the issue of bonus shares.

In brief, from the above interpretation, it is clear that the overall financial position of the company is satisfactory.

Comparative Income Statement

The income statement shows the results of the operations of a business concern. The comparative income statement gives an idea of the progress of a business over a period of time. The changes in absolute data in money values and percentage will be determined to examine the profitability of the business. Income statêment has four columns. First two columns show figures of various items for two years. Third and fourth columns are used to show increase or decrease in figures in absolute amounts and percentage respectively.

Guidelines for Interpretation of Income Statement

The analysis and interpretation of Income Statement will involve the following steps.

The increase or decrease in sales should be compared with the increase or decrease in cost of goods sold. An increase in sales may not increase in profit always. The profitability will improve if increase in sales is more than the increase in cost of goods sold. In the first stage, the amount of gross profit will be studied. Then, there will be an analysis of operational profits. The operating expenses such as office and administrative expenses, selling expenses, distribution expenses will be deducted from gross profits to find out operating profits. An increase in operating profit will result from the increase in sales and control of operating expension. A decrease in operating profit may be due to an increase in operating expenses or decrease in sales. The change in individual expenses should also be studied.

The increase or decrease in net profit gives an idea about the overall profitability of the concern. Non-operating expenses such on payment of tax, losses from sale of assets, writing off deferred expenses, interest paid etc. decrease the figue of operating profits. When all non-operating expenses will be deducted from operational profit, the result will be net profit. An increase in net profit will give us an idea about the progress of the concern. Finally, an opinion should be formed about profitability of the concerns. and it should be stated whether the overall profitability is good or not.

Example 2

The income statements of a concern are given for the year ending, on 31st Dec., 2005 and 2006. Rearrange the figures in a comparative form and study the profitability position of the concern.

	2005	*2006*
	Rs ('000)	Rs. ('000)
Net Sales	785	900
Cost of goods sold	450	500

Operating Expenses :		
General and administrative expenses	70	72
Selling Expenses	80	90
Non-operating expenses :		
Interest paid	25	30
Income tax	70	80

Solution

Comparative Income Statements
for the year ending 31st Dec., 2005 and 2006

	31st December		Increase/	Increase
Decrease	2005 Rs ('000)	2006 Rs ('000)	Decrease Rs ('000)	Decrease (Percentage)
Net Sales	785	900	(+) 115	+ 14.65
Less: Cost of Goods Sold	450	500	+ 50	+ 11.0
Gross profit	335	400	+ 65	+ 19.40
Operating Expenses :				
General & Administrative Expenses	70	72	+ 2	+ 2.8
Selling Expenses	80	90	+ 10	+ 12.5
Total operating expenses	150	162	+ 12	+ 8.0
Operating profit	185	238	+ 53	+ 28.65
Less: Other deductions :				
Interest paid	25	30	+ 5	+ 20
Net profit before tax	160	208	+ 48	+ 30.0
Less: Income tax	70	80	+ 10	+ 14.3
Net profit after tax	90	128	+ 38	+ 42.22

Interpretation

The comparative income statement given above reveals that there has been an increase in net sales of 14.65%. While the Cost of Goods Sold has increased nearly by 11% thereby resulting in an increase in the gross profit of 19.4%. Although the operating expenses have increased by 8%, the increase in gross profit is sufficient to compensate for the increase in operating expenses and hence there has been an overall increase in operational profit amounting to Rs. 53,000 *i.e.* 28.65% in spite of an increase in financial expenses of Rs. 5,000 for interest and Rs 10,000 for income-tax. There is an increase in net profits after tax amounting to Rs. 38,000 *i.e.* 42.22%. It may be concluded that there is a satisfactory progress in the company and the overall profitability of the company is good.

Example 3

Following are the Income Statement and Balance Sheet of XYZ & Co. for the years 2005 and 2006. Prepare the comparative income statement and comparative balance sheet for these two years.

Income Statements
for the year 2005 and 2006

(Rs.)

	2005 Rs.	2006 Rs.		2005 Rs.	2006 Rs.
To General Expenses	10,000	10,000	By Net Sales	4,00,000	5,00,000
To Cost of good sold	3,00,000	3,75,000			
To Selling expenses	15,000	20,000			
To Net Profit	75,000	95,000			
	4,00,000	5,00,000		4,0\0,000	5,00,000

Balance Sheet
as on 31st Dec.,

Liabilities	2005 Rs.	2006 Rs.	*Assets*	2005 Rs.	2006 Rs.
Outstanding Expenses	50,000	75,000	Cash	50,000	70,000
Secured loans	50,000	75,000	Plant	1,50,000	1,35,000
Capital	3,50,000	3,50,000	Land	50,000	50,000
Creditors	1,00,000	1,37,500	Furniture	50,000	70,000
Reserves	1,00,000	1,22,500	Building	1,50,000	1,35,000
			Debtors	1,00,000	1,50,000
			Stores	1,00,000	1,50,000
	6,50,000	7,60,000		6,50,000	7,60,000

Solution

Comparative Income Statement
for the years ending 2005 and 2006

	2005 Rs.	2006 Rs.	Change in 2006 Rs.	% change in 2006
Net Sales	4,00,000	5,00,000	1,00,000	+ 25
Less: Cost of Goods Sold	3,00,000	3,75,000	75,000	+ 25
Gross profit (1)	1,00,000	1,25,000	25,000	+ 25
Less: General expenses	10,000	10,000	—	—
Selling expenses	15,000	20,000	5,000	+ 33.3
Total expenses (2)	25,000	30,000	5,000	+ 20
Net profit (1 – 2)	75,000	95,000	20,000	+ 26.7

Comparative Balance Sheet
as on 31st Dec.,

	2005 Rs.	2006 Rs.	Change in 2005 Rs.	% change in 2006
Furniture	50,000	70,000	20,000	+ 40
Building	1,50,000	1,35,000	−15,000	− 10
Land	50,000	50,000	—	—
Plant	1,50,000	1,35,000	−15,000	− 10
Total Fixed Assets (1)	4,00,000	3,90,000	−10,000	− 2.5
Stock	1,00,000	1,50,000	50,000	50
Debtors	1,00,000	1,50,000	50,000	50
Cash	50,000	70,000	20,000	40
Total Current Assets (2)	2,50,000	3,70,000	1,20,000	48
Creditors	1,00,000	1,37,500	37,500	37.5
O/S Expenses	50,000	75,000	25,000	50
Total liabilities (3)	1,50,000	2,12,500	62,500	41.7
Net working capital (2 – 3)	1,00,000	1,57,500	57,500	57.5
Total Assets (1 + 2)	6,50,000	7,60,0000	1,10,000	16.9
Capital	3,50,000	3,50,000	—	—
Reserves	1,00,000	1,22,500	22,500	22.5
Proprietor's Fund (4)	4,50,000	4,72,500	22,500	5
Secured Loans (5)	50,000	75,000	25,000	50
Capital employed (4 + 5)	5,00,000	5,47,500	47,500	9.5
Total Assets (1 + 2)	6,50,000	7,60,000	1,10,000	16.9
Capital + Total liabilities (3 + 4 + 5)	6,50,000	7,60,000	1,10,000	16.9

Interpretation

On the basis of comparative income statements it can be said that Gross profit for the year 2006 has increased by 25% over the profit for the year 2005. The Net sales during the same period has increased by 25% which was coupled with increase in the cost of goods sold which also increased by same 25%. This means that input/output ratio or the production efficiency level has been maintained during 2006.The same increase of 25% in net sales and the cost of goods sold has resulted in increase in gross profit by 25%. The increase in Net profit is more pronounced *i.e.* by 26.7%. The reason for a higher increase is Net profit is the comparatively less increase in total expenses (only 20%). The general expenses during 2005 and 2006 were same but the increase in selling expenses by $33^1/_3$% has resulted in increase of total expenses by 20%.

The comparative balance sheets also reveals many facts about the composition of assets and the financial structure of the firm. The fixed assets have decreased over the period by 2.5%, though this decrease has primarily resulted by the amount of depriciation @ 10% on Building and Plant. However, the current assets have increased by 48%, this increase of 48% is too much in view of increase in Net sales by 25% only. Moreover, the current liabilities have increased by 41.7%. The net working capital has increased by 57.5%. This clearly indicates that the working capital of the firm is not properly managed. Had the increase in current assets restricted to 25% or the increase in current liabilities was also achieved at 48% or so, then the situation would not have been so alarming. However, the decrease in fixed assets has been offset by increase in Net Working Capital and consequently the total assets have increased by 16.9%. The firm has not raised any capital during the period and the increase in proprietor's funds has resulted because of increase in retained profits by Rs. 22,500. The secured loans have also increased by 50%. The fund provided by the retained earnings and the secured loans seem to have been utilized in financing the current assets. This has, on one hand, increased the short term paying capacity of the firm and on the other hand, will affect the earnings capacity of the firm as the current assets are less or non-productive. The increase in total assets by 16.9% is matched with the increase in total liabilities (proprietor's fund plus the secured loans) by 16.9%.

So, the comparative financial statements (CFS) explains about the changes in different items of the financial statement. However, despite these revelation, the CFS fails to highlight the component changes in relation to total assets or total liabilities. The CFS does not throw light on the variations in each assets as a percentage of total assets for a particular period or changes in diferent liabilities in relation to total liabilities for that period etc. This drawback of CFS is taken care of by the common size statement.

Example 4

The Following is the P/L A/c of XYZ Ltd. for the years 2005, 2006. Prepare comparative income statement and comment on the profitability of the undertaking.

(Rs)

Particulars	*2005*	*2006*	*Particulars*	*2005*	*2006*
To Selling expenses	45,912	57,816	By Discount on purchases	2,125	1,896
To Income tax	21,519	40,195	By Others incomes Int. & dividends	1,898	1,310
To Loss on sale of fixed assets	627	175			
To Net profit	35,371	44,425	By Profit on sale of land	1,500	—
To Cost of good sold	2,31,625	2,41,950	By Sales	3,60,728	4,17,125
To Int. paid	2,137	1,750	Less: Returns	(5,794)	(6,952)
To Office expenses	23,266	27,068			
	3,60,457	4,13,379		3,60,457	4,13,379

XYZ Ltd.

Comparative Income Statement for the years ending 2005 & 2006

Particulars	*2005 (Rs.)*	*2006 (Rs.)*	*Increase (+) Decrease (–) Amount (Rs.)*	*Increase (+) Decrease (–) Percentage*
Sales	3,60,728	4,17,125	+ 56, 397	+ 15.63
Less: Sales returns	5,794	6,952	+ 1,158	+ 19.98
	3,54,934	4,10,173	+ 55,239	+ 15.56
Less: Cost of goods sold	2,31,625	2,41,950	+ 10,325	+ 4.46
Gross Profit	1,23,309	1,68,223	+ 44,914	+ 36.42
Operating Expenses				
Office Exp.	23,266	27,068	+ 3,802	+ 16.34
Selling Expenses	45,912	57,816	+ 11,904	+ 25.93
Total Operating Expenses	69,178	84,884	+ 15,706	+ 22.70
Operating Profit	54,131	83,339	+ 29,208	+ 53.96
Add: Other Incomes	5,523	3,206	– 2,317	– 41.95
	59,654	86,545	+26,891	+ 45.08
Less : Other expenses	2,764	1,925	– 839	– 30.35
Profit Before Tax	56,890	84,620	+ 27,730	+ 48.74
Less: Income Tax	21,519	40,195	+ 18,676	+ 86.79
Net Profit After Tax	35,371	44,425	+ 9,054	+ 25.60

2. Common Size Statement

The common size statements represents the relationship of different items of a financial statement with some common item by expressing each item as a percentage of the common items. The common-size statements, Balance sheet and Income statement, are shown in analylised percentages. The figures are shown as percentages of total assets, total liabilities and total sales. The total assets are taken 100 and different assets are expressed as a percentage of the total. Similarly, various liabilities are taken as part of total liabilities. These statements are also known an component percentage or 100 per cent statements because even individual item is stated on a percentage of the total 100. The common-size statement may be prepared in the following way :

— The total of assets or liabilities are taken by 100.

— The individual assets are expressed on a percentage of total assets *i.e.* 100 and different liabilities are calculated in relation to total liabilities. For examples, if total assets are Rs. 5,00,000 and inventory value is Rs. 1,00,000, then it will be 5% of total assets $\frac{1,00,000 \times 100}{5,00,000}$

Common Size Balance Sheet

In common size Balance sheet, each item of the Balance sheet is stated as a percentage of the total of the Balance sheet. Thus, a statement in which Balance sheet items are expressed as the ratio of each asset to total assets and one ratio of each liability is expressed as a ratio of total liabilities is called common size Balance sheet. For example following assets are shown in a common size Balance sheet.

	Rs.	Percentage
Cash in hand and at bank	5,000	5.00
Sundry Debtors	10,000	10.00
Stock	30,000	30.00
Land and Building	50,000	50.00
Plant and Machinery	15,000	15.00
Total Assets	1,00,000	100.00

The total figure of assets Rs 1,00,000 is taken as 100 and all other assets are expressed as a percentage of total assets. The relation of each assets to total assets is expressed in the statement. The relation of each liability to total liabilities is similarly expressed.

The common size Balance sheet can be used to compare companies of diferent sizes. The comparison of figures in diferent periods is not useful because total figures may be affected by a number of factors. It is not possible to establish standard norms for various assets. The trends of figures from year to year may not be studied and even they may not give proper results.

Example 5

The Balance sheets of Sukhvirs Ltd. and Devendra Ltd. are given as follows.

Balance Sheets
as on 31st December, 2005

Liabilities	*Sukhvirs Ltd.* *Rs*	*Devendra Ltd.* *Rs*
Preference Share Capital	1,20,000	1,60,000
Equity Share Capital	1,50,000	4,00,000
Reserves & Surplus	14,000	18,000
Long-Term Loans	1,15,000	1,30,000
Bills Payable	2,000	–

(Contd...)

Sundry Creditors	12,000	4,000
Outstanding Expenses	15,000	6,000
Proposed Dividend	10,000	90,000
	4,38,000	8,08,000
Land and Builings	80,000	1,23,000
Plant and Machinery	3,34,000	6,00,000
Temporary Investments	1,000	40,000
Inventories	10,000	25,000
Book Debts	4,000	8,000
Prepaid expenses	1,000	2,000
Cash and Bank Balances	8,000	10,000
	4,38,000	8,08,000

Compare the financial positiions of two companies with the help of common-size Balance sheet.

Solution

Common-Size Balance Sheets
as on 31st Dec., 2005

Assets	*Sukhvirs & Co.* *Amount Rs.*	*%*	*Devendra & Co.* *Amount Rs.*	*%*
Fixed Assets				
Land and Buildings	80,000	18.26	1,23,000	15.22
Plant and Machinery	3,34,000	76.26	6,00,000	74.62
Total Fixed Assets	4,14,000	94.52	7,23,000	89.48
Current Assets				
Temporary Investments	1,000	0.23	40,000	4.95
Inventories	10,000	2.28	25,000	3.08
Book Debt	4,000	0.91	8,000	0.99
Prepaid Expenses	1,000	0.23	2,000	0.25
Cash and bank balances	8,000	1.83	10,000	1.25
Total Current Assests	24,000	5.48	85,000	10.52
Total Assets	4,38,000	100.00	8,08,000	100.00
Share Capital & Reserves				
Preference Share Capital	1,20,000	27.39	1,60,000	19.80
Equity Share Capital	1,50,000	34.25	4,00,000	49.50
Reserves and Surplus	14,000	3.19	18,000	2.23
Total Capital & Reserves	2,84,000	64.83	5,78,000	71.53
Long-Term Loans	1,15,000	26.25	1,30,000	16.09
Current Liabilities				
Bills Payable	2,000	0.46	–	–
Sundry Creditors	12,000	2.74	4,000	0.49
Outstanding Exp	15,000	3.44	6,000	0.74
Proposed dividend	10,000	2.28	90,000	11.15
	39,000	8.92	1,00,000	12.38
Total Liabilities	4,38,000	100.00	8,08,000	100.00

Interpretation

Analysis of pattern of financing of both the companies shows that Devendra & Co. is more tranditionally financed as compared to Sukhvirs & Co. The former company has depended more on its own funds as is shown by Balance sheet. Out of total Investments, 71.53% of the funds are proprietors funds and outsiders funds account only for 28.47%. In Sukhvir & Co. proprietor's funds are 64.83%, while outsiders share is 35.17%. Which shows that this company has depended more upon outsiders funds. In the present day, generally companies depends more upon outsiders funds. In this context both the companies have good financial planning.

Both the companies are suffering from inadequaty of working capital. The percentage of current liabilities is more than the percentage of current assets in both the companies. The first company is suffering more from working capital position than the second company because current liabilities are more than current assets by 3.4% and this percentage is 1.86%, in the case of second Company.

The analysis indicates that Investements in fixed assets have been financed from working capital in the both the companies. In Sukhvir & Co. fixed assets account for 94.52% of total assets while long-term funds account for 91.08% of total funds. In Devendra & Co. fixed assets account for 89.48% where long term funds account for 87.62% of total funds. It indicates that both the companies have used working capital for purchasing fixed assets.

In brief, both the companies are facing working capital problem and immediate steps should be taken to issue more capital or raise long-term loans to improve working capital position.

Common-Size Income Statement

The Items in income statement can be shown as percentage of sales to show the relations of each item to sales. A significant relationship can be developed between items of Income Statement and volume of sales. The increase in sales will increase selling expenses and not administrative or financial expenses. In case the volume of sales increases to a considerable extent, administrative and financial expenses may go up. In case the sales are declining, the selling expenses should be reduced. Thus, in common-size Income statement, each item is stated an percentage of the net sales. The percentage for different items are computed by deviding the absolute amount of that item by the common base (*i.e.* the Balance Sheet total or the Net Sales as the case may be) and then multiplying by 100. The percentage so calculated can be easily comapared with the corresponding percentage in some other period.

Example 6

The following are the Income statements of a company for the year ending 31st Dec., 2005 and 2006.

	2005 (Rs. in '000)	2006 (Rs. in '000)
Sales	500	700
Miscellaneous Income	20	15
	520	715
Expenses		
Cost of Sales	325	510
Office Expenses	20	25
Selling Expenses	30	45
Interest	25	30
Total exp.	400	610
Net profit	120	105
	520	715

Solution

Common-Size Income Statement
for the year ending 31st Dec., 2005 and 2006

	2005		2006	
	Amount (in Rs.)	*%*	*Amount (in Rs.)*	*%*
Sales	500	100.00	700	100.00
Less : Cost of Sales	325	65.00	510	72.80
Gross profit	175	35.00	190	27.14
Operating Expenses :				
Office Expenses	20	4.00	25	3.58
Selling Expenses	30	6.00	45	6.42
Total Operating Expenses	50	10.00	70	10.00
Operating Profit	125	25.00	120	17.14
Miscellaneous Income	20	4.00	15	2.14
Total Income	145	29.00	135	19.28
Less : Non-Operating expenses	25	5.00	30	4.28
Net Profit	120	24.00	105	15.00

Interpretation

The sales and gross profit have increased in absolute figure in 2006 as compared to 2005 but the percentage of gross profit to sales has gone down in 2006. The Increase in cost of sales as a percentage of sales has brought the profitability from 35 to 27.14%. Operating expenses have remained the same in both the years but non-operating expenses have decreased on a percentage in 2006. There is a slight decrease in non-operating expenses in the latter year but it could not help to improve profits.

Net profit have decreased both is absolute figure and as a percentage in 2006 as compared to 2005. The overall profitability has decreased in 2006 and the reason is a rise in cost of sales. The company should take immediate steps to control its cost of sales otherwise the company will be in trouble.

3. Trend Analysis

The financial statements may be analysed by computing trend of series of information. This method evaluates the direction upwards or downwards and involves the computation of the percentage relationship that each statement item bears to the same item in base year. The information for a number of years is taken up and one year, generally the first year, is taken as a base year. The figures of the base year are taken as 100 and trend ratios for other years are calculated on the basis of base year. The analysts is able to see the trend figures, whether upward or downward. For example, if sales figures for the years 2000 to 2005 are to be studied, then sale of year 2000 will be taken as 100 and the percentage of sales for all other years will be calculated in relation to the base year *i.e.* 2000.

2000	100
2001	130
2002	120
2003	125
2004	135
2005	150

The trends of sales shows that sales have been more in all the year since 2000.

The sales have shown as upward trend except in the year 2002 when sales were less than the pervious year *i.e.* 2001. A study of trends shows that rate of increase in sales is less is the years 2004 and 2005. The increase in sales is 5% in 2003 as compared to 2002. Though the sales are more as compared to the base year but still the rate of increases has not been constant and requires a study by comparing these trends to other items like cost of production etc.

Procedure for Calculating Trends

— One year is taken as a base year. Generally, the first or the last is taken as base year.
— The figure of base year are taken as 100.
— Trend percentage are calculated in relation to base year.

Example 7

Calculate the trend percentages from the following figure of X Ltd. taking 2000 as the base year and interpret them.

(Rs. in lakhs)

Year	*Sales*	*Stock*	*Profit before Tax*
2000	1,881	709	321
2001	2,340	781	435
2002	2,655	816	458
2003	3,021	944	527
2004	3,768	1,154	672

Solution

Trend Percentage
(Base year 2000 = 100)

Year	*Sales*		*Stock*		*Profit before tax*	
	Amount Rs. in Lakhs	*Trend %age*	*Amount Rs. in Lakhs*	*Trend %age*	*Amount Rs*	*Trend %age*
2000	1,881	100	709	100	321	100
2001	2,340	124	781	110	435	136
2002	2,655	141	816	115	458	143
2003	3,021	161	944	133	527	164
2004	3,768	200	1,154	162	672	209

Interpretation

The sales have continuously increased in all the years up to 2004. The percentage in 2004 is 200 as compared to 100 on 2000. The increase in sales is quite satisfactory. The figure of stock have also increased from 2000 to 2004. The Increase in stock is more in 2003 and 2004 as compared to earlier years. Profit before tax has substantially increased. In five year period it has more than doubled. The comparative increase in profits is much higher in 2003 and 2004 as compared to 2002.

Thus, the growth of the firm is good and it has doubled its sales and profits in just five years time. The profits percentage have increased more than sales which shows that there is a proper control over cost of goods sold. The over all performance X Ltd. is satisfactory.

Example 8

From the following data relating to the XXX & Co. for the year 2003 to 2006, Calculate the trend percentages (Taking 2003 as base year).

(Rs.)

	2003	2004	2005	2006
Net Sales	2,00,000	1,90,000	2,40,000	2,60,000
Less: Cost of goods sold	1,20,000	1,17,800	1,39,200	1,45,600
Gross Profit	80,000	72,200	1,00,800	1,14,400
Less : Expenses	20,000	19,400	22,000	24,000
Net Profit	60,000	52,800	78,800	90,400

Solution

Trend Percentages

	2003	2004	2005	2006
Net Sales	100	95.0	120.0	130.0
Less: Cost of goods sold	100	98.2	115.8	121.3
Gross Profit	100	90.3	126.0	143.0
Less : Expenses	100	97.0	110.0	120.0
Net Profit	100	88.0	131.3	150.6

Interpretation

On the whole, the 2004 was a bad year but the recovery was made during 2005 with increase in volume as well as profits. The figures of 2004 when compared with 2003 reveal that the sales have reduced by 5%, but the cost of Goods sold and the expenses have decreased only by 1.8% and 3% respectively. This means.that a substantial portion of the cost of goods sold and expenses is fixed in nature. This resulted in decrease in Net Profit by 12%. The position was recovered in 2005 and not only the decline was arrested but the positive growth was visible both in 2005 and 2006. Again, the increase in net profit by 31.3%(2005) and 50.6%(2006) is much more than the increse in sales by 20% and 30% respectively. This again proves that a substantial portion of the cost of Goods sold and expeneses is of fixed nature.

So, the Trend Percentage Analysis (TPA) is an important tool of historical analysis. It can be of immense help in making a comparative analysis over a series of years. The TPA provides brevity and easy readability to several financial statements as the percentages figures disclose more than the absolute figures. However, some precautions must be taken while using the TPA as a technique of the financial statement analysis which are as follows :

(*i*) There should not be a significant and material changes in accounting policies over the years. This consistency is necessary to ensure meaningful comparatibility.

(*ii*) Proper care must be taken while selecting the base year. It must be a normal and a representative year. Generally the initial year is taken as base year, but intervening year can also be taken as the base year, if the initial year is not found to be normal year.

(*iii*) The trend percentages should be analyzed *via-a-vis* the absolute figure to avoid any misleading conclusions.

(*iv*) If possible, the figures for different years should be adjusted for variations in price level also. For example, increase in Net sales by 30% (from 100 in 2003 to 130 in 2006) over 3 years might have resulted primarily because of increase in selling price and not because of increase in volume.

Quite often, it may be difficult to interpret the increase or decrease in any item (in absolute terms or in percentages terms) as a desirable change or an undesirable change. For example, decrease in cash may be discouraging if it is going to affect the liquidity but may be encouraging if it has resulted out of better cash management. Similarly, increase in inventory may result because of decrease in sales or because of necessity to maintain a minimum level of stock. In such cases, therefore, the techniques of CFS, CSS and TPA may not be of much help. Ratio Analysis can be used as a technique of financial statement analysis to overcome drawbacks of comparative financial statements, common size statement and trend percentage analysis.

LIMITATIONS OF FINANCIAL STATEMENT ANALYSIS

Financial statement analysis in a powerful mechanism of determining financial strength and wearness of a firm. However, the analysis is based on the information available in the financial statements. Therefore, the financial statement analysis suffers from some limitations.

Some of the limitations of financial statement analysis are given below.

— Shareholders, investors etc. are more interested in knowing the likely prospects in the future. The financial statements are not of much help as information given in these statements does not reflect the future.

— Financial Statements are the outcomes of accounting concepts and conventions. However, some valuation like stock, treatment of deferred revenue expenditure, provision for depreciation etc. are based on personel judgement and therefore are not free from bias.

— The financial statement can be drawn up on the basis of different accounting policies, *e.g.* depreciation can be provided either on straight line basis or on written down value basis.

— Financial statements displays the position is monetary terms. This statement do not include a very important asset, namely human resources.

— It does not consider changes in price levels.

— As the financial statements are prepared on the basin of a going concern, it does not give exact position. Thus, accounting concepts and conventions cause a serious limitations to financial analysis.

— Analysis is only a means and not an end in itself. The analysts has to make interpretation and draw his own conclusions. Different people may interpret the same analysis in differently.

THEORY QUESTIONS

1. What do you mean by the term financial statements ?
2. Explain the term financial statement analysis.
3. What are the objectives of financial statement analysis ?
4. Explain the different types of financial statement analysis.
5. Discuss external and internal analysis of financial statement analysis.
6. Explain (i) Horizontal analysis (ii) Vertical Analysis.
7. What are the procedures of financial statement analysis ?
8. Explain the techniques of financial statement analysis.
9. Explain fully the following methods of financial statement analysis
   (i) Comparative statement
   (ii) Common-size statement
   (iii) Trend analysis
10. What is trend analysis ? What is its significance ?
11. How is trend analysis conducted ?
12. Explain the importance of common-size statement.
13. What are the benefits of comparative statement ?
14. Discuss the limitations of financial statement analysis.

PROBLEMS

1. The following are the Balance sheet of Devendra Ltd. for the year ending 31st Dec., 2005 and 2006.

Liabilities	*2005 Rs.*	*2006 Rs.*	*Assets*	*2005 Rs.*	*2006 Rs.*
P/L Ac	25,000	30,000	Fixed Assets Less		
Bank overdraft	60,000	60,000	Depreciation	4,40,000	5,50,000
Provision for taxation	30,000	35,000	Stock	50,000	60,000
Preposed Dividend	25,000	35,000	Debtors	3,00,000	3,25,000
Creditors	50,000	60,000	Cash at Bank	20,000	40,000
Reserves	30,000	40,000	Cash in hand	60,000	73,000
Preference Share Capital	3,00,000	3,50,000	Prepaid Expenses	20,000	22,000
Equity Share Capital	4,00,000	5,30,000	Bills Receivables	30,000	70,000
	9,20,000	11,40,000		9,20,000	11,40,000

Prepare a Comparative Balance Sheet of the company and study its financial position.

2. The Balance sheets of a company are given as under. Explain the significance of changes in assets and liabilities of these comparative Balancé sheets.

	31st March, 2005	*31st March, 2006*
Profit and Loss A/c	3,00,000	4,00,000
Outstanding Expenses	60,000	60,000
Accounts Payable	2,00,000	3,00,000
General Reserves	2,00,000	3,50,000
Preference Share Capital	2,00,000	3,00,000
Equity Share Capital	6,00,000	11,00,000
	15,60,000	25,10,000
Cash	60,000	1,10,000
Inventories	2,00,000	5,00,000
Receivables	3,00,000	5,00,000
Investment	4,00,000	2,00,000
Fixed Assets	6,00,000	12,00,000
	15,60,000	25,10,000

3. With the help of Company Balance Sheets, study the financial position of DKS Ltd. Delhi for the years 2005 and 2006.

Balance Sheets

for the years ending 31st Dec., 2005 and 2006 **(Rs. in '000)**

Liabilities	*2005*	*2006*	*Assests*	*2005*	*2006*
Customer Credit Balance	2,603	3,079	Fixed Assets		
Accruals (Instcrest on Securities)	795	337	*Less:* Dep.	10705	12032
Unclaimed Dividend	16	117	Investments	2947	3429
Provision for Proposed Dividend	3,113	2,420	Current Assets :		
Provision for Contingent Liability	85	91	Receivables	2217	2584
Provision for Gratuity	—	298	Advance Payment		
Provision for Taxation	6,012	5,578	of Tax	2818	1500
Sundry Creditors	37,122	24,734	Prepaid expenses	17957	13772
Loan and Advances	81,745	61,282	Stores spare parts		

(Contd...)

Profit and Loss A/c	316	199	and tools, etc.	3890	4042
Reserves	3,500	4,450	Stock in trade	62334	46769
Ordinary Share Capital	6,500	14,200	Sundry debtors	39700	37951
6½% Redeemable cum-pref. share capital	—	4,000	Cash and Bank Balance	2739	2206
6% Redeemable cum-pref. share capital	3,500	3,500			
	1,45,307	1,24,285		1,45,307	1,24,285

4. The following are the Income Statements of D.K.S. Ltd. Delhi, for the years 2005 and 2006. Prepare, a Comparative Income Statement and Comment on the profitability of company.

Income Statement

	2005 Rs.	*2006 Rs.*		*2005 Rs.*	*2006 Rs.*
To Opening Stock	95,000	2,10,000	By Closing Stock	3,00,000	3,25,000
To Purchases Less Returns	6,00,000	6,50,000	By Sales less Returns	11,49,000	13,49,000
To Wages	70,000	90,000	By Dividend Received	7,000	9,500
To Salaries	52,000	74,000	By Income from Investments	14,000	17,000
To Discount allowed	6,000	8,000			
To Int. paid	13,000	15,000			
To Selling Expenses	13,000	13,000			
To Depreciation	50,000	70,000			
To Rent, Rates and Insurance	45,000	50,000			
To Loss on Sale of Plant	—	8,000			
To Net Profit	5,26,000	5,12,500			
	14,70,000	17,00,500		14,70,000	17,00,500

5. The following are the Balance Sheets of D.K.S. & Company for the years 2005 and 2006. Comments on the financial position of the business with the help of comparative Balance sheets technique :

Balance Sheets

As on 31st Dec. 2005 and 2006

Liabilities	*2005 Rs.*	*2006 Rs.*
P & L A/c	3,00,000	3,25,000
Long-term Loans	4,00,000	12,00,000
Bills Payable	80,000	1,00,000
Outstanding Expenses	20,000	25,000
Preference Share Capital	5,00,000	9,00,000
Equity share Capital	6,00,000	12,00,000
General Reserves	4,00,000	5,00,000
	23,00,000	42,50,000
Assets	*Rs.*	*Rs.*
Fixed Assets :		
Gross Block	18,50,000	40,50,000
Less : Dep.	8,00,000	15,00,000
	10,50,000	25,50,000

(Contd...)

Investments	4,50,000	3,50,000
Current Assets :		
Bill Receivables	2,50,000	4,00,000
Inventories	4,50,000	6,50,000
Cash	1,00,000	3,00,000
	23,00,000	42,50,000

6. Following income statements of a business are given for the years ending 31st Dec., 2005 and 2006. Rearrange them in a comparative form and make comments.

Income Statements
for the years ending on 31st December

	2005 *Rs.*	*2006* *Rs.*		*2005* *Rs.*	*2006* *Rs.*
To Cost of goods sold	10,00,000	10,50,000	By Sales	18,25,000	20,00,000
To Admn. Expenses	93,250	95,980	By Int. and Dividend	17,500	16,200
To Selling Expenses	2,90,000	3,09,000	To Profit from Sale of Land	7,000	9,000
To Int. Paid	18,000	17,000			
To Loss on Sale on Machinery	3,500	1,800			
To Income-Tax	85,000	1,68,000			
To Net Profit	3,59,750	3,83,420			
	18,49,500	20,25,200		18,49,500	20,25,200

7. The comparative income statements of K.P. Singh Ltd. are given for the year 2005 and 2006. Analyse and interpret the significance of changes in these statements.

	31st Dec., 2005	*31st Dec., 2006*
Sales	10,82,400	8,27,650
Less: Discounts, Returns etc.	13,260	11,750
Net Sales	10,69,140	8,15,900
Less: Cost of goods sold	7,15,460	5,35,640
Gross Profit	3,53,680	2,80,260
Less: Admn. & General Expn.	80,700	63,215
Less: Selling Expn.	1,68,250	1,52,440
Net. Op. Profit.	1,04,730	64,605
Less: Ints. on loans	16,215	20,600
Net Profit before Taxes	88,515	44,005
Corporation Tax	22,100	6,000
Net Profit for the year	66,415	38,005

8. From the following information, interpret the result of operations of a manufacturing concern, using trend ratios:

(Rs. in Lakhs)

	2003	2004	2005	2006
Sales (Net)	10,000	9,000	12,000	15,000
Less: Cost of Goods Gold	6,000	6,000	7,000	8,000
Gross Profit	4,000	3,000	5,000	7,000
Less: Operating Exp.	1,000	1,000	1,500	2,000
Net Operating Profit	3,000	2,000	3,500	5,000
Less Taxes	1,500	1,000	1,750	2,500
Profit after tax	1,500	1,000	1,750	2,500

9. Convert the following Balance Sheets into Common-Size Balance Sheet and interpret the results.

Balance Sheets
as on 31st Dec., 2005 and 2006

Liabilities	*2005 Rs.*	*2006 Rs.*	*Assets*	*2005 Rs.*	*2006 Rs.*
Equity Share Capital	2,000	2,200	Current Assets :		
Capital Reserves	190	285	Debtors	1,450	1,390
General Reserves	1,500	1,450	Cash	1,200	1,015
Sinking Fund	190	200	Stock	4,200	3,500
Debenture	1,450	1,650	Investment	4,000	1,250
Sundry Creditors	2,200	2,150	Fixed Assets :		
Others	1,015	1,020	Building	8,000	14,000
			Land	1,980	3,150
			Furniture	7,700	10,500

10. Following are the Balance Sheets of DKSG Industries Ltd. for the year ending Dec., 31, 2005 and 2006.

Liabilities	*2005 Rs.*	*2006 Rs.*	*Assets*	*2005 Rs.*	*2006 Rs.*
Equity Share Capital	5,00,000	7,00,000	Land & Buildings	3,70,000	2,70,000
Debenture	1,50,000	2,00,000	Plant & Machinery	4,10,000	8,86,000
Reserve & Surplus	4,12,000	4,54,000	Furniture & Fixture	9,000	18,000
Long-term loans on Mortgage	2,50,000	3,55,000	Other Fixed Assets	1,20,000	1,30,000
Account Payable	3,55,000	2,17,000	Long-term Loans	1,46,000	1,59,000
Other Current liabilities	1,07,000	1,10,000	Cash in Hand & at Bank	2,18,000	1,10,000
			Receivables	1,09,000	90,000
			Inventory	2,60,000	2,30,000
			Prepared Expenses	3,000	3,000
			Other Current Assets	1,29,000	1,40,000
	17,74,000	20,36,000		17,74,000	20,36,000

Analyse the financial position of the company with the help of common-size Balance sheet.

11. The following figures relate to the activities of K.P.S. Ltd., New Delhi for the year ending 31st March, 2006

	Rs.
Sales	8,50,000
Purchases	4,75,000

Opening Stock	1,70,000
Closing Stock	1,80,000
Selling and Distributive Expenses :	
Salaries	1,18,000
Advertising	16,000
Commission on Sales	17,500
Discount	12,000
Non-operating Expenses :	
Interest	15,000
Loss on Sales of Assets	1,11,500
Non-operating Income :	
Profit on Sale of investment	19,500
Administrative Expenses :	
Salaries	1,37,000
Rent	1,12,000
Postage and Stationery	15,000
Provision for taxation	1,50,000

You should study the Income Statement of the concern with the help of common-size statements.

12. Common-Size Balance Sheet and Income Statement of two companies are given as follows. You are required to study the comparative final position of the companies.

Common-Size Balance Sheets
as on 31st Dec., 2006

(in thousands of Rs.)

Assets	*D.K.S.G. Co. Ltd.*		*K.P.S.Co. Ltd.*	
	Amount	*% of Total*	*Amount*	*% of Total*
	Rs.		Rs.	
Current Assets				
Cash	2,000	2.22	4,200	3.80
Sundry Debtors	20,000	22.22	1,90,000	17.28
Closing Stock	1,20,000	13.33	1,50,000	13.66
Prepared Exp.	1,500	1.67	2,500	2.27
Other Current Assets	2,500	2.78	3,500	3.18
Total Current Assets	38,000	42.22	44,200	40.19
Fixed Assets after Dep.	52,000	57.78	65,800	59.81
Total Assets	90,000	100.00	1,10,000	100.000
Liabilities and Capital				
Current Liabilities :				
Sundry Creditors	5,500	6.1	15,500	14.09
Other Current Liabilities	6,500	7.2	7,500	6.81
Total Current Liabilities	12,000	13.3	23,000	20.90
Fixed Liabilities	13,000	14.4	17,000	15.46
Total Liabilities	25,000	27.7	40,000	36.36
Capital	65,000	72.3	70,000	63.64
Total Liabilities and Capital	90,000	100.00	1,10,000	100.00

Common Size Income Statement
for the year e ıding 31st Dec., 2006

(*in thousands of Rs.*)

Assets	D.K.S.G. Co. Ltd.		K.P.S.Co. Ltd.	
	Amount	*% of Total*	*Amount*	*% of Total*
	Rs.		Rs.	
Sales less returns	1,07,000	100.00	1,32,000	100.00
Cost of good sold	62,000	57.94	85,000	64.39
Gross Profit	45,000	42.06	47,000	35.61
Office and Admn. Expenses	8,400	7.85	9,000	6.81
Selling & Distributive Exp.	25,000	23.36	19,000	14.40
Total Operating Expenses	33,400	31.21	28,000	21.21
Operating Profit	11,600	10.85	19,000	14.40
Other Incomes	2,000	1.87	3,000	2.27
	13,600	12.72	22,000	16.67
Non-operating Expenses	2,400	2.24	2,600	1.97
Income before Tax	11,200	10.84	19,400	14.70
Tax	3,700	3.46	6,500	4.92
Net income after tax	7,500	7.02	12,900	9.78

CHAPTER 3

Ratio Analysis

Ratio analysis is an important means of expressing the relationship between two numbers. A ratio can be computed from any pair of numbers. To be useful, a ratio must represent a meaningful relationship, but use of ratios cannot take the place of studying the underlying data.

Ratios are guides or shortcuts that are useful in evaluating the financial position and operations of a company and in comparing them to previous years or to other companies. The primary purpose of ratios is to point out areas for further investigation. They should be used in connection with a general understanding of the company and its environment.

Comparison of income statement and balance sheet numbers, in the form of ratios, can create difficulties due to the timing of the financial statements. Specifically, the profit and loss account covers the entire fiscal period, whereas the balance sheet is for a single point in time, the end of the period. Ideally then, to compare an income statement figure such as sales to a balance sheet figure such as receivable, we usually need a reasonable measure of average receivables for the year that the sales figure cover. However, these data are not available to the external analyst. In some cases, the analyst should take the next best approach, by using an average of beginning and ending balance sheet figures. This approach smooths out changes from beginning to end, but it does not eliminate problem due to seasonal and cyclical changes. It also does not reflect changes that occur unevenly throughout the year.

FOCUS OF RATIO ANALYSIS

Ratio Analysis involves evaluating different aspects of a business enterprise which are of great importance to different users such as management, investors, creditors, bankers, analysts, investment advisers etc. Generally, the following ratios analyses are made while making financial statement analysis :

I. Liquidity or Short-Term Solvency Analysis
IL Profitability Analysis
III. Capital Structure or Gearing Analysis
IV. Market Strength or Investor Analysis
V. Growth and Stability Analysis

I. LIQUIDITY OR SHORT-TERM SOLVENCY ANALYSIS (OR RATIOS)

Liquidity or short-term solvency analysis aims to determine the ability of a business to meet its financial obligations during the short-term and to maintain its short-term debt-paying ability. The aim of liquidity analysis is for a company to have adequate funds on hand to pay bills when they are due and to meet unexpected needs for cash. If a business enterprise cannot maintain its short-term debt paying ability, obviously it cannot maintain a long-term debt-paying ability or long-term solvency. Shareholders also will not be satisfied with such a state of affairs of the company. Even a business enterprise on a very profitable course will find itself bankrupt if it fails to meet its obligations to short-term creditors.

Liquidity analysis mainly focuses on balance sheet relationships that indicate the ability of a business to liquidate current and non-current liabilities. The ratios that evaluate liquidity relate to working capital or some part of it, because it is out of working capital that debts are paid as they mature. The comparisons and ratios related to evaluating liquidity or short term solvency are as follows:

1. Working Capital Position

The working capital of a business is the excess of current assets over current liabilities; this is computed by subtracting current liabilities from the current assets. The resulting working capital figure is taken as one of the primary indications of the short-term solvency of the business. The working capital formula is as follows :

Working Capital = Current assets – Current liabilities

The current working capital amount should be compared with past amounts to determine if working capital is reasonable. Caution must be exercised, because the relative size of the firm may be expanding or contracting. Further, the absolute amounts of working capital are difficult to use in comparing companies of different sizes or in comparing such amounts with industry figures.

2. Current Ratio

Current ratio is sometimes referred to as working capital ratio or banker's ratio. Current ratio expresses the relationship of current assets to current liabilities. It is widely used as a broad indicator of a company's liquidity and short-term debt-paying ability. The current ratio formula is as follows :

$$\text{Current ratio} = \frac{\text{Current assets}}{\text{Current liabilities}}$$

Current ratio is a more dependable indication of solvency than is working capital. For many years the guideline for the minimum current ratio has been 2:1. The assumption is even if the value of current assets declines by 50%, the firm can still pay its current liabilities. But now-a-days there has been a decline in the liquidity of many firms. It can be said that in some industries, a current ratio substantially below 2 is adequate, while some other industries may require a ratio much larger than 2. In general, the shorter the operating cycle, the lower the normal current ratio. The longer the operating cycle, the higher the normal current ratio. A higher current ratio enables a firm to pay off current obligations and thus provides adequate margin of safety to the creditors.

A company's current ratio can be compared with the company's past current ratios and with industry averages as well. Such comparisons can help in determining if the current ratio is high or low at this period in time. However, these comparisons do not indicate why the current ratio is high or low. Possible reasons for unsatisfactory current ratio can be found from an analysis of the individual accounts and items which make up the current assets and current liability.

Example

The following are the current assets and current liabilities in respect of two companies. Company A and Company B.

	Company A	*Company B*
Current assets	Rs. 4,50,000	Rs. 1,60,000
Current liabilities	Rs. 1,50,000	Rs. 80,000

The current ratio will be as follows :

Current ratio =

$$\text{Company A} = \frac{\text{Rs } 4{,}50{,}000}{\text{Rs } 1{,}50{,}000} = 3:1$$

$$\text{Company B} = \frac{\text{Rs } 1{,}60{,}000}{\text{Rs } 80{,}000} = 2:1$$

3. Acid Test Ratio or Quick Ratio

The current ratio is generally used to evaluate an enterprise's overall short-term solvency or liquidity position. The current ratio does not take into account the make-up or composition of current assets. For example, a rupee of cash or debtor is considered more readily available to meet obligations than a rupee of inventory. The quick ratio is designed to overcome this problem by relating the most liquid assets to current liabilities. Cash, marketable securities or short-term investments, receivables and prepaids are included within the meaning of most liquid assets; inventory is excluded. The acid test ratio is as follows :

$$\text{Acid Test} = \frac{\text{Current Assets} - \text{Inventory}}{\text{Current Liabilities}}$$

It may be preferable to have a better view of liquidity by excluding some other items in current assets that may not represent relatively current cash flow. Examples of items to be excluded are prepaids and miscellaneous items such as assets held for sale: This is considered a more conservative manner of computing the acid test ratio and the formula of acid test ratio in this situation will be as follows :

$$\text{Acid Test} = \frac{\text{Cash} + \text{Marketable Securities} + \text{Net Receivable and Debtors}}{\text{Current Liabilities}}$$

Inventory should be removed from current assets when computing the acid test ratio. Some of the reasons for this are that inventory may be slow moving or possibly obsolete and parts of the inventory may have been pledged to specific creditors. For example, a winery has inventory that requires considerable time for aging and therefore a considerable time before sale. To include the wine inventory in the computation would overstate the liquidity. There is also a valuation problem with inventory, because it is stated at a cost figure that is likely to be materially different from a fair current valuation. In summary inventory should be left out of the computation because of possible misleading liquidity indications.

The usual guideline for the acid test ratio is 1.00. However, some industries may find that a ratio less than 1.00 is adequate, while others need a ratio greater than 1.00. For example, a typical grocery store sells only for cash and therefore does not have receivables. This type of business can have an acid test substantially below the 1.00 guideline and still have adequate liquidity.

Example:

A firm has the following current assets and current liabilities :

Debtor	**Rs.**	**5,000**
Inventory	**Rs.**	**20,000**
Cash	**Rs.**	**5,000**
Total current assets	**Rs.**	**40,000**

Total current liabilities Rs. 20,000

The acid test or quick ratio is as follows :

$$\text{Quick ratio} = \frac{\text{Quick assets}}{\text{Current liabilities}}$$

= 0.5:1

4. Cash Ratio.

Liquidity of a firm can be viewed from an extremely conservative point of view and the short-term liquidity of a company may be measured through cash ratio.

The cash ratio relates cash and marketable securities to current liabilities. The cash ratio is computed as follows :

$$\text{Cash Ratio} = \frac{\text{Cash + Marketable Securities}}{\text{Current liabilities}}$$

Cash ratio is not given much importance unless a firm is in deep financial trouble. It is not considered pragmatic to expect a business enterprise to have enough cash and marketable securities to cover current liabilities. However, in the case of very slow-moving inventories and receivables and highly speculative companies, cash ratio is of great importance. A high cash ratio indicates that a business enterprise is not using its resource cash to best advantage. A low cash ratio reflects an immediate problem with paying bills.

5. Receivables Turnover

The ability of a company to collect for credit sales in a timely way affects the company licuidity. The relationship between credit sales and accounts receivables may be stated as the receivable turnover. Receivables or debtors turnover determines the liquidity of one item of current assets and finds out how faster debts are being collected. The formula for computing receivables turnover is as follows:

Receivable Turnover =

Receivables turnover shows how many times, on average, the receivables were turned into cash during the period. A high debtors turnover ratio indicates shorter time span between credit sales and cash collection. This ratio requires one balance sheet account and one profit and loss account item. In case, credit sales figure is not given, total sales figure can be used to compute receivables turnover.

Example:

A firm has opening and closing debtors of Rs. 40,000 and Rs. 75,000 respectively and credit sales of Rs. 3,45,000. The debtors turnover ratio is as follows:

$$\text{Debtors turnover ration} = \frac{\text{Credit Sales}}{\text{Average Debtors}}$$

$$= \frac{\text{Rs } 3,45,000}{\text{Rs } 57,500}$$

$$= \text{6 times per year}$$

$$\text{Debt Collection period} = \frac{\text{12 months}}{\text{Debtors turnover}}$$

$$=$$

$$= \text{2 months}$$

6. Inventory turnover

Inventory turnover measures the relative size of inventory and influences the amount of cash available to pay liabilities. A smaller, faster-moving inventory means that the company has less cash tied up in inventory. On the contrary, a build up in inventory means that a recession or some other factor is preventing sales from keeping pace with purchasing and production. Ideally, inventory should be maintained at an optimum level to support production and sales. Inventory turnover ratio is calculated by using the following formula:

Inventory turnover =

Average inventory is obtained using a simple average process by dividing the opening and closing inventory by the two. Cost of goods sold is obtained by deducting gross profit from sales.

Example:

A firm has opening and closing inventory of Rs. 56,000 and Rs. 44,000 respectively. The firm has sold goods for Rs. 5,00,000 at gross profit margin of 20%. The inventory turnover ratio is as follows:

$$\text{Inventory Turnover} = \frac{\text{Cost of goods sold}}{\text{Average inventory}}$$

$$= \frac{\text{Rs. } 5{,}00{,}000 - \text{Rs. } 1{,}00{,}000}{1/2\ (\text{Rs. } 56{,}000 - 44{,}000)}$$

$$= \frac{\text{Rs. } 4{,}00{,}000}{\text{Rs. } 50{,}000}$$

$$= 8 \text{ times per year}$$

II. PROFITABILITY ANALYSIS (OR RATIOS)

The long-term survival of a business enterprise depends on satisfactory income earned by it. An evaluation of a company's past profits may give the investors, creditors and others a better understanding for decision-making. The profitability position also affects the liquidity position which is vital to creditors as well. These ratios are :

1. Earnings margin

It is the ratio of net income to turnover, expressed as a precentage.

$$\text{Earnings Margin} = \frac{\text{Net income}}{\text{Turnover}} \times 100\%$$

Earnings margin is not the same as margin of profits. Margin of profits refers to the direct operating results only and is the amount before income-tax and before non-operating income and charges. In earnings margin, only the final net profit is used.

2. Return on Capital Employed

This ratio measures profitability in relation to the total capital employed in a business enterprise. The terms invested capital, capital funds and total capital may be used interchangeably. It is a useful ratio when comparing the overall performances of companies particularly where they have different proportions of debt in their capital structure.

Return on Capital = × 100

According to some analysts, short-term borrowings, such as bank loans, commercial paper, and deferred tax liability, should be included under capital. Current accrued payables which are not interest bearing should be excluded because their interest component is not observable.

3. Return on Equity

Return on equity is derived by taking net income and dividing it by the shareholders equity. This indicates the return which the management is realising from the shareholders' equity and shows how effectively ordinary shareholder funds are being utilised by the management. As long as it is above the current interest rates, a company is doing fairly well.

$$\text{Return on Equity} = \frac{\text{Profit after taxation} - \text{Preference Dividends}}{\text{Ordinary shareholders' funds}} \times 100\%$$

It is obvious that both the ratios — return on capital and return on equity — will be influenced when a company has raised new capital during the course of the year. That is, in other words, the ratios will be artificially low. Also, the ratios do not take into account the effect of financial leverage which undesirably tends to increase the variability of earnings for the ordinary shares. In fact, ordinary shareholders of a company having higher dose of borrowings expect large returns to compensate for the high levels of risk.

4. Asset turnover ratio

This ratio reveals the number of times the net tangible assets (*i.e.*, total assets less current liabilities less intangibles) are turned over during the year. Strictly speaking, average net tangible assets should be used in calculating this ratio. But, invariably net tangible assets at the end of the year is used.

Asset Turnover =

An improvement in asset turnover ratio as compared to the previous year indicates that the turnover of the company has improved. In cases where assets are not revalued or replaced, its magnitude will be decreasing over the years due to depreciation. Then obviously, the ratio will be higher as the turnover figures for the future will reflect an increasing trend.

III. CAPITAL STRUCTURE OR GEARING ANALYSIS (RATIOS)

Gearing ratio, *i.e.*, the relationship of long-term debt to total capital is considered the most important by many investors and financial analysts. Popularly know as debt-equity ratio, this ratio has utility to many including shareholders, creditors, business managers, suppliers and other user groups. Gearing ratios are used to indicate :

(i) The cushion of assets/profits available to holders of fixed income capital should assets/profits decline.

(ii) The gearing advantage of potentially higher assets/profits attributable to ordinary shareholders and the correspondingly higher risk which is incurred.

(iii) The scope for raising additional fixed-income capital at reasonable cost from the point of view of the company.

The debt-equity ratio is computed as follows :

$$\text{Debt-equity ratio} = \frac{\text{Loan capital + Preference share capital}}{\text{Net tangible assets}} \times 100$$

Net tangible assets (or total capital) is obtained by subtracting the intangible assets and the current assets from total assets. Loan capital plus preference capital constitute the amount of long-term debt. Alternatively, long-term debt can be derived by subtracting current liabilities from total liabilities.

Sometimes capital gearing is calculated in terms of debt to equity ratio and not total capital. Capital gearing ratios, calculated in these two manners, provide essentially the same information. It is desirable that the investors select a standard method and follow it consistently throughout. It is, said that as a rule of thumb, one should not opt for a company whose long-term debt exceeds two- thirds of its total capitalisation Debt equity ratio is very helpful in assessing a company — whether the company is marching steadily into or out of debt. In younger and aggressive companies, comparatively speaking the long-term debts may at times exceed the shareholders equity which means that a company will not be able to get out of the difficult situation easily. A company depending on large amounts of debt should manage and perform well to avoid any worse contingencies. Debt equity ratios should be analysed not for one but for many years to determine a trend. If it is found that equity component is continuously increasing than the long-term debt, there may not be any cause for concern.

Interest Coverage Ratio

Interest coverage ratio determines the debt servicing capacity of a business enterprise keeping in view fixed interest on long-term debt. The formula for this ratio is :

$$\text{Interest Coverage ratio} = \frac{\text{Earnings before Interest and taxes (EBIT)}}{\text{Interest}}$$

If a business enterprise is able to earn a return on the assets higher than the rate of interest on long-term debt, the enterprise makes an overall profit. However, if the enterprise runs the risk of not earning a return on assets equal to the interest cost of the long-term loan, the enterprise makes an overall loss. The interest coverage ratio measures the degree of protection creditors have from default on the payment of interest by the company.

IV. MARKET STRENGTH ANALYSIS OR INVESTOR ANALYSIS

The market strength analysis or investor analysis are especially important for investors while analysing information about a company. This analysis helps the investors to decide about a company as an investment opportunity at a point of time. These ratios are also known as stock market ratios, investment ratios or market test ratios. The ratios under this category are as follows :

1. Earnings per share

Earnings per share is derived by dividing the profit of a company by the total number of shares outstanding. Earnings here means the net profit, net income or the net earnings. This is the amount by which the total revenues exceed the total expenses for the year.

$$\text{Earnings After Tax} = \frac{\text{Earnings after tax} - \text{Preference dividends}}{\text{Number of ordinary shares}}$$

The net earnings figure is the amount which is completely free from any obligations and the company can plough it back into the company, pay to the ordinary shareholders as dividends or a combination of both. This amount is also known as the earnings available for ordinary shareholders.

Earnings per share can either be primary or diluted. Primary earnings per share is the earnings per share for the number of ordinary shares outstanding as on the beginning of the report period. Diluted earnings per share, on the other hand, is calculated after taking into account convertible debentures, bonds etc. (which have been converted into ordinary shares) during the year. It is computed in the same manner as primary earnings per share except that it assumes that all investments with the convertibility clause were converted at the beginning of the year. In case a company has bonds and debentures which are convertible into ordinary shares, it is always useful to compute fully diluted earnings per share (assuming full conversion) as well as earnings per share on a normal basis. This implies adding back the interest paid on the convertibles, recalculating the numerator and then dividing by the total number of ordinary shares on the assumption that conversion has taken place.

2. Dividend per share

The dividend per share can be net or gross. Net dividend per share is the dividend declared on a single ordinary share for the year, the net of basic rate tax.

$$\text{Net Dividend Per share} = \frac{\text{Ordinary dividends paid to ordinary shareholders}}{\text{Number of ordinary shares}}$$

Gross dividend per share is net dividend per share together with the associated tax credit.

$$\text{Gross Dividend per share} = \frac{\text{Net dividend per share}}{1 - \text{Basic rate of tax}}$$

Alternatively,

Gross Dividend Per share = Net Dividend Per share + Associated Tax Credit

3. Gross Dividend yield

The gross dividend yield is the gross dividend per share divided by the ordinary share price, expressed as percentage.

$$\text{Gross Dividend yield} = \frac{\text{Gross dividend per share}}{\text{Ordinary share price}} \times 100$$

The gross dividend yield indicates the current level of income from a share. Dividend yields are normally calculated using gross dividends rather than net dividends because it helps in better analysis and comparison with other types of investments. Also, investors pay income-tax at rates other than the basic rate. If the dividend yield is calculated on a net basis, the level of tax rate which has been deducted should be made clear.

Besides indicating the general level of the market, dividend yield reflects the market estimates of future dividend growth and risk. The higher the dividend growth expectations for a given share, the lower the current yield; the higher the market's estimate of risk, the greater the current yield.

4. Dividend Cover

Dividend cover denotes the number of times the dividend per share is covered by earnings per share

$$\text{Dividend Cover} = \frac{\text{Earnings per share}}{\text{Dividend per share}}$$

Dividend cover helps in assessing the prospects for dividend increases. Or, alternatively, the possibility of a dividend cut, should profits decline. For the purpose of dividend cover, full distribution earnings per share is normally taken into account. In other words, it is assumed that all profits are distributed as dividends. The gross dividends per share should be taken to ensure consistency in the resulting figure of dividend cover.

5. Payout ratio

Payout ratio measures the proportion of earnings per share which are paid out as dividends.

$$\text{Payout ratio} = \frac{\text{Net dividend per share}}{\text{Net earnings per share}} \times 100$$

The percentage of available earnings paid out as ordinary dividends has a vital influence on the market's behaviour towards those issues which are not in the growth category. For those companies which have paid dividends in the form of stock dividends and cash, only the cash dividend should be included in calculating the payout ratio. In the case of dividends paid out as stock dividends, the investor receives nothing that was not already owned and the company gives up nothing of value.

6. Dividends to Cashflow

Dividends to cash flow' is a more useful ratio than the payout ratio. It helps in understanding the past trend in this regard and is greatly helpful in estimating future dividends, than the conventional payout ratio.

$$\text{Dividend to Cash flow} = \frac{\text{Dividend paid on ordinary shares}}{\text{Net earning available for ordinary share}}$$

7. Price/Earnings (P/E) ratio

It is the market price of shares expressed as a multiple of earnings per share.

$$\text{Parice Earnings (P/E) Ratio} = \frac{\text{Price per ordinary share}}{\text{Earnings per share}}$$

Many investors consider P/E ratio as the best indicator of the ongoing performance of a company. This ratio along with the payout ratio indicates the market estimates of future dividend growth and risk. High growth shares have high P/E ratios as investors are willing to pay a greater multiple of current earnings to achieve a higher future growth. If high risk is found in a share, it reduces its market price and hence automatically reduces its P/E ratio. Payout ratios can have a positive influence on P/E ratio. High P/Es are not always bad. If investors are willing to pay a high price for a share in relation to its earnings, then they are doing so in the belief that the company has a bright future. That it will continue to strengthen and grow in future. Buying a share with a high P/E is described as buying a security with a high multiple. It should be understood that the common share dividends come out of the earnings per share. A drop in earnings could mean that a dividend is in trouble.

The elements which govern the P/E ratio are:

(i) Those factors that are fully reflected in the financial data (tangible factors)—Growth of earnings and sales in the past; profitability or rate of returns on invested capital; stability of past earnings; Dividend rate and record, and; financial strength or credit standing.

(ii) Those factors that are reflected to an indefinite extent in the data (intangible factors)—Quality of management; Nature and prospects of the industry, and competitive position and individual prospects of the company.

8. Net asset value per share

This ratio is also known as the book value per share. Net asset value per share is the value of net tangible assets attributable to one ordinary share. Net asset value is. simply put; the shareholders' equity. Net asset value or book value has nothing to do with the market value as shares usually sell in the stock market at several times its net asset or book value.

$$\text{Net Asset Value per share} = \frac{\text{Ordinary share capital} + \text{Reserves} - \text{Intangibles}}{\text{Number of ordinary shares outstanding at balance sheet date}}$$

Net asset value applies to ordinary shares only. However, it does not mean that investors can get that amount if the company is liquidated. The amounts attributed to the assets are only attempts at fair and systematic evaluation, not at guessing what these assets would bring if sold in the market place. Net asset or book value can be considered only as the theoretical value of ordinary shares if the assets of the company were liquidated at the amounts attributed to them on the balance sheet. It is not unusual for a share price to be very different from the net asset value per share, even where assets in the balance sheet have recently been revalued. In general, the market price of a share will be influenced by earnings and the dividend-paying potential. Share price will not be significantly influenced by the net asset value per share except where :

(a) The company is an investment vehicle for specific types of assets (*e.g.*, investment trusts, property companies).
(b) It seems probable that the company will be liquidated.
(c) A takeover bid of the company seems likely.

The net asset value per share figure is useful while comparing shares of one company with shares of other companies operating in the same industry. If it is found that a company is selling shares at a much lower ratio of market price to book value than other companies in the same industry, it indicates a good investment opportunity. When a share can be bought for less than its net asset value, it is an indication that share will have good value in the future. In case of mutual funds, net asset value ratio is important as it is determined at or near the price at which the mutual fund will buy and sell its shares. In the stock market, it is often found that a share is selling five times, seven times (and more) its book value. The lower the multiple, the greater will be probable value of the share.

9. Cash flow per share

Cash flow per share is a useful indicator of a company's general ability to leverage itself, to pay dividends, to covert accounting earnings into cash and to enjoy financial flexibility.

$$\text{Cash flow per share} = \frac{\text{Cash flow from operations after taxes}}{\text{Ordinary shares outstanding at balance sheet date}}$$

The amount of cash flow does not totally belong to ordinary shareholders, as the earnings belong; it is also meant to pay the expenses and claims prior to the payment of dividend.

V. GROWTH AND STABILITY ANALYSIS OR RATIOS

Growth and stability ratios measure the performance and financial strength of a company apart from market valuation. Stability ratios are useful in evaluating the quality of bonds, debentures, preference shares, etc. These ratios are calculated over time and relate to sales, total returns, and earnings per share. Such ratios are :

(1) $\text{Growth in sales} = \dfrac{\text{Sales in final period}}{\text{Sales in base period}}$

(2) $\text{Growth in Total Returns} = \dfrac{\text{Net earned for total capital in final period}}{\text{Net earned for total capital in base period}}$

(3) $\text{Growth in earnings} = \dfrac{\text{Earnings per share in final period}}{\text{Earnings per share in base period}}$

(4) Maximum decline in coverage of interest charges

$$= \frac{\text{Worst year (or lowest year)}}{\text{Average of previous three years}}$$

Normally interest charges may include any of the following combinations :

— Interest on short and long-term debts, including capital leases

— Interest on expenses plus an interest component for Operating leases

— Interest on expenses on short and long-term debts plus rentals on both capital and operating bases

— Total fixed charges, rentals and preferred dividends.

(5) Per cent decline in return on total capital

$$= \frac{\text{Worst year (or lowest year)}}{\text{Average of previous three years}}$$

(6) Per cent decline in return on ordinary capital

$$= \frac{\text{Worst year (or lowest year)}}{\text{Average of previous three years}}$$

(7) Percentage decline in earning per share

$$= \frac{\text{Worst year (or lowest year)}}{\text{Average of previous three years}}$$

LIMITATIONS OF FINANCIAL RATIOS

Financial statement analysis through ratios is useful because they highlight relationships between items in the financial statements. However, they have number of limitations which should be kept in mind while preparing or using them.

(1) Ratios are based on accounting figures given in the financial statements However, accounting figures are themselves subject to deficiencies, approxi-mations, diversity in practice or even manipulation to some extent. Therefore ratios are not very helpful in drawing reliable conclusions.

(2) Ratios have inherent problem of comparability. Companies otherwise similar may employ different accounting methods, which can cause problems in comparing certain key relationships. For example, inventory turnover can be different for a company using FIFO than for the other company using LIFO method of inventory valuation. Similarly the differences in accounting methods relating to depreciation, estimates of the life of asset, amortisation of intangibles and preliminary expenses, treatment of extraordinary items etc. can create the problem of comparability among the companies even in the same industry.

(3) Inflation may limit the utility of accounting ratios. Due to inflation, historical cost-based financial statements and accounting figures do not reflect current value figures, especially in the case of assets purchased at different dates by the different enterprises. Since financial statements are not adjusted in terms of inflation effect, accounting ratios calculated (using varying cost or prices) have distortions and become deceptive. Sometimes, gains (reflected through ratios) over time in sales, net income and other key figures disappear when the accounting data are adjusted for changes in price levels.

(4) Accounting ratios are not totally dependable and they must be used after giving due weightage to general economic conditions, industry situation, position of firms within the industry, mode of operations, size of firm, diversity of product which can make the business enterprises completely dissimilar and thus affect the computation of accounting ratios.

(5) The different methods of computation also influence the utility of accounting ratios. The different concepts used for determining numerator and denomi-nator in a particular accounting ratio will not help in drawing reliable conclu-sions even in identical situations.

Example 1

The working capital of ABC Ltd. has deteriorated in recent years and now stands as under

Current Assets	*Rs.*	*Current Liabilities*	*Rs.*
Inventory	5,60,000	Creditors	4,90,000
Debtors	3,50,000	Bank loan	2,10,000
Cash	70,000		
	9,80,000		7,00,000

(a) Compute the current and quick ratios.

(b) A further bank loan of Rs. 50,000 against debtors is under negotiation. Assuming the loan is received, calculate the revised current and quick ratios.

(c) There is also a negotiation going on for discounting the debtors of Rs. 3,50,000 for Rs. 3,15,000 to a collection agency for immediate cash. Also obsolete stocks worth Rs. 1;25,000 are being sold for Rs. 80,000. Of the cash to be realised by the two transactions, the bank loan is proposed to be reduced to Rs. 1,00,000. Calculate the current ratio after the transactions are put through.

Solution

(a) Current Ratio $= \dfrac{\text{Current assets}}{\text{Current liabilities}} = \dfrac{9{,}80{,}000}{7{,}00{,}000} = 1.4$

Quick Ratio $= \dfrac{\text{Liquid assets}}{\text{Current liabilities}} = \dfrac{4{,}20{,}000}{7{,}00{,}000} = 0.6$

(b) Revised current ratio $= \dfrac{10{,}30{,}000}{7{,}50{,}000} = 1.37$

Revised quick ratio $= \dfrac{4{,}70{,}000}{7{,}50{,}000} = 0.63$

(c) Financial position after the transactions:

Current Assets :	Rs.
Inventory	4,35,000
Debtors	—
Cash	3,55,000
	7,90,000
Current Liabilities :	
Creditors	4,90,000
Bank Loan	1,00,000
	5,90,000

New current ratio $= \dfrac{7{,}90{,}000}{5{,}90{,}000} = 1.34$

New quick ratio $= \dfrac{3{,}55{,}000}{5{,}90{,}000} = 0.6$

Cash balance = Rs. 70,000 + Rs. 3,15,000 + Rs. 80,000 – Rs. 1,10,000
= Rs. 3,55,000

Example 2

A company's stock turnover is 5 times. Stock at the end of the year is Rs. 4,000 more than the stock in the beginning of the year. Sales during the year (all credit) were Rs. 3,00,000. Rate of gross profit on sales is 20%. Current liabilities at the end of the year were Rs. 60,000. Quick ratio is 1 :1. Calculate the current assets at the end of the year. Show your calculations clearly.

Solution

Gross Profit = 3,00,000 × 20/100 = 60,000

Cost of Goods Sold = Sales – Gross Profit

= 3,00,000 – 60,000 = Rs. 2,40,000

Current Assets = Quick Assets + Closing Stock

$$\text{Quick Ratio} = \frac{\text{Quick Assets}}{\text{Current Liabilities}}$$

1:1 = Quick Ratio

Quick Assets = Current Liabilities = Rs. 60,000

$$\text{Stock Turnover Ratio} = \frac{\text{Cost of Goods Sold}}{\text{Average Stock}}$$

$$5 = \frac{2{,}40{,}000}{\text{Average stock}}$$

5 Average Stock = 2,40,000

$$\text{Average Stock} = \frac{2{,}40{,}000}{5} = \text{Rs. } 48{,}000$$

$$\text{Average Stock} = \frac{\text{Opening Stock} + \text{Closing Stock}}{2}$$

Let the Opening Stock = X

Closing Stock = X + 4,000

$$48{,}000 = \frac{X + X + 4{,}000}{2}$$

96,000 = 2 X + 4,000

2X = 96,000 – 4,000 = 92,000

$$\frac{92{,}000}{2}$$

X = 46,000 (Opening Stock)

Closing Stock = 46,000 + 4,000 = Rs. 50,000

Current Assets = Quick Assets + Closing Stock : 60,000 + 50,000 = 1,10,000

Example 3

X Ltd. has a current ratio of 4 : 1 and its liquid ratio is 3 : 1. If its inventory is Rs. 36,000, find out the value of total current assets; total quick assets and total current liabilities.

Solution

$$\text{Current Ratio} = \frac{\text{Current Assets (CA)}}{\text{Current Liabilities (CL)}} = \frac{4}{1}$$

or CA = 4 CL

or CA – 4 CL = 0 ...(*i*)

$$\text{Quick Ratio} = \frac{\text{Quick Assets}}{\text{Current Liabilities}} = \frac{3}{1}$$

or $$\frac{\text{Current Assets} - \text{Stock}}{\text{Current Liabilities}} = \frac{3}{1}$$

or CA – Stock = 3 CL

or CA – 36,000 = 3 CL

or CA – 3 CL = 36,000 .... (ii)

Now we have

CA – 4 CL = 0 .... (i)

CA – 3 CL = 36,000 .... (ii)

Subtracting (ii) from (i) we get,

CL = 36,000

CA = 36,000 × 4 = Rs. 1,44,000

Quick Assets = Current Assets - Stock

= 1,44,000 – 36,000 = Rs. 1,08,000

Example 4

Calculate the Debtors Turnover Ratio from the following :

Total Sales — Rs. 2,00,000; Cash Sales — Rs. 40,000; Debtors at the beginning of the year – Rs. 20,000; Debtors at the end of the year – Rs. 60,000.

Solution

$$\text{Debtors Turnover Ratio} = \frac{\text{Net Credit Sales}}{\text{Average Debtors}}$$

Net Credit Sales = Total sales – Cash sales = 2,00,000 – 40,000 = Rs. 1,60,000

$$\text{Average Debtors} = \frac{\text{Debtors in the beginning} + \text{Debtors at the end}}{2}$$

$$= \frac{20{,}000 + 60{,}000}{2} = \frac{80{,}000}{2} = \text{Rs. } 40{,}000$$

$$\text{Debtors turnover Ratio} = \frac{1{,}60{,}000}{40{,}000} = 4 \text{ Times}$$

Example 5

A factory engaged in an industry which is capital intensive has been in operation for five years. The capital employed is Rs. 170 lakhs out of which Rs. 100 lakhs represent equity capital and reserves, Rs. 50 lakhs long-term borrowings on debentures and Rs. 20 lakhs cash credit from banks. The working capital of the company Rs. 85 lakhs is made up of stocks: Rs. 30 lakhs; stores: Rs. 14 lakhs; debtors: Rs. 35 lakhs; and advances and deposits : Rs. 6 lakhs. Annual sale is Rs. 80 lakhs.

Calculate five financial ratios from the above for use of the management.

Solution

The Balance sheet of the company from the data given is as follows :

Balance sheet

(Rs. in lakhs)

Liabilities	*Amount*	*Assets*	*Amount*
Share Capital and Reserves	100	Fixed Assets *(balancing figure)*	85
Debentures	50	Current Assets:	
Cash Credit from Bank	20	Stock	30
		Stores	14
		Debtors	35
		Advances and Deposits	6
	170		170

The following five ratios are calculated which can be used by the management:

Current Ratio $= \dfrac{\text{Current Assets}}{\text{Current Liabilities}} = \dfrac{85}{20} = 4.25 : 1$

Liquid Asset Ratio $= \dfrac{\text{Liquid Assets}}{\text{Current Liabilities}} = \dfrac{41}{20} = 2.05 : 1$

Debt-equity Ratio $= \dfrac{\text{Outsiders Funds}}{\text{Shareholders' Fund}} = \dfrac{50}{100} = 0.5 : 1$

Proprietary Ratio $= \dfrac{\text{Shareholders' Fund}}{\text{Total Assets}} = \dfrac{100}{170} = 0.59 : 1$

Fixed Assets Ratio $= \dfrac{\text{Fixed Assets}}{\text{Long-term Funds}} = \dfrac{85}{150} = 0.57 : 1$

Example 6

A company has made plans for the next year. It is estimated that the company will employ total assets of Rs. 8,00,000, 50% of the assets being financed by borrowed capital at an interest rate of 16% per year. The direct costs for the year are estimated at Rs. 4,80,000 and all other operating expenses are estimated at Rs. 80,000. The goods will be sold to customers at 150% of .the direct costs. Income-tax rate is assumed to be 50%.

You are required to calculate— Net Profit margin; Return on-assets; Assets turnover, and Return on owner's equity.

Solution

Calculation of Profit after Tax (PAT) :

Sales (150% of Rs. 4,80,000)	7,20,000
Less: Direct Costs	4,80,000
Gross Profit	2,40,000
Less: Operating Expenses	80,000
Earnings before Interest and Tax (EBIT)	1,60,000
Less: Interest (16% on Rs. 4,00,000)	64,000
Profit before Tax (PBT)	96,000
Less: Tax @ 50%	48,000
Profit after lax (PAT)	48,000

The necessary computations are as follows :

Net Profit Margin	$= \frac{\text{PAT}}{\text{Sales}} \times 100$	$= \frac{48,000}{7,20,000} \times 100 = 6.7\%$
Return on assets	$= \frac{\text{PAT}}{\text{Total Assets}} \times 100$	$= \frac{48,000}{8,00,000} \times 100 = 6\%$
Assets Turnover	$= \frac{\text{Sales}}{\text{Total Assets}}$	$= \frac{7,20,000}{8,00,000} = 0.9 \text{ times}$
Return on owner's equity	$= \frac{\text{PAT}}{\text{Equity}} \times 100$	$= \frac{48,000}{4,00,000} \times 100 = 12\%$

Example 7

Calculate the following for the years 2000 and 2001 using figures given below.

Return on Capital employed; Current Ratio; Debt/Equity Ratio; Fixed Assets Turnover Ratio; Inventory Turnover Ratio; Earnings Per Share; and Dividend Cover.

Comparative Balance Sheet

(*Rs. in lakhs*)

Liabilities	*1999*	*2000*	*2001*	*Assets*	*7999*	*2000*	*2001*
Share Capital:				Fixed Assets:			
Shares of Rs. 10 each	800	1,000	1.000	Gross block	2,800	3,000	4,000
Reserves and Surplus	700	800	1,000	Less: Depreciation	920	1,400	2,000
Secured Term Loans	800	2.000	2.400		1,880	1,600	2,000
Cash Credits from banks	800	1,000	1,500	Stock	1,520	2,400	2,800
Sundry Creditors	1,200	900	1,100	Debtors	480	500	900
				Other Current Assets	420	1.200	1,300
					2,420	4,100	5,000
	4,300	5,700	7,000		4,300	5,700	7,000

(Extracts) Profit and Loss Account

(*Rs. in lakhs*)

Particulars	***2000***	***2001***
Sales	4,800	7,200
Profit before depreciation and interest on term loans	1,500	2.400
Depreciation	480	600
Interest on term loans	420	600
Tax	300	600
Dividends	100	150

Solution **Calculation of Average Capital Employed**

(Rs. in lakhs)

	1999		2000		2001	
Total assets		4,300		5,700		7,000
Less : Current liabilities :						
Cash credit from banks	800		1,000		1,500	
Sundry creditors	1,200	2,000	900	1,900	1,100	2,600
		2,300		3,800		4,400
Average capital employed				(2,300 + 3,800) ÷ 2 = 3,050		(3,800 + 4,400) ÷ 2 = 4,100
Calculation of Cost of goods sold :						
Sales				4,800		7,200
Less : Profit before depreciation, and interest on term loans				1.500		2.400
				3,300		4,800

The ratio for 2000 and 2001 are as follows:

	2000	2001
Return on capital employed :		
$\frac{\text{Profit before Interest and tax}}{\text{Average capital employed}} \times 100$	$\frac{1,020}{3,050} \times 100 = 33.44\%$	$\frac{1,800}{4,100} \times 100 = 43.90\%$
Current ratio :		
$\frac{\text{Current assets}}{\text{Current liabilities}}$	$\frac{4,100}{1,900} = 2.16$	$\frac{5,000}{2,600} = 1.92$
Debt equity ratio :		
$\frac{\text{Debt}}{\text{Equity}}$	$\frac{2,000}{1,800} = 1.11$	$\frac{2,400}{2,000} = 1.20$
Fixed assets turnover ratio :		
$\frac{\text{Sales}}{\text{Average fixed assets (Net)}}$	$\frac{4,800}{1,740} = 2.76$ times	$\frac{7,200}{1,800} = 4.00$ times
Inventory turnover ratio :		
$\frac{\text{Cost of goods sold}}{\text{Average inventory}}$	$\frac{3,300}{1,960} = 1.68$ times	$\frac{4,800}{2,600} = 1.85$ times
Earning per share :		
$\frac{\text{Profits available for equity shareholders}}{\text{Number of equity shareholders}}$	$\frac{300}{100} =$ Rs 3	$\frac{600}{100} =$ Rs 6
Dividend cover :		
$\frac{\text{Profits available for equity shareholders}}{\text{Dividend for equity shareholders}}$	$\frac{300}{100} = 3$ times	$\frac{600}{150} = 4$ times

Gross Profit Ratio = 36%

Cost of Goods Sold Ratio = (100 – 36)% = 64%

∴ Sales = 1,92,000 × 100/64 = Rs. 3,00,000

Net Profit after Tax	= 12% of Sales = Rs. 36,000	
Tax Rate	= 40%	
Profit before Tax	= 36,000 × 100/60 = Rs. 60,000	
Tax	= 60,000 – 36,000 = Rs. 24,000	

Trading and Profit and Loss Account

Dr			Cr
To Opening Stock	9,200	By Sales	3,00,000
To Purchases	1,92,800	By Closing Stock	10,000
To Gross Profit c/d	1,08,000		
	3,10,000		3,10,000
To Indirect Expenses (balancing figure)	48,000	By Gross Profit b/d	1,08,000
To Provision for Tax	24,000		
To Net Profit	36,000		
	1,08,000		1,08,000

Example 8

From the following informations, calculate (i) Current ratio and (ii) Net profit ratio :

	Rs.
Net sales	2,80,000
Gross profit	20,000
Salaries and other expenses	8,000
Bills receivable	4,000
Debtors	16,000
Cash	12,000
Creditors	20,800
Bills payable	20,800
Debentures	5,00,000
Long-term loans	1,00,000
Total sales	3,00,000
Sales returns	20,000
Buildings	10,00,000

Solution

(i) Current Ratio $= \dfrac{\text{Current Assets}}{\text{Current Liabilities}}$

Current Assets = Bills Receivable + Debtors + Cash

= Rs. 4,000 + Rs. 16,000 + Rs. 12,000 = Rs. 32,000

Current Liabilities = Creditors + Bills Payable

= Rs. 20,800 + Rs. 20,800 = Rs. 41,600

Current Ratio $= \dfrac{\text{Rs. } 32{,}000}{\text{Rs. } 41{,}600} = 10 : 13$ or $0.77 : 1$ or 77%

(ii) Net Profit Ratio $= \dfrac{\text{Net Profit}}{\text{Net Sales}} \times 100$

Net Profit = Gross Profit – Salaries and Other Expenses

= Rs. 20,000 – Rs. 8,000 = Rs. 12,000

Net Sales = Rs. 2,80,000 (given)

Net Profit Ratio $= \dfrac{\text{Rs. } 12{,}000}{\text{Rs. } 2{,}80{,}000} \times 100 = 4.29\%$

Example 9

A company sells its products on cash as well as credit (though not deferred instalment system); the following relevant information has been extracted from, its books:

	Rs.		Rs.
Opening Stock	1,00,000	Sales (Credit)	5,50,000
Total Gross Sales	1,00,000	Bill Receivable as on	
Cash Sales	20,000	31 December,	2,000
Sales Returns	7,000	Provision for Doubtful debts	
Total Debtors for Sales as on Dec 31	9,000	as on December 31,	1,000
		Total Creditors as on	
		December 31,	10,000

Calculate the average collection period.
Note : Total days in a year may be taken as 365.

Solution

Debtors's Turnover Ratio = Net Credit Sales/Average Debtors + Average Bills Receivable
Net Credit Sales = Rs. 1,00,000 – Rs. 27,000 (20,000 + 7,000) = Rs. 73,000
Average Debtors + Average Bills Receivable = Rs. 9,000 + Rs. 2,000 = Rs. 11,000
Debtors Turnover Ratio : Rs. 73,000/Rs. 11,000 = 6.64 Times
Average Collection Period = 365 Days/Debtors' Turnover
= 365 / 6.64 = 55 days

Example 10

M/s Alpha Manufacturing Company has drawn up the following profit and loss account for the year ended 31 March, 2007

	Rs.		Rs.
Opening Stock	26,000	Sales	1,60,000
Purchases	80,000	Stock	38,000
Wages	24,000		
Manufacturing Expenses	16,000		
Gross Profit	52,000		
	1,98,000		1,98,000
Selling and Distribution Expenses	4,000	Gross Profit	52,000
Administrative Expenses	22,800	Compensation for	
General Expenses	1,200	acquisition of land	4,800
Value of furniture lost by fire	800		
Net Profit	28,000		
	56,800		56,800

Required : (A) Operating Ratio (B) Ratio of Operating Net Profit to Net Sales.

Solution

(A) **Operating Ratio** = Cost of Goods Sold + Operating Expenses/Sales

	Rs.
(i) Cost of Goods Sold	
Opening Stock	26,000
Add : Purchases	80,000
Wages	24,000

Manufacturing expenses	16,000
	1,46,000
Less : Closing Stock	38,000
	1,08,000

(ii) Operating Expenses

Selling and Distribution Expenses	4,000
Administrative Expenses	22,800
General Expenses	1,200
	28,000

Operating Ratio = 1,08,000 + 28,000/1,60,000 × 100 = 85%

(B) **Operating Net Profit to Net Sales = Operating Net Profil/Sales × 100**

Operating Net Profit	Rs.
Net Profit	28,000
Add: Non-operating expenses	800
	28,800
Less : Non-operating income	4,800
	24,000

= Rs. 24,000/Rs. 1,60,000 × 100 = 15%

Example 11

Following is the Balance Sheet of Samson Project Limited on 31 March, 2006

Liabilities	*Rs.*	*Assets*	*Rs.*
Equity Share Capital	20,000	Fixed Assets	40,000
Capital Reserve	4,000	Stock	6,000
General Reserve (opening balance)	2,000	Debtors	6,000
Profit and Loss Account	6,000	Cash on hand	6,000
8% Loan on Mortgage	16,000	Cash at bank	2,000
Trade Creditors	8,000		
Bank Overdraft	2,000		
Provision for taxation	2,000		
	60,000		60,000

Calculate and comment upon the following ratios : (i) Current Ratio; (ii) Liquid Ratio; (iii) Proprietary Ratio; (iv) Return on Total Resources; (v) Return on Proprietors' Fund.

Solution

(i) *Current Ratio* = Current Assets/Current Liabilities
= Debtors + Cash on hand + Cash at Bank + Stock/Creditors + Bank Overdraft + Provision for Taxation = Rs. 20,000/Rs. 12,000 = 1.67 :1

(ii) *Liquid Ratio* = Quick Assets/Quick Liabilities
= Debtors + Cash in hand + Cash at Bank/Creditors + Provision for taxation
Note : Bank Overdraft is presumed to be paid after certain period
= Rs. 14,000/Rs. 10,000 = 1.4 : 1

(iii) *Proprietary Ratio* = Proprietors's Equity/Total Assets × 100
Equity Share Capital + Reserves/Total Assets × 100
= Rs. 32,000/ Rs.60,000 × 100 = 53.33%

(iv) Return on Total Resources = Net Profit/ Total Resources × 100
= Rs. 6,000/ Rs. 60,000 × 100 = 10%

(v) Return on Proprietors's Funds = Net Profit/Shareholders's Equity × 100
= Rs. 6,000/ Rs. 32,000 × 100 = 18.75%

Comments : The current ratio is below the required rule of thumb 2 :1, while the liquid ratio is quite satisfactory. The proprietary ratio indicates that more than 50% of the assets are financed by owners's funds which are sufficient to ensure the safety of the mortgage loan. In the absence of standard ratios, it is difficult to comment on the return on total resources and proprietors's funds.

Example 12

Working capital of a company is Rs. 1,35,000 and current ratio is 2.5. Liquid ratio is 1.5 (Quick Assets to Quick liabilities) and the proprietary ratio 0.75. Bank Overdraft is Rs. 30,000. There are no long-term loans and fictitious assets. Reserves and surplus amount to Rs. 90,000 and the gearing ratio (Equity Capital/ Preference Capital) is 2. (*C.A. Modified*)

From the above draw the Statement of Proprietary Fund.

Solution

Working capital = Current assets – Current liabilities
= 2.5 x – x = 1.5 x = Rs. 1,35,000

Current liabilities (x) $= \dfrac{1,35,000}{1.5}$ = Rs. 90,000

Current assets = 90,000 × 2.5 = Rs. 2,25,000

Bank overdraft = Rs. 30,000

Quick liabilities = 90,000 – 30,000
= Rs. 60,000

Liquid ratio = 1.5

Quick assets = 60,000 × 1.5 = Rs. 90,000

Stock = Current assets – Quick assets
= 2,25,000 – 90,000 = Rs. 1,35.000

Let, fixed assets = Z

Total assets = Fixed assets + Current assets
= Z + 2,25,000

Proprietary Ratio = Proprietors' Fund/Total Assets

Proprietor's fund = .75 (Z + 2,25,000) – I

Proprietor's fund = Total Liabilities – Current liabilities
= Total Assets – Current Liabilities
= Z + 2,25,000 – 90,000 – II

From I & II

x + 2,25,000 – 90,000= .75 (z + 2,25,000)

z = Rs. 1,35,000

Fixed assets, *i.e.* Net Block = 1,35,000

Proprietors fund = .75(1,35,000+2,25,000)
= .75(3,60,000)
= Rs. 2,70,000

Proprietors funds = Equity Share Capital + Preference Share Capital + Reserves and Surplus
= Rs. 2,70,000

Equity Share Capital + Preference Share Capital

$$= 2,70,000 - \text{Reserves and surplus}$$
$$= 2,70,000 - 90,000 = \text{Rs. } 1,80,000$$

Equity Share Capital $= 1,80,000 \times \frac{2}{3} = \text{Rs. } 1,20,000$

$$= 1,80,000 \times \frac{1}{3} = \text{Rs. } 60,000$$

Statement of Proprietary Funds

			Rs.
Fixed Assets			1,35,000
Current Assets:			
Stock		1,35,000	
Quick Assets		90,000	
		2,25,000	
Less: Current Liabilities			
Bank Overdraft	30,000		
Other Current liabilities	60,000	90,000	
Working Capital			1,35,000
Proprietors' Funds			2,70,000
Represented by:			
Equity Share Capital			1,20,000
Preference Share Capital			60,000
Reserves and Surplus			90,000
			2,70,000

Example 13

From the following annual accounts of New Horizon Limited you are required to calculate the following ratios and comment on the results, indicating what other information you require.

(i) Gross profit percentage
(ii) Net profit percentage
(iii) Return on total assets
(iv) Quick assets ratio
(v) Debtors collection period
(vi) Stock turnover
(vii) Fixed assets turnover
(viii) Return on shareholders funds
(ix) Current ratio
(x) Debt ratio

Balance Sheet at 31st December, 2002

	(Rs. '000)
Share capital	450
Retained profits	240
	690

12% Debentures	700
Trade creditors	620
Proposed dividend	45
	2,055
Fixed assets net of depreciation	875
Stocks	310
Debtors	770
Bank balance	100
	2,055

Extracts from year's Profit and Loss Account

	(Rs.)
Sales for the year	31,00,000
Gross profoit	17,25,000
Expenses	8,05,000
Depreciation	2,50,000

Solution

(i) Gross profit percentage $= \frac{1725}{3100} \times 100\% = 55.6\%$

(ii) Net profit percentage $= \frac{670}{3100} \times 100\% = 21.6\%$

(iii) Return on total assets $= \frac{670}{2055} \times 100\% = 32.6\%$

(iv) Quick ratio $= \frac{870}{665} = 1.3 : 1$

(v) Debtors collection period $= \frac{770}{3100} \times 365 = 91$ days

(vi) Stock: turnover $= \frac{3100}{310} = 10$ times

(vii) Fixed assets : turnover $= \frac{3100}{875} = 3.5$ times

(viii) Return on shareholders funds $= \frac{586}{690} \times 100\% = 84.9\%$

(ix) Current ratio $= \frac{1180}{665} = 1.8 : 1$

(x) Debt ratio $= \frac{1365}{2065} \times 100\% = 66.4\%$

Very few ratios have an absolute value but they are used in a relative way in intra and inter-firm comparisons. Both gross and net margins are calculated using the profit before tax and interest to identify the trading profit, irrespective of the capital structure in force. Both these figures seem satisfactory but knowledge of the industry is necessary. Also the returns on shareholders funds and on total assets both appear quite satisfactory.

The quick ratio exceeds the 1:1 norm and the current ratio is near the 2:1 norm, but this requirement varies widely. On the other hand the debt ratio seems high, as two-thirds of all assets are financed by debt.

Asset turnover ratio also need comparisons to make any judgment but the debtors collection period of 91 days would seem too long for most industries, specially if credit is granted on a net monthly basis.

Example 14

XYZ Company's financial statements contain the following information :

	2002 Rs.	2003 Rs.
Cash	2,00,000	1,60,000
Sundry debtors	3,20,000	4,00,000
Temporary investments	2,00,000	3,20,000
Stock	18,40,000	21,60,000
Prepaid expenses	28,000	12,000
Total current assets	25,88,000	30,52,000
Total assets	56,00,000	64,00,000
Current liabilities	6,40,000	8,00,000
Loans	16,00,000	16,00,000
Capital	20,00,000	20,00,000
Retained earnings	4,68,000	8,12,000

Statement of Profit for the current year

	Rs.
Sales	40,00,000
Less cost of goods sold	28,00,000
Less interest	1,60,000
Net profit	10,40,000
Less taxes @ 50%	5,20,000
Profit after taxes	5,20,000
Profit distributed	2,20,000

From the above, appraise the financial position of the company from the point of view of: (i) Liquidity, (ii) Profitability, and (iii) Activity.

Solution

1. Liabilities Ratios :

(a) Current Ratio (2003) $= \frac{\text{Current Assets}}{\text{Current Liabilities}} = \frac{\text{Rs. } 30{,}52{,}000}{\text{Rs. } 8{,}00{,}000} = 3.81$

(b) Acid test Ratio (2003) $= \frac{\text{Liquid Assets}}{\text{Current Liabilities}} = \frac{\text{Rs. } 30{,}52{,}000 - 21{,}72{,}000}{\text{Rs. } 8{,}00{,}000} = 1.1$

2. Leverage Ratios :

(a) Debt Equity Ratio (2003) $= \frac{\text{Long term debts}}{\text{Equity Funds}} = \frac{\text{Rs. } 16{,}00{,}000}{\text{Rs. } 28{,}12{,}000} = .57$

(b) Interest Coverage Ratio (2003) $= \frac{\text{EBIT}}{\text{Interest Charge}} = \frac{\text{Rs. } 12{,}00{,}000}{\text{Rs. } 1{,}60{,}000} = 7.5 \text{ times.}$

3. Profitability Ratios :

(a) Gross Profit Ratio (2003) $= \dfrac{\text{Gross Profit}}{\text{Sales}} \times 100 = \dfrac{\text{Rs. } 12{,}00{,}000}{\text{Rs. } 40{,}00{,}000} \times 100 = 30\%$

(b) Net Profit Ratio (2003) $= \dfrac{\text{Net Profit}}{\text{Sales}} \times 100 = \dfrac{\text{Rs. } 5{,}20{,}000}{\text{Rs. } 40{,}00{,}000} \times 100 = 13\%$

(c) Return on Total Assets (2003) $= \dfrac{\text{Profit after Tax}}{\text{Total Assets}} \times 100 = \dfrac{\text{Rs. } 5{,}20{,}000}{\text{Rs. } 64{,}00{,}000} \times 100 = 8.12\%$

(d) Return on Cap. Emp. (2003) $= \dfrac{\text{PAT + Int } (1-\text{T})}{\text{Total Cap. Emp.}} \times 100$

$= \dfrac{\text{Rs. } 5{,}20{,}000 + 80{,}000}{\text{Rs. } 44{,}12{,}000} \times 100 = 13.6\%$

(e) Return on Equity Funds (2003) $= \dfrac{\text{Profit after Tax}}{\text{Equity Funds}} \times 100 = \dfrac{\text{Rs. } 5{,}20{,}000}{\text{Rs. } 28{,}12{,}000} \times 100$

$= 18.5\%$

3. Activity Ratios :

(a) Debtors Turnover (2003) $= \dfrac{\text{Sales}}{\text{Average Debtors}} = \dfrac{\text{Rs. } 40{,}00{,}000}{\text{Rs. } 3{,}60{,}000} = 11.1 \text{ times.}$

(b) Stock Turnover (2003) $= \dfrac{\text{Cost of goods sold}}{\text{Average Stock}} = \dfrac{\text{Rs. } 28{,}00{,}000}{\text{Rs. } 20{,}00{,}000} = 1.4 \text{ times.}$

(c) Total Assets Turnover (2003) $= \dfrac{\text{Sales}}{\text{Average Assets}} = \dfrac{\text{Rs. } 40{,}00{,}000}{\text{Rs. } 60{,}00{,}000} = .67 \text{ times.}$

On the basis of the above ratios, it can be said that the firm's positions is sound from the point of view of liquidity, solvency and profitability. However, its activity ratios do not represent a satisfactory position. Better position will be reflected only if the ratios are compared with the performance of other firm in the same industry.

Example 15

The Balance sheet of XYZ company is given below:

(*Rs. in lacs*)

Liabilities	*Amount*	*Assets*	*Amount*
Equity Share Capital	250	Fixed Assets	400
General Reserve	280	Investment	50
P&L A/c (current year)	30	Stock	460
Secured loans - Long term	300	Debtors	460
Secured loans - Short term	360	Cash in hand	10
Creditors	150	Misc. expenditure (not written off)	20
Other liabilities	30		
	1400		1400

Additional Information :

(a) From the Profit and Loss Account Rs. 90 lacs was transferred to Gene Reserve during the year.
(b) Interest cost amounted to Rs. 120 lacs.

(c) Taxation @ 40%

You are required to calculate (i) Debt equity ratio (ii) Current ratio (iii) Interest coverage ratio.

Solution

Current Ratio $= \frac{\text{Current Assets}}{\text{Current Liabilities}} = \frac{\text{Rs. 930 lacs}}{\text{Rs. 540 lacs}} = 1.73$

Debt Equity Ratio $= \frac{\text{Debt}}{\text{Equity}} = \frac{\text{Rs. 300 lacs}}{\text{Rs. 560 lacs}} = 0.54$

Interest Coverage Ratio $= \frac{\text{EBIT}}{\text{Interest}} = \frac{\text{Rs. 320 lacs}}{\text{Rs. 120 lacs}} = 2.66$

Working Notes:

Current Assets	*Rs.*	*Debt*	*Equity*	*Rs.*
Stock	460 lacs	Term loan Rs. 300 lacs	Capital	250 lakhs
Debtors	460 lacs		Reserve	280 lakhs
Cash	10 lacs		P & L A/c	30 lakhs
	930 lacs			560 lakhs

Current Liabilities	*Rs.*	*EBIT*	*Rs.*
Short term loan	360 lacs	Profit for the year (30+90)	120 lakhs
Trade Credit	150 lacs	Interest	120 lakhs
Other Liabilities	30 lacs	Tax @ 40% $\frac{120 \times 40}{60}$	
	540 lacs		320 lakhs

Example 16

Calculate the P/E ratio from the following:

	Rs.
Equity Share Capital (Rs. 20 each)	50,00,000
Reserves and Surplus	5,00,000
Secured Loans at 15%	25,00,000
Unsecured Loans at 12.5%	10,00,000
Fixed Assets	30,00,000
Investments	5,00.000
Operating Profit	25.00.000
Income-tax rate	50%
Market price/share	Rs. 50

Solution

		Rs.
Operating Profit		25,00,000
Less: Interest on:	Rs.	
Secured loans @ 15%	3,75,000	
Unsecured Loans @ 12.5%	1,25,000	5,00,000
Profit before Tax (PBT)		20,00,000

Less: Income Tax @ 50%	10,00,000
Profit after tax (PAT)	10,00,000
No. of Equity Shares	2,50,000

$$\text{EPS} = \frac{\text{Profit after tax}}{\text{No. of Equity shares}} = \frac{\text{Rs. } 10,00,000}{2,50,000} = \text{Rs. } 4$$

P/E ratio = Market Price per share/EPS = Rs. 50/Rs.4 = 12.50

Example 17

ABC Distributors has the following Balance Sheet and Income Statement:

Balance Sheet

Liabilities	*Amount*	*Assets*	*Amount*
	Rs.		Rs.
Shareholders Equity (50,000 shares)	3,00,000	Long Term Assets	3,50,000
Long term Debt	1.00,000	Cash	25,000
Account payable	80.000	Accounts Receivables	60.000
Other Current Liabilities	20,000	Inventory	65,000
	5,00,000		5,00,000

Income Statement

Particulars	*Amount*
	Rs.
Sales	9,00,000
Cost of Goods Sold	4,00,000
General, Administrative and Selling Expenses	1,00,000
Other expenses	2,50,000
Net Income (PAT)	16,50,000

You are required to :

(a) Determine ABC Distributor's liquidity position by calculating the Current ratio. Working Capital, the ratio of Current Assets to Total Assets, the ratio of Current Liabilities to Total Assets and the Cash Conversion cycle.

(b) Calculate the current market price per share of ABC's Stock if its P/E ratio is eight.

Solution:

Various Ratios of ABC Distributors may be found as follows :

Current assets	= Cash + Accounts receivable + Inventory
	= 25,000 + 60.000 + 65,000 = 1.50,000
Current liabilities	= Accounts payable + Other current liabilities
	= 80.000 + 20,000 = 1,00.000
Current Ratio	= Current assets/Current liabilities
	= 1,50,000/1,00,000 = 1.5
Net working capital	= 1,50,000-1,00,000 = 50,000.
Current assets/Total assets	= 1,50,000/5.00.000 = 0.30
Current liabilities/Total assets	= 1,00,000/5,00,000 = 0.20
Receivables Turnover	= Sales/Accounts receivables = 15.00

Inventory Turnover	= Cost of goods sold/Inventory == 6.15
Payable Turnover	= $\frac{\text{Cost of goods sold}}{\text{Accounts Payable}}$ = 5.00
Average collection period	= 365/Receivables turnover = 24.33 days
Inventory conversion period	= 365/Inventory turnover = 59.35 days
Payable Deferral period	= 365/Payables turnover =73 days
Cash conversion cycle	= 10.68 days (24.33+59.35-73)

Calculation of Market price of Share of ABC Distributors

EPS = PAT/No. of shares = 1,50,000/50,000 = 3.00

Price = (EPS) × (P/E) = (3.00 × 8) = Rs. 24.00

Example 18

Following is the Balance Sheet of M/s Bintex Co. Ltd. Bangalore, as on 31 st December, 2002.

Liabilities	*Rs.*	*Assets*	*Rs.*
Share Capital:		Land	4,00,000
Authorised, issued and fully paid up:		Building	21,00,000
50,000 9% preference		Plant and machinery	1,19,00,000
shares of Rs. 100 each	50,00,000	Furniture and Fittings	1,50,000
5,00,000 equity shares of Rs. 10 each	50,00,000	Office cars, trucks	1,50,000
	1,00,00,000	Stock	1,50,00,000
Capital reserves	5,00,000	Accounts receivable	6,00,000
General reserves	10,00,000	Cash and bank	2,00,000
Sinking fund reserves	15,00,000		
7% Debentures	50,00,000		
Bank Overdraft	85,00,000		
Notes payable	15,00,000		
Account payable	25,00,000		
	3,05,00,000		3,05,00,000

Compute the following from the above balance sheet:

(1) Net worth
(2) Total value of equity
(3) Shareholders reserves
(4) Total fixed assets
(5) Total current assets
(6) Working capital
(7) Long-term liabilities
(Show the workings, where necessary)

Solution:

(1) Net Worth

This represents the net assets of the company. It is also equivalent to proprietors' fund, *viz.*, paid up capital plus reserves. This can be obtained by calculating both ways Assets Approach and Liabilities Approach as given below:

	Rs.	Rs.
(a) Gross assets as per balance sheet		3,05,00,000
Less: Liabilities		

7% Debentures	50,00,000	
Bank overdraft	85,00,000	
Notes payable	15,00,000	
Accounts payable	25,00,000	
		1,75,00,000
Net worth		1,30,00,000

Alternatively

(a) Paid up capital		
Preference share capital	50,00,000	
Equity share capital	50,00,000	1,00,00,000
Reserves:		
Capital reserve	5,00,000	
General reserve	10,00.000	
Sinking fund reserve	15.00,000	30,00,000
Net worth		1,30,00,000

(2) Total value of equity

This can be obtained by adding up Equity Paid up Capital with reserves and surpluses belonging to equity shareholders. Alternatively the same can be obtained by subtracting from net worth of the company what is due to preferences shareholders:

	Rs.
Net worth as calculated under (1)	1,30,00,000
Less: Preference share capital	50,00,000
Total value of equity	80,00,000

(3) Shareholders' reserves

Capital reserve	50,00,000
General reserve	10,00,000
Sinking fund reserve	15,00,000
Total	30,00,000

(4) Total fixed assets

Land	4,00,000
Building	21,00,000
Plant and machinery	1,19,00,000
Furniture and fittings	1,50,000
Office cars and trucks	1,50,000
Total	1,47,00,000

(5) Total current assets

Stock	1,50,00,000
Account receivable	6,00,000
Cash at bank	2,00,000
Total	1,58,00,000

(6) Working capital

This represents excess of current assets over current liabilities:

Current assets as calculated under (5)	1,58,00,000

	Rs.	
Less: Current liabilities		
Bank overdraft	85,00,000	
Notes payable	15,00,000	
Accounts payable	25,00,000	1,25,00,000
Working capital		33,00,000
(7) Long-term liabilities		
7% debentures		50,00,000
		50,00,000

Example 19

Calculate and comment on the rate of return on total assets from the following data of two companies:

	Go Slow Co.	*Go Fast Co.*
Sales		2,52,75,000
Total assets	42,50,000	
Net profit in sales	6%	4%
Turnover of assets	6 times	6 times
Gross margin	20,68,000	12%

Solution

	Rs.	Rs.
Sales	Rs. 42,50,000 × 6 = 2,55,00,000	Rs. 2,52,75,000
Total assets	Rs. 42,50,000	Rs. 2,52,75,000 ÷ 6 = 42,12,500
Net profit in sales	6% of Rs. 2,55,00.000 = Rs. 15,30,000	4% of Rs. 2,52,75,000 = Rs. 10,11,000
Rate of return on total assets	Rs. 15,30,000 / Rs. 42,50,000 = 36%	Rs. 10,11,000 / Rs. 42,12,500 = 24%

The rate of return on total assets in respect of Go Fast Co. is less than that of Go Slow Co. as the total assets are same (approx.) in both the Cos. Net profit in sales in Go Fast Co. is 2/3 rd of net profit of Go Slow Co. and similar is the case of rate of return on total assets.

Example 20

The following are the ratios relating to the activities OF National Traders Ltd.:

Debtors velocity	3 months
Stock velocity	8 months
Creditors velocity	2 months
Gross profit ratio	25%

Gross profit for the current year ended 31 December amounted to Rs. 4,00,000 Closing stock of the year is Rs. 10,000 above the opening stock. Bills Receivable amount to Rs. 25,000 and bills payable to Rs. 10,000. Find out:

(a) Sales
(b) Sundry debtors
(c) Closing stock
(d) Sundry creditors.

Solution:

(a) Determination of sales:

$$\text{Gross profit ratio} = \frac{\text{Gross profit}}{\text{Sales}} \times 100$$

$$25 = \frac{\text{Rs. } 4,00,000}{\text{Sales}} \times 100$$

$$\text{Sales} = \frac{\text{Rs. } 4,00,000}{25} \times 100 = \text{Rs. } 16,00,000$$

(b) Determination of sundry debtors:

Debtors velocity is 3 months. In other words, debtors collection period 3 months, or debtors turnover ratio is 4. Assuming all sales to be credit sales and debtors turnover ratio being calculated on the basis of the year end figures, debtors would be determined as follows:

$$\text{Debtors turnover ratio} = \frac{\text{Credit sales}}{\text{Closing debtors + Bill receivable}}$$

or

$$\text{Closing debtors + Bills receivables} = \frac{\text{Credit sales}}{\text{Debtors turnover ratio}}$$

$$= \frac{\text{Rs. } 16,00,000}{4}$$

$$= \text{Rs. } 4,00,000$$

$$\text{Closing debtors} = \text{Rs. } 4,00,000 - \text{Rs. } 25,000$$

$$= \text{Rs. } 3,75,000$$

(c) Determination of closing stock:

Stock velocity of 8 months signifies that the turnover is 8 months. In other words, stock turnover ratio is 1.5 == (12 months ÷ 8).

$$\text{Stock turnover} = \frac{\text{Cost of goods sold (Sales} - \text{Gross Profit)}}{\text{Average stock}}$$

$$\text{Average stock} = \frac{\text{Rs. } 12,00,000}{1.5} = \text{Rs. } 8,00,000$$

$$\text{Closing stock} - \text{Opening stock} = \text{Rs. } 10,000 \quad (1)$$

$$\frac{\text{Closing stock + Opening stock}}{2} = \text{Rs. } 8,00,000 \quad (2)$$

or

$$\text{Closing stock + Opening stock} = \text{Rs. } 16,00,000 \quad (3)$$

Substracting equation (1) from equation (3) *i.e.*, Rs. 16,00,000 -10,000)

	Rs.
Opening stock	15,90,000
Opening stock	7,95,000
Closing stock	8,05,000

(d) Determination of sundry creditors:

Credit velocity of 2 months signifies that the credit payment period is 2 months. In other words, creditors turnover ratio is 6 (12 months ÷ 2). Assuming all purchases to be credit purchases and creditors turnover is based on year-end figures, we have:

$$\text{Creditors turnover ratio} = \frac{\text{Credit purchases}}{\text{Creditors + Bills payable}}$$

$$6 = \frac{\text{Rs. 12,10,000}}{\text{Creditors + Rs. 10,000}}$$

$$\text{Creditors + Rs. 10,000} = \frac{\text{Rs. 12,10,000}}{6} = \text{Rs. 2,01,667}$$

Creditors = Rs. 2,01,667 - Rs. 10.000 = Rs. 1,91,667

Credit purchases are calculated as follows :

Cost of goods sold = Opening stock + Purchases – Closing stock
Rs. 12,00,000 = Rs. 7,95,000 + Purchases – Rs. 8,05,000
Rs. 12,00,000 + Rs. 10,000 = Purchases
Rs. 12,10,000 = Purchases (credit)

Example 21

The capital of E. Co. Ltd., is as follows:

	(Rs.)
9% Preference shares of Rs. 10 each	3,00,000
Equity shares of Rs. 10 each	8,00,000
	11,00,000

The accountant has ascertained the following information:

Profit (after tax at 60%) Rs. 2,70,000: Depreciation Rs. 60,000; Equity dividend paid 20%: market price of equity shares Rs. 40. You are required to state the following, showing the necessary workings:

(a) Dividend yield on the equity shares.
(b) Cover for the preference and equity dividends.
(c) Earnings for equity shares.
(d) Price-earnings ratio.

Solution:

(a) Dividend yield on the equity shares:

$$= \frac{\text{Dividend per share}}{\text{Market price per share}} \times 100$$

$$= \frac{\text{Rs. 2(20\% of Rs. 10)} \times 100}{\text{Rs. 40}} \times 100 = 5\%$$

(b) Dividend coverage ratio:

(i) Preference
$$= \frac{\text{Profits after taxes}}{\text{Dividend payable to preference shareholders}}$$

$$= \frac{\text{Rs. 2,70,000}}{\text{Rs. 27,000 (9\% of Rs. 3,00,000)}}$$

= 10 times

(ii) Equity
$$= \frac{\text{Profits after taxes} - \text{Preference share dividends}}{\text{Dividend payable to equity shareholders at current rate of Rs. 2 per share}}$$

$$= \frac{\text{Rs. } 2{,}70{,}000 - \text{Rs. } 27{,}000}{\text{Rs. } 1{,}60{,}000 \text{ (80,000 shares} \times \text{Rs. 2)}}$$

$$= \frac{\text{Rs. } 2{,}43{,}000}{\text{Rs. } 1{,}60{,}000} = 1.52 \text{ times}$$

(c) Earnings for equity shares:

$$= \frac{\text{Earnings available to equity shareholders}}{\text{Number of the equity share outstanding}}$$

$$= \frac{\text{Rs. } 2{,}43{,}000}{80{,}000} = \text{Rs. 3.04 per share}$$

(d) Price-earning (P/E) ratio :

$$\text{P/E ratio} = \frac{\text{Market price per share}}{\text{Earnings per share}}$$

$$= \frac{\text{Rs. 40.00}}{\text{Rs. 3.04}} = 13.2 \text{ times}$$

Example 22

With the help of the following ratios draw the Balance Sheet of the Company for the year 2002:

Current Ratio	2.5
Liquidity Ratio	1.5
Net Working Capital	Rs. 3,00,000
Stock Turnover Ratio (cost of sales/closing stock)	6 times
Gross Proflt Ratio	20 per cent
Fixed Assets Turnover Ratio (on cost of sales)	2 times
Debt Collection Period	2 months
Fixed assets to shareholders net worth	0.80
Reserve and surplus to capital	0.50

Solution

Balance Sheet as on...

Liabilities	*Rs.*	*Assets*	*Rs.*
Share capital	5,00,000	Fixed assets	6,00,000
Reserve and surplus	2,50,000	Stock	2,00,000
Long-term borrowings		Debtors	2,50,000
(balancing figure)	1,50,000	Bank	50,000
Current liabilities	2,00,000		
	11,00,000		11,00,000

Working Notes:

If Current Liabilities	= 1
Current assets	= 2.5
It means the difference of working capital	= 1.5

Working Capital is 1.5	= Rs. 3,00,000
Therefore, Current Assets	= Rs. 5,00,000
Current Liabilities	= Rs. 2,00,000
Liquidity ratio	= 1.5
Therefore, the liquid assets (Bank and debtors (2,00,000 × 1.5)	= 3,00,000
Stock (5,00,000 – 3,00,000, *i.e.*, current assets – liquid assets)	= 2,00,000
Cost of sales (as stock turnover ratio is 6)	= 12,00,000
Sales as G/P ratio is 20 per cent, 12,00,000 + 20/80 × 12,000)	= 15,00,000
Fixed Assets are Rs. 12,00,000/2 since fixed assets turnover is ratio 2	= 6,00,000
Debtors are Rs. 15,00,000/6 since debt collection period is 2 months	= 2,50,000
Shareholders Net worth $\left(\dfrac{6,00,000 \times 1}{0.80}\right)$	= 7,50,000
Out of Shareholders net worth, reserves and surplus	= 2,50,000
Therefore, sharé capital	= 5,00,000

Example 23

With the following ratios and further information given below prepare a Trading Account, Profit and Loss account and Balance Sheet of Shri Narain:

(i) Gross Profit Ratio	25 per cent
(ii) Net Profit/Sales	20 per cent
(iii) Stock-turnover Ratio	10
(iv) Net Profit to Capital	1/5
(v) Capital to Total Liabilities	1 /2
(vi) Fixed Assets/capital	5/4
(vii) Fixed Assets/Total Current Assets	5/7
(viii) Fixed Assets	Rs. 10,00,000
(ix) Closing Stock	Rs. 1,00,000

Solution:

Trading and Profit and Loss Account for the year ended...

	Rs.		Rs.
To Opening stock	20,000	By Sales	8,00,000
To Purchases (balancing figure)	6,80,000	By Closing stock	1,00,000
To Gross Profit c/d	2,00,000		
	9,00,000		9,00,000
To Expenses	40,000	By Gross Profit b/d	2,00,000
To Net Profit	1,60,000		
	2,00,000		2,00,000

Balance Sheet as on...

Capital	Rs.		Rs.
Opening Balance	6,40,000	Fixed Assets	10,00,000
Add: Net Profit	1,60,000	Closing Stock	1,00,000
	8,00,000	Other Current Assets	13,00,000
Liabilities	16,00,000	(Balancing figure)	
	24,00,000		24,00,000

Working Notes:

1. Fixed Assets are Rs. 10,00,000

$$= \frac{\text{Fixed assets}}{\text{Capital}} = \frac{5}{4}$$

$$\text{Capital} = \frac{1,00,000}{5} \times 4 = \text{Rs. } 8,00,000$$

2. Capital is 1 /2 of total liabilities
   Liabilities = 8,00,000 × 2 = 16,00,000
3. Net profit is 1/5 of Capital
   Net profit = 8,00,000 × 1/5 = Rs. 1,60,000
4. Net Profit is 20 per cent of sales
   Sales = 1,60,000 × 100/20 = Rs. 8,00,000
5. Gross Profit Ratio is 25 per cent of Sales
   Gross Profit = Rs. 2,00,000
6. Stock Turnover Ratio (*i.e.*, Cost of Sales/Average Inventory) is 10
   Cost of Sales = Sales – Gross Profit
   = Rs. 8,00,000 – 2,00,000
   = Rs. 6,00,000
   Average Inventory is Rs. 60,000
7. Closing Stock is Rs. 1,00,000
   Average Inventory is Rs. 60,000
   Opening Stock is Rs. 20,000
8. Fixed Assets are Rs. 10,00,000
   Fixed Assets/Total Current Assets = 5/7
   Total Current Assets are 10,00,000 × 7/5
   = Rs. 14,00,000
   Stock is Rs. 1,00,000
   Other Current Assets are Rs. 13,00,000.

Example 24

From the following ratios extracted from the books of a company as at 31st December, 2001, draw up the Balance Sheet of the company:

Current Ratio	2.5:1	Gross Profit Ratio	20%
Working Capital	Rs. 3,00.000	Debt Collection period	2 months
Liquidity Ratio	1.5:1	Shareholders' Funds	Rs. 37,50,000
		Reserve and surplus	50% of share capital
Stock Turnover Ratio (Based on closing stock)	6 Times	Fixed Asset Turnover (on cost of sales)	2 Times

Solution

Shareholders fund = Rs. 7,50,000
Reserve and surplus = 50% of share capital = 50/150 × 7,50,000 = Rs. 2,50,000
Share capital = 7,50,000 – 2,50,000 = Rs. 5,00,000
Current Assets – Current Liabilities = Working Capital
2.5 x – x = Rs. 3,00,000
∴ x = Rs. 2,00,000 = Current Liabilities
Current Assets = 2.5 × 2,00,000 = Rs. 5.00,000

Assuming excess of current assets over liquid assets is represented by stock:
Stock = Current Assets – Liquid Assets
i.e. Rs. 5,00.000 – (1.5 × 2,00,000) = Rs. 2,00,000
Stock turnover ratio is = Cost of Sales/Closing Stock
Therefore, Cost of sales = 6 × 2,00,000 = Rs 12,00,000
Sales = 12,00,000 × 100/80 = Rs. 15,00,000
Debt Collection Period : 2 months.
Debtors = 2/12 X Sales = Rs. 2,50,000
Bank Balance = Liquid Asset – Debtors = Rs. 50,000.
Fixed Assets Turnover = 2 = Cost of sales/Fixed Assets – 12,00,000/Fixed Assets
Fixed Assets = Rs. 6,00,000

Balance sheet as at 31st December, 2001

Liabilities	*Amount*	*Assets*	*Amoini*
Share Capital	5,00.000	Fixed Assets	6,00,000
Reserve and Surplus	2,50,000	Stock	2,00,000
Term Loan (Balancing Figure)	1,50,000	Debtors	2.50,000
Current Liabilities	2,00,000	Bank	50,000
	11,00,000		11,00,000

Example 25

Prepare a Balance Sheet from the particulars furnished hereunder:

Stock Turnover	: 6
Gross Profit Margin	: 20%
Capital Turnover Ratio	: 2
Fixed Assets Turnover Ratio	: 4
Debt Collection Period	: 2 months
Creditors Payment Period	: 73 days

Gross Profit was Rs. 60,000
Excess of closing stock over opening stock was Rs. 5,000.
Difference in balance sheet represents bank balance.
The entire sales and purchases are made on credit basis.

Prepare the balance sheet. Capital turnover and fixed asset turnover are based on :

(i) cost of sales
(ii) Net sales.

Solution

$$\text{Gross Profit Ratio} = \frac{\text{Gross Profit} \times 100}{\text{Sales}}$$

$$20 = \frac{60{,}000 \times 100}{\text{Sales}} \text{ or Sales} = \text{Rs. } 3{,}00{,}000$$

Cost of Goods Sold = Sales – Gross Profit = 3,00,000 – 60,000 = Rs. 2.40,000

$$\text{Stock Turnover} = \frac{\text{Cost of Goods Sold}}{\text{Average Stock}}$$

$$6 = \frac{\text{Rs. } 2,40,000}{\text{Average Stock}}$$

Average stock = Rs. 40,000

Closing stock – Opening stock = Rs. 5,000

Opening stock = Rs. 37,500 (80,000 – 5,000)/2

Closing stock = Rs. 42,500

$$\text{Capital Turnover Ratio} = \frac{\text{Cost of Sales}}{\text{Capital}}$$

$$2 = \frac{\text{Rs. } 2,40,000}{\text{Capital}} \text{ or Capital} = \text{Rs. } 1,20,000$$

$$\text{Fixed Assets Turnover ratio} = \frac{\text{Cost of Sales}}{\text{Fixed Assets}}$$

$$4 = \frac{\text{Rs. } 2,40,000}{\text{Fixed Assets}}$$

Fixed Assets = Rs. 60,000

Debt collection period = 2 months

$$\text{Debtors Turnover Ratio} = \frac{\text{12 months}}{\text{Debt collection period}} = 12/2 = 6 \text{ times}$$

$$\text{Also, Debtors Turnover Ratio} = \frac{\text{Credit Sales}}{\text{Average Debtors}}$$

$$\text{Debtors} = \frac{\text{Rs. } 3,00,000}{6} = \text{Rs. } 50,000$$

Creditors' payment period = 73 days

Creditors' Turnover Ratio = 365/73 = 5 times

The amount of credit purchases is determined as follows :

Cost of Goods Sold = Opening Stock + Purchases – Closing Stock

2,40,000 = Rs. 37,500 + Purchases - Rs. 42,500

Purchases = Rs. 2,45,000

$$\text{Creditors' Turnover Ratio} = \frac{\text{Credit Purchases}}{\text{Creditors}}$$

$$5 = \frac{2,45,000}{\text{Creditors}} \text{ or Creditors} = \text{Rs. } 49,000$$

Balance Sheet as at.........

Liabilities	*Amount*	*Assets*	*Amoini*
Capital	1,20,000	Fixed Assets	60,000
Creditors	49,000	Closing Sleek	42,500
		Debtors	50,000
		Bank (Bakincing figure)	16,500
	1,69,000		1,69,000

Alternatively if, Capital Turnover and Fixed Assets Turnover ratios are based on net sales, the working is as follows:

Capital Turnover Ratio = Net Sales/Capital = 2 = 3.00,000/Capilal or Capital == Rs. 1,50,000
Fixed Assets Turnover Ratio = Net Sales/Fixed Assets = 4 = 3,00,000/Fixed Assets
Fixed Assets = Rs. 75.000

The Balance Sheet figures under this alternative would be as given below :

Balance Sheet as at............

Liabilities	*Amount*	*Assets*	*Amoini*
Capital	1,50,000	Fixed Assets	75,000
Creditors	49,000	Closing Stock	42,500
		Debtors	50,000
		Bank (Balancing figure)	31,500
	1,99,000		1,99,000

THEORY QUESTIONS

1. Discuss the importance of financial ratios.
2. Explain the financial ratios:
   (a) Liquidity ratios
   (b) Profitability ratio
   (c) Capital structure ratio
3. In what way market strength ratios are useful to investors?
4. Discuss the computation and significance of the following financial ratios:
   (a) Current ratio (b) Quick ratio
   (c) Inventory turnover ratio (d) Debt-equity ratio
   (e) Accounts receivables ratio (f) Earnings margin
   (g) Earning per share.
5. What are the limitations of accounting ratios?
6. What is asset turnover? What influence does a higher asset turnover tend to have on the rate of return on assets?
7. What is the key question in assessing liquidity? What ratios are used in this regard?
8. Discuss the significance of equity ratio and'explain how it is computed.
9. What similarities and differences exist in the objectives of investors and creditors in using ratios analysis.
10. Company A and Company B both have net income of Rs. 10,00,000. Is it possible to say that these companies are equally successful? Why or why not ?

PROBLEMS

1. The Balance Sheets of Y Ltd. stood as follows :

(Rs. in lakhs)

Liabilities	*31 -3-2001*	*31-3-2000*	*Assets*	*31-3-2001*	*31-3-2000*
Capital	250	250	Fixed assets	400	300
Reserves	116	100	*Less*: Depreciation	140	100
Loans	100	120		260	200
Creditors and other			Investments	40	30
current liabilities	129	25	Stock	120	100
			Debtors	70	50

			Cash and Bank	20	20
			Other current assets	25	25
			Miscellaneous expenditure	60	70
	595	495		595	495

You are given the following information for the year 2000-2001:

Sales	600
PBIT	150
Interest	24
Provision for tax	60
Proposed dividend	50

All the figures given above are rupees in lakhs.

From the above particulars, calculate for the year 2000-2001 :

(a) Return on Capital Employed Ratio. (b) Stock Turnover Ratio.
(c) Return on Net Worth Ratio. (d) Current Ratio.
(e) Proprietary Ratio.

2. A company is capitalised as follows:
Rs. 6,00,000 7% Preference Shares, Re. 1 each
Rs. 16,00.000 Ordinary Shares, Re. 1 each

The following information is relevant as to its financial year just ended:

Profit after taxation at 50 per cent Rs. 5,42,000; Ordinary dividend paid 20%; Depreciation Rs. 1,20,000; Market price of Ordinary Shares Rs. 4: and Capital commitments Rs. 2,40,000.

You are required to state the following showing the necessary workings:
(1) the dividend yield on the Ordinary Shares;
(2) the cover for the Preference and Ordinary dividends;
(3) the earnings yield;
(4) the price-earning ratio; and
(5) the net cash flow.

3. Calculate cost of goods sold from the following details :

Working Capital	Rs. 45,000
Current Ratio	1.5
Quick Ratio	0.9
Inventory Turnover (cost of sales/closing stock)	6 Times

4. Calculate sundry debtors and sundry creditors from the following information:

Debtors Velocity	2 months
Creditors Velocity	3 months
Cost of Sales	Rs. 2,00.000
Profit Margin	20% of cost
Bill Receivable	Rs. 2,000
Bills Payable	Rs. 10,000

Hint: Asssume no stock of goods is maintained and therefore, cost of sales and purchases are same.

5. Compute the Debtors Turnover Ratio from the following:

	Year I	Year II
Groos Sales	9,00,000	7,50,000
Debtors in the beginning	83,000	1,17,000
Debtors at the end	1,17,000	83,000
Sales Return	1,00,000	50,000

6. Compute the Debtors Turnover Ratio from the following:

	Rs.
Total Sales for the year	5,00,000
Cash Sales for the year	1,00,000
Debtors in the beginning of the year	50,000
Debtor at the end of the ycar	80,000

Also state the significance of this ratio.

7. Following figures have been extracted from a company accounts

Stock in the beginning of the year	Rs. 60,000
Stock at the end of the year	Rs. 1,00,000
Stock Turnover ratio	8 times
Selling price	25% above cost.

Compute the amount of gross profit and sales.

8. Calculate the current assets of a company from the following information:
   (a) Stock Turnover Ratio — 5 Times
   (b) Stock at the end is Rs. 15,000 more than stock in the beginning.
   (c) Sales — Rs. 2,00,000
   (d) Gross Profit Ratio — 25%
   (e) Current Liabilities — Rs. 50,000
   (f) Quick Ratio — 0.75

9. Following is the Balance Sheet of Y Ltd. as at December 31, 2001 :

Liabilities	*Amount*	*Assets*	*Amount*
Share Capital	8,00,000	Plant and Machinery	5,00.000
Reserves	1,20,000	Land and Building	5,00:000
Net Profit for 2001	90,000	Stock	2,00.000
15% Debentures	1,00,000	Debtors	1,50,000
Creditors	2,00.000	Cash	50,000
Bills Payable	70,000	Preliminary Expenses	10,000
Outstanding Expenses	30,000		
	14,10,000		14,10,000

You are required to calculate the following ratios:
1. Interest Coverage Ratio, 2. Debt Equity Ratio, 3. Current Ratio, 4. Quick Ratio, 5. Debt to Tolal Fund Ratio, 6. Proprietary Ratio, 7. Return on Shareholders Funds, and 8. Return on Investment.

10. From the following particulars, prepare the Balance Sheet of a Company:

Current Ratio	2
Working Capital	Rs. 4,00,000
Capital Block to Current Assets	3 : 2
Fixed Assets to Turnover	1 : 3
Sales Cash/Credit	1 : 2
Stock Velocity	2 months
Creditors Velocity	2 months
Debtors Velocity	3 months
Capital Block:	
Net Profit	10% of Turnover
Reserve	2.5% of Turnover
Debentures/Share Capital	1 : 2
Gross Profit Ratio	25% (to Sales)

11. With the help of the following information, complete the Balance Sheet of XYZ Ltd.:

Owners' Equity	Rs. 1,00,000
Current Debt to Total Debt	.40
Total Debt to Owner Equity	.60
Fixed Assets to Owners Equity	.60
Total Assets Turnover	2
Inventory Turnover	8 Times

12. Based on the following information of the financial ratios, prepare Balance sheet of Vinod Ltd. as on 31st March, 2000. Explain your workings and assumptions.
Current ratio 2.5; Liquidity ratio 1.5
Net Working Capital Rs. 6,00,000; Stock turnover ratio: 5
Ratio of gross profit to sales : 20%
Turnover ratio to net fixed assets: 2
Average debt collection period : 2.4 months
Fixed assets to net worth: 0.80
Long-term debt to capital and reserve 7/25

13. From the following annual statement of Pioneer Ltd. calculate the following ratios:
(a) Gross Profit Ratio; (b) Current Ratio; (c) Liquid Ratio; (d) Debt-Equity Ratio; and (e) Return on Equity Ratio.

Trading and Profit and Loss Account for the Year ended 31st December, 2002

	Rs.		Rs.
Materials Consumed:		Sales	85,000
Opening Stock	9,050	Profit on Sale of Investments	600
Purchases	54,525	Interest on Investments	300
	63.575		
Closing Stock	14,000		
	49,575		
Carriage Inwards	1,425		
Office Expenses	15,000		
Sales Expenses	3,000		
Financial Expenses	1,500		
Loss on Sale of Assets	400		
Net Profit	15,000		
	85,900		85,900

Balance Sheet as on 31st December, 2002

		Rs.			Rs.
Share Capital:			Fixed Assets :		
2,000 Equity Shares of Rs. 10 each		20,000	Buildings	15,000	
Reserves		9,000	Plant	8,000	
Profit and Loss account		6,000	Current Assets:		23,000
Bank overdraft		3000	Stock in trade	14,000	
Sundry creditors:			Debtors	7,000	
for expenses	2,000		Bills Receivable	1,000	
for others	8,000	10,000	Bank	3,000	25,000
		48,000			48,000

Ans: (a) Gross Profit Ratio 40%; (b) Current Ratio 1.92 :1; (c) Liquid Ratio 1.1:1 Bank overdraft has not been taken as a current liability (d) Debt-Equity Ratio:

(i) $\dfrac{\text{All Debts}}{\text{Equity}} = 0.371 : 1$

(ii) $\dfrac{\text{All Debts}}{\text{All Debts + Equity}} = 0.271 : 1$

(iii) Return on Investment Ratio = $\dfrac{\textbf{Net Profit}}{\textbf{Capital Employed}}$

$= \dfrac{15{,}000}{35{,}000} = 42.85$

14. Following is the Profit and Loss Account and balance sheet of A Limited for the year ended 31 December, 2002 and balance sheet as on that date. Calculate the different ratios and comment on the financial position of the company.

Profit and Loss Account for the ended 31st December, 2002

		Rs.
Net sales		3,00,000
Less: Cost of Goods sold		2,58,000
Gross profit		42,000
Operating Expenses:		
Selling	2,200	
General and administration	4,000	
Rent of Office	2,800	
		9,000
Gross Operating profit		33,000
Depreciation		10,000
		23,000
Other Income:		
Interest on Government Securities		1,500
Gross Income		24,500
Other expenses:		
Interest on bank overdraft	300	
Interest on debentures	4,200	
		4,500
Net Income before Tax		20,000
Tax @ 50 per cent on Net Income		10,000
Net Income after tax		10,000

Balance Sheet as on 31 December, 2002

Liabilities	*Rs.*	*Assets*		*Rs.*
Sundry Creditors	6,000	Cash		5,000
Bills Payable	10,000	Investments (Govt. Securities)		15,000
Outstanding Expenses	1,000	Sundry Debtors		20,000
Provision for Taxation	13,000	Stock		30,000
Total current liabilities	30,000	Total Current Assets		70,000
6 per cent Mortgage Debentures	70,000	Fixed Assets	1,80,000	
7 per cent preference shares	10,000	*Less*: Provision for dep.	50,000	1,30,000

Equity Shares	50,000		
Reserve and surplus	40,000		
Total Claim on Assets	2,00,000		2,00,000

Ans: Gross Profit Ratio 14 per cent. Net Profit Ratio (after considering interest on bank overdraft): 7.56 per cent ROI 13.53 per cent, stock turnover Ratio 8.6. Debt Collection Period 24 days. Fixed Assets Turnover 2.3, Fixed Assets Ratio 7.6, Debt-equity ratio 70/100 = .7, Current ratio 2.3).

15. Following is the balance sheet of C Ltd. as on 31st December, 2002

Liabilities		*Rs.*	*Assets*	*Rs.*
Equity share capital		20,000	Goodwill	12,000
Capital reserve		4,000	Fixed Assets	28,000
8% Loan on mortgage		16,000	Stocks	6,000
Trade creditors		8,000	Debtors	6,000
Bank overdraft		2,000	Investments	2,000
Taxation : Current		2,000	Bank	6,000
Future		2,000		
Profit and loss A/c:				
Profit for 2002 after taxation and interest on fixed deposits	12,000			
Less: Transfer to Reserve	4,000			
Dividend	2,000	6,000		
		60,000		60,000

Sales amounted to Rs. 1,20,000

Calculate ratio for:

1. Testing liquidity
2. Testing solvency
3. Testing profitability
4. Testing capital gearing and
5. Comment on the significant thereof.

16. From the following particulars extracted from the financial statements of Sun and Co, Ltd. Compute: (a) Current Ratio (b) Acid Test Ratio (c) Stock Turnover Ratio (d) Debtor Turnover Ratio and (e) Creditors Turnover Ratio for the two years 2002 and 2003 independently and comment on the liquidity position of the company:

	2002 Rs.	*2003 Rs.*
Opening stock	47,000	53,000
Closing stock	53.000	67,000
Sales less returns	2,52,000	3,65,000
Provision for bad debts	2,000	3,000
Sundry creditors	32,000	35,000
Purchases	1,80,000	1,90.000
Sundry debtors	42,000	63,000
Cash	10,000	15,000
Bank	8,000	10,000
Bills Receivable	15,000	20,000
Bilk Payable	29,000	30000
Marketable Securities	8,000	8,000

17. A. Ltd. and B. Ltd. produce and sell the same product but under different brand names. Their profit and loss statements and Balance Sheets are given below for the year ending 2002.

Profit and Loss Statement

(Figures in Rs. lakhs)

	A. Ltd.	B.Ltd.
Sales	25.00	30.00
Less: Costs: Materials	4.00	2.00
Labour	2.00	7.00
Overheads: Fixed	9.00	2.00
Variable	2.00	9.00
Total cost	17.00	20.00
Gross margin	8.00	10.00
Interest	2.00	4.00
Profit before taxes	6.00	6.00
Taxes	3.00	3.00
Profit after taxes	3.00	3.00
Dividends declared	2.00	2.00
Retained earnings	1.00	1.00

Balance Sheet

(Fig. in Rs. lakhs)

	A. Ltd.	B.Ltd.
A. Capital Liabilities:		
1. Equity Capital	10.00	20.00
2. Debenture Capital	8.00	20.00
3. Creditors	5.00	15.00
4. Reserves	17.00	5.00
	40.00	60.00
B. Assets:		
1. Plant and machinery	8.00	34.00
2. Buildings	6.00	16.00
3. Inventories	18.00	2.00
4. Debtors	7.00	1.00
5. Cash	1.00	7.00
	40.00	60.00

Required: Evaluate the performance of two organisations for the current year and assess the expected problem by using the relevant ratios.

18. A condensed balance sheet and other financial data for Alpha Company appear below :

Alpha Company Balance Sheet December 31, 2001

Assets :	(Rs.)
Current Assets	1,00,000
Plant Assets	1,40,000
Total Assets	2,50,000
Liabilities and Equity	
Current Liabilities	1,00,000
Long-term Liabilities	75,000

Total Liabilities	1,75,000
Common Equity	75,000
Total Liabilities and Equity	2,50,000

Income Statement Data

Net Sales	3,75,000
Interest Expense	4,000
Net Income	22.500

The following account balances existed at December 31,2000. Total Assets, Rs. 2,00,000; Equity, Rs. 65.000. The tax rate is 35 per cent.

Industry norms as of December 31, 2001 were:

Debt-equity ratio	1.75
Prof it margin	0.12
Return on total assets	0.15
Return on stockholders' equity	0.30
Total asset turnover	1.71

Calculate and evaluate the following ratios for Alpha Company as of December 31, 2001:

(a) Debt-equity ratio (b) Profit margin
(c) Return on total assets (d) Return on stockholders' equity
(e) Total asset turnover

19. Here are the income statements and balance sheets of A Company and B Company, taken from their annual reports for the year ended December 31, 2001.

Income Statement
For the year 2001

	A Company	*B Company*
Sales	Rs. 80,00,000	Rs. 70,00,000
Cost of goods sold	60,00,000	47,00.000
Selling, general, and administrative expenses	12,00,000	19.00,000
Interest on debt		70,000
Income before taxes	8,00,000	3,30,000
Income taxes	3,90,000	1,60,000
Net income	4,10,000	1,70,000
Dividends declared	1,00,000	70,000

Condensed Balance Sheets
As of December 31, 2001

	A Company	*B Company*
Assets :	Rs.	Rs.
Cash	3,00,000	3,00,000
Accounts receivable	8,00,000	6,50,000
Inventory	13,00,000	8,50,000
Net plant and equipment	21,00,000	15,00,000
Total assets	45,00,000	33,00,000
Liabilities and equity		
Accounts payable	7,10,000	4,00,000

Taxes payable	3,90,000	1,60,000
Long-term debt	—	14,00,000
Common equity	22,00,000	8,00,000
Retained earnings	12,00,000	5,40,000
Total liabilities and equity	45,00,000	33,00,000

On the basis of the available information, which do you consider to be (1) more liquid, (2) more solvent, (3) more profitable? Explain your conclusions.

20. From the following information you are required to prepare a Balance Sheet:
  1. Current Ratio — 1.75
  2. Liquid Ratio — 1.25
  3. Stock Turnover Ratio (cost of sales/closing stock) — 9
  4. Gross Profit Ratio — 25 per cent
  5. Debt Collection Period — 1½ months
  6. Reserves and surplus to capital — 2
  7. Turnover to fixed assets — 1.2
  8. Capital gearing ratio — 0.6
  9. Fixed assets to net worth — 1.25
  10. Sales for the year Rs. 12,00,000.

Ans.

	Rs.		Rs
Share capital	5,00,000	Stock	1,00,000
Long-term liabilities	3,00,000	Debtors	1,50,000
Reserves and Surplus	1,00,000	Cash and Bank balance	1,00,000
Current liabilities	2,00,000	Balance sheet total	11,00,000
Fixed assets	7,50,000		

21. The following are the summarised profit and loss account and Balance Sheet of a company:

Dr. **Profit and Loss Account for file year ended December 31, 2001** Cr.

To Opening Stock	20,000	By Sales	1,50,000
To Purchases	1,05,000	By Closing Stock	35,000
To Direct Expenses	10,000		
To Gross Profit c/cl	50,000		
	1,85,000		1,85,000
To Administrative Expenses	20,000	By Gross Profit b/d	50,000
To Selling Expenses	10,000		
To Non-Operating Expenses	5,000		
To Net Profit	15,000		
	50,000		50,000

Balance Sheet as at December 31, 2001

Share Capital	2,00,000	Plant & Machinery	50.000
Profit and Loss A/c	50,000	Building	70.000
Current Liabilities	6,000	Motor Car	80.000
		Furniture	10,000
		Stock	50,000
		Debtors	20,000

		Cash	10.000
		Bank	20,000
	3,10,000		3,10,000

Calculate the following ratios:

(i) Gross Profit Ratio
(ii) Operating Profit Ratio
(iii) Current Ratio
(iv) Liquid Ratio
(v) Stock Turnover Ratio
(vi) Fixed Asset Turnover Ratio
(vii) Return on Investment
(viii) Fixed Asset—Proprietors Funds Ratio

CHAPTER 4

Statement of Changes in Financial Position (SCFP)

Financial statement of a business enterprise, *i.e.*, income statement and balance sheet are important statements to judge the results of business operation and financial position at the beginning and end of year. The income statement sets forth the enterprise's revenues, expenses, gains and losses. The balance sheet portrays the overall financial position of a business enterprise at a specific date. The income statement, however, does not show the effects of all the events which affected an enterprise's liquidity — its ability to meet its cash obligations on time — nor does it reflect all the flows of resources into or out of the enterprise during the period. Also, the correct appraisal of performance requires knowledge about movement of funds during a year and their impact on the financial position; this is not achieved in balance sheet as it depicts only summarised financial position on a particular date. To overcome these deficiencies, a second performance related statement needs to be prepared which is popularly known as Statement of Changes in Financial Position, or Funds Statement.

CONCEPT OF STATEMENT OF CHANGES IN FINANCIAL POSITION (SCFP)

A statement of changes in financial position (funds statement) helps us to understand how and why a business enterprise has acquired its resources and what those resources were used for. The objectives of funds statement are (1) to summarise the financing and investing activities of the entity, including the extent to which the enterprise has generated funds from operations during the period and (2) to complete the disclosure of changes of financial position during the period.

CONCEPT OF FUNDS

A statement of changes in financial position can be prepared using different concepts of funds as a basis. For instance, statement of changes in financial position may focus on changes in working capital, cash, or total financial resources of a business enterprise. Accordingly, this chapter discusses the preparation of the following types of statement of changes in financial position :

(1) Statement of changes in working capital, popularly known as Funds Flow Statement or Statement of Sources and Applications of Funds.

(2) Statement of Changes in Cash, popularly known as Cash Flow Statement,

(3) Statement of Changes in Total Financial Resources.

FUNDS DEFINED AS WORKING CAPITAL

In common usage, the term funds means cash. However, accountants and financial executives think of 'funds' in a broader sense. They view the funds available to a business enterprise as its working capital. Working capital is defined as current assets minus current liabilities and thus, is a broader definition of funds than is cash. The basic objective of the statement of changes in financial position, working capital basis, is to explain the changes in the working capital for a specified period of time. In the process of achieving this objective, the statement should enable the user to identify the changes as they relate to three basic causes.

(a) Amount of changes in working capital associated with ihe operating activities of the firm.
(b) Long term financing or other sources that cause an increase in the working capital.
(c) Long term investment activities or other uses that cause a reduction in the working capital.

If the amount of working capital increased during a given fiscal period, this means that more working capital was generated than was used for various business purposes; if a decrease in working capital occurred the reverse is true.One of the key purposes of statement of changes in financial position is to explain fully the increase or decrease in working capital during an accounting period.

SOURCES AND USES OF WORKING CAPITAL

Any transaction that increases the amount of working capital is a source of working capital. For example, the sale or merchandise at a price greater than its cost is a source of working capital, because the increase in cash or receivable from the sale is greater than the decrease in inventory. Any transaction that decreases working capital is a use of working capital. For example, either incurring current liability to acquire a non-current asset or using cash to pay expenses represents a decrease in working capital.

The principal sources and uses of working capital are listed below :

Sources of Working Capital

The following are the sources of working capital:

1. Funds from Business Operations

If the inflow of funds from sales exceeds the outflow of funds to cover the cost of merchandise purchases and expenses of doing business, current operatios will provide a net source of funds. If the inflow of funds from sales is less than these outflows, operation will result in a net use of funds. Working capital provided by operations is the net increase or decrees in working capital resulting from the normal business activities of earning revenue and paying expenses. However, not all the expenses require the use of funds in the current period; therefore the amount of funds provided by operations is not the same as the amount of net income earned during the period.

The following points explain this situation :

(i) Some expenses do not reduce working capital. Some expenses, such as depreciation and amortisation of intangible assets reduce net income but have no immediate effect on the amount of working capital provided bv operations, ie., these items do not reduce working capital. The net income figure therefore understates the amount of working capital provided bv operations by amount of depreciation expense recorded during ihe period. Thus funds provided by operations would be computed in the following manner :

Funds from Operations :	
Net income	—
Add: Depreciation expense	—
Funds provided by operations	—

The addition of depreciation expense to the net income figure has led some people to believe that depreciation expenses is a source of funds. However, it is important for the users of financial statement to understand that depreciation is neither a source nor a use of working capital (funds). No funds flow into business as a result of recording depreciation expense. It is shown in the statement of changes in financial position merely to explain one of the differences between the concept of net income and the concept of working capital provided by operations.

(ii) Some items increase income but do not increase working capital — some items in the income statement increase net income without increasing working capital; such items must be deducted from net income in arriving at working capital provided by operations.

(iii) Non-operating gains and losses — non-operating gains and losses, if material in amount, should be eliminated from net income in order to show the working capital provided by 'normal' operations. For example, assume that plant costing Rs. 1,00,000 is sold at Rs. 1,20,000, at a net gain of Rs. 20,000. In the statement of changes in financial position, the entire Rs. 1,20,000 as proceeds from sale will be reported as funds provided by the sale of plant. The Rs. 20,000 non-operating gain, however, is already included in the net income for the period. In determining the amount of working capital provided by operations, this Rs. 20,000 non-operating gain must be deducted from the net income figure because the entire proceeds from sale of the plant are reported in the statement of changes in financial position.

As a separate example, assume that the same plant is sold for Rs. 90,000; then the non-operating loss of Rs. 10,000 should be added back to net income to arrive at working capital provided by operations and the working capital provided through sale of plant should be reported at Rs. 90,000.

Briefly, the procedure of computing funds provided by operations can be summarised as follows :

Funds from Operations

Net profit (or loss) as per the profit and loss account

Add: (i) Depreciation expense.
(ii) Amortisation of goodwill, patents and other intangible assets.
(iii) Amortisation of extraordinary losses occurred in previous periods.
(iv) Amortisation of discount on debentures.
(v) Loss on sale of non-current assets such as plant, equipment etc.

Less : (i) Gain on sale of non-current assets such as plant, équipment etc.
(ii) Profit or revaluation surplus of non-current assets.
(iii) Dividends and interest on investments (earned but not received)
(iv) Amortisation of premium received on debentures
= Fund from Business Operations

2. Sales of Non-current Assets

A business may obtain working capital by selling non-current assets, such as plant and equipment or long term investments, in exchange for current asset. As long as current assets are received, the sale is a source of funds regardless of whether the non-current assets are sold at a gain or loss. For example, assume that a business firm sells for Rs. 2,50,000 a plant which cost Rs. 3,00,000. Although the plant was sold at a loss, the firm has increased its current assets by Rs. 2,50,000 by selling the plant. Thus, the transaction is a source of working capital.

3. Long-term borrowing

Long-term borrowing, such as issue of debentures and bonds result in an increase in current assets, thereby increasing working capital. Short-term borrowing, however, does not increase working capital. When a company borrows cash on short term credit or by signing a short-term note payable, working capital is unchanged because the increase in current assets is offset by an increase in current liabilities of the same amount.

4. Issue of additional equity capital

The issue of additional equity shares results in an inflow of current assets, thereby increasing working capital. In a similar manner, additional investments of current assets by owners represent source of funds in single proprietorship and partnership.

Uses of Working Capital

The following are the uses of working capital :

1. Declaration of Cash dividend

The declaration of a cash dividend results in a current liability (dividend payable) and is therefore a use of funds. It should be understood that it is the declaration of dividend, rather than the payment of the dividend which is the use of funds. Actual payment of the dividend reduces current assets and current liabilities by the same amount and thus has no effect upon the amount of working capital. Issue of shares in lieu of dividend does not involve any distribution of assets and, therefore, are not a use of funds.

2. Purchase of non-current assets

Purchases of non-current assets, such as plant and equipment, reduce current assets or increase current liabilities. In either case, working capital is reduced.

3. Repayment of long-term debt

Working capital is decreased when current assets are used to repay long-term debt. However, repayment of short-term debt is not a use of funds, since current assets and current liabilities decrease by the same amount.

EFFECT OF TRANSACTIONS ON WORKING CAPITAL

In preparing a statement of changes in financial position, on working capital basis, it is convenient to classify business transactions into three categories :

1. Transactions affecting only Current Asset or Current Liability Accounts

These transactions produce changes in working capital accounts but do not change the amount of working capital. For example, the purchase of merchandise increases inventory and accounts payable but has no effect on working capital; it may therefore be ignored in preparing a statement of changes in financial position. Similarly, paying accounts payable affects cash, so this transaction would be reflected in cash basis statement of changes in financial position. However, the transaction has no effect on working capital since a current asset (cash) and a current liability (accounts payable) decrease by the same amount. Hence, the transaction would not be reflected as a source or use in a working capital basis statement of changes in financial position. Other transactions like collection of receivables, short-term borrowing, purchase of short-term Government securities also fall in this category of transactions.

2. Transactions affecting Current Asset or Current Liability Account and a Non-Working Capital (Non-current) Account

These transactions bring about either an increase or a decrease in the amount of working capital. The issue of long-term bonds, for example, increases current assets and increases loan on bonds, a non-working capital account; therefore the issue of bonds is a source of working capital. Similarly, when the bonds approach maturity they are transferred to the current liability classification in the balance sheet. This causes a reduction (a use) of working capital. If changes in non-working capital accounts are analysed, these events are brought to light, and their effect on working capital will be reported in the statement of changes in financial position.

3. Transactions affecting only Non-current Accounts

These transactions have no direct effect on the amount of working capital. The entry to record depreciation is an example of such a transaction. Other transaction in this category, such as issue of share capital in exchange for plant assets, are called exchanged transactions involving only non-current accounts and are viewed as both a source and a use of working capital, but do not change the amount of working capital. Alternatively, such exchange transactions may not be considered in preparing a statement of changes in financial position on working capital basis.

MAIN STEPS IN PREPARING THE STATEMENT

In order to prepare a statement of changes in financial position on a working capital basis, it is necessary to have balance sheets at two points in time and an income statement covering that span of time. The steps involved in preparing the statement are as follows :

1. Determine the change (increase or decrease) in working capital.
2. Determine the adjustments account to be made to net income.
3. For each non-current account on the balance sheet, establish the increase or decrease in that account. Analyse the change to decide whether it is a source (increase) or use (decrease) of working capital.
4. Be sure that total of all sources including those from operations minus the total of all uses equals the change found in working capital in step 1.

General Rules for Preparing Funds Flow Statement

The following general rules should be observed while preparing funds flow statement :

(1) Increase in a current asset means increase (plus) in working capital.
(2) Decrease in a current asset means decrease (minus) in working capital.
(3) Increase in a current liability means decrease (minus) in working capital.
(4) Decrease in a current liability means increase (plus) in working capital.
(5) Increase in current asset and increase in current liability does not affect working capital.
(6) Decrease in current asset and decrease in current liability does not affect working capital.
(7) Changes in fixed (non-current) assets and fixed (non-current) liabilities affects working capital.

SCHEDULE OF CHANGES IN WORKING CAPITAL

Many business enterprises prefer to prepare another statement, known as schedule of changes in working capital, while preparing a funds flow statement, on a working capital basis. This schedule of changes in working capital provides information concerning the changes in each individual current assets and current liabilities accounts (items). This schedule is a part of the funds flow statement and increase (decrease) in working capital indicated by the schedule of changes in working capital will be equal to the amount of changes in working capital as found by funds flow statement. The schedule of changes in working capital can be prepared by comparing the current assets and current liabilities at two periods. The format of schedule of changes in working capital is as follows :

Schedule of Changes in Working Capital

Items	*As on*	*As on*	*Changes* Increase	Decrease
A. Current Assets:				
Cash balance				
Bank balance				
Accounts receivable (Debtors)				
Marketable Securities				
Stock				
Prepaid expenses				
B. Current liabilities:				
Bank overdraft				
Accounts payables (creditors)				
Outstanding expenses				
Total				
Net increase/decrease in working capital				

Format of Funds Flow Statement

A funds flow statement can be prepared in statement form or 'T' form. Both the formats are being given below :

Funds Flow Statement (Statement Form)

A. Sources of Funds :	
(i) Funds from business operations	
(ii) Sale of fixed asset	
(iii) Issue of shares	
(iv) Issue of debentures	
(v) Long-term borrowings	
Total Sources	—
B. Application of Funds :	
(i) Loss from business operation	
(ii) Payment of dividend	
(iii) Payment of tax	
(iv) Purchase of fixed asset	
(v) Payment of long-term loans	
(vi) Redemption of debentures	
(vii) Redemption of preference shares	
Total uses	—
Net increase/decrease in Working capital (Total sources minus Total uses)	—

Funds Flow Statement ("T" Form)

Source of Funds	*Rs.*	*Application of Funds*	*Rs.*
(i) Funds from business operations		(i) Loss from business operations	
(ii) Sale of fixed assets		(ii) Payment of dividend	
(iii) Issue of shares		(iii) Payment of tax	
(iv) Issue of debentures		(iv) Purchase of fixed assets	
(v) Long-term borrowings		(v) Payment of long-term loans	
(vi) Decrease in working capital (If application amount is more than the sources amount)		(vi) Redemption of debentures	
		(vii) Redemption of preference shares	
		(viii) Increase in working capital (if sources are more than the application amount)	
Total		Total	

TREATMENT OF PROVISION FOR TAXATION AND PROPOSED DIVIDENDS

Provision for Taxation

There are two possible treatment about the provision for taxation :

(1) Provision for taxation can be treated as a current liability and it will decrease the working capital in the schedule of changes in working capital. However, payment of tax does not affect working capital because it involves both current asset and current liability account, *i-e.,* payment decreases cash or bank balance on the one hand and decreases the current liability (tax provision) by the equivalent amount on the other hand.

(2) Provision for taxation may be considered as non-current item. Such a treatment does not change working capital position. Provisions made for taxation during the current year is transferred to adjusted profit and loss account. The amount paid as tax is shown as an application of fund.

Proposed Dividends

There are also two treatments about the proposed dividend.

(1) Proposed dividends can be considered as current liability and hence will decrease working capital in the schedule of changes in working capital. However, when dividends are paid, it is not treated as uses of funds.

(2) Proposed dividend can be treated as non-current item. In this case, proposed dividend for current year is added back to retained profit in order to find out funds from operations. Then, payment of dividend, will be shown as application of funds. Generally, it is treated as non-current item.

Example 1

Compute funds from Operations from the following income statement :

Income Statement

	Rs.		Rs.
To Salaries	10,000	By G/P b/d	2,000
To Rent	4,000	By Rent	10,000
To Depreciation	2,000	By Interest amount	8,000
To Preliminary expenses	4,000	By Net loss	10,000
To Loss on sale of furniture	10,000		
	30,000		30,000

Solution :

Funds from Operations

Net loss as per Income statement		(10,000)
Add: Items which do not decrease funds :		
Depreciation	Rs. 2,000	
Preliminary expenses	Rs. 4,000	
Loss on sale of furniture	Rs. 10,000	16,000
Funds from operations		6,000

Notes : Rent and interest on investment, alternatively can be considered as non-operating income and in such case, they will have to be excluded (deducted) while calculating funds from operations. Also, then, these items will be shown under, 'non-operating income' in the funds flow statement.

Example 2

Explain the following balance sheets for the years 2002 and 2003, find out funds from operations

	2002 (Rs.)	2003 (Rs.)
General reserve	10,000	12,500
Goodwill	5,000	2,500
Provision for depreciation on plant	5,000	6,000
Preliminary expenses	3,000	2,000
Profit and loss appropriation A/c	15,000	20,000

Solution

Funds from Operations

	Rs.
Profit and loss appropriation account as on December 31, 2003	20,000
Add: Items not decreasing funds :	
Transfer to general reserve	2,500
Goodwill written off	2,500
Provision for depreciation on Plant	1,000
Preliminary expenses written off	1,000
	27,000
Less: Profit and Loss appropriation account balance as on December 31, 2002	15,000
Funds from operations	12,000

The funds from operations can also be found by preparing adjusted profit and loss account as given below :

Adjusted Profit and Loss Account

	Rs.		Rs.
To Transfer to general reserve	2,500	By balance b/d	15,000
To Goodwill written off	2,500	By funds from operations (balancing figure)	12,000
To Preliminary expenses written off	1,000		
To Provision for depreciation	1,000		
To Balance c/d	20,000		
	27,000		27,000

Example 3

Calculate funds from operations from the following Profit and Loss Account:

Profit and Loss Account

		Rs.		Rs.
To Opening stock		64,000	By Sales	2,00,000
To purchases	80,000		By Closing Stock	1,60,000
Less: Returns	16,000	64,000		
To Wages paid	40,000			
Add : Outstanding	20,000	60,000		
To Gross profit c/d		1,72,000		
		3,60,000		3,60,000
To Rent		30,000	By Gross profit b/d	1,72,000
To Salary	60,000			
Less : prepaid	10,000	50,000		
To Depreciation on furniture		6,000		
To Discount on issue of share		20,000		
To Goodwill written off		20,000		
To preliminary expenses		12,000		
To Net profit		34,000		
		1,72,000		1,72,000

Solution

Computation of Fund from Operations

1st Method		Rs.	2nd Method		Rs.
			Sources :		
Net profit made during the year		34,000	Sales	2,00,000	
Add : Expenses and items not resulting in the			Stock at the end	1,60,000	3,60,000
Application of funds			Less : Application :		
Depriciation	6,000		Opening stock	64,000	
Discount on shares	20,000		Net purchases	64,000	
Goodwill written off	20,000		Wages	60,000	
Preliminary Expenses	12,000	58,000	Rent	30,000	
			Salary	50,000	2,68,000
Fund from oepration		92,000			92,000

Example 3

Calculate funds from operations from the following Profit and Loss Account :

Profit and Loss Account

Particulars	*Rs.*	*Particulars*	*Rs.*
To Expenses paid and out standing	3,00,000	By Gross profit	4,50,000
To Depreciation	70,000	By Gain on sale of land	60,000
To Less on Sale of Machine	8,000		
To Discount on issue of Shares	400		
To Goodwill written off	20,000		
To Net Profit	1,11,600		
	5,10,000		5,10,000

Solution :

Statement Showing Funds From Operations

		Rs.
Net profit as per profit and loss A/c		1,11,600
Add : Non-Cash Charges		
Depreciation	Rs. 70,000	
Discount on issue of Shares	400	
Goodwill written off	20,000	
Loss on sale of Machine	8,000	98,400
		2,10,000
Less : Non-trading incomes/gains :		
Gain on sale of land		60,000
Funds from operations		1,50,000

Example 5

During the year 2006, Soni Ltd. earned a profit of Rs. 1,85,720 after adjusting the following :

	Rs.
Provision for Bad Debts	4,000
Salaries	8,000
Depreciation written off	15,300
Profit on sale of Fixed Assets	14,000
Discount on debentures written off	20,000
Loss on Sale of Investments	10,000
Preliminary Expenses Written off	50,000
Proposed Dividend	20,000
Transfer to Debenture Redemption fund	20,000
Dividend Received	9,000

Calculate funds from operations.

Solution :

Calculation of Funds from Operations

		Rs.
Profit as per profit & Loss Account :		1,85,720
Add : Non-Cash charges :	Rs.	
Depreciation	15,300	
Discount on Debentures	20,000	
Loss on Investment	10,000	
Preliminary Expenses	50,000	
Proposed Dividend	20,000	
Debenture Redemption Fund	20,000	1,35,300
		3,21,020
Less : Non-trading gains/incomes :		
Profit on sale of fixed Assests	14,000	
Dividend Received	9,000	23,000
Funds from operations		2,98,020

Example 6

From the following, Calculate funds from operation.

	Rs.
Net Profit for the year 2005-2006	15,000
Profit on sale of land	25,000
Goodwill written off	10,000
Transfer to General Reserve	4,000
Depreciation Provision on Machine :	
Beginning of the year	26,000
End of the year	20,500

In addition, a machine costing Rs. 20,000 (Accumulated Depreciation thereon Rs. 8,500) was sold for Rs. 11,500 during the year 2005-2006.

Solution

Statement of Showing Fund From Operations

	Rs.	Rs.
Net profit for the year 1990-91		15,000
Add : Non-cash Charges :		
Goodwill written off	10,000	
General Reserve	4,000	
Depricoation for the year	3,000	17,000
		32,000
Less : Non-trading gains/incomes :		
Profit on sale of land		25,000
Fund from operations		7,000

Working Notes

Calculation of Depreciation

Machinery Sold Account

	Rs.		Rs.
To Balance b/d Mach. A/c	20,000	By Depreciation A/c	8,500
(Balance Taken)		By Cash-sale	11,500
	20,000		20,000

Depriciation Account

	Rs.		Rs.
To Machinery sold A/c	8,500	To Balance b/d	26,000
To Balance c/d	20,500	By Profit & Loss A/c (Bal. fig.)	3,000
	29,000		29,000

Example 7

The following are the summarised balance sheets of M/s. Preeti Ltd. as on March 31. 2001 and 2002.

	2001 Rs.(000')	2002 Rs.(000')
Share Capital :		
10% Preference Share Capital	100	110
Equity Share Capital	220	250
Security Premium	20	26
Profit and Loss Account	104	134
Liabilities (Non-Current):		
12% Debetures	70	64
Current Liability:		
Creditors	38	46
Bill payable	5	4
Provision for Taxation	10	12
Dividends Payable	7	8
	574	654
Non current Assests:		
Machinery (Net)	200	230
Buildings (Net)	150	176
Land	18	18
Current Assets:		
Cash	42	32
Debtors	38	38
Bills-Receivable	42	62
Stock-on-hand	84	98
	574	654

Required :

(*i*) Schedule of changes in Working Capital.

(*ii*) Fund-flow statement.

Solution

Schedule of changes in Working Capital

Items	*2001 Rs.('000)*	*2002 Rs.('000)*	*Change in Working Capital Increase (Rs. '000)*	*Decrease (Rs.'000)*
Cash	42	32	—	—
Debtors	38	38	—	—
Bills Receivable	42	62	20	—
Stock on hand	84	98	14	—
Creditors	38	46	—	8
Bills Payable	5	4	1	—
Net Increase in Working Capital	—	—	—	17
			35	35

Preference Share Capital Account

	Rs.		Rs.
Balance c/d	110	Balance b/d	100
		Bank(Source)	10
	110		110

Securities Premium Account

	Rs.		Rs.
Balance c/d	26	Balance b/d	20
		Bank (Source)	6
	26		26

12% Debenture Account

	Rs.		Rs.
Bank (Application)	6	Balance b/d	70
Balance c/d	64		70
	70		70

Equity Share Capital Account

	Rs.		Rs.
Balance c/d	250	Balance b/d	220
		Bank (Source)	30
	250		250

Machinery Account

	Rs.		Rs.
Balance b/d	200	Balance c/d	230
Bank Application	30		
	230		230

Building Account

	Rs.		Rs.
Balance b/d	150	Balance c/d	176
Bank (Application)	26		
	176		176

Example 8

From the following Balance Sheets of Yamini Ltd. Prepare Fund flow statement. (Rs)

	Year I	*Year II*		*Year I*	*Year II*
Equity Share Capital	80,000	85,000	Land and Building	50,000	50,000
Profit and Loss A/c	14,500	24,500	Pland and Machinery	24,000	34,000
Mortage Loan	–	50,000	Stock	9,000	7,000
Creditors	9,000	5,000	Debtors	16,500	19,500
			Cash	4,000	9,000
	1,03,500	1,19,500		1,03,500	1,19,500

Depriciation provided on land and Building Rs. 5,000

Solution

Schedule of changes in Working Capital

Items	*2001*	*2002*	*Change in Increase*	*Working Capital Decrease*
	Rs.	Rs.	Rs.	Rs.
Stock	9,000	7,000	—	2,000
Debtors	16,500	19,500	3,000	—
Cash	4,000	9,000	5,000	—
Creditors	9,000	5,000	4,000	—
	—	—	12,000	2,000
Increase in Working Capital		—		10,000
			12,000	12,000

Yamini Ltd.
Fund Flow Statement
for the year ended 31st December, 2002

Sources of Funds	*Rs.*	*Uses of Funds*	*Rs.*
From Operations	15,000	Purchases of Plant	10,000
Issue of Share Capital	5,000	Purchases of Land & Building	5,000
From Mortage Loan	5,000	Increase in Working Capital	10,000
	25,000		25,000

Land & Building Account

	Rs.		Rs.
Balance b/d	50,000	Depreciation	50,000
Cash(use)	5,000	Balance c/d	5,000
	55,000		55,000

Plant and Machinery Account

	Rs.		Rs.
Balance b/d	24,000	Balance c/d	34,000
Cash(use)	10,000		
	34,000		34,000

Equity Share Capital A/c

	Rs.		Rs.
Balance c/d	85,000	Balance b/d	80,000
		Cash(Source)	5,000
	85,000		85,000

Mortgage Loan Account

	Rs.		Rs.
Balance c/d	5,000	Balance b/d	—
		Cash(Source)	5,000
	5,000		5,000

Adjusted Profit and Loss Account

	Rs.		Rs.
Depreciation	5,000	Balance b/d	14,500
Balance c/d	24,500	Funds or Working capital from operations (Balancing Figure)	15,000
	29,500		29,500

Example 9

From the following Comparative Balance sheets of Anshita Ltd., Make out : (*i*) Schedule of changes in working capital. (*ii*) Statements of Fund-Flow.

Liabilities	*2001*	*2002* Rs.	*Assets* Rs.	*2001* Rs.	*2002* Rs.
Equity Share Capital	3,00,000	4,00,000	Goodwill	1,15,000	90,000
Preference Share Capital	1,50,000	1,00,000	Land and Building	2,00,000	1,70,000
General Reserve	40,000	70,000	Plant	80,000	2,00,000
Profit and Loss Account	30,000	48,000	Debtors	1,60,000	2,00,000
Proposed Dividend	42,000	50,000	Stock	77,000	1,09,000
Creditors	55,000	83,000	Bills Receivable	20,000	30,000
Bills payable	20,000	1,6000	Cash	15,000	10,000
Provision for Taxation	40,000	50,000	Bank	10,000	8,000
	6,77,000	8,17,000		6,77,000	8,17,000

Supplementary Data :

(*i*) Depreciation of Rs. 10,000 and Rs. 20,000 have been charged on plant and Land and Building respectively in 2002.

(*ii*) An interim Dividend of Rs. 20,000 has been paid in 2002.

(*iii*) Income Tax Rs. 35,000 has been paid during the year 2002.

Solution

Schedule of Changes in Working Capital

Items	*2001*	*2002*	*Change in Increase*	*Working Capital Decrease*
	Rs.	Rs.	Rs.	Rs.
Creditors	55,000	83,000	—	28,000
Bills Payable	20,000	16,000	4,000	—
Debtors	1,60,000	2,00,000	40,000	—
Stock	77,000	1,09,000	32,000	—
Bills Receivable	20,000	30,000	10,000	—
Cash	15,000	10,000	—	5,000
Bank	10,000	8,000	—	2,000
Net Increase in Working Capital				51,000
			86,000	86,000

Anshita Ltd.
Fund Flow Statements
For the year ending on 2002

		Rs.
Sources of Working Capital : from Operations		2,18,000
Issue of Equity Share Capital		1,00,000
Sale of Land & Building		10,000
Total Sources		3,28,000
Uses of Working Capital :		
Purchase of Plant		1,30,000
Redemption of Preference Shares		50,000
Payments of Dividends		
(*i*) Previous Year	42,000	
(*ii*) Interim Dividend	20,000	62,000
Payment of Tax		35,000
Total use's		2,77,000
Net Increase in Working Capital		51,000
		3,28,000

Land and Building Account

	Rs.		Rs.
Balance b/d	2,00,000	Depreciation	20,000
		Bank (Balancing figure-source)	1,70,000
		Balance c/d	10,000
	2,00,000		2,00,000

Plant Account

	Rs.		Rs.
Balance b/d	2,00,000	Depreciation	10,000
Bank(Bal. Fig. Application)	1,30,000	Balance c/d	2,00,000
	2,10,000		2,10,000

Provision for Taxation Account

	Rs.		Rs.
Bank(Application)	35,000	Balance b/d	40,000
Balance c/d (Bal. Fig.)	50,000	Profit and Loss Account	45,000
	85,000		85,000

Proposed Dividend Account

	Rs.		Rs.
Bank (Application)	42,000	Balance b/d	42,000
Balance c/d	50,000	Profit & Loss Account	50,000
	92,000		92,000

Interim Dividend

	Rs.		Rs.
Balance (Application)	20,000	Profit and Loss Account	20,000

Goodwill Account

	Rs.		Rs.
Balance b/d	11,500	Profit and Loss Account	25,000
		Balance c/d	90,000
	1,15,000		1,15,000

Preference Share Capital Account

	Rs.		Rs.
Bank (Bal. fig. Application)	50,000	Balance c/d	1,50,000
Balance c/d	1,00,000		
	1,50,000		1,50,000

(Adjusted) Profit and Loss Account

		Rs.		Rs.
Amortization of Goodwill		25,000	Balance b/d	30,000
General Reserve		30,000	Working Capital from Operations	2,18,000
Interim Dividends		20,000		
Depreciation :				
Building	20,000			
Plant	10,000	30,000		
Provision for Taxation		45,000		
Balance c/d		48,000		
		2,48,000		2,48,000

Example 10

Following are the Balance Sheets of the Tanu Ltd. as on 31 March, 2001 and 2002.

	Rs.	Rs.		Rs.	Rs.
Preference Share Capital	–	2,00,000	Goodwill	20,000	30,000
Equity Share Capital	4,20,000	5,20,000	Buildings	6,00,000	5,80,000
General Reserve	1,00,000	1,10,000	Machinery	3,00,000	3,38,000
Profit and Loss Account	61,000	71,200	Stock	2,00,000	1,48,000
14% Debentures	2,00,000	–	Debtors	1,40,000	1,08,000
Creditors	4,40,000	2,68,000	Cash	20,600	37,200
Unclaimed Dividends	–	2,000			
Provision of Tax	60,000	70,000			
	12,81,000	12,41,600		12,81,000	12,41,600

(*i*) Dividends paid in cash Rs. 50,000 during the year (*ii*) Assets acquired for Rs. 1,00,000 payable in equity shares; Stock Rs. 50,000. Machine Rs. 40,000 and Goodwill Rs 10,000 (*iii*) Machine Purchased for Cash Rs. 12,000. (*iv*) Provision for Tax During the year Rs. 66,000. (*v*) Debenture holder accept preference shares in settlement of their claims. (*vi*) Depreciation on Building Rs. 20,000. Prepare Fund flow statement and Schedule for charges in Working Capital.

Solution

Schedule for Changes in Working Capital

	2001	*2002*	*Change in Increase*	*Working Capital Decrease*
	Rs.	Rs.	Rs.	Rs.
Stock	2,00,000	1,48,000	—	52,000
Debtors	1,40,400	1,08,400	—	32,000
Cash	20,600	37,200	16,600	—
Creditors	4,40,000	2,68,400	1,71,600	—
Unclaimed Dividends	—	2,000	—	2,000
Increase in Working Capital	—		—	1,02,200
			1,88,200	1,88,200

Machinery A/c

	Rs.		Rs.
Balance b/d	3,00,000	Depreciation (Bal. fig.)	14,000
Cash (use)	12,000	Balance c/d	3,38,000
Equity Share Capital Account	40,000		
	3,52,000		3,52,000

Goodwill A/c

	Rs.		Rs.
Balance b/d	20,000	Balance c/d	30,000
Equity Share Capital A/c	10,000		
	30,000		30,000

Buildings A/c

	Rs.		Rs.
Balance b/d	6,00,000	Depreciation	20,000
		Balance c/d	5,80,000
	6,00,000		6,00,000

Preference Share Capital A/c

	Rs.		Rs.
Balance c/d	2,00,000	Balance b/d	—
		14% Debenture A/c	2,00,000
	2,00,000		2,00,000

Equity Share Capital A/c

	Rs.		Rs.
Balance c/d	5,20,000	Balance b/d	4,20,000
		Machinery A/c	40,000
		Stock A/c (Source)	50,000
		Goodwill A/c	10,000
	5,20,000		5,20,000

14% Debenture A/c

	Rs.		Rs.
Preference Share Capital	2,00,000	Balance b/d	2,00,000

Unclaimed Dividends A/c

	Rs.		Rs.
Balance c/d	2,000	Balance b/d	–
		Dividends A/c	2,000
	2,000		2,000

Provision for Tax A/c

	Rs.		Rs.
Cash (use)	56,000	Balance b/d	60,000
Balance c/d	70,000	Profit and Loss A/c	66,000
	1,26,000		1,26,000

Dividend A/c

	Rs.		Rs.
Cash (use)	50,000	Profit and Loss A/c	52,000
Unclaimed Dividends	2,000		
	52,000		52,000

General Reserve A/c

	Rs.		Rs.
Balance c/d	1,10,000	Balance b/d	1,00,000
		Profit & Loss A/c	10,000
	1,10,000		1,10,000

Adjusted Profit and Loss A/c

	Rs.		Rs.
Depreciation on Machine	14,000	Balance b/d	61,000
Depreciation on Building	20,000	Funds from Operations	1,72,200
General Reserve	10,000	(Bal. Fig.)	
Provision for Tax	66,000		
Dividends (50,000 + 2,000)	52,000		
Balance c/d	71,200		
	2,33,200		2,33,200

Tanu Ltd.
Fund-Flow Statement
for the year ending 31 December, 2002

Sources of Funds	*Rs.*	*Uses of Funds*		*Rs.*
From Operations	1,72,200	Purchase of Machinery		12,000
Issue of Shares Capital		Payment of Tax		56,000
(for Purchase of Stock)	50,000	Payment of Dividend		
		Cash	50,000	
		Unclaimed	2,000	52,000
		Increase in Working Capital		1,02,200
	2,22,200			2,22,200

Notes:

(*i*) Unclaimed dividend has been shown as Current Liability in the Schedule of changes in Working Capital.

(*ii*) Unclaimed dividend has also been shown in the fund flow statement. The reason is that dividends paid in cash is Rs. 50,000 and the unclaimed portion is Rs. 2,000 in addition to those paid. Thus, profits have been appropriated for Rs. 52,000. Since it is a non-operating item, Rs. 52,000 has been added to the current years profit for calculating the funds from operations. Similarly Rs. 52,000 have been shown in the fund flow statement because Rs. 50,000 paid in cash decrease the working capital as also the outstanding liability for dividend decreases the working capital. Alternately, unclaimed dividend may be simply taken to schedule of changes in working capital and, then the same need not be added back to current year's profit and then need not be shown in the fund flow statement as use of working capital.

(*iii*) Exchange transactions such as purchase of Machine and goodwill by issue of share capital and conversion of Debentures into preference shares need not be shown in the fund-flow statement. They are required to be shown only in the statement of changes in Financial Position — working capital basis, because that tittle (SCFP) defines funds as working capital using all financial resources.

(*iv*) Issue of Share Capital has been shown as source of working capital to the extent o the amount of stock purchased because this transactions directly increases the working capital.

Example 11

From the following Comparative Balance sheets and Information of RPL Ltd. Prepare fund flow statement and Schedule of changes in Working Capital.

Balance sheet as on 31 March., ...

Liabilities	*2005*	*2006*	*Assets*	*2005*	*2006*
Equity Share Capital	40,000	70,000	Land	80,000	80,000
Profit and Loss A/c	13,420	16,000	Building	40,000	36,000
General Reserve	13,180	14,200	Furniture	5,000	7,000
Loan(Long term)	16,400	14,000	Sundry Debtors	12,200	16,600
Sundry Creditors	36,720	17,000	Bills Receivable	2,000	13,000
Bills payable	13,900	4,200	Goodwill	19,000	16,000
Provision for Tax	9,000	12,000	Cash in hand	620	5,400
Proposed Dividend	15,000	25,000			
Provision for Doubtful	1,200	1,600			
	1,58,820	1,74,000		1,58,820	1,74,000

Additional Information :

(*i*) Additional land was purchased at a Cost of Rs. 1,20,000 and later on sold at a profit of Rs. 20,000 during the year (*ii*) furniture with a Depreciated value of Rs. 2,000 was sold for Rs. 1,000. (*iii*) An Interim Dividend of Rs. 5,000 was paid durin the year. (*iv*) Income Tax paid Rs. 8,500. (*v*) Show all your Calculations properly.

Solution

Schedule of Changes in Working Capital

Items	*2005*	*2006*	*Change in Increase*	*Working Capital Decrease*
	Rs.	*Rs.*	*Rs.*	*Rs.*
Sundry Debtors	12,200	16,600	4,400	–
Bills Receivable	2,000	13,000	11,000	–
Cash in hand	620	5,400	4,780	–
Sundry Creditors	36,720.	17,000	19,720	–
Bill Payable	13,900	21,200	9,700	–
Provision for Doubtful Debts	1,200	1,600	–	400
Increase in Working Capital				49,200
			4,96,00	4,96,00

Land A/c

	Rs.		Rs.
Balance b/d	80,000	Cash(Source)	1,40,000
Cash (use)	1,20,000	Balance c/d	80,000
Profit and Loss A/c (Profit on sale)	20,000		
	2,20,000		2,20,000

Building A/c

	Rs.		Rs.
Balance b/d	40,000	Depreciation A/c (Balancing Fig.)	4,000
		Balance c/d	36,000
	40,000		40,000

Furniture A/c

	Rs.		Rs.
Balance b/d	5,000	Cash(Source)	1,000
Cash (use) (Balancing Figure)	4,000	Profit and Loss A/c (Loss on Sale)	1,000
		Balance c/d	7,000
	9,000		9,000

Equity Share Capital A/c

	Rs.		Rs.
Balance c/d	70,000	Balance b/d	40,000
		Cash (Source)	30,000
	70,000		70,000

General Reserve A/c

	Rs.		Rs.
Balance c/d	14,200	Balance b/d	13,180
		Profit and Loss A/c	1,020
	14,200		14,200

(Long term) Loan A/c

	Rs.		Rs.
Cash (use) (Bal. Fig.)	2,400	Balance b/d	16,400
Balance c/d	14,000		
	16,400		16,400

Provision for Tax A/c

	Rs.		Rs.
Cash(use)	8,500	Balance b/d	9,000
Balance c/d	12,000	Profit & Loss A/c (Bal. Fig.)	11,500
	20,500		20,500

Proposed Dividend A/c

	Rs.		Rs.
Cash(use)	15,000	Balance b/d	15,000
Balance c/d	25,000	Profit and Loss A/c	25,000
	40,000		40,000

Adjusted Profit and Loss A/c

	Rs.		Rs.
Depreciation on Building	4,000	Balance b/d	13,420
Furniture A/c	1,000	Land A/c (Profit on sale)	20,000
(Loss on sale)		Funds from operations Bal. Fig.	33,100
General Reserve A/c	1,020		
Provision for Tax A/c	11,500		
Proposed Dividend A/c	25,000		
Interim Dividend A/c	5,000		
Goodwill Written on	3,000		
Balance c/d	16,000		
	66,520		66,520

Goodwill A/c

	Rs.		Rs.
Balance b/d	19,000	Profit and Loss A/c (Bal. Fig.)	3,000
		Balance c/d	16,000
	19,000		19,000

Interim Dividend A/c

	Rs.		Rs.
Cash (use)	5,000	Profit and Loss A/c	5,000

Notes : Since the land Costing Rs. 1,20,000 has been sold at a profit of Rs. 20,000, the sale price is Rs. 1,40,000 (Rs. 1,20,000 + Rs. 20,000)

RPL Ltd.
Fund Flow Statement
for the year ended 31st March, 1993

Source of Funds	*Rs.*	*Uses of Funds*	*Rs.*
From Operations	33,100	Purchase of Land	1,20,000
Issue of Share Capital	30,000	Purchase of Furniture	4,000
Sale of Land	1,40,000	Repayment of Long Term Loan	2,400
(Rs.1,20,000 + 20,000)		Payment of Tax	8,500
Sale of Furniture	1,000	Payment of Dividend :	
		Interim	5,000
		Final	15,000
		Increased in Working Capital	49,200
	2,04,100		2,04,100

Example 13

Prepare funds flow statement from the following balance sheets and additional information:

Liabilities	*1998*	*1999*	*Assets*	*1998*	*1999*
Equity Share Capital	7,50,000	9,00,000	Goodwill	20,000	15,000
13% Debentures	2,50,000	2,00,000	Plant & Machinery	3,50,000	4,50,000

(Contd...)

Profit and Loss A/c	40,000	50,000	Land & Building	6,50,000	6,59,000
General Reserve	40,000	50,000	Investments	40,000	1,28,000
Creditors	50,000	60,000	Debtors	50,000	30,000
Bills payable	30,000	20,000	Stock	80,000	90,000
Provision for Tax	50,000	60,000	Bills Receivable	70,000	50,000
Provision for Depreciation			Bank	40,000	30,000
on Land and Building	1,00,000	1,40,000	Preliminary Expenses	10,000	8,000
	13,10,000	14,80,000		13,10,000	14,80,000

Additional Information:

(*i*) Provision for Depreciation on Plant and Machinery was Rs. 40,000 on 31 March, 1998 and Rs. 45,000 on 31 March 1999. (*ii*) Machinery costing Rs. 36,000 (accumulated Depreciation Rs. 12,000) was sold for Rs. 20,000. (*iii*) Investment costing Rs. 30,000 were sold at a profit of 20% on cost. (*iv*) Tax of Rs. 30,000 were paid. Prepare Fund Flow Statement and schedule of Changes in Working Capital. Show Working Notes.

Solution

Schedule of Changes in Working Capital

Items	*31st March* 1998 Rs.	1999 Rs.	*Change in Working Capital* *Increase* Rs.	*Decrease* Rs.
A. Current Assets				
Debtors	50,000	30,000	–	20,000
Stock	80,000	90,000	10,000	–
Bills Receivable	70,000	50,000	–	20,000
Bank	40,000	30,000	–	10,000
	2,40,000	2,00,000		
B. Current Liabilities				
Creditors	50,000	60,000	–	10,000
Bills payable	30,000	20,000	10,000	–
	80,000	80,000		
C. Working Capital (A–B)	1,60,000	1,20,000		
D. Decrease in Working Capital	–	40,000	40,000	–
	1,60,000	1,60,000	60,000	60,000

Plant & Machinery A/c

	Rs.		Rs.
Balance b/d(Gross) (Rs. 3,50,000 + Rs. 40,000)	3,90,000	Bank A/c(Source)	20,000
		Provision for Depreciation on Plant & Machinery	12,000
Bank Account(use) (Bal. Fig.)	1,41,000	P & L A/c (Loss)	4,000
		Balance c/d (Gross) (Rs. 4,50,000 + Rs. 45,000)	4,95,000
	5,31,000		5,31,000

Provision for Depreciation on Plant and Machinery A/c

	Rs.		Rs.
Plant and Machinery	12,000	Balance b/d	40,000
Balance c/d	45,000	P & L A/c (Bal. Fig.)	17,000
	57,000		57,000

Provision for Tax A/c

	Rs.		Rs.
Bank (Tax Paid-use)	30,000	Balance c/d	50,000
Balance c/d	60,000	P & L A/c (Provision Made)	40,000
	90,000		90,000

Investment A/c

	Rs.		Rs.
Balance b/d	40,000	Bank A/c (Source)	36,000
P&L A/c (Profit)	6,000	[30,000 + 20% of Rs. 30,000]	
Bank A/c (Use)	1,38,000	Balance c/d	1,48,000
	1,84,000		1,84,000

Goodwill A/c

	Rs.		Rs.
Balance b/d	20,000	P&L A/c	5,000
		Balance c/d	15,000
	20,000		20,000

Land & Building A/c

	Rs.		Rs.
Balance b/d	6,50,000	Balance c/d	6,59,000
Cash(use)	9,000		
	6,59,000		6,59,000

Premilinary Expense A/c

	Rs.		Rs.
Balance b/d	10,000	Proit & Loss A/c	2,000
		Balance c/d	8,000
	10,000		10,000

Equity Share Capital A/c

	Rs.		Rs.
Balance c/d	9,000	Balance b/d	7,50,000
		Cash (source)	1,50,000
	9,00,000		9,00,000

13% Debentures A/c

	Rs.		Rs.
Cash(use)	50,000	Balance b/d	2,50,000
Balance c/d	2,00,000		
	2,50,000		2,50,000

General Reserve A/c

	Rs.		Rs.
Balance c/d	50,000	Balance b/d	40,000
		Profit & Loss A/c	10,000
	50,000		50,000

Provision for Depreciation on Land & Building A/c

	Rs.		Rs.
Balance c/d	1,40,000	Balance b/d	1,00,000
		P & L A/c	40,000
	1,40,000		1,40,000

Adjusted Profit & Loss A/c

	Rs.		Rs.
Loss on Sale of Plant & Machinery	4,000	Balance b/d	40,000
Provision for Depreciation on Plant & Machinery	17,000	Profit on Sale of Investment	6,000
Provision for Taxation	40,000	Funds from operations	1,22,000
General Reserve A/c	10,000		
Provision for Depreciation on Land & Building	40,000		
Goodwill Written off	5,000		
Preliminary Expenses Written off	2,000		
Balance c/d	50,000		
	1,68,000		1,68,000

Fund Flow Statement
for the year ending on 31st March 1999

Source of Funds	*Rs.*	*Uses of Funds*	*Rs.*
From Operations	1,22,000	Purchase of Plant & Machinery	1,41,000
Issue of Share Capital	1,50,000	Payment of Tax	30,000
Sale of Plant & Machinery	20,000	Purchase of Investment	1,38,000
Sale of Investment	36,000	Purchase of land & Blg.	9,000
Decrease in Working Capital	40,000	Redemption of Debentures	50,000
	3,68,000		3,68,000

Example 14

Balance of X Ltd.
As on 31st December 1994 & 1995

Liabilities	*1994*	*1995*	*Assets*	*1994*	*1995*
	Rs.	*Rs.*			*Rs.*
Equity Share Capital	2,00,000	2,50,000	Bank	35,000	16,000
12% Debentures	1,00,000	80,000	Stock	40,000	75,000
10% Preference Share Capital	50,000	80,000	Bills Receivable	20,000	50,000
Public Deposits	20,000	30,000	Debtors	70,000	1,00,000
Loans	50,000	80,000	Machinery	75,000	60,000
Reserves	20,000	25,000	Furniture	10,000	8,000
P & L A/c	50,000	60,000	Land	1,70,000	28,000
Provision for Depreciation on Machinery	10,000	15,000	Buildings	1,40,000	99,000
Proposed Dividend	20,000	25,000	Goodwill	30,000	25,000
Creditors	40,000	50,000			
Bills payable	30,000	18,000			
	5,90,000	7,13,000		5,90,000	7,13,000

Additional Information :

(*i*) Depreciation charges during 1995 was Rs. 4,000 on Furniture Rs. 12,000 on Machinery and Rs. 20,000 on Buildings.

(*ii*) Redemption of debentures was made at 10% Premium.

(*iii*) Part of Machinery was sold for Rs. 15,000 at a loss of Rs. 4,000.

(*iv*) During 1995, Interim Dividend was paid Rs. 10,000 and Income Tax was paid Rs. 5,000.

You are required to prepare Fund Flow Statement and schedule of change in Working Capital from the above particulars. Working notes are also required.

Solution

Schedule of Charges in Working Capital

Items	*1994*	*1995*	*Change in Increase*	*Working Capital Decrease*
	Rs.	Rs.	Rs.	Rs.
Bank	35,000	16,000	–	19,000
Stock	40,000	75,000	35,000	–
Bills Receivable	20,000	50,000	30,000	–
Debtors	70,000	1,00,000	30,000	–
Creditors	40,000	50,000	–	10,000
Bills Payable	30,000	18,000	12,000	–
Net increase in W.C.				78,000
			1,07,000	1,07,000

X Ltd.
Fund Flow Statement
for the year ended 31st Dec., 1995

Source of Funds	*Rs.*	*Uses of Funds*	*Rs.*
Funds from Operations	1,02,000	Purchase of Furniture	2,000
Sale of Machinery	15,000	Machinery Purchased	11,000
Sale of Building	21,000	Redemption of Debentures	22,000
Issue of Equity Share	50,000	(20,000 + 2,000)	
Issue of Preference Share	30,000	Land Purchased	1,10,000
Public Deposits	10,000	Payment of Dividend	20,000
Loans	30,000	Payment of Interim Dividend	10,000
		Tax Paid	5,000
		Increase in Working Capital	78,000
	2,58,000		2,58,000

Although the Debentures have been redeemed at a premium, premium on Redemption account does not appear in the Balance Sheet. It means that the same has been written off to Profit and Loss Account. Hence premium on redemption account being non-fund account, has been added back to current year profit.

Example 15

Prepare (*i*) Statement of changes in Working Capital and (*ii*) Statement of Sources and Applications of funds, from the following Balance sheets :

Liabilities	*2002*	*2001*
	Rs.	Rs.
Capital	10,000	10,000
Profit and Loss Account	15,400	5,200
Long-term loan	8,000	6,000
Short-term Loan	2,400	2,400
Creditors	3,600	3,600
Outstanding wages	800	1,400
Income tax payable	3,400	3,800
	43,600	32,400
Assets		
Cash	5,400	5,600
Debtors	6,600	3,400
Stock	9,200	5,400
Long-term investment	12,000	7,000
Plant	9,600	10,600
Prepaid Insurance	800	400
	43,600	32,400

Solution

Statement of Sources and Application of Funds

	Rs.
Sources :	
Funds from operations	11,200
Long-term Loan	2,000
Total Sources	13,200
Applications :	
Purchase of Long-term investment	5,000
Total applications	5,000

Net Increase in Working capital = 13,200 – 5,000 = Rs. 8,200

Profit and Loss Account

	Rs.		Rs.
To Depreciation on Plant	1,000	By Balance b/d (profit)	5,200
To Net profit c/d	15,400	By Funds from operations (Balancing Figure)	11,200
	16,400		16,400

Statement of Changes in Working Capital

	2001 *Rs.*	*2002* *Rs.*	*Changes in current assets and current liabilities* *Dr.*	*Cr.*
	Rs.	Rs.	Rs.	Rs.
Current assets :				
Cash	5,600	5,400		200
Debtors	3,400	6,600	3,200	
Stock	5,400	9,200	3,800	
Prepaid Insurance	400	800	400	
	14,800	22,000		
Current liabilties :				
Outstanding wages	1,400	800	600	
Income tax payable	3,800	3,400	400	
	5,200	4,200		
Working Capital	9,600	17,800		
Net Increase in Working Capital	8,200			8,200
	17,800	17,800	8,400	8,400

Example 16

From the following Balance Sheets of A Ltd. make out :

(*i*) Statement of changes in the Working Capital; and

(*ii*) Funds Flow Statement.

Liabilities	*2001* Rs.	*2002* Rs.
Equity Share Capital	6,00,000	8,00,000
Profit & Loss A/c	1,00,000	1,60,000
General Reserve	50,000	70,000
Provision for Taxation	50,000	40,000
Sundry Creditors	1,10,000	1,30,000
Bills Payable	80,000	90,000
Outstanding Rent	10,000	25,000
	10,00,000	13,15,000

Assets	*2001* Rs.	*2002* Rs.
Land and Buildings	1,80,000	2,20,000
Plant and Machinery	5,00,000	8,00,000
Stock	1,00,000	85,000
Bills Receivable	50,000	30,000
Debtors	1,50,000	1,60,000
Cash in Hand	20,000	20,000
	10,00,000	13,15,000

Additional Information :

(*i*) Depreciation on Plant and Machinery in 2002 Rs. 50,000.

(*ii*) A piece of machinery costing Rs. 12,000 was sold for Rs. 8,000 during 2002 (depreciation of Rs. 7,000 had been provided on it).

(*iii*) An interim dividend of Rs. 6,000 was paid during the year.

(*iv*) Income tax paid during 2002 Rs. 45,000.

Solution

Statement of Changes in Working Capital

	2001 Rs.	*2002* Rs.	*Increase* Rs.	*Decrease* Rs.
Current Assets :				
Stock	1,00,000	85,000	–	15,000
Debtors	1,50,000	1,60,000	10,000	–
B/R	50,000	30,000	–	20,000
Cash	20,000	20,000	–	–
Current Liabilities :				
Sundry Creditors	1,10,000	1,30,000	–	20,000
Bills Payable	80,000	90,000	–	10,000
Outstanding Rent	10,000	25,000	–	15,000
Net Decreasee in Working Capital	–	–	70,000	–
			80,000	80,000

Funds Flow Statement

Sources	*Rs.*	*Application*	*Rs.*
Funds from operations	1,68,000	Tax paid	45,000
Equity Share capital	2,00,000	Purchase of Plant & Machinery	3,55,000
Sale of Machinery	8,000	Interim dividend	6,000
Decrease in Working Capital	70,000	Purchase of Land, Building	40,000
	4,46,000		4,46,000

Working Notes :

Adjusted Profit and Loss Account

Particulars	*Rs.*	*Particulars*	*Rs.*
To General Reserve	20,000	By Balance b/d	1,00,000
To Interim Dividend	6,000	By Profit on sale of	
To Provision for Taxation	35,000	Plant and Machinery	3,000
To Dep. on Plant	50,000	By Funds from operation	1,68,000
To Balance c/d	1,60,000		
	2,71,000		2,71,000

Plant and Machinery A/c

Particulars	*Rs.*	*Particulars*	*Rs.*
To Balance b/d	5,00,000	By Depreciation	50,000
To Profit and Loss A/c		By Bank	8,000
(profit on sale)	3,000	By Balance c/d	8,00,000
To Bank	3,55,000		
	8,58,000		8,58,000

Provision For Taxation

Particulars	*Rs.*	*Particulars*	*Rs.*
To Bank	45,000	By Balance b/d	50,000
To Balance c/d	40,000	By Profit & Loss A/c	35,000
	85,000		85,000

Example 17

The following are the balance sheet of a company for the years 2002 and 2003 and income statement for the year 2003.

Balance Sheets as on December 31, 2002 and December 31, 2003

	Dec. 31, 2003	*Dec. 31, 2002*	*Increase (decrease)*
Assets :	Rs.	Rs.	Rs.
Current assets:			
Cash	19,000	17,400	1,600
Debtors	24,600	24,000	600

	Inventory	33,000	34,000	(1,000)
	Prepaid insurance	4,000	3,600	400
	Long-term assets :			
	Machinery	3,60,000	3,50,000	10,000
Less:	Accumulated depreciation	(1,68,800)	(1,66,000)	(2,800)
	Total assets	2,71.800	2,63,000	8,800
Liabilities and Equity				
Current liabilities:				
	Creditors	33,600	32,400	1,200
	Salaries payable	600	1,000	(400)
	Income-taxes payable	4,400	3,400	1,000
	Long-term loan	46,000	40,000	6,000
	Equity Capital	1,00,000	1,00,000	
	Retained earnings	87,200	86,200	1,000
	Total Liabilities	2,71,800	2,63,000	8,800

Income Statements for the year ending 2003

		Rs.
Sales		63,800
Expenses:		
	Cost of goods sold	45,600
	Salaries	8,400
	Rent	1,200
	Depreciation	2,800
	Insurance	600
	Interest	400
	Income-lax	1,000
	Total expenses	60,000
	Net Income	3,800

	Rs.
Statement of Retained Earnings	
Retained earnings for the year 2002	86,200
Add: Net income for the year 2003	3,800
	90,000
Less: Dividends	2,800
	87,200

You are required to prepare a Funds Flow Statement, on a working capital basis.

Solution:

Funds Flow Statement
(Working Capital Basis)

		Rs.	Rs.	Rs.
(A)	**Sources of Funds :**			
	(i) Funds from operations :			
	Net income	3,800		
	Add: Non-cash charges:			
	Depreciation	2,800		
	Funds provided by operations		6,600	

(*Contd...*)

	(ii) Other sources:		
	Long-term borrowings	6,000	12,600
(B)	**Uses of funds :**		
	(i) Purchase of machinery	10,000	
	(ii) Dividends	2,800	
	Total uses		12,800
	Changes in Working Capital		(200)

The above statement presentation is a two parts statement; the sources are first detailed and then totalled, followed by the detail information and total for uses. The difference between the sources and uses must equal the change in working capital.

It can be noticed that sources of funds (working capital) is sub-divided into two parts; the first part is concerned with sources from operations, and the second part deals with other sources.

Uses of working capital in the above statement do not include any uses for operations, such as salaries and rent, because these have been included automatically by starling the funds flow statement with the net income rather than with revenue. Generally, the most common uses of funds shown are for the firm's investment activities such as the purchase of the new equipment, declaration of dividends, or payment of long-term liabilities.

Using the figures given in the Problem the Schedule of Changes in Working capital can be prepared as follows :

Schedule of Changes in Working Capital (Changes in Current Assets and Current Liabilities)

	December 31, 2003	*December 31, 2002*	*Increase (Decrease)*
Current assets:	*Rs.*	*Rs.*	*Rs.*
Cash	19,000	17,400	1,600
Accounts receivable	24,600	24,000	600
Inventory	33,000	34,000	(1,000)
Prepaid insurance	4,000	3,600	400
Total current assets	80,600	79,000	1,600
Current liabilities:			
Accounts payable	33,600	32,400	1,200
Salaries payable	600	1,000	(400)
Income-taxes payable	4,400	3,400	1,000
Total current liabilities	38,600	36,800	1,800
Working capital	42,000	42,200	(200)

Example 18

Following are the summarised Balance Sheets of A. Co. Ltd. as on 31st December, 2002 and 2003 :

Liabilities	*2002* Rs.	*2003* Rs.	*Assess*	*2002* Rs.	*2003* Rs.
Share Capital	2,00,000	2,50,000	Land & Buildings	2,00,000	1,90,000
General Reserve	50.000	60,000	Machinery & Plant	1,50,000	1,69,000
Profit & Loss A/c	30,500	30,600	Stock	1,00.000	74,000

(*Contd...*)

Bank loan	70,000	—	Sundry debtors	80,000	64,200
Sundry Creditors	1,50,000	1,35.200	Cash	500	600
Provision for taxation	30.000	35.000	Bank	—	8,000
			Goodwill	—	5,000
	5,30,500	5,10,800		5,30,500	5,10,800

Additional information supplied

During the year ended 31st December, 2003

(a) Dividend of Rs. 23,000 was paid :

(b) Assets of another company were purchased for a consideration of Rs. 50,000 payable in shares. The following assets were purchased: Stock Rs. 20,000 : Machinery Rs. 25,000.

(c) Machinery was purchased for Rs. 8,000

(d) Depreciation written off : Building Rs. 10,000, Machinery Rs. 14,000.

(e) Income-tax paid during the year Rs. 28,000. Provision of Rs. 33,000 was charged to profit and loss A/c.

Prepare a Statement of Sources and Applications of Funds for the year ended 31st December, 2003.

Solution

Statement of Sources and Applications of Funds

Sources	Rs.	*Applications*	Rs.
Issue of shares	20,000	Dividend paid	23,000
Funds from operation	90,100	Purchase of Machinery	8,000
		Income-tax paid	28,000
	1,10,100	Bank loan paid	70,000
Decrease in working capital (as per statement)	18,900		
	1,29,000		1,29,000

Statement of Changes In Working Capital

	2002 Rs.	*2003* Rs.	*Increase* Rs.	*Decrease* Rs.
Current Assets:				
Stock	1,00,000	74,000		26,000
Sundry debtors	80,000	64,200		15,800
Cash	500	600	100	
Bank	—	8,000	8,000	
Total (A)	1,80,500	1,46,800		
Current Liabilities:				
Sundry Creditors	1,50,000	1,35,200	14,800	
Total (B)	1,50,000	1,35,200		
Working Capital (A - B)	—	18,900	18,900	
	30,500	30,500	41,800	41,800

Adjusted Profit & Loss A/c

	Rs.		Rs.
To Depreciation:		By Balance b/d	30,500
Land & Building	10,000	By Funds from operation (balancing figure)	90,100
Machinery	14,000		
To General Reserve	10,000		
To Dividend	23,000		
To Provisions for tax	33,000		
To Balance c/d	30,600		
	1,20,600		1,20,600

Share Capital A/c

	Rs.		Rs.
To Balance c/d	2,50,000	By Balance b/d	2,00,000
		By Machinery purchase	25,000
		By Stock	20,000
		By Goodwill (balancing figure)	5,000
	2,50,000		2,50,000

Machinery A/c

	Rs.		Rs.
To Balance b/d	1,50,000	By depreciation	14,000
To Share Capital (purchase)	25,000	By Balance c/d	1,69,000
To Cash (purchase)	8,000		
	1,83,000		1,83,000

Provision for Income-tax

	Rs.		Rs.
To Cash (tax paid)	28,000	By Balance b/d	30,000
To Balance c/d	35,000	By P&LA/c	33,000
	63,000		63,000

Example 19

The non-current assets and equities of Norman Tools Ltd. are given at the beginning and at the end of the year.

	End of year Rs.	*Beginning of year* Rs.
Plant assets, net of depreciation	2,85,000	1,27,000
Investment in the stock of Bosin Equipment Company	5,80,000	2,64,000
Bonds Payable	14,00,000	5,00.000
Capital Stock	8,00,000	8,00,000
Retained earnings	8,21,000	4,76.000

You are unable to obtain complete balance sheet data or an income statement for the year, but you have obtained the following information :

(i) Dividends of Rs. 75,000 were paid,

(ii) A gain on the sale of equipment of Rs. 26,000 has been included in net income. The gross plant assets increased by Rs. 1,86,000 even though equipment costing Rs. 58,000 with a net book value of Rs. 38,000 was sold.

Prepare a statement of sources and uses of net working capital from the limited information available.

Solution

Adjusted Profit & Loss Account

	Rs.		Rs.
To retained earnings	3,45,000	By gain on sale of equipment	26,000
To dividend paid	75,000	By funds from operations	4,42,000
To depreciation on plant	48,000		
	4,68,000		4,68,000

Retained Earnings A/c

	Rs.		Rs.
To closing balance	8,21,000	By opening balance	4,76,000
		By Adjusted P & L A/c	3,45,000
	8,21,000		8,21,000

Plant Asset A/c

	Rs.		Rs.
To opening balance	1,27,000	By Dep. (Bal. figure)	48,000
To gain on sale	26.000	By sale	64,000
To Bank (Purchases) (1,86.000+58,000)	2,48,000	By closing balance	2,85,000
	3,97,000		3.97,000

Funds Flow Statement

	Rs.		Rs.
Sale of plant assets	64,000	Dividend paid	75,000
Funds from operation	4,42,000	Investment in the stock of B	3,16,000
Bonds payable	9,00,000	Plant Assets	2,44,000
		Increase in working Capital	7,71,000
	14,06,000		14,06,000

Example 20

From incomplete data given for Terry Company, you have been asked to prepare a statement of sources and uses of net working capital for 2001. Non-current Balance sheet account balances are given as follows:

	December 31	
	2001	*2000*
	Rs.	Rs.
Plant assets, net of depreciation	1.81,000	1,36,000
Long-term debt	—	45.000
Capital stock	1,50,000	1,25,000
Retained earning	2,16,000	1,68,000

Dividends of Rs. 34,000 were paid during the year. Depreciation of Rs. 19,000 was deducted on the income statement,

Equipment having a net book value of Rs. 48,000 was sold. A gain of Rs. 3,000 on the sale was included on the income statement.

Required: Prepare a statement of sources and uses of net working capital for 2001.

Solution

Retained Earnings A/c

	Rs.		Rs.
To dividend paid	34,000	By balance	1,68,000
To balance c/d (given)	2,16,000	By gain (on sale of plant)	3,000
		By Profit (bal. figure)	79,000
	2,50,000		2,50,000

Plant A/c

	Rs.		Rs.
To balanced b/d	1,86,000	By depreciation	19,000
To gain on sale of plant	3,000	By sale of plant	51,000
To cash (purchases)	62,000	By balance c/d (given)	1,81,000
	2,51,000		2,51,000

Statement of Sources and uses of Net Working Capital

	Rs.	Rs.
I. Sources of Working Capital		
(i) Funds from operations		
Net profit	79,000	
Add: depreciation	19,000	98,000
(ii) Other sources:		
Sales of equipment	51,000	
Increase in capital Stock	25,000	76,000
Total sources		1,74,000
II. Uses of net working capital:		
(i) Dividends paid		34,000
(ii) Payment of long-term debt		45,000
(iii) Purchase of new plant		62,000
(iv) Increase in working capital		33,000
		1,74,000

Note: Increase in net working capital is a balancing figure although it can also be calculated as given here.

Increase in net working capital can be calculated although no information is given about current assets and current liabilities. General Formula is:

Non-current liabilities — Non-current assets = Net working capital.

2000

Non-current liabilities = Long term debt + Capital Stock + Retained earnings

ie., Rs. 45,000 + 1,25,000 + 1,68,000	= Rs. 3,38,000
Non-current assets *i.e.*, Plant	= Rs. 1,86,000
Net working capital for 2000	= Rs. 1,52,000

2001

Non-current liabilities = Capital Stock + Retained earnings

ie., Rs. 1,50,000 + 2,16,000	= Rs. 3,66,000
Non-current assets *i.e.*, Plant	= Rs. 1,81,000
Net working capital for 2001	= Rs. 1,85,000
Increase in net working capital in 2001 over 2000	= Rs. 1,85,000 – 1,52,000
	= Rs 33,000

SIGNIFICANCE OF STATEMENT OF CHANGES IN FINANCIAL POSITION-WORKING CAPITAL BASIS

A better understanding and analysis of the affairs of a business enterprise, requires the knowledge about the movements in assets, liabilities and capital which have taken place during the year and their consequent effect on its financial position. This information is not specifically disclosed by a profit and loss account and balance sheet but can be made available in working capital based funds flow statement.

The funds flow statement is in no way a replacement for the profit and loss account and balance sheet although the information which it contains is a selection, reclassification and summarisation of information contained in these two statements. The balance sheet gives a "snapshot" view at a point in time of the sources from which a firm has acquired its funds and the uses which the firm has made of these funds- The equities side of the balance sheet delineates these sources, and the asset side shows the uses. The income statement is a flow statement; it explains changes that occurred in the retained earnings account by summarizing the increases (revenues) and decreases (expenses) in retained earnings during the accounting period. A funds flow statement explains the changes that took place in a balance sheet account or group of accounts during the period between dates of two balance sheets "snapshots." It shows the manner in which the operations of an enterprise have been financed and in which its financial resources have been used. It also distinguishes the use of funds for the long-term from the short-term. For example, it distinguishes the use of funds for the purchase of new fixed assets from funds used in increasing the working capital of the company. Thus, it provides a meaningful link between the balance sheets at the beginning and at the end of a period and profit and loss account for that period. It should be understood, however, that a funds statement does not purport to indicate the requirements of a business for capital.

The concept of working capital is in conformity with normal accrual accounting procedures. Hence, a funds flow statement based on the concept of net working capital fits well with other statements. Above all, working capital is also a measure of the short-term liquidity of the firm. Therefore, an analysis of factors bringing about a change in the amount of net working capital is useful for decision-making by shareholders, creditors, lenders and management.

LIMITATIONS OF STATEMENT OF CHANGES IN FINANCIAL POSITION — WORKING CAPITAL BASIS

The working capital concept of funds enlarges the problem of valuation because it includes inventory and prepaid items. Thus, the measurement of working capital flows is less precise than for cash. A fund statement based on the working capital concept is usually a brief presentation, and many significant inter-firm transactions are not disclosed. For example, significant addition to inventories financed by short-term credits would not be shown because the two items are offset in the computation of the net change in working capital. Furthermore, transactions not affecting working capital, such as the acquisition of plant and equipment by the issuance of equity capital, would not be included in the statement. Therefore, the funds statement in this presentation would not disclose structural changes in the financial relationships in the firm or major changes in policy regarding investments in current assets and short-term financing.

RELATIONSHIP BETWEEN WORKING CAPITAL BASIS STATEMENT OF CHANGES IN FINANCIAL POSITION AND INCOME STATEMENT

The income statement is based on the accrual principle; Cash significant events are reported, whether or not they coincide with actual cashflows. The accrual principle necessarily involves the use of estimates and artificial allocations in seeking to predict future cash effects of current events, and attempting to measure the current consequences of the past cash flows.

Working Capital provided by operations is derived from the income statement by omitting certain items that do not affect working capital. For this reason, working capital provided by operations depends on many of the same estimates and conventions that enter into the measurement of net income. Over time, cumulative amounts of income, working capital, and cash should coincide — the only difference should be the timing of the reported flows. Because most financial decisions must be based on annual data, and timing differences between the reported annual flows can be substantial, these differences have a significant impact on the actions taken by decision-makers.

CASH FLOW STATEMENT. (OR STATEMENT OF CHANGES IN FINANCIAL POSITION — CASH BASIS)

A cash flow statement discloses net increase (or decrease) in cash during an accounting period. It provides information about the flow of cash into and out of a company. According to AS-3, "the statement deals with the provision of information about the historical changes in cash and cash equivalents of an enterprise by means of a cash flow statement which classifies cash flows during the period from operating, investing and financing activities."

ICAI's AS-3 Cash Flow Statement contains the following explanations on the utility of cash flow statement:

1. Information about the cash flows of an enterprise is useful in providing users of financial statements with a basis to assess the ability of the enterprise to generate cash and cash equivalents and the needs of the enterprise to utilise those cash flows. The economic decisions that are taken by users require an evaluation of the ability of an enterprise to generate cash and cash equivalents and the timing and certainty of their generation.
2. Users of an enterprise's financial statements are interested in how the enterprise generates and uses cash and cash equivalents. This is the case regardless of the nature of the enterprise's activities and irrespective of whether cash can be viewed as the product of the enterprise, as may be the case with a financial enterprise. Enterprises need cash for essentially the same reasons, however different their principal revenue-producing activities might be. They need cash to conduct their operations, to pay their obligations, and to provide returns to their investors.
3. A cash flow statement, when used in conjunction with the other financial statements, provides information that enables users to evaluate the changes in net assets of an enterprise, its financial structure (including its liquidity and solvency) and its ability to affect the amounts and timing of cash flows in order to adapt to changing circumstances and opportunities. Cash flow information is useful in assessing the ability of the enterprise to generate cash and cash equivalents and

enables users to develop models to assess and compare the present value of the future cash flows of different enterprise. It also enhances the comparability of the reporting of operating performance by different enterprises because it eliminates the effects of using different accounting treatments for the same transactions and events.

4. Historical cash flow information is often used as an indicator of the amount, timing and certainty of future cash flows. It is also useful in checking the accuracy of past assessments of future cash flows and in examining the relationship between profitability and net cash flow and the impact of changing prices.

DEFINITIONS IN AS-3

The following terms are used in this Statement with the meanings specified :

Cash comprises cash on hand and demand deposits with banks.

Cash equivalents are short-term, highly liquid investments that are readily convertible into known amounts of cash and which are subject to an insignificant risk of changes in value.

Cash flows are inflows and outflows of cash and cash equivalents.

Operating activities are the principal revenue-producing activities of the enterprise and other activities that are not investing or financing activities.

Investing activities are the acquisition and disposal of long-term assets and other investments not included in cash equivalents.

Financing activities are activities that result in changes in the size and composition of the owners capital (including preference share capital in the case of a company) and borrowings of the enterprise.

Cash and Cash Equivalents

1. Cash equivalents are held for the purpose of meeting short-term cash commitments rather than for investment or other purposes. For an investment to qualify as a cash equivalent, it must be readily convertible to a known amount of cash and be subject to an insignificant risk of changes in value. Therefore, an investment normally qualifies as a cash equivalent only when it has a short maturity of, say, three months or less from the date of acquisition. Investments in shares are excluded from cash equivalents unless they are, in substance, cash equivalents; for example, preference shares of a company acquired shortly before their specified redemption date (provided there is only an insignificant risk of failure of the company to repay the amount at maturity).
2. Cash flows exclude movements between items that constitute cash or cash equivalents because these components are part of the cash management of an enterprise rather than part of its operating, investing and financing activities. Cash management includes the investment of excess cash in cash equivalents.

CLASSIFICATION OF CASH INFLOWS AND OUTFLOWS

A cash flow statement focuses on various activities and items which bring about changes in the cash balance between two balance sheet dates. This statement covers all items which increase or decrease the cash of a business enterprise, For example, this statement includes items like receipts from debtors and payments lo creditors. On the contrary, this statement will not cover items which have no immediate effect on cash increase or decrease. For instance, goods purchased on credit and goods sold on credit will not be included in this statement as these transactions have no effect on inflow and outflow of cash,

A cash flow statement aims to determine the effects on cash of different types of cash inflows and outflows. In this process, all cash flows. *i.e.*, activities resulting into cash flows are classified into different categories. The ICAI's AS-3 'cash flow statement' has classified cash flows into three categories:

(1) Operating Activities (or Flows)
(2) Investing Activities (or Flows)
(3) Financing Activities (or Flows)

Figure 4.1 displays the classification of cash inflow sand cash outflows relaling to operating activities, investing activities and financing activities.

(1) **Operating Activities.** Operating activities are those transactions which are considered in the determination of net income. Examples of cash inflows in this category are cash received from debtors for goods and services, interest and dividend received on loans and investment. Examples of cash outflows in this category are cash payments for goods and services: merchandise; wages; interest; taxes; supplies and others.

Classification of Cash Inflows and Cash Outflows

Cash Inflows

Cash received from debtors for goods and services

Interest and dividends on loans and investments

Cash sales of property, plant, equipment, other long-term assets, and intangibles

Cash sales of investments in shares, debentures and other securities

Cash collection (loan repayments) from borrowers

Proceeds from issue of shares

Proceeds from short-term and long-term debt

Operating Activities

Investing Activities

Financing Activities

Cash Outflows

Cash payments for goods and services merchandise

Cash payments for wages

Cash payments for interest to creditors

Payments to Government for taxes

Payments to others for expenses

Purchase of shares, debentures and securities of other enterprises

Purchase of property, plant, equipment and other long term assets

Loans given to other firms

Repayment of loans

Payment to owners, including cash dividend

Reacquiring preference or equity shares

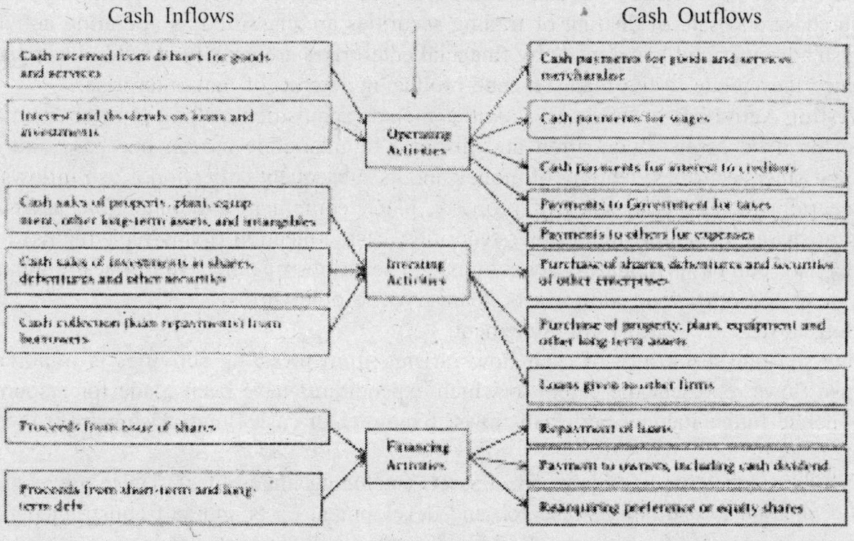

Fig. 4.1. Classification of cash inflows and outflows relating to operating activities, investing activities and financing activities

AS 3 Cash flow Statement states:

1. The amount of cash flows arising from operating activities is a key indicator of the extent to which the operations of the enterprise have generated sufficient cash flows to maintain the operating capability of the enterprise, pay dividends, repay loans and make new investments without recourse to external sources of financing. Information about the specific components of historical operating cash flows is useful, in conjunction with other information, in forecasting future operating cash flows.
2. Cash flows from operating activities are primarily derived from the principal revenue-producing activities of the enterprise. Therefore, they generally result from the transactions and other events that enter into the determination of net profit or loss. Examples of cash flows from operating activities are:

   (a) cash receipts from the sale of goods and the rendering of services;
   (b) cash receipts from royalties, fees, commissions and other revenue;
   (c) cash payments to suppliers for goods and services;
   (d) cash payments to and on behalf of employees;
   (e) cash receipts and cash payments of an insurance enterprise for premiums and claims, annuities and other policy benefits;

(f) cash payments or refunds of income-taxes unless they can be specifically identified with financing and investing activities; and

(g) cash receipts and payments relating to future contracts, forward contracts, option contracts and swap contracts when the contracts are held for dealing or trading purposes.

3. Some transactions, such as the sale of an item ol plant, may give rise to a gain or loss which is included in the determination of net profit or loss. However, the cash flows relating to such transactions are cash flows from investing activities.
4. An enterprise may hold securities and loans for dealing or trading purposes, in which case they arc similar to inventory acquired specifically for resale. Therefore, cash flows arising from the purchase and sale of dealing or trading securities arc classified as operating activities. Similarly, cash advances and loans made by financial enterprises are usually classified as operating activities since they relate to the main revenue-producing activity of that enterprise.

(2) **Investing Activities** — Investing activities include acquisition of long-term or fixed assets; disposal of long-term or fixed assets; acquisition and disposal of intangible assets; purchase and sale of shares, debentures and other securities; lending of money and its subsequent collection. Cash inflows from investing activities generally include cash sales of property, plant, equipment and intangible assets, cash sales of investments in shares, debentures and other securities, cash collection (loans repayments) from borrowers. Cash outflows arc purchase of shares, debentures and securities of other enterprises, purchase of property, plant, equipment and other long-term assets, loan given to other firms.

According to AS — 3 Cash Flow Statement:

(i) The separate disclosure of cash flows arising from investing activities is important because the cash flows represent the extent to which expenditures have been made for resources intended to generate future income and cash flows. Examples of cash flows arising from investing activities are :

(a) cash payments to acquire fixed assets (including intangibles). These payments include those relating to capitalised research and development costs and self constructed fixed assets;

(b) cash receipts from disposal of fixed assets (including intangibles);

(c) cash payments to acquire shares, warrants or debt instruments of other enterprises and interests in joint ventures (other than payments for those instruments considered to be cash equivalents and those held lor dealing or trading purposes),

(d) cash receipts from disposal of shares warrants or debt instruments of other enterprises and interests in joint ventures (other than receipts from those instruments considered to be cash equivalents and those held for dealing or trading purposes);

(e) cash advances and loans made to third parties (other than advances and loans made by a financial enterprise);

(f) cash receipts from the repayment of advances and loans made to third parties (other than advances and loans of a financial enter-prise);

(g) cash receipts from future contracts, forward contracts, option contracts and swap contracts except when the contracts are held for dealing or trading purposes, or the payments are classified as financing activities; and

(h) cash receipts from future contracts, forward contracts, option contracts and swap contracts except when the contracts are held for dealing or trading purposes, or the receipts are classified as financing activities.

(ii) When a contract is accounted for as a hedge of an identifiable position, the cash flows of the contract are classified in the same manner as the cash flow of the position being hedged.

(3) **Financing Activities** — Financing activities relate to long-term liability and equity capital. A firm engages in financing activities when it obtains resources from owners, returns resources to owners, borrows

resources from creditors and repays amounts borrowed. Cash inflows include proceeds from issue of shares and short-term and long-term borrowings. Cash outflows include repayment of loans and payments to owners, including cash dividends. Repayment of accounts payable or accrued liabilities are not considered repayment of loans under financing activities but are classified as cash outflows under operating activities. AS-3 Cash Flow Statement observes:

The separate disclosure of cash flows arising from financing activities is important because it is useful in predicting claims on future cash flows by providers of funds (both capital and borrowings) to the enterprise. Examples of cash flows arising from financing activities are:

(a) cash proceeds from issuing shares or other similar instruments;
(b) cash proceeds from issuing debentures, loans, notes, bonds and other short or long-term borrowings; and
(c) cash repayments of amounts borrowed.

CASH FLOW STATEMENT AND CASH RECEIPTS AND DISBURSEMENTS

A cash flow statement differs from the summary of cash receipts and disbursements. A cash flow statement is prepared by a rearrangement of items on the income statement and balance sheet, rather than from entries made to the cash account. Cash flow statement may also highlight the amount of cash generated by the firm's operations. This is not reported in statement of cash receipts and disbursements.

CASH FLOW AND INCOME STATEMENT

Cash flow statement apparently differs from income statement. An income statement includes adjustments in respect of expenses accrued in the calculation of periodic income, whereas cash flow statement excludes such adjustments. The largest item of difference between them is the allocation of fixed assets costs as depreciation. Also, the procedures adopted in the two statements are reflected in changes in balance sheet items. These would include changes in balances of trade debtors and trade creditors.

CASH PROFIT (CASH NET INCOME)

Accrual-based profit and loss account reveals accrual net income. By adjusting the items on the profit and loss account, one can arrive at cash profit or cash net income. It should be noted that cash profit relates to operating activities in the same way as profit and loss account focuses on net income determination from operating activities. But profit and loss account does not show cash inflow and outflow relating to operating activities because profit and loss account is prepared on accrual basis.

Cash profit and cash flow is not the same thing. Cash profit is confined to indicating cash flow relating to operating activities. But cash flow is a total concept indicating total inflows and outflows. For example, issue of equity shares is a source of cash inflow but will not be used for determining cash profit. Similarly, plant purchased will be cash outflow for its full value, but will not be used for determining cash profit.

PRESENTATION OF CASH FLOW STATEMENT

A cash flow statement can be presented in either the direct or indirect format. The investing and financing sections will be the same under either format. However, the operating section will be different.

Direct Method

Direct method is that method whereby major classes of gross cash receipts and gross cash payments are disclosed. Enterprises that utilise the direct method should report separately the following classes of operating cash receipts and payments :

1. Cash collected from customers, including lessees, licensee, and other similar items
2. Interest and dividends received
3. Other operating cash receipts, if any

4. Cash paid to employees and other suppliers of goods or services, including supplies of insurance, advertising, and other similar expenses
5. Interest paid
6. Income-taxes paid
7. Other operating cash payments, if any.

Companies that use the direct method must provide a reconciliation of net income to net cash flow from operating activities in a separate schedule in the financial statements.

According to AS-3 cash flow Statement:

The direct method provides information which may be useful in estimating future cash flows and which is not available under the indirect method and is, therefore, considered more appropriate than the indirect method. Under the direct method, information about major classes of gross cash receipts and gross cash payments may be obtained either :

(a) from the accounting records of the enterprise; or

(b) by adjusting sales, cost of sales (interest and similar income and interest expense and similar charges for a financial enterprise) and other items in the statement of profit and loss for :

(i) changes during the period in inventories and operating receivables and payables;

(ii) other non-cash items; and

(iii) other items for which the cash effects are investing or financing cash flows.

Indirect Method

Under the indirect method, the net cash flow from operating activities is determined by adjusting net profit or loss for the effects of :

(a) changes during the period in inventories and operating receivables and payable;

(b) non-cash items such as depreciation, provisions, deferred taxes, and unrealised foreign exchange gains and losses; and

(c) all other items for which the cash effects are investing or financing cash flows.

Alternatively, the net cash flow from operating activities may be presented under the indirect method by showing the operating revenues and expenses excluding non-cash items disclosed in the statement of profit and loss and the changes during the period in inventories and operating receivables and payables.

The indirect method starts with net income and reconciles it to net cash flow from operating activities. The cash flow from operating activities is found by adjusting net income for (1) changes in current assets and current liabilities and (2) depreciation expense. Depreciation expense is not a cash flow. Because it decreases net income, il is added back to net income in order to arrive at the operating cash flow. The following summarizes the process :

Change	*Adjustment to Net Income*
Decrease in a current asset	Add
Increase in a current asset	Subtract
Decrease in a current liability	Subtract
Increase in a current Stability	Add

The indirect method is more widely used, since it shows the relationship between the income statement and the balance sheet and therefore aids in the analysis of these statements.

Reporting Cash Flows from Investing and Financing Activities

An enterprise should report separately major classes of gross cash receipts and gross cash payments arising from investing and financing activities.

Both the approaches, direct and indirect result in the same amount for cash flow from operations after making necessary adjustments. However, both the approaches have the arguments, pros and cons.

The arguments in favour of direct approach are that it identifies the major categories of cash receipts and cash payments arising from operating activities; it provides a mure useful basis for estimating future cash flows; and it provides information that is not otherwise available in the balance sheet and profit and loss account- The direct method is a better indicator of company solvency, has a sounder conceptual framework and reflects accepted business practice. It permits an evaluation of cash flow relating to specific line items of income-statement such as sales and cost of goods sold. The empirical evidence indicates that the direct method is superior over the indirect method in predicting future operating cash flows and future net operating cash flows.

On the other hand, followers of the indirect approach argue that indirect method is less costly and more convenient to use by firms. It is argued that the direct approach would require information that is hard to collect and sensitive. One difficulty with the direct approach is that some of the cash flows may have characteristics of more than one category of cash flow.

However, [he indirect method has also been criticised on two grounds. First, it contains unnecessary detail and may confuse the users. Another limitation of the indirect method is that the adding of expenses such as depreciation suggests that expenses are a source of cash. The conceptual and practical problems which underlie the indirect method are as follows ·

(i) Ambiguity in the definition of "operations."
(ii) Diversity in reporting practices,
(iii) Impact of changes in the reporting entity on the non-cash current accounts.
(iv) Use of absorption costing in accounting for manufactured inventory.
(v) Measurement of current portion of long-term leases.
(vi) Reclassifications between current and non-current accounts.

Figure 4.2 and 4.3 show respectively direct and indirect method of preparing cash flow statement.

ABC Company

for the year ended December 31, 2003

	Rs.	Rs.
(A) Cash Flow from Operating Activities :		
Cash Receipts from :		
Sales		
Interest Received		
Cash Payments for:		
Purchases		
Operating Expenses		
Interest Payments		
Income Taxes		
Net Cash Flow from Operating Activities		
(B) Cash Flows from Investing Activities		
Sale of Plant Assets		
Sale of Investments		
Purchase of Plant Assets		
Purchase of Investments		
Net Cash Flows Used by Investing Activities		

(C) Cash Flows from Financing Activities
Repayment of Bonds and Debentures
Issue of Common shares
Dividends Paid
Net Cash Flows from Financing Activities
Net Increase (Decrease) in Cash

Fig. 4.2. Cash Flow Statement (Direct Method)

ABC Company

for the year ended December 31, 2003

	Rs.	Rs.
(A) Cash Flows from Operating Activities		
Net Income		
Adjustments to Reconcile Net Income to Net Cash provided by Operating Activities		
Depreciation		
Gain on Sale of Investments		
Loss on Sale of Plant Asset		
Decrease in Accounts Receivable		
Increase in Inventory		
Decrease in Prepaid Expenses		
Increase in Accounts Payable		
Increase in Accrued Liabilities		
Decrease in Income Taxes Payable		
Net Cash Flows from Operating Activities		
(B) Cash Flows from Investing Activities		
Sale of Plant Assets		
Sale of Investments		
Purchase of Plant Assets		
Purchase of Investments		
Net Cash Flows Used by Investing Activities		
(C) Cash Flows from Financing Activities		
Repayment of Bonds and debentures		
Issue of common shares		
Dividends Paid		
Net Cash flows from Financing Activities		
Net Increase (Decrease) in cash		

Fig. 4.3. Cash Flow Statement (Indirect Method)

PREPARING CASH FLOW STATEMENT

Before preparing cash flow statement, first of all, the following three steps have to be completed:

(1) Determining cash flows from operations or operating activities.
(2) Determining cash flows from investing activities.
(3) Determining cash flows from financing activities.

After obtaining information regarding the above, a cash flow statement can be prepared. The three steps have been discussed below :

Cash flow from operations

The profit and loss account focuses on net income determination from operating activities. However, it does not show cash inflow and outflow relating to operating activities because the profit and loss account is prepared on accrual basis. In preparing profit and loss account, revenues are recorded even though cash for them has not been received. Similarly, expenses are recorded even though they may not have been paid. Therefore, to find cash flows from operations, one need to convert accrual basis income statement figures to cash basis by making adjustments. By way of adjustments, earned revenues will be converted into cash received from sales or customers and incurred expenses will be converted into cash expended, i.e., expenses actually paid in cash.

The conversion process can be described as follows, using a short-cut calculation :

Accrual-Basis Net Income

↓

Deduct Increase in Accounts Receivable (or Add Decrease in Accounts Receivable)
Deduct Increase in Merchandise Inventory (or Add Decrease in Merchandise Inventory)
Deduct Increase in Prepaid Expenses (or Add Decrease in Prepaid Expenses)
Add Increase in Accounts Payable (Or Deduct Decrease in Accounts Payable)
Add Increase in Accrued Expenses (or Deduct Decrease in Accrued Expenses)
Add Depreciation and Amortization Expenses for the year

↓

Cash-Basis Net Income

While making conversion, one should know the relationship between income statement accounts and balance sheet changes. Each individual item on the income statement should be viewed as it relates to a balance sheet account. On the accrual basis of accounting, the explanation for the difference between ihe amount of sales revenue and the receipts from those sales is found in ihe changes in accounts receivable and debtors account. Similarly, the difference between the amount of an expense and the amount of payments fur lhal expense is found in the changes of its associated asset or liability, such as prepaid rent or rent payable. If there is no associated balance sheet account for in item on the income statement, it is presumed that the amount shown un the income statement resulted in a cash flow exactly equal to that revenue or expense. Figures 4.4 shows relationship between some income statement accounts and balance sheet accounts.

Financial Statement Relationship

	Income Statement Account	*Related to Balance Sheet Accounts*
1.	Sales	Debtors
2.	Cost of goods sold	(Inventory) (Creditors)
3.	Salaries Expenses	Salaries payable
4.	Rent expense	Rent payable
5.	Depreciation expense	Accumulated depreciation
6.	Insurance expense	Prepaid insurance
7.	Interest expense	Interest payable
8.	Income-tax expense	Income-taxes payable

Fig. 4.4. Relationship between Income Statement and Balance Sheet

PROVISIONS OF AS-3 ON CASH FLOW STATEMENT

In addition to suggestions stated earlier, AS-3 contains some more explanations on cash flow statement which have been discussed here.

1. Reporting Cash Flows on a Net Basis

(i) Cash flows arising from the following operating, investing or financing activities may be reported on a net basis :

(a) cash receipts and payments on behalf of customers when the cash flows reflect the activities of the customer rather than those of the enterprise; and

(b) cash receipts and payments for items in which the turnover is quick, the amounts are large, and the maturities are short,

(ii) Examples of cash receipts and payments referred to in point (i)(a) are :

(a) the acceptance and repayment of demand deposits by a bank;

(b) funds held for customers by an investment enterprise; and

(c) rents collected on behalf of, and paid over to, the owners of properties.

Examples of cash receipts and payments referred to in point (i)(b) are advances made for, and the repayments of :

(a) principal amounts relating to credit card customers;

(b) the purchase and sale of investments; and

(c) other short-term borrowings, for examples, those which have a maturity period of three months or less.

(iii) Cash flows arising from each of the following activities of a financial enterprise may be reported on a net basis :

(a) cash receipts and payments for the acceptance and repayment of deposits with a fixed maturity dale

(b) the placement of deposits with and withdrawal of deposits from other financial enterprises; and

(c) cash advances and loans made to customers and the repayment of those advances and loans.

2. Foreign Currency Cash Flows

(i) Cash flows arising from transactions in a foreign currency should be recorded in an enterprise's reporting currency by applying to the foreign currency amount the exchange rate between the reporting currency and the foreign currency at the date of the cash flow. A rate that approximates the actual rate may be used if the result is substantially the same as would arise if the rates at the dates of ihe cash flows were used. The effect of changes in exchange rates on cash and cash equivalents held in a foreign currency should be reported as a separate part of the reconciliation of the changes in cash and cash equivalents during the period.

(ii) Cash flows denominated in foreign currency are reported in a manner consistent with Accounting Standard (AS)11, Accounting for the Effects of Changes in Foreign Exchange Rates. This permits the use of an exchange rate that approximates the actual rate. For example, a weighted average exchange rate for a period may be used for recording foreign currency transactions.

(iii) Unrealised gains and losses arising from changes in foreign exchange rates are not cash flows. However, the effect of exchange rate changes on cash and cash equivalents held or due in a foreign currency is reported in the cash flow statement in order to reconcile cash and cash equivalents at the beginning and the end of the period. This amount is presented separately from cash flows from operating, investing and financing activities and includes the differences, if any, had those cash flows been reported at the end-of-period exchange rates.

3. Extraordinary Items

(i) The cash flows associated with extraordinary items should be classified as arising from operating, investing or financing activities as appropriate and separately disclosed.

(ii) The cash flows associated with extraordinary items are disclosed separately arising from operating, investing or financing activities in the cash flow statement, to enable users to understand their nature and effect on the present and future cash flows of the enterprise. These disclosures are in addition to the separate disclosures of the nature and amount of extraordinary items required by Accounting Standard (AS) 5, Net Profit or Loss for the Period, Prior Period Items and Changes in Accounting Policies.

4. Interest and Dividends

(i) Cash flows from interest and dividends received and paid should each be disclosed separately. Cash flows arising from interest paid and interest and dividends received in the case of a financial enterprise should be classified as cash flows arising from operating activities. In the case of other enterprises, cash flows arising from interest paid should be classified as cash flows from financing activities while interest and dividends received should be classified as cash flows from investing activities. Dividends paid should be classified as cash flows from financing activities.

(ii) The total amount of interest paid during the period is disclosed in the cash flow statement whether it has been recognised as an expense in the statement of profit and loss or capitalised in accordance with Accounting Standard (AS)10, Accounting for Fixed Assets.

(iii) Interest paid and interest and dividends received are usually classified as operating cash flows for a financial enterprise. However, there is no consensus on the classification of these cash flows for other enterprises. Some argue that interest paid and interest and dividends received may be classified as operating cash flows because they enter into the determination of net profit or loss. However, it is more appropriate that interest paid and interest and dividends received are classified as financing cash flows and investing cash flows respectively, because they are cost of obtaining financial resources or returns on investments.

(iv) Some argue that dividends paid may be classified as a component of cash flows from operating activities in order to assist users to determine the ability of an enterprise to pay dividends. Others argue that dividends paid should be classified as cash flows from financing activities because they are cost of obtaining financial resources.

5. Taxes on Income

(i) Cash flows arising from taxes on income should be separately disclosed and should be classified as cash flows from operating activities unless they can be specifically identified with financing and investing activities.

(ii) Taxes on income arise on transactions that give rise to cash flows that are classified as operating, investing or financing activities in a cash flow statement. While tax expense may be readily identifiable with investing or financing activities, the related tax cash flows are often impracticable to identify and may arise in a different period from the cash flows of the underlying transactions. Therefore, taxes paid are usually classified as cash flows from operating activities. However, when it is practicable to identify the tax cash flow with an individual transaction that gives rise to cash flows that are classified as investing or financing activities, the tax cash flow is classified as an investing or financing activities as appropriate. When tax cash flow are allocated over more than one class of activity, the total amount of taxes paid is disclosed.

6. Investments in Subsidiaries, Associates and Joint Ventures

When accounting for an investment in an associate or a subsidiary or a joint venture, an investor restricts its reporting in the cash flow statement to the cash flows between itself and the investee/joint venture, for example, cash flows relating to dividends and advances.

7. Acquisitions and Disposals of Subsidiaries and Other Business Units

(i) The aggregate cash flows arising from acquisitions and from disposals of subsidiaries or other business units should be presented separately and classified as investing activities.

(ii) An enterprise should disclose, in aggregate, in respect of both acquisition and disposal of subsidiaries or other business units during the period each of the following:

(a) the total purchase or disposal consideration; and

(b) the portion of the purchase or disposal consideration discharged by means of cash and cash equivalents.

(iii) The separate presentation of the cash flow effects of acquisitions and disposals of subsidiaries and other business units as single line items helps to distinguish those cash flows from other cash flows. The cash flow effects of disposals are not deducted from those of acquisitions.

8. Non-Cash Transactions

(i) Investing and financing transactions that do not require the use of cash or cash equivalents should be excluded from a cash flow statement. Such transactions should he disclosed elsewhere in the financial statements in a way that provides all the relevant information about these investing and financing activities.

(ii) Many investing and financing activities do not have a direct impact on current cash flows although they do affect the capital and asset structure of an enterprise. The exclusion of non-cash transactions for the cash flow statement is consistent with the objective of a cash flow statement as these items do not involve cash flows in the current period. Examples of non-cash transactions are :

(a) the acquisition of assets by assuming directly related liabilities;
(b) the acquisition of an enterprise by means of issue of shares; and
(c) the conversion of debt to equity.

9. Components of Cash and Cash Equivalents

(i) An enterprise should disclose the components of cash and cash equivalents and should present a reconciliation of the amounts in its cash flow statement with the equivalent items reported in the balance sheet.

(ii) In view of the variety of cash management practices, an enterprise discloses the policy which it adopts in determining the composition of cash and cash equivalents.

(iii) The effect of any change in the policy for determining components of cash and cash equivalents is reported in accordance with Accounting Standard; (AS)5, Net Profit or Loss for the Period, Prior Period Items and Changer in Accounting Policies.

10. Other Disclosures

(i) An enterprise should disclose, together with a commentary by management, the amount of significant cash and cash equivalent balances held by the enterprise that are not available for use by it.

(ii) There are various circumstances in which cash and cash equivalent balances held by an enterprise are not available for use by it. Examples include cash and cash equivalent balances held by a branch of the enterprise that operates in a country where exchange controls or other legal restrictions apply as a result of which the balances are not available for use by the enterprise.

(iii) Additional information may be relevant to users in understanding the financial position and liquidity of an enterprise. Disclosure of this information, together with a commentary by management, is encouraged and may include :

(a) the amount of undrawn borrowing facilities that may be available for future operating activities and to settle capital commitments, indicating any restrictions on the use of these facilities; and
(b) the aggregate amount of cash flows that represent increases in operating capacity separately from those cash flows that are required to maintain operating capacity.

(iv) The separate disclosure of cash flows that represent increases in operating capacity and cash flows that are required to maintain operating capacity is useful in enabling the user to determine whether the enterprise is investing adequately in the maintenance of its operating capacity. An enterprise that does not invest adequately in the maintenance of its operating capacity may be prejudicing future profitability for the sake of current liquidity and distributions to owners.

Example 21

Electron Company, a wholesaler of electronic supplies, has been in business for four years. The company has had modest profits and has experienced few operating difficulties until this year. The President, Hari Kapoor, has come to Citi Bank, where you are a loan officer, to discuss his company's working capital problems. Kapoor explains that expanding his firm has created difficulties in meeting obligations when they become due and the firm has been unable to take cash discounts offered by manufacturers for timely payment. He would like to borrow Rs. 40,000 from the Citi Bank. At your request, Kapoor submits the following financial data for the past two years:

	2003 Rs.	*2002* Rs.
Net sales	5,20,000	4.00,000
Net income (after income-taxes)	12,200	7,200
Interest expenses	6,000	5,800
Income-taxes	4.200	2,400

Assets	*December 31*	
	2003 Rs.	*2002* Rs.
Cash	16,300	18,100
Accounts receivable (net of allowance of Rs. 4,000 last year and Rs. 6,000 this year)	1,14,500	72,000
Inventory	1,12,200	80,000
Prepaid expenses	2,200	1,900
Plant assets (net)	1,20,000	1,25,000
	3,65,200	2,97,000
Liabilities and Shareholders' Equity		
Notes payable — Banks	24,500	15,000
Accounts payable	88,300	66,800
Taxes payable	4.200	2,400
Accrued liabilities	5,000	1,200
7% Mortgage payable	69,400	72,000
Equity share capital	1,50,000	1,25,000
Retained earnings	23,800	14,600
	3,65,200	2,97,000

You decide to prepare a statement of changes in financial position with cash as basis showing clearly the sources and uses divided into operating activities, financing activities and investing activities.

Based upon your analysis, decide whether and under what circumstances you would grant Mr. Kapoor's request for loan. Prepare a draft, explaining the reasons for your decision, to be placed before the Loan Committee of your bank.

Solution

Working:

Plant A/c

	Rs.		Rs.
To balance b/d	1,25,000	By depreciation (balancing figure)	5,000
		By balance c/d	1,20,000
Total	1,25,000		1,25,000

Cash from Operations:

		Rs.	Rs.
Net income (increase in retained earnings)			9,200
Add: (i)	Depreciation		5,000
(ii)	Increase in allowances for accounts receivables		2,000
(iii)	Increase in current liabilities:		
	Notes payable	9,500	
	Accounts payable	21,500	
	Taxes payable	1,800	
	Accrued liabilities	3,800	36,600
			52,800
Less:	Increase in current assets:		
	Accounts receivable (after including allowances amount *i.e.*, 1,20,500-76,000)	44,500	
	Inventory	32,200	
	Prepaid expenses	300	77,000
	Cash used by operations		(24,200)

Cash Flow Statement

	Rs.
Cash flows from operating activities :	
Cash used by operations	(24,200)
Cash flows from financing activities :	
Proceeds from issue of equity capital	25,000
Repayment of mortgage payable	(2,600)
Net cash used in financing activities	22,400
Cash at end of period	(1,800)

Comments:

The cash basis SCFP shows that cash has decreased by Rs. 1,800. The company raised equity capital of Rs. 25,000 and paid mortgage payable of Rs. 2,600. Thus, the financing activities provided a net cash inflow of Rs. 22,400 (Rs. 25,000-Rs. 2,600). But the operating activities have adverse impact on cash resources to the extent of Rs. 24,200. This depleted not only the financial inflows, but also resulted in decline in cash.

There has been increase in inventories and accounts receivables. Although short term borrowings have increased, but they do not match the increasing requirements of current assets.

The above situation requires investigation. If the company's poor situation is due to temporary sales difficulty or temporary rush procurement of materials, it can be expected that in future situations will improve and therefore loan can be granted. The management should also be advised to better manage current assets and current liabilities.

However, if it is concluded that the company will continue to have unsatisfactory operating situation, poor management of current assets and current liabilities, loan may not be granted.

Example 22

A comparative balance sheet and income statement of ABC Company Ltd. for the year ended December 31, 2003 are presented as follows:

ABC Company Ltd.
Comparative Balance Sheet as on December 31, 2003

	2004 (Rs.)	*2003* (Rs.)	*Change Increase/ Decrease* (Rs.)
Assets			
Cash	74,000	98,000	24,000 Decrease
Accounts Receivable	52,000	72,000	20,000 Decrease
Prepaid Expenses	12.000	0	12,000 Increase
Long-Term Investments	1,000	2,000	1,000 Decrease
Land	1,40,000	0	1,40,000 Increase
Building	4,00,000	0	4.00,000 Increase
Accumulated Depreciation—Building	(22,000)	0	22,000 Increase
Equipment	1,36,000	0	1,36,000 Increase
Accumulated Depreciation—Equipment	(20,000)	0	20.000 Increase
Total	7,73,000	1,72,000	
Liabilities and stockholders' equity			
Accounts Payable	81,000	12,000	69,000 Increase
Bonds Payable	3,00,000	0	3,00,000 Increase
Common equity	1,20,000	1,20,000	0
Retained Earnings	2,72,000	40,000	2,32,000 Increase
Total	7,73,000	1,72,000	

ABC Company Ltd.
Income Statement for the year ended December 31, 2004

	(Rs.)	(Rs.)
Revenues		9,84,000
Operating Expenses (excluding depreciation)	5,38,000	
Depreciation Expenses	42,000	5,80,000
Income from Operations		4,04,000
Income Tax Expense		1,36,000
Net Income		2,68,000

During 2004, the Company paid Rs. 36,000 in cash dividends.

Prepare a statement of cash flows using (a) the direct method and (b) the indirect method.

Solution

(a) Statement of cash flows-Direct Method

ABC Company Ltd.
Statement of Cash Flows for the year ended December 31, 2004

	(Rs.)	(Rs.)
Cash Flows from Operating Activities:		
Cash Received from Customers	10,04,000	
Cash Payments for Operating Expenses	(4,69,000)	
Cash Payments for Prepaid Expenses	(12,000)	
Cash Payments for Taxes	(1,36,000)	
Net Cash Provided by Operating Activities		3,87,000
Cash Flows from Investing Activities:		
Cash Paid to Purchase Land	(1,40,000)	
Cash Paid to Purchase Building	(4,00,000)	
Cash Paid to Purchase Equipment	(t,36,000)	
Sale of Long-Term Investment	1,000	
Net Cash used in Investing Activities		(6,75,000)
Cash Flows from Financing Activities:		
Cash Received from the Issuance of Bonds	3,00,000	
Cash Paid for Dividends	(36,000)	
Net Cash Provided by Financing Activities		2,64,000
Net Decrease in Cash and Cash Equivalents		(24,000)
Cash and Cash Equivalents at the Beginning of the year		98,000
Cash and Cash Equivalents at the end of the year		74,000

Under this method, the Rs. 10,04,000 in cash received from customers represents Rs. 9,84,000 in sales increased by a reduction in accounts receivable of Rs. 20,000. Accounts receivable was reduced due to a conversion into cash. The cash outflow of Rs. 4,69,000 was determined by reducing the Rs. 5,38,000 in expenses by the increase to accounts payable of Rs. 69,000. All other amounts were obtained either directly from the balance sheet or from the income statement.

Under the direct method, a separate schedule reconciling net income to net cash would be presented as follows:

ABC Company Ltd.
Statement of Cash Flows for the year ended December 31, 2004

	(Rs.)	(Rs.)
Cash Flows from Operating Activities:		
Net Income		2,68,000
Add: Adjustments to Reconcile Net Income to Net Cash:		
Depreciation Expense	42,000	
Decrease in Accounts Receivable	20,000	
Increase in Prepaid Expenses	(12,000)	
Increase in Accounts Payable	69,000	1,19,000
Net Cash Provided by Operating Activities		3,87,000

(*b*) *Statement of Cash Flows: Indirect Method*

ABC Company Ltd.

Statement of Cash Flows for the year ended December 31, 2004

	(Rs.)	(Rs.)
Cash Flows from Operating Activities:		
Net Income		2,68,000
Add: Adjustments to Reconcile Net Income to Net Cash Earnings		
Depreciation Expense	42,000	
Decrease in Accounts Receivable	20,000	
Increase in Prepaid Expenses	(12,000)	
Increase in Accounts Payable	69,000	1,19,000
Net Cash Flow Provided by Operating Activities		3,87,000
Cash Flows from Investing Activities:		
Cash Paid to Purchase Land	(1,40,000)	
Cash Paid to Purchase Building	(4,00,000)	
Cash Paid to Purchase Equipment	(1,36,000)	
Sale of Long-Term Investment	1,000	
Net Cash Used in Investing Activities		(6,75,000)
Cash Flows from Financing Activities:		
Cash Received from the Issuance of Bonds	3,00,000	
Cash Paid for Dividends	(36,000)	
Net Cash Provided by Financing Activities		2,64,000
Net Decrease in Cash and Cash Equivalents		(24,000)
Cash and Cash Equivalents at the Beginning of the year		98,000
Cash and Cash Equivalents at the end of the year		74,000

Example 23

The President of Wallis Engines Inc., has been looking at the financial statements of competitor. Roderick Parts Company. The President observes that the company invested over Rs. 50,00,000 in new plant and equipment in 2002 and did not finance it by the issuance of debt or capital stock. Furthermore dividend payments to stockholders were not reduced. The President asks you to determine how the competitor was able to finance these additions without borrowing or issuing stock.

In 2001 equipment having a net book value of Rs. 5,85,000 was sold at a gain of Rs. 3,20,000 net of income taxes. No other plant assets were sold. Financial data for the three years period were as follows :

	Year Ended (In thousand of Rupees)		
	2002 (Rs.)	*2001* (Rs.)	*2000* (Rs.)
*Net income	834	812	746
Depreciation deduced for the year	593	576	582
Dividends declared and paid	300	300	300

*Excludes effect of gain on sale of equipment.

Comparative balance sheets for Roderick Parts Company are given below :

Balance Sheets, December 31

	Year Ended (In thousand of Rupees)		
	2002 (Rs.)	2001 (Rs.)	2000 (Rs.)
Assets:	2002	2001	2000
Cash	1,494	1,575	865
Marketable securities	800	4,000	3,000
Accounts receivable	980	989	973
Inventory	1,068	1,330	1,042
Plant and equipment net of depreciation	10,529	5,972	7,133
Total assets	14,871	13,846	13,013
Equities:			
Accounts payable	1,921	1,817	1,608
Other current payables	936	549	757
Capital Stock	4,000	4,000	4,000
Paid-in capital in excess of par	1,800	1,800	1,800
Retained earnings	6,214	5,680	4,848
Total equities	14,871	13,846	13,013

Required:

(1) Prepare statement of changes in financial position for 2001 and 2002 that will show how net working capital was obtained and put to use.

(2) Explain to the president how net working capital was acquired for the-plant additions made by Roderick Parts Company.

Solution

Schedule of Changes in Working Capital (2001)

(Amounts in thousands of Rs.)

	Dr.	*Cr.*
Current assets:		
Cash (Rs. 1575-865)	710	
Marketable securities (Rs. 4,000-3,000)	1,000	
Accounts receivable (Rs. 969-973)		4
Inventory (Rs. 1,330-1,042)	288	
Current liabilities :		
Accounts payable (Rs. 1,817-1,608)		209
Other current payable (Rs. 549-757)	208	
Increase in working capital		1,993
Total	2,206	2,206

Schedule of Changes in Working Capital (2002)
(Amounts in thousands of Rs.)

Current assets :		
Cash (Rs. 1,494-1,575)	—	81
Marketable Securities (Rs. 800-4,000)		3,200
Accounts Receivable (Rs. 980-969)	11	
Inventory (Rs. 1,068-1,330)		262
Current Liabilities:		
Accounts Payable (Rs. 1,921-1,817)		104
Other Current Payables (936-549)		387
Decrease in Working Capital	4,023	
	4,034	4,034

Statement of Changes in Financial Position (2001)

Sources		*Rs.*	*Uses*	*Rs.*
Funds from operations:	Rs.			
Net income	8,12,000			
Add: Depreciation	5,76,000	13,88,000	Dividends	3,00,000
Other sources :				
Sale of equipment	5,85,000		Net increase in working capital	19,93,000
Add: Gain on sale	3,20,000	9,05,000		
Total		22,93,000		22,93,000

Statement of Changes in Financial Position (2002)

Sources		*Rs.*	*Uses*	*Rs.*
Funds from operations:	Rs.			
Net income	8,34,000		Dividends	3,00,000
Add: Depreciation	5,93,000	14,27,000	Investment in New plant and equipment	51,50,000
Net decrease in working capital		40,23,000		
Total		54,50,000		54,50,000

Plant Account

Dr.	*(Rs.)*	*Cr.*	*Rs.*
To balance	59,72,000	By depreciation	5,93,000
cash a/c (Purchase)	51,50,000	By balance	1,05,29,000
	1,11,22,000		1,11,22,000

Net working capital was acquired for the plant additions from the sale of marketable securities, net income, amount of depreciation.

Example 24

"Net income is fine", President of Oliver Parts Company exclaims, "but what I want to know is how much cash is coming to keep us solvent?"

An income statement for the year 2002 for Oliver Parts Company is give below:

Income Statement for the year ended December 31, 2002

	(Rs.)
Net sales	72,15,000
Cost of goods sold	41,26,000
Operating expenses	9,73,000
Income-tax	8,46,000
	59,45,000
Net Income	12,70,000

Depreciation of Rs. 1,76,000 is included in operating expenses.
Current assets and current liabilities as on December 31, 2001 and 2002 are given below:

	December 31	
	2002 (Rs.)	*2001 (Rs.)*
Current assets:		
Cash	9,32,000	13,40,000
Accounts receivable	9,21,000	7,46.000
Inventory	14,64.000	8,72,000
Prepaid expenses	26,000	28,000
Total current assets	33,43,000	29,86,000
Current liabilities:		
Accounts Payable	6,32,000	9,24,000
Accrued operating expenses payable	82,000	97,000
Income-taxes payable	1,57,000	3,24,000
Dividends payable	70,000	85.000
Total current liabilities	9,41,000	14,30,000

Dividends of Rs. 6,00,000 were declared in 2002. Aside from depreciation, net income, and dividends, no transactions affected non-current assets or equities.

Required:

(a) Prepare a statement of the flow of cash.

(b) In the President justified in being concerned about the case position.

Solution

Provision for Taxation

			(Rs.)
To Tax paid (bal. figure)	10,13,000	By balance b/d	3,24,000
To balance c /d	1,57,000	By P & L A/c	8,46,000
	11,70,000		1 1,70,000

Dividends Payable A/c1

To dividends paid	6,15,000	By bal. b/d	85,000
To bal. c/d	70,000	By P & L a/c	6,00,000
	6,85,000		6,85,000

Funds from operations

			(Rs)
I.	Net sales		72,15,000
	Less : (i) cost of goods sold		(41,26,000)
	(ii) Operating expenses		(9,73,000)
			50,99,000
	Net income before taxes		21,16,000
	Add: Depreciation		1,76,000
	Funds generated from operations		22,92,000
II.	Adjustments for changes in current assets/current liabilities:		
	(i) *Less*/Increase in current assets:		
	Accounts receivable (9,21,000 – 7,46,000)	= 1,75,000	
	Inventory (14,64,000 – 8,72,000)	= 5,92,000	
	(ii) *Less*: Decrease in current liabilities:		
	Accounts payable (9,24,000 – 6,32,000)	= 2,92,000	
	Accrued expenses payable (97,000 – 82,000)	= 15,000	10,74,000
			12,18,000
	(iii) *Add:* Decrease in current assets : Prepaid Expenses (28,000-26,000)		2,000
	Cash generated from operations		12,20,000

Cash Flow Statement

		(Rs)
Cash flows from operating activities :		
Cash generated from operations	12,20,000	
Income-tax paid	(10,13,000)	
Net cash from operating activities		2,07,000
Cash flows from investing activities	Nil	Nil
Cash flows from financing activities :		
Dividend paid	(6,15,000)	
Net cash from financing activities		(6,15,000)
Net increase in cash		(4,08,000)
Cash at beginning of period		13,40,000
Cash at end of period		9,32,000

Example 25

Usha Limited bad the following condensed Trial Balance at the end of 31 March, 2002:

	Rs.		Rs.
Cash	7,500	Current Liabilities	15,000
Accounts Receivable	30,000	Long-Term Notes Payable	25,500
Investments	20,000	Bonds Payable	25,000
Plant Assets	67,500	Capital Stock	75,000
Land	40,000	Retained Earnings	24,500
	1,65,000		1,65,000

During 2002-03 the following transactions took place:

(i) A tract of land was purchased for Rs. 7,750 cash.
(ii) Bonds payable in the amount of Rs. 6,000 were retired for cash at face value.
(iii) An additional Rs. 20,000 equity shares were issued at par for cash.
(iv) Dividends totalling Rs. 9,375 were paid.
iv) Net income for 2002-2003 was Rs. 28,450 after allowing for depreciation of Rs. 9,500.
(vi) Land was purchased through the issuance of Rs. 22,500 in bonds.
(vii) Usha Ltd. sold apart of its investments portfolio for Rs. 12,875 cash. The transactions resulted in a gain of Rs. 1,375 for the firm.
(viii) Current liabilities increased to Rs. 18,000 at 31-3-2003.
(ix) Accounts receivable at 31 March, 2003 total Rs. 38,000.

Prepare a statement of cash flows fur 2002-2003 with the indirect method as per AS 3 (Revised). Comment on the statement.

Solution:

Usha Ltd.

Cash Flow Statement for the year ended 31-3-2003

	Rs.	Rs.
Cash Flows from operating Activities		
Net income	28,450	
Adjustment for:		
Depreciation	9,500	
Gain on sale of investment	(1,375)	
Operating profit without working Cap, Changes	36,575	
Increase in Accounts Receivable	(8,000)	
Increase in Current Liabilities	3,000	
Cash Flows From Operating Activities		31,575
Cash Flows from Investing Activity		
Purchase of Land	(7,750)	
Sale of investments	12,875	
Cash Flows from Investing Activities		5,125
Cash Flows from Financing Activities		
Issue of Share Capital	20,000	
Redemption of bonds	(6,000)	
Dividend Paid	(9,375)	
Net Cash From Financing Activities		4,625
Net. Cash & Cash equivalents Increase:		41,325
Cash & Cash equivalents at the beginning of the period:		7,500
Cash & Cash equivalent at the end of the period:		48,825

SIGNIFICANCE OF CASH FLOW STATEMENT

Cash basis funds flow statements is important for a number of reasons.

(1) First, by focusing on cash flows, it explains the nature of the financial events which have affected the cash position. This statement explains the reason for the difference between opening and closing cash balance.

(2) The statement is important for financial planning purposes, For example, budgeted cash statements are a crucial element in the process of budget plans. These surpluses and shortfalls are expressed sequentially over the planning period and require management to deal with the forecasted cash

surplus or deficit, the former involving a short-term investment of surplus cash, the latter a short-term borrowing arrangement.

(3) This statement brings into sharp focus the enterprise's earning capacity with its spending and operating activity. Accounting principles restrict the income statement to matching periodic revenues with the cost of earning those revenues. Statement of changes in cash is not restricted in this way; hence, it provides an extended view of the financial inflows and outflows by including both capital and revenue flows.

(4) Cash flow statement provides an insight into the critical areas of financial management by identifying two important classes of cash flows, namely, operating cash flows and financing cash flows. This distinction draws attention to the net cash flows from operations and the net financing cash flows. The net operating cash flows classify the capability of the firm to support dividend payments to shareholders. It is these net cash flows which are of critical importance to investors and shareholders in predicting the amount of cash likely to be distributed in the future in the form of liquidation distributions or repayment of principal and in the evaluation of risk.

(5) The significance of cash flow statement lies in the increased complexity of business activity. This complexity results in a greater disparity between the time when income and expense items are reported and the time when the related cash flows occur. It may also result in a greater variability of cash flows.

LIMITATIONS OF CASH FLOW STATEMENT

Cash flow can be more precisely measured than can other concepts of funds because the valuation problem of cash are not as great as for other financial resources. However, movement of cash may be easily influenced. For example, payment of liabilities, may be temporarily delayed or marketable securities may be sold, increasing cash flow for a given period. This statement, since it does not cover non-cash items, is not useful in analysing changes in financial position of an enterprise. Cash and changes in cash are not adequate to measure change in financial position. For instance, an enterprise may possess very satisfactory financial (cash) position during a particular month. But if the firm the firm has to pay creditors next month, or make payments for the plant purchased in the near future the cash position of the firm will be adversely affected. In this way statement of changes in financial position measured through cash only has drawbacks and does not indicate accurately the changes in financial position. The statement has utility for making short-term financial planning but for long-term planning this statement would not be useful. Because of the limited usefulness of statement of changes in cash, the preparation of statement of changes in working capital (popularly known as funds flow statement) has been suggested.

STATEMENT OF CHANGES IN TOTAL FINANCIAL RESOURCES

One of the limitations of working capital concept of funds is that it omits a few major financial and investment transactions. Important information regarding changes in the resources of the firm and in the financial structure of the firm are omitted. Such items do not, of course, affect net working capital, but if included, would certainly provide quantitative and analytical information for decision-making. For example, issuing equity shares, or debentures for purchase of buildings or plant and machinery has no effect on working capital, but are significant financial transactions that should be disclosed.

Under the total financial resources concept of funds, the statement is not limited to transactions affecting working capital but would also be extended to cover all significant financial transactions that would otherwise be omitted under the other concepts of funds. That is the total financial resources concept requires that all material financial transactions he disclosed in the statement of changes in financial posilion. Transactions that technically do not increase or decrease funds (regardless of the concept of funds employed) but that represent significant financing and investing activities entered into by an entity must also be disclosed within the statement. Disclosure of a significant transaction that does not increase or decrease funds is made by showing one side of the transaction as a source of funds and the other side of the transaction as a corresponding use of funds. Transactions that affect financial position but do not increase or decrease funds include the following :

(a) Purchase of non-current assets *e.g.*, property and equipment by issuing share capital or debenture or long term debt.

(b) Reduction of a long-term liability by the issuance of share capitl or the incurrence of another long-term liability or a reduction in a non-current asset.

The above statement would be more useful in summarising the resources from which the funds have been obtained and the uses to which they have been put. The statement can analyse sources and uses in two categories of items (i) those which affect working capital (ii) those which do not affect working capital. Such a statement is, certainly, more informative and, therefore, potentially more useful in disclosing the firm's financing and investing activities during the two balance sheet dates. The fact that items which do not affect working capital are separately dealt with implies that it retains all the advantages of the working capital concept and, in addition, has the additional advantage of providing a complete picture of the total financial and investment activities of the firm.

As stated earlier, this statement includes significant transactions involving flows of non-cash resources even if cash itself is not affected. To recognize changes in all resources, these transactions are reported as both sources and uses of cash.

The following illustration explain it:

1. Purchased a Rs. 5,00,000 building for Rs. 1,00,000 cash and Rs. 4,00,000 mortgage note.

Source of Cash:	
Cash	Rs. 1,00,000
Issuing Mortgage note	Rs. 4,00,000
Use of Cash:	
Purchase-of Building	Rs. 5,00,000

2. Issued a promissory note to acquire land at a cost of Rs. 50,000

Source of Cash:	
Issuing promissory note	Rs. 50,000
Use of Cash:	
Purchase of land	Rs. 50,000

3. Issued 10,000 shares in exchange for 1,000 convertible debentures with Rs, 10,000 book value and Rs. 1,00,000 face value.

Source of Cash:	
Issue of Shares	Rs. 1,00.000
Use of Cash	
Retirement of debentures	Rs. 1,00,000

It can be noticed that each side of the transaction has a significant impact on the company's financial position. By applying the total resources concept, the statement of changes in financial position reflect more fully these significant events.

LIMITATIONS OF STATEMENT OF CHANGES IN FINANCIAL POSITION, ON TOTAL RESOURCES BASIS

The statement of changes in financial position, on total resources basis, has the following limitations:

Firstly, the concept of financial resources is vague and illdefined. The separate items included in the classification of sources and applications of funds do not necessarily represent increases and decreases of resources. Therefore, there is no direct disclosure of the extent to which the total resources of the firm have changed during the period.

Secondly, acquisitions of property in exchange for shares cannot be measured with the same degree of reliability as assets acquired for cash. Therefore, the summation of gross additions to plant and equipment for example, may result in misleading interpretations of the amount of resources acquired.

PREPARING FUNDS FLOW STATEMENT — TOTAL RESOURCES BASIS

In order to prepare funds flow statement, on total resources basis, successive balance sheets are compared and changes in each balance sheet item is recorded and further designated as a source of funds or a use of funds. The comparison of successive balance sheets will generally lead to following sources and uses of funds:

Sources of Funds

(i) Increase in owner's equity
(ii) Increase in liability
(iii) Decrease in an asset.

Uses of Funds

(i) Decrease in owner's equity
(ii) Decrease in a liability
(iii) Increase in an asset.

It is important to note that when funds are defined as total resources basis, the sources of funds are equal to the uses of funds as assets are always equal to owners equity plus liabilities.

Example 26

The following is the balance sheets of a company for the years 2002 and 2003 and an income statement for the year 2003.

Balance sheets as at Dec., 31, 2002 and 2003

	2002 Rs.	*2003* Rs.		*2002* Rs.	*2003* Rs.
Share Capital:			Fixed Assets:		
Equity	240	240	Gross block	1128	1210
Preference	100	100	Accumulated depreciation	(702)	(752)
Reserves and surplus	360	430	Net fixed assets	426	458
Long-term debt:			Long-term investment	30	70
Debentures	100	100	Current Assets:		
Current liabilities and provisions:			Cash and bank	146	146
Loans and advances	294	262	Marketable securities	12	12
Creditors	638	660	Debtors	320	378
Provisions	126	138	Stock	768	710
			Other current assets	134	134
			Intangible assets	22	30
	1,858	1,930		1,858	1,930

Income Statement for the year 2003

		(Rs. '000)
Sales		1,808
Cost of goods sold:		
Materials	732	
Wages	376	
Other manufacturing expense	320	
		1,428
Gross Profit		380
Operating expenses:		
Selling and administration	142	
Depreciation	50	
		192
Operating profit		188
Non-operating income (or expenses)		98
Net income before interest and tax		286
Interest:		
Debentures	8	
Borrowings	58	
		66
Profit before lax		220
Tax		116
Profit after tax		104
Dividend:		
Equity Capital	28	
Preference capital	6	34
Net income		70

Solution

Before preparing funds flow statement, changes in balance sheet items are analysed.

Changes in Balance Sheet Items

(Rs. '000)

	2002	*2001*	*Increase*	*Decrease*
Assets:				
Net fixed assets	426	458	32	—
Long-term investments	30	70	40	—
Cash and Bank	146	146	—	—
Marketable securities	12	12	—	—
Debtors	320	378	58	—
Stock	768	710	—	58
Other current assets	134	126	—	8
Intangible assets	22	30	8	—
Equity and liabilities:				
Equity capital	120	120	—	—
Preference capital	100	100	—	—
Reserves and surplus	360	430	70	—
Debentures	100	100	—	—
Loans and advances	294	262		32
Creditors	638	660	22	—
Provisions	126	138	12	—

Sources and Uses of Funds for the year 2003

		(Rs. '000)
Source of Funds:		
Increase in equity:		
Reserve and surplus		70
Increase in liabilities:		
Creditors	22	
Provisions	12	34
Decrease in assets:		
Stocks	58	
Other current assets	8	66
Total		170
Uses of Funds:		
Decrease in equity	—	—
Decrease in Liabilities:		
Loan and Advances	32	32
Increase in assets:		
Net fixed assets	32	
Long-term investments	40	
Debtors	58	
Intangible assets	8	138
		170

The sources and uses of funds statement can be prepared in a different manner using the information given in income statement of the company. This is given below:

Sources and Uses of Funds Statement for the year 2003

		(Rs. '000)
Sources of Funds:		
Profit before tax		220
Depreciation		50
Issue of equity capital		—
Increase in liabilities:		
Creditors	22	
Provisions	12	
		34
Decrease **in assets:**		
Stocks	58	
Other current assets	8	
		66
Total		370
Uses of Funds		
Taxes		116
Dividends		34
Decrease in liabilities:		
Loans and advances		
	32	32
Increase in assets:		
Fixed assets (gross)	82	
Long-term investments	40	
Debtors	58	
Intangible assets	8	188
		370

The above funds flow statement contains more detailed information than the previous one. This statement contains the following additional information:

(i) Change in reserve and surplus, which is equal to net income, is expressed as follows :
Profit before lax
Less: taxes
Less: dividends
Profit before tax is a source of funds, and taxes and dividends have been, therefore, shown as uses of funds.

(ii) Gross increase in fixed assets has been shown as uses of funds.

(iii) Depreciation for the year 2003 is shown as source of funds.

THEORY QUESTIONS

1. Explain why an adequate amount of working capital is essential to the successful operation of a business enterprise.
2. What are the primary ways in which an enterprise generates working capital and the primary ways in which a firm uses working capital?
3. What information can a reader gain from a statement of changes in financial position that is not apparent from reading an income statement?
4. If you were given the option to prepare statement of changes in financial position (SCFP) either on working capital basis or cash basis which one would you prefer? Why? Explain keeping in view the objective of financial statement of business enterprise.
5. Explain the different concepts of funds used in the preparation of statement of changes in financial position. Which concept of funds is appropriate under what circumstances and objectives?
6. How docs a funds flow differ from a balance sheet and an income statement? Distinguish between a cash basis funds flow statement and disbursement statement.
7. What additional information is required to convert a statement of sources and uses of net working capital into a statement of changes in financial position?
8. Why is cash flow statement a useful statement?
9. Identify the three major types of activities classified on a cash flow statement and give examples of cash inflow and cash outflow in each classification.
10. What limitations of funds flow statement are overcome by a cash flow statement?
11. What are the purposes of cash flow statement?
12. Discuss the procedures in preparing a funds flow statement.
13. Discuss the procedures in preparing a cash flow statement.
14. What are the three classifications of cash flows and give some examples of each?
15. Explain the statement of changes in financial position, prepared on total resources basis.
16. What are the two methods of determining cash flows from operation? Generally, which of these methods is preferable?
17. Why is the change in the cash balance so important for financial reporting and managerial decisions?
18. "A cash flow statement is required to explain changes in cash account balances between balance sheet dates. Explain this statement.
19. Explain in general how the cash balance is increased or decreased by income statement transactions.
20. List the common sources and uses of cash in each activity area; operating, investing and financing.
21. What are the different meanings of funds in relation to statement of changes in financial position?
22. What are the purposes of statement of changes in financial position?
23. How does a funds flow differ from balance sheet and income statement?

24. Discuss the guidelines as contained in AS-3 on Cash Flow Statement.
25. (a) Why are businesses now using the Statement of Cash Flows ?
    (b) Distinguish amongst cash flows from operating, investing and financing activities. Provide examples for each type of activity as per AS 3 (Revised) issued by the ICAI. Show a Proforma statement of cash flows.
    (c) How are significant non-cash financing and investing transactions reported as per AS 3 (Revised)?
26. Discuss in brief the main features of Accounting Standard (AS-3). What changes have been made in this standard ?
27. In what respects is AS-3 (revised) is an improvement over AS-3 (old). Is it permissible that a company follows the requirements of both the standards simultaneously?
28. Distinguish between 'cash' and 'cash equivalent'.

PROBLEMS

1. From the following Balance Sheet of company you are required to prepare (i) a statement showing changes in the working capital, and (ii) a statement of sources and applications of funds.

Particulars	*January*	*December*
	Rs	Rs.
Cash	40,000	44,400
Accounts receivable	10.000	20,700
Inventories	15,000	15,000
Land	4,000	4,000
Buildings	20,000	16,000
Equipment	15.000	17,000
Accumulated Depreciation	(5,000)	(2,800)
Patents	1,000	900
	1,00,000	1,15,200
Current Liabilities	30,000	32,000
Bonds Payable	22,000	22,000
Bonds Payable Discount	(2,000)	(1,800)
Capital Stock	35.000	43,500
Retained Earnings	15,000	19,500
	1,00,000	1,15,000

Additional Information:
(a) Income for the period Rs. 10,000.
(b) A building that cost Rs. 4,000 and which had a book value of Rs. 1,000 was sold for Rs. 1,400.
(c) The depreciation charge for the period was Rs. 800.
(d) There was Rs. 5,000 issue of common stock.
(e) Cash dividends Rs. 2,000 and a Rs. 3,500 stock dividend were declared.
(**Ans.** Increase in Working Capital Rs. 13,100. Sources Rs. 17,100, Applications Rs. 4,000).

2. From the following Balance Sheets of X Ltd. on 31st December, 2002 and 2003, you arc required to prepare:
   (a) A schedule of changes in working capital.
   (b) A funds flow statement

Liabilities	*2002* Rs.	*2003* Rs.	*Assets*	*2002* Rs.	*2003* Rs.
Share Capital	1,00,000	1,00,000	Goodwill	12,000	12.000
General Reserve	14,000	18,000	Building	40,000	36,000
Profit & Loss A/c	16,000	13,000	Plant	37,000	36,000
Sundry Creditors	8,000	5,400	Investments	10,000	11,000
Bill payable	1,200	800	Stock	30.000	23,400
Provision for Taxation	16,000	18,000	Bills Receivable	2,000	3,200
Provision for doubful debts	400	600	Debtors	18,000	19,000
			Cash at Bank	6,600	15,200
	1,55,600	1,55,800		1,55,600	1,55,800

The following additional information has also been given:

(a) Depreciation Charge on Plant was Rs. 4,000 and on building Rs. 4,000.

(b) Provision for taxation of Rs. 19,000 was made during the year.

(c) Interim dividend of Rs. 8,000 was paid during the year 2003.

Ans. Increase in working capital Rs, 7,000, Funds from operations Rs. 36,000.

3. Find out cash from operations from the following profit and loss account.

Profit and Loss Account for the year ending December, 2002

	Rs.		Rs.
To Rent	500	By Gross Profit	12,500
To Salaries	2,500	By Gain on sale of plant	2,500
To Depreciation	1,000	By Income-tax refund	1,500
To Loss on sale of Plant	500		
To Goodwill written off	2,000		
To Proposed dividends	2,500		
To Provision for taxation	2,500		
To Net profit	5,000		
	16,500		16,500

Ans. Cash from operations Rs. 9,500.

4. The details about the current assets of a company are as follows:

	2002 (Rs.)	*2003* (Rs.)
Debtors	20,000	24,000
Provision for bad debts	2,000	2,400
Bills receivable	8,000	6,000
Bills payable	10,000	12,000
Creditors	16,000	18,000
Inventories	10,000	16,000
Short-term investments	20,000	24,000
Outstanding expenses	2,000	3,000
Prepaid expenses	4,000	2,000
Accrued Income	6,000	8,000

Find out cash from operations

Ans. Rs. 15,400

5. A Ltd. Supplies you the following Balance Sheet on 31st December:

Liabilities	*2002* Rs.	*2003* Rs.	*Assets*	*2002* Rs.	*2003* Rs.
Share capital	1,40,000	1,48,000	Cash	18,000	15,600
Bonds	24,000	12,000	Debtors	29,800	35,400
Sundry Creditors	20,720	23,680	Stock	98,400	85,000
Provision for bad debt	1,400	1,600	Land	40,000	55,000
Reserves & Surplus	22,080	21,120	Goodwill	20,000	15,000
	2,06,200	2,06,400		2,06,200	2,06,400

Following additional information has also been supplied to you:

(i) Dividends amounting Rs. 7,000 were paid during the year 2003.

(ii) Depreciation on land was provided at the rate of 5% p.a.

You are required to prepare a Cash Flow Statement.

6. From the following information, calculate cash from operations

Total Sales	Rs. 2,40,000
Net profit for the year	Rs. 70,000
Debtors outstanding at the end of the year	Rs. 40,000
Debtors outstanding at the begining of the year	Rs. 20,000

7. Calculate cash from operations from the following information :

Sales of the year	Rs.10,00,000
Purchase of the year (including credit purchase of Rs. 2,00,000)	Rs. 7,00,000
Expenses of the year	Rs. 1,00,000

8. From the following information calculate cash from operations by using actual concept.

Expenses outstanding on 1-1-2006	Rs. 1,00,000
Expenses outstanding on 31-12-2006	Rs. 15,00,000
Net profit for the year 2006	Rs. 80,00,000
Int. received in advance on 1-1-2006	Rs. 50,000
Int. received in advance on 31-12-2006	Rs. 1,00,000

9. Following information is given to you.

Depreciation charged to P/L A/c	Rs. 10,00,000
Loss on sale of machinery written off-to P/L A/c	Rs. 2,00,000
Net profit after Tax	Rs. 16,00,000

	Opening Balance Rs.	*Closing Balance* Rs.
Debtors	40,000	50,000
Inventory	2,00,000	2,20,000
Outstanding Expenses	50,000	40,000
Creditors	70,000	80,000

From the above information, ascertain cash from operations using actual concept.

10. From the following Balance Sheets you are required to prepare a cash flow statements.

Liabilities	*2005* Rs.	*2006* Rs.	*Assets*	*2005* Rs.	*2006* Rs.
P and L A/c	1,10,000	1,23,000	Land	1,50,000	1,66,000
Share Capital	4,00,000	4,50,000	Cash	1,30,000	1,47,000
Trade Creditors	1,70,000	1,45,000	Stock	1,80,000	1,90,000
			Debtors	2,20,000	2,15,000
	6,80,000	7,18,000		6,80,000	7,18,000

11. The comparative Balance sheet of a company is as follows :

Liabilities	*2005* *Rs.*	*2006* *Rs.*	*Assets*	*2005* *Rs.*	*2006* *Rs.*
Capital	2,50,000	2,75,000	Land and Building	2,10,000	2,50,000
Creditors	85,000	93,000	Stock	1,50,000	1,45,000
Laon from Banks	3,60,000	3,00,000	Cash	1,15,000	1,22,000
Outstanding Expenses	15,000	17,000	Machinery	3,00,000	2,40,000
Bills Payable	1,50,000	1,40,000	Debtors	70,000	80,000
Loan	–	25,000	Prepaid Expenses	15,000	13,000
	8,60,000	8,50,000		8,60,000	8,50,000

Additional Information :

(i) Net profit for the year 2006 amounted to 60,000.

(ii) During the year a Machine costing Rs. 25,000 (accumulated depreciation Rs. 10,000) was sold for Rs. 13,000. The provision for depreciation against machinery as on 31-12-2005 was Rs. 50,000 and on 31-12-2006 was 85,000.

You are required to prepare a cash flow statement.

12. The comparative balance sheets for DKS Ltd. are given below :

	31st Dec., 2005 Rs.	31st Dec., 2006 Rs.
Asseets		
Cash	1,82,000	1,22,000
Stock	2,12,000	1,60,000
Debtors	2,04,000	1,24,000
Prepaid Expenses	32,000	24,000
Plant & Machinery	5,80,000	5,60,000
Goodwill	56,000	60,000
	12,66,000	10,50,000
Liabilities		
Creditors	50,000	34,000
Provision for Dep.	2,00,000	1,60,000
Debentures	2,02,000	2,02,000
Premium on Debentures Issue	22,000	28,000
Share capital	2,90,000	1,90,000
Share premium	30,000	—
Reserves and Surpluses	4,72,000	4,36,000
	12,66,000	10,50,000

The following additional information is available from the accounting records 2005.

(i) Net profit for the year Rs. 66,000.

(ii) Debenture Premium of Rs. 6,000 was amortised during the year.

Prepare a statement of chages in Financial Position on cash basis.

13. The DKSG Ltd. has prepared the following Balance sheets.

Balance Sheets
as on 31st December

(Rs. '000)

Liabilities	*2005* *Rs.*	*2006* *Rs.*	*Assets*	*2005* *Rs.*	*2006* *Rs.*
Equity Capital	1,400	1,400	Fixed Assets (Net)	1,000	1,820
Retained Earnings	140	200	Inventory	300	800
Sundry Creditors	280	780	Sundry Debtors	100	400
Mortage Payable	–	800	Prepaid Expenses	40	80
Tax payable	20	60	Cash	400	140
	1,840	3,240		1,840	3,240

Other information for the year ended 2006 is as under : (Rs.'000)

Sales	2,000
Cost of Goods sold	1,460
Expenses:	
General	220
Depreciation	160
Property Tax	80
Dividends	20
Retained Earnings	60

DKSG Ltd. carried out an expansion programme and had paid Rs. 18,000 cash and signed Rs, 80,000 mortage on a New Building. Prepare a cash Flow Statement.

Hint: (Rs. '000)

Opening Stock	300
+ Purchase	1960
	2260
Less: Closing Stock	800
Cost of goods sold	1460

14. Following are the Balance sheets of Good Luck Ltd.

Liabilities	*2005* Rs.	*2006* Rs.	*Assets*	*2005* Rs.	*2006* Rs.
Equity Share Capital	2,00,000	2,42,000	Land	1,24,000	1,48,000
7% Preference Share Capital	1,80,000	1,80,000	Buildings & Equipment	2,80,000	3,88,000
P/L A/c	1,75,900	1,81,900	Debtors	1,84,000	1,84,000
Creditors	2,20,000	2,08,000	Inventory	2,32,000	1,48,000
Outstanding Expenses	22,000	34,000	Prepaid Rent	11,800	12,400
Provision for Taxation	16,000	16,600	Prepaid Insurance	12,100	12,100
			Provision for Dep.	80,000	86,000
			Cash	50,000	56,000
	8,93,900	9,48,500		8,93,900	9,48,500

Additional Information:

(i) The company declared and paid equity dividend of Rs. 36,000 during the year 2006.
(ii) The provision for Taxation for 2006 is included in creditors.
(iii) A Truck costing Rs. 36,000 and with accumulated depreciation of Rs, 24,000 was sold at a profit of Rs. 600.
(iv) Prepared (a) Statement of Sources and Application of funds for year 2006, and (b) Cash Flow Statements.

15. From the following information you are required to prepare a cash flow statement of K.P.S Ltd. for the year ended 31st December, 2006.

Balance Sheet

Liabilities	*2005* Rs.	*2006* Rs.	*Assets*	*2005* Rs.	*2006* Rs.
Share Capital	1,70,000	1,70,000	Plant and Machinery	1,50,000	2,91,000
Secured Loans (Repayable in 2007)	—	1,40,000	Inventory	25,000	50,000
Creditors	1,14,000	1,39,000	Debtors	15,000	30,000
Tax Payable	11,000	13,000	Cash	1,20,000	1,07,000
P&L A/c	17,000	20,000	Prepaid Capital Exp.	2,000	4,000
	3,12,000	4,82,000		3,12,000	4,82,000

Profit and Loss Account
for the ended 31st Dec., 2006

			Rs.
To Opening Inventory	25,000	By closing stock	50,000
To Purchases	98,000	By Sales	1,00,000
To Gross Profit c/d	27,000		
	1,50,000		1,50,000
To General Exp.	11,000	By Gross Profit b/d	27,000
To Depreciation	8,000		
To Taxes	4,000		
To Net profit c/d	4,000		
	27,000		27,000
To Dividend	1,000	By Balance b/f	7,000
To Balance c/f	10,000	By Net Balance b/d	4,000
	11,000		11,000

16. Prepare a Cash Flow statement for 2006 from the following information.

Income statement for 2006	Rs	Rs	Rs
Sales		2,00,000	
Less : Cost of Sale (Including Rs. 2,000 depreciation)		1,50,000	
Gross Profit		50,000	
Less : Selling and Administrative expenses	10,000		
Interest on loan	1,000		
Other Expneses	5,000		16,000
			34,000

Balance Sheet

Assets	*2005* Rs.	*2006* Rs.
Cash in hand and at bank	15,000	13,000
Investments	5,000	15,000
Debtors	40,000	30,000
Stock	65,000	80,000

	2005	2006
Plant and Machinery	2,50,000	2,98,000
	3,75,000	4,36,000
Liabilities	*2005*	*2006*
	Rs.	Rs.
Creditors	55,000	45,000
Outstanding Expenses (Selling & Admn)	5,000	10,000
Accumulated Depreciation	8,000	10,000
Loans	15,000	25,000
Share Capital	1,72,000	2,00,000
Reserves	1,20,000	1,54,000
	3,75,000	4,36,000

17. The following are the Balance Sheet of Sukhvir Ltd.

Liabilities	*2005* Rs.	*2006* Rs.	*Assets*	*2005* Rs.	*2006* Rs.
Equity Capital	3,000	4,000	Property	2,000	2,500
Share premium	–	100	Plant and Machinery	4,000	4,500
			Less depreciation	(1,400)	(1,500)
P&L A/c Balance	1,000	1,000	Loan to subsidiary	–	150
Profit for the year	–	2,000	Shares in subsidiary	200	120
6% Debentors	1,500	1,000			
Profit on Redemption of Debentures	–	20	Stock	1,400	1,500
			Debtors	1,000	1,500
Sundry Creditors	1,400	1,100	Bank	350	1,570
Provision for Tax	500	1,000			
Proposed Dividend	150	200			
	7,550	10,420		7,550	10,420

Prepare Cash Flow Statement.

18. From the following balance, you are required to calculate cash from operations.

	2005 Rs.	*2006* Rs.
Debtors	50,000	47,000
Bills Receivable	10,000	12,500
Creditors	20,000	25,000
Bills payable	8,000	6,000
Outstanding Expenses	1,000	1,200
Prepaid expenses	800	700
Accrued Income	600	750
Income received in Advance	300	250
Profit made during the year	–	1,30,000

19. The following details are available from a company.

Liabilities	*2005* Rs.	*2006* Rs.	*Assets*	*2005* Rs.	*2006* Rs.
Share Capital	70,000	74,000	Cash	9,000	7,800
Debentures	12,000	6,000	Debtors	14,900	17,700
Reserves for doubtful debts	700	800	Stock	49,200	42,700
Trade creditors	10,360	11,840	Land	20,000	30,000
P/L A/c	10,040	10,560	Goodwill	10,000	5,000
	1,03,100	1,03,700		1,03,100	1,03,700

In addition you are given
- Dividend paid is Rs. 3,500
- Land was purchased for is Rs. 10,000 Amount provided for amortisation of goodwill is Rs. 5,000
- Debentures paid off Rs. 6,000

Prepare Cash Flow Statement

20. From the following information, prepare cash flow statement:

	1-1-2001 Rs.	*31-12-2001* Rs.		*1-1-2001* Rs.	*31-12-2001* Rs.
Share Capital	3,00,000	4.00.000	Goodwill	1.00,000	90.000
Profit and Loss A/c	1,10,000	1,50,000	Machinery	2,98,000	4,30,000
Debentures	1.50,000	1,00,000	Investment	1,00,000	60,000
Creditors	90,000	70,000	Stock	50,000	80,000
Provision for Taxation	80,000	80,000	Debtors	1.60,000	1,10,000
			Cash at Bank	10.000	20.000
			Preliminary Expenses	12,000	10,000
	7,30,000	8,00,000		7,30,000	8,00,000

During the year (i) investment were sold at a profit of Rs. 10,000 (ii) Debenture were redeemed at 10% premium (iii) Rs. 75.000 was paid as income-tax (iv) Depreciation charged amounted to Rs. 70,000.

Ans. Cash flow from operating activities (after tax) Rs. 1,17,000
Financing activities : Issue of shares Rs. 1,00,000, Redemption of debentures Rs. 55,000
Investing activities : Purchase of machinery Rs. 2,02,000, Sale of Investments Rs. 50,000.

21. From the following information prepare a cash flow statement

	1-1-2001 Rs.	*31-12-2001* Rs.		*1-1-2001* Rs.	*31-12-2001* Rs.
Share Capital	2,00,000	3,00,000	Fixed Assets	4,00,000	7,00,000
Share Premium	—	1,00,000	Dcblof.	50,000	1.00,000
Profit and Loss A/c	1,00,000	2.00,000	Stock	1,00,000	1.70.000
Debentures	2.00,000	—	Cash	5,000	—
Provision for Taxation	30,000	50.000	Bank	45,000	—
Loan	20,000	1.50.000			
Creditors	50,000	70,000			
Bank Overdraft	—	1,00,000			
	6,00,000	9,70,000		6,00,000	9,70,000

Net profit for the year after charging Rs. 50,000 as depreciation was Rs. 1,50,000. Dividend paid on shares was Rs. 50.000. Tax provision created during the year amounted to Rs. 60,000.

Ans. Cash flow from operating activities after lax) Rs. 1,20,000
Fixed assets purchased Rs. 3,50,000, Issue of shares Rs. 2,00,000, Redemption of Debentures Rs. 1,30,000. Loan raised Rs. 1,30,000, Dividend paid Rs. 50,000.

22. The differences in Bharat Co.'s Balance Sheet accounts at December 31, 2001 and 2002, are presented below.

	Increase (Decrease)
Assets :	Rs.
Cash and cash equivalents	1,20,000
Short-term investments	3,00,000
Accounts receivable, net	—
Inventory	80,000
Long-term investments	(1,00,000)
Plant assets	7,00,000
Accumulated depreciation	—
	11,00,000
Liabilities and Stockholders' Equity :	Rs.
Accounts payable and accrued liabilities	(5,000)
Dividends payable	1,60,000
Short-term bank debt	3,25,000
Long-term debt	1,10,000
Common stock. Rs. 10 par	1,00,000
Additional paid-in capital	1,20,000
Retained earnings	2,90,000
	11,00,000

The following additional information relates to 2001 :

- Net income was Rs. 7,90,000.
- Cash dividends of Rs. 5,00,000 were declared.
- Building costing Rs. 6,00,000 and having a carrying amount of Rs. 3,50,000 was sold for Rs. 3,50,000.
- Equipment costing Rs. 1,10,000 was acquired through issuance of long-term debt
- A long-term investment was sold for Rs. 1,35,000. There were no other transactions affecting long-term investments.
- 10,000 shares of common stock were issued for Rs. 22 a share.

Required:

In Bharat's 2001 statement of cash flows,

(i) Net cash provided by operating activities was
(a) Rs. 11,60,000 (b) Rs. 10,40,000
(c) Rs. 9,20,000 (d) Rs. 7,05,000

(ii) Net cash used in investing activities was
(a) Rs. 10,05,000 (b) Rs.11,90.000
(c) Rs. 12,75,000 (d) Rs. 16,00,000

(iii) Net cash provided by financing activities was
(a) Rs. 20,000 (b) Rs. 45.000
(c) Rs. 1,50,000 (d) Rs. 2,05,000

Ans. (i) (c) (ii) (a) (iii) (d)

23. The following is the Balance Sheet of a company.

Balance Sheets

	December 31, 2001 (Rs.)	2000 (Rs.)
Assets		
Current assets:		
Cash	3,00,000	2,00,000
Accounts receivable—net	8,40.000	5,80,000
Merchandise inventory	6,60,000	4,20,000
Prepaid expenses	1,00,000	50,000
Total current assets	19,00,000	12,50,000
Long-term investments	80,000	—
Land, buildings, and fixtures	11,30,000	6,00,000
Less: accumulated depreciation	1,10,000	50,000
	10,20,000	5,50,000
Total assets	30,00,000	18,00,000
Equities		
Current liabilities:		
Accounts payable	5,30,000	4,40,000
Accrued expenses	1,40,000	1,30,000
Dividends payable	70,000	—
Total current liabilities	7,40,000	5,70,000
Note payable—due 2003	5,00,000	
Stockholders' equity :		
Common stock	12,00,000	9,00,000
Retained earnings	5,60,000	3,30,000
	17,60,000	12,30,000
Total liabilities and stock-holders' equity	30,00,000	18,000

Income Statements

	Year ended December 31, *2001* Rs.	*2000* Rs.
Net credit sales	64,00,000	40,00,000
Cost of goods sold	50,00,000	32,00,000
Gross profit	14,00,000	8,00,000
Expenses (including income taxes)	10,00,000	5,20,000
Net income	4,00,000	2,80,000

Additional information available included the following :

- All accounts receivable and accounts payable related to trade merchandise. Accounts payable are recorded net and always are paid to take all of the discount allowed. The allowance for doubtful accounts at the end of 2001 was the same as at the end of 2000; no receivables were charged against the allowance during 2001.
- The proceeds from the note payable were used to finance a new store building Capital stock was sold to provide additional working capital.

(i) Cash collected during 2001 from accounts receivable amounted to
(a) Rs. 55,60.000 (b) Rs. 58,40,000
(c) Rs. 61,40,000 (d) Rs. 64,00,000

(ii) Cash payments during 2001 on accounts payable to suppliers amounted to
(a) Rs. 46,70,000 (b) Rs. 49,10,000
(c) Rs. 50,00,000 (d) Rs. 51,50,000

(iii) Net cash provided by financing activities for 2001 totalled
(a) Rs. 1,40,000 (b) Rs. 3,00,000
(c) Rs. 5,00,000 (d) Rs. 7,00,000

(iv) Net cash used in investing activities during 2001 was
(a) Rs. 80,000 (b) Rs. 5,30,000
(c) Rs. 6,10,000 (d) Rs. 6,60.000

Ans. (i) (c) (ii) (d) (iii) (d) (iv) (c)

CHAPTER 5

Marginal (Variable) Costing

CONCEPT OF MARGINAL COST, MARGINAL COSTING

Marginal cost, in cost accounting, means variable production costs, *i.e.* the costs which tend to vary in direct proportion to the changes in the production level. If an extra unit of output is produced, the costs which could be incurred for producing this extra unit, will only be marginal (variable) costs since fixed costs remain constant.

Marginal costing is a costing-techinque in which only variable manufacturing costs are considered and used while valuing inventories and determining cost of goods sold. That is, only variable manufacturing costs are considered product costs and are allocated to products manufactured. These costs include direct materials, direct labour and variable factory overhead. Fixed factory (manufacturing) overheads are not considered product costs and are not used to value inventories and determine the cost of goods sold and are excluded from the cost of product. Fixed manufacturing costs are treated as period costs in marginal costing, *i.e.* costs which are a function of a time rather than of production. In marginal costing, fixed manufacturing overheads are written off to the profit and loss account in the period in which are incurred.

ABSORPTION COSTING

Absorption costing, also known as full costing, is a costing technique in which all manufacturing costs, variable and fixed, are considered as costs of production and are used in determining the cost of goods manufactured and inventories. All manufacturing costs are fully absorbed into finished goods.

DIFFERENCE BETWEEN MARGINAL COSTING AND ABSORPTION COSTING

Marginal costing and absorption costing differ from each other in the following respects :

1. *Cost element in product cost* Marginal costing and absorption costing differ only in the treatment of fixed factory (manufacturing) overheads in the accounting records and financial statement. In both the costing techniques it is agreed that selling and administrative expenses, whether variable or fixed, are period costs and these costs are not treated as product costs with the result that selling and administrative expenses are not included in the costs of inventories and costs of goods sold. Similarly, it is also agreed that variable manufacturing costs are prodcuts costs, *i.e.*, costs to be charged to the product. The disagreement between the two, is only in regard to the treatment of fixed manufacturing costs.
2. *Inventory values* Marginal costing and absorption costing do influence inventory values differently. The value of inventories under marginal costing is relatively at a lower figure as inventories are determined in terms of only variable production costs. In absorption costing the value of inventories is comparatively at a higher figure because it considers fixed factory overhead also besides the variable production costs.

3. *Difference in net income* The treatment of fixed factory overhead brings differences in the net income figures in the two costing techniques. The magnitude of any difference in net income is function of fixed manufacturing costs per unit and the change in inventory levels.

The question of difference in net income has been further explained in the following pages while discussing income statement under absorption costing and marginal costing.

INCOME STATEMENTS UNDER ABSORPTION COSTING AND MARGINAL COSTING

Income Statement under Absorption Costing

Under absorption costing all costs are divided into three categories: manufacturing, selling, and administrative costs. In the income statement, all manufacturing costs (variable and fixed) are subtracted from the sales revenue to get a gross margin/gross profit on sales: and selling and administrative expenses (fixed and variable) are deducted from gross margin to arrive at the net income.

It should be clearly understood that fixed manufacturing overhead are charged to units produced on the basis of per unit fixed manufacturing overhead rate obtained by dividing the standard fixed manufacturing overhead by normal output level as follows:

$$\frac{\text{Standard fixed manufacturing overhead}}{\text{Normal output (Capacity)}}$$

If production is above or below the normal or standard output, adjustments are made for volume (capacity) variances. If the volume (capacity) variance is favourable, *i.e.*, over-absorption (actual production being higher than normal capacity production), the amount of over-absorption is deducted from the total cost of goods manufactured and sold. If the volume (capacity) variance is unfavourable, *i.e.*, under-absorption (actual production being lesser than normal capacity production), the amount of under-absorption is added to the cost of goods manufactured and sold. A proforma of income statement prepared under absorption costing is given in Fig. 5.1.

Income Statement (Absorption Costing)

		Amount *Rs*
Sales		—
Less:	Manufacturing costs:	
	(1) Variable production costs:	
	Direct material cost	—
	Direct labour cost	—
	Variable manufacturing overhead	—
	(2) Fixed factory (manufacturing) overhead	—
	Cost of goods manufactured	—
Add:	Beginning inventory	—
	Cost of goods available for sate	—
Less:	Closing inventory	—
	Cost of goods sold	—
	Over- or under-applied factory (manufacturing) overhead (Over-absorption to be deducted and under-absorption to be added)	—
	Cost of goods sold at actual	—
	Gross profit on sales	—
Less:	Fixed selling and administrative expenses	(—)
	Variable selling and administrative expenses	(—)
	Net Income	—

Fig. 5.1. Income Statement Proforma (Absorption Costing)

Income Statement under Marginal Costing

Under marginal costing, only variable costs of production (direct material, direct labour and variable manufacturing) are subtracted from sales revenue to determine a balance which is known by different names, such as marginal contribution, marginal income (profit), marginal revenue, marginal balance, profit pick-up, etc. All fixed costs, and variable selling, distribution and administrative costs are deducted from this balance to arrive at the net income. Since fixed manufacturing costs are not charged to products under marginal costing, there can be no volume (capacity) variance. Marginal contribution/marginal income under marginal costing is greater than the gross profit/gross margin under absorption costing. Figure 5.2 depicts a proforma of income statement prepared under marginal costing.

Under marginal costing, fixed manufacturing overhead are excluded and therefore inventory values are lower than inventory value computed under absorption costing. Income may be higher or lower depending upon whether inventories are built up or liquidated. That is, the income statement under absorption costing may reflect higher profit if the production is more than the normal capacity produc-tion and also lower sales has been made. This happens because above normal capacity production has over-absorbed its actual fixed manufacturing overhead.

Absorption/full costing and marginal costing influence differently gross profit, net profit, and inventory values of different month/periods. The following data and income statement prepared under both costing techniques explain this situation.

Data:

Normal capacity 20,000 units per month
Variable costs (direct materials, direct labour, variable factory overhead) per unit Rs 6.
Fixed factory overhead Rs 25,000 per month or Rs 1.25 per unit at normal capacity.
Fixed selling and administrative expenses are Rs 5,000 p.m.
Variable selling and administrative expenses are Re 1.00 per unit sold.
Sales prices per unit is Rs 10.

Actual production, sales and inventories in units are:

Income Statement (Marginal Costing)

	Amount Rs
Sales	—
Less: Variable production costs:	
Direct material costs	—
Direct labour cost	—
Variable manufacturing (factory) overhead	—
Cost of goods manufactured	—
Add: Beginning inventory	—
Cost of goods available for sale	—
Less: Closing inventory	—
Cost of goods sold	—
Marginal contribution	—
Less: Fixed manufacturing overhead	—
Variable selling and administrative expenses	—
Fixed selling and administrative expenses	—
Net Income	—

Fig. 5.2. Income Statement Proforma (Marginal Costing)

	First month	*Second month*	*Third month*	*Fourth month*
Unit in beginning inventory	—	—	3,000	1,000
Units produced	17,500	21,000	19,000	20,000
Units sold	17,500	18,000	21,000	16,500
Units in closing inventory	—	3,000	1,000	4,500

Solution

Income Statement (Absorption Costing)

	First month	*Second month*	*Third month*	*Fourth month*
Sales	Rs 1,75,000	1,80,000	2,10,000	1,65,000
Variable cost per unit Rs 6	1,05,000	1,26,000	1,14,000	1,20,000
Fixed factory overhead @ Rs 1.25	21,875	26,250	23,750	25,000
Cost of goods manufactured	1,26,875	1,52,250	1,37,750	1,45,000
Add: Beginning inventory			21,750	7,250
Cost of goods available for sales	1.26,875	1,52,250	1,59,500	1,52,250
Less: Ending inventory	—	21,750	7,250	32,625
Cost of goods sold	1.26,875	1,30,500	1,52,250	1,19,625
Over- or under-applied factory overhead	3,125	(1,250)	1,250	—
Cost of goods sold at actual	1,30,000	1,29,250	1.53,500	1,19,625
Gross profit on sales	45,000	50.750	56,500	45,375
Selling and administrative expenses (fixed and variable)	22,500	23,000	26,000	21,500
Net income for the month	22,500	27.750	30.500	23.S75

Note: In absorption costing income statement, fixed factory expenses arc included in the unit cost and also in the inventory values.

(i) Ending inventory: Second month $\frac{3,000}{21,000} \times 1,52,250 = \text{Rs } 21,750$

Third month $\frac{1,000}{22,000} \times 1,50,500 = \text{Rs } 7,250$

Fourth month $\frac{4,500}{21,000} \times 1,52,250 = \text{Rs } 32,625$

(ii) In first month, *Rs* 3,125 is under-absorbed factory overhead due to production less than normal capacity and should be added to the cost of goods sold.

(iii) In the second month, Rs 1,250 is over-absorbed due to higher production and has, therefore been subtracted.

(iv) In the third month, Rs 1,250 is under-absorbed and has been added back to cost of goods sold.

(v) In the fourth month, production is at normal capacity and there is no under- or over-absorption.

Income Statement (Marginal Costing)

	First month	*Second month*	*Third month*	*Fourth month*
Sales (Rs)	1,75,000	1,80,000	2,10,000	1,65,000
Variable production cost:				
Variable manufacturing costs				
Rs 6 per unit	1,05,000	1,26,000	1,14,000	1,20,000
Cost of goods manufactured	1,05,000	1,26,000	1,14,000	1,20,000
Add: Beginning inventory	—	—	18,000	6,000
Cost of goods available for sale	1,05,000	1,26,000	1,32,000	1,26,000
Less: Closing inventory	—	18,000	6,000	27,000
Cost of goods sold	1,05,000	1,08,000	1,26,000	99,000
Contribution	70,000	72,000	84,000	66,000
Less: Fixed factory overhead	25,000	25.000	25,000	25,000
Fixed selling and administrative expenses	5,000	5.000	5,000	5,000
Variable selling and administrative expenses	17,500	18,000	21,000	16,500
Total fixed costs and non-manufacturing variable costs	47,500	48,000	51,000	46,500
Net income for the month	22,500	24,000	33,000	19,500

Note: Under marginal costing, fixed factory (manufacturing) overhead costs are not included in the product unit costs and costs of inventories.

(i) Valuation of closing inventory

Second month = 3,000 × Rs. 6 = Rs 18,000
Third month = 1,000 × Rs. 6 = Rs 6,000
Fourth month = 4,500 × Rs. 6 = Rs 27,000

(ii) The question of under- or over-absorption of factory overhead does not arise under marginal costing.

A comparison of the income statements leads to the following conclusions:

1. Under variable costing, the closing inventory is costed at a smaller figure because only variable costs are charged to the product.
2. Both costing methods report the same amount of profit in periods in which production and sale are equal and there is no inventory change (first month). This is because the amount of fixed factory overhead costs charged to the period was the same in each case. Under marginal cost Rs 25,000 was deducted from sales as period costs. Under absorption costing Rs 25,000 was charged to the sales in two parts; (a) Rs 21,875 as part of the cost of sales (17,500 units × Rs. 1.25); and (b) Rs 3,125 as unfavourable volume (capacity) variance.
3. When inventory of manufactured goods fluctuates from period to period, net income will differ somewhat under the two methods because absorption costing requires that part of the period costs be included in inventory, whereas marginal costing excludes period costs. Therefore:
   (i) When production exceeds sales (the inventory is increased), the net income reported *under* absorption costing is higher than reported under variable costing. This follows because under absorption costing, a portion of the fixed costs budgeted for the period is shifted to the following period in the closing inventories whereas under marginal costing the total fixed costs are charged against income. This is clear from comparing the net income of the *second* and fourth month.

(ii) When sale exceeds production (the inventories are decreased), marginal costing shows a higher profit because only current period costs are being charged aganist current revenues whereas under absorption costing the period costs previously included in inventory are now being charged against current revenues. This situation is illustrated by the income of the third month.

4. Under marginal costing profits always move in the same direction as sales volume. They cannot, of course, increase or decrease in direct proportion because unit fixed costs do not remain constant. Profit reported under absorption costing behave irregularly and sometimes in the opposite direction from sales. For example, sales of the fourth month are lower than the sales of the first month, yet the net income reported for the fourth month is higher than the net income for the first month.
5. The above income statements are prepared on the assumption that selling prices remained constant and that there were no changes in either the manufacturing costs or the selling and administrative expenses. Further, it has been assumed that overheads costs are absorbed at predetermined rates based on normal capacity.
6. The aggregate net income (of different months or periods taken together) will be the same under both costing methods provided production and sales, in total, are equal. In the above example, total production are 77,500 units and total sales are 73.000 units. Since production and sales are unequal, the combined net income is not the same.

Reconciliation of Net Income

The differences in the net income between absorption costing and marginal costing are due to: (i) amount of fixed factory overhead charged to inventory, (ii) Over or under-absorbed fixed factory overhead having been deferred in absorption costing. The entire difference in net income can be explained by the amount of fixed factory overhead that is included in the beginning and closing inventories.

Reconciliation of Differences between Absorption and Marginal Costing Income

	Second month (Rs)	*Third month* (Rs)	*Fourth month* (Rs)
Marginal costing income	24,000	33,000	19,500
Absorption costing income	27,750	30,500	23,875
Difference to be explained	(3,750)	2,500	(4,375)
1. Differences in the value of opening and closing inventories:			
(a) Second month:			
Opening	0	—	—
Closing 18,000 – 21,750	(3,750)		
(b) Third month:			
Opening 18,000 – 21,750	—	3,750	
Closing 6,000 – 7.250	—	(1,250)	—
(c) Fourth month:			
Opening 6,000 – 7,250	—	—	(1,250)
Closing 27,000 – 32,625	—	—	(5,625)
	(3,750)	2,500	(4,375)

Inventory Values

Differences between the net incomes reported under absorption costing and marginal costing are also reflected in inventory values. As stated earlier, inventories under absorption costing absorb a part of the fixed manufacturing costs of a period, whereas inventories under marginal costing include only the variable manufacturing costs. Closing inventories calculated from the data given above would be as follows:

Closing Inventories

	First month	*Second month*	*Third month*	*Fourth month*
Absorption costing @Rs 7.25 per unit	—	21,750	7,250	32,625
Margin costing @Rs 6.00 per unit	—	18,000	6,000	27,000

The following summarises the differences between marginal costing and absorption costing with regard to effect on net income:

1. If production = sales; absorption profit = marginal costing profit.
2. If production > sales; absorption profit > marginal costing profit.
3. If production < sales; absorption profit < marginal costing profit.
4. If production fluctuates and sales are constant; absorption profit fluctuates and marginal costing. Profit is constant.
5. If production is constant and sales fluctuates; both profits vary in the direction of sales.

COST BEHAVIOUR

Cost behaviour can be defined as the manner in which costs changes due to changes in volume or activity In relation to cost behaviour analysis, fixed and variable cost classifications are basically found. A proper analysis of cost behaviour patterns is the basis of all profit planning and cost control. The separation of costs into fixed, variable and semi-variable is necessary in order to determine, analyse, control, measure or evaluate the following:

1. Departmental expenses allowed at various levels of production.
2. Operating efficiency of a department.
3. Use of variable costing method,
4. Utilisation of facilities.
5. Break-even point.
6. Relative profitability of territories, departments and customers.
7. Company profit position.
8. Cost-profit-volume analysis.
9. Marginal or differential cost for various decision making purposes.
10. Effect of proposed capital expenditures.
11. Effect of alternative courses of action.

METHODS OF DETERMINING COST BEHAVIOUR

Several methods are used for segregating semi-variable costs into fixed and variable. There are four major techniques that are found in practice and they may be listed as follows:

1. High and low points method
2. Scattergraph method
3. Least squares regression method
4. Accounting or analytical approach.

High and Low Points Method

This approach considers the difference in total cost between two different volumes, and divides the incremental cost by the volume. As the words 'high' and 'low' imply, the two levels of volume chosen are the highest and the lowest for the period under review. The result of this division is the estimated variable cost per unit. Then, the average activity level is computed together with the average cost for the periods in the data base. The fixed cost is estimated by taking the total average cost and subtracting the variable cost for the average activity level. The variable cost is computed by multiplying the average activity level by the variable cost per unit as determined above.

As a simple illustration, assume that a company incurred the following costs in two periods (high a low) in which 5,000 units and 10,000 units were produced:

	Cost incurred	
	5,000 units	10,000 units
Insurance on factory building	Rs 30,000	30,000
Indirect material	45,000	70,000

Since insurance remained constant at the two volumes, there is no variable component. Indirect materials contain both a fixed and variable components.

Separation is made as follows:

Variable components:

Indirect material cost of 10,000 units	Rs 70,000
Indirect material cost of 5,000 units	Rs 45,000
Cost of production of additional 5,000 units	Rs 25,000
Variable cost per unit Rs 25,000 ÷ 5,000 units	Rs 5

Fixed components:	5,000 units	10,000 units
Total indirect material cost	Rs 45,000	Rs 70,000
Variable components @ Rs 5 per unit	25,000	50,000
Fixed costs for period	Rs 20,000	Rs 20,000

Scattergraph Method

In this method, various costs are plotted on a vertical line, the *y*-axis, and measurement Figures (activity levels such as direct labour hours, units of output, percentage of capacity or direct labour cost) are plotted along a horizontal line, the x-axis. A straight line is fitted to this scatter of points by visual approximation. The slope of the line is used to estimate the variable costs and the intercept of the line with the vertical axis is considered as the estimated fixed cost.

Least Squares Regression Method

The method of least squares uses the equation for a straight line:

$Y = a + bx$, with a as the fixed element, and b the degree of variability. For many accounting applications, regression provides an accurate estimate of fixed and variable costs.

Accounting or Analytical Approach

This approach to cost behaviour analysis is a close scrutiny of the chart of accounts and a classification of costs into their fixed and variable components according to their basic characteristics determined by the accountant using good judgement, knowledge, and experience. This approach is simple and inexpensive but in its simplicity lies its inherent weakness. The results obtained are not accurate and may happen to be mere guesses.

Example 1

The following are the maintenance costs incurred in a machine shop for six months with corresponding machine hours :

Month	*Machine hours*	*Maintenance costs* Rs.
January	2,000	30,000
February	2,200	32,000
March	1,700	27,000
April	2,400	34,000
May	1,800	28,000
June	1,900	29,000
Total	12,000	1,80,000

Analyse the Maintenance Cost which is semi-variable into fixed and variable element.

Solution

Computation of Variable Cost and Fixed Cost has been done according to Range Method.

	Machine hours	*Maintenance costs*
Highest point, April	2,400	34,000
Lowest point, March	1,700	17,000
	700	7,000

$$\text{Variable cost per machine hour} = \frac{\text{Change in maintenance costs}}{\text{Change in hours}}$$

$= 7{,}000/700 = \text{Rs } 10$

Total variable cost for 2,400 machine hours will be 2,400 × Rs 10 = Rs 24,000

Hence, fixed cost is (Rs 34,000 – Rs 24,000) = Rs 10,000

Analysis of Maintenance Cost into Fixed and Variable Element

	Machine hours (Rs)	*Maintenance cost (Rs)*	*Fixed cost (Rs)*	*Variable cost (Rs)*
January	2,000	30,000	10,000	20,000
February	2,200	32,000	10,000	22,000
March	1,700	27,000	10,000	17,000
April	2,400	34,000	10,000	24,000
May	1,800	28,000	10,000	18,000
June	1,900	29,000	10,000	19,000

COST-VOLUME PROFIT (CVP) ANALYSIS

Profits of business firms are the result of many factors such as: (i) selling prices, (ii) volume of sales (iii) unit variable costs (iv) total fixed costs, (v) combinations in which the various product lines are sold, etc. To do an affective job in planning, management must have analyses which allow reasonably correct predictions of how profits will be affected by a change in any one of these factors. A cost volume profit (CVP) analysis is useful to management in knowing how profit is influenced by sales volume, sale price, variable expenses and fixed expenses.

Broadly, CVP analysis uses the techniques of (i) Break-even analysis and (ii) Profit-volume (P/V) analysis.

Break-even Analysis

A break-even analysis indicates at what level cost and revenue are in equilibrium. It is a simple and easily understandable method of presenting to management the effect of changes in volume on profits Detailed analysis of break-even data will reveal to management the effect of alternative decisions which reduce or increase costs and which increase sales volume and income. It is a device which portrays the effects of any type of future planning by evaluating alternative courses of action.

Break-even Point

The break-even point can be defined as the point or sales level at which profit are zero and there is no loss. That is, break-even point is that point at which total costs are equal to total sales revenue. At the break-even point profit being zero, contribution (sales-variable cost) is equal to the fixed cost. If the actual volume of sales is higher than the break-even volume, there will be a profit. Beyond the break-even point, all the marginal contribution represents income.

Assume that a company manufactures and sells a single product as follows:

Selling price per unit = Rs 20
Variable cost per unit = Rs 10
Total fixed cost = Rs 1,00,000

The break-even sales to cover fixed costs will be 10,000 units,

Selling price per unit = Rs 20
Variable cost per unit = Rs 10
Contribution = Rs 10

$$\text{Break-even volume} = \frac{\text{Rs 1,00,000 fixed cost}}{\text{Rs 10 contribution margin}}$$

$$= 10{,}000 \text{ units.}$$

If the company can sell more than 10,000 units, it will earn profits because fixed costs remain constant. If less than 10,000 units are sold, a loss will be incurred. The profits will be equal to the number of units sold in excess of 10000 units multiplied by the unit contribution margin. For example, if 25,000 units are sold the company will be operating at 15,000 units above its break-even point and will earn a profit of Rs 1,50,000 (15,000 units × Rs 10 contribution margin).

Break-even Formula

The break-even point can be obtained directly by a mathematical formula. The basic formula to find out the break-even point is:

$$\text{Break-even sales (units)} = \frac{\text{Fixed cost}}{\text{Contribution margin per unit}}$$

$$\text{Break-even sales (volume)} = \frac{\text{Fixed cost}}{\text{C / S ratio (also known as P / V ratio*)}}$$

$$\text{Break-even sales volume} = \frac{\text{Total fixed expenses}}{1 - \text{Total variable expenses / Total sales volume}}$$

$$\text{Cash break-even point (units)} = \frac{\text{Cash fixed cost}}{\text{Cash contribution per unit}}$$

* C/S ratio is popularly known as P/V ratio because after fixed costs are fully recovered, *i.e.* after break-even point all contributions (sales-variable costs) become profit. However, before break-even point all contributions will not become profit since fixed costs are yet to be recovered.

Break-even Chart

Total revenues and total costs at different sales volume can be estimated and plotted on a break-even chart. This chart is constructed as follows:

1. A horizontal base line, the x-axis, is drawn and spaced into equal distances representing either plant capacity, sales volume or number of units.
2. A vertical line, the y-axis is drawn on the left side of the chart and also spaced into equal parts This line indicates sales revenue and also costs.
3. A line parallel to the horizontal line (x-axis) is drawn for fixed costs.
4. A total cost line is drawn starting at the y-axis fixed cost point and moving to the right. This total cost line represents the total of all items of cost, fixed and variable.
5. The sales line is drawn starting at the zero point on the vertical axis and ending at the top on the right side.
6. The total cost line intersects the sales line at a point which is known as the break-even point.
7. The area to the left of the break-even point between the total cost line and the sales line is the loss area; the profit area lies to the right of the break-even point above the total cost line.

The data from the previous example are presented on the break-even chart (see Fig. 5.3). From Fig. 3 it can be observed that the break-even point occurs when sales are 10,000 units at Rs 2,00,000.

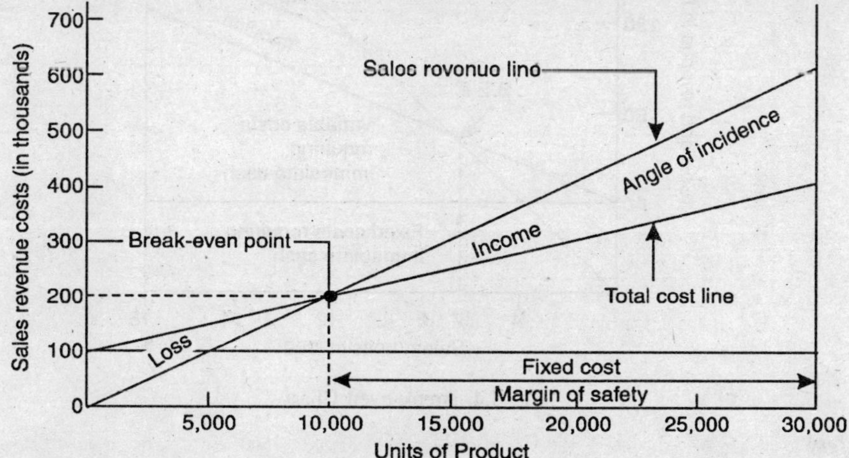

Fig. 5.3. Break-even Chart

Cash Break-Even Point

If a firm has a minimum of available cash or the opportunity cost of holding excess cash is high, management may want to know the volume of sales that will cover all cash expenses, during a period. This is known as the cash break-even point.

Not all fixed operating costs involve cash payments. For example, depreciation expense is a non-cash charge. To find the cash break-even-point, the non-cash charges must be subtracted from total fixed operating costs. Therefore, the cash break-even point is lower than the usual break-even point. The formula is:

$$\text{BEP} = \frac{\text{FC} - d}{\text{P} - \text{V}}$$

where P = selling price per unit
V = unit variable cost
FC = Fixed operating costs
d = depreciation expenses

Thus, cash break-even-point indicates break-even sales to cover only the fixed costs involving cash payments and to break even.

This is illustrated below:

Let Sales be 20,000 units at Rs 10 per unit
Variable costs, Rs 4 per unit
Fixed cost Rs 50,000 including depreciation, Rs 10,000
Preference dividend to be paid Rs 20,000
Taxed to be paid Rs 25,000
Assume that there are no lags in payment.

Break-even point (in units) will be 6,667 units as displayed in Figure 5.4 below.

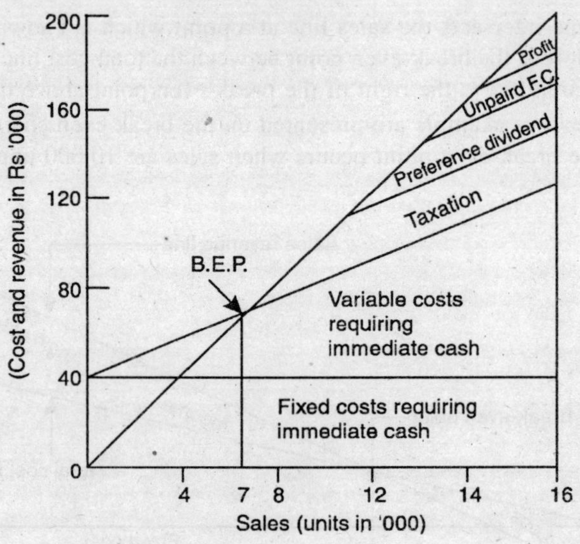

Fig 5.4. Break-even Chart

Margin of Safety

This is the difference between sales and the break-even point. If the distance is relatively short, it indicates that a small drop in production or sales will reduce profits considerably. If the distance is long, it means that the business can still make profits even after a serious drop in production. It is important that there should be a reasonable margin of safety, otherwise a reduced level of production may prove dangerous. The margin of safety can be found by using the following formula:

$$\text{Margin of safety} = \text{Profit} \div \text{P/V ratio}$$

$$\text{or} \quad \text{Margin of safety} = \frac{\text{Profit} \times \text{Sales}}{\text{Sales} - \text{Variable cost}}$$

Angle of Incidence

This is the angle at which the sales line cuts the total cost line. Management's aim will be to have as large an angle of incidence as possible because a large angle of incidence shows a high rate of profit. A narrow angle would show that even fixed overheads are absorbed and profit accrues at a relatively low rate of return, indicating that variable costs form a large part of cost of sales.

Sales Formula

Often, it is necessary to know what level of sales is required to achieve a desired level of profit. The desired sales can be expressed in various ways:

Sales = Fixed cost + Variable cost + Profit

or

Sales = (Profit + Fixed cost)/P/V ratio

Basic Assumptions In Break-even Analysis

Break-even analysis is based on several assumptions, listed as follows:

1. Selling prices and pricing policy will remain constant at all sales levels. If this is not ture, sales revenue cannot be plotted as a straight line.
2. All costs and expenses can be separated into fixed and variable components.
3. The total of the fixed costs is constant at all sales levels; the unit variable costs remain the same If this is not true, straight lines cannot be drawn.
4. Production and sales quantities are equal.
5. Managerial policies, technological methods, and efficiency of men and machines will not change and cost côntrol will neither be strengthened nor weakened.
6. Volume is assumed to be the only important factor affecting cost behaviour. Other influencing factors such as unit prices, sales-mix, labour strikes, and production methodology remain constant
7. In case of multiple products being manufactured by the enterprise, the sales-mix should remain unchanged. That is, the calculation of the break-even point in the case of multiple product predetermines the number of units to be sold in respect of each product. This multiproduct sales mix should remain unchanged.

Profit/Volume (P/V) Analysis

A P/V graph is sometimes used in place of or along with a break-even chart. Profits and losses are given on a vertical scale; and units of products, sales revenue or percentage of activity are given on a horizontal line. The horizontal line is drawn on the graph to separate profits from losses. The profits and **loss** at various sales levels are plotted and connected by the profit line. The break-even point is measured at the point where the profit line intersects the horizontal line. The P/V graph may be preferred to the break-even chart because profit and losses at any point can be read directly from the vertical scale; but the P/V graph does not clearly show how costs vary with activity.

Data used earlier to prepare the break-even chart are also used in preparing the P/V graph (see Fig. 5.5).

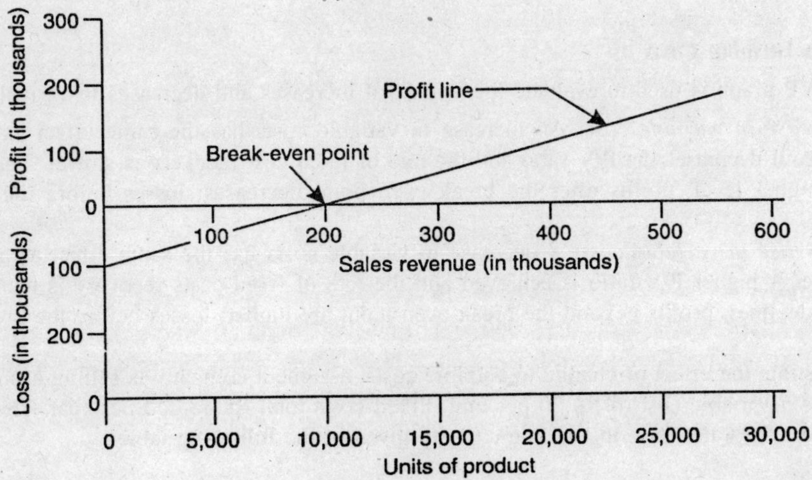

Fig. 5.5 Profit Volume (P/V) Graph

Role of CVP Analysis

A cost-volume profit analysis can be used to measure the effect of factor changes and management decision alternatives on profits. These factors include possible changes in selling prices, changes in variable or fixed cost, expansion or contraction of sales volume, or other changes in operating methods or policies. Cost-volume profit analysis is also useful for problems of product pricing, sales-mix, adding or deleting product lines, and accepting special orders.

Changes in Selling Prices

The CVP graph is frequently used to illustrate the potential profit effects of contemplated price changes. Effects on the profit pattern are as follows:

1. *Increase in selling price* If the selling price is increased, it increases the P/V ratio, and the rate of fixed costs recovery is increased. The break-even point (break-even volume) declines, profit beyond the break-even point increases, losses below the break-even point decreases.
2. *Decrease in selling price* If the selling price decreases, it decreases the P/V ratio and the rate of fixed cost recovery declines. The break-even point increases.

Assume, for example, that a company produces a product with a selling price of Rs 10 per unit and a variable cost of Rs 4 per unit. Fixed costs are Rs 36,000 per year. The effect of a 20% increase and 20% decrease in the present selling price is given below:

	Selling price		
	Present	*20% Increase*	*20% Decrease*
Selling price per unit	Rs 10.00	Rs 12.00	Rs 8.00
Variable cost per unit	4.00	4.00	4.00
Marginal contribution per unit	6.00	8.00	4.00
P/V ratio	60%	$66\frac{2}{3}\%$	50%
Fixed costs	36,000	36,000	36,000
Break-even point in units	6,000	4,500	9,000
In volume	60,000	54,000	72,000
Changes in break-even point			
In units	0%	– 25%	+ 50%
In sales volume	0%	– 10%	+ 20%

Changes In Variable Costs

The CVP graph is used to evaluate the impact of increases and decreases in variable costs per unit.

1. *Increase in variable costs* An increase in variable costs has the same effect as a decrease in the selling price. It decreases the P/V ratio and the rate of fixed cost recovery is slower. The break-even point moves to higher level; profits after the break even point decreases; losses before the break even point increases.
2. *Decrease in variable costs A* decrease in variable costs has the same effect as an increase in the selling price. A higher P/V ratio is achieved and the rate of fixed costs recovery is increased. The break-even point declines, profits beyond the break-even point are higher; losses before the break-even point are lower.

To illustrate the effect of change in variable costs, assume a company is selling a product for Rs. 40 a unit and has a variable cost of Rs 20 per unit. Fixed costs total Rs 48,000 per year. The effects of a 20% increase and a 20% decrease in variable cost are given in the following table:

	Present variable cost (Rs)	*20% Increase (Rs)*	*20% Decrease (Rs)*
Unit selling price	40.00	40.00	40.00
Variable cost per unit	20.00	24.00	16.00
Marginal contribution	20	16.00	24.00
P/V ratio	50%	40%	60%
Fixed costs	48,000	48,000	48,000
Break-even point:			
Sales volume	96,000	1,20,000	80,000
Units	2,400	3,000	2,000

Changes In Fixed Cost

Increases and decreases in the fixed cost do not have any impact on the P/V ratio but they change the break-even point. With the same P/V ratio, the rate of the fixed costs recovery remains the same.

1. *Increase in fixed costs* If fixed costs are increased, the break-even point (break-even-volume) is higher. Profits above the break-even point are lower by the amount of the increase in fixed costs; below the break-even point losses increase by the amount of increase.
2. *Decrease in fixed costs* If fixed costs are decreased, it lowers the break-even point. The profits are greater by the amount of the decrease, and losses are smaller by the amount of the decrease in fixed costs.

Assume that a company has a P/V ratio of 40% and present fixed costs of Rs 50,000. The effects of change in the fixed costs by Rs 10,000 are as follows:

	Present fixed cost	*Increase by* Rs.10,000	*Decrease by* Rs. 10,000
Fixed costs	Rs 50,000	Rs 60,000	Rs 40,000
P/V ratio	40%	40%	40%
Break-even point (Rs)	1,25,000	1,50,000	1,00,000
Decrease	0	+25,000	–25.000

From the above example, it is clear that the P/V ratio is the same in each situation and break-even point can be determined by dividing the amount of the change by the P/V ratio:

$$\frac{\text{Change in fixed costs}}{\text{P / V ratio}}$$

$$= \frac{\text{Rs } 10{,}000}{40\%} = \text{Rs } 25{,}000$$

Desired or Target Profit

Sometimes, management faces two decisions: (i) to increase sales volume through reduction in selling prices, and (ii) to increase selling prices in case the P/V ratio is low, with the expectation that a higher profit will be earned. These decisions should be taken carefully after studying the profit pattern and other factors, otherwise the results can be harmful particularly for those companies whose P/V ratios are already low. Also, if reduction in selling prices does not increase the sales volume, the price reduction will result only in lower profits.

The increase in sales volume required to overcome the effect of a price reduction is relatively greater when the rate of the contribution margin per unit is relatively greater as compared to when the rate of the contribution margin per unit is relatively low. If a product makes only a small contribution, then a reduction in selling price makes it all the more difficult to recover the fixed costs and to earn profits.

Similarly, a business firm may think of increasing the selling price if the P/V ratio is low. However, increase in selling price may reduce the sales volume.

Multi-product Situations

When there are multiple products with different contribution margins, the mix of the product has a direct effect on the fixed costs recovery and total profits of the firm. Different products have different P/V ratios because of different selling prices and variable costs. The total profits depend to some extent upon the proportions in which the products are sold.

For example, assume that a company with fixed costs of Rs 25.000 per year manufactures two products A and B with P/V ratios as follows:

	Product A	*Product B*
Unit selling price	Rs 10	Rs 20
Variable costs	4	16
Marginal contribution	6	4
P/V ratio	60%	20%

With comparatively low variable costs, product A has a relatively high P/V ratio: each unit of product A sold contributes Rs 6 to fixed costs recovery and profit. Product B, with comparatively high variable costs, has a low P/V ratio: each unit sold contributes only Rs 4 to fixed costs recovery and profit. Other things being equal, the sale of product A is more profitable than that of product B, despite the fact that the selling price of product B is twice that of product A. It is correct to say that profits will decline as the sales mix shifts from product A to product B. This also implies, however, that new analyses of profit volume relationship must be made as the product-mix changes.

LIMITATIONS OF CVP ANALYSIS

CVP analysis is a useful planning and control device, usually in the form of a chart, showing how revenue, costs, and profit fluctuate with volume. The CPV technique is useful to management in areas of budgeting, cost control and decision making. In spite of CVP being a useful technique, it suffers from some limitations. Firstly, because of the many assumptions, CVP is only an approximation at best. If prices, unit costs, sales-mix, operating efficiency, or other relevant factors change, then the overall CVP analysis and relationships also must be modified. Because of these assumptions, cost data are of limited significance.

In a multi-product situation, 'different products typically yield different contribution margins and produced in various volumes with differing costs. As a result neither the revenue curve nor the curve is necessarily straight and the break-even point is difficult to find.

Therefore, while preparing or interpreting cost-volume profit analysis, all assumptions and limitations should be carefully considered. A series of CVP analysis based on different sets of assumptions and circumstances may be prepared to reflect situations prevailing in different business enterprises When circumstances change, CVP analysis should also be revised to reflect the changing situations; It is also necessary to have up-to-date analysis so that it can act as a useful, device in profit forecast, budgeting, cost control and managerial decision-making.

Example 2

Prepare Income Statements under Absorption costing and under Marginal costing from the following information relating to the year 1997- 98:

Opening Stock = 1,000 units valued at Rs 70,000 including variable cost of Rs 50 per unit.
Fixed Cost = Rs 1,20,000
Variable Cost = Rs 60 per unit
Production =10,000 units

Sales = 7,000 units @ Rs 100 per unit.
Stock is valued on the basis of FIFO.

Solution

Income Statement (Absorption Costing)

	(Rs)	(Rs)
Sales		7,00,000
Less: Cost of goods sold:		
Opening stock (1,000 units × Rs 70)	70,000	
Variable cost (10,000 units × Rs 60)	6,00,000	
Fixed cost	1,20,000	
Cost of goods available for sales	7,90,000	
Less: Closing stock (4000 units)	2,88,000	
4,000 units × Rs 72 =		5,02,000
Net Income		1,98,000

Income statement (Marginal Costing)

	Rs.	Rs.
Sales		7,00,000
Less: Cost of good sold :		
Opening stock (1,000 units × Rs 50)	50,000	
Variable cost (10,000 units × Rs 60)	6,00,000	
	6,50,000	
Less: Closing stock (4000 units × Rs 60)	2,40,000	4,10,000
Contribution margin		2,90,000
Less: Fixed Cost		1,20,000
Net Income		1,70,000

Difference in Net Income = Rs 198000 - 1,70.000
= Rs 28,000

This difference in net income is due to difference in inventony values:

	Absorption costing	*Marginal costing*
	Rs.	Rs.
Opening stock	70,000	50,000
Closing stock	2,88,000	2,40,000
Difference	2,18,000	1,90,000

Net difference = 2,18,000 - 1,90,000
= Rs 28,000

Note: 1. It has been assumed that fixed cost is fixed production cost.
2. It has been assumed that variable cost (Rs 60 per unit) is variable production cost.

Example 3

Your company has a production capacity of 12.500 units and normal capacity utilisation is 80%. Opening inventory of finished goods on 1-1-1999 was 1,000 units. During the year ending 31-12-1999, it produced 11,000 units while it sold only 10,000 units.

Standard variable cost per unit is Rs 6.50 and standard fixed factory cost per unit Rs 1.50. Total fixed selling and administration overhead amounted to Rs 10,000. The company sells its product at Rs 10 per unit.

Prepare Income Statements under Absorption Costing and Marginal Costing. Explain the reasons for difference in profit, if any.

Solution

Income statement for the year ended 31st Dec., 1999
(Under Absorption Costing Method)

	Rs.	Rs.
Sales: 10,000 Units @ Rs. 10 per unit		1,00,000
Less : Cost of goods sold:		
Variable Production Costs:		
11,000 units @ Rs. 6.50 per unit	71,500	
Fixed factory cost @ Rs. 1.50 per unit 11000 × 1.50 =	16,500	
	88,000	
Add : Opening stock: 1000 units @ Rs. 8 per unit (*i.e.* Rs. 6.50 + Rs. 1.50)	8,000	
Costs of goods available for sales	96,000	
Less : Closing stock: 2000 units valued at current cost. $\frac{96,000 \times 2,000}{12,000}$	16,000	80,000
	Gross Profit	20,000
Less : Fixed selling and administrative overhead		10,000
Net Profit		10,000

Income statement for the year ended 31st Dec., 1999
(Under Marginal Costing Method)

	Rs.	Rs.
Sales: 10,000 Units @ Rs. 10 per unit		1,00,000
Less : Marginal Cost:		
Variable Production Costs:		
11,000 units @ Rs. 6.50 per unit	71,500	
Variable cost of opening stock of finished stock (1000 units @ Rs. 6.50 per unit)	6,500	
Cost of goods available for sales	78,000	
Less : Closing stock of finished goods: (2000 units @ Rs. 6.50 per unit)	13,000	
	65,000	65,000
Contribution		35,000
Less : Fixed selling and administrative overhead	10,000	
Fixed factory cost @ Rs. 1.50 per unit	16,500	26,500
Net Profit		8,500

Reason for difference. The difference in profits, Rs 1.500 (*i.e.* Rs 10,000 - Rs 8,500), as arrived at under absorption and marginal costing methods is due to the element of fixed cost included in the valuation of opening and closing stock under the absorption costing method.

Example 4

'LMN' limited sells its product at Rs 3 per unit. The company uses a First-in, First-out actual costing system. A new fixed manufacturing overhead allocation rate is computed each year by dividing the actual fixed manufacturing overhead cost by the actual production costs. The following simplified data are related to its first two years of operation:

	Year I	Year II
Unit Data		
Sales	1,000	1,200
Production	1,400	1.000
Cost	Rs	Rs
Variable manufacturing	700	500
Fixed manufacturing	700	700
'Variable marketing and administration	1,000	1,200
Fixed marketing and administration	400	400

Required:

(i) Prepare income statements based on:

(a) absorption costing and (b) variable costing for each year.

(ii) Give reasons for the differences in the answer.

Solution

(i) Income Statement (Absorption Costing)

	Year I (Rs)	Year II (Rs)
Sales	3,000	3,600
Less: Cost of goods sold:		
Opening stock	Nil	400
Variable manufacturing	700	500
Fixed manufacturing	700	700
Cost of goods available for sales	1,400	1,600
Less: Closing inventory $\frac{400}{1,400}$ × Rs 1,400 (Year I)	400	240*
Cost of goods sold	1,000	1,360
Gross Profit	2,000	2,240
Less: Variable marketing & Administration	(1,000)	(1,200)
Fixed marketing and Administration	(400)	(400)
Net Income	600	640

Note: In year II, FIFO method of inventory valuation is used. That is, closing inventory of 200 units belong to current production lot. Therefore, value of 200 units will be

$$\frac{200}{1000} \text{ Rs } 1200 = \text{Rs } 240$$

Income Statement (Marginal Costing)

	Year I (Rs)	Year II (Rs)
Sales	3,000	3,600
Less : Cost of goods sold:		
Opening stock	Nil	200
Variable manufacturing	700	500
Cost.of goods available for sales	700	700

(*Contd.*)

Less:	Closing stock. @ Re 0.50 (400 units, 200 units)	200	100
	Cost of goods sold	500	600
	Contribution margin	2,500	3,000
Less:	Fixed manufacturing	(700)	(700)
	Variable marketing & Administration	(1,000)	(1,200)
	Fixed marketing & Administration	(400)	(400)
	Net Income	400	700

(ii) The difference in profit figures between absorption costing and variable costing is due to the factory cost attached to inventory. Difference in Net Income is due to difference in inventoy values. This is explained as below:

		Year I (Rs)	*Year II* (Rs)
Absorption costing net income		600	640
Marginal costing net income		400	700
		200	60
Absorption costing inventory:	Opening	Nil	400
	Closing	400	240
Difference		400	160
Marginal costing inventory:	Opening	Nil	200
	Closing	200	100
Difference		200	100
Net difference		200	60

Example 5

Hind General Corporation produces only one product which had the following costs.

Variable manufacturing costs — Rs 4 per unit
Fixed Manufacturing costs — Rs 2,00,000 per year

The normal capacity is set at 2,00,000 units. There are no work-in-progress inventories.

In 2001, the company produced 2,00,000 units and sold 90 per cent of them at a price of Rs 7 per unit. In 2002, the company produced 2,10,000 units and sold 2,15,000 units at the same price.

You are required to prepare income statements for 2001 and 2002 based on absorption costing and marginal costing.

Solution

Hind General Corporation
Income Statement (Marginal costing basis)

Particulars	*2001*	*2002*
	Rs.	Rs.
Sales at Rs 7	12,60,000	15,05,000
Inventory-opening at Rs 4	Nil	80,000
Variable manufacturing costs at Rs 4	8,00,000	8,40,000
Standard variable cost of goods available for sales	8,00,000	9,20,000
Inventory-closing at Rs 4	80,000	60,000
Standard variable cost of sales	7,20,000	8,60,000
Contribution margin	5,40,000	6,45,000
Fixed manufacturing costs	2,00,000	2,00,000
Net Income	3,40,000	4,45,000

Income Statement (Absorption Costing Basis)

Particulars	*2001*	*2002*
	Rs.	Rs.
Sales at Rs 7	12,60,000	15,05,000
Inventory opening at Rs 5	Nil	1,00,000
Variable manufacturing costs at Rs 4	8,00,000	8,40,000
Fixed manufacturing costs at Re 1	2,00,000	2,10,000
Total goods at standard cost	10,00,000	11,50,000
Inventory closing at Rs 5	1,00,000	75,000
Standard cost of sales	9,00,000	10,75,000
Under (over) absorbed fixed costs	Nil	(10,000)
Actual cost of sales	9,00,000	10,65,000
Net Income	3,60,000	4,40,000

Example 6

The following cost information relates to factory X for two years.

	2001	*2002*
Installed capacity (units)	10,000	10,000
Opening stock (units)	Nil	1,000
Closing stock (units)	1,000	Nil
Output (units)	10,000	9,000
Selling price per unit	14	14
Fixed costs for the year	85,000	85,000
Variable cost per unit	2.90	2.90

Work out the profit under absorption costing and marginal costing for the two years. Also state any abnormality in the results disclosed by absorption costing. Assume FIFO basis.

Income Statement (Absorption Costing)

	2001 (Rs)	*2002 (Rs)*
Sales	1,26,000	1,40,000
Less : Cost of goods sold:		
Opening stock	Nil	11,400
Variable production cost	29,000	26,100
Fixed cost	85,000	85,000
Cost of goods available for sales	1,14,000	1,22,500
Less: Closing stock	11,400	Nil
Cost of goods sold	1,02,600	1,22,500
Net profit	23,400	17,500
Net profit as percentage of sales	18.6%	12.5%

Note: It has been assumed that variable cost and fixed cost are production cost.

Income Statement (Marginal Costing)

	2001 (Rs)	2002 (Rs)
Sales	1,26,000	1,40,000
Less : Cost of goods sold:		
Opening stock	Nil	2,900
Variable production cost	29,000	26,100
Cost of goods available for sales	29,000	29,000
Less: Closing stock	2,900	Nil
Cost of goods sold	26,100	29,000
Contribution margin	99,900	1,11,000
Less: Fixed Cost	85,000	85,000
Net profit	14,900	26,000
Net profit as percentage of sales	11.8%	18.6%

Example 7

Using the information below prepare profit statements for the months of June and July using (i) marginal costing (ii) full absorption costing. Also, explain why the two methods disclose different amounts of profit for June and July.

Data per unit:	Rs
Selling price	50
Direct material cost	18
Direct labour cost	4
Variable production overheads	3
Monthly costs:	
Fixed production overheads	99,000
Fixed selling expenses	15,000
Fixed administration expenses	25,000

Variable selling costs are 10% of sales revenue and normal production capacity is 11,000 units per month.

	Sales (units)	*Production (units)*
June	10,000	12,000
July	12,000	10,000

Solution

Profit Statement—Marginal Costing

	June	*July*
Sales units	10,000	12,000
Production units	12,000	10,000
Sales at Rs 50	5,00,000	6,00,000
Less: Cost of goods sold:		
Variable production costs at Rs 25	3,00,000	2,50,000
Add: Opening stock	—	50,000
Cost of goods available for sales	3,00,000	3,00,000

(*Contd.*)

Less: Closing stock	50,000	—
Cost of goods sold	2,50,000	3,00,000
Contribution	2,50,000	3,00,000
Less: Fixed costs:		
Production overheads	(99,000)	(99,000)
Selling expenses	(15,000)	(15,000)
Variable selling expenses	(50,000)	(60,000)
Administration expenses	(25,000)	(25,000)
Net profit	61,000	1,01,000

Working Note:

Variable production costs:	
Direct material cost	18
Direct wages	4
Variable production overheads	3
	Rs 25

Profit Statement—Absorption Costing

	June	*July*
Sales units	10,000	12,000
Production units	12,000	10,000
Sales at Rs 50	5,00,000	6,00,000
Less: Cost of goods sold:		
Production casts absorbed at Rs 34	4,08,000	3,40,000
Add: Opening stock	—	68,000
Cost of goods available for sales	4,08,000	4,08,000
Less: Closing stock	68,000	—
Cost of goods sold (over) under-absorbed fixed	3,40,000	4,08,000
Production overheads at Rs 9	(9,000)	9,000
Adjusted cost of goods sold	3,31,000	4,17,000
Gross profit	1,69,000	1,83,000
Less: Variable selling expenses	(50,000)	(60,000)
Fixed selling expenses	(15,000)	(15,000)
Fixed administration expenses	(25,000)	(25,000)
Net profit	Rs 79,000	Rs 83,000

Working Note:

	Rs	
Production costs:		
Direct material cost	18	
Direct wages	4	
Variable production overheads	3	
Fixed production overheads	9	(Rs 99,000 ÷ 11,000 units)
	Rs 34	

Taken together, the two costing techniques disclose the same total profit for the two months.

In June marginal costing discloses Rs 18,000 less profit than full absorption costing. This difference is caused by 2,000 units being in stock. Under absorption costing the fixed production overheads absorbed by these units cost Rs 18,000 (2,000 × Rs 9), and this amount is carried forward in the cost of stock rather than being written off against profit in June as with the marginal costing.

In July, sales exceed production by 2,000 units, and the Rs 18,000 of fixed production overheads is charged against revenue, as the stocks created in June have been sold.

Example 8

ABC Motors assembles and sells motor vehicles. It uses an actual costing system, in which unit costs are calculated on a monthly basis. Data relating to March and April, 2000 are:

	March	*April*
Unit data:		
Beginning Inventory	0	150
Production	500	400
Sales	350	520
Variable-cost data:		
Manufacturing Costs per unit produced	Rs 10,000	Rs 10,000
Distribution costs per unit sold	3,000	3,000
Fixed-cost data:		
Manufacturing Costs	Rs 20,00,000	Rs 20,00,000
Marketing Costs	6,00,000	6,00,000

The selling price per motor vehicle is Rs 24,000

Required:

(*i*) Present income statements for ABC Motors in March and April of 2000 under (a) variable costing, and (b) absorption costing.

(*ii*) Explain the differences between (*a*) and (*b*) for March and April.

Solution

(i) Income Statement (Variable Costing)

	March (Rs)	*April (Rs)*
Sales	84,00,000	1,24,80,000
Less: Variable cost of goods sold:		
Opening stock	Nil	15,00,000
Variable manufacturing cost	50,00,000	40,00,000
Cost of goods available for sales	50,00,000	55,00,000
Less: Closing stock	15,00,000	3,00,000
Cost of goods sold	35,00,000	52,00,000
Contribution Margin	49,00,000	72,80,000
Less: Other costs:		
Fixed manufacturing	(20,00,000)	(20,00,000)
Fixed marketing	(6,00,000)	(6,00,000)
Variable distribution	(10,50,000)	(15,60,000)
Net Income	12,50,000	31,20,000

Income Statement (Absorption Costing)

		March (Rs)	April (Rs)
Sales		84,00,000	1,24,80,000
Less:	Cost of goods sold:		
	Opening stock	Nil	21,00,000
	Variable manufacturing cost	50,00,000	40,00,000
	Fixed manufacturing cost	20,00,000	20,00,000
	Cost of goods available for sales	70,00,000	81,00,000
Less:	Closing stock	21,00,000	4,50,000
	Cost of goods sold	49,00,000	76,50,000
	Gross profit	35,00,000	48,30,000
Less:	Distribution Cost	(10,50,000)	(15,60,000)
	Fixed marketing	(6,00,000)	(6,00,000)
	Net Income	18,50,000	26,70,000

Note: The company follows actual costing system and calculates unit costs on monthly basis. Therefore, for April month, inventory of 30 units has been valued as follows:

Variable manufacturing cost 30 × Rs 10.000	=	30,00,000
Fixed manufacturing cost @ Rs 5000 × 30	=	15,00,000
(Rs 20,00,000 ÷ Current Production 400 units)		
That is, inventory at Rs 15,000 per unit	=	45,00,000

For March month, inventory of 150 units has been calculated as follows :

Variable manufacturing Rs 10,000 × 150	=	Rs 15,00,000
Fixed manufacturing Rs 4000 × 150	=	Rs 6,00,000
That is, inventory at Rs 14,000 per unit	=	Rs 21,00,000

(ii) Difference in Profit

	March	April
Absorption Costing profit	Rs 18,50,000	Rs 26,70,000
Variable costing profit	↑ 12,50,000	↓ 31,20,000
	6,00,000	4,50,000

Difference in profit is due to difference in inventory values in the two costing techniques.

	March (Rs)	April (Rs)
Absorption costing:		
Opening stock	Nil	21,00,000
Closing stock	21,00,000	4.50,000
Difference	21,00,000	16.50.000
Variable costing:		
Opening stock	Nil	15,00,000
Closing stock	15,00,000	3,00,000
Difference	15,00,000	12,00,000
Net difference (effect)	6,00,000	4,50,000

Example 9

The ratio of variable cost to sales is 70%. The break-even point occurs at 60% of the capacity sales. Find the capacity sales when fixed costs are Rs 90,000. Also compute profit at 75% of the capacity sales.

Solution

Basic Calculations

$$\frac{\text{Variable Cost}}{\text{Sales}} = 70\%$$

Hence $$\frac{\text{Contribution}}{\text{Sales}} = 30\% \text{ or P/V Ratio} = 30\%$$

Computation of Capacity Sales

Break-even Point $= \frac{\text{Fixed cost}}{\text{P / V ratio}} = \frac{\text{Rs } 90{,}000}{30\%} = \text{Rs } 3{,}00.000$ (i)

Break-even Point (as given) = 60% of capacity sales

Hence Capacity Sales $= \frac{\text{Rs } 3{,}00{,}000}{60\%} = \text{Rs } 5{,}00{,}000$

Computation of Profit at 75% of the Capacity Sales

	Rs
75% of Capacity sales (75% × Rs 5,00,000)	3,75,000
Less: Variable Cost (70% × Rs 3,75,000)	2,62,500
Contribution	1,12,500
Less: Fixed Cost	90,000
Profit	22,500

Example 10

Profit/Volume Ratio of a company is 50%, while its margin of safety is 40%. If sales volume of the company is Rs 50 lakhs, find out its break-even point and net profit.

Solution

$$\text{Margin of safety} = \frac{\text{Excess Sales over Break - even Sales}}{\text{Actual Sales}}$$

$$40\% = \frac{x}{50 \text{ lakhs}}$$

or $x = 20$ lakhs

Hence (*i*) Break sales = 50 lakhs – 20 lakhs = 30 lakhs

Variable Cost of Break-even Sales = Rs 15 lakhs.

Hence Fixed Costs = Rs 15 lakhs.

(*ii*) Net Profit = Contribution – Fixed Cost

= 50 lakhs × 50/100-15 lakhs

= 25 lakhs – 15 lakhs = Rs 10 lakhs.

Example 11

X Ltd. has earned contribution of Rs 2,00,000 and net profit of Rs 1,50,000 on sales Rs 8,00,000. What is its margin of safety?

Solution

P/V Ratio $= \frac{\text{Contribution}}{\text{Sales}} \times 100$

$$= \frac{\text{Rs } 2,00,000}{\text{Rs } 8,00,000} \times 100 = 25\%$$

$$\text{Margin of Safety} = \frac{\text{Profit}}{\text{P / V Ratio}} = \frac{\text{Rs } 1,50,000}{25\%}$$

$$= \text{Rs } 6,00,000$$

Example 12

If margin of safety is Rs 2,40,000 (40% of sales) and P/V ratio is 30%. Calculate its (1) Break-even Sales and (2) Amount of profit on sales of Rs 9,00,000.

Solution

Basic Calculation

(i) Margin of Safety or Profit $= \frac{\text{Profit}}{\text{P / V Ratio}}$

= Margin of Safety × P/V Ratio

= Rs 2,40,000 × 30% = Rs 72,000

(ii) Total Sales $= \frac{\text{Margin of Safety}}{40\%}$

$= \frac{\text{Rs } 2,40,000}{40\%} = \text{Rs } 6,00,000$

(iii) Contribution = Sales × P/V Ratio

= Rs 6,00,000 × 30% = Rs 1,80,000

(iv) Fixed Cost = Contribution – Profit

= Rs 1,80,000 – Rs 72,000

= Rs 1,08,000

Computation of Break-even Sales $= \frac{\text{Fixed Cost}}{\text{P / V Ratio}} = \frac{\text{Rs } 1,08,000}{30\%} = \text{Rs } 3,60,000$

Computation of Profit on Sales of Rs 9,00,000

= Sales × P/V Ratio – Fixed Cost

= Rs 9,00,000 × 30% – Rs 1,08,000

= Rs 2,70,000 – Rs 1,08,000 = Rs 1,62,000

Example 13

(i) Ascertain profit, when sales = Rs 2,00,000
Fixed Cost = Rs 40,000
BEP = Rs 1,60,000

(ii) Ascertain sales, when fixed cost = Rs 20,000
Profit = Rs 10,000
BEP = Rs 40,000

Solution

(i) P/V ratio $= \frac{\text{Fixed Cost} \times 100}{\text{B.E.P.}} = \frac{\text{Rs } 40,000 \times 100}{\text{Rs } 1,60,000} = 25\%$

Contribution = Sales × P/V Ratio = F.C. + Profit

= Rs 2,00,000 × 25% = Rs 50,000 = Rs 40,000 + Profit

or Rs 50,000 = Rs 40,000 + Profit

or Profit = Rs 10,000

(ii) Contribution = F.C. + Profit = Rs 20,000 + Rs 10,000 = Rs 30,000

P/V ratio $= \frac{\text{Rs } 20{,}000}{\text{Rs } 40{,}000} \times 100 = 50\%$

Also, P/V ratio $= \frac{\text{Contribution}}{\text{Sales}} \times 100$

or Sales $= \frac{C}{P / V \text{ ratio}} \times 100 = \frac{\text{Rs } 30{,}000}{50\%} = \text{Rs } 60{,}000$

Example 14

The profit volume ratio of X Ltd. is 50% and the margin of safety is 40%. You are required to calculate the net profit if the sales volume is Rs 1,00,000.

Solution

Margin of Safety $= \frac{\text{Excess Sales Over Break-even Sales}}{\text{Actual Sales}}$

40/100 = X/1,00,000

or 100X = 40,00,000

or X = Rs 40,000

Break-even Sales = Rs 1,00,000 – Rs 40,000 = Rs 60,000

Profit Volume Ratio = 50%

Variable Cost = 50%

Hence, Variable Cost is Rs 60,000 – 60,000 × 50/100 = Rs 30,000

Fixed Cost = Rs 60,000 – Rs 30,000 = Rs 30,000

Contribution on Sales of Rs 1,00,000 = Rs 50,000

Less: Fixed Cost = Rs 30,000

Profit = Rs 20,000

Example 15

A. company sells its product at Rs 15 per unit. In a period, if it produces and sells 8,000 units, it incurs a loss of Rs 5 per unit. If the volume is raised to 20,000 units, it earns a profit of Rs 4 per unit. Calculate break-even point in terms of rupees as well as in units.

Solution

I.	Sales = 8,000 Units × Rs 15 per Unit =	Rs 1,20,000
	Loss = 8,000 Units × Rs 5 per Unit =	Rs 40,000
II.	Sales = 20,000 Units × Rs 15 per Unit =	Rs 3,00,000
	Profit = 20,000 Unit × Rs 4 per Unit =	Rs 80,000

	Sales	*Profit/Loss*
I.	1,20,000	(–) 40,000
II.	3,00,000	(+) 80,000

P/V Ratio $= \frac{\text{Change in Profit}}{\text{Change in Sales}}$

$= \frac{1{,}20{,}000}{1{,}80{,}000} = \frac{2}{3} \text{ or } 66\frac{2}{3}\%$

Sales at Break-even point (in Rs)

Fixed Cost = S × PV Ratio – Profit

(On the basis raised volume II)

$$\text{Fixed Cost} = \text{Rs. } 3{,}00{,}000 \times \frac{2}{3} - 80{,}000$$

Fixed Cost = Rs 2,00,000 – Rs 80,000 = Rs 1,20,000

$$\text{B.E.P.} = \frac{F}{P/V \text{ ratio}} = \frac{1{,}20{,}000 \times 3}{2} = \text{Rs. } 1{,}80{,}000$$

$$\text{Sales at Break-even point (in units)} - \frac{\text{Sales in Rs}}{\text{Selling price per unit}}$$

$$= \frac{\text{Rs } 1{,}80{,}000}{15} = 12{,}000$$

Note: (1) Rs 5 per unit loss is given is the question, in the indirect way it is a variable cost per unit.

(2) Change in Profit is computed by adding loss of Rs 40,000 in the profit of Rs 80,000 because loss of Rs 40,000 has also been covered in the second period of time or in the second option if the volume is raised to 20,000 units.

Example 16

A company has earned a contribution of Rs 2,00,000 and net profit of Rs 8,00,000. What is the margin of safety?

Solution

Given

Contribution = Rs 2,00,000

Net Profit = Rs 1,50,000

Sales = Rs 8,00,000

$$\text{P/V ratio} = \frac{\text{Contribution}}{\text{Sales}} \times 100$$

$$= \frac{2{,}00{,}000}{8{,}00{,}000} \times 100 = 25\%$$

$$\text{Margin of safety} = \frac{\text{Profit}}{P/V \text{ Ratio}} = \frac{1{,}50{,}000}{25} \times 100$$

= Rs 6,00,000

Margin of safety = Rs. 6,00,000

Or

We know

$S - V = F + P$

or $S - V = C$

∴ $C = F + P$

Putting the values = 2,00,000 = F + 1,50,000

F = 2,00,000 – 1,50,000

= Rs 50,000

$$\text{Break-even point} = \frac{\text{Fixed cost}}{P/V \text{ Ratio}}$$

$$= \frac{\text{Rs } 50,000}{25} \times 100 = \text{Rs } 2,00,000$$

Margin of safety = Actual sales – Break-even sales = Rs 8,00,000 – Rs 2,00,000
= Rs 6,00,000

Example 17

B & Co. has recorded the following data in the two most recent periods:

Total Cost of Production (Rs)	*Volume of Production (units)*
14,600	800
19,400	1,200

What is the best estimate of the firm's fixed costs per period?

Solution

	Period 1	*Period 2*	*Difference*
Total Cost of Production (Rs)	14,600	19,400	4,800
Volume of Production (Units)	800	1,200	400

$$\text{Variable Cost per unit} = \frac{\text{Difference in Total Cost of Production}}{\text{Difference in Volume of Production}}$$

$$= \frac{\text{Rs } 4,800}{400 \text{ units}} = \text{Rs } 12$$

Fixed Cost = Total Cost of Production of a period – Total Variable Cost
= Rs 14,600 – 800 units × Rs 12
= Rs 14,600 – Rs 9,600 = Rs 5,000

Example 18

A Ltd. maintains a margin of safety of 37.5% with an overall contribution to sales ratio of 40%. Its fixed costs amount to Rs 5 lakhs. Calculate the following:

(i) Break-even Sales;
(ii) Total Sales;
(iii) Total Variable Costs;
(iv) Current Profit;
(v) New "Margin of Safety" if the sales volume is increased by $7\frac{1}{2}$%.

Solution

(i) $\text{Break-even Sales} = \frac{\text{Fixed cost}}{\text{P / V Ratio}}$

$$\frac{\text{5 Lakhs}}{40\%} = 12.50 \text{ lakhs}$$

(ii) Total Sales = Break-even Sales + Margin of Safety
Margin of Safety = Actual Sales – Break-even Sales
Let Actual Sales be Rs 100
Margin of Safety is Rs 37.5
Hence, Break-even Sales will be Rs 62.5
In case Break-even Sales are 62.5; Actual Sales are Rs 100
Hence, if Break-even Sales are Rs 12.5 lakhs

Actual sales will be = $\frac{100}{62.5} \times 12.5$

= Rs 20 lakhs

(iii) Contribution = Sales – Variable Costs

Hence, Total Variable Costs = 60% of Rs 20 lakhs

= Rs 12 lakhs

(iv) Current Profit = Sales – (Variable Costs + Fixed Costs)

= Rs 20 lakhs – (Rs 12 lakhs + Rs 5 lakhs)

= Rs 20 lakhs – Rs 17 lakhs

= Rs 3 lakhs

(v) New Margin of Safety if sales volume is increased by 7.5%

New Sales Value = Rs 20 lakhs + 7.5% of 20 lakhs = Rs 21.50 lakhs

Hence, New Margin of Safety = 21.50 lakhs – B.E. Sales of Rs 12.50 lakhs – Rs 9 lakhs.

Example 19

A company has annual fixed costs of Rs 14,00,000. In 1996 sales amounted to Rs 60,00,000 as compared with Rs 45,00,000 in 1995 and profit in 1996 was Rs 4,20,000 higher than in 1995.

(i) At what level of-sales does the company break-even?

(ii) Determine profit or loss on a forecast sales volume of Rs 80,00,000.

(iii) If-there is a reduction in selling price in 1997 by 10% and the company desires to earn the same profit as in 1996, what would be the required sales volume?

Solution

$$\text{PV Ratio} = \frac{\text{Increase in Profit}}{\text{Increase in Sales}} \times 100$$

$$= \frac{4{,}20{,}000}{15{,}00{,}000} \times 100 = 28\%$$

(i) Break-even Sales $= \frac{\text{Fixed Cost}}{\text{PV Ratio}}$

$$= \frac{14{,}00{,}000}{28\%}$$

= Rs 50,00,000

(ii) Profit on sales of Rs 80,00,000

Total Contribution 80,00,000 × 28/100	= 22,40,000
Less: Fixed Cost	14,00,000
Profit	8.40,000

(iii)

If Present Selling Price is	Rs 100
Variable Cost is (100-28)	Rs 72
New Selling Price (100-10)	Rs 90
New Contribution	Rs 18
New PV Ratio	$\frac{18}{90} \times 100 = 20\%$

Profit in 1996:

Contribution 60,00,000 × 28/100 =	16,80,000
Less: Fixed Cost	14,00,000
Profit	2,80,000

$$\text{Sales for Desired Profit of Rs 2,80,000} = \frac{\text{Fixed Cost + Desired Profit}}{\text{New PV Ratio}}$$

$$= \frac{14,00,000 + 2,80,000}{20\%}$$

$$= \frac{16,80,000}{20\%} = \text{Rs } 84,00,000$$

Example 20

A Company manufactures radios, which are sold at Rs 1,600 per unit. The total cost is composed of 30% for direct materials, 40% for direct wages and 30% for overheads. An increase in material price by 30% and in wage rates by 10% is expected in the forthcoming year, as a result of which the profit at current selling price may decrease by 40% of the present profit per unit. You are required to prepare a statement showing current and future profit at present Selling Price.

How much Selling Price should be increased to maintain the present rate of profit?

Solution

Let X be the cost, Y be the profit and Rs 1,600 selling price per unit of radio manufactured by a company. Hence

$$X + Y = \text{Rs } 1,600$$

Statement of present and future cost of a radio

Particulars	*Present cost (Rs)*	*Increase in cost (Rs)*	*Anticipated future cost (Rs)*
	(a)	*(b)*	*(c) = (a) + (b)*
Direct material	0.3 X	0.09 X	0.39 X
Direct labour	0.4 X	0.04 X	0.44 X
Overheads	0.3 X	—	0.30 X
Total	X	0.13 X	1.13 X

An increase in material price and wage rates resulted into a decrease in current profit by 40 per cent at present selling price; therefore we have:

$$1.13\,X + 0.6\,Y = 1,600 \qquad \text{(ii)}$$

On solving (i) and (ii) we get:

$$X = \text{Rs } 1,207.55$$
$$Y = \text{Rs } 392.45$$

Current profit Rs 392,45 or 32.5% of cost

Future profit Rs 235.47

Statement of revised selling price to maintain the present rate of profit

	Rs.
Direct material cost 0.39 × Rs 1,207.55	470.94
Direct labour cost (0.44 × Rs 1207.55)	531.32
Overheads 0.30 × Rs 1,207.55	362.27
Total cost	1,364.53
Profit (32.5% of total cost)	443.47
Revised selling price	1,808.00

Example 21

XYZ Ltd. furnishes you the following income information:

Particulars	*Year 2006*	
	First-half (Rs)	*Second-half (Rs)*
Sales	8,10,000	10,26,000
Profit earned	21,600	64,8001

From the above, you are required to compute the following assuming that the fixed cost remains the same in both the periods:

(i) P/V Ratio
(ii) Fixed Costs
(iii) The amount of profit or loss where sales are Rs 6,48,000.
(iv) The amount of sales required to earn a profit of Rs 1,08,000.

Solution

(i) *Computation of PV Ratio*

(i) PV Ratio $= \dfrac{\text{Change in Profit}}{\text{Change in Sales}} \times 100$

$= \dfrac{43{,}200}{2{,}16{,}000} \times 100 = 20\%$

(ii) *Computation of Fixed Cost*

Fixed Cost = Contribution – Profit

For 1st half = 8,10,000 × 20% – 21.600
= 1,62,000-21,600
= Rs 1,40,400

(iii) Contribution = 20% × Rs 6,48,000 = Rs 1,29,600

Loss = Rs 1,29,600 – 1,40,400 = Rs 10,800

(iv) Computation of sales to earn a profit of Rs 1,08,000.

$= \dfrac{\text{Fixed Cost + Desired Profit}}{\text{PV Ratio}}$

$= \dfrac{1{,}40{,}400 + \text{Rs } 1{,}08{,}000}{20\%} = \text{Rs } 12{,}42{,}000$

Example 22

The following costs and sales of a manufacturing company for the first half and second half of 2005-06 are given:

	First-half Rs	*Second-half* Rs
Sales	24,00,000	30,00,000
Total Costs	21,80,000	26,00,000

You are asked to determine:

(i) Contribution/Sales Ratio of the firm.
(ii) Annual Fixed Costs.
(iii) Break-even Point.
(iv) Margin of Safety as Percentage of Sales.

Solution

(a) Computation of Contributions/Sales Ratio

Particulars	*First-Half Rs*	*Second-Half Rs*	*Change Rs*
Sales	24,00,000	30,00,000	6,00,000
Total Cost	21,80,000	26,00,000	4,20,000
Profit	2,20,000	4,00,000	1,80,000

$$\text{Contribution/Sales Ratio} = \frac{\text{Change in Profit}}{\text{Change in Sales}} = \frac{1,80,000}{6,00,000} = 0.3 \text{ or } 30\%$$

(b) *Computation of Fixed Cost for 2005-06*

Total Sales for the year = Rs 54,00,000
Total Costs = Rs 47,80,000
PV Ratio is = 30%
Total Variable Cost = 70% of Rs. 54,00,000
= Rs 37,80,000
Fixed Cost = Total Costs – Variable Costs
= Rs 47,80,000 – Rs 37,80,000
= Rs 10,00,000

(c) *Break-even Point*

$$= \frac{\text{Fixed Costs}}{\text{PV Ratio}} = \frac{\text{Rs } 10,00,000}{30\%} = \text{Rs } 33,33,333$$

(d) *Margin of Safety as a percentage of Sales*

Margin of Safety (MS) = Sales – Break-even Sales
= Rs 54,00,000 – Rs 33,33,333
= Rs 20,66,667

$$\text{Margin of Safety as \% of Sales} = \frac{20,66,667}{54,00,000} \times 100 = 38.3\%$$

Example 23

Raj Ltd. manufactures three products X, Y and Z. The unit selling prices of these products are Rs 100. Rs 160 and Rs 75 respectively. The corresponding unit variable costs are Rs 50, Rs 80 and Rs 30. The proportions (quantity-wise) in which these products are manufactured and sold are 20%, 30% and 50% 'respectively. The total fixed costs are Rs 14,80,000.

Calculate overall break-even quantity and the product-wise break up of such quantity.

Solution

Overall Break-Even Quantity

Products	*X*	*Y*	*Z*
Selling Price per unit (Rs)	100	160	75
Less: Variable Cost per unit (Rs)	50	80	30
Contribution per unit (Rs)	50	80	45
Share in Total Sales	20%	30%	50%
Proportionate Contribution per unit	10	24	22.50

Composite Contribution per unit = 56.5

$$\text{Composite Break-even Point} = \frac{\text{Total Fixed Cost}}{\text{Composite Contribution per unit}}$$

$$= \frac{\text{Rs } 14,80,000}{\text{Rs } 56.5} = 26.195 \text{ units.}$$

Product-wise break-up of overall break-even quantity:

Product X : 26,195 units × 20/100 = 5,239 units
Product Y : 26,195 units × 30/100 = 7,858 units
Product Z : 26,195 units × 50/100 = 13,098 units

Example 24

A single product company sells its products at Rs 60 per unit. In 1996, the company operated at a margin of safety of 40%. The fixed costs amounted to Rs 3,60,000 and the variable cost ratio to sales was 80%.

In 1997, it is estimated that the variable cost will go up by 10% and the fixed costs will increase by 5%.

Find the selling price required to be fixed in 1997 to earn the same P/V ratio as in 1996.

Assuming the same selling price of Rs 60 per unit in 1997, find the number of units required to produced and sold to earn the same profit as in 1996.

Solution

Basic Calculations

1. P/V Ratio in 1996

$$\text{P/V Ratio} = \frac{\text{Selling Price per unit} - \text{Variable Cost per unit}}{\text{Selling Price per unit}} \times 100$$

$$= \frac{\text{Rs } 60 - \text{Rs } 48}{\text{Rs } 60} \times 100 = \frac{\text{Rs } 12}{\text{Rs } 60} \times 100 = 20\%$$

2. Number of units sold (in 1996)

$$\text{Break-even Point} = \frac{\text{Fixed Cost}}{\text{Contribution per unit}} = \frac{\text{Rs } 3,60,000}{\text{Rs } 12} = 30.000 \text{ units}$$

The margin of safety is 40%. Hence break-even point is at 60% of units sold.

$$\text{or} \quad \text{No. of units sold} = \frac{\text{Break-even point}}{60\%} = \frac{30,000 \text{ units}}{60} \times 100 = 50,000 \text{ units}$$

3. Profit earned in 1996

Profit = Units sold in 1996 × Contribution per unit – Fixed costs
= 50,000 units × Rs 12 – Rs 3,60,000
= Rs 6,00,000 – Rs 3,60,000 = Rs 2,40,000

Fixation of Selling Price in 1997

Variable Cost per unit in 1997 = Rs 48 + Rs 4.80 = Rs 52.80
Fixed cost in 1997 = Rs 3,60,000 + Rs 18,000 = Rs 3,78,000
P/V Ratio in 1996 = 20%
Since P/V ratio is 20%, Hence, Variable cost is 80%

$$\text{Hence, the required selling price} = \frac{\text{Rs } 52.80}{80\%} = \text{Rs } 66$$

Number of units to he produced and sold in 1997 to earn the same profit as in 1996

Profit in 1996 = Rs 2,40,000

Fixed cost in 1997 = Rs 3,78,000

Desired contribution in 1997

(Rs 2,40,000 + Rs 3,78,000) = Rs 6,18,000

Contribution per unit in 1997 = Selling price per unit – Variable cost per unit

= Rs 60 - Rs 52.80 = Rs 7.20

$$\text{Number of units to be produced and sold in 1997} = \frac{\text{Fixed cost in 1997}}{\text{Contribution per unit in 1997}}$$

$$= \frac{\text{Rs } 6,18,000}{\text{Rs } 7.20} = 85,833 \text{ units.}$$

Example 25

A company producing a single product sells it at Rs 50 per unit. Unit variable cost is Rs 35 and fixed cost amounts to Rs 12 lakhs per annum. With this data you are required to calculate the following, treating each independent of the other:

(a) P/V Ratio and Break-even Sales

(b) New Break-even Sales if variable cost increases by Rs 3 per unit, without increase in selling price.

(c) Increase in sales required if profits are to be increased by Rs 24 lakhs.

(d) Percentage increase/decrease in sales volume units to off-set

  (i) an increase of Rs 3 in the variable cost per unit.

  (ii) a 10% increase in selling price without affecting existing profits quantum.

(e) Quantum of advertisement expenditure permissible to increase sales by Rs 1.2 lakhs, without affecting existing profits quantum.

Solution

(a) P/V Ratio

$$= \frac{\text{Contribution per unit}}{\text{Selling Price per unit}}$$

$$= \frac{50-35}{50} = 30\%$$

Break-even sales

$$= \frac{\text{Fixed Cost}}{\text{P.V. Ratio}} = 30\%$$

$$= \frac{12.00}{30\%} = \text{Rs 40 lakhs}$$

(b) Revised PV ratio

$$= \frac{\text{Existing contribution per unit}}{\text{Selling price per unit}}$$

$$= \frac{15-3}{50} = \frac{12}{50} = 24\%$$

Revised break-even sales

$$= \frac{12}{24\%} = \text{Rs 50 lakhs}$$

(c) Increase in sales required

$$= \frac{\text{Increase in Contribution}}{\text{PV Ratio}}$$

$$= \frac{24}{30\%} = \text{Rs 8 lakhs}$$

(d) (i) Percentage in sales volume (units)

$$= \frac{\text{Reduction in contribution}}{\text{New contribution per unit}}$$

$$= \frac{3}{12} \times 100$$

$$= 25\%$$

(ii) Percentage Decrease in Sales Volume (units)

$$= \frac{\text{Increase in Contribution per unit}}{\text{New Contribution per unit}}$$

$$= \frac{5(i.e.\ 10\% \text{ of Rs } 50)}{20\ i.e.\ (55-35)}$$

$$= 25\%$$

(e) The contribution by sales arising out of advertisement expenses should be equal to amount of Rs 1.2 lakhs the sale increase to avoid profit or loss. Hence, 30% of 1.2 lakhs or Rs 36,000 should be the maximum permissible advertisement expenditure for being incurred to get an increase of sale of Rs 1.2 lakhs without affecting existing profits.

Example 26

A company has three factories situated in North, East and South with its Head Office in Mumbai. The Management has received the following summary report on the operations of each factory for a period:

(Rs in 1000)

Particulars	*Sales*		*Profit*	
	Actual	*Over/(Under) Budget*	*Actual*	*Over/(Under) Budget*
North	1,100	(400)	135	(180)
East	1,450	150	210	90
South	1,200	(200)	330	(110)

Calculate for each factory and for the company as a whole for the period:
(i) Fixed Costs, (ii) Break-even Sales

Solution

Computation of Profit Volume Ratio

(Rs in '000)

Particulars	*Sales*			*Profit*			*P/V Ratio*
	Actual	*Over/ (Under) Budget*	*Budget Sales*	*Actual*	*Over/ (Under) Budget*	*Budget Sales*	*(Diff. between Profit) / Diff. between Sales*
North	1,100	(400)	1,500	135	(180)	315	45% (180/400 × 100)
East	1,450	150	1,300	210	90	120	(60%) (90/150 × 100)
South	1,200	(200)	1,400	330	(110)	440	55% (110/200 × 100)

(i) Computation of Fixed Costs

(Rs '000)

Particulars	*Actual Sales*	*P/V Ratio %*	*Contribution*	*Actual Profit*	*Fixed Cost*
	(1)	(2)	(3) = (1) × (2)	(4)	(5) = (3) – (4)
North	1,100	45	495	135	360
East	1,450	60	870	210	660
South	1,200	55	660	330	330
Total	3,750	54	2,025	675	1,350

(ii) Computation of Break-even Sales

(Rs '000)

Particulars	*Fixed Cost*	*P/V Ratio%*	*Break-even Sales*
	(a)	*(b)*	*(a)/(b)*
North	360	45	800
East	660	60	1,100
South	330	55	600
			2,500

$$\text{Break-even Sales (company as whole)} : \frac{\text{Fixed Cost}}{\text{Composite P / V Ratio}} = \frac{1350}{54} = 2{,}500 \text{ (in Rs,'000)}$$

Example 27

A company wants to buy a new machine to replace one which is having frequent breakdown. It received offers for two models M 1 and M2. Further details regarding these models are given below:

	M1	M2
Installed capacity (units)	10,000	10,000
Fixed overhead per annum (Rs)	2,40,000	1,00,000
Estimated profit at the above capacity (Rs)	1,60,000	1,00,000

The product manufactured using this type of machine (Ml or M2) is sold at Rs 100 per unit. You are required to determine:

(a) Break-even level of sales for each model.

(b) The level of sales at which both the models will earn the same profit.

(c) The model suitable for different levels of demand for the product.

Solution

(a) *Basic Calculations*

Statement showing Comparative Parameters of two Machines

	Type of Machines	*Model M1*	*Model M2*
1.	Installed Capacity (units)	10,000	10,000
2.	Fixed Overhead per annum (Rs)	2,40,000	1,00,000
3.	Selling Price of the Product (Rs)	100	100

(*Contd.*)

4.	Estimated Profit at the above Capacity (Rs)	1.60,000	1,00,000
5.	Total Sales Value (Rs)	10,00,000	10,00,000
6.	Total Contribution (Rs) (2) + (4)	4,00,000	2,00,000
7.	Variable Cost	6,00,000	8,00,000
8.	Variable Cost per unit	Rs 60	Rs 80
9.	P/V Ratio = Contribution/Sales	0.40	0.20

Computation of Break-even Sales

	Model M1	Model M2
Break-even Sales	$\frac{\text{Fixed Cost}}{\text{P / V Ratio}}$	$\frac{\text{Fixed Cost}}{\text{P / V Ratio}}$
	= $\frac{\text{Rs } 2,40,000}{.40}$	$\frac{\text{Rs } 1,00,000}{.20}$
	= Rs 6,00,000	Rs 5,00,000
BEP in units	= 6,000 units	5,000 units

(b) *Sales at which both models will earn the same profit.*

Let the units sold be taken as x

Total Cost for Model 1 = 60x = 2,40,000

Total Cost for Model 2 = 80x = 1,00.000

On putting these figures in the form of a simultaneous equation:

$$60 \times 2,40,000 = 80\,x + 1,00,000$$

or $$20\,x = 1,40,000$$

or $$x = 7,000 \text{ units}$$

Thus, at 7,000 units of output, the total costs under both the machines will be the same and hence earn the same profit.

(c) *Model Suitable for different levels of Demand* In view of the above staled comparative parameters Model M2 is suitable for low demand since it has a lower Break Even Point anil Lower Fixed Cost and makes higher profit between 5,000 units and 7,000 units than Model M 1. In case the level of demand for the product exceeds 7,000 units. Model M 1 is belter since it makes higher profit.

This can be substantiated by profitability of two models of Machines at different levels (6,000 units and 8,000 units) as being depicted below:

Levels of Demand	*6,000 units*		*8,000 units*	
Types of Machines	*M1*	*M2*	*M1*	*M2*
Total Contribution (Rs)	2,40,000	1,20,000	3,20,000	1,60,000
Less : Fixed Cost (Rs)	2,40,000	1,00,000	2,40,000	1,00,000
Profit		20,000	80,000	60,000

Example 28

The variable cost structure of a product manufactured by a company during the current year is as under:

	Rs per unit
Material	120
Labour	30
Overheads	12

The selling price per unit is Rs 270 and the fixed cost and sales during the current year are Rs 14 lakhs and Rs 40.5 lakhs respectively.

During the forthcoming year, the direct workers will be entitled to a wage increase of 10% from the beginning of the year and the material cost, variable overhead and fixed overhead are expected to increase by 7.5%, 5% and 3% respectively. The following are required to be computed:

(a) New sale price in the forthcoming year if the current P/V ratio is to be maintained.

(b) Number of units that would require to be sold during the forthcoming year so as to yield the same amount of profit in the current year, assuming that selling price per unit will not be increased.

Solution

Current Year's Statement of Profitability

Units sold 15,000

Particulars		*Rs*	*Total*
Selling Price per unit (Rs)		270	
Less: Variable Cost per unit:			
Material	120		
Labour	30		
Overheads	12		
		162	
Contribution per unit		108	
Total Contribution (15,000 units × Rs 108)			16,20,000
Less: Fixed Cost			14,00,000
Profit			2,20,000
P/V Ratio	(108/270)		40%

(a) Statement Showing New Selling Price for the Forthcoming Year (Retaining Current Year's P/V Ratio)

	Particulars		*Rs*
(1)	Variable Cost per unit :		
	Material	129.00	
	Labour	33.00	
	Overheads	12,60	
			174.60
(2)	Selling Price (174.60 × 100/60)		291.00
(3)	Contribution (2) – (1)		116.40
(4)	P.V. Ratio		40%

(b) Computation of Number of Units to be Sold during Forthcoming Year (Maintaining the current Year's Profit)

	Particulars	*Rs*	*Rs*
(i)	Current Year Profit	2,20,000	
(ii)	Revised Fixed Cost	14,42,000	16,62,000
(iii)	Required Contribution (Rs 270 – Rs 174.60)		95.40
(iv)	Number of Units to be sold (16,62,000/95.40)		17,422 units

Working Note:

Computation of Variable Cost per unit

	Current Year	Forthcoming Year	
	Rs	Increase %	Total (Rs)
Material	120.00	7.5 (120 × 1.075)	129.00
Labour	30.00	10 (30 × 1.10)	33.00
Overhead	12.00	5 (12 × 1.05)	12.60
	162.00		174.60
Fixed Cost	Rs. 14,00,000	3 (14,00,000 × 1.03)	14,42,000

Example 29

The comparative profit statement of two quarters of a firm is as under:

	Quarter I	Quarter II
Units sold	2,500	3,750
	Rs	Rs
Direct materials	87,500	?
Direct wages	62,500	?
Fixed and variable factory overheads	75,000	95.000
Sales	2,75,000	?
Profit	50,000	66,250

In the second quarter, the direct material price has increased by 20%. There was a saving of Rs 5.000 in fixed overheads in the second quarter. The other costs and selling price remained the same. Determine die quantity that should have been sold in the second quarter to maintain the same amount of profit per unit as in the first quarter.

Solution

Working Notes:

1. *Direct material, Direct wages, Selling price and Profit per unit*

$$\text{Direct material (p.u)} = \frac{\text{Rs } 87{,}500}{2{,}500 \text{ units}} = \text{Rs } 35$$

$$\text{Direct wages (p.u)} = \frac{\text{Rs } 62{,}500}{2{,}500 \text{ units}} = \text{Rs } 25$$

$$\text{Selling price (p.u)} = \frac{\text{Rs } 2{,}75{,}000}{2{,}500 \text{ units}} = \text{Rs } 110$$

$$\text{Profit (p.u)} = \frac{\text{Rs } 50{,}000}{2{,}500 \text{ units}} = \text{Rs } 20$$

2. *Variable factory overhead per unit and Fixed factory overheads for II Quarter*

$$\text{Variable factory overhead (p.u)} = \frac{\text{Changes in semi-variable overheads}}{\text{Changes in production volume}}$$

$$= \frac{\text{Rs } 1{,}00{,}000^{**} - \text{Rs } 75{,}000}{3{,}750 \text{ units} - 2{,}500 \text{ units}}$$

$$= \frac{\text{Rs } 25{,}000}{1{,}250 \text{ units}} = \text{Rs } 20$$

** In fact the fixed and variable factory overheads during the quarter (II) were Rs 1,00,000 but due to saving of Rs 5,000 the balance amount of Rs 95,000 was paid.

Fixed factory overheads for II Quarter

	Rs
Total factory overheads of II quarter	1,00,000
Less: Variable factory overheads (3,750 units × Rs 20)	75,000
Total fixed factory overheads for II quarter	25,000
Less: Saving of fixed factory overheads	5,000
Net fixed factory overheads for II quarter	20,000

Statement of quantity of units to be sold In second quarter to maintain same amount of profit per unit as In the first Quarter

	Rs	Rs
Selling price per unit: (A) *(Refer to working note 1)*		
Variable costs: (per unit) :		
Direct materials $\left(\text{Rs } 35 \times \frac{120}{100}\right)$	42	
Direct wages	25	
Variable factory overheads *(Refer to working note 2)*	20	
Total variable cost: (B)		87
Contribution per unit: {(A - D)}		23
Less: Profit per unit (*Refer to working note I*)		20
Balance for fixed cost per unit		3
Total fixed cost		20,000

Hence the number of units to be sold in the second quarter to maintain the same amount of profit p.u.

$$\text{as in the first quarter} = \frac{\text{Total fixed cost}}{\text{Balance for fixed cost p.u.}}$$

$$= \frac{\text{Rs } 20{,}000}{\text{Rs } 3 \text{ per unit}} = 6{,}667 \text{ units (approx.)}$$

Example 30

A Company manufactures a product, currently utilisirg 80% capacity with a turnover of Rs 8 00 000 at Rs 25 per unit. The cost data are as under:

Material cost Rs 7.50 per unit.

Labour cost Rs 6.25 per unit.

Semi-variable cost (Including variable cost of Rs 3.75 per unit) Rs 1,80,000.

Fixed cost Rs 90,000 upto 80% level of output, beyond this an additional Rs 20,000 will be incurred.

Calculate:

(i) Activity level at Break-even-Point

(ii) Number of units to be sold to earn a net income of 8% of sales

(iii) Activity level needed to earn a profit of Rs 95.000

(iv) What should be the selling price per unit, if break-even-point is to be brought down to 40% activity level?

Solution

Working Notes:

1. (i) *Number of units sold at 80% capacity*

$$= \frac{\text{Turnover}}{\text{Selling price}} = \frac{\text{Rs } 20,000}{\text{Rs } 25} = \text{Rs } 32,000 \text{ units}$$

(ii) *Number of units sold at 100% capacity*

$$= \frac{\text{Rs } 32,000}{\text{Rs } 80} \times 100 = 40,000 \text{ units}$$

2. *Component of fixed cost included in semi-variable cost of 32,000 units*

Fixed cost = {Total semi-variable cost – Total variable cost}
= Rs. 1,80,000 – 32,000 units × Rs 3.75
= Rs 1,80,000 – Rs 1,20,000
= Rs 60,000

3. (i) *Total fixed cost beyond 80% capacity*

= Fixed cost + Component of fixed cost included in semi-variable cost (Refer to working note 2)
= Rs 90,000 + Rs 60,000 = Rs 1,50,000

(ii) *Total fixed cost beyond 80% capacity*

= Total fixed cost at 80% capacity + Additional fixed cost to be incurred
= Rs 1,50,000 + Rs 20,000 = Rs 1,70,000

4. *Variable cost and contribution per unit*

Variable cost per unit = Material cost + Labour cost + Variable cost component in semi-variable cost
= Rs 7.50 + Rs 6.25 + Rs 3.75 = Rs 17.50

Contribution per unit = Selling price per unit – Variable cost per unit
= Rs 25 – Rs 17.50 = Rs 7.50

5. *Profit at 80% capacity level*

= Sales revenue – Variable cost – Fixed cost
= Rs 8,00,000 – Rs 5,60,000 (32,000 units × Rs 17.50) – Rs 1,50,000
= Rs 90,000

(i) *Activity lev el at Break-even Point*

$$\text{Break-even point (units)} = \frac{\text{Fixed cost}}{\text{Contribution per unit}} = \frac{\text{Rs } 1,50,000}{\text{Rs } 7.50} = 20,000 \text{ units}$$

(*Refer to working notes 3 & 4*)

$$\text{Activity level at Break-even Point} = \frac{\text{Break-even point (units)}}{\text{No. of units at 100\% capacity level}} \times 100$$

(*Refer to working note 1(ii)*)

$$= \frac{20,000 \text{ units}}{40,000 \text{ units}} \times 100 = 50\%$$

(ii) *Number of units to be sold to earn a net income of 8% of sales*

Let x be the number of units sold to earn a net income of 8% of sales.

Mathematically, it means that:

(Sales revenue of x units) = Variable cost of x units + Fixed cost + Net income

$$\text{or Rs } 25x = \text{Rs } 17.5x + \text{Rs } 1{,}50{,}000 + \frac{8}{100} \times (\text{Rs } 25x)$$

$$\text{or Rs } 25x = \text{Rs } 17.5x + \text{Rs } 1{,}50{,}000 + \text{Rs } 2x$$

$$\text{or } x = (\text{Rs } 1{,}50{,}000/\text{Rs } 5.5) \text{ units}$$

$$\text{or } x = 27{,}273 \text{ units}$$

(iii) *Activity level needed to earn a profit of Rs 95,000*

The profit at 80% capacity level, is Rs 90,000 which is less than the desired profit of Rs 95,000, therefore the needed activity level would be more than 80%. Thus the fixed cost to be taken to determine the activity level needed should be Rs 1,70,000 (*Refer to Working note 3(ii)*).

$$\text{Units to be sold to earn a profit of Rs 95,000} = \frac{\text{Fixed cost + Desired profit}}{\text{Contribution per unit}}$$

$$= \frac{\text{Rs } 1{,}70{,}000 + \text{Rs } 95{,}000}{\text{Rs } 7.5}$$

$$= 35{,}333.33 \text{ units}$$

$$\text{Activity level needed to earn a profit of Rs 95,000} = \frac{35{,}333.33}{40{,}000 \text{ units}} \times 100$$

$$= 88.33\%$$

(iv) *Selling price per unit, if break-even-point is to be brought down to 40% (16,000 units) activity level*

Let x be the selling per unit

Units at Break-even-point = 16,000 units

$$\text{Break-even-point} = \frac{\text{Fixed cost}}{\text{Contribution per unit}}$$

$$\text{At 16,000 units} = \frac{\text{Rs } 1{,}50{,}000}{(x - \text{Rs } 17.50)}$$

$$\text{or } (x - \text{Rs } 17.50) = \frac{\text{Rs } 1{,}50{,}000}{16{,}000 \text{ units}}$$

$$\text{or } (x - \text{Rs } 17.50) = \frac{\text{Rs } 75}{8 \text{ units}}$$

$$\text{or } 8x - 8 \times \text{Rs } 17.50 = \text{Rs } 75$$

$$\text{or } 8x - \text{Rs } 140 = \text{Rs } 75$$

$$\text{or } 8x = \text{Rs } 215$$

$$\text{or } x = \text{Rs } 26.875$$

Hence, S.P. (per unit) = Rs. 26.875

Example 31

Fill in the blanks for each of the following independent situations:

	A	B	C	D	E
Selling Price per unit	—	Rs 50	Rs 20	—	Rs 30

Variable Cost as % of Selling Price	60	—	75	75	—
No. of units sold	10,000	4,000	—	6,000	5,000
Marginal contribution	Rs 20,000	Rs 80,000	—	Rs 25,000	Rs 50,000
Fixed Cost	Rs 12,000	—	Rs 1,20,000	Rs 10,000	—
Profit/Loss	—	Rs 20,000	Rs 30,000	—	Rs 15,000

Solution

Independent situation	*Blank space to be filled*	*Figure of blank*
A	Profit/(Loss) [Refer to working note 1(i)]	Rs 8,000
	Selling price per unit [Refer to working note 1(ii)]	Rs 5
B	Fixed costs [Refer to working note 2(i)]	Rs 60,000
	Variable cost as % of seeling price [Refer to working note 2(ii)]	60%
C	No. of units sold [Refer to working note 3(ii)]	30,000 units
	Marginal contribution *[Refer to working note 3(i)]*	Rs 1,50,000
D	Selling price per unit *[Refer to working note 4 (ii)]*	Rs. 16.66
	profit (Loss) *[Refer t working note 4(i)]*	Rs. 15,000
E	Variable cost as % of selling price *[Refer to working note 5(ii)]*	66.66%
	Fixed costs *[Refer to working note 5(i)]*	Rs. 35,000

Working Notes :

1. (i) Profit/(Loss) = Contribution — Fixed costs
   = Rs. 20,000 – Rs. 12,000 = Rs. 8,000

   (ii) Let selling price per unit be (x)

   (Selling price per unit — Variable cost per unit) No. of units sold = Marginal contribution

   or $\left(x - \frac{3}{5}x\right) \times 10{,}000$ units = Rs. 20,000

   Variable cost as %

   or $\frac{2}{5}x$ = Rs 2

   or x = Rs 5

2. (i) Fixed costs = Marginal contribution — Profit
   = Rs. 80,000 – Rs. 20,000 = Rs. 60,000

   (ii) Variable Cost as % of selling price

$$= \frac{\text{Selling price per unit} - \text{Marginal contribution per unit}}{\text{Selling price per unit}} \times 100$$

$$= \frac{\text{Rs } 50 - \text{Rs } 20}{\text{Rs } 50} \times 100 = 60\%$$

3. (i) Marginal contribution= Fixed costs + Profit
= Rs. 1,20,000 + Rs. 30,000 = Rs 1,50,000

(ii) No. of units sold $= \frac{\text{Marginal Contribution}}{\text{Contribution per unit}}$

$$= \frac{\text{Rs } 1,50,000}{(\text{Rs. } 20 - \text{Rs}15)} = \frac{\text{Rs } 1,50,000}{\text{Rs } 5}$$

= 30,000 units

4. (i) Profit/(Loss) = Marginal contribution – Fixed costs
= Rs. 25,000 – Rs. 10,000 = Rs. 15,000

(ii) Selling price per unit (x)
(Selling price per unit – Variable cost per unit) No. of units sold = Marginal contribution

or $\left(x - \frac{3}{4}x\right)$ 6,000 units = Rs. 25,000

or $\frac{x}{4} \times 6,000 =$ Rs. 25,000

or $x =$ Rs. 16.66 per unit

5 (i) Fixed costs = Marginal contribution – Profit
= Rs. 50,000 – Rs. 15,000 = Rs. 35,000

(ii) Variable costs per unit = Selling price — Marginal contribution per unit
= (Rs. 30 – Rs. 50,000/5,000)
= Rs. 20

Variable costs as % of selling price $= \frac{\text{Variable costs per unit}}{\text{Selling price per unit}} \times 100$

$$= \frac{\text{Rs. } 20}{\text{Rs. } 30} \times 100 = 66.66$$

Example 32

ABC Ltd. which produces three products furnishes the following data for the year 2006.

	Products		
	Alfa	*Beta*	*Gamma*
Selling price per unit	Rs. 100	75	50
Profit/Volume Ratio	10%	20%	40%
Maximum Sales Potential (units)	40,000	25,000	10,000
Raw Material as % of Variable Cost	50%	50%	50%

The company uses the same raw material for all the three products. Raw material is in short supply and the company has a quota for supply of raw material of the value of Rs. 18,00,000 for the year 2006 for manufacture of its products to meet its sales. Total fixed costs is Rs. 6,80,000.

You are required to :

(a) Determine a sales max which will give the maximum overall profit keeping in view the short supply of raw material.

(b) Compute the maximum profit.

Solution

Particulars		*Products* *Alfa*	*Beta*	*Gamma*
Selling price per unit	Rs	100	75	50
Profit Volume Ratio		10%	20%	40%
Contribution per unit	Rs	10	15	20
Variable Cost per unit	Rs	90	60	30
Raw Material per unit	Rs	45	30	15
Contribution per rupee of raw material	=	10/45	15/30	20/15
	=	2/9	1/2	4/3
Ranking		3	2	1

(a) Computation of Sales Mix

Products	*Units* Rs	*Sales* Rs	*Raw Material used*
Gamma	10,000	5,00,000	1,50,000
Beta	25,000	18,75,000	7,50,000
Alfa	20,000	20,00,000	9,00,000
Balance	55,000	43,75,000	18,00,000

(b) Computation of Profit

Products	*Sales* Rs	*P/V Ratio*	*Contribution*
Gama	5,00,000	40	2,00,000
Beta	18,75,000	20	3,75,000
Alfa	20,00,000	10	2,00,000
			7,75,000
	Less : Fixed Cost		6,80,000
	Net Profit		95,000

Example 33

A company has two Plants at Locations I and II, operating at 100% and 75% of their capacities respectively. The company is considering a proposal to merge the two plants at one location to optimise available capacity. The following details are available in respect of the two plants, regarding their present performance/operations:

Particulars	*Location I*	*Location II*
Seles (Rs in lakhs)	200	75
Variable Cost (Rs in lakhs)	140	54
Fixed Cost (Rs in lakhs)	30	14

For decision-making pruposes you are required to work out the following information:

(a) The capacity at which the merged pant will break-even.

(b) The profit of the merged plant working at 80% capacity.

(c) Sales required if the merged plant is required to earn an overall profit of Rs 22 lakhs.

Solution

Comparative Performance of Plant at 100% Capacity

Rs in lakhs

Plants	*Plants Location-I*	*Plant Location-II*	*Merged Plant*
Capacity Levels	100%	100%	100%
Sales	200	100	300
Less : Variable Cost	140	72	212
Contribution	60	28	88
Less: Fixed Cost	30	14	44
Profit (Loss)	30	14	44
P/V Ratio: (%): Contribution/Sales)	30%	28%	29.33
Break-even Sales (Fixed Cost/P/V Ratio)	44/29.33%		150

(a) Capacity at BEP (%) : $\frac{150}{300} \times 100 = 50\%$

(b) Computation of Profitability of the Merged Plant at 80% Capacity

(Rs in lakhs)

Particulars	*Rs.*
Sales (80% of 300)	240.00
Less: Variable Cost	169.60
Contribution	70.40
Less : Fixed Cost	44.00
Profit	26.40

(c) Computation of sales required to earn Desired Profit of Rs. 22 lakhs:

Contribution required (Rs in lakhs) :

Fixed Cost	44.00	
Desired Profit	22.00	66.00
P/V Ratio (%)		29.33%

Desired Sales Level (Rs. in lakhs) $\frac{66 \times 100}{29.33} = 225.00$

Example 34

An automobile manufacturing company produces different models of cars. The budget in respect of model 118 for the month of September, 2006 is as under :

Budgeted Output	*(Rs in lakhs)*	*40,000* units *(Rs in lakhs)*
Net Realisation		700
Variable Costs :		
Materials	264	
Labour	52	
Direct Expenses	124	440
Specific Fixed Costs	90	
Allocated Fixed Costs	112.50	202.50
Total Costs		642.50
Profit		57.50
Sales		700.00

Calculate:

(i) Profit with 10 per cent increase in selling price with a 10 per cent reduction in sales volume.

(ii) Volume to be achieved to maintain the original profit after a 10 per cent rise in material costs, at the originally budgeted selling price per unit.

Solution

(i) Statement of profit

(with 10 per cent increase in selling price with a 10 per cent reduction in sales-volume)

	(Rs. in Lakhs)
Sale Revenue: (A) (*See WN 1*)	693
Less: Variable Costs: (B) (*See WN 2*)	396
Contribution [(A) – (B)]	297
Less: Total Fixed Costs	202.5
Profit	94.5

Working Notes :

1. Selling Price (per unit) $= \frac{\text{Rs } 7,00,00,000}{40,000 \text{ units}} = \text{Rs } 1,750$

   New Selling Price (per unit) = Rs. 1,750 + Rs 175 = Rs 1,925

   Reduced Sales Volume = 36,000 units

   Total Sales Revenue = Rs. 1,925 × 36,000 = Rs 693 lakhs

2. (i) *Variable Costs per unit*

		Rs
Materials Cost	=	660
Labour Cost	=	130
Direct Expenses	=	310
Total Variable Cost	=	1,100

(ii) *Volume to be achieved to maintain original profit*

	Rs.	Rs.
Selling Price (per unit) (as per Working Note)		1,750
Less: Variable Costs		
Materials Cost (Rs. 660 + Rs. 66)	736	
Labour Cost	130	
Direct Expenses	310	1,166
Contribution per unit		584

Desired Contribution = Fixed Cost + Original Profit
= Rs. 202.50 + Rs. 57.50
= Rs. 260 lakhs

No. of cars to be sold to maintain original profit at original sales price $= \frac{\text{Rs } 260 \text{ lakhs}}{\text{Rs } 584}$

= 44,520.547 or say 44,521 cars.

Example 35

(a) A Company had incurred fixed expenses of Rs. 4,50,000, with sales of Rs 15,00,000 and earned a profit of Rs 3,00,000 during the first half year. In the second half, it suffered a loss of Rs 1,50,000.

Calculate :

(i) The profit-volume ratio, break-even point and margin of safety for the first half year.

(ii) Expected sales volume for the second half year assuming that selling price and fixed expenses remained unchanged during the second half year.

(iii) The break-even point and margin of safety for the whole year.

(b) A company manufactures and markets three products X, Y and Z. All the three products are made from the same set of machines. Production is limited by machine capacity. From the data given below, indicate priorities for Products X, Y and Z with a view to maximising profits:

Particulars		*Products*		
		X	*Y*	*Z*
Raw Material Cost per unit	(Rs)	11.25	16.25	21.25
Direct Labour Cost per unit	(Rs)	2.50	2.50	2.50
Other Variable Cost per unit	(Rs)	1.50	2.25	3.55
Selling Price per unit	(Rs)	25.00	30.00	35.00
Standard Machine time required per unit in minutes		39	20	28

Solution

(a) (i) *Computation of Profit-Volume Ratio, Break-even Point and Margin of Safety: (for the first half year)*

$$\text{Profit-volume ratio} = \frac{\text{Contribution}}{\text{Sales}} \times 100$$

$$= \frac{\text{Fixed Expenses} + \text{Profit}}{\text{Sales}} \times 100$$

$$= \frac{\text{Rs } 4{,}50{,}000 + \text{Rs } 3{,}00{,}000}{\text{Rs } 15{,}00{,}000} \times 100$$

$$= 50\%$$

$$\text{Break-even point} = \frac{\text{Fixed Expenses}}{\text{P / V Ratio}}$$

$$= \frac{\text{Rs } 4{,}50{,}000}{50\%}$$

$$= \text{Rs } 9{,}00{,}000$$

Margin of Safety = Actual Sales – Break-even sales

= Rs 15,00,000 – Rs. 9,00,000

= Rs 6,00,000

(ii) *Computation of Expected Sales Volume*

$$\text{Expected Sales Volume} = \frac{\text{Fixed Expenses - Loss}}{\text{P / V Ratio}}$$

$$= \frac{\text{Rs } 4{,}50{,}000 - \text{Rs } 1{,}50{,}000}{50\%}$$

$$= \text{Rs } 6{,}00{,}000$$

(iii) *Computation of Break-even point and Margin of Safety (for the whole year)*

$$\text{Break-even point} = \frac{\text{Fixed expenses for the whole year}}{P/V \text{ Ratio}}$$

$$= \frac{\text{Rs } 9{,}00{,}000}{50\%} = \text{Rs } 18{,}00{,}000$$

$$\text{Margin of safety} = \frac{\text{Profit for the year}}{P/V \text{ Ratio}}$$

$$= \frac{\text{Rs } 3{,}00{,}000 - \text{Rs } 1{,}50{,}000}{50\%}$$

$$= \text{Rs } 3{,}00{,}000$$

(b) Statement showing Priorities for Products X, Y and Z to Maximise Profits

Products			*X*	*Y*	*Z*
Selling Price per unit	(Rs)		25.00	30.00	35.00
Less: Variable Cost per unit *(See working note)*	(Rs)		15.25	21.00	27.30
Contribution per unit	(Rs)	(A)	9.75	9	7.70
Std. Machine time required in minutes per units		(B)	30	20	28
Contribution per minute	(Rs)	(A)/(B)	0.25	0.45	0.275
Priorities for Products			III	I	II

Working Notes:

Computation of Variable Cost per Unit

Particulars	*Products*		
	X	*Y*	*Z*
	Rs	Rs	Rs
Raw Material Cost	11.25	16.25	21.25
Direct Labour Cost	2.50	2.50	3.55
Other Variable Cost	1.50	2.25	3.55
Total Variable Cost per unit	15.25	21.00	27.30

Example 36

Two firms A & Co. and B & Co. sell the same stype of product in the same market. Their budgeted Profit & Loss Account for the year ending 31st March, 2006 are as follows :

Particulars	*A & Co.*		*B & Co.*	
	Rs	*Rs*	*Rs*	*Rs*
Sales		5,00,000		6,00,000
Variable Costs	4,00,000		4,00,000	
Fixed Costs	30,000	4,30,000	70,000	4,70,000
Net Profit		70,000		1,30,000

Required :

1. Calculate at which sales volume both the firms will earn equal profit.
2. Sales which firm is likely to earn greater profits in conditioin of:

(i) heavy demand for the product, and

(ii) low demand for the product

Give reasons.

Solution

1. Computation of Sales Volume for Equal Profits

Particulars	*A & Co.*	*B & Co.*
Sales (Rs.)	5,00,000	6,00,000
Less : Variable Costs (Rs)	4,00,000	4,00,000
Contribution (Rs)	1,00,000	2,00,000
P/V Ratio (C/S × 100)	20%	33:33%

$$\text{Sales Volume} = \frac{\text{Difference in Fixed Cost}}{\text{Difference in P / V Ratio}}$$

$$\text{(for both the firms to earn equal profit)} = \frac{\text{Rs } 40{,}000}{13.33\%}$$

$$= \text{Rs } 3{,}00{,}000$$

The P/V ratio of B & Co. at 33.33% is higher than that of A & Co. at 20% and therefore B & Co. will earn higher profit if the sales volume exceeds the level of Rs 3,00,000.

As a matter of fact for each additional unit of product's sale above Rs 3,00,000 the profit of B & Co. will rise by Rs 33.33 which exceeds by Rs 13.33, the profit of A & Co. under similar circumstances. However, below that level, Profit for A & Co. will be greater. Hence, it can generally be concluded that B & Co. is likely to earn higher profits under conditions of heavy demand for the product above Rs 3,00,000. On the other hand A & Co. is expected to make higher profits under conditions of low demand for the product below sales volume of Rs. 3,00,000.

Example 37

A manufacturing company has an installed capacity of 1,20,000 units per annum. The cost structure of the product manufactured is as under :

	Rs
(i) Variable cost per unit—	
Materials	8
Labour (Subject to a minimum of Rs 56,000 per month)	8
Overheads	3

(ii) Fixed overheads – Rs. 1,68,750 per annum.

(iii) Semi-variable overheads Rs 48,000 per annum at 60% capacity, which increase by Rs 6,000 per annum for increase of every 10% of the capacity utilisation or any part thereof for the year as a whole.

The capacity utilisation for the next year is estimated at 60% for two months, 75% for six months and 80% for the remaining part of the year. If the company is planning to have a profit of 25% on the selling price, calculate the selling price per unit. Assume that there are no opening and closing stocks.

Solution

Statement of Selling Price and Profit

	Rs.
Materials 89,000 units × Rs 8 per unit (WN 1)	7,12,000
Labour Cost (WN 2)	7,28,000
Variable Overheads (89,000 units × Rs. 3)	2,67,000
Semi-variable overheads (WN 3)	60,000
Fixed Overheads	1,68,750
Total Cost	19,35,750
Add: Profit @ 25% of selling price or 33 1/3% on cost	6,45,250
Total Sales Value	25,81,000
Selling Price per unit (Rs 25,81,000/89,000 units)	29.00

Working Notes :

1. *Computation of Capacity Utilisation (for the next year) :*

60% of capacity for first two months	= 2 months × 6,000 units	= 12,000 units
75% of capacity for next six months	= 6 months × 7,500 units	= 45,000 units
80% of capacity for the remaining four months	= 4 months × 8,000 units	= 32,000 units
Total capacity utilisation		= 89,000 units

Capacity utilisation $= \dfrac{89{,}000 \text{ units}}{1{,}20{,}000 \text{ units}} \times 100 = 74\tfrac{1}{6}\%$

2. *Computation of labour cost (subject to a minimum of Rs 56,000 p.m.)*

	Rs
Labour Cost of first two months 12,000 units × Rs 8 = Rs 96,000 However Minimum in 56,000 × 2	1,12,000
Labour cost of next six months 45,000 units × Rs 8	3,60,000
Labour cost of last four months 32,000 units × Rs 8	2,56,000
Total Labour Cost	7,28,000

3. *Computation of semi-variable overheads (per annum) :*

	Rs
Semi-variable Overheads (at 60% capacity)	48,000
Semi-variable Overheads for additional (14 – 1/6% capacity are the same as that for 20% of the capacity utilisation for the entire year)	12,000
	60,000

Example 38

Indian Plastics make plastic buckets. An analysis of their accounting reveals :

Variable cost per bucket	Rs 20
Fixed cost	Rs 50,000 for the year
Capacity	2,000 buckets per year
Selling price per bucket	Rs 70

Required :

(i) Find the break-even point.

(ii) Find the number of buckets to be sold to get a profit of Rs 30,000.

(iii) If the company can manufacture 600 buckets more per year with an additional fixed cost of Rs 2,000, what should be the selling price to maintain the profit per bucket as at (ii) above ?

Solution

(i) BEP = Fixed cost/contribution per unit

= 50,000/50 = 1,000 buckets.

(ii) Buckets to be sold for desired profit of Rs 30,000.

$$\text{Sales for Desired Profit} = \frac{\text{Fixed cost + Desired profit}}{\text{Contribution per unit}}$$

$$= \frac{50{,}000 + 30{,}000}{50}$$

= 80,000/50

= 1,600 buckets

(iii) Computation of new selling price :

		Rs
Profits per bucket at sales of 1,600 buckets:		
Sales (1,600 × 70)		1,12,000
Less: Variable cost 1,600 × 20		32,000
	Contribution	80,000
Less:	Fixed costs	50,000
	Profit	30,000
Profit per bucket 30,000/1,600 =		18.75
Total sales 1,600 + 600 = 2,200 buckets		
Total profit desired = 2,200 × 18.75 =		Rs 41,250

Let selling price be '*x*'

The following equation can be made:

Total sales = Total cost + Profit

$2{,}200x$ = 20(2,200) + 52,000 + 41,250

$2{,}200x$ = 1,37,250

or x = Rs 62.39 per bucket

Note : It has been assumed that 600 more buckets to be manufactured are in addition to 1,600 buckets as computed under (ii) above.

Example 39

A retail dealer in garments is currently selling 24,000 shirts annually. He supplies the following details for the year ended 31st December, 2005

	Rs
Selling price per shirt	40
Variable cost per shirt	25
Fixed Cost: Staff salaries for the year	1,20,000
General office costs for the year	80,000
Advertising costs for the year	40,000

As a cost accountant of the firm, you are required to answer the following each part independntly:

(i) Calculate the break-even point and margin of safety in sales revenue and number of shirts sold.

(ii) Assume that 20,000 shirts were sold in a year. Find out the net profit of the firm.

(iii) If it is decided to introduce selling commission of Rs 3 per shirt, how many shirts would require to be sold in a year to earn a net income of Rs 15,000.

(iv) Assuming that for the year 2006 an additional staff salary of Rs 33,000 is anticipated, and price of a shirt is likely to be increased by 15% what should be the break-even point in number of shirts and sales revenue?

Solution

(i) BEP = Fixed cost/Contribution per unit
= 2,40,000/15 = 16,000 units or
= 16,000 × 40 = Rs 6,40,000

Margin of Safety (MS) = Actual sales – Break-even sales
= 24,000 × 40 – 6,40,000
= 9,60,000 – 6,40,000
= Rs 3,20,000

(ii) Net profit when 20,000 shirts are sold :

Contribution: 20,000 × 15	Rs 3,00,000
Less: Fixed costs	Rs 2,40,000
Profit	Rs 60,000

(iii) Sales for desired profit :

$$= \frac{\text{Fixed cost + Desired profit}}{\text{New contribution per unit}}$$

$$= \frac{2,40,000 + 15,000}{15 - 3}$$

$$= \frac{2,55,000}{12} = 21,250 \text{ shirts}$$

(iv) New break-even point :

In units: New fixed cost/New contribution per unit

$$= \frac{2,40,000 + 33,000}{46 - 25}$$

= 2,73,000/21 = 13,000 shirts

In Rs = 13,000 × 46 = Rs. 5,98,000

Example 40

An enthusiastic marketing manager suggests to his managing director that only if he is permitted to reduce the selling price of a product by 20%, he would be able to achieve a 30% increase in sales volume. The managing director, finding that the sales volume increase exceeds in percentage the extent of requested reduction in price, given the clearance.

You are given the following information :

Present selling price per unit	Rs	7.50
Present volume of sales		2,00,000 Nos.
Total variable costs	Rs	10,50,000
Total fixed costs	Rs	3,60,000

Assuming no changes in the costs pattern in the coming period.

(i) Examine the consequences of the managing director's decision assuming that 30% increase in sales is realised.

(ii) At what volume of sales can the present quantum of profits be sustained, after effecting the price reduction.

Solution

Statement Showing the present Result and Result after Price Reduction

	Present result	*Proposed results*
	Rs	Rs
Selling price per unit	7.50	6.00
Sales volume	2,00,000 units	2,60,000 units
Variable cost per unit	5.25	5.25
Contribution per unit	2.25	0.75
Total contribution	4,50,000	1,95,000
Total fixed costs	3,60,000	3,60,000
Profit (loss)	90,000	(1,65,000)

(i) The above statement shows that on account of reduction in the selling price there will be loss of Rs 1,65,000 as compared to the present profit of Rs 90,000, in spite of increase in the sales volume. Thus, there will be an effective drop of profit of Rs 2,55,000 on account of the decision taken by the managing director on the suggestion made by the marketing manager.

(ii) Statement showing the volume of sales at which the present profit can be retained after price reduction.

$$\text{Volume of sales for the profit} = \frac{\text{Fixed cost} + \text{Desired profit}}{\text{Contribution per unit}}$$

$$= \frac{3,60,000 + 90,000}{0.75*} = 60,00,000 \text{ units}$$

*Rs 6 – Rs 5.25

The above statement shows that 200 per cent increase is required to justify a reduction of selling price by 20% without in any way affecting the present profit.

Example 41

Cadbury Schweppes Limited, a British chocolate and soft drink company, is planning to establish a subsidiary company in India to produce, Schweppes Mineral Water.

Based on the estimated annual sales of 40,000 bottles of the mineral water, cost studies produced the following estimates for the Indian subsidiary:

	Total annual costs	*Per cent of total annual cost that is variable*
Material	Rs 1,93,600	100%
Labour	90,000	70%
Overhead	80,000	64%
Administration	30,000	30%

The Indian production will be sold by manufacturer's representatives who will receive a commission of 8 per cent of the sale price. No portion of the British office expenses is to be allocated to the Indian subsidiary.

It is required to:

(i) compute the sale price per bottle to enable management to realise an estimated 10 per cent profit on sale proceeds in India, and

(ii) calculate the break-even point in rupee sales for the Indian subsidiary on the assumption that the sale price is Rs 11 per bottle.

Solution

(i) Computation of Selling Price per Unit

Let the selling price per unit be x

Total sales	$40,000\,x$
Total commission	$3,200\,x$
Total profit	$4,000\,x$

Total sales = Total cost + Profit

$$40,000\,x = 1,93,600 + 90,000 + 80,000 + 30,000 + 3,200x + 4,000\,x$$

or $\quad 40,000\,x = 3,93,600 + 7,200\,x$

or $\quad 32,800\,x = 3,93,600$

x = Rs. 12

(ii) Computation of Break-even Point

Sales (40,000 × 11)		Rs 4,40,000
Less: Marginal cost :		
Material	Rs 1,93,600	
labour 90,000 × 70/100	63,000	
Overhead 80,000 × 64/100	51,200	
Administration $30,000 \times \dfrac{30}{100}$	9,000	
Sales commission 4,40,000 × 8/100	35,200	3,52,00
Total contribution		88,000

$$\text{Break-even sales} = \frac{\text{Fixed cost} \times \text{Total sales}}{\text{Total contribution}}$$

$$= \frac{27,000 + 28,800 + 21,000 \times 4,40,000}{88,000}$$

$$= \frac{76,800}{88,000} \times 4,40,000 = \text{Rs } 3,84,000$$

Example 42

A factory engaged in manufacturing plastic buckets is working to 40% capacity and produces 10,000 buckets per annum.

The present cost break-up for one bucket is as under :

Material	Rs 10
Labour cost	3
Overheads	5 (60% fixed)

The selling prices is Rs 20 per bucket.

If it is decided to work the factory at 50% capacity the selling price falls by 3%. At 90% capacity, the selling price falls by 5% accompanied by a similar fall in the prices of material.

You are required to calculate the profit at 50% and 90% capacities and also calculate break-even points for the same capacity productions.

Solution

Statement Showing Profit and Break-even point at Different Capacity Levels

Capacity levels		*50%*		*90%*
Production (units)		*12,500*		*22,500*
	Per unit	*Total*	*Per unit*	*Total*
(i) Sales	Rs 19.40	Rs 2,42,500	Rs 19.00	Rs 4,27,500
Variable cost:				
Materials	10.00	1,25,000	9.50	2,13,750
Wages	3.00	37,500	3.00	67,500
Variable overheads	2.00	25,000	2.00	45,000
(ii) Total variable cost	15.00	1,87,500	14.50	3,26,250
(iii) Contribution (i – ii)	4.40	55,000	4.50	1,01,250
(iv) Fixed costs		30,000		30,000
(v) Net profit (iii – iv)		25,000		71,250

Break-even point; at 50% capacity $\dfrac{\text{Fixed cost}}{\text{Contribution per unit}}$ at 90% capacity $\dfrac{\text{Fixed cost}}{\text{Contribution per unit}}$

Units $\dfrac{30,000}{4,40} = 6,818$ units $\dfrac{30,000}{4.50} = 6,667$ units

Sales value Rs 1,32,270 Rs 1,26,673

Example 43

Triple X company produces these products with the following characteristics:

	Product I	*Product II*	*Product III*
Price per unit	Rs 5	Rs 6	Rs 7
Variable cost per unit	3	2	4
Expected sales (units)	100,000	150,000	250,000

Total fixed costs for the company are Rs 12,40,000.

Assuming that the product mix would be the same at the break-even point, compute the break-even point in :

(a) Unit (total and by product line)

(b) Sales Rupees (Total and by product line)

Solution

(a) Compute weighted-average contribution margin :

	Product I	*Product II*	*Product III*
Product mix	$\frac{1,00,000 \text{ units}}{5,00,000 \text{ units}}$	$\frac{1,00,000 \text{ units}}{5,00,000 \text{ units}}$	$\frac{2,50,000 \text{ units}}{5,00,000 \text{ units}}$
	= .20	= .30	= .50

Weighted-average
contribution margin = .20 (Rs 2) + .30(Rs 4) + .50(Rs 3) = Rs 3.10

or

$$\frac{(1,00,000 \text{ units})(\text{Rs } 2) + (1,50,000)(\text{Rs } 4) + (2,50,000)(\text{Rs } 3)}{5,00,000 \text{ units}}$$

$$= \text{Rs } 3.10$$

$$x = \frac{\text{Rs } 12,40,000}{\text{Rs } 3.10}$$

$$x = 4,00,000 \text{ units}$$

(b) To compute break-even sales Rupees, find the weighted-average price and variable costs :

P = (.20) (Rs 5) + (.30) (Rs 6) + .50 (Rs 7)
= **Rs 6.30**

V = (.2) (Rs 3) + (.30) (Rs 2) + (.50) (Rs 4)
= Rs 3.20

$$\text{Break-even point} = \frac{F}{\frac{P-V}{P}} = \frac{\text{Rs } 12,40,000}{\text{Rs } 3.10 / \text{Rs } 6.30} = \text{Rs } 12,40,000$$

$$= \frac{\text{Rs } 12,40,000}{.492}$$

= Rs 25,20,000 approx.

(Check 4,00,000 units × Rs 6.30 = 25,20,000)

Product line amounts:

	Total	*Product I*	*Product II*	*Product III*
	(100%)	(20%)	(30%)	(40%)
Units	4,00,000	80,000	1,20,000	2,00,0000
Units price (Rs)	6.30	5	6	7
Sales Rupees	25,20,000	4,00,000	7,20,000	14,00,000

Example 44

The Chief Cost Accountatn of Vikas Limited found to his surprise that the actual profit for the period ending 30th June, 2006 was the same as budgeted in spite of realising 10% more than the budgeted selling prices. The following were the results :

Particulars	*Budget* *Rs*	*Actuals* *Rs*
Sales	5,00,000	8,25,000
Variable costs of sales	3,00,000	5,75,000

Fixed costs	1,00,000	1,50,000
Profit	1,00,000	1,00,000

You are required to assist the Chief Cost Accountant in preparing the necessary explanations as to why the profit remained the same despite an increase in sales.

Solution

In order to assist the Chief Accountant of Vikas Ltd., in prepaing the necessary explanations, for the profit remaining the same, in spite of an increase in sale revenue, the following factors may be considered :

Factors contributing to the increase in profit :

	Rs
(i) Increase in sales revenue due to increased selling price (Working Note 1)	75,000
(ii) Increase in contribution on account of increased sales volume (Working Note 4)	1,00,000
	1,75,000

Factors contributing to the increase in cost:

(i) Increase in variable costs: (working Note 5)	1,25,000
(ii) Increase in fixed cost	50,000
	1,75,000

Working Notes:

1. Increase in sales revenue due to price increase (10% more than the budgeted)

$$= \frac{\text{Rs } 8,25,000 \times 100}{110} = \text{Rs } 75,000$$

2. Increase in sales volume = (Actual sales-Sales revenue due to increased selling price — Budgeted sales)

= Rs 8,25,000 – Rs 75,000 – 5,00,000
= Rs 2,50,000

3. Budgeted P/V Ratio $= \frac{\text{Budgeted contribution}}{\text{Budgeted sales}} \times 100$

$$= \frac{\text{Rs } 5,00,000 - \text{Rs } 3,00,000 \times 100}{\text{Rs } 5,00,000}$$

= 40%

4. Increase in contribution due to higher sales volume = Rs 2,50,000 × 40% = Rs 1,00,000
5. Budgeted proportion of variable cost (on the sale of Rs 7,50,000)

$$= \frac{\text{Budgeted cost}}{\text{Budgeted sales}} \times \text{Actual sales volume}$$

$$= \frac{\text{Rs } 3,00,000}{\text{Rs } 5,00,000} \times \text{Rs. } 7,50,000$$

= Rs 4,50,000

Increase in variable cost

= (Actual variable cost of sales – Budgeted proportion of variable cost)
= Rs 5,75,000 – Rs 4,50,000 = Rs 1,25,000

A Perusal of the above mentioned factors clearly shows that the profit of M/s Vikas Ltd., has increased by Rs 1,75,000 due to increase in selling price (Rs 75,000) and contribution on increased volume (Rs. 1,00,000). At the same time the cost of the firm has also increased to the tune of Rs 1,75,000 (increase in variable cost Rs 1,25,000 and increase in fixed cost Rs. 50,000). Since the increase in profit equals to the increase in cost, therefore, the profit of the firm has remained the same as shown in the budget.

Example 45

Taurus Ltd. Prduces three products — A, B and C, from the same manufacturing facilities. The cost and other details of the three products are as follows :

	A	B	C
Selling price/unit (Rs)	200	160	100
Variable cost/unit (Rs)	120	120	40
Fixed expenses/month (Rs)			2,76,000
Maximum production per mouth (units)	5,000	8,000	6,000
Total hours available for the month 200 hours			
Maximum demand per month (units)	2,000	4,000	2,400

The processing hours cannot be increased beyond 200 hours per month.

You are required to:

(a) Compute the most profitable product-mix:

(b) Compute the overall break-even sales of the company for the month based on the mix calculated in (a) above.

Solution

M/s Taurus Limited

(a) Computation of Most Profitable Product Mix:

Products	*Number of units to be produced (Note I)*	*Contribution per unit* Rs.	*Total contribution* Rs.
A	2,000	80	1,60,000
B	1,600	40	64,000
C	2,400	60	1,44,000
	Total contribution:		3,68,000
	Less: Fixed expenses:		2,76,000
	Profit:		92,000

(b) Computation of Over all Break-even Sales

$$\text{Break-even sales} = \frac{\text{Fixed costs}}{\text{Total contribution}} \times \text{Total sales}$$

$$= \frac{\text{Rs } 2{,}76{,}000}{\text{Rs } 3{,}68{,}000} \times \text{Rs } 8{,}96{,}000$$

$$= \text{Rs } 6{,}72{,}000$$

Working Notes:

1. Statement showing units to be produced

	Products A	B	C
(i) Selling price per unit (Rs)	200	160	100
(ii) Variable cost per unit (Rs)	120	120	40
(iii) Contribution per unit (i) – (ii)	80	40	60
(iv) Maximum products per hour (units)	$\frac{5,000}{200}$ = 25	$\frac{8,000}{200}$ = 40	$\frac{6,000}{200}$ = 30
(v) Contribution per hour (Rs) (Maximum production per hour × Contribution per unit)	Rs 80 × 25 2,000	Rs 40 × 40 1,600	Rs 60 × 30 1,800
(vi) Ranking	I	III	II
(vii) Units to be produced	2,000	1,600	2,400
(viii) Time required for the units to be produced (hrs)	80	40	80

(2) Statement of Contribution

Products	*Units*	*Selling price per unit*	*Variable cost per unit*	*Sales revenue*	*Variable cost*	*Contribution*
(i)	*(ii)*	*(iii)*	*(iv)*	*(v)*	*(vi)*	*(vii)*
A	2,000	200	120	4,00,000	2,40,000	1,60,000
B	1,600	160	120	2,56,000	1,92,000	64,000
C	2,400	100	40	2,40,000	96,000	1,44,000
Total				8,96,000	5,28,000	3,68,000

Example 46

The budgeted income statement by product lines of Multiproducts Ltd. for 2001 is as follows :

	Product A	*Product B*	*Product C*
	Rs	Rs	Rs
Sales	2,00,000	5,00,000	3,00,000
Variable Expenses :			
Cost of goods sold	90,000	2,70,000	1,50,000
Selling	30,000	90,000	45,000
Fixed Expenses:			
Overhead	36,000	90,000	54,000
Administrative	16,000	40,000	24,000
Income before tax	28,000	10,000	27,000
Income tax @ 40%	11,200	4,000	10,800
Net income	16,800	6,000	16,200

All products are manufactured in the same facilities under common administrative control. Fixed expenses are allocated among the products in proportion of their budgeted sales volume:

(a) Compute the budgeted break-even point of the company as a whole, from the data provided.

(b) What would be the effect on Budgeted Income, if half of the budgeted sales volume of product B were shifted to product A and C in equal rupee amounts, so that the total budgeted sales in rupees remain the same.

(c) What would be the effect of the shift in the product mix suggested in (b) above on the budgeted break-even point of the whole company?

Solution

(a) Budgeted BEP for the company as a whole

$$\text{Composite PV ratio} = \frac{\text{Total contribution}}{\text{Total sales}} \times 100$$

$$= \frac{80{,}000 + 1{,}40{,}000 + 1{,}05{,}000}{10{,}00{,}000}$$

$$= \frac{3{,}25{,}000}{10{,}00{,}000} \times 100 = 32.5\%$$

$$\text{BEP for the company} = \frac{\text{Total fixed costs}}{\text{Composite PV ratio}}$$

$$= \frac{52{,}000 + 1{,}30{,}000 + 78{,}000}{32.5\%}$$

$$= \frac{2{,}60{,}000}{32.5} \times 100 = \text{Rs } 8{,}00{,}000$$

(b) Effect on Budgeted Income if half the sales of Product B are shifted equally to Products A and C.

	Product A	*Product B*	*Product C*
	Rs	Rs	Rs
Sales (i)	3,25,000	2,50,000	4,25,000
Variable Expenses			
Cost of goods sold	1,46,250	1,35,000	2,12,500
Selling	48,750	45,000	63,750
Fixed Expenses (Apportioned according to sales) :			
Overhead	58,500	45,000	76,500
Administrative	26,000	20,000	34,000
Total Cost (ii)	2,79,500	2,45,000	3,86,750
Income before tax (i) – (ii)	45,500	5,000	38,250
Income tax @ 40%	18,200	2,000	15,300
Net Income	27,300	3,000	22,950
Total Net Income			Rs 53,250

The original budgeted income is Rs 39,000. Hence, the income would increase by Rs 14,250 as a result of the proposed change.

(c) Break-even after shift in the product mix

$$\text{Composite PV Ratio} = \frac{\text{Total contribution}}{\text{Total sales}} \times 100$$

$$= \frac{1{,}30{,}000 + 70{,}000 + 1{,}48{,}750}{10{,}00{,}000} \times 100$$

$$= \frac{3{,}48{,}750}{10{,}00{,}000} \times 100 = 34.875\%$$

Break-even point of the company as a whole

$$= \frac{\text{Total fixed expenses}}{\text{Composite PV ratio}}$$

$$= \frac{2,60,000}{34.475\%}$$

= Rs 7,45,520

Thus, the break-even point will stand reduced to sales of Rs 7,45,520 from Rs 8,00,000 as a result of shift in the total production-mix.

Example 47

A company manufactures a single product with a capacity of 1,50,000 units per annum. The summarised profitability statement for the year is as under :

	Rs	Rs
Sales: 1,00,000 units @ Rs 15 per unit		15,00,000
cost of Sales:		
Direct Materials	3,00,00	
Direct Labour	2,00,000	
Production Overhead: Variable	60,000	
Fixed	3,00,000	
Administration Overheads (Fixed)	1,50,000	
Selling and Distribution Overheads: Variable	90,000	
Fixed	1,50,000	12,50,000
Profit		2,50,000

You are required to evaluate the following options:

(i) What will be the amount of sales arequired to earn a target profit of 25% on Sales, if the packing is improvied at a cost of Re. 1 per unit ?

(ii) There is an offer from a large retailer for purchasing 30,000 units per annum, subject to providing a packing with a different brand name at a cost of Rs 2 per unit. However, if this case there will be no selling and distribution expenses. Also this will not, in any way, affect the company's existing business. What will be the break-even price for this additional offer?

(iii) If an expenditure of Rs 3,00,000 is made on advertising, the sales would increase from the present level of 1,00,000 units to 1,20,000 units at a price of Rs 18 per unit. Will that expenditure be justified ?

(iv) If the selling price is reduced by Rs 2 per unit, there will be 100% capacity utilization. Will the reduction in selling price be justified ?

Solution

Working Notes :

(1) *Contribution per unit :*	Rs
Selling price per unit: (A)	15,00
Variable cost per unit:	
Direct materials (Rs 3,00,000/1,00,000 units)	3.00
Direct labour (Rs 2,00,000/1,00,000 units)	2.00
Variable production overheads (Rs. 60,000/1,00,000 units)	0.60

Variable selling and distribution overheads (Rs 90,000/1,00,000 units)	0.90
Total variable cost per unit: (B)	6.50
Contribution per unit: [(A) – (B)] (Rs15 – Rs 6.50)	8.50

(2) *Total fixed cost:*

	Rs
Production overheads	30,00,000
Administration overheads	1,50,000
Selling and distribution overheads	1,50,000
Total fixed cost	6,00,000

(i) Amount of sales required to earn a target profit of 25% on sales after improving the packing

	Rs
Present variable cost per unit (*Refer to working note 1)*	6.50
Improved packing cost per unit	1.00
Revised variable cost per unit	7.50

$$\text{P/V ratio} = \frac{\text{Contribution}}{\text{Sales}} \times 100 = \left\{\frac{\text{Rs } 15 - \text{Rs } 7.50}{\text{Rs } 15} \times 100\right\} = 50\%$$

Let x be the desired sales revenue to earn a target profit of 25% on sales: then the desired contribution would be: Total fixed cost + 25% × x

$$\text{Since P/V ratio} = \frac{\text{C}}{\text{S}} \times 100 = \frac{\text{Fixed Cost + Profit}}{x} \times 100$$

$$\therefore x = \frac{\text{Rs } 6{,}00{,}000 + 25\%\, x}{50\%} \quad \textit{(Refer to working note 2)}$$

$$\text{or } x \times 50\% = \text{Rs } 6{,}00{,}000 + 25\%\, x$$

$$\text{or } \left[\frac{x}{2} - \frac{x}{4}\right] = \text{Rs } 6{,}00{,}000$$

$$\text{or } x = \text{Rs } 24{,}00{,}000$$

Hence, the desired amount of sales required to earn a target profit of 25% on sales is Rs 24,00,000. On the sale of Rs 24,00,000, the desired contribution is 50% of sales *i.e.* Rs 12,00,000 and profit is 25% of sales *i.e.* Rs 6,00,000.

(ii) Evaluation of an offere of purchasing 30,000 units per annum (subject to providing a packing with a different brand name at a cost of Rs 2 per unit) from a large retailer. Determine also the break-even price for this additional offer.

	Rs
Present variable cost per unit	6.50
Less: Variable selling and distribution overheads per unit	0.90
	5.60
Add : Special packing cost per unit	2.00
Revised variable cost per unit	7.60

The break-even price per unit for this additional offer of 30,000 units would be Rs 7.60 per unit.

In other words the break-even price for this additional offer here means the price per unit at which 30,000 units offer can be accepted without earning any profit on it.

Note: The existing business will bear the impact of fixed cost. Fixed costs will not affect this additional offer of 30,000 units.

(iii) Justification of incurring advertisement expenses of Rs 3,00,000 for increasing the sale from 1,00,000 units to 1,20,000 units.

	Rs
New selling price per unit	18.00
Less: Variable cost per unit *(Refer to working note 1)*	6.50
Contribution per unit	11.50
Total contribution *(1,20,000 units × Rs 11.50)*	13,80,000
Less: Present fixed cost	(6,00,000)
Less: Additional expenditure on advertising	(3,00,000)
Profit	4,80,000

Justification: The amount of profit on the sale of 1,00,000 units was Rs 2,50,000 *(Refer to statement of the question)*. On increasing the sale of product units from 1,00,000 to 1,20,000 profit of the concern increased from Rs 2,50,000 to Rs 4,80,000 therefore, the expenditure advertisement is justifiable and the proposal under consideration is viable.

(iv) Justification of reduction in selling price to increase capacity utilisation to 100%

	Rs
Revised selling price per unit	13.00
Less: Variable cost per unit *(Refer to working note 1)*	6.50
Contribution per unit	6.50
Total contribution at 100% capacity utilization *(1.50,000 units x Rs 6.50)*	9,75,000
Less: Fixed cost	6,00,000
Profit	3,75,000

Justification: A reduction in selling price by Rs 2 per unit for 100% capacity utilization, increases the present profit of Rs 2,50,000 to Rs 3,75,000. Hence the reduction in selling price is justified.

Example 48

The PTO Division of XYZ manufacturing company produces power take-off units for the farm equipment business. The PTO Division headquartered in Mumbai has a newly renovated, automated plant in Mumbai and an older, less-automated plant in Pune. Both plants produce the same power take-off units for farm tractors that are sold to most domestic and foreign tractor manufacturers.

The PTO Division expects to produce and sell 1,92.000 power take-off units during the coming year. The division production manager has the following data available regarding the unit costs, unit prices and production capacities for the two plants:

- All fixed costs are based on a normal year of 240 working days. When the number of working days exceed 240, variable manufacturing costs increase by Rs 3 per unit in Mumbai and Rs 8 per unit in Pune. Capacity for each plant is 300 working days.
- XYZ manufacturing Co. charges each of its plants a per unit fee for administrative services such

as payroll, general accounting and purchasing, because management considers these services to be a function of work performed at the plants. For each of the plants at Mumbai and Pune. the fee is Rs 6.50 and represents the variable portion of general and administrative expense.

Wishing to maximize the higher unit profit at Pune, the PTO's production manager has decided to manufacture 96,000 units at each plant. This production plan results in Pune's operating at capacity and Mumbai's operating at its normal volume. XYZ's Corporate Controller is not happy with this plan, because he does not believe it represents optimal usage of PTO's plants.

	Mumbai	Pune
Selling price	Rs 150.00	Rs 150.00
Variable manufacturing cost	72.00	88.00
Fixed manufacturing cost	30.00	15.00
Commission (5%)	7.50	7.50
General & Administrative expenses	25.50	21.00
Total unit cost	135.00	131.50
Unit profit	Rs 15.00	Rs 18.50
Production rate per day	400 units	320 units

Required:

(i) Determine the annual break-even units for each of the PTO's plants.

(ii) Determine the operating income that would result from the division production manager's plan to produce 96,000 units at each plant.

(iii) Determine the optimal production plan to produce the 1,92,000 units at PTO's plants in Mumbai and Pune and determine the resulting operating income for the PTO Division.

Solution

Working Note:

Total fixed cost based on a normal year of 240 working days

	Mumbai Plant	*Pune Plant*
Production rate per day (units)	400	320
No. of days	240	240
Total production (units) in 240 days	96,000 (400 units × 240 days)	76,800 (320 units × 240 days)
Fixed manufacturing cost per unit (Rs)	30	15
Total fixed manufacturing cost based on a normal year of 240 working days (Rs): (A)	28,80,000 (96,000 units × Rs 30)	11,52,000 (76,800 units × Rs 15)
Fixed General & Administrative expenses (Rs): (B)	18,24,000 (96,000 units × 19)	11,13,600 (76,800 × Rs 14.50)
Total fixed cost (Rs): {(A) + (B)}	47,04,000	22,65,600

(i) Annual Break-even units for each of the P.T.O's plants

	Mumbai Plant	*Pune Plant*
Selling price p.u. (Rs): (A)	150.00	150.00
Total variable cost:		
Variable manufacturing cost at normal volume (p.u.) (Rs)	72.00	88.00
Commission (p.u.) (Rs)	7.50	7.50

(*Contd...*)

Variable General & Administrative expenses (p.u.): (Rs)	6.50	6.50
Total variable cost (p.u.) (Rs): (B)	86.00	102.00
Contribution (p.u.) (Rs): {(A) – (B)}	64.00	48.00
Annual-break-even (units)	73,500	47,200
Fixed cost/Contribution (p.u.)	(Rs 47,04,000/Rs 64)	(Rs 22,65,600/Rs 48)
(Refer to working note)		

(ii) Operating Income Statement
(as a result of Divisional Production Manager's plan to produce 96,000 units at each plant)

	Mumbai Plant	*Pune Plant*
Normal capacity (units)	96,000	76,800
	(400 units × 240 days)	(320 units × 240 days)
Full capacity (units)	1,20,000	96,000
	(400 units × 300 days)	(320 units × 300 days)
Sales revenue (Rs): (A)	1,44,00,000	1,44,00,000
	(96,000 units × Rs 150)	(96,000 units × Rs 150)
Variable costs:		
Variable manufacturing cost (Rs)	69,12,000	92,16,000
	(96,000 units × Rs 72)	(96,000 units × (Rs 88 + Rs 8)
Commission (Rs)	7,20,000	7,20,000
	(96,000 units × Rs 7.50)	(96,000 units × Rs. 7.50)
Variable general & administrative expenses (Rs)	6,24,000	6,24,000
	(96,000 units × Rs 6.50)	(96,000 units × Rs 6.50)
Total variable cost (Rs): (B)	82,56,000	1,05,60,000
Contribution margin (Rs): {(A) – (B)}	61,44,000	38,40,000
Less: Fixed cost (Rs)	47,04,000	22,65,600
(*Refer to working note 3*)		
Operating Income (Rs)	14,40,000	15,74,400

Total Operating income of both the plants= Rs 14,40,000 + Rs 15,74,400
= Rs 30,14,400

Note: The question does not clarify that whether the variable cost will increase in respect of additional units only when the working days exceeds 240 days or against all the units. Operating income in the above statement of Pune plant, has been arrived at by assuming an increase in variable cost by Rs 8 on all the units produced in the plant. An alternative operating income figure of Pune plant can also be obtained by considering increase in varaible cost on only 19,200 units. In the alternative case the operating income of Pune plant will come to Rs 21,88,800 (Rs 15,74,400 + 76,800 units × Rs 8)

	Mumbai Plant	*Pune Plant*
Optimal production plan		
Capacity of production (units)	1,20,000*	72,000
Sales revenue (Rs): (A)	1,80,00,000	1,08,00,000
	(1,20,000 units × Rs 150)	(72,000 units × Rs 150)
Variable cost:		
Variable manufacturing cost (Rs)	90,00,000	63,36,000
	(1,20,000 units × Rs 72 + Rs 3)	(72,000 units × Rs 88)
Commission	9,00,000	5,40,000
	(1,20,000 units × Rs 7.50)	(72,000 units × Rs 7.50)

(Contd...)

Variable general & administrative expenses (Rs)	7,80,000	4,68,000
	(1,20,000 units × Rs 6.50)	(72,000 units × Rs 6.50)
Total variable cost (Rs): (B)	1,06,80,000	73,44,000
Contribution margin (Rs): {(A) – (B)}	73,20,000	34,56,000
Less: Fixed cost (Refer to working note)	47,04,000	22,65,600
Operating Income	26,16,000	11,90,400
Total Operating Income for PTO's division = Rs 38,06,400		

*Mumbai plant is utilized at full capacity level because the variable cost of manufacturing is lower vis-a-vis Pune plant.

Note: The operating income of the Mumbai plant in the above statement has been arrived at by assuming increase in variable cost by Rs 3 on all the units produced in the plant. An alternative operating income figure of the Mumbai plant can also be obtained by considering increase in variable cost on only 24,000 units (*i.e.* in respect of additional units when working days exceeds 240 days). In the alternative case the operating income of Mumbai plant will come to Rs 29,04,000 (Rs 26,16.000 + 96,000 units × Rs 3).

THEORY QUESTIONS

1. What do you mean by marginal costing? Discuss its usefulness and limitations.
2. Write a lucid note on marginal costing indicating its effect on profit computations.
3. What are the most important areas of management decisions opened up by the application of the margin (direct) costing method? Answer briefly and to the point.
4. Marginal costs reveal the lowest price at which a product can be sold during a trade depression, but they also reveal to management the most profitable lines during the period of intense trade activity. Explain with examples, the second part of this statement.
5. Discuss the following terms in relation to marginal costing.
   (a) Key factor, (b) P/V ratio, and (c) Margin of safety.
6. (a) What do you understand by the term "margin of safety" with reference to volume of production?
   (b) How do the following reflect on a break-even volume and on a P/V ratio; (i) increase in total fixed cost (ii) increase in total physical sales; (iii) decrease in variable costs per unit.
7. What do you understand by the term "break-even analysis"? Enumerate its uses.
8. How do income statements prepared under the absorption costing and marginal costing concepts differ ?
9. Compared with absorption costing when will variable costing report lower profits, higher profits, same profits?
10. In what ways is variable costing better adapted to managerial use in profit planning, decision-making and control?
11. Why do the supporters of marginal costing state that fixed costs are not to be included in inventories?
12. Discuss the uses of CVP analysis and its significance to management.
13. "In classifying a particular cost as fixed or variable, the volume or activity level is extremely important." Discuss and illustrate this statement.
14. "The contribution approach is the foundation of CVP logic and related techniques." Discuss.
15. Discuss the role of contribution in marginal costing in decisions relating to fixation of selling price.
16. State with reasons whether the following propositions are correct.
    (a) In an undertaking with a high fixed cost, break-even point can be attained at a lower level of; activity.
    (b) Profit is represented by the product of the margin of safety and the P/V ratio.
    (c) In relation to normal sales, a low margin of safety along with a high P/V ratio is generally an indication of high fixed costs.
17. Distinguish between "marginal costing" and "absorption costing".
18. "The effect of a price reduction is always to reduce the P/V ratio, to raise the break-even point, and to shorten margin of safety." Explain with a suitable illustration.
19. Define break-even point. How can the break-even point be computed?

20. How is a break-even chart prepared? What information does the break-even chart give?
21. What are the basic assumptions in cost-volume-profit analysis under (a) absorption costing, and (b) variable costing?
22. Describe how a P/V chart is drawn. How does the P/V chart differ from a break-even chart?
23. For product-mix decisions, what criteria can be used to select products that will maximise net income?
24. Break-even analysis assumes that variable costs and revenues are linear and that fixed costs are fixed. Briefly explain why these assumptions may not be realistic.
25. Can there be two break-even points. Show with the help of a graph
26. Distinguish between contribution and profit.

PROBLEMS

1. The following data has been taken from the records of a company. You are required to find out net profit using the technique of marginal costing.

		Rs
Sales		75,000
Variable costs:		
Direct materials	Rs 22,500	
Direct wages	12,500	
Factory overheads	5,250	
Administration, selling and distribution overheads	8,000	
	48,250	
Fixed costs:		
Factory overheads	2,000	
Administrative and other overheads	3,350	
	5,350	
Total cost		53,600
Profit		21,400

2. Using the information given below, calculate the net income for the months of October, November and December and the value of finished goods on hand at the end of period using absorption costing and marginal costing. Also, comment on the differences in profits under these two methods.

	October	November	December
Production	45,000	36,000	45,000
Sales	36,000	42,000	48,000
Opening stock	-	9,000	3,000
Closing stock	9,000	3,000	

Additional information:

Selling price per unit	Rs 50
Variable cost per unit	Rs 30
Fixed cost per unit	Rs 10
Total fixed costs per month	Rs 3,90,000
Normal output per month	39,000 units

Ans. Profit under absorption costing, October Rs 4,20.000, November Rs 3,90,000. December Rs 5,40,000. Profit under marginal costing, October Rs 3,30,000, November Rs 4,50,000. December Rs 5,70,000. Difference in profits of different months is due to differences in values of closing stocks which are determined differently under both the methods.

3. The following data were taken from the cost and production records of a company at the end of an accounting period:

		Rs
Sales revenue		1,28,000
Cost of goods manufactured:		
Fixed	32,000	
Variable	48,000	80.000
Selling and administrative expenses:		
Fixed	20,000	
Variable	0	20,000
Opening inventory of finished goods		NIL
Normal and actual production		10,000 units
Closing inventory of finished goods		2,000 units

Calculate the net income for the period and the value of the finished goods on hand at the end of the period using (a) absorption costing, and (b) marginal costing.

Ans. Net profit. Absorption costing Rs 44,000. Variable costing Rs 37,600, Closing stock absorption costing Rs 16,000, Variable costing Rs 9,600.

4. A company produces a single product that sells for Rs 150 per unit. Standard capacity is 1,00,000 units per year. On Jan. 1, 2002 there was no inventory of finished goods, production and sales for the year were as follows:

	Number of units	
	Produced	*Sold*
First	2,00,000	1,00,000
Second	3,00,000	2.50,000
Third	2.00,000	2,50,000
Fourth	3.00.000	4,00,000
	10,00,000	10,00,000

Manufacturing costs and selling and administrative expenses were as follows:

	Fixed	*Variable (per unit)*
Raw material	—	27
Direct labour	—	25
Indirect manufacturing cost	Rs 2,00,000	18
Selling and administrative expenses	80,000	20
	Rs 2,80,000	90

Prepre: (a) Quarterly income statements under absorption costing and variable costing; (b) account for the difference between the net incomes reported under each concept.

5. The directors of a company have been studying the following condensed profit reports for the years 2001 and 2002.

Data	2001	2002
Sales (Rs)	3,00,000	4,50,000
Profit (or loss) (Rs)	55,000	35,000

The directors are perturbed over the trend, for a 50% increase in sales resulted in a decrease in profit in 2002. The chief cost accountant explains that unabsoibed overhead was charged to 2002 operations. His statement was based on the following data:

Data	*2001*	*2002*
Sales (units)	20,000	30,000
Production (units)	30,000	20,000
Sales price per unit (Rs)	15	15
Variable cost per unit (Rs)	5	5
Fixed faciory overhead (Rs)	1,80,000	1,80,000

Fixed factory overhead per unit (standard)	6	6
Fixed selling and administrative expenses	25,000	25,000

Prepare: (a) income statement by the conventional method to which the chief cost accountant referred; (b) income statements by variable costing method.

Ans. Net profit. Absorption costing 2001, Rs 55.000; 2002, Rs 35000. Variable costing 2001, Rs 5,000 loss 2002 Rs 95,000.

6. From the following data calculate:
   (i) P/V ratio
   (ii) Profit when sales are Rs 20,000
   (iii) New break-even point if selling price is reduced by 20%

Fixed expenses	Rs 4,000
Break-even point	Rs 10,000

Ans. P/V ratio 40%; Profit Rs 4,000; BEP Rs 16,000.

7. Calculate from the following data (i) the value of output at which the business breaks-even and (ii) the percentage capacity at which it breaks-even:

	Budget for year 2003 based on 100% capacity (Rs)	*Estimated shut-down expenditure (Rs)*
Direct wages	2,09,964	
Direct materials	2,44.552	
Works expenses	1,81.820	93,528
Selling and distribution expenses	61,188	40,188
Administration expenses	30,000	20,508
Net sales	8,40,000	

Ans. (i) BHP sales Rs 4,85,746
(ii) 57.83%
shutdown expenditures should be treated as fixed costs.

8. The following figures are available from the records of Venus Enterprises as at 31 st March:

	2001 Rs lakhs	2002 Rs lakhs
Sales	150	200
Profit	30	50

Calculate:
(a) The P/V ratio and total fixed expenses;
(b) The break-even level of sales:
(c) Sales required to earn a profit of Rs 90 lakhs;
(d) Profit or loss that would arise if the sales were Rs 280 lakhs.

Ans. (a) 40% 130 lakhs (b) Rs 75 lakhs
(c) Rs 300 lakhs (d) Rs 82 lakhs

9. Two manufacturing companies which have the following operating details decide to merge.

	Company No. I	*Company No. 2*
Capacity utilization %	90	60
Sales (Rs lakhs)	540	300
Variable cost (Rs lakhs)	396	225
Fixed costs (Rs lakhs)	80	50

Assuming that the proposal is implemented, calculate:
(i) Break-even sales of the merged plant and the capacity utilization at that stage.
(ii) Profitability of the merged plant at 80% capacity utilization.
(iii) Sales turn over of the merged plant to earn a profit of Rs 75 lakhs.

(iv) When the merged plant is working at a capacity to earn a profit of Rs 75 lakhs what percentage increase in selling price is required to sustain an increase of 5% of fixed overheads.

Ans. (i) 25.909% P/V ratio. Rs 501.67 lakhs, 45.6% (ii) Rs 98 lakhs (iii) Rs 791.23 lakhs (iv) 0.821%.

10. Company A and Company B, both under the same management, make and sell the same type of product Their budgeted profit and loss accounts for January—June 2002 are as under:

	Company A		*Company B*	
	Rs.	Rs.	Rs.	Rs.
Sales		3,00,000		3,00,000
Less: Variable cost	2,40,000		2,00,000	
Fixed costs	30,000	2,70,000	70,000	2,70,000
		30,000		30,000

You arc required to

(i) Calculate the break-even point for each company.

(ii) Calculate the sales volume at which each of the two companies will make a profit of Rs 10,000

(iii) Assess how their profitability will change with decrease or increase in volume.

Ans: (i) A Rs 1,50,000 B Rs 2,10,000 (ii) A Rs 2,00,000 B Rs 2,40,000

11. The following figures relate to a company manufacturing a varied range of products:

	Total cost	*Total sales*
Year ending 31st Dec., 2001	19,83,600	22,23,000
Year ending 31st Dec., 2002	21,43,200	24,51,000

Assuming stability in prices, with variable costs carefully controlled to reflect predetermined relationships, and an unvarying figure for fixed costs, calculate:

(a) The profit/volume ratio, to reflect the rates of growth for profit and sales

(b) Fixed cost

(c) Fixed cost % to sales

(d) Break-even point

(e) Margin of safety for the year 2001 and the year 2002.

Ans: (a) 30% (b) Rs 4,27,500

(c) 2001,19.23%, 2002, 17.44% (d) Rs 14,25,000

(e) 2001, Rs 7,98,000, 2002, Rs 10,26,000

12. A company has a P/V ratio of 40 per cent. By what percentage must sales be increased to offset—

(i) 10 per cent reduction in selling price, and

(ii) 20 per cent reduction in selling price?

Ans: *Hint*

Let the present units sold be 100 @ Re 1 per unit	Rs
Present total sales	100
Present variable cost	60
Present contribution	40
(P/V ratio 40%)	
(i) If selling price is reduced by 10%	
Selling price per unit	0.90
Variable cost per unit	0.60
Contribution per unit	0.30

In order to maintain the same contribution, *viz* Rs 40 the volume of sales should be:

$$\frac{\text{Present total contribution}}{\text{New contribution per unit}} \times \text{New selling price per unit}$$

$$\frac{40}{30} \times 90 = 120 \text{ or } \frac{1200}{.90} \text{ units or } 133\frac{1}{3} \text{ units}$$

Thus, the volume of sales will have to be increased by 33% from the existing level if the selling price is reduced by 10%.

(ii) If the selling price is reduced by 20%

	Re
Selling price per unit	0.80
Variable cost per unit	0.60
Contribution per unit	0.20

For maintaining the same contribution the volume of sales should be:

$$\frac{40}{0.20} \times 0.80 = \text{Rs } 160 \text{ or } \frac{160}{.80} = 200 \text{ units}$$

Thus, the volume of sale will have to be increased by 100% over the existing, if the selling price is reduced by 20%.

13. Two competing companies ABC Ltd. and XYZ Ltd. produce and sell in the same type of product in the same market. For the year ending March 2006, their forecasted profit and loss accounts arc as follows:

		ABC Ltd.		*XYZ Ltd.*
Sales		Rs 2,50,000		Rs 2,50,000
Less: Variable costs of sales	Rs 2,00,000		1,50,000	
Fixed costs	25,000	2,25,000	75,000	2,25,000
Forecasted net profit before tax		25,000		25,000

You are required to compute:

1. P/V ratio
2. Break-even sales volume

You are also required to state which company is likely to earn greater profits in conditions of:

(a) low demand, and

(b) high demand.

Ans. P/V Ratio ABC Ltd. 20%, XYZ Ltd. 40%; Break-even sales volume ABC Ltd. Rs 125000, XYZ Ltd, Rs 187500. In case of low demand, profit situation for ABC Ltd. will be better as it has a larger safety margin and lower amount of fixed costs. In case of high demand, XYZ will do better since additional sales will give profit at 40% (P/V ratio) whereas in case of ABC Ltd. additional sales will give profit at 20% (P/V ratio).

14. The budgeted sales of three products are as follows :

	Product		
	X	*Y*	*Z*
Budgeted sales in units	10,000	15.000	20,000
Budgeted selling price per unit	4	4	4
Budgeted variable cost per unit	2.5	3	
Budgeted fixed expenses	12,000	9,000	7,500

From the information you are required to compute the following for each product:

(a) The budgeted profit

(b) The budgeted break-even sales

(c) The budgeted margin of safety in terms of sales value.

Ans.

	X	*Y*	*Z*
Profit	3,000	6,000	2,500
Break-even sales	Rs 32,000	36,000	60,000
Margin of safety	Rs 8,000	24,000	20,000

15. From the following data, calculate break-even point expressed in terms of units and also the new B.E.P. If selling price is reduced by 10%.

Fixed expenses:

Depreciation	Rs 1,00,000
Salaries	Rs 1,00,000

Variable expenses:

Materials	Rs 3 per unit
Labour	Rs 2 per unit
Selling price	Rs 10 per unit

Ans. (i) 40,000 units (ii) 50,000 units

16. From the following information relating to Quick Standards Ltd., you are required to find out (a) Contribution, (b) Break-even point in units, (c) Margin of safety, (d) Profit.

Total fixed costs	Rs 4,500
Total variable costs	7,500
Total sales	15,000
Units sold	5,000 (Units)

Also calculate the volume of sales to cam profit of Rs 6,000.

Ans. (a) Rs 75,000 (b) 3,000 units
(c) Rs 6,000, 40% (d) Rs 3,000

17. S. Ltd. furnishes you the following information relating to the half year ended 30th June. 2001 : Fixed expenses Rs 45,000 Sales value 1,50,000 Profit 30,000 During the second half of the year, the company has projected a loss of Rs 10,000.

Calculate:

(i) The break-even point and margin of safety for six months ending 30th June, 2001
(ii) Expected sales volume for second half of the year assuming that the P/V ratio and fixed expenses remain constant in the second half year also.
(iii) The break-even point and margin of safety for the whole year 2001.

Ans. (i) BEP Rs 90,000, margin of safety Rs 60000.
(ii) Sales Rs 70,000
(iii) BEPRs 1,80,000
Margin of safety Rs 40,000

18. S.M. Ltd. produces two products and the Budget for 60% level of activity for the year 2001-2002 gives the following information:

	Product A	*Product B*
	Rs	Rs
Raw material cost per unit	7.50	3.50
Direct labour cost per unit	4.00	3.00
Variable overheads per unit	2.00	1.50
Fixed overheads per unit	6.00	4.50
Selling price per unit	20.00	15.00
Production and sales	4,000 units	6,000 units

The Managing Director not being satisfied with the projected results as stated above, referred the budget to the marketing director for improvement of the performance. The marketing director proposed that the sales quantities of Product A and B could each be increased by 50% provided the selling prices were reduced by 5% in the case of Product A and 10% in the case of Product B. The price reduction should be made applicable to the entire quantity of sales of each of the two products.

Required: (i) Present the overall profitability under the original budget and the revised budget after taking the increased sales into consideration. (ii) Find the over all break-even sales under the original budget and the revised budget.

19. Mansarovar Auto products Produces and sells two small components P and Q used in automobiles. The details regarding unit income and costs of these components arc as under :

	Products	
	P	*Q*
Selling price	Rs 12	Rs 20
Direct materials	2	4
Direct labour	2	1
Variable factory overhead	2	4
Fixed factory overhead	2	4
Total cost of goods sold	8	13
Gross profit per unit	4	7

Factory overheads, both fixed and variable, have been accounted for on a machine hour basis. As far as can be determined, the sales outlook is such that the plant could operate at full capacity on either or both products. Both P and Q are processed through the same cost centres. Selling costs are all fixed. Which product should be preferred? Give a brief explanation in support of your answer.

20. Delhi Equipments Ltd., manufactures four components, the cost particulars of which are given below:

Components	A	B	C	D
Elements of cost:				
Direct material	Rs 80	100	100	120
Direct labour	20	25	25	30
Variable overhead	10	12	15	10
Fixed overhead	15	23	20	20
	125	160	160	180
Output per machine hour (units)	4	2	3	3

The key factor is shortage of machine capacity.

You are required to advise management as to whether they should continue to produce all or some of the components (which are used in its main product) or they should buy them from a supplier who has quoted the following prices:

A = Rs 115; B = Rs 175; C = Rs 135; D = Rs 185.

Ans. Hint:

Statement of Profitability

	Components			
	A	*B*	*C*	*D*
Direct material	Rs 80	Rs 100	Rs 100	Rs 120
Direct labour	20	25	25	30
Variable overhead	10	12	15	10
Marginal cost per unit	110	137	140	160
Purchase price per unit	115	175	135	185
Excess of purchase price				
Over marginal cost	5	38	—	25
Excess of marginal cost over purchase price	—	—	5	—
Decline in profitability per machine hour				
if purchase is made from outside	5 × 4	38 × 2	—	25 × 3
Increase in profitability per machine	= 20	= 76		= 75
hour if purchase is made from outside			– 5 × 3 = 15	

The above analysis shows:

(i) Component C should be purchased from outside whether there is a key factor or not since its marginal cost is more than its purchase price. Purchasing from outside will push up the profitability by Rs 15 per machine hour.

(ii) Continue the production of components A, B and D is case shortage of machine capacity is not the key factor.

(iii) In case shortage of machine capacity is the key factor as given in the question, the management must decide about the ranking of the three components. The above analysis shows that ranking should be in the order of A, D and B.

This is because in case of A, if it is purchased from outside, the loss of profitability will be only Rs 20 per machine hour, while in case of D and B it will be Rs 75 and Rs 76 per machine hour respectively.

21. From, the following-data, which product would you recommend for manufacture in the factory?

Per unit of	*Product A*	*Product B*
Standard manufacturing time	2 hours	3 hours
Direct materials (Rs)	50	30
Direct labour @ Rs 10 per hour	20	30
Variable over head @ Rs 6 per hour	12	18
Selling price	200	240

Total machine hours available in the factory are 60,000.

Ans. Product A

22. Calculate the effect on profit of a proposed change in "Sales Mix" from the following data:

Existing sales mix	*M*	*N*	*0*	*P*	*Total*
Sales (in Rs)	80,000	1,00,000	40,000	20,000	2,40,000
Variable cost (in Rs)	48,000	68,000	32,000	8,000	1,56,000
Fixed cost (in Rs)	—	—	—	—	58,800
Proposed sales mix	Rs 60,000	88,000	80,000	12,000	2,40,000

Ans. Deline in profit Rs. 8640.

23. (a) The following particulars are extracted from the records of a company:

	Product A	*Product B*
Sales (per unit)	Rs 100	Rs 120
Consumption of material	2 kg	3 kg
Material cost	Rs 10	Rs 15
Direct wages cost	15	10
Direct expenses	5	6
Machine hours used	3	2
Overhead expenses:		
Fixed	5	10
Variable	15	20

Direct wage per hour is Rs 5. Comment on the profitability of each product (both use the same raw material) when (i) Total sales potential in units is limited; (ii) Total sales potential in value is limited; Raw material is in short supply; and (iv) Production capacity (in terms of machine hours) is the limit factor.

(b) Assuming raw material as the key factor, availability of which is 10,000 kg and maximum potential of each product being 3,500 units, find out the product mix which will yield the maximum profit.

Ans. *Hint:*

	Per unit of	
	A	*B*
Sales	Rs 100	Rs 120
Direct material	10	15
Direct wages	15	10
Direct expenses	5	6
Variable overhead	15	20
Marginal cost	45	51
Contribution per unit	55	69
P/V ratio	55%	57.5%
Contribution per kg of material	27.5	23
Contribution per machine hour	18.3	34.5

(i) In case total sales potential in units is a limiting factor, B is more profitable as it is making a larger contribution per unit as compared to A.

(ii) In case total sales potential in value is a limiting factor, still B is more profitable since its P/V ratio is higher than that of A.

(iii) In case raw material is in short supply, A is more profitable as its contribution per kg of material is higher than that of Product B.

(iv) In case production capacity is limited, B is more profitable since it gives higher contribution per machine hour than A.

Note: Best situation is obtained when contribution per unit of key factor is the maximum.

(b) In case raw material is the key factor, A is more profitable to produce as its contribution per kg of material is higher than that of B. If 3,500 units of A are manufactured, total material consumption will be 7,000 kg (*i.e.* 3,500 x 2 kg). The balance of 3,000 kg of material can be used to manufacture 1,000 units (3,000 ÷ 3) of B. The total profit by this product mix will be as follows:

Contribution:		
Product A 3,500 units @ Rs 55 each	Rs 1,92,500	
Product B 1,000 units @ Rs 69 each	69,000	
Total Contribution:		2,61,500
Total fixed costs:		
Product A 5 × 3,500	= Rs 17,500	
Product B 10 × 3,500	= 35,000	52,500
Total profit		2,09,000

24. A, B and C are three similar plants under the same management who want them to merge for better operation. The details are as under:

Plant	A	B	C
Capacity operated	100%	70%	
	Rs (in lakhs)	Rs (in lakhs)	Rs (in lakhs)
Turnover	300	280	150
Variable cost	200	210	75
Fixed cost	70	50	62

Find out:

(i) The capacity of the merged plant for break even.

(ii) The profit at 75% capacity of the merged plant.

(iii) The turnover, from the merged plant to give a profit of Rs 28 lakhs.

Ans. (i) 52%

(ii) Profit Rs 80.5 (lakhs)

(iii) Rs 600 lakhs.

25. Sunita Manufacturing Company produces chairs. An analysis of their accounting reveals:

Fixed cost	Rs 50,000 for the year
Variable cost	Rs 20 per chair
Capacity	2,000 chairs per year
Selling price	Rs 70 per chair

(i) Find the break-even point

(ii) Find the number of chairs to be sold to get a profit of Rs 30,000.

(iii) What will be the answer for (i) and (ii) if selling price changes to Rs 60 per chair?

(iv) If the company can manufacture 600 chairs more per year with an additional fixed cost of Rs 2,000, what should be the selling price to maintain the profit per chair as at (ii) above?

26. SV Ltd., a multi-product company furnishes you the following data relating to the year 2006 :

	First half of the year	*Second half of the year*
	Rs	Rs
Sales	45,000	50,000
Total Cost	40,000	43,000

Assuming that there is no change in prices and variable cost and that the fixed expenses are incurred equally in the two half year periods, calculate for the year 2006:

(i) The P/V ratio
(ii) Fixed expenses
(iii) Break-even sales
(iv) Percentage of margin of safety

Ans. (i) 40%
(ii) 26,000
(iii) 65,000
(iv) 31.58%.

CHAPTER 6

Differential Cost Analysis for Managerial Decisions

DECISION-MAKING

Decision-making is the process of evaluating two or more alternatives leading to a final choice, popularly known as Alternative Choices Decisions. Decision-making is closely associated with planning for the future and is directed towards a specific objective or goal.

DIFFERENTIAL ANALYSIS

Differential analysis may be defined as the use of relevant costs and relevant revenues in making-decisions. Relevant costs and benefits are very important in evaluating alternatives, in ascertaining the effect of various alternatives on profit and selecting the alternative with the greatest benefit. The relevant costs and revenues are the differences between the alternatives under consideration. The amount of such differenes are called differentials and the accounting analysis concerned with the effect of alternatives on revenues and costs is called differential analysis. Relevant revenues and relevant costs are also known as differential revenues and differential costs. Differential revenue is the amount of increase or decrease in revenue expected from a particular course of action as compared with an alternative. Differential analysis provides a decision role to managers in decision-making which is: the alternative that gives the greatest incremental profit should be selected. Incremental profit is the difference between the relevant revenues and relevant costs of each alternative.

In case, decision affects both revenue and costs, management must estimate the changes in each to estimate the change in profit. In many decisions, only costs will change. In this case, the most beneficial (profitable) decision will be the one with the lowest cost because the lowest cost alternative will give the highest profit, provided all other factors and situations remain constant.

RELEVANT COSTS

Whatever alternatives are evaluated, the decision-maker has to decide which costs are relevant. Relevant costs are those that are pertinent, and bear upon the decision to be made. Relevant costs are the costs that will change as a result of the decision. Relevant costs are also known as decision-making costs. The relevant costs vary with the type of decision. However, the following are the common characteristics of relevant costs:

1. Relevant costs are expected future costs
2. They differ between different decision alternatives.

Expected future costs imply that the costs are expected to occur during the time period covered by the decision. For example, new product will need the incurrence of direct material, direct labour and other costs. Relevant costs also differ between decision alternatives. For example, a graduate may choose between advanced education and immediate employment. The costs that are relevant in this decision and which differ between the two decisions are the costs of books, fees, etc., because these costs will not be incurred if the graduate takes up employment. However, irrelevant costs are costs of accommodation clothes, etc. which will have to be incurred under both the decisions.

Relevant costs arc also known as differential costs. Differential cost is the difference in the total costs between alternative choices. It is the difference in total costs between two volumes. When a decision results in an increased cost, the differential cost may be referred to as an incremental cost. The incremental cost includes the change in fixed component as well as the variable component. Assume that a company has physical facilities to manufacture 20,000 units of a product; production beyond that point would require the installation of additional equipment, that is, fixed costs as well as variable costs will have to be incurred if management desires to produce more than 20,000 units.

TYPES OF CHOICES DECISIONS

Most management decisions may be referred to as alternative choice decisions. Alternative choice decisions cover situations with two or more alternative courses of action from whch the manager (decision-maker) must select the best alternative. A decision involving more than two alternatives is called multiple alternative choice decision. Some examples of alternative choice decisions are: make or buy own or lease, retain or replace, repair or renovate, now or later, change versus status quo, slower or faster, export versus local sales, shutdown or continue, expand or contract, change the produce-mix take or refuse orders, place special orders, select sales territories, replace present equipment with new machinery, sell at split-up point or process further, etc.

Some of the above alternative choices decisions and the information relevant to the decisions are discussed below.

MAKE OR BUY

Make or buy decisions arise when a company with unused production capacity consider the **following** alternatives:

(a) To buy certain raw materials or subassemblies from outside suppliers.

(b) To use available capacity to produce the items within the company.

A make or buy decision is basically one of determining which alternative is economically most desirable and most effectively utilises the firm's resources. These decisions can effect the firm's production methods and capacities, available working capital, cost of borrowing funds, and competitive position Costs that will be incurred under both alternatives are not relevant to the analysis. The firm should make an analysis of the cost, quality and quantity considerations of the individual make or buy decisions. Differential cost analysis is especially useful if the company has idle capacity and idle workers that can be used to make the tools or parts. Other potential use of available capacity should also be considered and qualitative factors must be evaluated in the decision process. These considerations include price stability from suppliers, reliability of delivery and quality of the material or component involved. Qualitative factors are not included in differential cost analyses, but they should be used to test the reasonableness of any decision based purely on quantitative cost studies.

For example, assume that a company can make a part that it has been purchasing at a unit cost of Rs 30. The company has been operating at 75% of normal capacities and in the foreseeable future no use for the excess capacity is contemplated except for the possible production of the part. Fixed manufacturing cost amounts to Rs 17,00,000 a year whether the plant operates at 75% or 100% of capacity. The cost to manufacture 50,000 units of the part that will be needed has been estimated as follows:

	Units cost	*Total cost*
		Rs
Direct materials	12.5	6,25,000
Direct labour	8.0	4,00,000
Variable manufacturing overhead	5.0	2,50,000
Total incremental cost	25.5	12,75,000
Cost to purchase part	30.0	15,00,000
Net advantage in parts production	4.5	2,25,000

In the above analysis the fixed manufacturing overhead has not been considered because it has to be incurred under both alternatives. Logically, the costs that will be increased or decreased as a result of making the part should be considered. In some cases, both the variable and fixed costs will be affected.

Add or Drop Products

The decision to eliminate an unprofitable product is a special case of product profitability evaluation. To evaluate the financial consequences of eliminating a product, it is necessary to concentrate on the differential or incremental profit effect of the decision. An important factor in the decision to add or drop a product is whether it will increase or decrease the future income of the business. Appropriate cost and profit measures must be developed for each alternative.

Assume a company is considering dropping product *B* from its line because accounting statements show that product *B* is being sold at a loss.

	Product A	*Product B*	*Product C*	*Total*
	Rs	Rs	Rs	Rs
Sales revenue	50,000	7,500	12,500	70,000
Cost of sales:				
Direct material	7,500	1,000	1,500	10,000
Direct labour	15,000	2,000	2,500	19,500
Indirect manufacturing cost (50% of direct labour)	7,500	1,000	1,250	9,750
	30,000	4,000	5,250	39,250
Gross margin on sales	20,000	3,500	7,250	30,750
Selling and administrative expenses (allocation on arbitrary basis)	12,500	4,500	4,000	21,000
Net income (loss)	7,500	(1,000)	3,250	9,750

Additional Information

(i) Factory overhead costs are made up of fixed costs of Rs 5.850 and variable costs of Rs 3,900 Variable costs by products are; product A Rs 3,000, product B, Rs 400, and product C Rs 500

(ii) Fixed costs and expenses will not be changed if product B is eliminated.

(iii) Variable selling and administrative expenses to the extent of Rs 11,000 can be traced to the product as follows: A, Rs 7,500; B, Rs 1,500; C, Rs 2,000.

(iv) Fixed selling and administrative expenses are Rs 10,000.

The decision to drop product B cannot be reasonably made from the above data prepared under conventional income statement. This information together with the following statement may be helpful to management.

	Product A	Product B	Product C	Total
	Rs	Rs	Rs	Rs
Sales revenue	50,000	7,500	12,500	70,000
Less: Variables product Costs:				
Direct material	7,500	1,000	1,500	10,000
Direct labour	15,000	2,000	2,500	19,500
Factory overhead	3,000	400	500	3,900
Selling and administrative expenses	7,500	1,500	2,000	11,000
	33,000	4,900	6,500	44,400
Contribution margin	17,000	2,600	6,000	25,600
Less: Fixed costs:				
Factory overhead				5,850
Selling and administrative expenses				10,000
Total fixed costs				15,850
Net income				9,750

This statement shows that product B exceeds its variable costs by Rs 2,600. If the sale of product B were discontinued, this marginal contribution would be lost and the net income of the firm would be reduced by Rs 2,600. That is, net income will be Rs 7,150 (Rs 9,750 – Rs 2,600). In this illustration it has been assumed that sales of products A and C will not be increased after product B is dropped. Further, it has been assumed that dropping product B will not change the fixed costs and expense. If these assumptions are not true, new analysis must be made. Assume, for example, that after dropping product B, the sales of product A increase by 10%. The total profit of the firm will not increase by this sales increase. Product A makes only a marginal contribution of 34%.

Sales revenue	Rs 50,000	100%
Variable costs	33,000	66%
Marginal contribution	17,000	34%

On additional sales of Rs 5,000, the marginal contribution would be Rs 1,700;

Sales revenue	Rs 5,000
Variable costs (66%)	3,300
Marignal contribution (34%)	1,700

This contribution is less than Rs 2,600 now being realised on the sales of product B. It would take additional sales of product A of approximately Rs 7,647 to equal the marginal contribution of'Rs 2,600 now being made by product B:

$$\frac{\text{Marginal contribution of product B}}{\text{Marginal contribution of product A}} = \frac{2,600}{34\%} = \text{Rs } 7,647$$

It is possible that dropping product B may result in reduction in some of the fixed costs. Product B now contributes Rs 2,600 towards recovery of fixed costs and expenses. Only if the fixed costs and expenses can be reduced by more than this amount, will it be advisable to drop product B.

Sell or Process Further

The decision whether a product should be sold at the split-off point or processed further is faced by many manufacturers. The choice between selling a product at split-off or processing it further is a short-run operating decision. Additional processing adds value to a product and increases its selling price above the amount for which it could be sold at split-off. The decision to process further depends upon whether the increase in total revenues exceeds the additional costs incurred for processing beyond split-off. Generally speaking, there are two general conditions under which a sell or process further decision could occur.

1. The company is evaluating the possibility of processing beyond split-off and must incur certain equipment costs and other fixed costs if additional processing is to occur.
2. The company already processes a product beyond split-off and has invested in the equipment and required personnel.

The first situation is really a capital budgeting problem and here it is not sufficient to determine whether incremental revenues exceed incremental costs. Since new investments in machinery and building **are** involved, the rate of return on this investment must also be considered.

In the second situation, the relevent costs are only those costs which relate to the additional processing of each product beyond the split-off point. The joint costs are relevant to the further processing decisions. Certain fixed costs such as supervisory salaries are related to additional processing. If these costs are eliminated by selling products at split-off, they are incremental and should be included in the decision analysis. If salaried personnel are assigned other duties in the company when additional processing is discontinued, the salary costs are not incremental since they are incurred under either decision alternative. If the equipment used for additional processing sits idle or can be used in other processes, it should be ignored in the decision analysis. Depreciation expense is never relevant in short- run operating decisions, since depreciation is an allocation of costs incurred in a past period.

In deciding upon which course of action to follow, the company compares the contribution margin from the sale of the partially processed product with the contribution margin from the sale of the completely processed product. The revenue to be derived from the sale of the partially processed product is the opportunity cost attached to the decision of further processing. Assume, for example, a partially processed product can be sold for Rs 90 per unit which is manufactured at a cost of Rs 60. Further processing can be done at an additional cost of Rs 30 per unit and the final product can be sold at Rs 150 per unit. The firm can produce 10,000 units. The analysis is shown below:

	Sell	*Process and Sell*
Sales revenue (10,000 units)	Rs 9,00,000	Rs 15,00,000
Less: Manufacturing costs	6,00,000	9,00,000
	30,000	6,00,000

Net advantage in further processing Rs 6,00,000 – 3,00,000 = Rs 30,0000.

Thus, there is a net advantage of Rs 3,00,000 in processing the product further. The market value of the partially processed product (Rs 9,00,000) is considered to be the opportunity cost of further processing.

The figure of net advantage of Rs 3,00,000 can be arrived at in the following manner also:

Revenue from sale of final product (10,000 × 150)		Rs 15,00,000
Less: Additional processing cost (10,000 × 30)	3,00,000	
Revenue from sale of intermediate product	9.00,000	12,00,000
Net advantage in further processing		3,00,000

Operate or Shutdown

Differential cost analysis is also used when a business is confronted with the possibility of a temporary shutdown. This type of analysis has to determine whether in the short-run a firm is better off operating than not operating. As long as the products sold recover their variable costs and make a contribution towards the recovery of fixed costs, it may be preferable to operate and not to shutdown. Also management should consider the investment in the training of its employees which would be lost in the event of a temporary shutdown. Recruiting and training new workers would add to present costs. Another factor is the loss of established markets. Also, a temporary shutdown does not eliminate all costs. Depreciation, taxes, interest, and insurance costs are incurred during shutdown also. The other points (benefits) which should be considered are the following: avoiding operating losses, savings in maintenance and repair costs, savings in indirect labour costs, savings in fixed costs.

A company operating below 50% of its capacity expects that the volume of sales will drop below the present level of 10,000 units per month. Management is concerned that a further drop in sales volume will create a loss and has under consideration a recommendation that operations be suspended, until better market conditions prevail and also a better selling price. The present operating income statement is as follows:

Sales revenue (10,000 units @ Rs 3.00)		Rs 30,000
Less: Variable costs @ Rs 2.00 per unit	20,000	
Fixed costs	10,000	30.000
Net Income		0

The following income statements have been prepared for sales at different capacities:

	Units Produced					
	Shutdown	2,000	4,000	6,000	8,000	10,000
Sales revenue @ Rs 3	0	6,000	12,000	18,000	24,000	30,000
Variable costs @ Rs 2	0	4,000	8,000	12,000	16,000	20,000
Contribution	0	2,000	4,000	6,000	8,000	10,000
Fixed costs	4,000	10,000	10,000	10,000	10,000	10,000
Loss	4,000	8,000	6,000	4,000	2,000	0

It would appear that shutdown is desirable when the sales volume drops below 6,000 units per month, the point at which operating losses exceed the shutdown cost. This volume of 6,000 units could be arrived at without an income statement as follows:

Fixed costs if plant operates	Rs 10,000
Fixed costs if plant shutsdown	4,000
Additional cost to be recovered when operating	6,000

Each unit of product sold contributes Re 1.00 to fixed costs recovery:

Selling price per unit	Rs 3.00
Variable cost per unit	Rs 2.00
Contribution	Rs 1.00

Sale of 6,000 units is necessary to recover Rs 6,000 of fixed costs.

$$\frac{\text{Rs } 6{,}000}{\text{Re } 1.00} = 6{,}000 \text{ units}$$

If the selling price is cut to Rs 2.80, the contribution margin will be Re 0.80 per unit. Required sale to recover an additional Rs 6,000 of fixed costs.

$$\frac{\text{Rs } 6{,}000}{\text{Re } 0.80} = 7{,}500 \text{ units}$$

That is, sales of 7,500 units would be necessary to recover an additional Rs 6,000 of fixed costs.

Special Orders

The question of special orders or one time orders arises when a company has excess or idle production capacity and management considers the possibility of selling additional products at less than normal celling prices, provided that such a special order will not affect the regular sales of the same product.

The basic problem is to determine an acceptable price for the special order units. Cost analysis using the contribution approach is a useful technique to determine the short-run profit effects of special order transactions. In deciding the pricing of special orders where normal operations are not disturbed and where unused production capacity exists, it is not advisable to attach fixed costs to products. Price determination should take into account the recovery of incremental (variable) costs caused by accepting the special order. If the normal fixed costs are included in the price of the special order, the price may be too high and the business firm could lose the entire order and the contribution margin to be earned on the special order. Only the relevant (variable) costs should be used in the decision analysis to arrive at an appropriate price. Fixed costs are relevant only if incurred to facilitate the special order.

The following example illustrates the special order decisions.

A manufacturing company produces 20,000 units by operating at 60% of the capacity and sells at a price of 30 per unit. The budgeted figures for the year 2003 are as follows:

	Production (20,000 units)
Raw material @ Rs 4.25	Rs 85,000
Direct labour @ Rs 5.75	1,15,000
Variable factory overhead @ 7.75	1,55,000
Fixed factory overhead	1,25,000
Variable selling costs 2.75% of selling price	1,25,000
Fixed selling and administrative costs	72,500

The company receives a special order for 10,000 units from a firm. The company desires to earn a profit of Re 1.00 per unit and no selling expenses are to be incurred for the special order. The minimum price on the special order and income statements are as follows:

Pricing of Special Order

	(10,000 units) (Rs)
Variable costs to be incurred:	
Raw materials	4.25
Direct labour	5.75
Variable overhead	7.75
Variable cost per unit (no selling expenses)	17.75
Desired profit	1.00
Minimum price	18.75

Increase in sales = 10,000 units × Rs 18.75 = Rs 1,87,500

Income Statement

	Without special order (Rs)	*Special order* (Rs)	*With special order* (Rs)
Sales	6,00,000	1,87,500	7,87,500
Less: Variable costs:			
Raw materials	85,000	42,500	1,27,500
Direct labour	1,15,000	57,500	1,72,500
Variable factory overhead	1,55,000	77,500	2,32,500
Variable selling costs (2.75% of selling price)	16,500	—	16,500
Total variable costs	3,71,500	1,77,500	5,49,000

Less: Fixed costs:			
Fixed factory overhead	1,25,000	—	1,25,000
Fixed selling and administrative cost	72,500	—	72,500
Total fixed costs	1,97,500	—	1,97,500
Total costs	5,69,000	1,77,500	7,46,500
Net income before taxes	31,000	10,000	41,000

From the above analysis it is clear that the acceptance of the special order will increase the profit by Rs 10,000. Also the bid price (Rs 18.75) is significantly less than the normal price of Rs 30. However, before arriving at a proper decision, management should consider some qualitative factors other than just the immediate impact on income. An important point is the effect on regular customers. If regular customers are paying more for the products, they may demand price reduction or quit buying from the firm and seek another source of supply. Another consideration is the possibility of special order customers being the regular customers.

Replace or Retain

The decision to replace or retain plant and equipment is also an important decision and should be taken very carefully. The differential costs which are important in retain or replace decisions are the following: change in fixed overhead costs, loss on sale of old equipment, capital investment and related costs such as rate of return and interest. Management should also consider differential benefits likely to be derived such as higher production and increased sales, realisable value of old machine, savings in operating costs, tax advantages, if any. Suppose a company has purchased a plant for Rs 1,00.000 five years ago which has a life of 10 years with no salvage value. The present book value is Rs 50,000. Management is considering the replacement of this plant with a new plant costing Rs 80,000 having a life of five years with no scrap value at the end of its life. The costs of operating present plant and the proposed paint are as follows:

	Present plant (Rs)	*Proposed plant* (Rs)
Variable costs:		
Labour, supplies, power, etc.	80,000	48.000
Fixed costs: Insurance, taxes, etc.	10,000	12,000
Depreciation	10,000	16,000
	1,00,000	76,000

It appears that the proposed plant would result into cost savings of Rs 24,000 (Rs 1,00,000 – 76.000). However, the book value of the present equipment is a sunk cost and not relevant in the decision. The following table helps in making a better analysis of the data:

	Present plant (Rs)	*Proposed plant* (Rs)
Variable costs:		
Labour, supplies, power, etc.	80,000	48,000
Fixed costs: Insurance, taxes, etc.	10,000	12,000
Depreciation	0	16,000
	90,000	76,000

The purchase of the new plant results in a saving of Rs 14,000 (Rs 90,000 – 76,000). Management has to consider whether this benefit is enough to justify the investment of Rs 80,000 in new machinery.

LIMITATIONS OF DIFFERENTIAL COST ANALYSIS

Differential cost analysis helps in evaluating decision alternatives. Relevant costs arc the cost factors that differ between alternativers. The primary objective is to select the least costly alternative. However cost computations and profit estimates are one means of tackling such problems. Many projects and proposals are rejected simple because the costs involved are too high or relative income potential was lower than that of an alternative. Yet, the project may have been beneficial to the company in that it would havé allowed the company to balance its risk, or to offer a complete product line which would have attracted new customers to all the company's products. Perhaps this is the very reason why the cost accountant needs to be extremely careful in the translation of the data with which he works.

Managers must study carefully the data to be used in decision-making. Other qualitative factors besides cost should be given proper attention. The pressure of competition, the maintenance of sources of supply and of certain marketing outlets, and the maintenance of the existing personnel organisation and morale may often be the real determinants of business decisions. The quantitative information alone does not provide a solution to all business problems. Sometimes, other factors are more important than cost factors.

Example 1 (*Differential Cost Analysis*)

P Ltd., is at present operating at 80% capacity level, the production being 15,000 units per annum. The company operates a flexible budgetary control system. The following relevant cost data are obtained from the company's budget at different capacity utilisation levels:

	Capacity utilisation level	
	80%	*100%*
Sales	Rs 20,00,000	Rs 25,00,000
Variable overheads	Rs 2,25,000	Rs 2,50,000
Semi-variable Overheads	Rs 1,05,000	Rs 1,11,000
Fixed overheads	Rs 4,00,000	Rs 4,70,000
Output (in Units)	15,000	18,750

Material and labour cost per unit are constant under present conditions. The management expects profit margin of 10% on sales.

You are required to compute the differential cost of producing the additional 3,750 units by increasing the capacity utilization level to 100 per cent and the minimum price per unit at 10% profit on cost.

Solution

		Rs
Sales at 80% capacity		20,00,000
Less: Profit 10% $\left(\frac{20,00,000 \times 10}{100}\right)$		2,00,000
Cost of goods sold:		18,00,000
Less: Expenses	Rs	
Variable overheads	2,25,000	
Semi-variable overheads	1,05,000	
Fixed overheads	4,00,000	7,30,000
Cost of material and labour at 80% capacity		10,70,000

Therefore, material and labour cost at 100% capacity

$$\frac{10,70,000 \times 100}{80} = \text{Rs } 13,37,500$$

Differential cost analysis is as follows:

	80% Capacity 15,000 units	*100% Capacity 18,750 units*	*Differential cost*
	Rs	Rs	Rs
Material and Labour	10,70,000	13,37,500	2,67,500
Variable Expenses	2,25,000	2,50,000	25,000
Semi-variable Exp.	1,05,000	1,11,000	6,000
Fixed Expenses	4,00,000	4,70,000	70,000
Total Cost	18,00,000	21,68,500	3,65,500

(a) Differential Cost for 3750 Units = Rs 3,68,500

(b) Minimum Price = $\frac{\text{Rs } 3,68,500}{3750 \text{ units}}$ Rs 98,266

Add: 10% Profit on cost 9,826

1,08,092

Example 2 (*Deciding Mode of Conveyance*)

A company is considering three alternative proposals for conveyance facilities for its sales personnel 10 have to do considerable travelling, approximately 20,000 kilometres every year. The proposals are as follows:

(i) Purchase and maintain its own fleet of cars. The average cost of car is Rs 1,00,000.
(ii) Allow the Executive use his own car and reimburse expenses at the rate of Rs 1.60 paise per kilometre and also bear insurance costs.
(iii) Hire cars from an agency at Rs 20,000 per year per car. The company will have to bear costs of petrol, taxes and tyres.

The following further details are available:
Petrol Re. 0.60 per kilometre
Repairs and maintenance Re 0.20 per kilometre
Tyre Re 0.12 per kilometre
Insurance Rs 1,200 per car per annum
Taxes Rs 800 per car per annum
Life of the car : 5 years with annual milage of 20,000 kilometres.
Resale value : Rs 20,000 at the end of the fifth year.
You are required to work out the relative costs of the three proposals and rank them.

Solution

	Alternatives (Cost per km Rs)		
	(i) (Rs)	(ii) (Rs)	(iii) (Rs)
Petrol	0.60	—	0.60
Repairs and Maintenance	0.20	—	—
Tyres	0.12	—	0.12
Insurance (1200 ÷ 20,000 km)	0.06	0.06	—
Taxes (800 ÷ 20,000 km)	0.04	—	0.04
Depreciation: $\frac{1,00,000 - 20,000}{5 \times 20,000}$	0.80	—	—

Reimbursement of Expenses	—	1.60	—
Hire Charges (20,000 ÷ 20,000)	—	—	1.00
	1.82	1.66	1.76
Cost of 20,000 kms	36,400	32,200	35,200

∴ The Proposal should be selected in order of (ii), (iii) and (i)

Example 3 (*Differential Cost Computation*)

A company has an installed production capacity of 1,00,000 units and presently it is working at 70% capacity utilisation. As production capacity utilisation increases, cost per unit decreases as follows:

Capacity	*Cost per unit*
70%	Rs 97
80%	Rs 92
90%	Rs 87
100%	Rs 82

The company has received three export orders from different sources as under:
Source A – 5,000 units at Rs 55 per unit
Source B – 10,000 units at Rs 52 per unit
Source C – 10,000 units at Rs 51 per unit
Advise the company whether any or all the export orders should be accepted or not.

Solution

Statement showing Differential Costs at Different Capacity Utilisation Levels (Installed Capacity 1,00,000 units)

Capacity Utilisation	*Production at different levels capacity utilisation*	*Unit cost Rs*	*Total cost Rs*	*Differential cost Rs*	*Differential cost Rs*
Per cent	Units				
70	70,000 $\left(1,00,000 \times \frac{70}{100}\right)$	97	67,90,000	–	–
80	80,000 $\left(1,00,000 \times \frac{80}{100}\right)$	92	73,60,000	5,70,000	57 $\left[\frac{5,70,000}{10,000}\right]$
90	90,000 $\left(1,00,000 \times \frac{90}{100}\right)$	87	78,30,000	4,70,000	47 $\left[\frac{4,70,000}{10,000}\right]$
100	1,00,000	82	82,00,000	3,70,000	37 $\left[\frac{3,70,000}{10,000}\right]$

Statement Showing Profit or Loss Accepting the various Export Orders

Export order source	*Export order*	*Capacity utilisation*	*Differential costs per unit*	*Differential costs Total*	*Price per unit*	*Sales revenue from the export order*	*Profit or (loss)*
	Unit	*Per cent*	*Rs*	*Rs*	*Rs*	*Rs*	*Rs*
A	5,000	75	57	2,85,000	55	2,75,000	(10,000)
B	10,000	85	First 5,000 units being upto 80% @ Rs 57 Next 5,000 Units Rs @ Rs 47	5,20,000	52	5,20,000	Nil
C	10,000	95	First 5,000 units being upto 90% Next 5,000 units @Rs 7	4,20,000	51	5,10,000	90,000
Total	25,000	95%		12,25,000		13,05,000	80,000

It is clear from the above statement that it is advantageous for the Company only when it accepts all the export orders. If the company accepts export orders only from one or two of three sources, it will suffer a loss. Therefore, he company should accept export orders from all the three sources to earn additional profits.

Example 4 (*Material Procurement Decision*)

A company has the option to procure material from two sources:

Source I assures that dececties will not be more than 20% of supplied quantity.

Source II does not give any assurance, but on the basis of past experience of supplies received from it, it is observed that defective percentage is 2.8%.

The material is supplied in lots of 1,000 units. Source II supplies the lot at a price, which is lower by Rs 100 as compared to Source I. The defective units of material can be rectified for use at a cost of Rs 5 per unit.

You are required to find out which of the two sources is more economical

Solution

Comparative Statement of procuring Material from Two Sources

	Material source I	*Material source II*
Defectives (in%)	2 (*Future estimate*	2.8 (*Past experience)*
Units supplied (in one lot)	1,000	1,000
Total defective units in a lot	20 (*1,000 units × 2%)*	28 (*1,000 units × 2.8%)*
Additional price paid per lot (Rs) : (A)	100	–
Rectification cost of defect (Rs) (B)	100 (*20 units × Rs 5)*	140 (*28 units × Rs 5)*
Total additional cost per source (Rs) : {(A) + (B)]	200	140

Decision : On comparing the total additional cost incurred per lot of 1,000 units, we observe that it is more economical, if the required material units are procured from material Source II.

Example 5 (*Selling Price Decision*)

The accounts of a company are expected to reveal a profit of Rs 14,00,000 after charging fixed costs of Rs 1,00,000 for the year ended 31st March 2000. The selling price of the product is Rs 50 per unit and variable cost per unit is Rs 20.

Market investigations suggest the following responses to the price changes :

Alternatives	*Selling Price reduced by*	*Quantity Sold increased by*
I	5%	10%
II	7%	20%
III	10%	25%

Evaluate these alternatives and state which of the alternatives, on profitability consideration, should be adopted for the forthcoming year.

Solution

Statement for evaluating three alternatives on profitability consideration

	Alternatives		
	I	*II*	*III*
Selling price per unit (Rs)	47.50 (Rs 50 – 5% of Rs 50)	46.50 (Rs 50 – 7% of Rs 50)	45.00 (Rs 50 – 10% of Rs 50)
Less : Variable cost per unit (Rs)	20.00	20.00	20.00
Contribution per unit (Rs)	27.50	26.50	25.00
Revised quantity of units to be sold (*Refer to Working Note 3*)	88,000	96,000	1,00,000
Total contribution (Rs)	24,20,000 (88,000 units × Rs 27.50)	25,44,000 (96,000 units × Rs. 26.50)	25,00,000 (1,00,000 units × Rs 25)

Recommendation : An evaluation of the above three alternatives on profitability consideration clearly shows that alternative II is the best as it gives maximum contribution and hence profitability. Therefore this alternative should be adopted.

Working Notes :

1. *Contribution per unit*
   = Rs Selling price per unit – Variable cost per unit
   = Rs 50 – Rs 20 = Rs 30
2. *Expected quantity of units to be sold*

	(Rs)
Profit	14,00,000
Add: Fixed costs	10,00,000
Total contribution	24,00,000

$$\text{Quantity of units sold} = \frac{\text{Total contribution}}{\text{Contribution per unit}} = \frac{\text{Rs } 24{,}00{,}000}{\text{Rs } 30} = 80{,}000 \text{ units}$$

(*Refer to working note I*)

3. *Revised quantity of units to be sold*

Alternatives	*Units to be sold*
I	80,000 units + 10% of 80,000 units = 88,000 units
II	80,000 units + 20% of 80,000 units = 96,000 units
III	80,000 units + 25% of 80,000 units = 1,00,000 units

Example 6 (*Dropping a Product*)

The costs per unit of three products X, Y and Z are given below :

Products	X	Y	Z
Direct Material (Rs)	20	16	18
Direct Labour (Rs)	12	14	12
Variable Overheads (Rs)	8	10	6
Fixed Expenses (Rs)	6	6	4
	Rs 46	46	40
Profit	18	14	12
Selling Price (Rs)	64	60	52
No. of units produced	10,000	5,000	8,000

Production arrangements are such that if one product is given up the production of the others can be raised by 50%. The directors propose that product Z should be given up because the contribution from the product is the lowest. Present suitable analysis of the data indicating whether the proposal should be accepted.

Solution

1. *Computation of present Profit*

	Rs.
Product X (10,000 × 18)	1,80,000
Product Y (5,000 × 14)	70,000
Product Z (8,000 × 12)	96,000
	3,46,000

2. *Computation of Fixed Cost*

	Rs
Product X (10,000 × 6)	60,000
Product Y (5,000 × 6)	30,000
Product Z (8,000 × 4)	32,000
	1,22,000

3. Computation of Profit Under Proposed Situation (Product Z discontinued)

Product X (15,000 × 40)	Rs. 6,00,000
Producy Y (7,500 × 40)	3,00,000
	9,00,000
Add: Total Fixed Cost [as per calculation above]	1,22,000
Total Cost (1)	10,22,000
Sales:	
Product X (15,000 × 64)	9,60,000
Product Y (7,500 × 60)	4,50,000
Total Sales (2)	14,10,000
Profit = (2) – (1)	= 3,88,000

Thus, the profit under the proposed situation will increase by Rs 42,000 (*i.e.* 3,88000 – 3,46,000). Hence, the proposal for discontinuance of Product Z should be accepted.

Note: It has been assumed that fixed costs of Rs 1,22,000 are for the business as a whole. They have been simply apportioned to Product X, Y, and Z and they will continue to be same even after the Product Z is discontinued.

Example 7 (Decision to Increase Sales)

Quality Product Limited has drawn up the following budget for the year 2005-2006.

	Rs
Raw materials	20,00,000
Labour, stores, power and other variable costs	6,00,000
Fixed Manufacturing Overheads	7,00,000
Packing and variable distribution cost	4,00,000
Fixed general overheads including selling	3,00,000
	40,00,000
Sales Revenue @ Rs 50 per unit	50,00,000
Budgeted Profit	Rs 10,00,000

The General Manager suggests to reduce selling prices by 5% and expects to achieve an additional volume of 5%. The more intensive manufacturing programme will involve additional costs of Rs 15,000 for production planning. It will also be necessary to open an additional sales office at the cost of Rs. 1,00,000 per annum.

The Sales Manager, on the other hand, suggests to increase selling price by 10% which it is estimated will reduce sales volume by 10%. At the same time a saving in manufacturing overheads and general overheads of Rs 50,000 and Rs 1,00,000 per annum respectively is expected on this reduced volume.

Which of these two proposals would you accept and why? Show complete working.

Solution

Computation of Profit as per Proposal of General Manager

1.	New Sales Volume (Units 1,00,000 + 5%)		1,05,000
			Rs
2.	Sales Value (1,05,000 × 4,750)		49,87,500
3.	Cost of Sales :		
	Variable Costs = $\frac{30,00,000}{1,00,000} \times 1,05,000$		31,50,000
	Fixed Cost:		
	Present = 7,00,000 + 3,00,000		10,00,000
	Additional Fixed Cost		1,15,000
	Total Costs		42,65,000
	Profit (2) – (3) = (4)		7,22,500

Computation of Profit as per Proposal of Sales Manager

1.	Sales Volume (1,00,000 – 1,000)		9,00,000
			Rs
2.	Sales Value (90,000 × 55)		49,50,000
3.	Cost of Sales		
	Variable Cost = $\frac{30,00,000}{1,00,000} \times 90,000$		27,00,000
	Fixed Cost:		
	Present	10,00,000	
	Less: Saving in Fixed Cost	1,50,000	8,50,000
	Total Cost		35,50,000
	Profit = (2) – (3)		14,00,000

The profit as per the proposal of Sales Manager is much higher as compared to the proposal of the General Manager. Hence, the proposal of the Sales Manager should be accepted.

Example 8 (*Product profitability*)

The following particulars are taken from the records of a company engaged in manufacturing two products, A and B, from a certain material :

Particulars	Product A (per unit) Rs	Product B (per unit) Rs
Sales	2,500	5,000
Material cost (Rs 50 per kg)	500	1,250
Direct labour (30 per hour)	750	1,500
Variable overhead	250	500
Total fixed overheads: Rs 10,00,000		

Comment on the profitability of each product when:

(i) Total sales in value is limited.

(ii) Raw materials is in short supply.

(iii) Production capacity is the limiting factor.

(iv) Total availability of raw materials is 20,000 kg and maximum sales potential of each product is 1,000 units, find the product mix to yield maximum profit.

Solution

Basic Calculations

Statement of Evaluation of Products A and B

Particulars	Product A Rs	Product A Rs	Product B Rs	Product B Rs
Sales		2,500		5,000
Less: Variable Costs:				
Material Cost	500		1,250	
Direct Labour	750		1,500	
Variable Overhead	250	1,500	500	3,250
1. Contribution per unit		1,000		1,750
2. P/V Ratio	$\frac{1,000}{2,500} \times 100$ = 40%		$\frac{1,750}{5,000} \times 100$ 35%	
3. Material in kg per unit	$= \frac{\text{Rs } 500}{\text{Rs } 50}$ = 10 kg		$\frac{\text{Rs } 1,250}{\text{Rs } 50}$ 25 kg	
4. Contribution per kg of Material	= Rs 100		Rs 70	
5. Labour hour per unit	$= \frac{\text{Rs } 750}{30}$ = 25 hours		$\frac{1,500}{30}$ = 50 hours	
6. Contribution per Labour Hour	= Rs 40		Rs 35	

(i) *Comment on the Profitability of each product when total sales in value is limited*
Product A had a higher P/V ratio than Product B and hence Product A is more profitable.

(ii) *Comment on the Profitability of each product when raw materials is in short supply*
Product A has a higher contribution kg of raw materials than Product B. Hence, Product A is more profitable.

(iii) *Comment on the Profitability of each product when production capacity is the limiting factor*
Product A has a higher contribution per labour hour than Product B. Hence, Product A is more profitable.

(iv) *When raw material and sales quantity both are limiting factors*

Statement of Product Mix of Yield Maximum Profits
(when total availability of raw materials is 20,000 kg)

Products	*Units to be made*	*Raw material consumed (kg)*	*Contribution per unit (Rs)*	*Total Contribution (Rs)*	*Fixed Cost (Rs)*	*Profit (Rs)*
(I)	*(II)*	*(III)*	*(IV)*	*(V)*	*(VI)*	*(VII) = (V) – (VI)*
A	1,000	10,000 (1,000 units × 10 kg.)	1,000	10,00,000		
B	400	10,000 (400 units × 25 kg.)	1,750	7,00,000		
		20,000		17,00,000	10,00,000	7,00,000

Example 9 (*Replacement of a Product*)

A multi product company has the following costs and output data for the last year.

	Product X	Y	Z
Sales mix	40%	35%	25%
	Rs	Rs	Rs
Selling Price	20	25	30
Variable cost per unit	10	15	18
Total fixed cost			1,50,000
Total sales			5,00,000

The company proposes to replace product Z by product S. Estimated cost and output data are:

Sales mix	50%	30%	20%
Selling price	20	25	28
Variable cost per unit	10	15	14
Total fixed costs			1,50,000
Total sales			5,00,000

Analyse the proposed change and suggest what decision the company should take.

Solution

(1) Computation of Present Profit and BEP

Particular	*Products* X	Y	Z	
	Rs	Rs	Rs	
Selling price	20	25	30	
Variable cost	10	15	18	
Contribution	10	10	12	
P/V ratio	50%	40%	40%	
Sales mix	40%	35%	25%	100%
Contribution per rupee of sales: (P/V ratio × Sales mix)	20%	14%	10%	44%
Sales				Rs 5,00,000
Total contribution Rs (5,00,000 × 44/100)				2,20,000
Fixed costs				1,50,000
Profit				Rs 70,000
Break-even point (Rs 1,50,000 × 100/44)				Rs 3,40,909

(2) Computation of Proposed Profit and BEP

Particular	Products X	Y	Z	Total
	Rs	Rs	Rs	
Selling price	20	25	28	
Variable cost	10	15	14	
Contribution	10	10	14	
P/V Ratio	50%	40%	50%	
Sales mix	50%	30%	20%	100%
Contribution per rupee of sales (P/V ratio × Sales mix)	25%	12%	10%	47%
Sales				Rs 5,00,000
Total contribution 5,00,000 × 47/100				2,35,000
Fixed cost				1,50,000
Profit				Rs 85,000
Break-even point (1,50,00 × 100/47)				3,19,149

A comparison of the present situation and the proposed situation shows that if product Z is replaced by product S, profit would increase by Rs 15,000 and break-even point will reduce by Rs 21,760. The change is beneficial and, therefore, product Z may be dropped, provided all other relevant factors remain constant.

Example 10 (*Decision about Mechanisation*)

Management of a manufacturing unit is considering extensive modernisation of the factory through progressive mechanisation which would result in improved productivity and reduced strength. Through negotiations with the union, it was agreed that for every 1% increase in productivity, workers would be paid 0.5% incentive wages. It was also agreed that through voluntary retirement the staff strength would be reduced to

300 from the present level of 400. The following further comparative data are available before and after the proposed mechanisation :

	Before mechanisation	*After mechanisation*
No. of articles produced per month	50,000	48,000
Fringe benefits	50% of wages	
Wages paid per month	Rs 4,00,000	
Sales per month (value)	Rs 24,00,000	
P/V ratio	25%	

Based on the above data, you are required to work out the annual financial implication of proposal.

Solution

Improvement in productivity after mechinisation:

Proportionate output of 300 workers on the basis of existing productivity level —

$$\frac{50,000}{400} \times 300 = 37,500 \text{ units}.$$

Actual output of 300 workers envisaged after mechanisation = 48,000 units

$$\text{Improvement in productivity} = \frac{48,000 - 37,500}{37,500} \times 100\% = 28\%$$

Incentive wages payable :

Incentive wages for 28% improvement in productivity @ 1/2% for every 1% improvement) = 28% × 0.5% = 14%

Annual wages payable to 300 workers before incentive

$$= \frac{\text{Rs } 4,00,000}{4000} \times 300 \times 12$$

= Rs 3,60,000

Selling price per unit = Rs 24,00,000 ÷ 50,000 = Rs 48,00 per unit

Computation of savings (loss) after mechanisation

Particulars	*Before mechanisation* Rs	*After mechanisation* Rs
Wages payable per annum	48,00,000	36,00,000
Frings benefits @ 50% of wages	24,00,000	18,00,000
Incentives wages @ 14% of wages	–	5,04,000
	72,00,000	59,04,000
Savings per annum		13,96,000
Less: Loss of contribution due to lower sales:		
(50,000 units – 48,000 units) × 12 × $\frac{25}{100}$ of Rs 48		2,88,000
Increase in annual contribution due to mechanisation		Rs 11,08,000

Example 11 (*Make or Buy*)

Auto Parts Ltd. has an annual production of 90,000 units for a motor component. The component's cost structure is as below :

	Rs
Materials	270 per unit
Labour (25% fixed)	180 per unit
Expenses :	
Variable	90 per unit
Fixed	135 per unit
Total	675

(a) The purchase manager has an offer from a supplier who is willing to supply the component at Rs 5.40. Should the component be purchased and production stopped?

(b) Assume the resources now used for this component's manufacture are to be used to produce another new product for which the selling price is 485.

In the latter case the materials price will be Rs 200 per unit. 90,000 units of this product can be produced on the same cost basis as above for labour and expenses. Discuss whether it would be advisable to divert the resources to manufacture the new product, on the footing that the component presently being produced would, instead of being produced, be purchased from the market.

Solution

(a) Statement showing the Variable Cost and Purchase Cost of Component..... Used by Auto Parts Ltd.

Variable cost	*Per unit* *Rs*	*Total for 90,000 units* *Rs*
Materials	270	2,43,00,000
Labour	135	1,21,50,000
Expenses	90	81,00,000
Total variable cost (when component is produced)	495	4,45,50,000
Cost of purchase (when component is purchased)	540	4,86,00,000
Difference, excess of purchase price over variable cost	45	40,50,000

Fixed expenses not being affected, it is evident from the above statement that if the component is purchased from the outside supplier, the company will have to spend Rs 45 per unit more and on 90,000 units the company will have to spend Rs 40,50,000 more. Therefore, the company should not stop the production of the component.

(b) The following statement shows the cost implications of the proposal to divert the available facilities for a new product.

Statement showing the Contribution per unit if the Existing Resources are used for the Production of Another New Product

		Rs	Rs
Selling price of the new product per unit			
Less :	Materials cost	200	485
	Labour (variable)	135	
	Expenses (Variable)	90	425
Contribution per unit			60
Loss per unit if the present component is purchased:			
Purchase price of the existing product			
Less: Total variable cost of producing the existing component			540
Less: Total variable cost of producing the existing component			495
Excess cost			45

Thus, if the company diverts its'resources for the productive on another new product, it will benefit by Rs 15, *i.e.* Rs 60 – 45 per unit. On 90,000 units the company will save Rs 13,50,000. Therefore, it is advisable to divert the resources to manufacture. The new product and the component presently being produced should be purchased from the market. This is also brought out by the following figures:

	Rs
Total cost of producing the component (90,000 × 675) (A)	6,07,50,000
Cost of purchasing the component (90,000 × 540)	4,86,00,000
Fixed expenses, not having been saved	1,62,00,000
(90,000 × 180, i.e. 675 – 495)	6,48,00,000
Less: Contribution from the new product (90,000 × 60)	54,00,000
Total cost if component is purchased and new product is made (B)	5,94,00,000
Savings (A – B)	13,50,000

Example 12 (Special Order)

Nubo Manufacturing Company is presently operating at 50% of partical capacity producing about 50,000 units annually of a patented electronic component. Nubo recently received an offer from an overseas market to sell 30,000 components at Rs 6.00 per unit FOB Nubo's Plant. Nubo has not previously sold components in the market. Budgeted production costs for 50,000 and 80,000 units of output are as follows:

Units	50,000	80,000
Costs	Rs	Rs
Direct material	75,000	1,20,000
Direct labour	75,000	1,20,000
Factory overheads	2,00,000	2,60,000
	3,50,000	5,00,000
Cost per unit	Rs 7.00	Rs 6.25

The sales manager thinks the order should be accepted, even if it results in a loss of Re. 1.00 per unit because he feels the sales may build up future markets. The production manager does not wish to have the order accepted primarily because the order would show a loss of Re 0.25 per unit when computed on the new average unit cost. The cost account has made a quick computation indicating that accepting the order will actually increase profit.

You are required to :

(a) Explain what apparently caused the drop in cost from Rs 7.00 per unit to rs 6.25 per unit when

budgeted production increased from 50,000 to 80,000 units. Show supporting computations.
(b) should the order be accepted?

Solution

From the given data at two levels of production, the costs per unit at 50,000 and 80,000 units are ascertained as under:

Units of production	*Total cost (Rs)*	*50,000 C.P.U (Rs)*	*Total cost (Rs)*	*80,000 C.P.U.*
Direct material	75,000	1.50	1,20,000	1.50
Direct labour	75,000	1.50	1,20,000	1.50
Factory overhead	2,00,000	4.25	2,60,000	3.25
	3,50,000	7.25	5,00,000	6.25

(a) The reason for the difference in average units cost of factory overhead was caused by some of the overheads being fixed within the total overhead under different levels of output. The fixed portion may be ascertained first as follows:

Change in cost (overhead) at two levels = Rs 60,000
Change in output at two levels = 30,000 units

Thus, variable cost P.U. $= \frac{\text{Rs } 60,000}{30,000} = \text{Rs } 2$

Therefore, amount of variable cost at 50,000 units = 50,000 × 2 = Rs 1,00,000 variable cost
Fixed overhead (Rs 2,00,000 – Rs 1,00,000) = Rs 1,00,000 fixed cost.

So at 50,000 units, the cost P.U. of fixed portion of overhead = Rs 2 (Rs 1,00,000 ÷ 50,000) and at 80,000 units the cost P.U. of fixed portion of overhead = Rs 1.25 = (Rs 100,000 ÷ 80,000). Thus, there is a decrease in unit cost to the tune of Re 0.75. Hence there is a drop in cost from Rs 7 to Rs 6.25 due to the incidence of fixed overhead being spread over to increased number of production.

(b) So when the variable cost P.U. remains constant, the total variable cost will vary in direct proportion with the volume of production: but since the total amount of fixed overhead is the same at different levels of production; the impact of fixed overhead on the cost of production of more number of units is favourable, as C.P.U. comes down with the increase in production volume. Hence, the order for the overseas market is acceptable.

Example 13 (*Capacity Decision*)

A Ltd. Co. has capacity to produce 1,00,000 units of a product every month. It works cost at varying levels of production is as under :

Level	*Works cost per unit* Rs
10%	400
20%	390
30%	380
40%	370
50%	360
60%	350
70%	340
80%	330
90%	320
100%	310

Its fixed administration expenses amount to Rs 1,50,000 and fixed marketing expenses amount to Rs 2,50,000 per month respectively. The variable distribution cost amount to Rs 30 per unit.

It can market 100% of its output at Rs 500 per unit provided it incurs the following further expenditure:

(a) it gives gift items costing Rs 30 per unit of sale;

(b) it has lucky draws every month giving the first prize of Rs 50,000 ; 2nd prize of Rs 25,000, 3rd prize of Rs 10,000 and three consolation prizes of Rs 5,000 each to customers buying the product.

(c) it spends Rs 1,00,000 on refreshments served every month to its customers;

(d) it sponsors a television programe every week at a cost a of Rs 20,00,000 per month.

It can market 30% of its output at Rs 550 per unit without incurring any of the expense referred to in (a) to (d) above.

Advise the company on its course of course of action. Show the supporting cost sheets.

Solution

Statement of Cost

Capacity level	*30%*		*100%*	
Capacity level (Units)	*30,000*		*1,00,000*	
	Per unit Rs	*Total* Rs	*Per unit* Rs	*Total* Rs
Works cost	380.00	1,14,00,000	310.00	3,10,00,000
Add: Fixed Aministration Expenses	5.00	1,50,000	1.50	1,50,000
Cost of Production	385.00	1,15,50,000	311,50	3,11,50,000
Add: Fixed Marketing Expenses	8.33	2,50,000	2.50	2,50,000
Add: Variable Distribution Cost	30,00	9,00,000	30,00	30,00,000
Add: Special cost:				
Gift item cost	–	–	30,00	30,00,000
Customer's prizes	–	–	1,00	1,00,000
Refreshments	–	–	1,00	1,00,000
Television Programme Sponsorship cost	–	–	20.00	20,00,000
Cost of Sales	423.33	1,27,00,000	396.00	3,96,00,000
Profit	126.67	23,00,000	104.00	1,40,000
Sales	550.000	1,50,00,000	500.00	5,00,00,000

Advice

A Ltd. makes an extra profit of Rs 81 lacs (Rs 104 lacs – Rs 23 lacs) if it works at 100% capacity to produce 1,00,000 units of a product per month. Hence, the company is advised to produce 1,00,000 units and incur the special costs required for marketing its 100% output.

Example 14 (*Decision about Mechanisation*)

The present output details of a manufacturing department are as follows:

Average output per week	48,000 units from 160 employees
Saleable value of output	Rs 6,00,000
Contribution made by output towards fixed expenses and profit	Rs 2, 40,000

The Board of Directors plans to introduce more mechanisation into the department at a capital cost of Rs 1,60,000. The effect of this will be to reduce the number of employees to 120, and increasing the output per individual employee by 60%. To provide the necessary incentive to achieve the increased output, the Board intends to offer a 1% increase on the piece work rate of Re. 1 per unit for every 2% increase in average individual output achieved.

To sell the increased output, it will be necessary to decrease the selling price by 4%.

Calculate the extra weekly contribution resulting from the proposed change and evaluate for the Board's information, the desirability of introducing the change.

Solution

Working Notes

1. *Present average output per employee and total future expected output per week*

$$\text{Present average output per employee per week} = \frac{\text{Total present output}}{\text{Total number of present employees}}$$

$$= \frac{48{,}000 \text{ units}}{160 \text{ employees}}$$

$$= 300 \text{ units}$$

$$\text{Total future expected output per week} = \text{Total number of future employees}\left(\text{Present output} + \text{60\% of present output per employee}\right)$$

$$= 120 \text{ employees } (300 \text{ units} + 60\% \times 300 \text{ units})$$

$$= 57{,}600 \text{ units}$$

2. *Present and proposed piece work rate*

Present piece work rate	= Re 1.00 per unit
Proposed piece work rate	= Present piece work rate + 30% × Re. 1
	= Re 1.00 + 0.30 per unit
	= Rs 1.30 per unit

3. *Present and proposed sale price per unit*

Present sale price per unit (Rs 6,00,000/48,000 units)	= Rs 12.50
Proposed sale price per unit (Rs 12.50 – 4% × Rs 12.50)	= Rs 12

4. *Present marginal cost (excluding wages) per unit :*

$$= \frac{\text{Present sale value — Fixed expenses and profit – Contribution towards present wages}}{\text{Present output (units)}}$$

$$= \frac{\text{Rs } 6{,}00{,}000 - \text{Rs } 2{,}40{,}000 - \text{Rs } 48{,}000}{48{,}000 \text{ units}} = \text{Rs } 6.50 \text{ per unit}$$

Statement of extra weekly contribution (information resulting from the proposed change of mechanisation meant for Board's evaluation)

Expected sales units (*Refer to Working Note* 1)	Rs	57,600 Rs
Sales value: (A) (57,600 units × Rs 12) (*Refer to Working Note 3*)		6,91,200
Marginal costs (excluding wages) : (B) (57,600 units × Rs 6.50) (Refer to working Note 4)	3,74,400	
Wages: (C) (57,600 units × Rs 1.30) (*Refer to Working Note 2*)	74,880	
Total marginal cost: {(D) = (B) + (C)}		4,49,280
Marginal contribution : {(A) – (D)}		2,41,920
Less: Present contribution		2,40,000
Increase in contribution (per week)		1,920

Evaluation : Since the mechanisation has resulted in the increase of contribution to the extent of Rs 1.920 per week, therefore the proposed change should be accepted.

Example 15 (*Product Mix Decision*)

A company produces three products. The cost data are as under :

		A	B	C
Direct Materials		Rs 64	152	117
Direct Labour :				
Deptt.	Rate per hour Rs	Hrs.	Hrs.	Hrs.
1	5	18	10	20
2	6	5	4	7
3	4	10	5	20
Variable Overheads		Rs 16	9	21
Fixed Overheads		Rs 4,00,000 per annum		

The budget was prepared at a time, when the market was sluggish. The budgeted quantities and selling prices are as under :

Product	*Budgeted Qty.*	*Selling Price (Rs)/Unit*
A	9,750	270
B	7,800	280
C	7,800	400

Later the market improved and the sales quantities could be increased by 20% for product A and 25% each for products B and C. The sales manager confirmed that the increased quantities could be achieved at the prices originally budgeted. The production manager stated that the output cannot be increased beyond the budgeted level due to limitation of direct labour hours in Department 2.

Required :

(i) Present a statement of budgeted profitability.

(ii) Set optimal product mix and calculate the optimal profit.

Solution

Statement of Budgeted Profitability

Products		*A*	*B*	*C*	*Total*
Budgeted Quantity (Units)	(1)	9,750	7,800	7,800	
	(2)	Rs	Rs	Rs	
Selling Price per unit		270	280	400	
Variable Cost per unit:					
Direct Materials		64	152	117	
Direct Labour		160	94	222	
Variable Overheads		16	9	21	
Total Variable Cost per unit (3)		240	255	360	
Contribution per unit (4) = ((2) – (3))		30	25	40	
Total Contribution	(1) × (4)	2,92,500	1,95,000	3,12,000	7,99,500
Loss : Fixed Cost					4,00,000
Profit					3,99,500

(2) Statement of Optimal Product Mix and Profit

Products		*A*	*B*	*C*	*Total*
Contribution per unit	(1)	30	25	40	
Direct Labour hours in Department 2	(2)	5	4	7	
Contribution per direct labour hour (1)/(2)	(Rs)	6	6.25	5.71	
Ranking		II	I	III	
Optimal Product Mix Units	(3)	11,700 (58,500 hrs.)	9,750 (39,000 hrs.)	5,292 (37,044 hrs.)	
Total Contribution (Rs) (1) × (3)		3,51,000	2,43,750	2,11,680	8,06,430
Less: Fixed Cost (Rs)					4,00,000
Optimal Profit					4,06,430

Working Notes :

1. Total Hours available in Department 2

Products (a)	*Units (b)*	*Hrs per unit (c)*	*Total Hrs. (d) = (b) × (c)*
A	9,750	5	48,750
B	7,800	4	31,200
C	7,800	7	54,600
Total			1,34,550

2. Maximum Sales Quantities of Products (under improved market conditions)

Products	*Units*	*Increase in percentage*	*Total number of units*
A	9,750	20	11,700
B	7,800	25	9,750
C	7,800	25	9,750

Example 16 (*Product Mix Decision*)

M/s Mars Ltd. are manufactuaring three products. The cost details are as follows:

Particulars	*Products*					
	A		*B*		*C*	
	Units	*Rs*	*Units*	*Rs*	*Unit*	*Rs*
Direct Materials	4	12	5	15	6	18
Direct Labour		5		6		6
Direct Expenses		8		9		11
		25		30		35
Selling Price		35		40		50
		10		10		15
No. of Units sold	20,000		40,000		20,000	
Total Contribution		2,00,000		4,00,000		3,00,000
Total				Rs 9,00,000		
Less: Fixed Costs				Rs 7,50,000		
				Rs 2,50,000		

The direct materials were all imported. Due to foreign exchange restrictions, henceforth, the company can import only 3,00,000 units of raw materials. The company can produce in all 1,00,000 units maximum (all products). However, they can market only 20,000 units of product A & C each. There is a local substitute materials which is available at a price of Rs 3.75 per unit. Besides, the company has to spend Rs 50,000 on intermediaries and consumables, if local substitute material is used in the production process. There was also a thrid party who was willing to take a part of the plant on lease upto 50,000 units capacity of B and willing to pay lease charges of Rs 2,75,000.

You are required to advise the management :

(i) What should be the quantum of production/sales mix of products with existing import restrictions?

(ii) Whether the company can optimise production of 1,00,000 units with local substitute materials?

(iii) Whether the company can enhance profits by leasing out a part of the plant to the thrid party and restricting its own production?

Soution

(1) Statement of Quantum of productions/ Sales Mix of Products
(with existing import restrictions)

Products	*A*	*B*	*C*	*Total*
Selling aprice per unit (Rs)	35	40	50	
Less: Variable Cost per unit	25	30	35	
Contribution per unit of product (Rs) (1)	10	10	15	
Units of Materials (2)	4	5	6	
Contribution per unit of materials (Rs) = (1)/(2)	2.50	2	2.50	
Ranking	I	II	I	
Units made (4)	20,000	20,000	20,000	
(Materials consumed)	(80,000 units)	1,00,000 units)	1,20,000 units)	
Total Contribution (Rs) (5) = (1) × (4)	20,000	2,00,000	3,00,000	Rs 7,00,000
Less: Fixed Costs (Rs)				Rs 7,50,000
Profit (Loss)				Rs (50,000)

(ii) *Use of Local substitute of Material*

	(Output 1,00,000 units) Rs	Rs
Contribution per unit of product B on using local substitute material (Rs 10 – Rs 3.75)	6.25	
Total contribution on 40,000 units of product B (40,000 units × Rs 6.25)		2,50,000
Less: Intermediatries Expenses		50,000
Net additional Contribution		2,00,000
Loss on Present Output of 60,000 units (as per (1))		50,000
Net Profit		1,50,000

Thus, the company can have optimum production of 1,00,000 units by using local substitute of material.

(iii) *Evaluation of Leasing Out a part of the Plant*

Total contribution on sale of 20,000 units of Products A and C and 10,000 units of Product B by using imported material (20,000 units × Rs 10 + 10,000 units × Rs 10 + 20,000 units × Rs 15)	6,00,000
Less : Fixed Assets	7,50,000
Profit (Loss)	(1,50,000)
Add: Lease Rent received	2,75,000
Net Profit	1,25,000

Conclusion: The net profit is Rs 1,50,000 in case the company uses local substitute of material and the plant capacity fully for producing 1,00,000 units, whereas by leasing about the plant capacity upto 50,000 of Product B for a rent of Rs 2,75,000, the company makes a profit of Rs 1,25,000. A comparative study of the two alternatives suggests that it will be better for the company to have optimum production of 1,00,000 units by using local substitute of material.

Example 17 (Profitable Product Mix)

A manufacturing company produces and sells three products P, Q and R. It has an available machine hour capacity of one lakh hours, interchangeable among the three product. Presently, the company produces and sells 20,000 units of P and 15,000 units each of Q and R. The unit selling price of the three products are Rs 25, Rs 32 and Rs 42 for P, Q and respectively. With this price structure and the aforesaid sales-mix the company is incurring loss. The total expenditure exclusive of fixed charges (presently Rs 5 per unit), is Rs 13.75 Lakhs. The unit cost ratio among the products P, Q and R is 4 : 6 : 7. Since the company desires to improve its profitability without changing its cost and price structures, if has been considering the following three mixes so as to be within its total available capacity.

Products	*Mix I (in units)*	*Mix II (in units)*	*Mix III (in units)*
P	25,000	20,000	30,000
Q	15,000	12,000	5,000
R	10,000	18,000	15,000

You are required to compute the quantum of loss now incurred and advise the most profitable mix which could be considered by the company.

Solution

Basic Calculations

1. Computation of Equivalent Production

Production	*Present Production*	*Cost Ratio*	*Equivalent Units*
P	20,000	4	80,000
Q	15,000	6	90,000
R	15,000	7	1,05,000
	50,000		2,75,000

2. Computation of Variable Cost Per Unit

Total Variable Cost: Rs 13,75,000

Hence, Variable Cost per equivalent unit Rs 5 (*i.e.*, Rs 13,75,000/2,75,000)

Variable Cost of product P is Rs 20 per unit

Variable Cost of product Q is Rs 30 per unit

Variable Cost of product R is Rs 35 per unit

3. Computation of Present Profit (Loss)

			Rs
	Contribution from Products:		
P	20,000 × (25 – 20)	=	1,00,000
Q	15,000 × (32 – 30)	=	30,000
R	15,000 × (42 – 35)	=	1,05,000
Total Contribution			2,35,000
Less: Fixed Cost @ Rs 5 per unit for 50,000 units			2,50,000
Loss			(15,000)

Statement of Comparative Contribution for Different Mixes

Products	*Contribution*		
	Mix I	*Mix II*	*Mix III*
	Rs	Rs	Rs
P	1,25,000	1,00,000	1,50,000
Q	30,000	24,000	10,000
R	70,000	1,26,000	1,05,000
Total	2,25,000	2,50,000	2,65,000

Fixed cost of Rs 2,50,000 is constant at all levels of activity. Mix III is giving the highest contribution of the three and hence is the best and, therefore, recommended.

Note: It has been stated that the machine capacity is interchangeable and the company has selected the three mixes "so as to be within its total available capacity". No capacity constraint has been considered.

Example 18 (*Profitability Decision*)

A company produces a single product which is sold by it presently in the domestic market at Rs 75 per unit. The present production and sale is 40,000 units per month representing 50% of the capacity available. The cost data of the product are as under :

Variable costs per unit Rs 50

Fixed costs per unit per month Rs 10 lakhs.

To improve the profitability, the management has 3 proposals on hand as under :

(a) to accept an export supply order for 30,000 units per month at a reduced price of Rs 60 per unit, incurring additional variable costs of Rs 5 per unit towards export packing, duties, etc.:

(b) to increase the domestic market sales by selling to a domestic chain stores 30,000 units at Rs 55 per unit, retaining the existing sales at the existing price;

(c) to reduce the selling price for the increased domestic sales as advised by the sales department as under:

Reduce selling price per unit by Rs	*Increased in sales expected (in units)*
5	10,000
8	30,000
11	35,000

Prepare a table to present the results of the above proposals and give your comments and advice on the proposals.

Solution

The three proposals can be studied by differential cost analysis. The present capacity utilisation is only 50% and as such there is a scope to increase the sales up to another 4,000 units. The comparison of proposals will depend on contribution generated since the field cost is not affected upto full utilisation and as such not relevant for decision-making.

Statement showing Contribution at Various Price Levels

Particulars	*Proposal (a)*		*Proposal (b)*		*Proposal (c)*	
	Present Level	*Export Order*	*Present Level*	*Domestic Order*	*Price*	*Reduction*
Selling Price per unit Rs	75	60	55	70	67	64
Variable Cost per unit Rs	50	55	50	50	50	50
Contribution per unit Rs	25	05	05	20	17	14
Quantities in units	40,000	30,000 (addl.)	30,000 (addl.)	50,000 (total)	70,000 (total)	75,000 (total)
Existing Contribution (Rs in lakh)	10	—	—	—	—	—
Additional Contribution (Rs in lakh)		1.5	1.5			
Total Contribution for revised quantity (Rs in lakhs)				10.0	11.9	10.5
Total Contribution (Rs in lakhs)	10.00	11.5	11.5	10.0	11.9	10.5
Proposal		(a)	(b)	c(i)	c(ii)	c(iii)

Comments and Advice:

(1) In case only cost considerations are considered, proposal to reduce selling price by Rs 8 to get a gross sales of 7,000 units is most profitable since it yields a total contribution of Rs 11.9 lakhs.

(2) In between export order as per proposal (a) and increased domestic order as per proposal (b) there is no change in additional profitability since both yield same results.

(3) However keeping in mind the impact on other domestic sale, if a part of production alone is sold at a drastically reduced price of Rs 55 per unit, it is desirable to go for export order. This will also enable gaining valuable foreign exchange. Besided with exchange rate fluctuations it may result in higher profits, in case the selling price is quoted in foreign currency.

(4) Reduction in selling price against possible increased sales is full of doubt and has only a marginal effect of Rs 40,000 as additional profit.

Thus, on the whole it is better to go for export order.

Example 19 (*Product priority Decision*)

Sum Toys (P) Ltd. manufactures and sells children's toys of high quality over an extensive market, utilising the services of skilled artists who are paid at an average rate of Rs 15 per hour. The total no. of skilled labour hours available in a year is only 14,000. The details of planned production for 2005-06, estimated cost and unit selling prices are given below :

Toy	*Production Planned (unit)*	*Cost of Production per Unit*			*Selling Price per unit*
		Direct Materials Rs	*Direct Labour* Rs	*Fixed Overheads* Rs	Rs
A	3,000	20	10	15	70
B	4,000	24	12	18	92
C	4,000	32	12	18	95
D	3,000	40	16	24	110
E	2,400	60	20	30	180

Variable overhead costs amount to 50% of the direct labour cost.

The company has estimated the following maximum and minimum demands for each product :

	A	*B*	*C*	*D*	*E*
Maximum (units)	5,000	6,000	6,000	4,000	4,000
Minimum (units)	1,000	1,000	1,000	500	500

Solution

Basic Calculations

Statement of Priority Production Taking Labour Time as key Factor

Product	*Selling Price per unit*	*Total Variable Cost*				*Contribution*		
		Direct materials	*Direct labour*	*Variable overheads*	*Total*	*Per unit*	*Per Labour hour*	*Production priority*
	Rs	Rs	Rs	Rs	Rs	Rs	Rs	
A	70	20	10	5	35	35	52.50	IV
B	92	24	12	6	42	50	62.50	II
C	95	32	12	6	50	45	56.25	III
D	110	40	16	8	64	46	43.13	V
E	180	60	20	10	90	90	67.50	I

Contribution per labour hour has been derived as follows:

$$\frac{\text{Product per unit contributin} \times \text{Rs15 average labour rate}}{\text{Product direct labour cost}}$$

Product A = $\quad = 52.5$

$$B = \frac{50 \times 15}{12} = 62.5$$

$$C = \frac{45 \times 15}{12} = 56.25$$

$$D = \frac{46 \times 15}{16} = 43.13$$

$$E = \frac{90 \times 15}{20} = 67.50$$

(a) Statement of Estimated Profit for 2005-06
(As per Company's Production Plan)

Product	*Vol. of Sales (units)*	*Contribution per unit (Rs)*	*Total Contribution (Rs)*	*Total Fixed Cost (Rs)*	*Profit (Rs)*
A	3,000	35	1,05,000	45,000	60,000
B	4,000	50	2,00,000	72,000	1,28,000
C	4,000	45	1,80,000	72,000	1,08,000
D	3,000	46	1,38,000	72,000	66,000
E	2,400	90	2,16,000	72,000	1,44,000
			8,39,000	3,33,000	5,06,000

(b). Production Plan for Maximum Profits

Product	*Volume of Sales (units)*	*Hours required*	*Contribution per unit (Rs)*	*Total Contribution (Rs)*	*Priority*
E	4,000 (Max.)	5,334	90	3,60,000	I
B	6,000 (Max.)	4,800	50	3,00,000	II
C	3,331 (Balance)	2,665 (Bal. hrs.)	45	1,49,895	III
A	1,000 (Minimum)	667	35	35,000	IV
D	500 (Minimum)	534	46	23,000	V
		14,000		8,67,895	

(a) The maximum profit under plan (b) suggested would amount to Rs 8,67,895 – Rs 3,33,000 = Rs 5,34,895.

Example 20 (*Buy Decision*)

Stirling Industries Ltd. manufactures a product Z by making and assembling three components A, B and C. The components are made in a machine shop using three identical machines each of which can make any of the three components. However, the total capacity of the three machines is only 12,000 machine-hours per month and is just sufficient to meet the current demand. Labour for assembling is available according to requirements. Further details are given below :

Components	*Machine-hours required per unit*	*Variable cost per unit*	*Market price at which the component can be purchased if required*
A	4	Rs 48	Rs 64
B	5	60	75
C	6	80	110
Assembling (per unit of Z)	–	30	–

Fixed costs per month amount to Rs 50,000. Product Z is sold at Rs 300 per unit. From next month onwards the company expects the demand for Z to rise by 25%. As the machine capacity is limited, the company wants to meet the increase in demand by buying such numbers of A, B or C which is most profitable.

You are asked to find out the following :

(a) Current demand and profit made by the company.

(b) Which component and how many units of the same should be bought from the market to meet the increase in demand ?

(c) Profit made by the company if suggestion in (b) is accepted.

Solution

(a) Total Machine Hours required per unit of Z = 15 hrs.
Hence, with 12,000 hours available 800 units of Z can be produced.

Statement of Current Profit (Output and Sales 800 Units)

	Particulars	*Rs*
	Selling Price per unit	300
Less :	Variable cost including assembling	218
	Contribution per unit	82
	Total contribution from 800 units @ Rs 82	65,600
Less:	Fixed Costs	50,000
	Current Net Profit	15,600

(b) Statement of Additional Cost per Hour if Components are Purchased from the Market

	A	*B*	*C*
Market Price per unit	Rs 64	Rs 75	Rs 110
Less: variable Cost of making per unit	Rs 48	Rs 60	Rs 80
Additional Cost of purchasing per unit	Rs 16	Rs 15	Rs 30
Hours saved by purchasing	4	5	6
Additional cost per hour-saved	Rs 4	Rs 3	Rs 5

Thus, to save machine hours it is best to purchase B which has the least additional cost per hour. In the next month demand will be 25% more *i.e.*, (800 units + 25%) or 1,000 units. This can be met as follows:

	Hrs required
Make 1,000 units of C	6,000
Make 1,000 units of A	4,000
Make 400 units of B	2,000 (Balance)
	12,000 hours

The balance of 600 units (1,000 – 400) of B can be purchased from the market.

(c) Statement of Profit as per plan given in (b)

		Rs	Rs
Sale Value of 1,000 units of Z	@ Rs 300		3,00,000
Cost of making 1,000 units of C	@ Rs 80	Rs 80,000	
Cost of making 1,000 units of A	@ Rs 48	Rs 48,000	
Cost of making 400 units of B	@ Rs 60	Rs 24,000	
Cost of buying 600 units of B	@ Rs 75	Rs 45,000	
Assembling 1,000 units Z	@ Rs 30	Rs 30,000	2,27,000
Contribution			73,000
Fixed Costs			50,000
Net Profit			23,000

Example 21 (*Production Subcontracting Decision*)

New Bharat Industries is manufacturing several consumer durables which have good demand in the market. The firm has been established only very recently and currently it is in the final stage of production. It has ambitious plans to expand production after earning income in the market. However, the company is having a problems to get adequate power supply. Moreover, most of its labourers are casual workers and labour absenteeism is also affecting production. In view of these unstable conditions the firm has adopted the practice of preparing quarterly flexible budgets.

For the quarter ending 31st December, 2006 flexible budgets for three possible levels of production were prepared as follows. The company wanted to achieve 90% capacity utilisation as its products had good demand.

Particulars	*Flexible Budgets* 60%	80%	90%
		(in Lakhs of rupees)	
Budgeted Sales	50.00	66.00	75.00
Budgeted Costs:			
Direct Materials	12.00	16.00	18.00
Direct Labour	15.00	20.00	22.50
Production Overheads	11.80	14.00	15.10
Administration Overheads	2.00	2.00	2.00
Selling overheads	7.80	9.80	10.20

Soon after the decision to attain 90% capacity utilisation, available power was reduced by the State Electricity Board and the reduced supply was sufficient to meet 50% capacity production.

The position has been immediately reviewed and the firm is considering the following possible options to meet the situation.

(a) Stop production for the quarter. As regular employees are only very few, lay-off compensation payable will be only Rs 1.20 lakhs. Further, overheads can be reduced by as much as 60%.

(b) Continue production at 50% level. Estimated sales income at this level will be Rs 40 lakhs.

(c) A private agency in the area has offered surplus captive power available with it. With this additional supply production can be maintained at 90% level. However, the overall variable production overhead will increase by 40%.

(d) Sub-contract the balance 40% which cannot be made by the firm to two small industrial units in the area, which have the necessary facilities, equally at a cost of Rs 15 lakhs each.

Evaluate each of the above options and recommend the best plan. Indicate the other important points, if any, to be considered.

Solution

Flexible Budget

(In Rs lakhs)

Capacity Levels:	*50%*		*90%*	
Costs:	*Variable*	*Fixed*	*Variable*	*Fixed*
Direct Materials	10.00	–	18.00	–
Direct Labour	12.50	–	22.50	
Production Overheads	5.50	5.20	9.90	5.20
Administration Overheads	–	2.00	–	2.00
Selling & distribution Overheads	4.00	3.00	7.20	3.00
Total	32.00	10.20	57.60	10.20
Total Cost		42.20		67.80
Sales		40.00		75.00
Estimated Profit (Loss)		(2.20)		7.20

Results under different options

(a) *Stop Production*

Lay-off compensation	Rs 1.20 lakhs
Fixed Overheads at 40% of Rs 10.20 lakhs	4.08 lakhs
Loss	5.28 lakhs

(b) *Continue Production at 50% capacity:*
Loss incurred will be Rs 2.20 lakhs
(as shown in Flexible Budget above)

(c) *Purchase Power from external source:*

Production is now at 90% level		
Profit at 90% level Rs 7.20 lakhs	Rs 7.20 lakhs	(as shown in the Flexible Budget above)
Less: Additional Cost: Variable Production Overheads @ 40% of Rs 9.90 lakhs	3.96 lakhs	
Net Profit	3.24 lakhs	

(d) *Sub-contract Part of Production:*

Cost of Production at 50% level	Rs 42.20 lakhs
Payment to Sub-contract Firms towards Production	Rs 30.00 lakhs
Cost: Variable Selling and Distribution Overheards for balance 40% goods supplied by outsiders (Rs 7.20 lakhs – Rs 40 lakhs)	Rs 3.20 lakhs
	Rs 75.40 lakhs
Sales	Rs 75.00 lakhs
Net loss	Rs 0.40 lakhs

Comments: The firm is a growing firm which is trying to expand its production and sales. At present it is affected mainly by shortage of power which is working as a limiting factor. As its long term objective is to expand its activities, options (a) and (b) are not acceptable. Option (d), apart from the loss, entrusting production to another unit, may result in parting with technology and method of manufacture and creating a potential competitor. Hence, this is also not acceptable, even if it has been more profitable. The best course for the firm at present, therefore is to follow option (c) and build up its own captive power supply so that future production would in no way be affected.

THEORY QUESTIONS

1. What is meant by the term "differential costing"? Does differential cost mean the same thing as variable cost?
2. What is incremental cost? Does incremental cost mean the same thing as variable cost?
3. Give examples of how incremental costs are used in decision-making.
4. A departmental store is thinking of eliminating one of its departments because the accountant using the total cost basis to profitability analysis, says the department is operating at a loss. What should be investigated before the final decision is made?
5. Explain the meaning and features of relevant costs. Give suitable examples to support your explanation.
6. Ventilators Ltd. wants to stabilise its production through the year. The approaches recommended are :
   (a) Maintain production at an even pace throughout the year, and get the off-season producing stored on the premises.
   (b) Maintain production at an even pace but offer dealers a special discount for off-season purchases.
   (c) Extend special terms to dealers, but maintain prices at a level that will enable regular movement of goods throughout the year.

   Discuss the relative merits and disadvantages of the above proposals.
7. Cost-benefit analysis is needed for resolving many managerial problems. List the various items of cost and benefits that you will quantify in respect of managerial decisions:
   (a) change versus status quo;
   (b) retain or replace;
   (c) shutdown or continue

8. Explain the basic characteristics of costs involved in decision-making.
9. State the costing data required for (i) determining the priority of products, and (ii) make or buy decisions.
10. How would you go about determining the point at which a manufacturing company that is facing a period of operating losses should shut assuming that profitability of operations is the only point to be considered?
11. Why is the contribution that a product makes towards the recovery of non-escapable costs a better measure of its profitability than the profit or loss reported on its sale after it has been charged with its fair share of all costs?

PROBLEMS

1. Timeless products, a clock manufacturer, is operating at capacity. Constrained by machine time, the company has decided to drop the most unprofitable of its three product lines. The accounting department came up with the following data from last year's operations:

	Manual	*Electric*	*Quartz*
Machine time per unit	0.4 hour	2.5 hours	5.0 hours
Selling price per unit	Rs 20	30	50
Less: Variable costs per unit (Rs)	(10)	(14)	(28)
Contribution margin (Rs)	10	16	22

Which line should Timeless products drop?

Ans. Timeless products should drop the quartz line.

2. A factory is currently working at 50% capacity and produces 10,000 units of product P, the unit cost of which is Rs 180 comprised as follows:

	Rs
Direct materials	100
Direct labour	30
Factory overhead	30(40% fixed)
Administration overhead	30(50% fixed)

The selling price per unit is Rs 200

If the capacity is increased to 60% the raw material cost increase by 2% and selling price falls by 2% At 80% capacity, raw material cost increases by 5% and selling price falls by 5%.

You are required to work out the total cost and profit for the three capacity levels and prepare a brief note for the management on the profitability at these levels of performance with your recommendation.

Ans. Profit at 50% Rs 2,00,000 at 60%, Rs 2,12,000. at 80%, Rs. 2,12,000. It is advisable to run the factory at 60% capacity level. The total amount of profit at 60% and 80% capacity is the same. In fact it will be preferable to use the surplus capacity over 60% for some other purpose.

3. A firm is selling X product, whose variable cost per unit is Rs 10 and fixed cost is Rs 6,000. It has sold 1,000 articles during one month at Rs 20 per unit. Market research shows that there is a great demand for the product if the price can be reduced. If the price can be reduced to Rs 12.50 per unit it is expected that 5,000 articles can be sold in the expanded market. The firm has to take a decision whether to produce and sell 1,000 units at the rate of Rs 20 or to produce and sell for the growing demand of 5,000 units at the rate of Rs 12.50. Give your advice to the management in taking a decision.

Ans. Profit (a) 1,000 units, Rs 4,000
(b) 5,000 units, Rs 6,500

Proposal to manufacture and sell 5,000 units is preferable.

4. A manufacturer of a certain product has been selling exclusively in the Indian market up to now. He has just received his first export equity and wants to quote as competitively as the circumstances will allow.

His latest Indian cost sheet is:

Raw materials	Rs 34 per unit
Direct labour	13
Services	6

Works overhead	7
Office overhead	2
	62
Profit earned in India	6
Indian selling price	68

Management is thinking of quoting a selling price somewhere between Rs 62 and Rs 68 per unit for this export order. One of the directors suggests quoting an even lower price based on the principles of marginal costing. As the firm's accountant, you are requested to compute the lowest price the management could quote on these principles. State clearly any assumptions that you may make on the above facts, and also on any other costs or facts.

Ans. Marginal cost of product Rs 51. Any price above this amount can be quoted by the company.

5. On the basis of the following information in respect of an engineering company, what is the product-mix which will give the highest profit attainable? Do you recommend overtime working up to a maximum of 15,000 hours at twice the normal wages (overheads are ignored for the purpose of this question)?

Products	*A*	*B*	*C*
Raw materials per unit (kg)	10	6	15
Labour hours per unit @ Re 1 per hour	15	25	20
Sales price per unit (Rs)	125	100	200
Maximum production possible (Units)	6,000	4,000	3,000

1,00,000 kg raw materials are available @ Rs 10 per kg. Maximum production hours are 1,84,000 with facility for a further 15,000 hours on overtime basis at twice the normal wage rate.

6. A company manufactures three products A, B and C. There are no common processes and the sale of one product does not affect price or volume of sales of any other.
The company's budgeted profit/loss for 2002 has been abstracted as follows:

	Total	*A*	*B*	*C*
Sales	Rs 3,00,000	Rs 45,000	Rs 2,25,000	Rs 30,000
Production cost: Variable	1,80,000	24,000	1,44,000	12,000
Fixed	60,000	3,000	48,000	9,000
Factory cost	2,40,000	27,000	1,92,000	21,000
Selling and administration costs: Variable	24,000	8,100	8,100	7,800
Fixed	6,000	2,100	1,800	2,100
Total cost	2,70,000	37,200	2,01,900	30,900
	30,000	7,800	23,100	(–) 900

On the basis of the above, the Board had almost decided to eliminate product C, on which a loss was budgeted. Meanwhile, they have sought your opinion. As the company's Cost Accountant what would you advice? Give reasons for your answer.

Ans. P/V ratio, A 28.7%, B 32.4%, C 34%

It is found that product C, though has the highest P/V Ratio, seems to be non-profitable because it has to bear a higher percentage of fixed cost as compared to its total cost. The percentage comes to about 36 $\left(i.e. \frac{11{,}100}{30{,}900} \times 100\right)$ which in case of other products is too less. Since the surplus capacity generated by one product canot be used for other product, there seems to be no justification for discontinuing product C till some new product is developed which will have a higher P/V ratio than product C. In the present circumstances, since C has a higher P/V ratio, and if the sales continue to rise, C may start giving profit too.

7. A factory produces 24,000 units. The cost sheet gives the following information :

Direct material	Rs 1,20,000
Direct wages	84,000
Variable overheads	48,000
Semi-variable overheads	28,000
Fixed overheads	80,000
Total Cost	3,60,000

The product is sold at Rs 20 per unit. The management proposed to increase the production by 3,000 units for sales in the foreign market. It is estimated that semi-variable overheads will increase by Rs 1,000. But the product will be sold at Rs 14 per unit in the foreign market. However, no additional capital expenditure will be incurred. The management seeks you advice as cost accountant. What will you advise them?

Ans. Sales of additional units 3,000 in the foreign market will give a profit of Rs 9500. Hence the proposal should be accepted.

8. The budgeted results for X Co. include the following :

	Rs in lakhs	*Variable cost as % of sales value*
Sales: Product A	60	50%
Product B	50	60%
Product C	80	65%
Product D	40	80%
Product E	30	70%
	260	

Fixed overheads for the period Rs 100.00 lakhs.

You are required to (a) Prepare a statement showing the amount of loss expected, (b) assuming that the sale of only one product can be increased at a time, you are asked to a recommend a change in the sale volume of each product which will eliminate the expected loss.

Ans. (a) Total loss Rs 5,00,000.

(b) Additional sales required to break-even, assuming sales of only one product is increased at a time, to give the additional contribution of Rs 5,00,000, is calculated as follows:

$$\text{Sales required} = \frac{\text{Under – recovery of fixed overhead}}{\text{P / V ratio of the product}}$$

Product	*Rs*	*Rs*
A	$\frac{5,00,000}{50\%}$	10,00,000
B	$\frac{5,00,000}{40\%}$	12,50,000
C	$\frac{5,00,000}{45\%}$	14,28,571
D	$\frac{5,00,000}{20\%}$	25,00,000
E	$\frac{5,00,000}{30\%}$	16,66,667

The company should utilise the spare capacity available for Product 'A' to achieve maximum profitability as its P/V ratio is highest. Fixed costs remaining the same at every level of production, this combination will lead to maximum profitability.

9. Quality Products. Ltd. manufactures and markets a single product. The following data are available.

	Per unit		*Per unit*
Materials	Rs 16	Dealer's margin	Rs 4
Conversion costs (Variable)	12	Selling price	40

Fixed cost: Rs 5 lakhs

Present sales: 90,000 units

Capacity utilisation: 60 per cent

There is acute competition. Extra efforts are necessary to sell. Suggestions have been made for increasing sales:

(a) By reducing sales price by 5 per cent.

(b) By increasing dealer's margin by 25 per cent over the existing rate.

Which of these two suggestions you would recommend, if the company desires to maintain the present profit? (Give reasons)

Ans. Present profit Rs 2,20,000

(a) Units required to maintain the same profit 1,16,111 units

(b) Units required to maintain the same profit 102,875 units. Second proposal is recommended.

10. From the cost records of a company, for a specific period for product X, the information given in the first column is extracted. The second column can be ignored since it is only one of the projections of an assistant accountant; but it may be useful to you:

	This period activity	*One of the future projections*
Sales, in units	10,000	20,000
Profit (loss) (in Rs)	(10,000)	10,000
Fixed cost (in Rs)	30,000	30,000
Variable cost per unit (in Rs)	8	8

On the basis of the first column, determine:

(a) What increased sales volume is required to cover an extra attractive packaging cost of Re 0.50 per unit, to increase the sales, at the existing sales price, to yield zero profit?

(b) What increased sales volume is required, at the present sale price to cover an additional publicity expense of Rs 5,000 for that period while yielding a profit of Rs 5,000?

(c) What increased sales volume is required to reach a profit of Rs 4,000 while reducing the selling price by 3% per unit ?

Ans. (a) BEP if extra packaging cost is incurred is 20,000 units. Additional Sales Rs 1,00,000.

(b) Additional sales required Rs 1,00,000.

(c) Additional sales required Rs 94,000.

11. Yardley Corporation uses a joint process to produce products A, B and C. Each product may be sold at its split-off point or processed further. Additional processing costs are entirely variable and are traceable to the respective products produced. Joint production costs for 2002 were Rs 50,000.

Relevant data are as follows:

Sales value and additional costs if processed further

Product	*Units Produced*	*Sales value at split-off*	*Sales value*	*Additional costs*
A	20,000	Rs 45,000	Rs 60,000	Rs 20,000
B	15,000	75,000	98,000	20,000
C	15,000	30,000	62,000	18,000
		Rs 1,50,000		

Required:

To maximise profit, which products should Yardley subject to further processing? Why?

12. Alpha Company has the following budgeted figures for its various products for next year :

	Products		
	A	*B*	*C*
	(Rs '000)	(Rs'000)	(Rs'000)
Sales value	480	480	160
Variable costs	432	384	120
Fixed costs (allocated)	24	36	50

The company is concerned about product C and several alternatives are being considered:

Alternative 1

Cut C's selling price by 10%. it is estimated that this will increase C's unit sales by 40%.

Alternative: 2

Substitute a new product D for C. Estimated sales are Rs 1,40,000 in the first year. Variable costs are estimated at 55% of sales. Fixed cost directly attributable to C of Rs 10,000 will be eliminated but Rs 16,000 additional fixed costs directly attributable to D will be incurred.

Alternative: 3
Eliminate C entirely. This will reduce the fixed costs attributable to C by Rs 10,000.
Alternative: 4
Convert C into special finish by adding additional treatments, which will secure a price increase of 20%. The additional costs incurred will be 10% of the new increased price.
Management wants to know the effect of each alternative on the profit of the company and their ranking in order of preference.

Ans. The four alternatives have no relationship with products A and B. It can be assumed that these products will continue to make contribution whatever they are currently making. Therefore, there is no need to examine products A and B profitability.
For product C, the following ranking of alternatives is applicable :
Rank 1 — Alternative 2 — Increases profit by Rs 17,000
Rank 2 — Alternative 4 — Increases profit by Rs 12,800
Rank 3 — Alternative 1 — Increases profit by Rs 9,600
Rank 4 — Alternative 3 — Increases profit by Rs 30,000

13. A company is at present working at 90 per cent of its capacity and producing 13,500 units per annum. It operates a Flexible Budgetary control System. The following figures are obtained from its budget:

	90%	100%
	Rs	Rs
Sales	15,00,000	16,00,000
Fixed expenses	3,00,500	3,00,600
Semi-fixed expenses	97,300	1,00,500
Variable overhead expenses	1,45,000	1,49,500
Units made	13,500	15,000

Labour and material cost per unit are constant under present conditions. Profit margin is 10 per cent.
(a) You are required to determine the differential cost of producing 1,500 units by increasing capacity to 100 per cent.
(b) What would you recommend for an export price for these 1,500 units taking into account that overseas prices are much lower than indigenous prices?

14 A toy manufacturer earns an average net profit of Rs 30 per piece in a selling price of Rs 150 by producing and selling 60,000 pieces at 60% of the potential capacity. Composition of his cost of sales is:

Direct material	:	Rs 40
Direct wages	:	Re 10
Works overhead	:	Rs 60 (50% fixed)
Sales	:	Re 10 (25% variable)

During the current year, he intends to produce the same number but anticipates that:
(a) his fixed charges will go up by 10%
(b) rates of direct labour will increase by 20%
(c) rates of direct material will increase by 5%
(d) selling price cannot be increased.
Under these circumstances, he obtains an order for a further 20% of his capacity. What minimum price will you recommend for accepting the order to ensure the manufacturer an overall profit of Rs 1,87,000 ?

CHAPTER 7

Standard Costing

DEFINITION OF STANDARD COST, STANDARD COSTING

A standard cost is a planned cost for a unit of product or service rendered. Standard costs represent excellent target costs that should be obtained. The Institute of Cost and Management Accountants (UK) defines standard cost as "a predetermined cost which is calculated from management's standards of efficient operation and the relevant necessary expenditure. It may be used as a basis for price fixing and for cost control through variance analysis." Standard cost expresses what costs should be under attainable good performance.

Standard costing is the setting of predetermined cost estimates in order to provide a basis for comparison with actual costs. The Institute of Cost and Management Accountants (UK) defines standard costing as "the preparation and use of standard costs, their comparison with actual costs, and the analysis of variances to their causes and points of incidence."

ADVANTAGES OF STANDARD COSTING

Among the many advantages generally attributed to standard costing, the most important may be listed as follows:

1 *Managerial planning.* Planning is a process of using all resources in such a manner that maximises business profits. Standard costs, are more convenient than actual costs for budget preparation because the standard costs at different production levels and for different product-mixes are readily built up into total costs as called for by the budget. On the other hand, using actual costs requires a great deal of analysis and adjustment when extensive changes in product volume or product-mixes take place.

2. *Coordination* The establishment of standards coordinates all functions—manufacturing, marketing engineering, research, and accounting towards the achievement of a common goal. Setting standards involves defining and communicating targets so that they can work towards the attainment of the goal.

3. *Cost Control* Cost control and cost reduction are probably the most important aims of any costing system; and standard costing gives due recognition to this fact. Cost control has the objective of production of the required quality at the lowest cost attainable under existing conditions. Standards enable management to make periodic comparison of actual costs with standard costs in order to measure performance and to take action to maintain control over costs.

4. *Economical means of costing and record-keeping* The use of standard costs can reduce clerical labour and expense by avoiding the detailed record-keeping which is necessary when actual *costs* alone are used.

5. *Formulating price and production policies* Standard costs as compared to actual costs can be used for estimating selling prices. When standard unit costs are available, expected costs and sales prices can be computed on the basis of standard costs. Standards already established can easily be modified to reflect current conditions and changes in material prices or labour rates and the price of the product can be determined on a realistic basis.

Actual costs, on the other hand, may reflect excessive usage of material, abnormal labour: times or an inequitable charge for overhead. Actual overhead cost per unit at any given time may be so influenced by temporary fluctuations in production levels as to make actual cost entirely unusable for pricing.

6. *Standards as incentives to employees* If standards are reasonable and attainable they act as incentives to employees to improve their performances and to maintain the quality of the product, Standards motivate workers, supervisors and foremen to work more efficiently in the accomplishment of their respective standards.

DIFFERENT TYPES OF STANDARDS

The two principal consideration affecting the classification of standards are: (i) attainability of standards, that is, the ease with which it is possible to achieve the standards, and (ii) frequency with which the standards are revised. On the basis of these two factors, it is possible to classify standards as ideal normal, basic, current or expected actual standards.

Ideal, Perfect, Maximum Efficiency or Theoretic Standards

Ideal standards (costs) are the standards which can be attained under the most favourable conditions possible. The level of performance under ideal standards would be achieved through the possible combination of factors—the most favourable prices for materials and labour, highest output with best equipment and layout, and maximum efficiency in the utilisation of the production resources—in other words, maximum output at minimum cost. Such standards reflect only goals or targets without any hope of performance being currently achieved. These standards are extremely tight and do not provide for waste and inefficiency in any form; no material is wasted; no units are spoiled; there are no idle hours; operators work at predetermined speed; the available capacity is fully utilised.

Normal Standards

Normal standards are the average standards which (it is anticipated) can be attained during a future period of time, preferably long enough to cover one business cycle. These standards are not revised until the cycle has run its full course. This generally results in an incorrect valuation of inventories and consequent errors in the profit disclosed, as the inventories are understated in periods of high prices, and over-stated when prices are low. Normal standards are mainly used as a device to solve the problem of absorbing fixed overhead rather than in connection with material cost and wages. Since these standards do not reflect the goals to be attained, they are not often used.

Basic Standards

The Institute of Cost and Management Accountants (UK) defines a basic standard as the standard which is established for use unaltered for an indefinite period which may be a long period of time. Basic standards are seldom revised or updated to reflect current operating costs and price level changes .

Currently Attainable or Expected Actual Standards

Current standards are standards which are established for use over a short period of time, and are related to current conditions. They represent current costs to be expected *from* efficient operations. Currently attainable standards are formulated after making allowance for the cost of normal spoilage. cost of idle time due to machine breakdowns, and the cost of other events which are unavoidable in normal efficient operations. They take the place of actual cost and are recorded in account books and financial statements. Any deviation from these standards reflect inefficiencies in the production activities. unless the variances have occurred due to uncontrollable factors. These standards are most accurate and very useful to management in product costing, inventory valuations: estimates, analyses, performance evaluation, planning, employee motivation, and for managerial decision making and external financial reporting.

HOW TIGHT SHOULD STANDARD BE

It can be rightly said that a single standard may not be suitable for all purposes. For the purposes of cost control, tight standards need to be established. The attainable (good) performance standards are useful for purposes of inventory valuation, product costing and income determination.

High Standards

A high standard helps in cost reduction and motivating employees to try to reach the targets established. High standards represent the best possible performance and, if achieved, raise the levels of performance and efficiency as compared to poor or loose standards. High standards being unattainable in practice may not be good for the employees. Employees may not seriously accept them because they know that they are unattainable and impossible to achieve. High standards are also not realistic and therefore cannot be used in product costing, inventory valuation, financial statement, planning, and capital investment decisions.

Low (Loose) Standards

A Standard which is low or loose can be attained by poor performance. However, it defeats the purpose of standard costing and fails to disclose inefficiencies. Such standards do not help management in cost control as they are not accurate measures to compare actual results.

In conclusion, it can be said that accountants generally seem to favour currently attainable standards which are most appropriate for performance appraisal, accounting purposes, cost control and decision-making. Such standards produce good performance, promote employee motivation and include unavoidable elements, such as spoilage, lost time, capacity not utilised in setting standards.

REVISION OF STANDARDS

Standard costs require continuous review and. at times, frequent change. Changing prices, technological advances, new personnel, new machinery, changing quality of materials and new labour negotiations, all influence standards and make them obsolete resulting in unrealistic budgets, poor cost control and unreasonable unit cost for inventory valuation and income determination.

A company should establish a programme to revise standards whenever required so that standards can be set at a currently attainable level. Labour rate standards should be revised for any change in labour rates; material quantity standards for any change in type, quality of material or method of production. If a new machine is purchased to replace an old machine, labour time standards and material quantity standards should be updated. In addition to these obvious revisions, in every business firm there should be a system for revising standards for adequacy and suitability at least once a year. A periodic review of standards is desirable to accomplish the objectives of standard costing

VARIANCE ANALYSIS

The function of standards in cost accounting is to indicate variances between standard costs which are allowed and actual costs which have been recorded. The Institute of Cost and Management Accountants (UK) defines variance as the difference between a standard cost and the comparable actual cost incurred during a period. Variance analysis can be defined as the process of computing the amount of and isolating the cause of variances between actual costs and standard costs. Variance analysis involves two phases:

1. Computation of individual variances, and
2. Determination of the cause(s) of each variance

First, we concentrate on the computation of material, labour and factory overhead variances. Analysis of causes, reporting variances to managers, and accounting disposition of variances conclude the study of standard costing in this chapter.

Materials Variance

The following variances constitute materials variances:

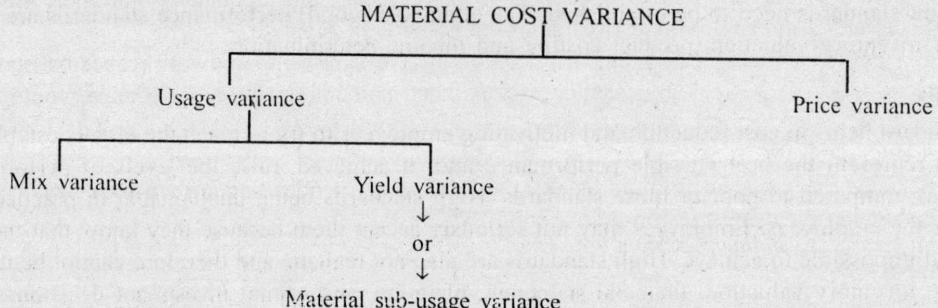

Material Cost Variance

Material cost variance is the difference between the actual cost of direct materials used and standard cost of direct materials specified for the output achieved. This variance results from differences between quantities consumed and quantities of materials allowed for production and from differences between prices paid and prices predetermined. This can be computed by using the following formula.

Material cost variance = $(AQ \times AP)\ \{SQ \times SP)$

where
AQ = Actual quantity
AP = Actual price
SO = Standard quantity for the actual output
SP = Standard price

Materials Usage Variance

The material quantity or usage variance results when actual quantities of raw materials used in production differ from standard quantities that should have been used to produce the output achieved. It is that portion of the direct materials cost variance which is due to the difference between the actual quantity used and standard quantity specified. As a formula this variance is shown as:

Materials quantity variance = (Actual quantity – Standard quantity) × Standard price

A material usage variance is favourable when the total actual quantity of direct materials used is less than the total standard quantity allowed for the actual output.

Example 1

Compute the materials usage variance from the following information:

Standard material cost per unit		Materials issued
Material A	2 pieces @ Re 1.00 = 2.00	Material A 2,050 pieces
Material B	3 Pieces @ Rs 2,00 = 6.00	Material B 2,980 pieces.
	Rs 8.00	
	Units completed 1,000	

Solution

Materials usage variance = (Actual quantity – Standard quantity) × Standard price

Material A = (2,050 – 2,000) x Re 1.00 = Rs 50 (Adverse or Unfavourable)

Material B = (2,980 – 3,000) × Rs 2.00 = Rs 40 (Favourable)

Total = Rs 10 (Unfavourable)

It should be noted that the standard rather than the actual price is used in computing the usage variance. Use of actual price would have introduced a price factor into a quantity variance. Because different departments are responsible, these two factors must be kept separate.

As a genèral principle, actuals (cost, quantity, price, output, etc.) are compared with respective standard data to compute variances. Therefore, any formula to calculate, mathematically, any variance would be as follows:

(Actual-Standard)

However, one may use variance formula as Standard-Actual as it does not influence in any way the variance figure calculated by using the formula 'Actual-Standard'.

Materials Price Variance

A materials price variance occurs when raw materials are purchased at a price different from standard price. It is that portion of the direct materials which is due to the difference between actual price paid and standard price specified and cost variance multiplied by the actual quantity. Expressed as a formula,

Materials price variance (Actual price – Standard price) × Actual quantity

Materals price variance is unfavourable when the actual pr:ce paid exceeds the predetermined standard price. It is advisable that materials price variance should be calculated at the time of materials purchase rather than when materials are used. Purchase of matrials is an earlier event than the use of materials. Therefore, a variance based on quantity purchased is basically an earlier report than a variance based on quantity actually used. This is quite beneficial from the viewpoint of performance measurement and corrective action.

Example 2

Assuming in Example 8.1 that material A was purchased at the rate of Re 1.00 and material B was purchased at the rate of Rs 2.10 the material price variance will be as follows:

Materials price variance = (Actual price – Standard price) × Actual quantity

Material A = (1,00 – 1,00) × 2,050 = Zero

Material B = (2.10 – 2.00) × 2.980 = Rs 298 (Unfavourable)

The total of materials usage variance and price variance is equal to materials cost variance.

Materials Mix Variance

The materials usage or quantity variance can be separated into mix variance and yield variance.

A mix variance will result when materials are not actually placed into production in the same ratio as the standard fomula. For instance, if a product is producèd by adding 100 kg of raw material A and 200 kg of raw material B, the standard material mix ratio is 1 : 2. Actual raw materials used must be in this 1 : 2 ratio, otherwise a materials mix variance will be found.

Materials mix variance is that portion of the materials quantity variance which is due to the difference between the actual composition of a mixture and the standard mixture. It can be computed by using the following formula:

Materials mix variance = (Standard cost of actual quantity of the actual mixture – Standard cost of actual quantity of the standard mixture)

or

Materials mix vàriance = (Actual mix – Revised standard mix of actual input) × Standard price

Revised standard proportion is calculated as follows :

$$\frac{\text{Standard mix of a particular material}}{\text{Total standard quantity}} \times \text{Actual input}$$

Example 3

A product is made from two raw materials, materials A and materials B. One unit of finished product tequires 10 kg of material. The following is standard mix:

Material A	20%	2 kg @	Rs 2.00 =	Rs 4.00
Material B	80%	8 kg @	Rs 1.00 =	Rs 8.00
	100%	10 kg	Rs 1.20	Rs 12.00

During a period one unit of product was produced at the following costs:

Material A	8 kg @	Rs 2.00	= Rs 16.00
Material B	4 kg @	Rs 1.25	= Rs 5.00
	12 kg	Rs 1.75	Rs 21.00

Compute the materials mix variance.

Solution

Material mix variance = (Actual proportion – Revised standard proportion of actual input) × Standard price

Revised standard proportion:

$$\frac{\text{Standard of a particular mix}}{\text{Total standard quantity}} \times \text{Actual input}$$

Revised standard proportion :

$$\text{Material A} = \frac{2}{10} \times 12 = 2.40 \text{ kg}$$

$$\text{Material B} = \frac{8}{10} \times 12 = 9.60 \text{ kg}$$

Materials mix variance :

Material A = (8 kg – 2.40 kg) x 2.00
= 5.60 × 2.00 = Rs 11.20 (Unfavourable)

Material B = (4 kg – 9.60) × 1.00
= 5.60 × 1.00 = Rs 5.60 (Favourable)

Total mix variance = Rs 5.60 (Unfavourable)

Materials Yield Variance

Materials yield variance explains the remaining portion of the total materials quantity variance. It is that portion of materials usage variance which is due to the difference between the actual yield obtained and standard yield specified (in terms of actual inputs). In other words, yield variance occurs when the output of the final product does not correspond with the output that could have been obtained by using the actual inputs.

The total of materials mix variance and materials yield variance equals materials quantity or usage variance. When there is no materials mix variance, the materials yield variance equals the total materials quantity variance.

The formula for computing yield variance is as follows :

Yield variance = (Actual yield – Standard yield specified) × Standard cost per unit

or

Yield variance = (Actual loss – Standard loss on actual input) × Standard cost per unit

Example 4

Standard input = 100 tonnes, standard yield = 90 tonnes, standard cost per. tonne of output = Rs . 20 Actual input 200 tonnes, actual yield 182 tonnes. Compute the yield variance.

Solution

Standard yield for the actual input $\frac{90}{100} \times 200 = 180$ tonne

Yield variance = (Actual yield – Standard yield for the actual input) x Standard cost per unit.
= (182 – 180) × Rs 20
= 2 × 20 = 40 (Favourable)

The above yield variance can be computed by using another formula also, e.g.,

Yield variance = (Actual loss – Standard loss on actual input) × Standard cost per unit
= (18 tonnes – 20 tonnes) × Rs 20
= Rs 40 (Favourable)

In this example there is no mix variance and therefore, the materials usage variance will be equal to the materials yield variance.

The above formula uses output or loss as the basis of computing the yield variance. Yield variance can also be computed on the basis of input factors only. The fact is that loss in inputs equals loss in output. A lower yield simply means athat a higher quantity of inputs have been used and the anticipated or standard output (based on actual inputs) has not been achieved. Yield, in such a case, is known as subusage variance (or Revised usage variance) which can be computed by using the following formula: sub-usage or revised usage variance = (Revised standard proportion of actual input — Standard quantity) × Standard cost per unit of input.

Example 5

Standard material and Standard price for manufacturing one unit of a product is given below :

	Standard Material	Standard price
Material A	5 kg	@ Rs 4
Material B	3 kg	@ Rs 6

The actual production of the product is 400 units.
The actual material A 2,500 kg @ Rs 3.90
B 1,000 kg @ Rs 6.25
Calculate the materials subusage variance.

Solution

Revised standard production of actual input :

Material A = $\frac{5}{8} \times 3500 = 2187.\ 5$ kg

Material B = $\frac{5}{8} \times 3500\quad 1312.5$ kg

Material sub-usage variance:
(Revised standard proportion of actual input – Standard quantity) × St. cost per unit of Material A
= (2, 187.5 – 2,000) × 4
= 187.5 × 4 = Rs 750 (Unfavourable)

Material B = (1,312.5 – 1,200) × 6
= 112.5 × 6 = Rs 675 (Unfavourable)

Total materials subusage variance = Rs 1,425 (Unfavoaurable)

or

$$= (3,500 - 3,200) \times \text{Rs } \frac{15,200}{3,200}$$

$$= 300 \times \frac{15,200}{3,200} = \text{Rs } 1,425 \text{ (Unfavourable)}$$

Materials yield variance always equals subusage variance. The difference lies only in terms of calculation. The former considers the output or loss in output and the latter considers standard **input** and actual input used for the actual output,

Example 6

From the following particulars compute: (a) materials cost variance; (b) materials price variance (c) materials usage variance:

Quantity of materials purchased	3,000 units
Value of materials purchased	Rs 9.000
Standard quantity of materials required per tonne of output	30 units
Standard rate of material	Rs 2.50 per unit
Opening stock of materials	Nil
Closing stock of materials	500 units
Output during the period	80 tonnes

Solution

Materials consumed = 3,000 – 500 = 2,500 units

Actual rate of material $= \text{Rs } \frac{9,000}{3,000} = \text{Rs } 3 \text{ per unit}$

Standard quantity of actual output = 30 × 80 = 2,400 units

Materials cost variance = Actual cost – Standard cost
= (Actual price × Actual quantity) – (SP × Standard quantity)
= Rs 3 × 2,500 – Rs 2.50 × 2,400
= 7,500 – 6,000
= Rs 1,500 Adverse

Materials price variance = Actual quantity (Actual price – Standard price)
2,500 × (Rs 3 – Rs 2.50) = Rs 1250 (Adverse)

Materials usage variance = Standard price × (Actual quantity – Standard quantity)
= Rs 2.50 (2,500 – 2,400)
= Rs 250 (Adverse)

Example 7

The standard materials cost to produce a tonne of chemical X is:

300 kg of material A @ Rs 10 per kg
400 kg of material B @ Rs 5 per kg
500 kg of material C @ Rs 6 per kg

During a period, 100 tonnes of mixture X was prduced from the usage of :

35 tonnes of material A at a cost of Rs 9,000 per tonne
42 tonnes of material B at a cost ofRs 6,000 per tonne
53 tonnes of material C at a cost of Rs 7,000 per tonne

Calculate the price, usage and mix variances.

Solution

Material	*Standard*			*Actual*		
	Qty (Kg)	*Rate (Rs)*	*Amount (Rs)*	*Qty (Kg)*	*Rate (Rs)*	*Amount (Rs)*
A	30,000	10	3,00,000	35,000	9	3,15,000
B	40,000	5	2,00,000	42,000	6	2,52,000
C	50,000	6	3,00,000	53,000	7	3,71,000
	1,20,000		8,00,000	1,30,000		9,38,000

Materials cost variance = Actual cost – Standard cost for actual output
= Rs 9.38.000 – Rs 8,00,000
= Rs 1,38,000 (Adverse)

Materials price variance= Actual quantity × (Actual price – Standard price)

A = 35,000 × (9 – 10) = Rs 35,000 (F)
B = 42,000 × (6 – 5) = Rs 42,000 (A)
C = 53,000 × (7 – 6) = Rs 53,000 (A)
Total Rs 60,000 (A)

Materials price variance = Standard price × (Actual quantity – Standard quantity for actual output)

A = 10 × (35,000 – 30,000) = Rs 50.000 (A)
B = 5 × (42,000 – 40,000) = Rs 10,000 (A)
C = 6 × (53,000 – 50,000) = Rs 18.000 (A)
Total Rs 78,000 (A)

Materials mix variance = Standard price x (Actual quantity – Revised standard quantity)

A = Rs 10 × (35,000 – 32,500)
= 10 × 2.500 = Rs 25,000 (A)

B $= 5 \times \left(42{,}000 - \frac{1{,}30{,}000}{3}\right)$

$= 5 \times \frac{4{,}000}{3}$ = Rs 6,667(F)

C $= 6 \times \left(53{,}000 - \frac{1{,}62{,}500}{3}\right)$

$= 6 \times \frac{3{,}500}{3}$ = 7,000 (F)

Total = 11,333 (A)

Working Notes :

1. Revised standard quantity $= \frac{\text{Standard quantity of a mix} \times \text{Total actual quantity}}{\text{Total Standard quantity of mixture}}$

$$A = \frac{30{,}000}{1{,}20{,}000} \times 1{,}30{,}000 = 32{,}500 \text{ kg}$$

$$B = \frac{40,000}{1,20,000} \times 1,30,000 = \frac{1,30,000}{3}$$

$$C = \frac{50,000}{1,20,000} \times 1,30,000 = \frac{1,62,000}{3}$$

2. Standard cost per unit of output $= \dfrac{\text{Total standard cost}}{\text{Total standard output}}$

$$= \frac{\text{Rs } 8,00,000}{100} = \text{Rs } 8,000 \text{ per tonne}$$

3. Standard output for actual mix $= \dfrac{\text{Standard output}}{\text{Standard mix}} \times \text{Actual mix}$

$$= \frac{100}{1,20,000} \times 1,30,000$$

$$= \frac{1,300}{12} \text{ tonnes}$$

Materials yield variance (although not asked for in the question) would be calculated as follows:
Materials yield variance = (Actual output – Standard output for actual mixture) × Standard cost per unit output

$$= \left(100 - \frac{1300}{12}\right) \times \text{Rs } 8,000$$

$$= \frac{100}{12} \times \text{Rs } 8,000$$

$$= \text{Rs } 66,667$$

Example 8

A company manufacturing 'distempers' operates a costing system. The standard cost of one of the products of the company shows the following standards:

Materials	*Quantity*	*Standard price per kg (Rs)*	*Total Rs*
A	40 kg	75	3,000
B	10 kg	50	50
C	50 kg	20	1,000
Material cost per unit (Total)			4,500

The standard input mix is 100 kg and the standard output of the finished product is 90 kg. the actual results for period are:

Materials used

A = 2,40,000 kg @ Rs 80/kg
B = 40,000 kg @ Rs 52/kg
C = 2,20,000 kg @ Rs 21/kg

Actual output of the finished product = 4,20,000 kg

You are required to calculate the material price, mix and yield variances.

Solution

Material	*Standard*			*Actual*		
	Qty (Rs)	*Rate (Rs)*	*Amount (Rs)*	*Qty (Rs)*	*Rate (Rs)*	*Amount (Rs)*
A	2,00,000	75	1,50,00,000	2,40,000	80	1,92,00,000
B	50,000	50	25,00,000	40,000	52	20,80,000
C	2,50,000	20	50,00,000	2,20,000	21	46,20,000
	5,00,000		2,25,00,000	5,00,000		2,59,00,000

Standard output 4,50,000 kg
Actual output 4,20,000 kg

Materials cost variance = (Actual cost – Standard cost of actual output)
= 2,59,00,000 – 4,20,000 × 50
= 2,59,00,000 – 2,10,00,000
= Rs 49,00,000 (A)

Materials price variance = Actual quantity × (Actual rate – Standard rate)
A = 2,40,000 × (80 – 75) = 12,00,000 (A)
B = 40,000 × (52 – 50) = 80,000 (A)
C = 2,20,000 × (21 – 20) = 2,20,000 (A)
Rs 15,00,000

Material usage variance = Standard rate × (Actual quantity – Standard quantity for actual output)
A = 75 × (2,40,000 – 2,00,000 × 42/45) =40,00,000 (A)
B = 50 × (40,000 – 50,000 × 42/45)= 3,33,333 (F)
C = 20 × (2,20,000 – 2,50,000 × 42/45) = 2,66,667 (F)
Rs 34,00,000 (A)

Material mix variance = Standard rate × (Actual quantity– Revised standard quantity)
A = 75 (2,40,000 – 2,00,000) = 30,00,000 (A)
B = 50(40,000 – 50,000) = 5,00,000 (F)
C = 20 (2,20,000 – 2,25,000) = 6,00,000 (F)
Rs 19,00,000 (A)

Materials yield variance = Standard Cost per unit × (Actual output – Standard output for actual mix)
= 50 (4,20,000 – 4,50,000)
= Rs 15,00,000 (A)

Example 9

S. V. Ltd. manufactures a single product, the standard mix of which is:
Material A 60% at Rs 20 per kg
Material B 40% at Rs 10 per kg

Normal loss in production is 20% of input. Due to shortage of Material A, the standard mix was changed. Actual results for March 2002 were;

Material A	105 kg at Rs 20 per kg
Material B	95 kg at Rs 9 per kg
Input	200 kg
Loss	35 kg
Output	165 Kg

Calculate:

(i) Material Price Variance (ii) Material Usage Variance

(iii) Material Mix Variance (iv) Material Yield Variance

Solution

Workings :

1. Standard quantity for actual production —

$$\text{Material A} = \frac{60 \times 165}{80} = \frac{495}{4} \text{ kg}$$

$$\text{Material B} = \frac{40 \times 165}{80} = \frac{165}{2} \text{ kg}$$

2. Calculation of revised Standard quantity —

$$\text{Material A} = 200 \times \frac{3}{5} = 120 \text{ kg}$$

$$\text{Material B} = 200 \times \frac{3}{5} = 80 \text{ kg}$$

3. Calculation of standard quantity—

$$\text{Material A} = \frac{120 \times 165}{160} = \frac{495}{4}$$

$$\text{Material B} = \frac{80}{160} \times 165 = \frac{165}{2}$$

4. Calculation of standard cost per unit of output—

Material A = 60 × 20 = Rs 1,200

$$\text{Material B} = \frac{40}{100} \times 10 = \frac{\text{Rs } 400}{1{,}600}$$

Less loss 20% = 100 – 20 = 80

$$\text{Cost per unit} = \frac{1{,}600}{80} = \text{Rs } 20$$

(i) Calculation of Variances :

Material price variance = (AP – SP) × AQ

Material A = (Rs 20 – 20) × 105 = Nil

Material B = (Rs 9 – 10) × Rs 95 (F)

Total Rs 95 (F)

(ii) Material usage variance = (AQ – SQ) × SP

$$\text{Material A} = \left(105 - \frac{495}{4}\right) \times \text{Rs } 20 = \text{Rs } 375 \text{ (F)}$$

$$\text{Material B} = \left(95 - \frac{165}{2}\right) \times \text{Rs } 10 = \text{Rs } 125 \text{ (A)}$$

Total Rs 250 (F)

(iii) Material mix variances = (AQ – RSQ) × SP
Material A = (105 – 120) × Rs 20 = Rs 300 (F)
Material B = (95 – 80) × Rs 10 = Rs 150 (A)
Total Rs 150 (A)

(iv) Material yield variance = (Actual output – Std. output) × Std. cost per unit of outputs
= (165 – 160) × Rs 20 = Rs 100 (F)

Example 10

The standard cost of a certain chemical mixture is:

35% Material A at Rs 25 per kg

65% Material B at Rs 36 per kg

A standard loss of 5% is expected in production

During a period there is used :

125 kg of Material A at Rs 27 per kg and

275 kg of Material B at Rs 34 per kg

The actual output was 365 kg

Calculate:

(a) Material Cost Variance

(b) Material Price Variance

(c) Material Mix Variance

(d) Material Yield Variance

Solution

Material	*Standard*			*Actual*		
	Qty (Rs)	*Rate (Rs)*	*Amount (Rs)*	*Qty (Rs)*	*Rate (Rs)*	*Amount (Rs)*
A	140	25	3,500	125	27	3,375
B	260	36	9,360	275	34	9,350
	400		12,860	400		12,725

Standard output = 400 – 20 = 380 kg

Actual output = 365 kg

Standard cost per kg = 12,860/380 = Rs 33.84

The various variances can now be calculated as follows :

(a) Material cost variance = (Actual cost – Standard cost for actual output)
= 12,725 – 365 × 33.84
= 12,725 – 12,352 = Rs 373 (Adverse)

(b) Material price vriance = Actual quantity × (AR – SR)
A = 125 × (27 – 25) = 250 (A)
B = 275 × (34 – 36) = 350 (F)
= Rs 300 (Favourable)

(c) Material mix variance = Standard rate × (AQ – Revised standard quanity)
Material A = 25 × (125 – 140) = 375 (F)
Material B = 30 × (275 × 260) = 540 (A)
= 165 (Adverse)

(d) Material yield variance = Standard cost × (Actual output for actual mix – Standard output)
= 33.84 × (365 – 380)
= Rs 508 (Adverse)

Workings Notes:

1. Standard quantity for actual mix
   Material A : 400 × 35/100 = 140 kg
   Materil B : 400 × 65/100 = 260 kg
2. Since Standard mix and Actual mix are the same, the Revised standard quantity and Standard quantity will also be the same.

Example 11

The standard material inputs required for 1,000 kgs of a finished product are given below:

Material (in kg)	*Quantity (in Kg)*	*Standard Rate per kg (in Rs)*
P	450	20
Q	400	40
R	250	60
	1,100	
Standard Loss	100	
Standard Output	1,000	

Actual production in a period was 20,000 kgs. of the finished product for which the actual quantities of material used and the prices paid thereof are as under :

Material	*Quantity used (in kgs.)*	*Purchased price per kg (in Rs.)*
P	10,000	19
Q	8,500	42
R	4,500	65

Calculate :

(i) Material Cost Variance (MCV)
(ii) Material Price Variance (MPV)
(iii) Material Usage Variance (MUV)
(iv) Material Mix Variance (MMV)
(v) Material Yield Variance (MYV)

Present a reconciliation among the variances.

Solution

Material	*Standard Qty (Kgs)*	*Standard Rate (Rs)*	*Standard Amount (Rs)*	*Actual Qty (Kgs)*	*Actual Rate (Rs)*	*Actual Amount (Rs)*
P	9,000	20	1,80,000	10,000	19	1,90,000
Q	8,000	40	3,20,000	8,500	42	3,57,000
R	5,000	60	3,00,000	4,500	65	2,95,500
Total	22,000		8,00,000	23,000		8,39,500

Variances

(i) MCV = Standard Cost for Actual Output – Actual Cost
= 8,00,000 – 8,39,500 = Rs. 39,500 (A)

(ii) MPV = Actual Qty. × (SR – AR)
P = 10,000 × (20 – 19) = Rs. 10,000 (F)

Q = 8,500 × (40 – 42) = Rs 17,000 (A)
R = 4,500 × (60 – 65) = Rs 22,500 (A)
Rs. 29,500 (A)

(iii) MUV = SR × (Std. Qty. for Actual Output – Actual Qty.)
P = 20 × (9,000 – 10,000) = 20,000 (A)
Q = 40 × (8,000 – 8,500) = 20,000 (A)
R = 60 × (5,000 – 4,500) = 30,000 (F)
10,000 (A)

(iv) MMV = SR × (RSQ – AQ)

$$P = 20 \times \left(\frac{9,000}{22,000} \times 23,000\right) - 10,000$$

= 20 × (9,409 – 10,000) = Rs 11,820 (A)

$$Q = 40 \times \left(\frac{8,000}{22,000} \times 23,000\right) - 8,500$$

= 40 × (8,364 – 8,500) = 5,440 (A)

$$R = 60 \times \left(\frac{5,000}{22,000} \times 23,000\right) - 4,500$$

= 60 × (5,227 – 4,500) = 43,620 (F)
26,360 (F)

(v) MYV = Std. Cost per unit × (Std. Output for Actual Mix – Áctual Output)
= 40 × (20,909 – 20,000)
= Rs. 36,360 (Adverse)

Statement of Reconcillation of Variances

Particulars	*Rs.*	*Rs.*
(i) Material Price Variance		29,500(A)
(ii) Material usage Variance:		
(a) Material Mix Variance	26,363 (F)	
(b) Material Yield Variance	36,363 (A)	10,000 (A)
Material Cost Variance		39,500 (A)

Example 12

Pragati Company manufactures a product P by mixing three raw materals. For every 100 kg of output 125 kg of raw material input are used. In April 2006, there was an output of 5,600 kg. of P. The Standard and actual particulars of April, 2006 are as follows:

Raw Material	*Standard*		*Actual*	
	Mix	*Price per kg*	*Mix*	*Price per kg*
I	50%	Rs. 40	60%	Rs. 42
II	30%	Rs. 20	20%	Rs. 16
III	20%	Rs. 10	20%	Rs. 12

Calculate all material Variances. The actual quantity of material used was 7,000 kg

(*B.Com. Hons. Delhi 1997*)

Solution

Raw-material	*Standard for output of 5,600 kg.*			*Actual for output of 5,600 kg.*		
	Qty (Rs)	*Rate (Rs)*	*Amount (Rs)*	*Qty (Rs)*	*Rate (Rs)*	*Amount (Rs)*
I	3,500	40	1,40,000	4,200	42	1,76,400
II	2,100	20	42,000	1,400	16	22,400
III	1,400	10	14,000	1,400	12	16,800
Total	7000*		1,96,000	7,000		2,15,600

$$\frac{*5{,}600}{100} \times 125$$

DMCV = Std. Cost for Actual Output – Actual Cost
= 1,96,000 – 2,15,600 = Rs. 19,600 (A)

DMPV = Actual Qty. × (SR – AR)

I = 4,200 × (40 – 42) = 8,400 (A)
II = 1,400 × (20 – 16) = 5,600 (F)
III = 1,400 × (10 – 12) = 2,800 (A)
5,600 (A)

DMUV = SR × (Std. qty. for actual output – Actual qty.)

I = 40 × (3,500 – 4,200) =28,000 (A)
II = 20 × (2,100 – 1,400) =14,000 (F)
III = 10 × (1,400 – 1,400) = NIL
14,000 (A)

DMMV = SR × (SRQ – AQ)

Since total Std. Mix and Actual Mix are the same, the RSQ will be the same as Std. qty.

I 40 × (3,500 – 4,200) = 28,000 (A)
II 20 × (2,100 – 1,400) = 14,000 (F)
III 10 × (1,400 – 1,400) = 0
14,000 (A)

The DMYV will be *Nil.*

Example 13

Vinak Ltd. produces an article by blending two raw materials. It operates a standard costing system and the following standards have been set for raw materials:

Material	*Standard mix*	*Standard price per kg*
A	40%	Rs 4.00
B	60%	Rs 3.00

The standard loss in processing is 15%.

During April 2001 the company produced 1,700 kg of finished output. The position of stocks and purchases for the month of April 2001 is as under :

Materials	*Stock on 1.4.01 (kg)*	*Stock on 30.4.01 (kg)*	*Purchasing during April 2001* (kg)	Cost (Rs)
A	35	5	800	3,400
B	40	50	1,200	3,000

Calculate the following variances:

(i) Materials price variance
(ii) Materials usage variance
(iii) Materials yield variance
(iv) Materials mix variance
(v) Total materials cost variance.

Solution

Standard cost of standard mix:

Type of material material	*Standard quantity of material required Rs.*	*Standard price per kg Rs.*	*Standard quantity*
A	800	4	3,200
B	1,200	3	3,600
Total	2,000		6,800

Note: 1. The loss being 15% to produce 85 kg of an article, the standard quantity of material required is 100 kg. Therefore, to produce 1,700 kg of the article the standard quantity of material required is

$\frac{100}{85} \times 1{,}700$ kg or 2,000 kg

2. Out of 2,000 kg of material used, 40% is type A and 60% is type B, i.e. 800 kg of A and 1,200 kg of B are the standard quantities.

Actual costs

Type of materials	*Actual quantity of material used* kg	*Actual price per kg* Rs	*Actual quantity X actual price* Rs
A	830	4.25	3,518.75
B	1,190	2.50	2,995.50
Total	2,020		6,513.75

*Actual quantity of material A is 830 kg out of this 35 kg is available at the standard price of Rs 4 per kg and remaining 795 kg at Rs 4.25 per kg.

Actual quantity of material B used is 1,190 kg; out of this 40 kg is available at the standard price Rs 3 per kg and the remaining 1,150 kg at Rs 2.50.

(i) Materials price variance = Actual quantity × (Actual price – Standard price)

A. Standard price of 830 units @ 4		3,320.00
Actual price of 35 units @ Rs 4	140.00	
795 units @ Rs 4.25	3,378.75	3,518.75
		198.75 (A)

B. Standard price of 1, 190 units @ Rs.		3.570.00
Actual price of 40 units @ Rs 3	120,00	
1,150 units @ Rs 2.50	2,875.00	2,995.00
		575.00 (F)
Total		376.75 (F)

(ii) Materials (total) usage variance = Standard price × (Actual quantity – Standard quantity)

	Rs
A :4 × (830 – 800)	120.00 (A)
B: 3 × (1,190 – 1,200)	30.00 (F)
	90.00 (A)

(iii) Materials yield variance = Standard rate × (Actual yield – Standard yield)

$$\text{Standard rate} = \frac{\text{Total standard cost}}{\text{Standard yield}} = \text{Rs } \frac{6,800}{1,700} = \text{Rs 4 per kg}$$

Yield variance = 4 (1,700 – 1,717*) or Rs 68 (A)

*By using 2,000 kg of material, standard yield is 1,700 kg. Therefore, the standard yield by using 2,020 kg of material will be (1,700/2,000 × 2,020 or 1.71 kg)

(iv) Material mix variance = Actual quantity × (Per unit standard cost of standard mix – per unit standard cost of actual mix)

$$= 2,020 \left(\frac{6,800}{2,000.} - \frac{6,890}{2,020} \right)$$

= 2,020 (3.4 – 3.410) or Rs. 22 (A)

(v) Materials cost variance = (Actual cost – Standard cost)
= Rs 6,513.75 – 6,800
= Rs 286.25 (F)

Labour Variances

Direct labour variances arise when actual labour costs are different from standard labour costs. Labour variances constitute the following:

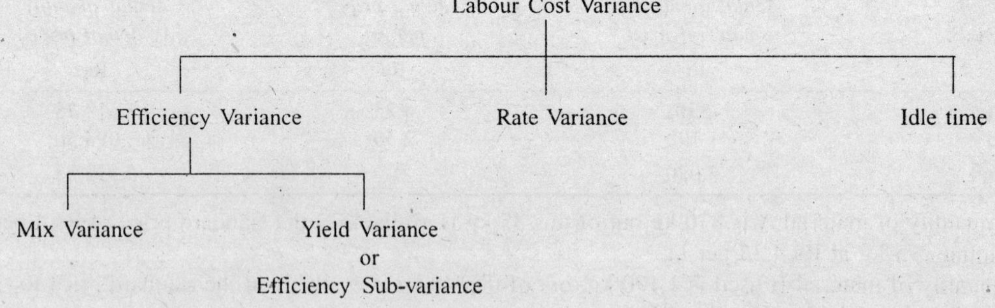

Labour Cost Variance

Labour cost variance denotes the difference between the actual direct wages paid and the standard direct wages specified for the output achieved. This variance is calculated by using the following formula:

Labour cost variance = (AH × AR – SH × SR)

where AH = Actual hours
AR = Actual rate

SH = Standard hours
SR = Standard rate

Labour Efficiency Variance

The calculation of labour efficiency or usage variance follows the same pattern as the computation of materials usage variance. If actual direct labour hours required to complete a job differ from the number of standard hours specified, a labour efficiency variance results; it is the difference between actual hours expended and standard labour hours specified multiplied by the standard labour rate per hour. The formula is:

Labour efficiency variance = (Actual hours – Standard hours for the actual output) × *Std.* rate per hour.

It may be noted that the standard labour hour rate and not the actual rate is used in computing labour efficiency variance. If quantity variances are calculated, changes in prices/rates are excluded, and when price variances are calculated, standard quantities are ignored.

Labour Rate Variance

Labour rate variance is computed in the same manner as materials price variance. When actual direct labour hour rates differ from standard rates, the result is a labour rate variance. It is that portion of the direct wages variance which is due to the difference between the actual rate paid and standard rate of pay specified. The formula for its calculation is

Labour rate variance = (Actual rate – Standard rate) × Actual hours

Favourable rate variance arise whenever actual rates are less than standard rates; unfavourable variances occur when actual rates exceed standard rates.

Labour Mix Variance

Labour mix variance is computed in the same manner as materials mix variance. Manufacturing or completing a job requires different types or grades of workers and production will be completed if labour is mixed according to standard proportions. Standard labour mix may not be adhered to under some circumstances and substitution will have to be made. There may be changes in the wage rates of some workers; there may be a need to use more skilled or expensive types of labour, e.g. employment of men instead of women;. sometimes workers and operators maybe absent. These lead to the emergence of a labour mix variance which is calculated by using the following formula:

Labour mix variance = (Actual labour mix – Revised standard labour mix in terms of actual total hours) × Standard rate per hour

To take an example, suppose the following were the standard labour cost data per unit in a factory :

Class	*Proportion* %			*Cost* Rs
A	50	3 hours @	Rs 4.00	12
B	50	3 hours @	Rs 2.00	6
	100	6 hours	Rs 3.00	18

In a period, many class B workers were absent and it was necessary to substitute class B workers. Since the class A workers were less experienced with the job more labour hours were used. The recorded costs of a unit were:

Class	*Proportions* %			*Cost* Rs
A	75	6 hours @	Rs 4.00	24.00
B	25	2 hours @	Rs 2.00	4.00
	100	8 hours	Rs 3.50	28.00

Labour mix variance will be calculated as follows:

Labour mix variance = (Actual proportion – Revised standard proportion of actual total hours) × Standard rate per hour

Revised standard proportion :

$$\text{Class A} = \frac{3}{6} \times 8 = 4 \text{ hours}$$

$$\text{Class B} = \frac{3}{6} \times 8 = 4 \text{ hours}$$

Applying the formula:

Class A = (6 – 4) × Rs 4 = 8 (Unfavourable)

Class B = (2 – 4) × Rs 2 = 4 (Favourable)

Total labour mix variance = Rs 4 (Unfavourable)

Labour Yield Variance

The final product cost contains not only material cost but also labour cost. Therefore, higher or lower output than the standard output should take into account labour yield variance also. A lower output psimply means that final output does not correspond with the production units that should have been produced from the hours expended on the inputs. It can be computed by applying the following formula:

Labour yield variance = (Actual output – Standard output based on actual hours) × Average standard labour rate per unit of output

or

Labour yield variance = (Actual loss – Standard loss on actual hours) × Average standard labour rate per unit of output

Labour yield variance is also known as labour efficiency sub-variance which is computed in terms of inputs, i.e. standard labour hours and revised labour hours mix (in terms of actual hours). Labour efficiency sub-variance is computed by using the following formula:

Labour efficiency sub-variance (Revised standard mix — Standard mix) × Standard labour rate

Substitution Variance This type of variance arises in the case of labour, due to the substitution of labour, that is when one grade of labour is substituted by another. This variance in fact represent the difference between the actual hours at standard rate of standard worker and the actual hours at standard rate of actual worker.

The formula for compulation is:

Substitution variance = (Standard hours × Standard rate for standard worker)
– (Standard hours × Standard rate of actual worker)

Idle Time Variance

Idle time variance occurs when workers are not able to do the work due to some reason during the hours for which they are paid. Idle time can be divided according to causes responsible for creating idle time e.g. idle time due to breakdown, lack of materials or power failures. Idle time variance will be equivalent to the standard labour cost of the hours during which no work has been done, but for which workers have been paid for unproductive time. Suppose, in a factory 2.000 workers were idle because of a power failure. As a result of this a loss of production of 4.000 units of product A and 8,000 units of product B occurred. Each employee was paid his normal wage (a rate of Rs 20 per hour). A single standard hour is needed to manufacture four units of product A and eight units of product B. Idle time variance will be computed in the following manner:

Standard hours lost:

$$\text{Product A} = \frac{4{,}000}{4} = 1{,}000 \text{ hr.}$$

$$\text{Product B} = \frac{8{,}000}{8} = 1{,}000 \text{ hr}$$

Total hours lost = 2,000 hr

Idle time variance (power failure)

2,000 hours @ Rs 20 per hour = Rs 40.000 (Adverse)

Example 14

Standard hours for manufacturing two products M and N are 15 hours per unit and 20 hours per unit respectively. Both products require identical kind of labour and the standard wages rates per hour is Rs 5. In the year 2001, 10,000 units of M and 15,000 units of N were manufactured. The total of labour hours actually worked were 4,50,000 and the actual wage bill came to Rs 23,00,000. This include 12.000 hours paid for @ Rs 7 per hour and 9,400 hours paid for @ Rs 7.50 per hour, the balance having been paid at Rs 5 per hour. You are required to compute the labour variances.

Solution

Labour cost variance = (Actual labour cost – Standard labour cost for actual output)

Standard cost:

For product M	= 10,000 × 15 × 5 =	7,50,000
For product N	= 15,000 × 20 × 5 =	15,00,000
Total standard cost		22,50,000

Total actual labour cost = Rs 23,00,000

Labour cost variance = Rs 23,00,000 – 22,50,000 = Rs 50,000 (Adverse)

Labour rate variance	= Actual hours × (Actual rate – Standard rate)	
	= 12,000 × (Rs 7 – Rs 5)	= 24,000 (A)
	– 9,400 × (Rs 7.50 – Rs 5)	= 23,500 (A)
	= 4,29,100 × (Rs 5 – Rs 5)	= —
	Total	47, 500 (A)

Labour efficiency variance = Standard rate × (Actual time – Standard time)

= Rs 5 × (4,50,500 – 4,50,000)

= Rs 2.500 (Adverse)

Example 15

The Standard cost card for a product shows:

Material cost 2 kg @ Rs 2.50 each	Rs 5.00 per unit
Wages 2 hours @ Rs 10 each	Rs 20 per unit

The actuals which have emerged from business operations are as follows:

Production	8,000 units
Material consumed 16,500 kg @ Rs 2.40 each	Rs 39,600
Wages paid 18,000 hours @ Re 8 each	Rs 1,44,000

Calculate the appropriate material and labour variances.

Solution

Materials cost variance = (Actual cost – Standard cost)

= 16,500 × 2.40 – 16,000 × 2.50)

= Rs 39,600 – Rs 40,000

	= 400 (Favourable)
Material price variance	= Actual quantity × (Actual price – Standard price)
	= 16,500 × (2.40 – 2.50)
	= Rs 1,650 (Favourable)
Materials usage variance	= Standard price × (Actual quantity – Standard quantity)
	= 2.50 × (16.500-16,000)
	= Rs 1,250 (Adverse)
Labour cost variance	= (Actual labour cost – Standard labour cost)
	= (Rs 1,44,000 – Rs 1,60.000)
	= Rs 16,000 (Favourable)
Labour rate variance	= Actual hours × (Actual rate – Standard rate)
	= 18,000 × (Rs 8 – Rs 10)
	= Rs 36,000 (Favourable)
Labour efficiency variance	= (Actual hours – Standard hours for actual production) × SR
	= (18,000 – 16,000) × Rs 10
	= Rs 20,000 (Adverse)

Example 16

The standard output of production 'EXE' is 25 units per hour in manufacturing department of a company employing 100 workers. The standard wage rate per labour hour is Rs 6.

In a 42 hour week. the department produced 1,040 units of 'EXE' despite 5% of the time paid was lost due to an abnormal reason. The hourly wage rate actually paid were R.s 6.20, Rs 6 and Rs 5.70 respectively to 10, 30 and 60 of the workers.

Compute relevant variances.

Solution

Basic Calculations

1. Standard man hours per unit:
   25 units is the standard output when 100 workers work for 1 hour. Hence, standard man hours per unit are 100/25 = 4.

2. Standard Output: 1,040 units			*Actual Output: 1.040 units*				
Man hours for actual output	*Rate per hr.*	*Amount*	*Actual hours paid for*	*Idle time hrs.*	*Prod. hrs.*	*Rate per hour*	*Amount paid for production*
		Rs	Rs			Rs	Rs
4.160	6	24.960	420	21	399	6.20	2,604
(1.040 units × 4 hrs.)			1,260	63	1,197	6.00	7,560
			2,520	126	2,394	5.70	14.364
		24,960	4,200	210	3,990		24,528

Computations of Variances

Labour Cost Variance:

= Standard Labour Cost – Actual Labour Cost
= Rs 24,960 – Rs 24,528 = Rs 432 (F)

Labour Rate Variance:

= Actual Time paid for × (Standard Rate – Actual Rate)

(i) 420 × (6 – 6.20) = 84 (A)
(ii) 1,260 × (6 – 6) = —
(iii) 2,520 × (6 – 5.70) = 756 (F)
672 (F)

Labour Efficiency Variance (after segregating Idle Time Variance);
= Standard Rate × (Standard Time for actual output – Actual Time worked)
= Rs 6 × (4,160 hrs. – 3,990 hrs.) = Rs 1,020 (F)

Labour Idle Time Variance:
= Idle Time hrs. × Standard Rate
= 210 hrs. × Rs 6 = Rs 1,260 (A).

Example 17

The following standards have been set to manufacture a product:

Direct materials:

2 units of A at Rs 4 per unit	8.00
3 units of B at Rs 3 per unit	9.00
15 units of C at Rs 1 per unit	15.00
	32.00
Direct labour 3 hrs @ Rs 8 per hour	24.00
Total standard prime cost	56,00

The company manufactured and sold 6,000 units of the product during the year. Direct material cost were as follows:

12,500 units of A at Rs 4.40 per unit.
18,000 units of B at Rs 2.80 per unit.
88,500 units of C at Rs 1.20 per unit.

The company worked 17,500 direct labour hours during the year. For 2,500 of these hours the company paid at Rs 12 per hour while for the remaining the wages were paid at the standard rate. Calculate materials price and usage variances and labour rate and efficiency variances.

Output 6,000 units

	Standard			Actual		
	Qty Units	*Rate (Rs)*	*Amount (Rs)*	*Qty Units*	*Rate (Rs)*	*Amount (Rs)*
A	12,000	4.00	48,000	12,500	4.40	55,000
B	18,000	3.00	54,000	18,000	2.80	50,400
C	90,000	1.00	90,000	88,500	1.20	1,06,200
Total	1,20,000		1,92,000	1,19,000		2,11.600

Material price variance = Actual quantity × (Actual rate – Standard rate)

A = 12,500 × (4.40 – 4) = 5,000 (A)
B = 11,000 × (2.80 – 3) = 3,600 (F)
C = 88,500 × (1.20 – 1) = 17,700 (A)
Total 19,100 (Adverse)

Material usage variance = Standard rate × (Actual quantity – Standard quantity for actual output)

A = 4× (12,500 – 12,000) = 2,000 (A)
B = 3 × (18,000 – 18,000) = Nil
C = 1 × (88,500 – 90,000) = 1,500 (F)
Total Rs 500 (Adverse)

Labour rate variance = Actual hrs × (Actual rate – Standard rate)
(i) = 2,500 × (12 – 8) = 10,000 (A)
(ii) = 15,000 × (8 – 8) = Nil
Total = Rs 10,000 (Adverse)

Labour efficiency variance = Standard rate × (Actual time – Standard time for actual output)
= 8 × (1 7,500 – 6,000 × 3)
= Rs 4,000 (Favourable)

Example 18

From the following data of A and Co. Ltd. relating to budgeted and actual performance for the month of March, 2002, compute the Direct Material and Direct Labour Cost Variances.

Budgeted data for March:	
Units to be-manufactured	1,50,000
Units of direct material required (based on standard rates)	4,95,000
Planned purchase of raw materials (Units)	5,40,000
Average unit cost of direct material	Rs 8
Direct labour hours per unit of finished goods	3/4 hr
Direct labour cost (Total)	Rs 29,92,500

Actual data at the end of March:	
Units actually manufactured	1,60,000
Direct material cost (Purchase cost based on units actually issued)	Rs 43, 41,900
Direct material cost (Purchase cost based on units actually purchased)	Rs 45,10,000
Average units cost of direct material	Rs. 8.20
Total direct labour hours for March	1,25,000
Total direct labour cost for March	Rs 33,75,000

Solution

Direct Material Variances

MCV = Actual material cost – Standard material cost of actual output
= 43,41,900 – 1,60,000 × 3.3 × 8
= 43,41,900 – 42,24,000
= 1,17,900 (Adverse)

MPV = Actual quantity × (Actual rale – Standard rate)
= 5,29,500 × (8.20-8)
= Rs 1,05,900 (Adverse)

MUV = Standard rate × (Actual quantity – Standard quantity for actual output
= 8 × (5,29,500 – 1,60,000 × 3.30)
= 8 × (5,29,500 – 5,28,000)
= Rs 12,000 (Adverse)

Direct Labour Variances

LCV = Actual labour cost – Standard labour cost for actual output
= 33,75.000 – 1,60,00 × 3/4 × 26.60
= 33,75,000 – 31,92,000
= Rs 1,83,000 (Adverse)

LRV = Actual time × (Actual rate – Standard rate)
= 1,25,000 × (27 – 26.60)
= Rs 50,000 (Adverse)

LEV = Standard rate × (Actual time – Standard time for actual output)
= 26.60 × (1,25,000 – 1,60,000 × 3/4)
= 26.60 × (1,25,000 – 1,20,000)
= Rs 1,33,000 (Adverse)

Working Notes :

(i) Standard units of direct material required per unit of output;

$$= \frac{4,95,000}{1,50,000} = 3.30 \text{ units}$$

(ii) Total actual quantity of direct materials used

$$= \frac{43,41,900}{8.20} = 5,29,500 \text{ units}$$

(iii) Standard direct labour cost per hour

$$= \frac{29,92,500}{1,50,000 \times 3/4} = \frac{29,92,500}{1,12,500} = \text{Rs } 26.50$$

(iv) Actual direct labour cost per hour

$$= \frac{33,75,000}{1,25,000} = \text{Rs } 27$$

OVERHEAD VARIANCES

The analysis of factory overhead variances is more complex than variance analysis for direct materials and direct labour. Generally, overhead variances constitute the following variances:

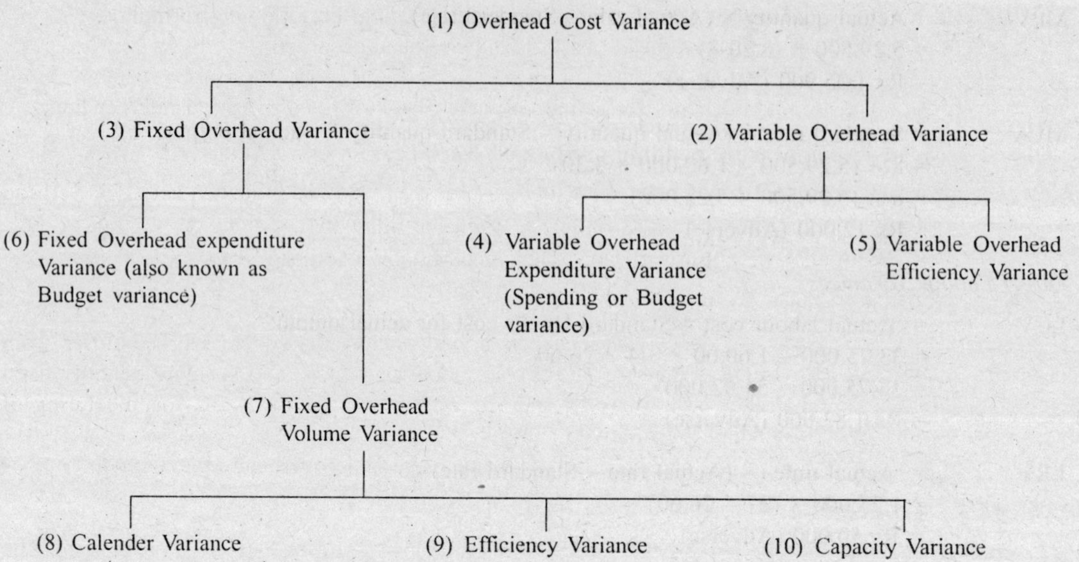

1. Total Overhead Cost Variance

This overall overhead variance is the difference between the actual overhead cost incurred and the standard cost of overhead for the output achieved. This can be computed by applying the following formula :

(Actual overhead incurred – Standard hours for the actual output × Standard overhead rate per hour)

or

Actual overhead incurred – (Actual output × Standard overhead rate per unit)

To illustrate the overall overhead variance, assume that the actual overhead for a department amouts to Rs 10,00,000 for the month of January, 2002 and standard (or allowed) hours for work performed total 4,500 hours, while actual hours used are 5,000. If overhead rate is Rs 200 per hour, the overall overhead variance will be the following:

Actual department overhead	Rs 10,00,000
Overhead charged to production (4,500 hr × Rs 200)	Rs 9,00,000
Overall or net overhead variance (Unfavourable)	Rs. 1,00,000

2. Variable Overhead Variance

It is the difference between actual variable overhead cost and standard variable overhead allowed for the actual output achieved. The formula for computing this variance is as follows:

Actual overhead cost – (Actual output × Variable overhead rate per unit)

or

Actual overhead cost – (Standard hours for actual output × Standard variable overhead rate per hour)

3. Fixed Overhead Variance

This variance indicates the difference between the actual fixed overhead cost and standard fixed over head cost allowed for the actual output. This variance is found by using the following formula.

Fixed overhead variance = Actual overhead cost – Fixed overhead absorbed

or

Actual overhead cost – (Standard hours for actual output × Standard fixed overhead rate per hour).

4. Variable Overhead Expenditure (Spending or Budget) Variance

This variance indicates the difference between actual variable overhead and budgeted variable overhead based on actual hours worked. This variance is found by using the following formula:

(Actual variable overhead – Budgeted variable overhead)

5. Variable Overhead Efficiency Variance

This variance is like labour efficiency variance and arises when actual hours worked differ from standard hours required for good units produced. The actual quantity produced and standard quantity fixed might be different because of higher or lower efficiency of workers employed in the manufacturing of goods. This variance is found by using the following formula:

(Actual hours – Standard hours for actual output) × Standard variable overhead rate per hour

6. Fixed Overhead Expenditure (Spending or Budget) Variance

This variance indicates the difference between actual fixed overhead and budgeted fixed overhead. The formula for computing this variance is as follows:

(Actual fixed overhead – Budgeted fixed overhead)

If actual fixed overhead costs are greater than budgeted fixed costs, an unfavourable variance results because actual costs exceed the budget. Actual overhead costs seldom equal budgeted costs because property tax rates may change, insurance premiums may increase or equipment charges may affect depreciation rates. As an illustration, assume that a company completed 36,000 units (equal to 18,000 standard productive hours) in 18,500 hours at the recorded fixed cost of Rs 75.100. The standard fixed cost rate per hour is Rs 4. Therefore,

Expenditure variance = (Actual overhead costs – Budgeted overhead costs)

That is = (75,100 – 18,500 × 4) = (75,100 – 74,000)

= Rs 1,100 (unfavourable)

The expenditure or budget variance provides management with information which helps in controlling costs. The budget variance is usually prepared on a departmental basis and the factors that cause the budget variance are, therefore, controllable by departmental managers.

7. Fixed Overhead Volume Variance

Volume variance relates to only fixed overhead. This variance arises due to the difference between the standard fixed overhead cost allowed (absorbed) for the actual output and the budgeted fixed overhead based on standard hours allowed for actual output achieved during the period. The variance shows the over-or-under-absorption of fixed overheads during a particular period. If the actual output is more than the standard output, there is over-absorption and variance is favourable. If actual output is less than the standard output, the volume variance is unfavourable. The formula for computing this variance is a follows:

(Budgeted overhead applied to actual output – Budgeted fixed overhead based on standard hours allowed for actual output)

or

(Actual production – Budgeted production) × Standard fixed overhead rate per unit

Volume variance is further sub-divided into three variances.

8. Fixed Overhead Calender Variance

It is that portion of volume variance which is due to the difference between the number of actual working days in the period to which the budget is applicable and budgeted number of days in the budget period.

If actual working days is more than the budgeted working days, the variance is favourable as work has been done on days more than budgeted or allowed and vice-versa. The formula is as follows:

(No. of actual working days – No. of budgeted working days) × Standard fixed overhead rate per day

Calander variance can be computed based on hours or output. Then the formulae are:

Hours Basis

Calander variance = (Revised budget capacity hours – Budgeted hours) × Standard fixed overhead rate per hour

If revised budgeted capacity hours are more than the budgeted hours, the variance will be favourable In the reverse situation, the variance will be unfavourable.

Output Basis

Calander variance = (Revised budgeted quantity in terms of actual number of days worked – Budgeted quantity) × Standard fixed overhead rate per unit

If revised budgeted quantity is more than the budgeted quantity the variance is favourable; if revised budgeted quantity is less, the variance will be unfavourable.

9. Fixed Overhead Efficiency Variance

It is that portion of volume variance which arises when actual hours of production used for actual output differ from the standard hours specified for that output. If actual hours worked are less than the standard hours, the variance is favourable and when actual hours are more than the standard hours, the variance is unfavourable. The formula is:

Fixed overhead efficiency variance = (Actual hours – Standard hours for actual production) × Standard fixed overhead rate per hour

or

Fixed overhead efficiency variance = (Actual production – Standard production as per actual time available) × Standard fixed overhead rate per unit

10. Fixed Overhead Capacity Variance

It is that part of fixed overhead volume variance which is due to the difference between the actual capacity (in hours) worked during a given period and the budgeted capacity (expressed in hours). The formula is:

Capacity variance = (Actual capacity hours – Budgeted capacity hours) × Standard fixed overhead rate per hour

This variance represents idle time also. If actual capacity hours are more than the budgeted capacity hours, the variance is favourable and if actual capacity hours less than the budgeted capacity hours, the variance will be unfavourable.

In case actual number of days and budgeted number of days are also given, then budgeted capacity hours will be calculated in terms of actual number of days and it will be known as revised budgeted capacity hours, i.e. budgeted hours for actual days worked. In this situation, the formula for calculating capacity variance will be as follow:

Capacity variance = (Actual capacity hours – Revised budgeted capacity hours) × Standard fixed overhead rate per hour

In the above formula, the variance will be favourable if actual capacity hours are more than the revised budgeted hours. However, if actual capacity hours are lesser than the revised budgeted hours, the variance will be adverse as lesser hours means that lesser actual hours have been worked taking the actual days utilised into account.

Two-way, Three-way and Four-way Variance Analysis

The above overhead variances are also classified as Two-way, Three-way and Four-way variance. The different variances under these categories are listed below. The formulae for computing these variances are similar to as explained in the preceding section.

A. Two-way Variance Analysis

1. Controllable variance (Budget variance)
2. Volume variance (Uncontrollable variance)

B. Three-way Variance Analysis

1. Expenditure variance (Spending variance)
2. Capacity variance
3. Efficiency variance

C. Four-way Variance Analysis

1. Expenditure variance (Spending variance)
2. Variable overhead efficiency variance
3. Fixed overhead efficiency variance
4. Capacity variance

Example 19

From the following data, calculate overhead variances:

	Budget	*Annul*
Output	15,000 units	16,000 units
No. of working days	25	27
Fixed overheads	Rs 30,000	Rs 30,500
Variable overheads	Rs 45,000	Rs 47,000

There was an increase of 5% in capacity.

Solution

1. Total overhead cost variance:
   (Actual overhead cost – Actual units × Standard rate)
   (Rs 30,500 + 47,000 – 16,000 × Rs 5)
   Rs 77.500 – Rs 80,000 = Rs 2,500 (Favourable)

   $$\text{Standard rate} = \frac{\text{Standard overhead}}{\text{Standard output}}$$

2. Variable overheads expenditure variance:
   (Actual variable cost – Actual units × Standard rate)
   (47,000 – 16,000 × Rs 3)
   47,000 – Rs 48,000 = Rs 1,000 (Favourable)

3. Fixed overhead variance:
   Actual fixed overhead cost – (Actual units × Standard rate of fixed overhead)
   30,500 – (16,000 × 2)
   30,500 – 32,000 = Rs 1,500 (Favourable)
4. Volume variance:
   Actual units × Standard rate – Budgeted fixed overheads
   16,000 × Rs 2 – Rs 30,000 = Rs 2,000 (Favourable)
5. Expenditure variance:
   Actual fixed overheads – Budgeted fixed overheads
   Rs 30,500 – Rs 30,000 = Rs 500 (Unfavourable)
6. Capacity variance:
   Standard rate (Revised budgeted units – Budgeted units)
   Revised budgeted units = Budgeted units + Increase in capacity

$$= 15{,}000 + \frac{5}{10} \times 15{,}000 = 15{,}750 \text{ units}$$

   Capacity variance
   = Rs 2 (15,750 units –15,000 Units)
   = Rs 2 × 7 50 – Rs 1,500 (Favourable)
7. Calendar variance:
   Increase or decrease in production due to more or less working days × Standard rate per unit
   Within 25 days. Standard production with increased capacity = 15,750 units

   Within 2 days (27 – 25), production will be increased by $= \frac{15{,}750 \times 2}{\cdot 25} = 1{,}260$ units

   Calendar variance = 1,260 units × Rs 2
   = Rs 2,520 (Favourable)
8. Efficiency variance:
   Standard rate (Actual production– Standard production)
   Standard production:

Budgeted production	= 15,000 units
Production increased due to increase in capacity	= 750 units
Production increased due to 2 more working days	= 1,260 units
	17,010 units
Efficiency variance	= Rs 2 (16.000 units – 17,010 units)
	= Rs 2 (– 1,010 units) = Rs 2,020 (Unfavourable)

Example 20

The following information was obtained from the records of a manufacturing unit using Standard Costing Systeme

	Standard	*Actual*
Production	4,000 units	3,800 units
Working days	20	21
Fixed overhead Rs	40,000	39,000
Variable overhead Rs	12,000	12,000

You are required to calculate the following overhead variances:

(a) Variable overhead variance

(b) Fixed overhead variance

(i) Expenditure variance

(ii) Volume variance

(iii) Efficiency variance

(iv) Calendar variance

(c) Also prepare a Reconciliation Statement for the standard fixed expenses worked out at Standard fixed overhead rate and the Actual fixed overhead.

Solution

Basic calculations	*Budgeted data*	*Actual data*
Variable overhead (Rs)	12,000	12,000
Fixed overhead (Rs)	40,000	39,000
Production (units)	4000	38,00
Working (days)	21	20

Standard variable overhead rate per unit $= \frac{12,000}{4,00o \text{ units}} =$ Rs 3

Standard production per day $\frac{4,000 \text{ units}}{20 \text{ days}} = 200$ units

Standard fixed overhead per day = 200 × Rs 10 = Rs 2,000

(a) Variable overhead cost variance = Actual variable overhead – Recovered variable overhead
= 12.000 – 3,800 × 3
= 12,000 – 11,400=Rs 600 (A)

(b) Fixed overhead variance = (Actual fixed overheads – Recovered fixed overheads)
= 39,000 – 3,800 × 10
= 39,000 – 38,000 = Rs 1,000 (A)

(i) Fixed overhead expenditure variance = Actual overheads – Budgeted overheads
= 39,000 – 40,000 = Rs 1,000 (F)

(ii) Fixed overhead volume variance = Recovered overheads – Budgeted overheads
= 38,000 – 40,000 = Rs 2,000 (A)

(iii) Fixed overhead efficiency variance = Standard fixed overhead rate per day × (Actual time – Standard time for actual output)
= 2,000 × (21 – 3,800/200)
= 2.00 (21 – 19) = 4,000 (A)

(iv) Fixed overhead calendar variance = Standard fixed overhead rate per day × (Actual days – Budgeted days)
= 2.000 × (21 – 20)
= Rs 2.000 (F)

or

Standard fixed overhead rate per day × Extra days/Deficit worked
= 2,000 × 1 = 2,000 (F)

(c) Reconciliation statement

Standard fixed overheads 3800 × 100		Rs 38,000
Less: Fixed overhead expenditure variance	1,000 (F)	
Less: Fixed overhead calendar variance	2,000 (F)	3,000 (F)
		35,000
Add: Fixed overhead efficiency variance (A)		4,000
Actual Fixed Overheads		39,000

Example 21

A Company has normal capacity of 100 machines working 8 hours per day of 25 days in a month. The budgeted fixed overheads of a month are Rs 1,50,000. The Standard time required to manufacture one unit of product is 4 hours. In a particular month, the Company worked for 24 days of 750 machine hours per day and produced 4,500 units of the product. The actual fixed overheads incurred were Rs. 1,45,000. compute:

(a) Efficiency variance,
(b) Capacity variance,
(c) Calendar variance,
(d) Expenditure variance,
(e) Volume variance, and
(f) Total fixed overhead variance

Solution

Standard/Budgeted data		**Actual data**	
Budgeted fixed overhead (Rs)	1,50,000	Actual fixed overhead (Rs)	1,45,000
Budgeted output units	5,000	Actual output units	4,500
Budgeted hours	20,000	Actual hours	18,000
Budgeted days	25	Actual days	24
Standard labour hours per unit	4		
Standard hours worked per day	800		
Standard rate per unit (Rs)	30		
Standard rate per hour (Rs)	7.50		
Standard fixed overhead rate per day (Rs.)	6,000		

Computation of variances :

(a) *Efficiency variance:*

$$= \text{Standard fixed overhead rate per unit} \begin{Bmatrix} \text{Actual quantity} \\ \text{of output} \end{Bmatrix} - \begin{Bmatrix} \text{Standard quantity} \\ \text{of output} \end{Bmatrix}$$

= Rs 30 {4,500 units – 4,500 units} = Nil

(b) *Capacity variance:*

= Standard fixed overhead rate per hour {Actual capacity hours – Budgeted capacity hours}
= Rs 7.50 (18,000 hours – 24 days × 800 hours)
= Rs 7.50 (18,000 hours – 19,200 hours)
= Rs 9,000 (Adverse)

(c) *Calendar variance:*

= Standard fixed overhead rate per day {Actual days – Budgeted days}
= Rs 6,000 (24 days – 25 days)
= Rs 6,000 (Adverse)

(d) *Expenditure variance:*
= {Budgeted fixed overhead-Actual fixed overhead}
= {Rs 1,50,000 – Rs 1,45,000}
= Rs 5,000 (Favourable)

(e) *Volume variance:*
= Standard fixed overhead rate per unit {Actual output – Budgeted output}
= Rs 30 (4,500 units – 5,000 units)
= Rs 15,000 (Adverse)

(f) *Total fixed overhead variance*
= {Fixed overhead recovered on actual output – Actual fixed overhead incurred}
= {4,500 units × Rs 30 – Rs 1,45,000}
= Rs 10,000 (Adverse)

Verification:

Total fixed overhead variance = Expenditure variance + Volume variance
or Rs. 10,000 (Adverse) = Rs 5,000 (Favourable) + Rs 15,000 (Adverse)
and
Volume variance = Efficiency variance + Capacity variance + Calendar variance
Rs 15,000 (Adverse) = Nil + Rs 9,000 (Adverse) + Rs 6,000 (Adverse)

Example 22

The following data has been collected from the cost records of a unit for computing the various fixed overhead variances for a period:

Number of Budgeted Working Days	25
Budgeted Man-hours per day	6,000
output (budgeted) per man hour (in units)	1
Fixed Overhead cost as budgeted	Rs 1,50,000
Actual Number of Working days	27
Actual man-hours per day	6,300
Actual Output per man-hour (in units)	0.9
Actual Fixed Overhead	Rs1,56,000

Calculate Fixed Overhead Variances:

(a) Expenditure Variance:
(b) Calendar Variance;
(c) Capacity Variance;
(d) Efficiency Variance;
(e) Volume Variance;
(f) Fixed Cost Variance.

Solution

(a) FOEXV = Budgeted Fixed Overheads – Actual Fixed Overheads
= Rs 1,50.000 – Rs 1,56,000
= Rs 6,000 (Adverse)

(b) FOCALV = No. of Excess Working Days × Fixed Overhead Rate per Day
= 2 × 6,000 = Rs 12,000 (Favourable)

Or = Possible Overheads – Budgeted Overheads
= 27 × 6.000 – 25 × 6,000
= Rs 1,52,000 – 1,50,000 = Rs 12,000 (Favourable)

(c) FOCAPV (Revised) = Standard Overheads – Possible Overheads
= Re 1 × 6,300 × 27 – 1,62,000
= Rs 1,70,100 – 1,62,000
= Rs 8,100 (Favourable)

(d) FOEFFV = Recovered Overheads – Standard Overheads
= 9 × 6,300 × 27 – 1,70,100
= Rs 1,53,090 – 1,70,100
= Rs 17,010 (Adverse)

(e) FOCV = FOEXPV + FOVV
= FOEXPV + FOCALV + FORCAPV + FOEFFV
= Rs 6,000(A) + Rs 12,000 (F) + 8,100 (F) + 17,010 (A)
= Rs 2,910 (Adverse)

Control Ratios

Control ratios are useful to management to know whether the deviations of actuals from budgeted results are favourable or unfavourable. These control ratios are expressed in percentage. The ratio is taken as favourable if it is 100% or more. In case it is less than 100%, the ratio is considered as unfavourable Control ratios are as follows:

1. *Activity Ratio Activity* ratio is used to measure the level of activity achieved over a period. It is obtained when the number of standard hours equivalent to the output produced are expressed at a percentage of the budgeted hours.

$$\text{Activity ratio} = \frac{\text{Standard hrs for actual production}}{\text{Budgeted hours}} \times 100$$

2. *Capacity Ratio* This ratio points out to what extent budgeted hours have been utilised. This ratio shows the relationship between actual working hours and budgeted working hours.
3. *Efficiency Ratio* Efficiency ratio shows the degree of efficiency achieved in production. It is derived when the standard hours equivalent to the output produced, are expressed as a percentage of the actual hours spent in producing the output.

$$\text{Efficiency ratio} = \frac{\text{Standard hours for actual production}}{\text{Actual hours worked}} \times 100$$

Example 23

In a manufacturing shop product X requires 2.5 man-hours and product Y requires 6 man-hours. In month of 25 working days of 8 hours a day, 2,000 units of X and 1,000 units of Y were produced. The company employs 50 workers in the shop and the budgeted man-hours are 1,08,000 for the year. You are required to work out the capacity ratio, activity ratio and efficiency ratio.

Solution

Standard man-hours produced:

Product X : 2,000 units @	2.5 Man-hours	=	5,000 Man-hours
Product Y : 1,000 units @	6 Man-hours	=	6,000 Man-hours.
	Total	=	11,000 Man-hours

Budgeted man-hours per month = 1,08,000/12
= 9,000

Actual man-hours worked = 50 workers × 25 days × 8 hours = 10,000 man-hours

Ratios:

$$\text{Capacity ratio} = \frac{\text{Actual Man - hours worked}}{\text{Budgeted Man - hours}} \times 100$$

$$= \frac{10{,}000}{9{,}000} \times 100 = 111.11\%$$

$$\text{Activity ratio} = \frac{\text{Standard man - hours produced}}{\text{Budgeted man - hours}} \times 100$$

$$= \frac{11{,}000}{9{,}000} \times 100 = 122.22\%$$

$$\text{Efficiency ratio} = \frac{\text{Standard man - hours produced}}{\text{Actual man - hours worked}} \times 100$$

$$= \frac{11{,}000}{10{,}000} \times 100 = 111.00\%$$

Example 24

If the 'activity ratio' and 'capacity ratio' of a company is 104% and 96% respectively, find out its 'efficiency ratio'.

Solution

The various ratios are calculated as under :

$$\text{(i) Activity Ratio} = \frac{\text{Standard hours for actual production}}{\text{Budgeted hours}} \times 100$$

$$\text{(ii) Capacity Ratio} = \frac{\text{Actual hours worked}}{\text{Budgeted hours}} \times 100$$

$$\text{(iii) Efficiency Ratio} = \frac{\text{Standard hours for actual production}}{\text{Actual hours worked}} \times 100$$

From the above, it is clear that the Efficiency Ratio can be obtained by dividing Activity Ratio by Capacity Ratio.

Hence,

$$\text{Efficiency Ratio (in percentage)} = \frac{\text{Activity Ratio}}{\text{Capacity Ratio}} \times 100$$

$$= \frac{104\%}{96\%} \times 100 = 108.33\%$$

Example 25

Calculate from the following figures:

(i) Efficiency ratio,

(ii) Activity Ratio, and

(iii) Capacity Ratio

Budgeted Production	880 units
Standard Hours Per Unit	10
Actual Production	750 units
Actual Working Hours	6,000

Solution

(i) Efficiency Ratio $= \dfrac{\text{Standard hours for actual production}}{\text{Actual hours worked}} \times 100$

$= \dfrac{750 \text{ units} \times 10 \text{ hours}}{6{,}000} \times 100 = 125\%$

(ii) Activity Ratio $= \dfrac{\text{Standard hours for actual production}}{\text{Budgered hours}} \times 100$

$= \dfrac{750 \text{ units} \times 10 \text{ hours}}{880 \text{ units} \times 10 \text{ hours}} \times 100 = 85.23\%$

(iii) Capacity Ratio $= \dfrac{\text{Actual hours worked}}{\text{Budgeted hours}} \times 100$

$= \dfrac{6{,}000 \text{ hours}}{880 \text{ units} \times 10 \text{ hours}} \times 100 = 68.18\%$

Revision Variance

When a budget is revised, but where, as a matter of policy the change is not incorporated in the standard cost rate, a variance will arise termed as a Revision Variance. Revision variance is the difference between the basic standard cost and the revised standard cost.

DISPOSITION OF VARIANCE

Variance may be disposed off in either of the following ways:

1. Inventories and the cost of goods sold may be adjusted to reflect the actual costs.
2. Variances may be transferred to the profit and loss account.

Under the first method, all variances are allocated between the inventory accounts and cost of goods sold account. This method, in fact, converts the accounts balances from standard costs to actual historical costs.

The following arguments are given in support of this method:

1. Only actual costs should be recorded in the cost of goods sold account and inventory accounts. The supporters of this method do not favour standard costs as true costs or costs suitable for use in the profit and loss account but as merely guides in factory management.
2. Variances from the standard are costs and not losses and therefore should be reflected in the inventory valuations and cost of goods sold.
3. If the variances are large, standard costs do not represent the actual costs and therefore are not good measures to determine the costs of goods sold and inventory.

Under the second method, the variances are considered as profit or loss items in the period in which they occurred. The work-in-process, finished goods inventory, and cost of goods sold are stated at standard costs. Unfavourable cost variances are deducted from the gross profit at standard costs. Favourable cost variances are added to the gross profit calculated at standard cost. The treatment of the cost variances under this method is shown on the income statement given below.

ABC Company
Income Statement for the Year Ending December 31, 2006

	Rs	Rs
Sales revenue		5,00,000
Cost of sales (standard)	3,00,000	
Selling and administrative expenses (standard)	1,50,000	4,50,000
Net Income (standard)		50,000
Deduct unfavourable variance from net income:		
Material price	200	
Material usage	800	
Labour efficiency	900	
Overhead:		
Volume	2,000	
Budget	1,100	5,000
Net income (actual)		45,000

The second method has the following arguments in its favour :

1. Standard costs help in the preparation of statements at the early date; actual cost delays the determination of inventory costs and cost of goods sold.
2. Standard costs avoid the inclusion of costs due to wastage, losses, inefficiencies, excessive overheads from low production volume. Standard cost represent normal costs and therefore inventory figures are conservative and acceptable for income determination and other purposes.
3. In a multi-product company, it may be difficult to determine accurately how much variance should be distributed to each product.
4. In taking corrective action managers may find it more useful when variance are depicted in the profit and loss account. Managerial attention is usually hampered when variances are combined with cost of goods manufactured.

It is difficult to suggest which method should be followed in accounting for variances. If the variance are large and significant, the first method, *i.e.*, distribution of variances to the respective accounts appears to be appropriate for financial reporting, tax and job and contract pricing purposes. The second method may be preferable when the variances are insignificant. Thus, the treatment of variances depends on many factors such as (i) size of variance, (ii) accuracy of standard costs, (iii) cause of variances such as incorrect standard costs, (iv) timing of variances, e.g. caused by seasonal fluctuation, (v) type of variance-material, — labour, and overhead.

MANAGERIAL USES OF VARIANCES

Determination of variances is only the first step in the process of standard cost variance analysis. Me computation of material, labour and overhead variances is useless for cost control and performance evaluation. The final objective of variance analysis is to determine the person(s) responsible for each variance and to pinpoint the cause(s) for incurrence of these variances. That is, before management can take effective action for improving control over costs, it needs to know not only the amount of variances, but also where the variances originated, who was responsible for them, and what caused them to arise.

Analysis of Variances by Responsibilities

Variances must be identified with the manager responsible for the costs incurred who should be held responsible for that cost. The cost factors which are directly controllable by operating supervision must be separated from those costs factors from which executive management is responsible.

Specific titles of individuals who are responsible for each type of variance differ among business enterprises. Generally speaking, the following personnel are held accountable for variances noted against them:

Responsibility for Cost Variances

Variance	*Personnel Responsible*
(i) Materials price variance	Purchasing agent or purchasing manager.
(ii) Materials quantity variance	Plant superintendent, departmental supervisors, machine operators, quality control department and material handlers.
(iii) Labour rate standard	Personnel (employment) department manager, departmental supervisor and plant superintendent.
(iv) Labour efficiency variance	Plant superintendent, departmental supervisors, production scheduling department, quality control department, material handlers and machine operators.
(v) Overhead expenditure variance	Variable portion is the responsibility of the individual foreman or supervisor, they are expected to keep actual expenses within the budget. Fixed portion is the responsibility of top management.
(vi) Overhead efficiency variance	Same personnel who are responsible for labour efficiency variance.
(vii) Overhead volume variance	Top management and production schedulers.

Analysis of Variances by Causes

Reasons for the variance should be determined and plans for necessary corrective action made either by discussing possible causes with the supervisors or by examining underlying data and records. The analysis of variances by causes is therefore an important aspect of the use of standard costs to attain effective cost control. For any standard cost variance, there are many possible causes. The following list is not all inclusive but does indicate causes responsible for variances.

Possible Causes of Standard Cost Variances

Materials Price Variance

1. Recent changes in purchase price of materials.
2. Failure to purchase anticipated quantities when standards were established resulting in higher prices owing to non-availability of quantity purchase discounts.
3. Not taking cash discounts anticipated at the time of setting standards resulting in higher prices
4. Substituting raw material differing from original materials specifications.
5. Freight cost changes and changes in purchasing and storekeeping costs if these are debited to the materials

Materials Quantity Variance

1. Poor materials handling.
2. Inferior workmanship by machine operator.
3. Faulty equipment.
4. Cheaper, defective raw material causing excessive scrap.
5. Inferior quantity control inspection.

6. Pilferage.
7. Wastage due to inefficient production method.

Labour Rate Variance

1. Recent labour rate changes within industry,
2. Employing a man of a grade different from the one laid down in the standard.
3. Labour strike leading to utilisation of unskilled help.
4. Labour layoff causing skilled labour to be retained at higher rates, so as to prevent resignations and job switching.
5. Employee sickness and vacation time.
6. Paying a higher overtime allowance than provided for in the standard.

Labour Efficiency Variance

1. Machine breakdown, use of defective machinery and equipment.
2. Inferior raw materials.
3. Poor supervision.
4. Lack of timely material handling.
5. Poor employee performance.
6. Inefficient production scheduling—delays in routing work, materials, tools and instructions.
7. Inferior engineering specifications.
8. New inexperienced employees.
9. Insufficient training of workers.
10. Poor working conditions—inadequate or excessive heating, lighting, ventilation, etc.,

Overhead Volume Variance

(Factors causing either idle time or overtime of plant and facilities)

1. Failure to utilise normal capacity.
2. Lack of sales order
3. Too much idle capacity
4. Inefficient or efficient utilisation of existing capacity
5. Machine breakdown
6. Defective materials
7. Labour troubles
8. Power failures.

Overhead Efficiency Variance

These included all causes which are listed under labour efficiency variance.

Analysis of Variances by Products

Since management usually wants current true costs when decisions are to be made with respect to priceing and related questions, variances are often analysed by products in order to arrive at current product costs. Companies producing non-standard goods according to customer's specifications may also help analyse variances by job orders. The analysis of variances by causes is useful in deciding whether or not cost variances should be allocated to products in arriving at product costs for pricing. Standard product *costs* should be reviewed periodically and revised when it is found that the standard product costs in use are no longer useful for the purpose.

Variance Reports to Management

Variance reports basically aim to inform managers responsible for the operation when actual performance differs from the standards. To be effective, the report must be timely, accurate and clearly under-.stood the recipients.

Control of production and costs is a matter of timing; the effectiveness of the control is often in direct proportion to the speed with which variances are reported. Timely reporting often requires daily and weekly reporting of performance information. Therefore, it is important to focus managerial attention on off-standard conditions immediately following each shift, day or week, rather than to accumulate and summarise variances from standards each month. A month, and generally even a week, is too long a period for many off-standard conditions to remain unchecked and uncorrected, because the time interval may prevent positive identification of employees who are responsible for the unsatisfactory work. Variance analysis reports are primarily control reports. In developing and reporting the variances, it should be remembered that the variance data must (i) deal with relevant distinctions, (ii) be understandable (iii) measure with reasonable accuracy what they are supposed to measure, (iv) be presented and plained concisely, (v) be timely, and (vi) provide the amount of details needed by different persons at each level of management.

LIMITATIONS OF STANDARD COSTING

Standard costs are not without their shortcomings. The first limitation is regarding the predetermined nature of standard costs. The accuracy of standard costs is limited by the knowledge and skill of the people who created them and they contain the prejudices of their makers. Such badly conceived standard costs do not enjoy the confidence of the users of the system.

Secondly, it is difficult to select a type of standard (ideal, currently attainable, normal, etc.) which can help in cost control and achieve other managerial purposes. If standards are too low, they defeat the objective of standard costing and bring the operating efficiency down. If they are too high. they can crcate ill-will and encourage employees to beat the system by fair means or foul.

Thirdly, a good programme of standard costing requires that both management and operating personnel should have lull confidence in it and standards should be fair and workable. Educating employees? necessary in this regard. However, lack of acceptability, education and communication is a major difficully in operating a standard costing system.

In spite of the above limitations, standard costing has developed into an extraordinary and very useful tool and has contributed much in providing different kinds of cost data for so many different purposes.

Thirdly, a good programme of standard costing requires that both management and operating personnel should have lull confidence in it and standards should be fair and workable. Educating employees is necessary in this regard. However, lack of acceptability, education and communication is a major difficully in operating a standard costing system.

In spite of the above limitations, standard costing has developed into an extraordinary and very useful tool and has contributed much in providing different kinds of cost data for so many different purposes.

THEORY QUESTIONS

1. Define and explain the concepts of standard cost and standard costing.
2. Discuss briefly the use of stamdard costs in the following management activities: cost reductions, operating performance evaluation, product pricing decisions and providing incentives.
3. Compare and contrast the usefulness of ideal standards, basic standards, and currently attain standards.
4. "Standard costs arc bases for a proper managerial control of manufacturing operation." Define stamdard cost and explain the above statement.
5. What is standard costing and how would you distinguish it from budgetary control?
6. What are (he points of similarity and difference between budgeted and standard costs.
7. "Variance analysis is an integral part of standard cost accounting." Explain this statement.
8. By purchasing low-grade materials, a company reports favourable material price variance, consistently experiences

unfavourable material quantity variances. What relationship may exist in these conditions? Is (he price variances really favourable?

9. What are the shortcomings of historical costs for managerial uses.?
10. Briefly explain the meaning of each of the following variances: material prices, material usage, labour efficiency, and labour rate.
11. Discuss some of the problems that might be created by standards which are set loo high and by standards which are loo loose.
12. What are the advantages and limitations of standard costing?
13. Discuss briefly some of the limitations of standard costs.
14. Explain why overhead variances are generally treated as period costs.
15. Discuss the information which a well-designed cost report should give to management from the point view of production and control. How should such information be given?
16. What is a two variance analysis" of factory overheads. Give a brief description.
17. Explain the term 'variance' and distinguish between controllable and uncontrollable variances.
18. Describe briefly the managerial use of variances.

PROBLEMS

1. The standard quantity and standard price of raw material required for one unit of Product A are give an as follows:

	Quantity	*Selling price*
Material X	2 kg	Rs 3 per kg
Material Y	4 kg	Rs 2 per kg
	6 kg	

The actual production and relevant data are as follows:

Output 500 units of Product A

Material	*Total quantity* for 500 units	*Total cost* (Rs)
X	1.100 kg	3,410
Y	1.800 kg	3,960

Calculate the variances.

Ans. Material cost variance R.s 370(A): usage variance Rs 100(F).
Material price variance Rs 470 (A)

2. From the data given below, calculate the materials price variance, the materials usage variance i materials mix variance. Consumption per 100 units of product:

Raw material	Standard	Actual
A	40 units @, Rs 50 per unit	50 units @ Rs 50 per unit
B	60 units @ Rs 40 per unit	60 units @ Rs 45'per unit

Ans. Material price variance Rs 300(A); Mix variance Rs 60(A); Usage variance Rs 500(A)

3. The following standard and actual data is given about a product.

Material	*Standard*			*Actual*		
	Qty *Units*	*Rule* *(Rs)*	*Amount* *(Rs)*	*Qty* *Units*	*Rate* *(Rs)*	*Amount* *(Rs)*
A	500	6	3,000	400	6	2,400
B	400	3.75	1,500	500	3.60	1,800
C	300	3.00	900	400	2.80	1.120
	1,200			1,300		
Less:			Actual loss 220			
10% loss	120					
	1,080		5,400	1,080		Rs 5,320

Calculate : (i) Material cost variance

(ii) Materials price variance

(iii) Materials mix variance

(iv) Materials yield variance

(v) Total material usage variance.

Ans. (i) Rs 80(A) (ii) Rs 155 (F) (iii) Rs 375 (F) (iv) Rs 450 (A) (v) Rs 75 (A).

4. The standard cost of a certain chemical mixture is:

   40% Material A at Rs 200 per kg

   60% Material B at Rs 300 per kg

   A standard loss of 10% is expected in production. During a period materials used are:

   90 kg Material A at the cost of Rs 180 per kg

   110 kg Material B at the cost of Rs 340 per kg

   The weight produced is 182 tonnes ofgood production.

   Calculate and present :

   (i) Materials price variance

   (ii) Materials usage variance

   (iii) Materials mix variance

   (iv) Materials yield variance

   Ans. (i) Rs 2,600 (A) (ii) Rs 1577.77 (F) (iii) Rs 1,000 (F) (iv) Rs. 577.77(F)

5. Mixers Ltd., is engaged in producing a 'standard mix' using 60 kg of chemical X and 40 kg of chemical Y. The standard loss of production is 30%. The standard price of X is Rs. 5 per kg and of Y is Rs 10 per kg. The actual mixture and yield were as follows:

   X 80 kg@Rs 4.50 per kg and

   Y 70 kg @ Rs 8.00 per kg

   Actual yield 115 kg

   Calculate material variances

   Ans. Material cost variance Rs. 230 (F)

   Material price variance Rs 180 (F)

   Material usage variance Rs. 50 (F)

   Material mix variance Rs. 50 (A)

6. From the data given below, calculate labour variances for the two departments:

	Deptt. A	*Deptt B*
Actual gross wages (Direct)	Rs 2,000	Rs 1,800
Standard hours produced	8,000	6,000
Standard rate per hour	Rs 30	Rs 35
Actual hours worked	8,200	5.800

7. The details regarding composition and the weekly wage rates of labour force engaged on a job scheduled to be completed in 30 hours are as follows:

Category of workers	*No. of labourers*	*Standard hourly wage rate*	*Actual no. of labourers*	*Hourly wage rate*
Skilled	75	60	70	70
Semi-skilled	45	40	30	50
Unskilled	60	30	80	20

   The work is actually completed in 32 hours. Calculate the various labour variances.

   Ans. Labour cost variance, Rs 13,000 (A), Rate variance Rs 6,400 (A), Labour efficiency 6,600 (A), Mix variance Rs 9,600 (F), Labour sub efficiency Rs 16,200 (A).

8. A chemical company gives you the following standard and actual data of its Chemical No. 1456. You are required to calculate variances.

(kg)	*Standard data* (Rs)	*Total* (Rs)	*Actual data*	*Total* (Rs)	
450	of Material A @ 20 per kg	9,000	450 kg @ 19 per kg	8,550	
360	of Material B @ per kg	3,600	360 kg @ 11 per kg	3,960	12,510
810		12,600	810		
	2,400 skilled hours @ Rs 20 per hour	4,8000	2,400 hrs @ 25	60,000	
	1,200 unskilled hours @ Re 10 per hour	1,2000 6,0000	1,200 hrs. @ 15	18,000	78,000
90	Normal loss		50 kg Actual loss		
720		72600	760 kg		90,510

9. The following data is supplied to you:

Input	*Material*	*Rs per kg*	*Rs*	*Standard Total Rs*	*Input kg*	*Actual Rs per kg*	*Rs*	*Total (Rs)*
400	A	50	20,000		420	45	18,900	
200	B	20	4,000		240	25	6,000	
100	C	15	1,500	25,500	90	15	1,350	26.250
700					750			
	Labour							
	100 man hours @ Rs 20 per hr		2,000		120 hr @ Rs 25per hr		3000	
	200 women hr @ Rs 15 per hr		3,000	5,000	240 hr @ Rs16 per hr		3840	6840
25 kg Normal loss					75 kgActual loss			
675 kg				30,500	675 kg			33,090

From the above information calculate variances.

10. Calculate standard labour time for machine part No. 2235 from the following data :

Standard batch size		100 pieces
Set-up time		64 minutes
Operating time (each piece) :		
Fixing job on machine	= 2 minutes	
Cutting time	= 10 minutes	
Removing job from machine	= 3 minutes	

Allow 10% on total operation time for inspection during process and allow further 5% on total time for fatigue.

Ans. Standard time for 100 pieces 1800 minutes.

11. Vinak Ltd. has furnished you the following information for the month of August. 2002 :

	Budget	*Actual*
Output (Units)	30,000	32,500
Hours	30,000	33,000
Fixed overhead	Rs 45,000	50,000
Variable overhead	Rs 60,000	68,000
Working days	25	26

Calculate the variances.

Ans. Total overhead cost variance Rs 4,250 (A)
Variable overhead cost variance Rs 3,000 (A)
Fixed overhead cost variance Rs 1,250 (A)
Expenditure variance Rs 1,250 (A)
Volume variance Rs 3,750 (F)
Efficiency variance Rs 750 (A)
Capacity variance Rs 4,500 (F)
Calender variance Rs 1,800 (F)

12. The following figures are extracted from the books of a company: Budgeted overhead Rs 10,000 (Fixed Rs 6,000; Variable Rs 4,000)

Budgeted hours	2,000
Actual overhead	10,400 (fixed Rs 6,100; variable Rs 4,300)

Actual hours Rs 2,100
Compute the overhead variances.
Ans. Overhead cost Rs 100 (F), Variable overhead 100 (A). Fixed overhead Rs 200 (F)

13. Narang Ltd., produces two commodities, Good and Better, in one of its departments. Each unit takes 5 hrs and 10 hrs as production time, respectively. 1,000 units of Good and 600 units of Better were produced during March 2002. Actual man-hours spent in this production were 10,000. Yearly budgeted hours are 96,000. Compute the various control ratios.

Ans. Capacity ratio	1.25
Efficiency ratio	1.10
Activity ratio	1.8

14. ABC Ltd. manufactures two products A and B. Product A takes 6 hours to make while product B take 12 hours. In a month of 25 days of 8 hours each. 1,200 units of A and 750 units of B were produced. The firm employs 75 men in the department responsible for producing these two products. The budgeted hours are 1,86,000 per annum. You are required to calculate activity ratio, capacity ratio and efficiency ratio.

Ans. Activity ratio	104.5%
Capacity utilisation ratio	96.8%
Efficiency ratio	108%

15. From the following data, calculate activity ratio. A factory manufactures two products A and B. Standard time to manufacture product A is 2 hours and product B 10 hours. The budgeted and actual production in December 2002 were as follows :

	Budgeted production	*Actual production*
Product A	125 units	100 units
Product B	30 units	24 units

Total hours worked were 660
Ans. Activity ratio 80%

CHAPTER 8

Budgeting

CONCEPT OF BUDGETING

One of the primary objectives of cost and management accounting is to provide information to business managements for planning and control. Budgeting acts as tool of both planning and control. Budgeting is a formal process of financial planning using estimated financial and accounting data. The Institute of Cost and Management. Accountants (UK) defines a budget as "a financial and/or quantitative statement, prepared and approved prior to a defined period of time, of the policy to be pursued during that period for the purpose of attaining a given objective. It may include income, expenditure and the employment of capital."

CONCEPT OF BUDGETARY CONTROL

Budgetary control is a means of control in which the actual state affairs is compared with the budget so that appropriate action may be taken with regard to any deviations before it is too late. Briefly, the use of a budget to control a firm's activities is known as budgeting control. Budgetary control has the following main objectives:

1. To provide an organised procedure for planning. It provides a detailed plan of action for a business over a definite period of time.
2. To coordinate all the activities of various departments of a business firm in such a manner that the maximum profit will be achieved for the minimum use of resources.
3. To provide a means of determining the responsibility for all deviations from the plan (budget), and to supply information on the basis of which necessary corrective action may be taken. Thus, budgetary control has the objective of controlling cost.

OBJECTIVES AND FUNCTIONS OF BUDGETING

An effective budgeting system is vital to the success of a business firm. Budgeting is needed in organizations to perform the following functions: (i) Planning, (ii) coordination, (iii) communication, and (iv) control and performance evaluation.

Planning

Almost all business activities require some planning to ensure efficient and maximum use of scarce resources. The budget is a formal planning framework that provides specific deadlines to achieve departmental objectives and contributes towards the overall objectives of an organization. A budget incorporates expected performance and present managerial targets.

Coordination

Coordination is a managerial function under which all factors of production and all departmental activities are balanced and integrated to achieve the objectives of the organization. The budgeting process provides the basis for individuals in all parts of the organization to exchange ideas on how best to achieve these objectives. According to Horngreen*, budgets help management to coordinate in the following ways:

1. The existence of a well-laid plan is the major step towards achieving coordination. Executives are forced to think of the relationships among individual operations, and the company as a whole.
2. Budgets help to restrain the empire-building efforts of executives. Budgets broaden individual thinking by helping to remove unconscious biases on the part of engineers, sales and production officers.
3. Budgets help to search out weaknesses in the organisational structure. The formulation and administration of budgets isolate problems of communication, of fixed responsibility, and of working relationships.

Communication

It is necessary in an efficient organisation that all people be informed about the objectives, policies, programmes and performances. This is made possible through their participation in the budgeting process. Budgets inform each manager of what others have agreed to do. They also inform managers of the resources available to achieve objectives and targets.

Control and Performance Evaluation

Budgeting enters into control at three points:

1. When a budget is being formulated, departments analyse their plans for the furture and submit estimates as per their requirements, justfying each of their demands by demonstrating a need.
2. After budgets of different departments have been reviewed and approved they become targets that set desirable limits on spending.
3. At the end of the budget period, a comparison of actual expenditures with budget expenditure is made as a means of judging performance and fixing responsibility for deviations.

ADVANTAGES OF BUDGETING

Budgeting plays an important role in the effective use of resources and achieving overall organisational goals. It has the following advantages:

1. Budgeting compels and motivates management to make an early and timely study of its problems. It generates a sense of caution and care, and adequate study among managers before decisions are made by them.
2. Budgeting provides a valuable means of controlling income and expenditure of a business as it is a "plan for spending".
3. Budgeting provides a tool through which managerial policies arid goals are periodically evaluated, tested and established as guidelines for the entire organisation.
4. Budgeting helps in directing capital and other resources into the most profitable channels.
5. Budgeting coordinates and correlates all business activites. It enables management to decentralise responsibility without losing control of the business. It reveals weaknesses, inefficiencies, deviations in the organisation very promptly which can be checked immediately to achieve a desired goal.

---

* Charles T. Horngreen, *Cost Accounting, A* Managerial Emphasis, Prentice-Hall of India, New Delhi, p. 123.

6. The use of budgeting in an organisation develops an attitude of "cost consciousness," stimulates the effective use of resources, and creates an environment of profit-mindedness throughout the organisation.
7. It provides a norm, basis or yardstick for measuring performance of departments and individuals working in organisations.
8. Budgeting encourages productive competition, provides incentive to perform efficiently and gives a sense of purpose to each individual in the organisation.
9. Budgeting provides a systematic and disciplined approach to the solution of problems in the organisation. Horngreen observes: "The uppermost point is that budgets provide a discipline that brings planning to the forefornt as a key managerial responsiblity."
10. Budgeting, if executed in nearly every enterprise, helps the total national economy by providing stability of employment, economic use of resources and effective prevention of waste.

LIMITATIONS OF BUDGETING

While budgeting has many advantages that are vital to an organisation, it has certain limitations which require careful consideration:

1. Planning, budgeting or forecasting is not an exact science; it uses approximations and judgement which may not be cent per cent accurate. At best, a budget is an estimate; no one knows precisely what will happen in the future.
2. The success and utility of budgeting depends on the cooperation and participation of all members of management. Many a time budgeting has failed because executive management has paid only lip service to its execution.
3. A budget is only a tool and does not eliminate nor take over the place of management. Executives generally feel "circled in" by a budget and its related figures. They fail to understand that budget is meant to provide detailed information, goals and targets which may help them in achieving the company objectives.
4. The establishment of a budgeting process takes time. Also, sometimes too much is expected from a budget and in case expectations are not fulfilled, the blame is put on the budget.
5. Excessive emphasis on budgeting may result in attempts by lower level management and employees to buck the system by providing inaccurate estimates of future costs and revenues. As the end of budget period approaches and employees realise that actual expenses have not been as great as allowed by the budget, there may be a temptation to spend excessive amounts in order to "use up" the budget allowance. Such activities result in sub-optimal profits for the company.

BUDGETING PROCESS

The budgeting process or programme varies widely from one organisation to another. Differences in management style, organisation objectives, structure of competition and similar factors affect the procedures companies adopt in budget preparations. However, there are a set of guidelines (procedures) which are used in the budgeting process by a large number of organisations. These common steps can be listed as follows:

1. *Obtaining estimates of sales, production levels, expected costs, and availability of resources from each sub-unit/division/department* The departmental heads or managers are required to provide estimates of future conditions and activities that will have an impact on the company.
2. *Coordinating estimates* In many organisations, the budget committee evaluates the different plans submitted by various organisational units to determine the potentiality of plans in the overall interest of the company and to estimate what resources are available and can be fairly allocated among the various units of the organisation.

3. *Communicating the budget to responsible managers and the concerned departments* After individual budget plans have been approved in the light of organisational goals and availability of resources, the budgets should be communicated to departments and responsible managers. Changes and modifications incorporated in the final budget should be made known to managers to obtain their cooperation and support for the budgets.
4. *Implementing the budget plan* The final budget is presented to the managers concerned and adopted as the plan of operation for the coming budget period.
5. *Reporting interim progress towards budgeted objectives* As a feedback in the budgeting process, performance reports are prepared to inform departmental managers and top management about the performances achieved in terms of budgeted figures. Such an investigation may call for a need to revise the budget during the year. This feedback of information can also be used as a basis for preparing the next year's budget.

ORGANISATION FOR BUDGETING (THE BUDGET COMMITTEE)

Responsibility for budget direction and execution is usually placed in the hands of a Budget Committee which reports directly to top management. In large companies the budget committee is composed of executives incharge of major functions of the business and includes the sales manager, personnel manager, finance manager, the production manager, the chief engineer, the treasurer and the chief accounts

The principal functions of the budget committee are to:

1. Decide the company's general policies and objectives.
2. Receive and review individual budget estimates concerning different departments/divisions.
3. Suggest changes, modifications in accordance with organisational objectives.
4. Approve budgets which act as an authority/target for departmental action.
5. Receive and analyse performance reports regarding the implementation of budgets.
6. Suggest corrective action to improve efficiency and achieve budgetary goals.

BUDGET MANUAL

A budget manual is a document which define the responsibilities of persons engaged in a budgetary programme and sets out the routine, the forms and records required under budgeting. Budget manuals specify the procedures to be followed in developing the budget. Since organisations differ in terms of structure, method of production, and operating requirements, it is difficult to prepare a budget manual suitable for use in all business enterprises.

THE BUDGET PERIOD

The budget period is an import factor in developing a comprehensive budgeting programme. The length of the budget period depends on the type of business, the length of the manufacturing cycle from raw material to finished product, the ease of difficulty of forecasting future market conditions and other factors. However, a business enterprise generally prepares a Short-range budget, and a Long-range budget.

Short-range Budget

Short-range budgets may cover periods of three, six or twelve months depending upon the nature of the business. Most manufacturing firms use one year as the planning period. Wholesale and retail firms usually employ a six-month budget which is related to their selling seasons. In determining the period of the short-range budget, the following factors should be considered:

1. The budget period should be long enough to cover complete production of various products.

2. For business of a seasonal nature, the budget period should cover at least one entire seasonal cycle.
3. The budget period should be long enough to allow for the financing of production well in advance of actual needs.
4. The budget period should coincide with the financial accounting period to compare actual results with budget estimates and thus to facilitate better interpretation of the performance.

Long-range Budget

A long-range budget or planning is defined as a systematic and formalised process for directing and controlling future operations towards a desired objective for periods extending beyond one year. Such budgets cover specific areas, such as future sales, future production, long-term capital expenditures, extensive research and development programmes, financial requirements, profit forecast. They evaluate the future implications associated with present decisions and help. management in making present decisions and select the most profitable alternative.

There are many factors which are duly considered while preparing long term budgets, such as market trends, economic factors, growth of population, consumption pattern, industrial production, national income, government economic and industrial policy. Quantitative sales can be budgeted for a three to five years period. After forecasting sales, a budgeted profit and loss account can be prepared relating anticipated sales to corresponding cost and thus net operating profit can be forecasted. Likewise, a balance sheet for many years can be prepared to forecast cash, inventory levels, accounts receivable, accounts payable, liabilities, etc. The forecasted profit and loss account and balance sheet for a long-range is a very useful tool in accomplishing the objectives of the organisation as a whole.

ELEMENTS OF A SUCCESSFUL BUDGETING PLAN

The success of the budgeting process in an organisation depends on the following essential elements:

1. *Accurate forecasting of business activities* Forecasting is a prerequisite in a budgeting process. It is not only the starting point, but is also critical to the development of an accurate budget.
2. *Coordinating business activities* Budgeting needs to coordinate all the individual budgets into integrated plan as each budget has certain implications for the other budgets. There must be coordination between sales, production, purchasing, personnel budgets.
3. *Communicating the budgets* The success of a comprehensive budgeting programme depends on communication of individual budgets to the different units in the organisation. Managers are not responsible for budget unless the budget is communicated clearly, concisely and in an authoritative manner to them.
4. *Acceptance and cooperation* Successful budgeting also requires that budgets should be accepted by the people who must execute them. Budgeting should have the active cooperation of the entire organisation from the top to the bottom.
5. *Reasonable flexibility* The budgeting programme should contain reasonable flexibility if the situation so demands. However, it should be noted that too much flexibility and too much tightness are both undesirable. Too much flexibility will weaken the cost control and the budget will become inoperative. Simillarly, too much rigidity not permitting reasonable deviations will create problems and restrictions in the implementation of the budget.
6. *Providing a framework for evaluation*. Budgeting provides a basis to evaluate the performance of different departments.

BUDGET CENTRES

An organisation is usually broken down into different budget centres for administrative and control purposes. A budget centre is the lowest level in an organisation for which detailed costs are budgeted, separately from those of other budget centres. The main factor in setting up budget centres is one of the fixing responsibility for action and inaction. To ensure, adequate cost control, the budget centres should fulfil the following conditions:

1. The budget of a particular budget centre should specify precisely the costs controllable by the person responsible for that centre.
2. Costs for which responsibility is joint, e.g., work carried out by a maintenance department, should be kept separate from costs which can be controlled by one manager.
3. Cost that are apportioned between two or more budget centres should also be controlled and for such costs one person should be made responsible.

LIMITING OR PRINCIPAL BUDGET FACTOR

When budgets are made, there is invariably some factor which governs or sets a limit to the quantity which can be made or sold. This is known as the limiting or principal budget factor. The Institute of Cost and Management Accountant (UK) defines a principal budget factor as "the factor the extent of whose influence must first be assessed in order to ensure that the functional budgets are reasonably capable of fulfilment." In the field of sales, the limiting factor is customer demand which is influenced by many factors, such as price and quality of the product, competition, the general purchasing power of the public, advertising, etc. In the field of production, the principal budget factor may be plant capacity, the supply of labour of the right quality, or the availability of scarce materials.

BUDGETS AND STANDARD COSTS

Standard costs and budgets are both vital tools in planning, operation and control of a business enterprise. Both differ in the following respects:

1. A standard costing system can operate without any comprehensive budgeting system. But budgets in absence of standard costs will only be fair estimates and cannot provide a reasonable base against which the actual results can be compared.
2. The objectives of budgeting are different from standard costing. A budget is a profit plan reflecting anticipated financial inflows and outflows. Budgets include both income and expenditure, but standards are set usually for expenses only. Standard costs are developed only for the production and related manufacturing cost.
3. Budgets project the volume of business and levels of costs which should be maintained. That is, they reflect cost ceilings which should not be exceeded if the budgeted profit is to be attained. Standard costs emphasise the cost levels to which cost should be reduced. If costs reach this level, profit will be increased. Standards are minimum targets which are to be attained by actual performance at specific efficiency.
4. Budgets covering the entire business present the forecasted profit and loss account and sometimes balance sheet also. Therefore, budgets act as guides for operating the business on a definite course of action. Standards are frequently used only in labour operation and do not represent expected costs but the cost that should be in a certain assumed conditions of performance. Horngreen* observes that the term "standard" is a unit concept and the term budgeted cost is a total concept. It may be helpful to think of a standard as a budget for the production of a single unit of output.

---

* Charles T. Horngreen, *Cost Accounting, A Managerial Emphasis,* Prentice-Hall of India, New Delhi p. 173.

5. Budgets if achieved by the organisation do not usually involve much variance analysis. Under standard costing detailed variance analysis is carried out to find out deviations so that corrective action may be taken.
6. Review and revision of budgets is more frequently based on the changing circumstances than those of standard costs. Standard costs are more static and subject to less change.
7. Budgets are equally important for planning, organisation, coordination and control functions of management. Standard costs contribute relatively more to the control function than other managerial functions although standards are used for all business functions.

In spite of the above differences, there are some similarities between standard costing and budgeting. Both have in common the establishment of predetermined measures of performance and the comparison of actual and planned performance so as to disclose deviations which are used for the purpose of cost control. Both help in the preparation of reports which compare actual costs and predetermined costs for management planning and control. Standards are almost indispensable to the work of establishing and operating a budget.

FIXED AND FLEXIBLE BUDGETING

Fixed Budgeting

The Institute of Costs and Management Accounts (UK) defines a fixed budget as the budget which is designed to remain unchanged irrespective of the level of activity actually attained. It is based on a single level of activity. A fixed budget performance report compares data from actual operations with the single level of activity reflected in the budget. Fixed budgets do not change when production level changes.

However, in practice, fixed budgeting is rarely used. The main reason is that actual output is often significantly different from the budgeted output. In such a case the budget cannot be used for the purpose of cost control. The performance report may be misleading and will not contain very useful information. For example, if actual production is 12,000 units in place of the budgeted 10,000 units, the costs incurred cannot be compared with the budget which relates to different levels of activity. Since, in fixed budgeting, units are overlooked, a cost to cost comparison without considering the units may give misleading results. The performance report prepared under fixed budgeting merely discloses whether actual costs were higher or lower than budgeted costs. Therefore, the fixed budget is unable to provide useful information when actual output differs significantly from expected or budgeted output. The fact that costs and expenses are affected by fluctuations in volume limits the use of the fixed budget. Clearly, the idea of comparing performance at one activity level with a plan that was developed at some other activity level is nonsense from the viewpoint of judging how efficiently the manager has produced any given output.

A fixed budget can be usefully employed when budgeted output is close enough to the actual output. If output can be estimated within close limits, the fixed budget can be a good basis for performance measurement. Maximum managerial control may be exercised by making comparisons with actual operating figures.

FLEXIBLE BUDGETING

A flexible budget is a budget that is prepared for a range, *i.e.*, for more than one level of activity. It is a set of alternative budgets to different expected levels of activity. The flexible budget is also known by other names, such as variable budget, dynamic budget, sliding scale budget, step budget, expenses formula budget and expenses control budget. The underlying principle of a flexible budget is that every business is dynamic, ever-changing, and never static. Thus, a flexible budget might be developed that would apply to a "relevant range" of production, say 8,000 to 12,000 units. Under this approach, if actual production slips to 9,000 units from a projected 10,000 units, the manager has a specific tool (*i.e.*, the flexible budget) that can be used to determine budgeted cost at 9,000 units of output. The flexible budget provides a reliable basis for comparisons because it is automatically geared to changes in production activity. A flexible budget has the following important features:

1. It covers a range of activity (output).
2. It is flexible, *i.e.*, easy to change with variation in production levels.
3. It facilitates performance measurement and evaluation.

Steps in Flexible Budgeting

The following steps (stages) are involved in developing a flexible budget:

1. Deciding the range of activity to which the budget is to be prepared.
2. Determining the cost behaviour patterns (fixed, variable, semi-variable) for each element of cost to be included in the budget.
3. Selecting the activity levels (generally in terms of production) to prepare budgets at those levels.
4. Preparing the budget at each activity level selected by associating the activity level with corresponding costs. The corresponding costs to be attached with each activity level are determined in terms of their behaviour, *i.e.*, fixed, variable, semi-variable.

ADVANTAGES OF FLEXIBLE BUDGETING

Flexible budgeting is budgeting that is automatically tailored to any level of activity. Although it is most often associated with the control of overhead, a flexible budget may also include direct materials and direct labour. Welsch* has listed three specific uses of the flexible budget.

1. To facilitate development of the departmental expense budgets for inclusion in the profit plans.
2. To provide expense goals for the managers of responsibility centres during the period covered by the profit plan.
3. To provide adjusted budget allowances for comparison purposes (against actual expenses) in the monthly performance reports.

In general, flexible budgeting has the following important advantages:

1. *Accurate budgeting.* The use of flexible budgets may result in the preparation of more accurate budgets. Flexible budgeting techniques require that consideration is to be given to the output factor in budget preparation. Since all costs do not behave in the same manner (as some costs rise faster than others when production increases) a budget giving consideration to the volume (output) factor is bound to be more accurate than one where volume is not considered.
2. *Accurate performance measurement.* The flexible budgeting technique incorporates changes in activity level and compares actual results with the budget in terms of output achieved. This facilitates more meaningful comparison and evaluation between actual and budgeted data as comparable data are compared.
3. *Coordination.* Flexible budgeting results in coordination between all activities/departments of a business. Production is planned in relation to expected sales, materials and labour are acquired to meet expected production requirements. Facilities are provided to achieve budgetary goals, and funds are made available for the investments necessary to have higher output.
4. *Control tool.* Flexible budgeting is an effective management control tool. Comparisons between the budgeted costs (at the actual production level) and actual costs form the basis for analysing cost variances and fixing responsibility for the same. In fact, managers themselves feel motivated in controlling costs for which they are responsible. This contributes to cost control throughout the organisation.

---

*Glenn A, Welsch, *Budgeting, Profit Planning and Control*, p. 22.

Example 1

From the following data, prepare a flexible budget for production of 40,000 units and 75,000 units, distinctly showing variable cost and fixed cost as well as total cost. Also indicate element-wise cost per unit. Budgeted output is 1,00,000 units and budgeted cost per unit is as follows :

Direct Material	95
Direct labour	50
Production overhead (variable)	40
Production overhead (fixed)	5
Administration overhead (fixed)	5
Selling overhead (10% fixed)	10
Distribution overhead (20% fixed)	15

Solution

Flexible Budget

	1,00,000 units		*40.000 units*		*75,000 units*	
	Per unit	*Total*	*Per unit*	*Total*	*Per unit*	*Total*
Variable cost:	Rs	Rs	Rs	Rs	Rs	Rs
Direct material	95	95,00,000	95	38,00,000	95	71,25,000
Direct labour	50	50,00,000	50	20,00,000	50	37,50.000
Production overhead	40	40,00,000	40	16,00.000	40	30,00,000
Selling overhead = $\frac{10 \times 90}{100}$	9	9,00,000	9	3,60,000	9	6,75,000
Distribution overhead = $\frac{15 \times 80}{100}$	12	12,00,000	12	4,80,000	12	9,00,000
Total variable cost	206	2,06,000	206	82,40,000	206	1,54,50,000
Fixed cost						
Production overhead	5	5,00,000	12.50	5,00,000	6.67	5,00,000
Administrative overhead	5	5,00,000	12.50	5,00,000	6.67	5,00,000
Selling overhead	1	1,00,000	2.50	1,00,000	1.33	1,00,000
Distribution overhead	3	3,00,000	7.50	30,00,000	3.00	3,00,000
Total fixed cost	14	14,00,000	35.00	14,00,000	17.67	14,00,000
Total cost	260	2,20,00,000	231.00	96,40,000	223.67	1,68,50,000

Example 2

Goldman Company Limited operates on a system of Flexible Budgets. With the aid of the following information, you are required to prepare Flexible Budget at 80%, 90% and 100% level of activity showing the profits that would result at these levels:

(i) The present sale of 8,00,000 units at Rs 10 each is at the normal level of 80%. If the output is increased to 90%, the selling price will be reduced by 2.5% and if the output reached 100%, the original selling price will be reduced by 5% in order to reach a wider market.

(ii) The prime cost per unit is Rs 5 made up of Direct Materials Rs 3.50, Direct Labour Rs 1.25 and Direct Expenses Re 0.25. If output reaches 90% level of activity and above, a saving of 5% can be effected in the purchase price of raw materials.

(iii) Variable Overhead—Salesmen's commission will be 5% of the sales value.

(iv) Semi-variable overhead at normal level of activity are:

	Rs
Supervision	80,000
Power	70,000
Heat and Light	40,000
Maintenance	50,000
Salesmen Expenses	60,000
Indirect Labour	1,00,000
Transport Costs	2,00,000

These are expected to increase by 5% if output reaches 90% level and by a further 10% if it reaches the 100% level.

(v) Fixed overheads are:

	Rs
Rent and Rates	1,00,000
Depreciation	4,00,000
Advertisement	5,00,000
Administration	7,50,000
Sales Department	2,00,000
General	50,000

Solution :

Goldman Company Limited
Flexible Budget

	Items	*Capacity Levels*		
		80%	*90%*	*100%*
1.	Sales (units)	8,00,000	9,00,000	10,00,000
2.	Selling Price (Rs)	10	9.75	9.50
3.	Sales (Rs)	80,00,000	87,75,000	95,00,000
4.	Costs:			
	A. Variable Costs			
	Direct materials	28,00,000 (8,00,000 × 3.50)	29,92,500 (9,00,000 × 3.325)	32,25,000 (10,00,000 × 3.325)
	Direct Labour (@Rs 1.25 per unit)	10,00,000	11,25,000	12,50,000
	Direct Expenses (@ Re 0.25 per unit)	2,00,000	2,25,000	2,50,000
	Variable Overhead: (Salesmen Commission @ 5% of Sales Value)	4,00,000	4,38,750	4,75,000

B. Semi-Variable Costs:			
Supervision	80,000	84,000	88,000
Power	70,000	73,500	77,000
Heat and Light	40,000	42,000	44,000
Maintenance	50,000	52,500	55,000
Salesmen Expenses	60,000	63,000	66,000
Indirect Labour	1,00,000	1,05,000	1,10,000
Transport Costs	2,00,000	2,10,000	2,20,000
C. Fixed Costs:			
Rent and Rates	1,00,000	1,00,000	1,00,000
Depreciation	4,00,000	4,00,000	4,00,000
Advertisement	5,00,000	5,00,000	5,00,000
Sales Department	2,00,000	2,00,000	2,00,000
General	50,000	50,000	50,000
Administration	7,50,000	7,50,000	7,50,000
Total Costs	70,00,000	74,11,250	79,60,000
5. Profit = (3) – (4)	10,00,000	13,63,750	15,40,000

Example 3

Goodluck Ltd. is currently operating at 75% of its capacity. In the past two years, the level of operations were 55% and 65% respectively. Presently, the production is 75,000 units. The company is planning for 85% capacity level during 1999-2000. The cost details are as follows:

	55%	65%	75%
	Rs	Rs	Rs
Direct Materials	11,00,000	13,00,000	15,00,000
Direct Labour	5,50,000	6,50,000	7,50,000
Factory Overheads	3,10,000	3,30,000	3,50,000
Selling Overheads	3,20,000	3,60,000	4,00,000
Administrative Overheads	1,60,000	1,60,000	1,60,000
	24,40,000	28,00,000	31,60,000

Profit is estimated @ 20% on sales. The following increase in costs are expected during the year.

	In percentage
Direct Materials	8
Direct Labour	5
Variable Factory Overheads	5
Variable Selling Overheads	8
Fixed Factory Overheads	10
Fixed Selling Overheads	15
Administrative Overheads	10

Prepare flexible budget for the period 1999-2000 at 85% level of capacity. Also ascertain profit and contribution.

Solution

Flexible Budget at 85% Capacity Level (85,000 Units)
(for the period 1999-2000)

Particulars	*Cost base on previous* Rs.	*Increase in Cost* Rs.	*Total Cost* Rs.
Variable Costs :			
Direct Materials (WN 1)	17,00,000	1,36,000 (8% × Rs. 17,00,000)	18,36,000
Direct Labour (WN 2)	8,50,000	42,500 (5% × Rs. 8,50,000)	8,92,500
Variable Factory Overheads (WN 3)	1,70,000	8,500 (5% × Rs. 1,70,000)	1,78,500
Variable Selling Overheads (WN 4)	3,40,000	27,200 (8% × Rs. 3,40,000)	3,67,200
Total Variable Costs : (1)			32,74,200
Fixed Costs :			
Fixed Factory Overheads (WN 5)	2,00,000	20,000 (10% × Rs. 2,00,000)	2,20,000
Fixed Selling Overheads (WN 6)	1,00,000	15,000 (15% × Rs. 1,00,000)	1,15,000
Administrative Overheads	1,60,000	16,000 (10% × Rs. 1,60,000)	1,76,000
Total Fixed Costs : (2)			5,11,000
Total Costs : (1) + (2)			37,85,200
Add : Profit : (20% on sale, or 25% on cost)			9,46,300
Sales Revenue :			47,31,500
Less : Total Variable Costs :			32,74,200
Contribution			14,57,000

Statement of Contribution and Profit

	Rs.
Sales Total cost Rs. 37,85,200 + Profit 25% on cost or 20% on sales	47,31,500
Less : Varirable Costs	32,74,200
Contribution	14,57,300
Less : Fixed Costs	5,11,000
Profit	9,46,300

Working Notes :

Particulars	*Capacity Levels*			
	55%	*65%*	*75%*	*85%*
	55,000 Units	*65,000 Units*	*75,000 Units*	*85,000 Units*
1. Direct Materials	11,00,000	13,00,000	15,00,000	17,00,000
2. Direct Labour	5,50,000	6,50,000	7,50,000	8,50,000
3. Variable Factor Overhead :	1,10,000	1,30,000	1,50,000	1,70,000
$\frac{(\text{Rs. } 3,30,000 - \text{Rs. } 3,10,000)}{10,000 \text{ units}}$ = Rs. 2 per unit				
4. Variable Selling Overhead	2,20,000	2,60,000	3,00,000	3,40,000
$\frac{(\text{Rs.}3,60,000 - \text{Rs.}3,20,000)}{10,000 \text{ units}}$ = Rs. 4 per unit				
5. Fixed Factory Overhead : (Total Factory Overheads – Variables Factory Overheads)	2,00,000	2,00,000	2,00,000	2,00,000
6. Fixed Selling Overheads : (Total Selling Overheads – Variable Sellsing Overheads)	1,00,000	1,00,000	1,00,000	1,00,000

Example 4

For production of 10,000 electrical automatic irons, the following are the budgeted expenses :

	Per unit
Direct materials	Rs. 60
Direct labour	30
Variable overheads	25
Fixed overheads (Rs. 1,50,000)	15
Variable expenses (direct)	5
Selling expenses (10% fixed)	15
Administration expenses (Rs. 50,000) rigid for all levels of production	5
Distribution expenses (20% fixed)	5
Total cost of sale per unit	160

Prepare a budget for production of 6,000; 7,000 and 8,000 irons, showing distinctly marginal cost and total cost.

Solution:

Flexible Budget of Electrical Automatic Irons

Production	*6,000 units*		*7,000 units*		*8,000 units*	
	Total (Rs.)	*per unit* (Rs.)	*Total* (Rs.)	*per unit* (Rs.)	*Total* (Rs.)	*per unit* (Rs.)
Direct material	3,60,000	60.00	42,20,000	60.00	4,80,000	60.00
Direct labour	1,80,000	30.00	2,10,000	30.00	2,40,000	30.00
Direct variable expenses	30,000	5.00	35,000	5.00	40,000	5.00

Variable Overheads:						
Production	1,50,000	25.00	1,75,000	25.00	2,00,000	25.00
Selling	81,000	13.50	94,500	13.50	1,08,000	13.50
Distribution	24,000	4.00	28,000	4.00	32,000	4.00
Marginal cost	8,25,000	137.50	9,62,500	137.50	11,00,000	137.50
Fixed production overheads	1,50,000	25.00	1,50,000	21.43	1,50,000	18.75
Administration overheads	50,000	8.33	50,000	7.14	50,000	6.25
Selling overheads	15,000	2.50	15,000	2.14	15,000	1.88
Distribution overheads	10,000	1.67	10,000	1.43	10,000	1.25
Fixed cost	2,25,000	37.50	2,25,000	32.14	2,25,000	28.13
Total cost (Marginal cost plus fixed cost)	10,50,000	175.00	11,87,500	169.64	13,25,000	165.63

Working Notes:

	Selling expenses	*Distribution expenses*
Total for 10,000 units	1,50,000	50,000
Variable : 90% and 80% respectively	1,35,000	40,000
Variable expenses per unit	13.50	4.00
Fixed expenses 10% and 20% of total, respectively	15,000	10,000

Example 5

The budget manager of Jaypee Electricals Ltd. is preparing a flexible budget for the accounting year commencing from 1st April 2001. The company produces one product, component—Peekay. Direct material costs Rs 7 per unit. Direct labour averages Rs 2.50 per hour and requires 1.60 hours to produce one unit of Peekay.

Salesmen are paid a commission of Re 1 per unit sold. Fixed selling and administration expenses amount to Rs 85,000 per year.

Manufacturing overhead has been estimated in the following amounts under specified conditions of volume:

Volume of production (in units)	1,20,000	1,50,000
Expenses:	(Rs)	(Rs)
Indirect material	2,64,000	3,30,000
Indirect labour	1,50,000	1,87,500
Inspection	90,000	1,12,500
Maintenance	84,000	1,02,000
Supervision	1,98,000	2,34,000
Depreciation—Plant and Equipment	90,000	90,000
Engineering services	94,000	94,000
Total manufacturing overhead	9,70,000	11,50,000

Normal capacity of production of the company is 1,25,000 units.

Prepare a budget of total cost at 1,40,000 units of output.

Solution

Flexible Budget for the Year April 2001 to March 2002 Production Volume 140000 Units

Items of cost	*Fixed costs (Rs)*	*Variable costs* Per unit	*Variable costs* Total	*Total cost (Rs)*
Direct materials	—	7.00	9,80,000	9,80,000
Indirect labour	—	4.00	5,60,000	5,60,000
Indirect materials	—	2.20	3,08,000	3,08,000
Indirect labour	—	1.25	1,75,000	1,75,000
Inspection	—	0.75	1,05,000	1,05,000
Maintenance	12,000	0.60	84,000	96,000
Supervision	54,000	1.20	1,68,000	2,22,000
Depreciation—Plant and Equipment	90,000	—	—	90,000
Engineering service	94,000	—	—	94,000
Sales commission	—	1.00	1,40,000	1,40,000
Fixed selling and distribution expenses	85,000	—		85,000
Total	3,35,000	18.00	25.20,000	28,55,000

Working Notes :

Segregation of semi-variable costs into fixed and variable components:

$$\text{Variable-cost per unit} = \frac{\text{Difference in cost}}{\text{Difference in output}}$$

Fixed cost = Total cost – Variable cost

(i) Maintenance—Variable cost per unit $= \frac{\text{Rs } 1{,}02{,}000 - 84{,}000}{1{,}50{,}000 - 1{,}20{,}000}$

$= \frac{\text{Rs } 18{,}000}{30000 \text{ unit}}$

= Re 0.60 per unit

Fixed cost = Rs 84,000 – (1,20,000 × .60)

= 12,000

Variable cost = 14,000 × .60 = Rs 84,000

(ii) Supervision

Variable cost per unit $= \frac{\text{Rs } 2{,}34{,}000 - 1{,}98{,}000}{1{,}50{,}000 - 1{,}20{,}000}$

$= \frac{\text{Rs } 36{,}000}{30{,}000 \text{ units}}$

= Rs 1.20 per unit

Fixed cost = Rs 1,98,000 – (1,20,000 × 1.20)

= 1,98,000 – 1,44,000

= 54,000

Variable cost = 1,40,000 units × Rs 1.20

= Rs 1,68,000

(iii) Indirect materials. Indirect labour. Inspection are fully variable costs. This can be proved by taking these elements of costs and following the above method of segregation. For instance, as an example, indirect materials is taken.

Indirect materials

Variable cost per unit $= \dfrac{\text{Rs } 3{,}30{,}000 - 2{,}64{,}000}{1{,}50{,}000 - 1{,}20{,}000}$

$= \dfrac{\text{Rs } 66{,}000}{30{,}000}$

= Rs 2.20 per unit

Fixed cost = Rs 2,64,000 (12,000 × 2.20)
= 2,64,000 – 2,64,00
= No fixed cost

Example 6

The profitability statement of Gourmet Co. Ltd. has been summarized as follows:

	Rs	Rs
Sales		15,00,000
Direct materials	4,50,000	
Direct wages	3,00,000	
Variable overheads	1,20,000	
Fixed overheads	4,40,000	13,10,000
Profit		1,90,000

The budgeted capacity of the company is Rs 20,00,000 but the key factor is sales demand. It is proposed that in order to utilise the existing capacity the selling price of this only product manufactured by the company should be reduced by 5%.

You are required to prepare a forecast statement which should show the effect of the proposed reduction in selling price and include any changes in costs expected during the coming year. The following additional information is given:

(i) Sales forecast Rs 19,00,000 (after reduction).
(ii) Direct material prices are expected to increase by 2%.
(iii) Direct wage rates are expected to increase by 5% per unit.
(iv) Variable overheads are expected to increase by 5% per unit.
(v) Fixed overheads will increase by Rs 20,000.

Solution

Forecast Statement of Profit

1.	Sales		19,00,000
2.	*Less:* Variable costs:		
	Direct material	4,50,000	
	Add: For increase on account of sales volume (1/3 × 4,50,000)	1,50,000	
		6,00,000	
	Add: Increase in price (2% of Rs 6,00,000)	12,000	
			6,12,000
	Direct wages	3,00,000	
	Add: For increase in sales volume (1/3 of Rs 3,00,000)	1,00,000	
		4,00,000	

Add: For increase in wage rates (5% of Rs 4.00.000)	20,000	4,20,000
Variable overheads	1,20,000	
Add: For increase in sales volume (1/3 ×1.20,000)	40,000	
	1,60,000	
Add: For increase in rates (5% of Rs 1,60,000)	8,000	1,68,000
Total variable costs		12,00,000
3. Contribution (1) – (2)		7,00,000
4. Fixed overheads	4,40,000	
Add: Expected increase in fixed overheads	20,000	4,60,000
Profit		2,40,000

Note :

Sales after price reduction = Rs 19,00,000

Sales before price reduction 19,00,000 × 100/95 = 20,00,000

Increase in sales volume from present sales without price reduction over existing sales

$$\frac{5,00,000 \times 100}{15,00,000} = 33\frac{1}{3}\%$$

Example 7

Paints Private Ltd. Company, manufacturing a single product, is facing severe competition in selling it at Rs 50 per unit. The company is operating at 60% level of capacity at which level the sales are Rs 12,00,000 and variable costs are Rs 30 per unit. Semi-variable costs may be considered as fixed at Rs 90,000 when output is nil and the variable elements in Rs 250 for each additional 1% level of activity. Fixed costs are Rs 1,50,000 at the present level of activity. But at 80% level of activity or above, these costs are expected to increase by Rs 50,000.

To cope with the competition, the management of the company is considering a proposal to reduce the selling price by 5%. You are required to prepare a statement showing the operating profit at levels of activity of 60%, 70%, 80%, 90% assuming that:

(a) The selling price remains at Rs 50

(b) The selling price is reduced by 5%

Paints Private Ltd. Flexible Budget

	60% (*24,000 units*) Rs	*70%* (*28,000 units*) Rs	*80%* (*32,000 units*) Rs	*90%* (*36,000 units*) Rs
Variable cost	7,20,000	8,40,000	9,60,000	10,80,000
Semi-variable:				
Fixed	90,000	90,000	90,000	90,000
Variable	15,000	17,500	20,000	22,500
Fixed cost	1,50,000	1,50,000	2,00,000	2,00,000
Total cost	9,75,000	10,97,500	12,70,000	13,92,500
(a) Sales (Selling price remaining at Rs 50)	12,00,000	14,00,000	16,00,000	18,00,000
Profit	2,25,000	3,02,500	3,30,000	4,07,500
(b) Sales (Selling price is reduced to Rs 47.50.5% reduction)	11,40,000	13,30,000	15,20,000	17,10,000
Profit	1,65,000	2,32,500	2,50,000	3,17,500

TYPES OF BUDGETS

Budgets are the end product of the budgeting process. The numbers and types of budgets in a business enterprise depend on the size and nature of the business. However, in a manufacturing concern, the following budgets are generally prepared:

(A) Operating and functional budgets:
1. Sales budget
2. Production budget
3. Production cost budget
   (i) Direct materials budget
   (ii) Direct labour budget
   (iii) Factory overhead budget
4. Ending inventories budget
5. Cost of goods sold budget
6. Selling expense budget
7. Administrative expense budget
8. Budgeted income statement

(B) Financial budgets:
1. Capital expenditure budget
2. Research and development budget
3. Cash budget
4. Budgeted balance sheet
5. Budgeted statement of the changes in financial position.

SALES BUDGET

The most important budget, which all other budgets are, contingent upon, is the sales budget.. All budgets, such as production budget, selling and distribution budget and others are all affected by the sales budget and are dependent upon the revenue derived from sales. Fig 1 illustrates a specimen of sales budget.

ABC Company Ltd.
Sales Budget for the year Ending December 31, 2002

Products	*Budgeted sales units*	*Budgeted sales price (Rs)*	*Total*
A	70,000	80,000	56,00,000
B	80,000	1,20,000	96,00,000
Total	1,50,000		1,52,00,000

Fig 1. Sales Budget

SALES FORECAST

Developing a sales budget requires forecasting future sales levels. The three main factors that should be considered by management in forecasting sales are: (a) information concerning past performance, (b) information about present conditions within the individual company and in each sales territory, and (c) data concerning the industry and general business conditions.

The information about past performance is the starting point for sales forecasting. The sales record for past years, and particularly for the year just ending should be available to management in minute detail.

The second essential step in forecasting sales is the accumulation of data regarding conditions within the company and in each sales territory. The management can obtain a good picture of sales prospects through information sent to the head office by salesmen, dealers, and sales officers of different territories.

A sales forecast is a prediction based on past sales performance and an analysis of expected market conditions. The true value in making a forecast is that it forces a company look at the future objectively. The company that takes note of the past stays aware of the present and precisely analyzes that information to see into the future.

Conducting a sales forecast will provide a business with an evaluation of past and current sales levels and annual growth, and allow to compare company to industry norms. It will also help establish policies so that a firm easily can monitor prices and operating costs to guarantee profits, and make aware of minor problems before they become major problems.

I. The Importance of Sales Forecasting

Sales forecasting is a self-assessment tool for a company. Managers have to keep taking the pulse of their company to know how healthy it is. A sales forecast reports, graphs and analyzes the pulse of a business. It can make the difference between just surviving and being highly successful in business. It is a vital cornerstone of a company's budget. The future direction of the company may rest on the accuracy of sales forecasting.

Companies that implement accurate sales forecasting processes realize important benefits such as:

1. Enhanced cash flow
2. Knowing when and how much to buy
3. In-depth knowledge of customers and the products they order
4. The ability to plan for production and capacity
5. The ability to identify the pattern or trend of sales
6. Determine the value of a business above the value of its current assets
7. Ability to determine the expected return on investment (This can be very helpful if the company is trying to obtain financing from investors or other lending institutions)

The combination of these benefits may result in:

- Increased revenue
- Increased customer retention
- Decreased costs
- Increased efficiency

For sales forecasting to be valuable to a business, it must not be treated as an isolated exercise. Rather, it must be integrated into all facets of an organization.

II. What Information is Needed to Prepare a Sales Forecast?

Since the forecast is based on a company's previous sales, it is necessary to know sales volume for the past several years. To complete a thorough sales forecast, we also need to take into consideration all of the elements, both internal and external, that can affect sales.

Mathematically, it is possible to forecast sales with some precision. Realistically, however, this precision can be doubtful because of external market and economic factors that are beyond a company's control. The following are some of the external factors that can affect sales:

Seasonality of the business
Relative state of the economy
Direct and indirect competition
Political events
Styles or fashions
Consumer earnings
Population changes
Weather
Productivity changes

Sales forecasting requires sufficiently detailed analysis of both the external and internal factors related to the sales function. Internal factors that can affect sales are somewhat more controllable, such as:

Labour problems
Credit policy changes
Sales motivation plans
Inventory shortages
Working capital shortage
Price changes
Change in distribution method
Production capability shortage
New product lines

The sales forecast must be qualified by asking the following questions:

1. What are the items to be forecasted (individual product lines or business units)?
2. How far in the future should the forecast extend?
3. How frequently should the forecast be made?
4. How frequently should the forecast be reviewed?
5. What would constitute an acceptable tolerance of forecast error?

The following internal data will be scrutinized and analyzed when conducting a sales forecast. Therefore, this data must be prepared on a consistent basis:

1. Accounting records
2. Financial statements
3. Sales-call reports
4. After-sales service demands from clients

It is significant to note that if a company sells more than one type of product or service, it should prepare a separate sales forecast for each service or product group. The more focused a sales forecast is, the more precise its outcome will be.

III. How Long and How Often Should One Forecast?

Sales forecast needs to be performed, reviewed and compared with actual performance results on a regular basis. It should be it as a routine tune-up that keeps the gears of a business running smoothly so that company can achieve a higher performance record.

Although every business owner's comfort level may be different, sales forecasts should be conducted monthly during the first year, and quarterly after that. The more often is a forecast, the better are chances of weeding out extreme variations in year-to-year sales. It will also possibly identify a trend or level of variations that is more realistically oriented to probable future sales patterns.

Although any forecast has a percentage of uncertainty, the farther into the future is projected, the greater will be uncertainty. As a rule, there are three lengths of time for sales forecasting:

1. Short-range forecasts are for fewer than three months. They are used to make continual decisions about planning, scheduling, inventory and staffing in production, procurement and logistics activities.
2. Intermediate forecasts have a span of three months to two years. They are used for budgetary planning, cost control, marketing new products, sales force compensation plans, facility planning, capacity planning and process selection and distribution planning.
3. Long-range forecasts cover more than two years. They are used to decide whether to enter new markets, develop new products or services, expand or create new facilities, or arrange long-term procurement contracts.

Perhaps the simplest method is to assume that, the percentage increase (or decrease) in sales will continue and that no market factors will influence sales performance more in the future than in the past.

IV. Sales Analysis

After collecting all relevant information for a sales forecast, a sales analysis or budget is prepared. The sales budget is usually prepared on the lines of (i) product, (ii) territory, and (iii) customer.

PRODUCTION BUDGET

After preparing the sales budget, the production budget is prepared. A production budget is stated in physical units. It specifies the number of units of each product that must be produced to satisfy the sales forecasts and to achieve the desired level of closing finished goods inventory. Essentially, the production budget is the sales budget adjusted for inventory changes as follows:

Units to produce = Budgeted sales + Desired closing inventory of finished goods – Beginning inventory of finished goods

A specimen production budget in given in Fig. 2.

ABC Company
Total Production Budget for the Month of December, 2002

	Products	
	A	*B*
Budgeted sales (units)	70,000	80,000
Add: Desired dosing finished goods inventory	20,000	30,000
	90,000	1,10,000
Less: Beginning finished goods inventory	40,000	50,000
Units to be produced	50,000	60,000

Fig. 2. Production Budget

The production budget, like other budgets, is detailed by months or quarters along with a tentative annual budget. Further, budgets are prepared for every production centre for comparison with actual production.

PRODUCTION COST BUDGET

A production cost budget summarises the materials budget, labour budget, the factory overhead budget, and may be expressed and analysed by departments and or products. A production cost budget, also known as a manufacturing budget is made up of three budgets: (i) materials, (ii) labour, and (iii) factory overhead.

DIRECT MATERIALS BUDGET

This budget specifies the cost of direct materials used and the cost of the direct materials purchased. Figure 3 explains the calculation of the direct materials budget. The usage part of the direct materials budget determines the cost of purchases of direct materials.

ABC Company
Direct Materials Budget for the Year Ending December 2002

A. *Usage Budget*	Products		
	A	*B*	*Total*
Budgeted production in units	50,000	60,000	
Direct materials requirements			
Product A 5 kg per unit	× 5		
Product B 8 kg per unit		× 8	
Direct materials usage (kg)	2,50,000	4,80,000	
Cost per kg	Re 1.00	Rs 1.50	
Cost of direct materials used	Rs 2,50,000	Rs 7,20,000	Rs 9,70,000

B. Purchase Budget

	Direct material (in kg)		
	A	*B*	*Total*
Direct materials usage	2,50,000	4,80,000	
Budgeted closing direct materials inventory	+50,000	+75,000	
Total requirements	3,00,00	5,55,000	
Beginning direct materials inventory	70,000	1,00,000	
Purchase of direct materials	2,30,000	4,55,000	
Cost per kg	× Re 1.00	× Rs 1.50	
Cost of purchase	Rs 2,30,000	Rs 6,82,500	Rs 9,12,500

Fig. 3. Direct Materials Budget

The direct materials budget is useful in the following ways :

1. It helps the purchasing department to prepare a schedule to ensure delivery of materials when needed.
2. It helps in fixing minimum and maximum levels of inventories in the stores department.
3. It helps the finance manager to determine the financial requirements to meet production targets.

The materials budget usually deals with direct materials only. Supplies and indirect materials are generally included in the factory overhead budget.

DIRECT LABOUR BUDGET

The labour budget estimates the labour, adequate in number and grades, to enable the production budget to be achieved. It is generally preferable to prepare a separate direct labour budget and to include indirect labour in the factory overhead budget. The labour budget prepared must disclose the following information: (i) the number of each type or grade of worker required in each period to achieve the budgeted output; (ii) budgeted cost of such labour in each period; and (iii) period of training necessary for different types of workers.

Figure 4 illustrates the preparation of a direct labour budget.

ABC Company
Direct Labour Budget for the Year Ending December 2002

	Products		
	A	*B*	*Total*
Budgeted production requirements (units)	50,000	60,000	
Direct labour hours per unit	3	2	
Total direct labour hours	1,50,000	1,20,000	2,70,000
Direct labour cost per hour	Rs 5.00	Rs 5.00	Rs 5.00
Total direct labour cost (Rs)	Rs 7,50,000	Rs 6,00,000	Rs 13,50.000

Fig. 4. Direct Labour Budget

FACTORY OVERHEAD BUDGET

The factory overhead budget is prepared on the basis of the chart of accounts which reflects different expense accounts and which properly classifies expenses accounts and details the cost centres or departments. Although expenses can be classified in different manners such as natural classification, variability, the preparation of the factory overhead budget requires that expenses should be classified by departments since expenses are incurred by various departments. In this way departmental beads should be held accountable for expenses incurred by their departments,

Figure 5 depicts the factory overhead budget where in overhead costs have been classified into fixed and variable components.

ABC Company
Factory Overhead Budget for the Year Ending December 2002
(Based on budgeted capacity of 2,70,000 direct labour hours)

	Items	*Direct labour*	*Rate per direct hour* Rs	*Total cost* Rs
A.	*Variable factory overhead:*			
	(i) Supplies	2,70,000	1.00	2,70,000
	(ii) Repairs	2,70,000	0.50	1,35,000
	(iii) Indirect labour	2,70,000	1.00	2,70,000
	(iv) Others	2,70,000	0.40	1,08,000
				7,83,000
B.	*Fixed factory overhead cost*			
	(i) Supervision		Rs 4,00,000	
	(ii) Depreciation		5,00,000	
	(iii) Property tax		2,50,000	
	(iv) Others		1,77,000	
	Total fixed factory overhead cost			13,77,000
	Total factory overheads cost			21,60,000

$$\text{Predetermined overhead rate Rs.} = \frac{\text{Rs. } 21,60,000}{2,70,000 \text{ hours}}$$

= Rs 8.00 per direct labour hour

Fig. 5. Factory Overhead Budget

ABC Company Ending
Inventory Budget for the Year Ending December 2002

		Rs.
Direct materials inventory		
Product A	5,000 kg × Re 1.00 per kg	50,000
Product B	75,000 kg × Rs 1.50 per kg	1,12,000
		1,62,500
Finished goods inventory		
Product A	20,000 units × Rs 25.00	5,00,000
Product B	30,000 units × Rs 30.00	9,00,000
		14,00,000

Fig. 6. Ending Inventories Budget

ENDING INVENTORIES BUDGET

An inventory budget can be prepared to find out the values of direct materials and finished goods inventory as shown in Fig. 6.

COST OF GOODS SOLD BUDGET

After preparing direct materials, direct labour, factory overhead, and ending inventory budgets, the cost of goods sold budget can be prepared. The cost of goods sold budget summarises all the above budgets as shown in Fig. 7.

SELLING EXPENSES BUDGET

Closely related with the sales budget is the selling and distribution cost budget which shows the budgeted costs of promoting sales for the budget period. It is also known as the marketing expense budget. The selling cost budget is made up of a number of cost items, some of which are fixed and some variable, The principal fixed expenses are salaries and depreciation; the principal variable expenses are commissions, travel, advertising and bad debts.

ABC Company
Cost of Goods Sold Budget for the Year Ending Dec. 31, 2002

	Rs.	Rs.
Direct materials		
Beginning inventory	2,00,000	
Purchases	9,12,500	
	11,12,500	
Less : Closing inventory	1,62,500	
Cost of direct materials used		9,50,000
Direct Labour		13,50,000
Factory Overhead		21,60,000
Total factory cost		44,60,000
Beginning finished goods inventory		25,00,000
Total goods available for sale		69,60,000
Closing finished goods inventory		14,00,000
Cost of goods sold		55,60,000

Fig. 7. Cost of Goods Sold Budget

Fig. 8 exhibits an annual selling expenses budget classified according to fixed and variable expenses. Separate budgets for each of these expenses may be prepared especially in the case of a large company.

ABC Company
Selling Expense Budget for the year Ending Dec. 31, 2002

	Items	*Costs* Rs	*Total costs* Rs
(A)	Variable selling expenses:		
	(i) Sales commission	35,000	
	(ii) Salary and wages	40,000	
	(iii) Advertising	15,000	
	(iv) Travelling	22,000	1,12,000
(B)	Fixed selling expenses:		
	(i) Warehousing	60,000	
	(ii) Advertising	30,000	
	(iii) Marketing Manager's Salary	60,000	
	(iv) Depreciation	27,000	1,77,000
Total selling expenses			2,89,000

Fig. 8. Selling Expenses Budget

Administrative Expenses Budget

The administrative expenses budget covers the administrative costs for non-manufacturing business activities. The administrative expense budget contains expenses like directors' remuneration, legal charges, audit fees. salaries, rent, office expenses, interest, property taxes, postage, telephone, telegraph, etc. These expenses should be properly classified under different headings to determine the responsibility of cost incurrence and control. For example, these expenses can be classified into different categories such as company administration, general accounting, general office, etc. Figure 9 presents an administrative expense budget.

ABC Company
Administrative Expenses Budget for the Year Ending December 31, 2002

Items	*Amount* Rs	*Amount* Rs
(A) Variable administrative expenses:		
(i) Supplies	35,000	
(ii) Clerical wages	60,000	
Total variable administrative expenses		95,000
Fixed administrative expenses:		
(i) Director's remuneration	1,20,000	
(ii) Legal charges	20,000	
(iii) Depreciation	25,000	
(iv) Salaries	30,000	
(v) Rent	60,000	
(vi) Postage, telephone, etc.	32,000	
Total fixed administrative expenses		2,87,000
Total administrative expenses		3,82,000

Fig. 9. Administrative Expense Budget

BUDGETED INCOME STATEMENT

A budgeted income statement summarises all the individual budgets, *i.e.,* sales budget, cost of goods sold budget, selling budget, and administrative expense budget. No new estimates are made; figures are taken from budgets previously prepared. This budget determines income before taxes. If the tax rate is available, net income after taxes can also be computed. Figure 10 exhibits a budgeted or projected income statement.

CAPITAL EXPENDITURE BUDGET

The budgeting of capital expenditure is one of the most important areas of managerial decisions. Capital expenditures represent long-term commitments. Also, the benefits of capital expenditure spread over a long period of time. Capital expenditure budgets are prepared for both short and long-range project depending on the requirements of the business firm. Short-range projects are implemented during the current accounting period. Long-range projects are not executed in the current period, they are expressed only in general terms. They become budget commitments only when the time for their implementation approaches.

ABC Company
Budgeted Income Statement for the Year Ending December, 2002

		Rs.
Sales		1,52,00,000
Cost of goods sold		55,60,000
Gross margin		96,40,000
Selling expenses	2,89,000	
Administrative expenses	3,82,000	6,71,000
Income before taxes		89,69,000
Income taxes (assuming 50%)		44,84,500
Net Income		44,84,500

Fig. 10. Budgeted Income Statement

RESEARCH AND DEVELOPMENT BUDGET

The research and development budget is the most important tool for planning and controlling research and development costs. It compels management to think in advance about the fairness of these expenses both in total amounts and in each field of a research programme. It helps in coordination with the company's other plans and projects. Since the research and development programmes compete with other desirable activities in allocation of funds, coordination is needed to balance financially immediate and long-term company plans. Also, this budget guides the research and development department to plan correctly the staff and equipment requirements and special facilities needed for the work.

CASH BUDGET

A cash budget contains detailed estimates of cash receipts (cash inflows) and disbursements (cash outflows) for the budget period or some other specific period. The preparation of a cash budget has the following objectives:

1. It indicates the effect on the cash position of seasonal requirements, large inventories, unusual receipts, and slowness in collecting receivables.
2. It indicates the cash requirements needed for a plant or equipment expansion programme.
3. It points up to the need for additional funds from sources such as bank loans or sales of securities and the time factors involved.
4. It indicates the availability of cash for taking advantage of discounts.
5. It assists in planning the financial requirements of bond redemption, income tax instalments, and payments to pensions and retirement funds.
6. It shows the availability of excess funds for short-term investments,

Period of Cash Budget

The period of time covered by a cash budget depends on the type of business, management planning needs, and cash position. A cash budget many generally be related to the following time periods:

1. *Operational cash planning.* Cash budgets may be prepared monthly, weekly or even daily to meet informational requirements of management.
2. *Short-range.* Short-range cash budgeting is prepared annually and is in correspondence with the annual profit plan. it indicates cash inflows and outflows as generated by the annual profit plan.
3. *Long-range.* Long-range budgeting does not disclose detailed estimates of revenue and expenses. The effects of business expansion and long-term trends are incorporated in long-range cash budgeting. Long-range cash projection is in accord with (i) the timing of the capital expenditure projects, and (ii) the timing of the long-range profit plan (usually five years).

Preparation of a Cash Budget

A cash budget may be prepared by following either of the three generally accepted procedures:

1. The receipts and disbursements method.
2. The adjusted profit and loss or adjusted net income method.
3. Balance sheet method.

In the first method, all anticipated cash receipts are carefully forecasted such as cash sales, cash collections from debtors, dividends, interest on investments, proceeds from sale of assets, royalties, bank loans, etc. Likewise, cash disbursements for materials purchases, supplies, salaries, repayment of loans, dividends, taxes, expenses, purchases of plant or equipment are also determined. This method is useful for short-range cash projection but is not appropriate for long-term cash budgeting. This methods is in accord with the annual profit plan.

The second approach is the profit and loss or adjusted net income method. The starting point in this approach is budgeted profit reflected in the income statement. Basically, projected profit is converted from an accrual basis to a cash basis. That is, the budgeted profit of a period is adjusted for non-cash transactions and expected cash-oriented changes in asset and liability accounts not affected by profit calculations. Using the budgeted profit for a period as a starting point, various non-cash transactions are added back to net profit for the period. Non-cash items are depreciation, bad and doubtful accounts, expired insurance premiums, expenses, and income tax accruals. After this, anticipated decreases in assets or increase in liabilities are further added and anticipated increases in assets or decreases in liabilities are deducted. The budgeted cash at the end of a period is the cash balance at the beginning of the period plus the net cash increase (or minus the net cash decrease) as indicated in the analysis of the adjusted profit method.

The third approach is the balance sheet method. In this approach closing balances of all (budgeted) balance sheet items except cash and bank balances are found and put in a budgeted balance sheet. If the total of liabilities side items is more than the total of asset side items. The balancing figure will be cash bank balance. On the contrary if the total of assets side items is more than the total of liabilities side items. the balancing figure will be bank overdraft or shortage in cash. Budgeted figures of closing balance sheet items can be found after adjusting the opening balance sheet items with the transactions anticipated for the year.

BUDGETED OR PROJECTED BALANCE SHEET

A projected balance sheet represents the expected financial position at a particular date. The projected balance sheet is prepared from the budgeted balance sheet at the beginning of the budget period and the expected changes in the account balances reflected in the operating budgets, capital expenditure budgets, and cash budget. The projected balance sheet also automatically determines the arithmetical accuracy of other budgets since they are used in preparing the forecasted balance sheet.

MASTER BUDGET

A master budget sometimes called a comprehensive budget, is the summary or total budget package for a business firm. It is the end product of the budget-making process. It shows the budgeted profit and loss account for the budget period and the budgeted balance sheet at the end of the period. It reveals the top management's goals of revenues, expenses, net income, cash flows, and financial position. The other budgets prepared by a business firm are specific, *i.e.* they deal with separate distinct activities of the organisation such as sales, production, selling and distribution and administrative activities. They incorporate plans and budgetory goals for a small segment of a business enterprise. However to achieve business objectives, it is necessary to have coordination among different budgets reflecting diverse activities of a business firm. For example, there should be coordination between sales and production departments and the goals of the production department should match the goals of the sales department. In the absence of coordination among the budgets, a business firm may have problems, such as surplus inventory, shortage of stock, non-availability of raw materials and other resources, employees dissatisfaction, etc. A master budget takes the macro (aggregate) view of the business enterprise and coordinates sales with production; raw materials, manpower, machinery and other resources with production targets, and the like. The master budget is an intergrative tool that cuts across divisional boundaries in order to coordinate the firms' diverse activities. While master budgets provide plans for an entire system, operating budgets provide plans for the organisation's sub-system, that is, operating budgets constitute the building blocks used to complete the master budget.

REVISION OF BUDGETS

As stated earlier in the chapter, successful budgets should have adequate flexibility to meet changing business conditions. Since budgets are used for planning, operation, coordination and control, they should be revised if changes occur in the environment Revision of budgets may be necessary due to the following factors some of which might have been considered earlier in the development of budgets:

1. Errors committed in preparing the budgets which may subsequently be known.
2. Emergence of unforeseen and unanticipated situations which may cause the budget to be revised.
3. Changes in internal factors, e.g. production, forecast, capacity utilisation, etc.
4. Changes in external factors, e.g., market trends, nature of the economy, prices of inputs and resources, consumers' tastes and fashions.

Changes in the above factors do not affect a firm's budgets if they are of minor significance. Some changes, however, considerably affect budgets and in this situation management is faced with two problems:

1. Whether only individual budgets should be changed; and
2. Whether the master budget be changed.

Regarding the first question, most business firms are in agreement and suggest that specific individual budgets should be changed. For instance, if there is likely to be a significant change in expected sales (increase or decrease), production and purchasing departments should be informed about this to avoid over-stocking or under-stocking.

A reversion of the master budget is debatable and sometimes is opposed mainly on two counts: (i) the master budget process is highly complex and expensive; (ii) the evaluation process may take care of these changes if the changes take place. The second argument is more or less on middle ground. While it argues for revision when changes do occur, it focuses on actual effects rather than projected changes. It is felt that this avoids making small changes in the plan that are of little consequence. Those who support the revision of the muster budget argue that the revised budget is a better and more effective basis for performance evaluation and control. By revising budget, all members of the organisation come to know of the expectations and standards for which they will be accountable.

Example 8 (Materials Requirement)

Bala Company expects to sell 84.000 units of finished goods over the next 3-months period. The company currently has 44.000 units of finished goods on hand and wishes to have an inventory of 48,000 units at end of the 3-month period. To produce 1 unit of finished goods requires 4 units of raw materials. The company currently has 2,00.000 units of raw materials on hand and wishes to have an inventory of 2,20,000 units of raw materials on hand at the end of the 3-months period. How many units of raw materials must the Bala Company purchase during the 3-months period?

Solution

Material Requirements

Finished units to be produced	=	(84,000 units) to be sold	+	(48,000 units in) Ending invetory	–	(44,000 units) Beginning inventory
Units to be produced	= 88,000					
Units of raw materials to be used	= 4 units of raw materials per Finished unit × 88,000 units = 3,52,000					
Units of raw materials to be purchased	=	3,52,000 units to be used	+	2,20,000 units desired in ending inventory	–	2,00,000 units in beginning inventory
	=	3,72,000 units				

Example 9 (Production Budget)

Gama Engineering Company Limited manufactures two products X and Y. An estimate of the number of units expected to be sold in the first seven months of 2001 is given below :

	Product X	*Product Y*
January 2001	500	1,400
February	600	1,400
March	800	1,200
April	1,000	1,000
May	1,200	800
June	1,200	800
July	1,000	900

It is anticipated that:

1. There will be no work-in-progress at the end of any month; and
2. Finished units equal to half and anticipated sales for the next month will be in stock at the end of each month (including December 2000).

The budgeted production and production costs for the year ending 31st December, 2001 are as follows:

	Product X	*Product Y*
Production (units)	11.000	12,000
Direct materials per unit (Rs)	12	19
Direct wages per unit (Rs)	5	7
Direct manufacturing charges apportionable to each type of product (Rs)	33,000	48,000

You are required to prepare:

(a) A production budget showing the number of units to be manufactured each month.
(b) A summarised production cost budget for the six-month period January to June 2001.

Solution

Gama Engineering Company Limited
(a) Production Budget (in Units) for the Six Months Ending 30th June, 2001

	Jan.	*Feb.*	*March*	*April*	*May*	*June*
Product X						
Closing stock	300	400	500	600	600	500
Sales	500	600	800	1,000	1,200	1,200
	800	1,000	1,300	1,600	1,800	1,700
Less: Opening stock	250	300	400	500	600	600
Production (in units)	550	700	900	1,100	1,200	1,100
Product Y						
Closing stock	700	600	500	400	400	450
Sales	1,400	1,400	1,200	1,000	800	800
	2,100	2,000	1,700	1,400	1,200	1,250
Less: Opening stock	700	700	600	500	400	400
Production (in units)	1,400	1,300	1,100	900	800	850

(b) Summarised Production Cost Budget for the Six Months Ending 30th June, 2001

	X		Y	
Production (in units)	5,550		6.350	
	Unit cost	*Total cost*	*Unit cost*	*Total cost*
Direct materials	Rs 12	Rs 66,600	Rs 19	Rs 1,20,650
Direct wages	5	27,750	7	44,450
Manufacturing charges	3	16,650	4	25,400
	20	1,11,000	30	1,90,500

Example 10

A single product company estimated its sales for the next year quarterwise as under:

Quarter	*Sales units*
I	30,000
II	37,500
III	41,250
IV	45,000

The opening stock of finished goods is 10,000 units and the company expects to maintain the closing stock of finished goods at 16,250 units at the end of the year. The production pattern in each quarter is based on 80% of the sales of the current quarter and 20% of the sales of the next quarter.

The opening stock of raw materials in the beginning of the year is 10,000 kg and the closing stock at the end of the year is required to be maintained at 5,000 kg. Each unit of finished output required 2 kg of raw materials.

The company proposes to purchase the entire annual requirement of raw materials in the first three quarters in the proportion and at the prices given below:

Quarter	*Purchase of raw materials % to total annual requirement in quantity*	*Price per kg Rs*
I	30%	2
II	50%	3
III	20%	4

The value of the opening stock of raw materials in the beginning of the year is Rs 20,000. You are required to present the following for the next year, quarterwise:

(i) Production budget in units.
(ii) Raw material consumption budget in quantity.
(iii) Raw material purchase budget in quantity and value.
(iv) Priced stores ledger card of the raw material using First in First out method.

Solution

Basic Calculations
Total Annual Production (In Units)

Sales in 4 Quarters (units)	1,53,750
Add: Desired Closing Balance (units)	16,250
	1,70,000
Less: Opening Balance (units)	10,000
Total Number of units to be produced in the next year.	1,60,000

(i) Production Budget (in Units)

Quarters	*I* Units	*II* Units	*III* Unils	*IV* Units	*Total* Units
Sales	30,000	37,500	41,250	45,000	1,53,750
Production in Current Quarter (*80% of the sale of current quarter*)	24,000	30,000	33,000	36,000	
Production for Next Quarter (*20% of the sale of next quarter*)	7,500	8,250	9,000	12,250*	
Total Production	31,500	38,250	42,000	48,250*	1,60,000

*Difference in Balancing Figure.

(ii) Raw Material Consumption Budget (in Quantity)

Quarters	*Qurters*				*Total*
	I	*II*	*III*	*IV*	
Units to be produced in each Quarter (1)	31,500	38,250	42,000	48,250	1,60,000
Raw material consumption per unit (kg) (2)	2	2	2	2	
Total raw material consumption (kg) (1 × 2)	63,000	76,500	84,000	96,500	3,20,000

(iii) Raw Material Purchase Budget (in Quantity)

Raw Material Required for Production (kg)	3,20,000
Add: Desired Closing Balance of Raw Material (kg)	5,000
	3,25,000
Less: Opening Balance (kg)	10,0000
Material to be Purchased (kg)	3,15,000

Raw Material Purchase Budget (in Quantity).

Quarters	*% of Annual Requirement (Qty.) for Purchasing Raw Material*	*Quantity of Rate Material to be purchased (kg)*	*Rate per kg (Rs)*	*Amount Rate (Rs)*
1	2	3	4	5 = 3 × 4
I	30	94,500 (3,15,000 × 30%)	2	1,89,000
II	50	1,57,500 (3,15,000 × 50%)	3	4,72,500
III	20	63,000 (3,15,000 × 20%)	4	2,52,000
Total		3,15,000		9,13,500

(iv) Priced Stores ledger Card
(of the raw material using FIFO method)

Particulars	I Kg.	I Rate Rs	I Value Rs	II (kg)	II Rate Rs	II Value Rs	III Kg	III Rate Rs	III Value Rs	IV Kg.	IV Rate Rs	IV Value Rs
Opening Balance (1)	10,000	2	20,000	41,500	2	83,000	1,22,500	3	3,67,500	38,500	3	1,15,500
										63,000	4	2,52,000
Purchases: (2)	94,500	2	1,89,000	1,57,500	3	4,72,500	63,000	4	2,52,000			
Consumption: (3)	63,000	2	1,26,000	41,500	2	83,000	84,000	3	2,52,000	38,500	3	1,15,500
				35,000	3	1,05,000				58,000	4	2,32,000
Balance: (4)	41,500	2	83,000	1,22,500	3	3,67,500	38,500	3	1,15,500	5,000	4	20,000
(4) = (1) + (2) – (3)							63,000	4	2,52,000			

Example 11

The following data pertains to Mr. *Y* for the month budget for November 2000:

	Rs.
Direct material used	847
Beginning finished goods inventory	?
Ending finished goods inventory	94
Direct manufacturing labour	389
Manufacturing overhead	?
Cost of goods manufactured	1,878
Cost of goods sold	?
Cost of goods available for sale	1,949

Prepare the cost of goods sold budget for the month of Nov. 2000 by filling the missing figures.

Solution

	Rs
Direct material used	847
Beginning finished goods inventory	71
Ending finished goods inventory	94
Direct manufacturing labour	389
Manufacturing overhead	642
Cost of goods manufactured	1878
Cost of goods sold	1855
Cost of goods available for sale	1949

As, we know that cost of goods manufactured is the aggregate of Direct material, Direct manufacturing labour and Manufacturing overhead.

∴ Rs 1878 =Rs 847 + 389 + Manufacturing overhead

∴ Rs 1878 - 847 - 389 = Manufacturing overhead

∴ Rs 642 = Manufacturing overhead

Cost of goods available for sale = Cost of goods manufactured + Opening balance of finished goods.

Rs 1,949 = Rs 1,878 + Opening balance of finished goods

Rs 1,949 – Rs 1,878 = 0penmg balance of finished goods

Rs 71 = Opening balance of finished goods.

Cost of goods sold = Cost of goods manufactured + Opening balance of finished goods – Closing balance of finished goods

Cost of goods sold + Rs 1,878 + Rs 71 – Rs 94

Cost of goods sold = Rs 1,855

Cost of goods sold budget for the month of November, 2000

	Rs
Direct material used	847
Direct manufacturing labour	389
Manufacturing overhead	642
Cost of goods manufactured	1878
Add: Opening balance of finished goods	71
Cost of goods available for sale	1949
Less: Closing stock of finished goods	94
Cost of goods sold	1855

Example 12

Nestley Ltd. has prepared the following sales budget for the first five months of 1998:

	Sales Budget (Units)
January	10,800
February	15,600
March	12,200
April	10,400
May	9,800

Inventory of finished goods at the end of every month is to be equal to 25% of sales estimate for the next month. On 1st Jan., 1998, there were 2,700 units of product on hand. There is no work-in-progress at the end of any month.

Every unit of product requires two types of materials in the following quantities:

Material A—4 kg

Material B—5 kg.

Materials equal to one half of thé requirement of next month's production are to be in hand at the end of every month. This requirement was met on 1st Jan., 1998.

Prepare the following budgets for the quarter ending 31st March, 1998:

(a) Production Budget (Quantitative)

(b) Material Purchase Budget (Quantitative).

Solution

Nestley Ltd.

Production Budget (In Units)

For quarter ending 31st March, 1998

Particulars	*Jan.*	*Feb.*	*March*
Sales	10,800	15,600	12,200
Add: Closing Stock	3,900	3,050	2,600
	14,700	18,650	14,800
Less: Opening Stock	2,700	3,900	3,050
	12,000	14,750	11,750

Materials Requirement Budget
For the quarter ending 31st March, 1998

Particulars	*Jan.*	*Feb.*	*March*
Production (units)	12.000	14,750	11,750
Material A	Kg	Kg	Kg
Required for Production	48,000	59,000	47,000
Add: Desired Closing Stock	28,500	23,500	20,500
	76,500	82,500	67,500
Less: Opening Stock	24,000	28,500	23,500
	52,500	54,000	44,000
Material B			
Required for Production	60,000	73,750	58,750
Add: Desired Closing Stock	36,875	29,375	25,625
	96,875	1,03,125	84,375
Less: Opening Stock	30,000	36,875	29,375
	66,875	66,250	55,000

Working Notes :

1. Production for April in Units

Sales	10,400
Add: Closing Stock	2,450
	12,850
Less: Opening Stock	2,600
	10,250

2. Material required for Production in April
   A 10,250 × 4 = 41,000 kg
   B 10,250 × 5 = 51,250 kg

Example 13

The following are the estimated sales of a company for eight months ending 30.11.1998:

Months		*Estimated Sales (units)*
April	1998	12,000
May	1998	13,000
June	1998	9,000
July	1998	8,000
August	1998	10,000
September	1998	12,000
October	1998	14,000
November	1998	12,000

As a matter of policy, the company maintains the closing balance of finished goods and raw materials as follows:

Stock item	Closing balance of month
Finished goods	50% of the estimated sales for the next month
Raw materials	Estimated consumption for the next month

Every unit of production requires 2 kg of raw material costing Rs 5 per kg.

Prepare Production Budget (in units) and Raw Material Purchase Budget (in units and cost) of the company for the half year ending 30 September, 1998. (*ICWA Inter, June 1999*)

Solution

Production Budget (In Units)
(for the half-year ending 30th September, 1998)

Month 1998	*Sales (in units)*	*Closing Balance 50% of the estimated Sales for the next month*	*Opening balance*	*Production*
1	*2*	3	4	*5 = (2) + (3) − (4)*
April	12,000	6,500	6,000	12,500
May	13,000	4,500	6,500	11,000
June	9,000	4,000	4,500	8,500
July	8,000	5,000	4,000	9,000
August	10,000	6,000	5,000	11,000
September	12,000	7,000	6,000	13,000
	64,000			65,000

Purchase Budget (In Cost and Units)
(for the half-year ending 30th September, 1998)

Month 1998	*Production in units*	*Consumption (kg) @ 2 kg per unit*	*Closing Balance*	*Opening Balance*	*Purchase in kg*	*Rate Rs*	*Amount Rs*
April	12,500	25,000	22,000	25,000	22,000	5	1,10,000
May	11,000	22,000	17,000	22,000	17,000	5	85,000
June	8,500	17,000	18,000	17,000	18,000	5	90,000
July	9,000	18,000	22,000	18,000	22,000	5	1,10,000
August	11,000	22,000	26,000	22,000	26,000	5	1,30,000
September	13,000	26,000	26,000	26,000	26,000	5	1,30,000
	65,000	1,30,000					6,55,000

Example 14 (Sales Overhead Budget)

You are requested to prepare a sales overhead budget from the estimates given below:

Advertisement	Rs 2,500
Sales of the sales department	5,000
Expenses of sales department	1,500
Counter salesmen's salaries and dearness allowance	6,000

Commission to counter salesmen at 1% on their sales

Travelling salesmen's commission at 10% on their sales and expenses at 5% on their sales. The sales during the period were estimated as follows:

Counter sales	*Travelling salesmen*
Rs 80,000	Rs 10,000
1,20.000	15,000
1,40,000	20,000

Solution

Sales Overhead Budget for the Period Ending

	Estimated sales		
	Rs 90,000	*Rs 1,35,000*	*Rs 1,60,000*
Fixed overheads:			
Advertisement	2,500	2,500	2,500
Salaries of sales department	5,000	5,000	2,500
Expenses of sales department	1,500	1,500	1,500
Counter salesmen's salaries and DA	6,000	6,000	6,000
	15,000	15,000	15,000
Variable overheads:			
Counter salesmen's commission @ 1% on sales	800	1,200	1,400
Travelling salesmen's commission @10%	1,000	1,500	2,000
Expenses @ 5%	500	750	1,000
	2,300	3,450	4,400
Total sales overheads	17,300	18,450	19,400

Example 15 (Cash Receipts Budget)

A company normally collects cash from credit customers as follows: 50 per cent in the month of sale, 30 per cent in the first month after sale, 18 per cent in the second month after sale, and 2 per cent are never collected. Sales, all on credit, are expected to be as follows:

	Rs
January	5,00,000
February	6,00,000
March	4,00,000
April	5,00,000

(a) Calculate the amount of cash expected lo be received from customers during March.
(b) Calculate the amount of cash expected to be received from customers during April.

Solution :

	Rs
(a) Budgeted cash collection in March:	
From January Sales (.18 × 5,00,000)	90,000
From February sales (.30 × 6,00,000)	1,80,000
From March sales (.50 × 4,00,000)	2,00,000
Total Budgeted Collections in March	4,70,000
(b) Budgeted cash collections in April:	
From February sales (.18 × 6,00,000)	1,08,000
From March sales (.30 × 4,00,000)	1,20,000
From April sales (.50 × 5,00,000)	2,50,000
Total budgeted collections in April	4,78,000

Example 16 (Cash Budget)

The January 1 cash balance of the Jay Company is Rs 5,000. Sales for the first four months of the year are expected to be as follows: January, Rs 65,000; February, Rs 54,000; March, Rs 66,000; and April,

Rs 63,000. On January 1, uncollected amounts for November and December of the previous year are Rs 13,500 and Rs 39,150, respectively. Collections from customers follow this pattern; 55% in the month of sale, 30% in the month following the sale, 13% in the second month following the sale, and 2% uncollectable.

Materials purchases for December were Rs 10,000, Forecast purchases for the coming year are;

Rs 12,500; February, Rs 16,500; March, Rs 13,000; and April, Rs 14,000. Purchases are usually paid by the 10th of the month following the month of purchase. Other cash expenditures of Rs 41,000 are forecasted for each month.

Calculate

(i) Expected cash collection during February
(ii) Expected cash balance, February 1
(iii) Expected cash balance, February 29.

Solution

Cash Budget of Jay Company for Months of January and February

	January (Rs)	*February (Rs)*
Opening Balance	5,000	27,550
Receipts—From customers	73,550	60,510
(A)	78,550	88,060
Payments:		
For purchases	10,000	12,500
Other expenditure	41,000	41,000
Total Payments (B)	51,000	53,000
Closing Balance (A) – (B)	37,550	34,560

Thus:

(i) Expected cash collections during February = Rs 60,150
(ii) Expected cash balance-February = Rs 27,550
(iii) Expected cash balance-February = Rs 34,560

Working Note:

Collections on account of sales

January

For November arrears 13,500 × 13/15 = Rs 11,700

For December arrears $\frac{39,150}{45} \times 30$ = 26,100

For January sales 65,000 × 55/100 = 35,750

73,550

February

For December arrears $\frac{39,150}{45} \times 13$ = Rs 11,310

For January sales 65,000 × 30/100 = 19,500

For January sales 54,000 × 55/100 = 29,700

60,510

Example 17 (Cash Budget)

ABC Co. wished to arrange overdraft facilities with its bankers during the period April to June 2001 when it will be manufacturing mostly for stock. Prepare a cash budget for the above period from the following data, indicating the extent of the bank facilities the company will require at the end of the each month:

(a)	*Sales* Rs	*Purchases* Rs	*Wages* Rs
February	1,80,000	1,24,800	12,000
March	1,92,000	1,44,000	14,000
April	1,08,000	2,43,000	11,000
May	1,74,000	2,46,000	10,000
June	1,26,000	2,68,000	15,000

(*b*) 50 per cent of the credit sales are realised in the month following the sales and the remaining 50 per cent in the second month following. Creditors are paid in the month of purchase.

(*c*) Cash at Bank on 1-4-2001 (estimated) Rs 25,000.

Solution

ABC Co.
Cash Budget for April to June 2001

	April Rs	*May* Rs	*June* Rs
Opening balance (Overdraft)	25,000	56,000	(47,000)
Receipts:			
Collections from debtors	1,86,000	1,50,000	1,41,000
	2,11,000	2,06,000	94,000
Payments:			
Payments to creditors	1,44,000	2,43,000	2,46,000
Wages	11,000	10,000	15,000
Closing balance (Overdraft)	56,000	(47,000)	1,67,000)
	2,11,000	2,06,000	94,000

The overdraft facilities required by ABC Co. for different months are as under :

(i) In May 2001 Rs 47,000
(ii) In June 2001 1,67,000

Working Notes:

Collections from Debtors

April 2001	Rs	
Sales for February	1,80,000 × 1/2	90,000
Sales for March	1,96,000 × 1/2	96,000
		1,86,000
May 2001		
Sales for March	1,92,000 × 1/2	96,000
Sales for April	1,08,000 × 1/2	54,000
		1,50,000

June 2001		
Sales for April	1,08,000 × 1/2	54,000
Sales for May	1,74,000 × 1/2	87,000
		1,41,000

Example 18

From the following budget data, forecast the cash position at the end of April, May and June 2002:

Month	*Sales*	*Purchase*	*Wages*	*Miscellaneous expenses*
February	1,20,000	84,000	10,000	7,000
March	1,30,000	1,00,000	12,000	8,000
April	80,000	1,04,000	8,000	6,000
May	1,16,000	1,06,000	10,000	12,000
June	88,000	80,000	8,000	6,000

Additional information:

Sales: 20% realised in the month of sales, discount allowed 2%. Balance realised equally in two subsequent months.

Purchase: These are paid for in the month following the months of supply.

Wages: 25% paid in arrears following month.

Miscellaneous expenses: paid a month in arrears.

Rent: Rs 1,000 per month paid quarterly in advance due in April.

Income Tax: First instalment of advance tax Rs 25,000 due on or before 15th June.

Income from investments: Rs 5,000 received quarterly, in April, July etc.

Cash in hand: Rs, 5,000 on 1st April 2002.

Solution

Cash Budget
for Three Months Ended 30th June, 2002

	April Rs	*May* Rs	*June* Rs
Receipts:			
Opening balance	5,000	5,680	—
Receipt from debtors	1,15,680	1,06,736	95,648
Income from investment	5,000	—	—
	1,25,680	1,12,416	95,648
Payments:			
Creditors	1,00,000	1,04,000	1,06,000
Wages	9,000	9,500	8,500
Rent	3,000	—	—
Miscellaneous expenses	8,000	6,000	12,000
Income tax	—	—	25,000
Opening balance	—	—	(–) 7,084
	1,20,000	1,19,500	1,58,684
Closing balance	5,680	(–) 7,084	(–)62,936

Notes:

Collection from debtors	Rs	Wages	Rs.
April			
20% of 80,000	16,000	25% of 12,000	3,000
Less: 2% discount	320	*Add*: 75% of 8,000	6,000
	15,680		9,000
Add: 40% of 1,20,000 + 1,30,000	1,00,000		
	1,15,680		
May:			
20% of 1,16,000	23,200	20% of 8,000	2,000
Less: 2% of 1,16,000	464	*Add*: 75% of 10,000	7,500
	22,736		9,500
Add: 40% of 1,30,000 + 80,000	84,000		
	1,06,736		
June:			
20% of 88,000	17,600	20% of 10,000	2,500
Less: 2% discount	352	*Add*: 75% of 8,000	6,000
	17,248		8,500
Add: 40% of 1,30,000 + 1,16,000	78,400		
	95,648		

ZERO BASE BUDGETING (ZBB)

Zero base budgeting (ZBB) is a method of budgeting whereby all activities are evaluated each time budget is formulated and every item of expenditure in the budget is fully justified. That is, ZBB involves starting from scratch or zero.

In traditional budgeting, departmental managers need justify only increases over the prior year's budget known as incremental budgeting. This implies that what is already being spent is automatically sanctioned. Under the ZBB concept, each department's functions are reviewed completely and ail expenditures, rather than only the increases, must be approved.

Also in some departments ascertainment of budgeted costs is easier that other departments. For example, in production departments, it is easier to determine costs of inputs to achieve a level of budgeted output. But, in other departments such as accounts, personnel, research and development, it is difficult to even identify the output, and therefore equally greater difficult to determine the cost of input to sustain (unidentifiable) output. Consequently, the budgets of previous year tend to be subjectively increased as the next year budgeted expenditure. However, the previous year's budgets may be inefficient and adjusting merely new year's budgets to the previous year's budget may result in wastage. ZBB overcomes this problem, to a certain extent. ZBB rejects the traditional view of annual budgeting as an incremental process which takes into account current expenditure plus an estimate of next year's expenditure to arrive at the next budget. Instead the projected expenditure for exiting programmes should start from base zero with each year's budgets being compiled as if the programme were being launched for the first time.

APPLICATION OF ZBB

ZBB involves the following stages (steps):

(1) Each separate activity of the organisation is identified and called a decision package. A decision package is a document that identifies and describes a specific activity in such a manner that management can (i) evaluate it and rank it against other activities competing for limited resources and (ii) decide whether to approve or disapprove it.

(2) Each decision package must be justified, *i.e.* it should be enquired into whether a decision package promotes the goals of an enterprise.

(3) If justified, then the cost of minimum efforts needed to sustain each decision package is determined.

(4) Alternatives for each decision package are considered in order to select better and cheaper options for the package.

(5) Incremental decision packages are also justified and costed in the above manner. These incremental packages describe the costs and benefits of additional work that would be done above that required by the base package for the minimum amount of work needed to carry out the activity.

(6) Managers rank their decision packages in order of priority for resource allocation.

(7) Resources are allocated to the packages.

ADVANTAGES OF ZBB

(1) It. represents a move towards allocation of resources by need and benefit and thus results in more efficient allocation of resources.

(2) It identifies and eliminates wastage and obsolete operations.

(3) It ensures that the best possible methods of performing jobs are used and that new ideas emerge.

(4) It creates a questioning attitude rather than one which accepts that current practices represent value for money.

(5) It leads to increased staff involvement which may lead to improved motivation and greater interest in the job,

(6) It increases communication and coordination within the organisation.

(7) Managers become more aware of the costs of inputs which helps them to identify priorities.

(8) The documentation of decision packages provides management with a deep, coordinated knowledge of a!l the organisation's activities.

(9) It is useful especially for service departments where it can be difficult to identify output.

DISADVANTAGES OF ZBB

(1) The cost involved in preparing a vast number of decision packages in a large firm are very high.

(2) It is very time-consuming and a large amount of additional paper work is involved.

(3) Managers develop fear and feel threatened by ZBB and therefore may oppose new ideas and changes.

(4) The ranking of decision packages and allocation of resources is subjective to a certain degree, which can result in departmental conflict.

(5) Administration and communication of ZBB process may become critical problems because more managers become involved in this process than in most budgeting and planning procedures and these problems are further compounded in large organisations.

PERFORMANCE BUDGETING

The concept of performance budgeting is used extensively in the Government and Public sector undertakings. A performance budget is essentially a projection of the Government activities and expenditure thereon for the budget period. It shows budgeted expenses classified by functions and activities and wherever practical, units cost also. In comparison to other budget forms, the objectives of performance budgeting are to provide a closer linkage between planning and action and to provide a more common basis for review, control and reporting.

The basic issues involved in the preparation of performance budgets are that of developing work programmes and performance expectations by assigning responsibilities necessary for the attainment of the goals of objectives of the enterprise. It also involves establishment of well defined centres of responsibility, establishment of targets for each responsibility centre in terms of physical units so that actual performance can be measured against the same, forecasting the amount of expenditure required to meet physical plan laid down and evaluation of actual with both physical targets and monetary targets performance.

THEORY QUESTIONS

1. Defint "budget" and "budgetary control". Give a description of two important budgets.
2. (a) Define budgetary control and explain its objectives.
   (b) Define how functional budgets are built up, taking any one specific example.
3. Explain the meaning of a business budget. How does it serve as an instrument of control?
4. Discuss the mode of operation of systems of budgets and budgetary control.
5. What do you understand by budgetary control? Explain the mechanism that would lead to effective control.
6. What are the advantages arising out of the budgetary control system? What do you think are the essentials of an effective budgetary control system?
7. Discuss the objectives and limitations of budgetary control.
8. Define budgetary control and discuss the objectives of introducing a budgetary control system in an organisation.
9. Discuss the cardinal features and objectives of budgetary control.
10. Explain the difference between a forecast and a budget. Give examples to illustrate the differences between:
    (a) Fixed budget,
    (b) Flexible budget, and
    (c) Functional budget.
11. What are functional budgets ? Which functional budgets are most commonly used by management?
12. Define budgetary control and distinguish it from standard costing. Discuss the inter-relationship between budgetary control and the standard costing system.
13. Discuss briefly the procedure for the preparation of a sales budget.
14. What do you understand by a "flexible budget"?
15. What is a sales budget? How is it prepared?
16. Describe briefly the fundamental functions of business budgets.
17. Explain the concept of a flexible budget. How is it prepared?
18. What is sales budget? How does the sales forecast differ from the sales budget?
19. What do you understand by 'Flexible Budget'? How is it prepared? Distinguish between fixed budgeting and flexible budgeting.
20. Explain the following:
    (a) Zero Base Budgeting (b) Master Budget

21. List the important functional budgets prepared by a business.
22. What is a cash budget? What are its uses:
23. State the important features of zero base Budgeting,
24. Distinguish between fixed and flexible budget.

PROBLEMS

1. A factory engaged in manufacturing plastic toys is working at 40% capacity and produces 10000 toys per month. The present cost breakup for one toy is as under:

Material	Rs 10
Labour	Rs 3
Overhead	Rs 5 (60% fixed)

The selling price is Rs 20 per toy. If it is decided to work the factory at 50% capacity, the selling price falls by 3%. At 90% capacity the selling price falls by 5% accompanied by a similar fall in the price of material. You are required to prepare a statement showing profit at 50% and 90% capacities.

Ans. Profit 40% capacity Rs 20,000, 50% capacity Rs 25,000, 90% capacity Rs 71,250.

2. Prepare a flexible budget for overheads on the basis of data given below. Ascertain the overhead rates at 50, 60 and 70 per cents capacity.

	At 50% capacity Rs	*At 60% capacity Rs*	*At 70% capacity Rs*
Variable overheads:			
Indirect material		6,000	
Indirect labour		18,000	
Semi-variable overheads:			
Electricity (40% fixed, 60% variable)		30,000	
Repairs and maintenance (80% fixed 20% variable)		3,000	
Fixed overheads:			
Depreciation		16,500	
Insurance		4,500	
Salaries		15,000	
Total overheads		93,000	

Estimated direct labour hours — 1,86,000

Ans. Overhead rates

Capacity level 50% = Rs 0.55
Capacity level 60% = Re 0.50
Capacity level 70% = Re 0.46

3. The budgeted cost of a factory specialising in the production of a single product at the optimum capacity of 6,400 units per annum amounts Rs 1,76,048 as detailed below:

Fixed cost		Rs 20,688
Variable costs:		
Power Rs	Rs. 1,440	
Repairs etc.	1,700	
Miscellaneous	540	
Direct material	49,280	
Direct labour	1,02,400	1,55,360
		1,76,048

Having regard to possible impact on sales turnover by market trends the company decided to have a flexible budget with a production target of 3,200 and 4,800 units (the actual quantity proposed to be produced being left to a later date before commencement of the budget period). Prepare a flexible budget for production levels at 50% and 75% capacity.

Assume selling price per unit is maintained at Rs 40 as at present, indicate the effect on net profit. Administration, selling and distribution expenses continue at Rs 3,600.

Ans: Net profit
(a) 100%. Rs 75,352
(b) 75% Rs 51,192
(c) 50% Rs 26,032

4. Draw up a flexible budget for overhead expenses on the basis of the following data and determine the overhead rates at 70%, 80% and 90% plant capacity levels.

	At 80% capacity
Variable overheads:	Rs
Indirect labour	12,000
Indirect material	4,000
Semi-variable overheads:	
Power (30% fixed, 70% variable)	20,000
Repairs & maintenance (60% fixed, 40% variable)	2,000
Fixed overheads:	
Depreciation	11,000
Insurance	3,000
Others	10,000
Total overhead	62,000
Estimated direct labour hours	1,24,000 hrs.

Ans. Overhead rate per direct labour hour
(a) 70% Re 0.5359
(b) 80% Re 0.5000
(c) 90% Re 0.4720

5. Draw a material procurement budget (quantitative) from the following information:
Estimated sales of a product 40,000 units. Each unit of the product requires 3 units of material A and 5 units of material B

Estimated opening balances at the commencement of the next year:	
Finished product	5,000 units
Material A	12,000 units
Materials B	20,000 units
Materials on order:	
Material A	7,000 units
Materials B	11,000 units
The desirable closing balances at the end of the next year:	
Finished product	7,000 units
Material A	15,000 units
Materials B	25,000
Material on order:	
Material A	8,000
Mterial B	10,000

Ans. Units to be procured A 1,30,000 B 2,14,000

6. Prepare a production budget for each month and a summarised production cost budget for the six-month period ending 31st December, 2002 from the following data of product X.

(i) The units to be sold for different months are as follows:

July 2002	1,100
August	1,100
September	1,700
October	1,900
November	2,500
December	2,300
January 2003	2,000

(ii) There will be no work-in-progress at the end of any month.

(iii) Finished units equal to half the sales for the next month will be in stock at the end of each month (including June 2002)

(iv) Budgeted production and production cost for the year ending 31st December, 2002 are as follows:

Production (units)	22,000	
Direct material per unit (Rs)		10.00
Direct, wages per unit (Rs)		4.00
Total factory overhead apportioned to product (Rs)	88,000	

Ans. Total production cost Rs 1,98,900

7. A company is drawing its production plan for the year 1997-98 in respect of two of its products 'Gamma' and 'Delta'. The company's policy is not to cany any closing WIP at the end of any month. However, its policy is to hold a closing stock of finished goods at 50% of the anticipated quantity of sales of the succeeding month. For the year 1997-98 the company's budgeted production is 20,000 units of 'Gamma' and 25,000 units of 'Delta'. The following is the estimated cost data:

Particulars	*Gamma* Rs.	*Delta* Rs.
Direct Materials per unit	50	80
Direct Labour per unit	20	30
Other Manufacturing Expenses apportionable to each type of product based on production	2,00,000	3,75,000

The estimated units to be sold in the first 7 months of the year 1997-98 are as under:

Particulars	*April*	*May*	*June*	*July*	*Aug.*	*Sept.*	*Oct.*
Gamma	900	1,100	1,400	1,800	2,200	2,200	1,800
Delta	2,900	2,900	2,500	2,100	1,700	1,700	1,900

You are required to

(a) prepare a production budget showing month-wise number of units to be manufactured:

(b) present a summarised production cost budget for the half-year ending 30.9.97.

Ans. Budgeted production Gamma total 10050 units Delta total 13300 units, total production cost Gamma Rs 8,04,000 Delta Rs 16,62,500.

8. From the information given below, prepare a cash budget of the Jaipur Refrigerators (P) Ltd. for the quarter January—March 2002.

	Dec. 2001	*Jan. 2002*	*Feb. 2002*	*March 2002*	*April 2002*
(a) Sales budget units	60	60	65	75	80
(b) Selling price per unit Rs	1,000	1,000	1,000	1,000	1,000
(c) Off-season discount	20%	20%	10%	—	
(d) End of mouth Inventory units	10	12	15	25	25

(e) Half the sales proceeds are collected in the month of sale and the other half in the month following.

(f) Materials amounting to Rs 300 per unit manufactured are purchased one month in advance of manufacture and paid for in cash, earning 5% cash discount on half of the material purchased.

(g) Direct labour budget was Rs 50 per unit and variable overheads Rs 100 per unit.

(h) Indirect labour budget was Rs 6,000 per month.
(i) Depreciation was provided uniformly at Rs 3,000 per month.
(j) The fixed overheads budget was Rs 6,000 per month during off season and Rs 7,000 during the season. Out of this the quarterly premium for fire insurance amounting to Rs 600 was payable in the first month of each quarter :
(k) Dividends for the year 2001 amounting to Rs 20,000 were expected to be declared in March 2002 and payments were to be made between March and April.
(l) A machine was sold for Rs 10,000 in December 2001 on 3 months credit.
(m) The company had overdraft arrangements with the State Bank of Jaipur and Bikaner up to Rs 50,000.

Ans. Balance January Rs 6,410
February Rs 12,797.50
March Rs 30,597.50

CHAPTER 9

Accounting for Price-Level Changes

The continuous inflation has an adverse effect on household budgets, as well as business and industry. Because of the continuous increases in prices, that is, decline in the value of Indian rupee, a demand has been made in accounting area that business enterprises should prepare inflation-adjusted financial statements in place of historical cost-based financial statements which are currently prepared by them. During the last few years, various accounting bodies, professional institutes, accountants, and academicians have conducted a great deal of research and experimentation on accounting for changing prices. This chapter aims to provide a comprehensive analysis of the concepts, issues, and techniques in inflation accounting. However, before discussing these aspects it would be proper to evaluate the strengths and weaknesses of financial statements under historical cost accounting, especially during periods of inflation.

HISTORICAL COST ACCOUNTING (HCA)

Historical Cost Accounting (HCA), also known as conventional accounting, record transactions appearing in both the balance sheet and the profit and loss account in monetary amounts which reflect their historical costs, *i.e.*, prices that are generally the result of arm's length transactions. The historical cost principle requires that accounting records be maintained at original transaction prices and that these values be retained throughout the accounting process to serve as the basis for values in the financial statements. HCA is based on the realisation principle which requires the recognition of revenue when it has been realised. Arguments which are advanced in favour of HCA are listed as follows:

1. Accounting data under HCA are generally considered free from bias, independently verifiable, and hence more reliable by the investing public, and other external users.
2. Historical accounting reduces to a minimum the extent to which the accounts may be affected by the personal judgements of those who prepare them.
3. Historical accounting is also defended on the ground that it is only the legally recognised accounting system accepted as a basis for taxation, dividend declaration, defining legal capital, etc.
4. Historical cost valuation is, among all valuation methods currently proposed, the method that is least costly to society considering the social costs of recording, reporting, auditing and settling disputes.

Limitations of Historical Cost Accounting

In an economic environment, where prices are constantly rising, as has been the case in most countries of the world, HCA suffers from some limitations. The drawbacks of HCA are listed as follows :

1. In times of inflation, the value of money declines and, therefore, the monetary unit (*e.g.*, rupee in India) which is used as a standard of measurement does not have a constant value and shrinks in value as the prices rise. The HCA ignores this decline in the value of rupee and keeps adding transactions acquired at different dates with rupees of varying purchasing power.
2. Secondly, HCA does not match current revenues with the current costs of operations. Revenues are measured in inflated (current) rupees whereas production costs are a mix of current and historical costs.
3. The 'inflated' profits resulting under HCA are not the real profits but exaggerated and illusory. This causes the depreciation allowance to become inadequate to replace fixed assets and finance growth and expansion. In periods of inflation, therefore, inflated profits result in substantial fall in the operating Capital and in turn, in the operating capability of a business enterprise.
4. Inflation causes many other problems and dislocations, such as the following, which are not considered in HCA. The result is that historical cost figures become of less and less significance and the value of accounts for decision-making is severely restricted.
   (i) Growing uncertainty about magnitude of future costs and price changes for materials, labour and capital equipment impair the company's ability to finance itself internally because corporate income-taxes are based on stated nominal profits rather than reals profits.
   (ii) Business responds by requiring higher returns on new capital projects than in lower inflationary periods. This usually requires significant increases in selling prices, which may be difficult to impose because of competition or price controls.
   (iii) During high inflationary periods, the economic situation becomes uncertain for common man as well as businessman. Businessmen attach more importance to the risks in new investments. Projects expected to give marginal return are given up and thus new productive activities are curtailed.
   (iv) There is no distinction in the historical cost accounts between real and fictitious growth. A rising figure for sales over a period of time might be seen to indicate a growth in sales, but the truth may be different. In order to determine the actual position, it is necessary to know how individual product prices have changed over the period.
5. HCA is defended on the ground of its assumed objectivity. Objectivity is claimed because historical cost numbers are derived from actual transactions that have been entered into by the enterprise itself rather than (sometimes) from transactions that are being entered into by others in the market-place. The objectivity that is claimed is largely unfounded because of the existance of alternative, generally, accepted methods for computing depreciation, inventory valuation and similar such items. As a result, there is a serious credibility gap in financial reporting.
6. Although historical cost generally represents 'current market value' at the time of transaction, however, as time passes, the cost(value) of non-monetary items in the balance sheets tends to move further and further from their current value due solely to changes in the value of money (inflation).
7. Since historical accounting is based on realisation principles, profit can easily be manipulated. By accelerating or retarding the timing of the realisation of gains, profits can be increased or decreased.

UTILITY OF INFLATION-ADJUSTED ACCOUNT

As stated in previous paragraphs, historical cost-based financial statements are not adequate in an inflationary period. Total capital requirements of the business go up and capital formation (cash flows) are not adequate to meet replacement of plant and equipment, and working capital requirements, Inflationary cost increases consume a progressively larger share of cash flows generated.

Some examples of ways in which inflation-adjusted informaton would help the decision-making are listed as follows :

1. By introducing a system of inflation accounting, the external users will be able to make better decisions; shareholders will be more realistic in their dividend expectations and investment valuations; employees will have a clearer view of what the company can afford in settling wage claims; and the Government will be aware of the impact of taxation on 'real' company profits.
2. Management will be better informed and, therefore, better equipped to tackle the problems caused by inflation. Management decisions may be influenced by the disclosure of 'real' growth.
3. Economic policy decisions concerning investment incentives, industry development schemes, and taxation are based in part on macro economic data; information about the effect of specific price changes on individual enterprises and by industry groupings are likely to provide insight to policy-makers on the different effects of inflation on each industry.

NATURE OF PRICE CHANGES

Price changes can be of the following types :

(1) General Price Changes
(2) Specific Price Changes
(3) Relative Price Changes

General Price Changes

A general price change is the result of a change in the value of the monetary unit during periods of inflation and deflation. Generally all prices would move together by the same percentage. However, if prices are moving at different rates, which is the usual case, a measure of general price changes can be obtained only by computing an average or index of prices to express the general level of current prices compared with some base period. The ratio of the current index of prices to the base-period index expresses the relative change in all prices included in the index. For example, if the price index increases from 100 to 200, prices would have doubled, but the purchasing power of the Rupee would have decreased to one half of its previous level.

Specific Price Changes

A change in the price of specific commodity represents a change in its exchange value. Changes in prices in an input market result in increase or decrease in costs or expenses of the firm, and changes of prices in the output market result in a shift in revenues (assuming that the price change does not affect the quantity sold).

Relative Price Changes

Most often, prices of goods and services move at different rates, and some even in different directions. The extent to which specific prices move at different rate or in a different direction from general price is known as relative price changes. This is explained with the help of the following example.

Example 1

If the market price of product A was Rs. 20 in 2001 and Rs. 30 in 2002; and further, if the market price of all the product comprising general prices index was Rs. 200 in 2001 and Rs. 240 in 2002, calculate :

(i) Specific price index for product A
(ii) General price index for all the products
(iii) Relative price index of product A

Solution

(i) Specific Price Index of product A, Rs. 30 – Rs. 20 = Rs. 10
i.e. 10/20 × 100 = 50%

(ii) General Price Index for all products, Rs. 240 – Rs. 200 = Rs. 40
i.e., 40/200 × 100 = 20%

(iii) Relative Price Index of Product A
Assuming price index of 100 in 2001 as a base, specific price index in 2002 will be 150, and General Price Index will be 120 in 2002.
Therefore, relative price index of product A is
Rs. 150 – Rs. 120 = Rs. 30
i.e., 30/120 × 100 = 25%

METHODS OF ACCOUNTING FOR CHANGING PRICES

Many alternatives have been proposed in accounting to minimise the limitations of historical cost-based financial statements and to recognise the effects of inflation on financial statements. Of the many proposals that have been put forward for inflation accounting, the following two methods need specific consideration.

(1) Current Purchasing Power Accounting (CPPA). Also known as Constant Purchasing Power Accounting, General Price-Level Accounting.
(2) Current Cost Accounting (CCA).

CURRENT PURCHASING POWER ACCOUNTING (CPPA)

Known by different names such as Constant Purchasing Power Accounting (CPPA), General Price Level Accounting (GPLA), Constant Dollar Accounting (in USA), General Purchasing Power Accounting, this method adjusts historical costs for changes in the general level of prices as measured by a general price-level index. Changes in the general level of prices represent changes in the general purchasing power of the monetary unit. Increases in the general level of prices (inflation) reduce the general purchasing power to purchase goods and services in general; decreases in the general level of prices (deflation) increase the general purchasing power to purchase goods and services in general.

Under CPPA, by restating historical cost financial statements for changes in the general purchasing power, the adjusted financial statements would reflect the original amounts in terms of current purchasing power, which, if spent today, would command the same general purchasing power as the original reported amounts.

Methodology of CPPA

To convert the historical cost financial statements, an acceptable general price level index representing the changes in the general purchasing power of the monetary unit (rupee) is needed. Generally the most broad based consumer goods price index is used. The historical cost figures are multiplied by a conversion factor which is the ratio of the price-level index at the date of conversion and price level index at the transaction date. A price level index is the ratio of the average price of a group of goods or services at a given date and the average price of a similar group of goods or services at another date, known as the base year when the price level index is equal to 100. For example, assume a plant has been purchased on January 1, 2001 for Rs. 60,00,000 when the general price index was 150. The general price index on January 1, 2006 was 200. The cost of the plant in terms of rupees on January 1, 2006 would be Rs. 80,00,000 (60,00,000 × 200/150). Since it is practically difficult to convert each figure in terms of the price-level index of the date of transaction, it is assumed that all transactions take place evenly throughout the year.

BALANCE SHEET UNDER CPPA

Monetary and Non-Monetary Items

The working of CPPA requires that, first of all, balance sheet items should be classified into Monetary Items, and Non-Monetary Items.

Monetary Items

Monetary items are those items which are fixed by contract or otherwise remain fixed irrespective of any change in the general level of price. Monetary items may be monetary assets as well as monetary liabilities. Examples of monetary assets are cash, debtors, bills receivable, etc. Similarly debentures, creditors etc., are monetary liabilities. Financial Accounting Standards Board of USA designate certain balance sheet items as monetary and the remainder as non-monetary. FASB's classification of such items is presented below.

Classification of Items as Monetary or Non-monetary

Assets	*Monetary Item*	*Non-monetary Item*
Cash on hand and demand bank deposits (U.S. dollars)	X	
Time deposits (U.S. dollars)	X	
Foreign currency on hand and claims to foreign currency	X	
Marketable securities:		
Stocks		X
Bonds (other than convertibles)	X	
Convertible bonds (until converted, these represent an entitlement to receive a fixed number of dollars)	X	
Accounts and notes receivable	X	
Allowance for doubtful accounts and notes receivable	X	
Inventories:		
Produced under fixed contracts and accounted for at the contract price	X	
Other inventories		X
Loans to employees	X	
Prepaid insurance, advertising, rent, and other prepayments		X
Long-term receivables	X	
Refundable deposits	X	
Advances to unconsolidated subsidiaries	X	
Equity investment in unconsolidated subsidiaries or other investors		X
Pension, sinking, and other funds under an enterprise's control		X
Property, plant, and equipment		X
Accumulated depreciation of property, plant, and equipment		X
Cash-surrender value of life insurance	X	
Purchase commitments (portion paid on fixed-price contracts)		X
Advances to a supplier (not on contract)	X	
Patents, trademarks, licenses, formulas		X
Goodwill	X	
Other intangible assets and deferred charges		X

(Contd...)

Liabilities	*Monetary Item*	*Non-monetary Item*
Accounts and notes payable	X	
Accrued expenses payable (for example, wages)	X	
Accrued vacation pay (if it is to be paid at the wage rates as of the vacation dates and if those rates may vary)		X
Cash dividends payable	X	
Obligations payable in foreign currency	X	
Sales commitments (portion collected on fixed-price contracts)		X
Advances from customers (not on contract)	X	
Accrued losses of firm purchase commitments		X
Deferred income	X	
Refundable deposits	X	
Bonds payable and other long-term debts	X	
Unamortized premiums or discounts and prepaid interest on bonds and notes payable	X	
Convertible bonds	X	
Accrued pension obligations		X
Obligations under warranties	X	
Deferred income-tax credits	X	
Deferred investment-tax credits		X
Preferred stock		
Carried at an amount equal to a fixed liquidation or redemption price	X	
Carried at an amount less than fixed liquidation or redemption price		X
Common stockholder's equity		X

Source : Adapted from FASB Statement No. 33.

It is obvious that in a period of inflation, the holders of cash or other monetary assets lose purchasing power because the cash they have or expect to receive represents amounts of less purchasing power. On the other hand, holders of monetary assets gain purchasing power during a period of deflation. These relationships are reversed for monetary liabilities. Holders of monetary liabilities gain general purchasing power during a period of inflation because they can repay the amounts due in rupees of lower purchasing power. However, holders of monetary liabilities lose purchasing power during a period of deflation. For example, suppose a firm has creditors of Rs. 20,000 on January 1, 2001, which are payable on December 31, 2001. It may be argued that the firm's liability of Rs. 20,000 represents less general purchasing power as on December 31, 2001 as compared to original liability (January 1, 2001) which possesses higher general purchasing power. Therefore, purchasing power gain arises from holding monetary liabilities during inflationary periods. Conversely, the holders of monetary assets lose in a period of inflation because of loss in general purchasing power, *i.e.*, because a given amount of money could buy fewer goods and services. For instance, suppose a firm has Rs. 40,000 as cash on hand on January 1, 2001 which remained intact until December 2001. Assume that 10 per cent inflation occurred during the year. This situation implies that the firm would need Rs. 44,000 on December 31,2001. The fact that the firm only holds Rs. 40,000 results in a loss of general purchasing power of Rs. 4,000. The same purchasing power loss would also arise from holding accounts receivable or debtors or any claims to a fixed quantity of money since the amount of money expected to be received commands a decreasing amount of general purchasing power during periods of general price level increases.

Calculation of Purchasing Power Gain or Loss on Monetary Items

The CPPA method suggests the computation of the purchasing power gain or loss made by an enterprise on holding net monetary items. Purchasing power gain or loss on monetary items can be calculated in two ways. One procedure calculates the purchasing power gain or loss associated with each monetary asset and each monetary liability and then sums up the individual gains and losses to determine the gain or loss. A second procedure calculates the gain or loss on holding all monetary items as if they were maintained in a single account:

Alternatively, under the second procedure, general purchasing power gain or loss can be computed in terms of net monetary assets (monetary assets — monetary liabilities) for which the following procedures may be used.

(i) Compute the net monetary asset position at the beginning of the period. For example, if cash and accounts payable at the beginning of the period are Rs. 50,000 and Rs. 30,000 respectively, the net monetary assets will be Rs. 20,000.

(ii) Restate net monetary asset position at the beginning of the period in terms of the purchasing power at the end of the period. For example, assume the general price-level index was 120 at the beginning of the period and 180 at the end of the period, The net monetary asset position at the beginning of the period, which was Rs. 20,000 would be restated to Rs. 30,000 (Rs. 20,000 × 180/120).

(iii) Restate all the monetary receipts of the year to the year end basis and add this to the restated net monetary position at the beginning of the period as calculated in (*ii*). Assume that sales of Rs. 40,000 occurred evenly during the year and the general average price index was 150, the adjusted monetary receipts would be restated to Rs. 48,000 (Rs. 40,000 × 180/150). This result is added to Rs. 30,000 as calculated in (ii) to arrive at a total restated net increase in monetary items of Rs. 78,000.

(iv) Restate all the monetary payments of the year to the year end basis and deduct the result from the total restated net increase in monetary items as calculated in (iii). Assume that purchases and expenses of Rs. 30,000 also occurred evenly during the year. The adjusted monetary payments would be restated to Rs. 36,000 (Rs. 30,000 × 180/150). This result is deducted from Rs. 78,000 as calculated in (iii) to arrive at the adjusted computed net monetary assets at the end of the period, which is Rs. 42,000.

(v) Deduct the actual net monetary assets at the end of the period from the adjusted net monetary asset at the end of the period as found in (iv) to obtain the purchasing power gain/loss. In this example, the net monetary assets at the end of the period is Rs. 30,000 (20,000 + 40,000 – 30,000) and adjusted net monetary assets as found in (iv) is Rs. 42,000. Therefore purchasing power loss on net monetary items is Rs. 12,000.

Treatment of Purchasing Power Gain and Loss

It has been widely suggested that the purchasing power gain or loss should be included in current income.

Example 2

Compute the net monetary result of X Company Ltd. as at 31st December, 2003. The relevant data are given below :

	1st January, 2003	*31st December, 2003*
	Rs.	Rs.
Cash	5,000	10,000
Book debts	20,000	25,000
Creditors	15,000	20,000
Loan	20,000	20,000

Retail Price Index Numbers :

January 1, 2003	200
December 31, 2003	300
Average for the year	240

Solution

Calculation of Purchasing Power Gain/Loss

Particulars	*Unadjusted* Rs.	*Conversion Factor*	*Adjusted* Rs.
Net monetary assets as at January 1, 2003	(–) 10,000	300/200	(–) 15,000
Add: Increase in monetary receipts	(+) 10,000	300/240	(+) 12,500
	Nil		(–) 2,500
Less: Increase in monetary liabilities	(–) 5,000	300/240	(–) 6,250
Net monetary assets (or net monetary liabilities)	(–) 5,000		(–) 8,750

Purchasing Power gain on monetary items Rs. 8,750 – Rs 5,000 = Rs 3,750.

Note: The amount of net monetary liabilities as on December 31, 2003 should be Rs. 8,750 during inflation. However, such liabilities are only Rs. 5,000. Therefore the company is making purchasing power gain of Rs. 3,750.

Alternate Solution

Purchasing power gain can be computed following another method, as shown below:

Statement showing the Net monetary Result on Account of Price Level Changes

Monetary Liabilities :		
(i) Monetary liabilities as on 1st January, 2003 should have gone up with increase in price indices (Rs. 35,000 × 1.5)	52,500	
(ii) Increases in monetary liabilities during 2003 which should have gone up with increase in price indices (5,000 × 1.25)	6,250	
Monetary liabilities on 31st December, 2003 should have stood at:	58,750	
However, the liabilities on 31st December, 2003 stood at:	40,000	
Gain on holding of monetary liabilities		18,750
Monetary Assets:		
(iii) Monetary assets as on 1st January, 2003 should have gone up with increase in price indices (Rs. 25,000 × 1.5)	37,500	
(iv) Increase in monetary assets during 2003 should have gone up with increase in price indices (Rs. 30,000 × 1.25)	12,500	
Monetary assets on 31st December, 2003 should have stood at:	50,000	
However, the monetary assets on 31st December, 2003 stood at:	35,000	
Loss on holding monetary assets		(–) 15,000
Net gain on monetary items		3,750

Working Notes :

(i) Conversion factors:

(a) For items as on 1st January, 2003 : 300/200 = 1.5

(b) For items arising during 2003 : 300/240 = 1.25

(ii) Increase in monetary assets/liabilities during 2003

	as on 1st January,	31st December,	Increase during
(a) Monetary assets	25,000	35,000	10,000
(b) Monetary liabilities	35,000	40,000	5,000

Non-Monetary Items

All assets and liabilities that lack the properties of monetary items are classified as non-monetary, Non-monetary assets include inventories, building, plant and equipment, and claims to cash in amounts dependent on future prices. Whereas the holding of monetary items (like cash and accounts receivable) results in purchasing power gain or loss, the mere holding of non-monetary items (like inventory and equipment) does not result in purchasing power gain or loss because they do not represent a fixed amount to be received or paid and thus their prices in terms of the monetary unit may change over time. While most liabilities are monetary, non-monetary liabilities include equity capital and retained earnings, Non-monetary liabilities do not represent fixed claims to pay cash. The monetary assets and liabilities at the end of the year will appear at the same amounts, whereas non-monetary items are reported at their adjusted amounts in the CPPA adjusted balance sheet. The restatement of non-monetary items is done by applying the following conversion factor.

$$\frac{\text{Current year index}}{\text{Index when the non-monetary items were acquired}}$$

For example, assume that a plant was purchased for Rs. 2,00,000 on January 1, 1999 when the general price index was 100. The estimated useful life of the asset was 10 years. If the general price level index on December 31, 2003 is 150, the adjustments of the plant amount would be as follows :

Adjustment of Plant Amount as on December 31, 2003

	Unadjusted (Rs.)	*Conversion Factor*	*Adjusted (Rs.)*
Plant	2,00,000	150/100	3,00,000
Accumulated depreciation	1,00,000	150/100	1,50,000
Net Plant	1,00,000		1,50,000

The adjustment of the owners equity, with the exception of retained earnings, is similar to the non-monetary items. The original invested capital is multiplied by the following conversion factor :

$$\frac{\text{Current year index}}{\text{Index when the capital was invested}}$$

Retained earnings, which cannot be adjusted by a single conversion factor represent net income after dividends accumulated since the business firm was created. Retained earnings may be restated as follows :

(i) The first time when historical cost financial statements are restated in terms of current general purchasing power, retained earnings may be determined simply as a residual after all other items in the balance sheet have been restated.

(ii) In the following periods, the adjusted end-of-period retained earnings may be determined by (a) net income as reported in the general price-level income statement (including general price-level gains and losses on monetary items), and (b) adjustments resulting from general price-level gains or losses on monetary shareholders equity items.

Profit and Loss Account Under CPPA

In CPPA profit and loss account, adjustments are needed about the following items:

(a) Opening inventory,
(b) Transactions during the year,
(c) Depreciation written off for the year and,
(d) Closing inventory

The method to be followed for restating historical cost-income statement under CPPA is basically the same as suggested for adjusting other historical amounts in terms of current purchasing power, usually applying the following conversion factor:

$$\frac{\text{Current year index}}{\text{Index applicable to the item at the beginning or when it was created}}$$

For example, for restating opening inventories, opening price level index is relevant whereas average price index for the year can be used for adjusting transactions occurring evenly throughout the year. Purchases are adjusted using price-level index when the purchases were made. Alternatively, average price index is used if specific price index relating to the purchases are not available. In order to calculate depreciation under CPPA, first of all, assets are restated in terms of CPPA, and then the depreciation rate is applied on the restated values of assets. Closing inventory is restated using a price level index depending on the cost flow assumption (FIFO, LIFO or average costing) used by a business firm.

Example 3

From the following information, find out (i) cost of sales, (ii) closing, inventory, under the CPP method assuming the firm is following FIFO method:

Opening stock on January 1, 2003	Rs. 40,000
Purchases during 2003	Rs. 2,00,000
Closing Stock	Rs. 30,000
Price level index:	
Opening	80
Average	125
Last quarter purchases resulting into closing stock	120
Closing Index	140

Solution:

Cost of Sales and Closing Inventory

	Historical cost	*Conversion factor*	*Adjusted under CPP*
Opening inventory	Rs. 40,000	140/80	Rs. 70,000
Add: Purchases	2,00,000	140/125	2,24,000
	2,40,000		2,94,000
Less: Closing inventory	30,000	140/120	35,000
Cost of goods sold	2,10,000		2,59,000

Example 4

From the following data, calculate cost of the sales and closing inventory under CPP method assuming that the firm is following LIFO method for inventory valuation:

Inventory as on January 1, 2003	Rs. 80,000
Purchases during 2003	4,80,000
Inventory as on 31st December, 2003	1,20,000
Price index, January 1, 2003	100
Price index, December 31, 2003	140
Average price index 2003	125

Solution :

Cost of Sales and Closing Inventory

	Historical cost	*Conversion factor*	*Adjusted under CPP*
Opening Inventory	Rs. 80,000	140/100	1,12,000
Add: Purchases	4,80,000	140/125	5,37,600
	5,60,000		6,49,600
Less: Closing inventory			
From Opening Inventory	80,000	140/100	1,12,000
From Current Purchases	40,000	140/125	44,800
Cost of goods sold	4,40,000		4,92,800

Example 5

The following is the Balance sheet of ABC company for the year ending December 31,2003 and December 31,2004

Balance Sheet for the year ending December 31, 2003 and Dec. 31, 2004

Liabilities	*2003 Rs.*	*2004 Rs.*	*Assets*	*2003 Rs.*	*2004 Rs.*
Liabilities (10%)	50,000	50,000	Monetary assets	30,000	60,000
Capital	1,00,000	1,00,000	Inventories (2003, 3000 units) (2004, 2000 units)	30,000	20,000
Retained earnings		10,000	Land	40,000	40,000
Accumulated depreciation		10,000	Plant & Equipment	50,000	50,000
	1,50,000	1,70,000		1,50,000	1,70,000

The income statement of ABC company for the year ending December 31,2004 is as follows :

	Rs	Rs
Sales (5000 units @ Rs. 40)		2,00,000
Less: Cost of goods sold :		
Beginning inventory (3000 units @ Rs. 10)	30,000	
Add: Purchases (4000 units @ Rs. 12)	48,000	
	78,000	
Less: Closing inventory (2000 units @ Rs. 10)	20,000	
		58,000
Gross margin		1,42,000
Less; Expenses:		
Interest expense	5,000	

Selling and administrative expenses	1,17,000	
Depreciation	10,000	
		1,32,000
Net Income		10,000

The following additional information is available :

(i) On December 31, 2003 the price-level index was 100. The price-level index as on December 31, 2004 was 180 and the average price index for 2004 had been 120.

(ii) The inventory purchases were made at a date when the price-level index was 150.

(iii) All revenues and costs were incurred evenly throughout the year, with the exception of the cost of goods sold and the depreciation expense.

(iv) LIFO has been assumed.

(v) Depreciation for plant and equipment was accumulated by the straight line mwthod on a five year life.

Solution:

Calculation of Purchasing Power Gains or Losses

	Unadjusted (Rs.)	*Conversion*	*Adjusted* (Rs.)
Net monetary assets on January 1, 2004	(20,000)	180/100	(36,000)
Add: Monetary receipts during 2004, sales	2,00,000	180/120	3,00,000
Net monetary items	1,80,000		2,64,000
Less: Monetary payments :			
Purchases	48,000	180/150	57,600
Interest	5,000	180/120	7,500
Selling and administrative expense	1,17,000	180/120	1,75,000
Total	1,70,000		2,40,600
Computed net monetary assets as on December 31,2004	10,000		23,400
Less: Actual net monetary assets December 31,2004			10,000
Purchasing power loss on monetary assets			13,400

Adjusted Income Statement of ABC Company for the year ending 2004

	Unadjusted (Rs.)	*Conversion* Factor	*Adjusted* (Rs.)
Sales (5,000 units @ Rs. 40)	2,00,000	180/120	3,00,000
Less: Cost of goods sold :			
Beginning inventory (3000 units)	30,000	180/100	54,000
Purchases (4000 units)	48,000	180/150	57,600
Goods available for sale	78,000		1,11,600
Closing inventory (2000 units)	20,000	180/100	36,000
Cost of goods sold	58,000		75,600
Gross margin	1,42,000		2,24,000
Other expenses:			
Interest expenses	5,000	180/120	75,000
Depreciation expense	10,000	180/120	18,000
Selling and administrative expense	1,17,000	180/120	1,75,500
	1,32,000		2,01,000
Net operating income	10,000		23,400

Reconciliation of Adjusted Retained Earnings

	Rs.
Retained earnings, January 1, 2004	—
Adjusted net operating income	23,400
Less: Purchasing power loss	13,400
Net Income transferred to Balance sheet	10,000

2003 Balance Sheet of ABC Company Adjusted to 2004 Price Levels

Liabilities	*Unadjusied (Rs.)*	*Factor*	*Adjusted (Rs.)*	*Assets*	*Unadjusted (Rs.)*	*Factor*	*Adjusted (Rs.)*
Liabilities	50,000	180/100	90,000	Monetary Assets	30,000	180/100	54,000
Capital	1,00,000	180/100	1,80,000	Inventories	30,000	180/100	54,000
Retained earnings				Land	40,000	180/100	72,000
				Plant & equiprnent	50,000	180/100	90,000
Total	1,50,000		2,70,000		1,50,000		2,70,000

2004 Balance Sheet of ABC Company Adjusted to 2004 Price Levels

Liabilities	Unadjusted	Factor	Adjusted	Assets	Unadjusted	Factor	Adjusted
Liabilities (10%)	50,000	180/180	50.000	Monetary assets	60,000	180/180	60,000
Capital	1,00,000	180/100	1,80,000	Inventories	20,000	180/100	36,000
Retained earnings	10,000		10,000	Land	40,000	180/100	72,000
				Plant & Equpnt.	50,000	180/100	90,000
				Accumulated Depreciation	(10,000)	180/100	(18.000)
Total	1,60,000		2,40,000		1,60,000		2,40,000

*Alternatively, adjusted retained earnings Rs. 23,400 could be written on the liabilities side and purchasing power loss of Rs. 13,400 on the asset side, However, the net result will be the same, *i.e.* Rs. 10,000.

Arguments in Favour of CPPA

A number of arguments have been advanced in favour of CPPA which are as follows :

(i) Inflation is concerned with changes in the general level of prices, therefore, only CPPA can be regarded as a true form of inflation accounting.

(ii) As CPPA uses uniform purchasing power as the measuring unit, it possesses the qualities of objectivity and comparability.

(iii) CPPA provides useful information about the comparable impact of inflation across firms. Inflation affects firms differently, depending on the age and composition of their assets and equities. Highly capital intensive firms are likely to report significantly larger depreciation expense under CPPA method than nominal depreciation expense. Highly leveraged firms will report a larger purchasing power gain during periods of increasing prices than firms that use relatively little debt. CPPA reports these differing effects of inflation across firms.

(iv) CPPA improves the relevance and measurement of net income as it provides a better matching of revenues and expenses because of a constant and common measuring unit. On the contrary, conventional historical accounting does not measure income properly as a result of the matching of rupees of different size (purchasing power) on the income statement.

(v) CPPA provides relevant information for management evaluation and use. Purchasing power gain and loss resulting from holding monetary items reflect management's response to inflation. The restated non-monetary items indicate the approximate purchasing power needed to replace the assets.

(vi) CPPA presents to users, in general, the impact of general inflation on profit and provides more realistic return on investment, Financial data adjusted for price-level changes provide a basis for a more intelligent, better informed allocation of resources, whether those resources are in the hands of individuals, business entities or government.

Arguments Against CPPA

The following arguments have been advanced against CPPA.

(i) CPPA accounts only for changes in the general price-level and does not account for changes in the specific price-level. Since specific price movements are not necessarily synchronised with movements of the general price level index, the restatement in terms of general purchasing power does not reflect the current value of the resources of the firm.

(ii) Furthermore, there is a problem of choice of an appropriate general price-level index. A general price-level index that is applied must necessarily be a broad measure of purchasing power for a comprehensive market basket of goods. Unfortunately, broad indices are generally not well suited to specific industries, *e.g.*, individual companies and investors do not buy market baskets but rather have specific spending and investment needs.

(iii) CPPA requires the identification and classification of assets and liabilities as monetary or non-monetary. The treatment of monetary items has been a source of criticism under CPPA. Not only is there conceptual disagreement, but there is strong objection to the idea of 'rewarding' highly leveraged (indebted) firms with a reported increase in profits based solely on indebtedness.

(iv) The capital maintenance concept of CPPA is a proprietary one, *i.e.,* maintenance of financial capital in real terms in contrast to entity approach to capital maintenance. CPPA does not solve the problem of gradual depletion of operating capital of an enterprise in periods of inflation. The balance sheet prepared on the basis of CPPA does not reflect the current worth of an enterprise.

CURRENT COST ACCOUNTING (CCA)

Current cost accounting uses value to the business as the measurement basis. Value to the business is defined as (a) net current replacement cost or, if a permanent diminution to below net current replacement cost has been recognised; (b) recoverable amount. Recoverable amount is the greater of net realisable value of an asset and, where applicable, the amount recoverable from its further use. The value to the business concept is illustrated in the following figure:

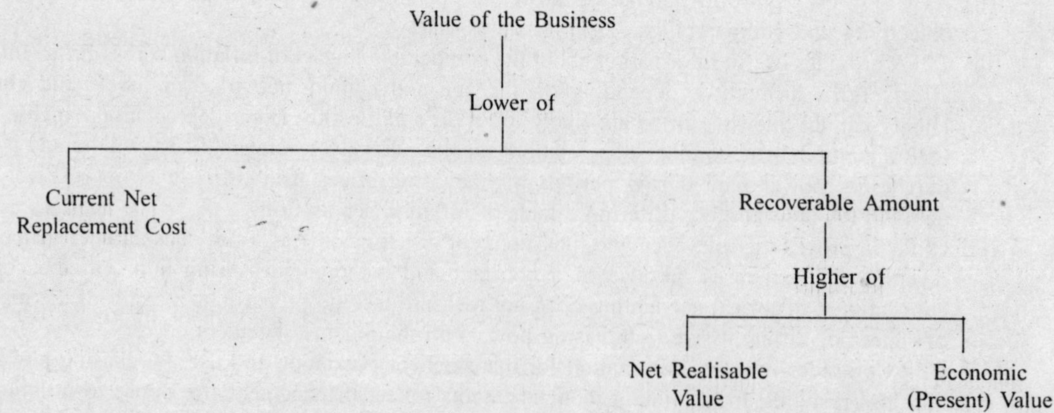

Where an asset will normally be replaced it is shown at the net current replacement cost, and charged on this basis in the profit and loss account. However, where it is not to be replaced or where replacement cost is higher than both net realisable value and present value, the higher of net realisable value and present value is usually used as the measurement basis. The replacement cost of a specific asset is normally derived from the current acquisition cost of a similar asset, new or used, or of an equivalent productive capacity or service potential. Net realisable value usually represents the net current selling price of the asset. Present value represents a current estimate of future net receipts attributable to the asset, appropriately discounted.

Objective of CCA

Current Cost Accounting (CCA) aims to maintain capital of a business enterprise in terms of its operating capability. Operating capability is denoted by the net operating assets of the enterprise in terms of shareholders funds. As an equation,

Net Operating assets = Total tangible assets + Net monetary working capital (current assets – current liabilities)

A change in the input prices of goods and services used and financed by the business will affect the amount of funds required to maintain the operating capability of the business enterprise. Therefore, maintaining the operating capability is the objective which is attempted to be achieved under CCA while preparing profit and loss account and balance sheet. CCA is based on UK accounting standard, SSAP 16-Current Cost Accounting, issued in 1980. CCA aims to prepare the following:

(A) Current Cost Profit and Loss Account (to determine Current Cost Operating profit)

(B) Current Cost Balance Sheet

Current Cost Profit and Loss Account

In CCA, the profit and loss account is prepared to determine the current cost operating profit (CCOP). CCOP is determined after allowing for the impact of price changes, on the funds needed to continue the existing business and maintain its operating capability whether financed by share capital or borrowing. CCOP is calculated before interest on net borrowings and taxation. CCOP is determined after making the following three adjustments to historical cost profit before interest and taxes:

(1) Depreciation Adjustment

(2) Cost of Sales Adjustment (COSA)

(3) Monetary Working Capital Adjustment (MWCA)

After determining CCOP, interest and taxes are considered in current cost profit and loss account to finally ascertain net income under CCA. Net income under CCA can be defined as the surplus amount which can be distributed to proprietor or shareholders after keeping the operating capability of an enterprise intact.

(1) *Depreciation Adjustment.* This reflects the difference between depreciation calculated on the current cost of fixed assets and depreciation charged in computing the historical cost income. The accounting policy adopted for the purposes of calculating the historical cost profit should be followed when calculating the depreciation on the current cost of fixed assets The current cost depreciation charge may be calculated by revising the depreciation charge in accordance with change in the appropriate index level between the year of purchase of the asset and current year. This is illustrated by the following example.

A plant was purchased on January 1, 2003 for Rs. 1,20,000 when the price index was 100. The life of the plant was estimated to be 10 years having no scrap value. On December 31, 2007 the relevant price index was 150.

The following calculations will be made to arrive at depreciation adjustment figure on December 31, 2007.

	Historical cost	Index factors	Current cost
	Rs		Rs
Value of plant	1,20,000	150/100	1,80,000
Accumulated depreciation	60,000		90,000
	60,000		90,000

Depreciation adjustment :		
Current cost depreciation p.a. 10% of Rs. 1,80,000	=	Rs 18,000
Historical cost depreciation p.a. 10% of Rs. 1,20,000	=	Rs 12,000
Depreciation Adjustment		Rs 6,000

When fixed assets are revalued every year, there will also be a shortfall of depreciation representing the effect of price rise during the current year on the accumulated depreciation till date. This shortfall is called backlog depreciation which is the amount needed to cover total depreciation provision based on current cost at the year end. This backlog depreciation arising out of increase in current costs could be charged either to the general reserves or against the related revaluation surplus on fixed assets. The former will ensure that the enterprise maintains its operating capital at the time of replacement of fixed assets. The latter procedure has been recommended in the UK Standard (SSAP 16).

(2) *Cost of the Sales Adjustment (COSA).* The cost of the sales adjustment refers to the difference between current cost of inventories at the date of sale and amount charged as the cost of goods sold in computing the historical cost profit. Theoretically, current cost of sales should be determined on an item by item basis. In a real world situation, however, it would be impracticable to do so and therefore, groups of similar items may be used.

The following example illustrates cost of sales adjustment. The following data relate to a company:

Opening inventory	Rs. 2,000
Add: Purchases	4,000
	Rs. 6,000
Less: Closing inventory	1,000
Cost of goods sold at historical cost	Rs. 5,000
Price levels during the year:	
Beginning	100
Closing	120
Average	110

Solution:

(1) Opening and closing inventory to be revised in terms of average cost of the year

Opening inventory Rs. 2,000 × 110/100 = Rs. 2,200

Closing inventory Rs. 1,000 × 110/100 = Rs. 917

(2) Computing current cost of sales using revised amounts for opening and closing inventories.

	Rs.
Opening inventory	2,200
Add: Purchases	4,000
	6,200
Less: Closing inventory	917
Cost of sales on current cost basis	5,283

(3) Calculating cost of sales adjustment

Cost of sale on current cost basis	5,283
Less: Cost of sales on historical cost basis	5,000
Cost of sales adjustment	283

(3) *Monetary Working Capital Adjustment (MWCA).* The MWCA reflects the amount of additional (or reduced) finance needed for monetary working capital as a result of changes in the input prices of goods and services used and financed by the business. Monetary working capital (usually represented by the difference between trade debtors and trade creditors) is an integral part of the net operating asset of the business. In times of rising prices, a business needs more funds to finance monetary working capital. The adjustment reflects this additional need for funds.

MWCA is calculated if debtors are more than the creditors. If creditors are more than the debtors, this is a minus net working capital. The minus excess (creditors-debtors) is not regarded as funding working capital and excluded. It is included in net borrowing for the purpose of calculating gearing ratio and gearing adjustment.

The MWCA is made in the calculation of current cost operating profit and takes the form of a charge or credit to profit and loss account with the corresponding credit or charge to the current cost reserve. SSAP 16 of UK requires that MWCA should include items used in day-to-day operating activities of the business. It includes trade debtors (including trade bills receivables, prepayments) and trade creditors (including, trade bills payable, accruals, expense creditors). MWCA should not include creditors or debtors relating to fixed assets bought or sold or under construction.

Calculating MWCA

(i) Determine the items to be included in MWCA.

(ii) Determine separately the relevant indices to be used in adjusting debtors and creditors:

(a) The index for debtors should reflect changes in the current cost of goods and services sold attributable to change in input prices over the period the debt is outstanding. Indices of selling prices may be used where these provide a fair approximation of cost changes in amount and time.

(b) The index for creditors should reflect similar changes in the cost of items which have been financed by those creditors over the period the credit is outstanding.

(c) Where the percentage changes in the indices to be used on debtors and creditors are similar, a single index can be used and the adjustment can be determined in one calculation.

(iii) Apply relevant index or indices to debtors and creditors to determine MWCA. In principle, in calculating the adjustment on debtors the profit element in debtors should be excluded. However, the total amount of debtors can be used where this gives a fair approximation.

(iv) An averaging method, compatible with the method used for COSA, may be used to calculate the adjustment.

The following example illustrates the calculation of monetary working capital adjustment:

Historical Cost Balance Sheet

		Jan. 1 (Rs.)	*Dec. 31 (Rs.)*
Trade Debtors		1,20,000	1,60,000
Trade Creditors		1,00,000	1,30,000
Net monetary working capital		20,000	30,000
Specific price index of Finished Goods	— Opening	100	
	— Closing	120	

Net Monetary Working Capital in terms of current cost (Jan. 1) 20,000 × 110*/100 = Rs. 22,000
(Dec. 31) 30,000 × 110/120 = Rs. 27,500

Change due to volume = Rs. 27,500 - Rs. 22,000 = Rs. 5,500
Total change = Rs. 30,000 - Rs. 20,000 = Rs. 10,000
Monetary working capital adjustment = Rs. 10,000 – Rs. 5,500 = Rs. 4,500

The following journal entry is made to record monetary working capital adjustment:

Profit and Loss A/c Dr. 4,500
To Current Cost Reserve A/c. 4,500
(Monetary Working Capital Adjustment)

*110 becomes the average price index.

Gearing Adjustment

The current cost operating profit (CCOP) determined after making the above three adjustments is the true amount of profit from operations (ordinary activities of an enterprise) which can help the enterprise to continue to maintain its operating capability. However, the net operating assets which are used to indicate operating capability of a firm are likely to be financed partly by borrowings. Therefore, the effect of the borrowings is considered while determining profit which can be distributed to shareholders. This effect is measured through calculating gearing ratio and subsequently the amount of gearing adjustment. No gearing adjustment arises, where a company is wholly financed by shareholder's capital. A company that has a large proportion of fixed interest and fixed dividend bearing capital to ordinary capital is said to be highly geared. While repayment obligations in respect of borrowings are normally fixed in monetary amount, the proportion of net operating assets so financed by borrowings increases or decreases in value to the business. Thus, when these assets have been realised either by sale or use in the business, repayment of borrowing could be made so long as the proceeds are not less than the historical costs of those assets, It is, therefore, suggested that the current cost profit attributable to shareholders should be determined by taking into account the method of financing the net operating assets. The current cost profit attributable to shareholders reflects surplus for the period after making allowance for the impact of price changes on funds needed to maintain the shareholder's proportions of the net operating assets.

Thus, gearing adjustment is made where a proportion of the assets of business is financed by borrowing. Net borrowing is defined as the amount by which liabilities exceed assets. Liabilities and assets for the purpose of gearing adjustment are defined as follows:

Liabilities are the aggregate of all liabilities and provisions (including convertible debentures and deferred tax but excluding dividends) other than those included within monetary working capital, Assets are the aggregate of all current assets other than those that are subject to a cost of sales adjustment and those that are included within monetary working capital.

The gearing adjustment itself results from the application of the gearing ratio to the net adjustment made in converting the historical cost income to current cost income. The gearing ratio is found in the relationship between net borrowings and average net operating assets. Average net operating assets is obtained from the opening and closing net operating assets divided by two. The gearing ratio formula is:

$$\text{Gearing Ratio} = \frac{\text{Average Net Borrowings}}{\text{Average net operating assets}}$$

Net borrowings = All liabilities and provisions including convertible debentures and deferred tax but excluding dividends and items included in MWCA

minus

All current assets* other than items included in MWCA and COSA.

* If the total of current assets (bank balance) is more than the current liabilities, no gearing adjustment is calculated.

Sometimes; gearing ratio is calculated using average equity capital, as follows:

$$\text{Gearing ratio} = \frac{\text{Average net borrowings}}{\text{Average net borrowings} + \text{Average equity capital}}$$

Current Cost Reserve

Current cost accounting suggests the creation of a reserve account, known as current cost reserve account. The current cost reserve includes (*i*) current cost adjustments, *i.e.,* depreciation backlog adjustment, cost of sales adjustment and monetary working capital adjustment, (*ii*) gearing adjustment, (*iii*) unrealised revaluations surpluses on fixed assets, closing stock and investment. The gearing adjustment amount is credited to profit and loss account and debited to Current Cost Reserve Account.

Example 7

Assume a company has a capital mix of 40 per cent debt and 60 per cent equity. The following amounts of adjustments have been found using CCA method:

Cost of sales adjustment	Rs. 10,000
Depreciation adjustment	Rs. 20,000
Monetary working capital adjustment	Rs. 25,000
Total	Rs. 55,000

In the above case debt constitutes 40 per cent of the total capital. Therefore, the amount of gearing adjustment will be Rs. 22,000 (Rs. 55,000 × 40%). It means only Rs. 33,000 which represents shareholders' share will be charged to Profit and Loss account. The Current Cost Reserve Account will be credited with the amount of Rs. 33,000 on account of three adjustments. Alternatively, more preferably, Rs. 55,000 is charged to Profit and Loss account. Since the amount of gearing adjustment is credited to Profit and Loss account, the net effect is that only Rs. 33,000 stands charged to Profit and Loss account. Also, gearing adjustment is debited to Current Cost Reserve account.

Preparation of Current Cost Balance Sheet

Under current cost accounting, current cost balance sheet is prepared. Balance sheet items are treated in the following manner:

(1) *Fixed Assets.* The fixed assets should be shown in the balance sheet at their value to the business. The value of the business of an asset is the amount which the business would lose if it were deprived of that asset. Determining the value to the business, *ie.,* generally the current cost of fixed assets, involves great difficulty, because usually the assets now in use were acquired long ago than is typically the case with inventory,' and the assets in use, if replaced currently, would be replaced by different assets.

Thus, if a used asset of like age and condition to the asset in use can be priced that will set the current cost. If a new asset has to be used as the basis for pricing the old asset, adjustments have to be made for the differences in life expectancy, productive capacity, quality of service, and operating costs between the new and the old asset. The concepts of gross and net current replacement cost are important in this context. The gross current replacement cost of an existing asset is the cost that would have to be incurred at the date of the valuation to obtain and install a substantial identical asset in new conditions. For example, if a plant purchased on January 1, 2001 for Rs. 80,000 can be purchased on December 31, 2003, for Rs.-1,00,000, its gross current replacement cost on December 31,2003, will be Rs. 1,00,000. The net current replacement cost of an existing asset refers to that part of the gross current replacement cost which represents its unexpired service potential. For example, suppose the plant in the above example is estimated to have an economic life of five years. Since it has been used for three years, its net current replacement cost would be Rs. 40,000 (assuming that the equipment will have a zero scrap value at the end of its economic life).

In circumstances, where the asset in use would not be replaced, if for any reason it were taken out of service, its value to the business is not its current cost but a lower recoverable amount. This recoverable amount is its value if sold or its value if used, whichever is higher. Its value if sold is its realisable value, net of selling costs. Its value in use is the net present value of future cash flows (including the ultimate proceeds of disposal) expected to be derived from the use of the asset by the enterprise.

(2) *Land and Buildings*. The land and buildings occupied by the owner himself, should be shown in the balance sheet at their value to the business which will normally be the open market value for their existing uses, plus estimated acquisition costs. However, in cases where an open market valuation of the land and buildings as a whole cannot be made, the net replacement cost of the buildings and the open market value of land for its existing use plus the estimated acquisition costs should be taken as their value to the business. The valuation should be made by professionally qualified valuers at periodic intervals.

(3) *Inventories*. In the balance sheet, inventories should normally be shown at the lower of the current replacement cost as on the date of balance sheet and the net realisable value.

Revaluation Surplus Transferred to Current Cost Reserve Account

Increase in the value of fixed assets like plant and machinery, land and building, closing stock, investment is credited to current cost reserve account. The increase in value of fixed asset is arrived at by deducting the net historical cost of the asset from its net current cost at the end of the year, both sums being calculated before taking depreciation into account.

To take an example, assume a plant was purchased for Rs. 1,20,000 having a useful life of ten years. Its replacement cost now is Rs, 1,80,000. In the fifth year, the amount to be transferred to current cost reserve account will be Rs. 36,000, calculated as follows :

	Net book value after 5 years (Rs.)	+	*Depreciation for 5th year*	=	*Net book value before depreciation (Rs.)*
Current cost	Rs. 90,000	+	Rs. 18,000	=	Rs. 1,08,000
Historical cost	Rs. 60,000	+	Rs. 12,000	=	Rs. 72,000
Net credit to current cost reserve a/c					Rs. 36,000

The profit and loss account, balance sheet and current cost reserve account under current cost accounting will appear as follows:

Current Cost Accounting (CCA) Profit and Loss Account

		Rs.
Historical profit before interest and tax		—
Less: Current cost operating adjustments;		
(i) Depreciation adjustment	—	
(ii) Cost of sales adjustment (COSA)	—	
(iii) Monetary working capital adjustment (MWCA)	—	—
Current cost operating profit		—
Less: Interest on borrowings including debentures and dividend on preference shares		—
Current cost profit after interest		—
Add: Gearing adjustment*		—
Current cost profit before tax		—
Less: Provision for tax		—
Current cost profit after tax (attributable to shareholders)		—
Less: Dividends proposed		—
Current cost profit retained		—

Note : Amount of gearing adjustment is generally deducted from interest.

***Notes:**

1. Alternatively, gearing adjustment amount could be deducted from the total of current cost operating adjustments (dep. adjustment, COSA and MWCA). The result will be the same if gearing adjustment is deducted from current cost adjustments, or if not deducted from current cost operating adjustment and subsequently added to current cost profit.
2. Gearing adjustment is calculated only when a firm is financed partly by borrowing. No gearing adjustment arises when a company is wholly financed by shareholders' capital. To find out the net borrowings, cash balance is deducted from total borrowings. Or if cash balance is more than the borrowings, there will be no gearing adjustment.

   The above profit and loss account (prepared in a statement format) can be shown in a 'T' format, as below.

PROFIT AND LOSS ACCOUNT

To Depreciation adjustment	—	—	By historical profit before interest and taxes	—
To current cost reserve			By current cost reserve (gearing adjustment)	—
COSA	—			
MWCA*	—	—		
To Interest		—		
To Profit before tax		—		
Total			Total	

* MWCA will be shown on credit side of profit and loss account in case of negative adjustment. In this case entry will be:

Current Cost Reserve A/c Dr.
  To Profit and Loss A/c

Entry for revaluation of assets is as follows:

Plant and Machinery A/c Dr.
  To Current Cost Reserve A/c

Balance Sheet under CCA

Profit and Loss a/c	—	Plant and Machinery	—
Current Cost Reserve (balance)		(or similar assets) (Revalued amount)	

Current Cost Reserve A/c

To P. & L. A/c (gearing adjustment)	—	By Fixed Assets (revalued surplus amount)	—
To depreciation (backlog)	—	By P & L A/c (COSA)	—
To balance c/d	—	By P & L A/c (MWCA)	—

Example 5

A company buys and sells goods. During the three months ending March 31, 2003 the company enter into the following transactions:

2003	
January 1	Buy 500 units costing Rs. 750
January 31	Sell 400 units for Rs. 2000 and replace them with units costing Rs.1,400.
February 28	Sell 200 units for Rs. 1000. Buy 50 units costing Rs. 200.
March 31	Sell 200 units for Rs. 1100. Buy 100 units costing Rs. 500.

The retail price index during the period was as follows:

January 1, 2003	200
January 31, 2003	220
February 28, 2003	230
March 31, 2003	240

You are required to prepare trading accounts under the following situations:7

(1) Historical Cost Accounting.
(2) Current Purchasing Power Accounting.
(3) Current Cost Accounting.

Solution

Trading A/c for the 3 months ending March 31, 2003

(1) **Historical Cost Accounts**

			Rs
Sales January 31			2,000
February 28			1,000
March 31			1,100
			4,100
Less: Cost of Sales			
January 31(4/5 × 750)		600	
February 28(1/5 × 750 + 1/4 × 1400)		500	
March 31(2/4 × 1400)		700	1,800
Gross Profit			2300

(2) Current Purchasing Power Accounting

			Rs.
Sales January 31	2000 × 240/220		2,182
February 28	1000 × 240/230		1,043
March 31			1,100
			4,325
			4,325
Less: Cost of sales			
January 1	Rs. 750 × 240/200 = 900		
January 31	Rs. 1050 × 240/220 = 1,145		
(3/4 × 1400)			2,045
Gross profit			2,280

(3) Current Cost Accounting

			Rs
Sales (as for historical cost)			4,100
Cost of sales			
31 Jan.		1,400	
28 Feb. $\left(\frac{200}{50}\times 200\right)$		800	–
31 Mar. $\left(\frac{200}{100}\times 500\right)$		1,000	3,200
Gross profit			900

Evaluation of Current Cost Accounting

The adoption of current cost or lower recoverable amount in place of historical cost as the attribute to be used for measuring assets and if relevant, liabilities also, would greatly increase the relevance of information conveyed in financial reports, and it would increase its utility and representational faithfulness. It is important that the value of an item to the business must be capable of being determined reliably; if this cannot be done, a surrogate for it must be found satisfactory.

The basic objective of current cost accounts is to provide more useful informa-tion than that available from historical cost accounts for the guidance of management of the business, the shareholders and others on such matters as the financial viability of the business, return on investment; pricing policy, cost control and distribution decisions; and gearing.

The current cost accounting possesses the merit of closely approximating the impact of specific price changes on the business enterprise because it makes use of specific indices. As such the method seeks to maintain the operating capability of the enterprise during inflation.

SSAP 16 points the limitations of CCA as follows:

> "As with historical cost accounts, CCA (based on value to the business concept) is not a substitute for forecasting when such matters as a change in the size or nature of the business are consideration. It assists cash flow forecasts, but does not replace them. It does not measure the effect of changes in the general value of money or translate the figures into currency of purchasing power at a specific date. Because of this it is not a system of accounting for general inflation. Further, it does not show changes in the value of the business as a whole or the market value of the equity."

An important weakness of this model is that is seems to possess an element of subjectivity inherent in periodic revaluations, specially where specific price indices are not generated by an authoritative agency.

Furthermore, perhaps the largest (problem) is the aggregation problem. The value to the firm principle has its theoretic roots in the valuation of the individual assets, not the firm as a whole, but accounts, whether balance sheets or profit and loss accounts, are aimed at the assessment of the performance of the business as a whole. Other important problems include the precise definition of replacement cost under conditions of economic and technological change: replacement cost is fundamental to the value to the firm method.

THEORY QUESTIONS

1. "Financial statements based on historical cost basis are meaningless and highly distorted". Discuss.
2. Distinguish between financial statements restated for general price-level changes and current value financial statements.

   Which of these two approaches would you suggest for making adjustments for price level changes in financial statements for a developing country like India ? Give reasons.
3. Define and present the computation procedures for general price level gain or loss.
4. Distinguish between monetary assets and liabilities and non-monetary assets and liabilities.
5. Distinguish between purchasing power gain and loss and monetary working capital adjustment.
6. Discuss the arguments in favour of and against current cost or lower recoverable amount accounting.
7. Explain the computation procedures and adjustment necessary under CCA.
8. What is the main objective of CCA ? Discuss briefly the rationale of various adjustments that are required in determining current cost profit for an accounting period.
9. What are the main points of criticism of Current Purchasing Power Accounting (CPPA) ? Can they be justified ?
10. Explain the meaning of monetary assets and Monetary liabilities. Give suitable examples.
11. Write notes on :

    (i) Purchasing Power gain and loss (ii) Depreciation Adjustment

    (iii) Gearing Adjustment (iv) COSA

    (v) Monetary Working Capital Adjustment
12. Explain the procedure of restating financial staqtements under CPPA.
13. How are purchasing power gain/loss determined.
14. Discuss the meaning of monetary assets and non-monetary assets under CPPA.

APPENDIX

Skill Development

ANALYSIS OF PUBLISHED FINANCIAL STATEMENTS OF INDIAN COMPANIES

1. The following is unaudited financial results of Steel Authority of India for the quarter/nine months ended on 31st December, 2006.

STEEL AUTHORITY OF INDIA

Unaudited Financial Results for the Quarter/Nine Months ended on 31st December, 2006 (Rs./Crores)

Sl. No.	*Particulars*	*Quarter Ended (Unaudited)*		*Nine Months Ended (unaudited)*		*Financial Year Ended 31.03.2006*
		31.12.2006	*31.12.2005*	*31.12.2006*	*31.12.2005*	*(Audited)*
1.	Gross sales/Income from operations	9841.65	7756.23	28356.57	22870.74	33173.72
	Less : Excise Duty	1304.58	1139.77	3715.44	3091.80	4429.91
2.	Net Sales/Income from operations	8537.07	6616.46	24641.13	19778.94	28743.81
3.	Interest Earned	192.29	107.19	537.56	359.26	461.49
4.	Other Income	30.80	13.19	62.86	45.50	118.96
5.	Total Income (2+3+4)	**8760.16**	**6736.84**	**25241.55**	**20183.70**	**29324.26**
6.	Expenditure					
	(a) Increase (-)/Decrease in stock-in-trade	-227.38	-654.45	-740.10	-2408.40	-1021.03
	(b) Consumption of Raw Materials	3165.98	3087.52	9087.56	8325.32	11404.74
	(c) Staff cost	1227.30	966.68	3456.04	3130.15	4156.69
	(d) Consumption of stores & spares	663.75	591.42	1927.91	1697.22	2311.58
	(e) Power & fuel	653.56	627.13	1923.27	1836.49	2489.74
	(f) Other Expenditure	622.22	649.23	1882.99	1889.99	2601.74
	Total Expenditure (a to f)	**6105.43**	**5267.53**	**17537.67**	**14470.77**	**21943.46**
7.	Profit before Depreciation, Interest & Tax (5-6)	2654.73	1469.31	7703.88	5712.93	7380.80

(*Contd...*)

8.	Interest	90.57	108.63	276.65	361.77	467.76
9.	Depreciation	329.94	324.26	929.28	903.17	1207.30
10.	Profit before tax (7-8-9)	2234.22	1036.42	6497.95	4447.99	5705.74
11.	Provision for Taxation					
	(a) Current tex	681.59	455.55	2293.96	1803.07	1915.40
	(b) Fringe Benefit Tax	6.10	7.24	18.30	21.44	24.33
	(c) Deferred Tax Liability /Assets(-)	75.10	-82.44	-83.87	-286.29	-245.37
	(d) Earlier years	0.24	0.00	-30.85	0.00	-1.59
	Sub-Total (a to d)	763.03	380.35	2197.54	1538.22	1692.77
12.	Net Profit after Tax (10-11)	1471.19	656.07	4300.41	2909.77	4012.97
13.	Paid up Equity share Capital (Face value Rs 10 per share)	4130.40	4130.40	4130.40	4130.40	4130.40
14.	Reserves (excluding revaluation reserve) & surplus					8471.01
15.	Earnings per share-Basic and Diluted (Not Annualised) (Rs.)	3.56	1.59	10.41	7.04	9.72
16.	Aggregate of public share holding					
	—No. of shares	58,41,17,725	58,40,39,325	58,41,17,725	58,40,39,325	58,40,48,325
	—Percentage of share holding	14.14	14.14	14.14	14.14	14.14

Required :

Analyse the financial strength (or weaknesses) and financial and operating condition of the company on the basis of above data, using relevant accounting ratios. Also, comment on the comparative performance of the company taking into account performance of the company for the years 2005 and 2006 as given in the above published financial results.

2. The following is the balance sheet and Profit and Loss Account of an Indian Company for the year ending March 31, 2005 and 2006.

BALANCE SHEETS AS ON 31 MARCH 2005 AND 2006

(Rupees in crores)

	2006	*2005*
LIABILITIES		
Non-Current Liabilities		
Share Capital	2800	1400
Reserves and Surplus	2010	1516
Debentures	1500	1800
Current Liabillties		
Sundry Crreditors	420	458
Working Capital Loan from Banks	240	224
Accrued Expenses	100	72
Income-tax Payable	600	360
Total Liabilities	**7670**	**5830**

ASSETS		
Non-Current Assets		
Net-Fixed Assets	3600	1600
Investments	800	560
Current Assets		
Cash-in-hand and in bank	1050	1500
Sunday Debtors	620	750
Inventories	1570	1384
Pre-paid Expenses	30	36
Total Assets	**7670**	**5830**

PROFIT AND LOSS ACCOUNT FOR THE YEAR ENDED 31 MARCH 2006

(Rupees in Crores)

Net Sales	6800	
Cost of Goods Sold	3840	
Gross Profit		2960
Depreciation	280	
Other Operating Expenses	1280	
		1560
		1400
Interest paid		120
Profit Before Tax (PBT)		1280
Provision for Income-Tax		586
Profit After Tax (PAT)		694
Dividend		200
Balance transferred		494

You are required to compute necessay financial ratios and comment on the financial position, profitability, liquidity of the company.

3. The following is the balance sheet and profit and loss account of ITC Ltd for the year ending 31st March 2005 and 2006.

ITC LTD.
Balance Sheet
as at 31st March, 2006

	31st March, 2006 *(Rs. in Crores)*		*31st March, 2005* *(Rs. in Crores)*	
I. SOURCES OF FUNDS				
1. Shareholder's Funds				
(a) Capital	375.52		248.22	
(b) Share Capital Suspense	—		1.21	
(c) Reserves and Surplus	8685.96	9061.48	7646.18	7895.61
2. Loan Funds				
(a) Secured Loans	33.67		88.69	
(b) Unsecured Loans	86.06	119.73	156.67	245.36
3. Deferred Tax-net		324.76		376.09
Total		**9505.97**		**8517.06**
II APPLICATION OF FUNDS				
1. Fixed Assets				
(a) Gross Block	6227.17		5746.27	
(b) Less : Depreciation	2065.44		1795.51	
(c) Net Block	4161.73		3950.76	
(d) Capital Work-in-Progress	243.40	4405.13	186.15	4136.91
2. Investments		3517.01		3874.68
3. Current Assets, Loans and Advances				
(a) Inventories	2636.29		2002.99	
(b) Sundry Debtors	547.96		527.76	
(c) Cash and Bank Balances	855.82		55.66	
(d) Other Current Assets	146.80		142.52	
(e) Loans and Advances	975.03		810.36	
	5161.90		3539.29	
Less :				
4. Current Liabilities and Provisions				
(a) Liabilities	2189.03		1925.64	
(b) Provisions	1378.07		3033.82	
	3578.07		3033.82	
Net Current Assets		1583.83		505.47
Total		**9505.97**		**8517.06**

ITC LTD.
Profit and Loss Account
For the year ended year ended 31st March,2006

		For the year ended 31st March, 2006 (Rs. in Crores)	*For the year ended 31st March, 2005 (Rs. in Crores)*
IA.	**Gross Income**	16510.51	13585.39
IB.	**Net Income**		
	Gross Sales	16224.43	13349.58
	less: Excise Duties and Taxes on Sales of Products and Services	6433.90	5710.13
	Net Sales [after considering Provision for Taxes of Rs. Nil (2005 - 214.75 Crores)	9790.53	7639.45
	Other Income	286.08	235.81
		10076.61	**7875.26**
II.	**Other Expenditure**		
	Raw materials etc.	3983.23	2769.55
	Manufacturing, Selling etc. Expenses	2491.85	2119.77
	Depreciation	332.34	312.87
		6807.42	**5202.19**
III.	**Profit**		
	Profit before Taxation and Exceptional items	3269.19	2673.07
	provision for Taxation	988.82	836.00
	Profit after Taxation before Exceptional items	2280.37	1837.07
	Exceptional items (net of tax)	(45.02)	354.33
	Profit after Taxation	2235.35	2191.40
	Profit brought forward	611.41	387.84
		2846.76	**2579.24**
	Release from Hotel foreign Exchange earnings Reserve	—	15.14
	Available for appropriation	2846.76	2594.38
IV.	**Appropriations**		
	General Reserve	1150.00	1100.00
	Proposed Dividend	995.12	773.25
	Income Tax on Proposed Dividend [Including Rs. 0.02 Crore (2005-Rs.1.27 Crores) for earlier years]	139.58	109.72
	Profit carried forward	562.06	611.41
		2846.76	**2594.38**

Required : Compute necessary accounting ratios and comment on liquidity, profitability and financial condition of the company as revealed by the accounting ratios.

4. Balance Sheets of Hindustan Lever Ltd. as on 31st Dec. 2004 and 2005 and Profit and Loss Account for the year ending 31 st Dec-2004 and 2005 are as follows:

HINDUSTAN LIVER LTD.

Balance Sheet as at 31st December, 2005

Figures in brackets represent deduction

		2005 Rs. lakhs		2004 Rs. lakhs
SOURCES OF FUNDS				
Sharepholders's funds				
Capital	220,12.44		220,12.44	
Reserves and suplus	2085,50.16		1872,58.51	
		2305,62.60		2092,70.95
Loan funds				
Secured loans	24,49.96		1453,05.78	
Unsecured loans	32,44.11	56,94.07	18,05.67	1471,11.45
		2362,56.67		3563,82.40
APPLICATION OF FUNDS				
Fixed assets				
Gross block	2375,11.02		2314,21.91	
Depreciation and impairment loss	(989,61.28)		(891,08.07)	
Net block	1385,49.74		1423,13.84	
Capital work-in-progress	98,03.29	1483,53.03	94,42.22	1517,56.06
Investments		2014,19.84		2229,56.27
Deferred Tax				
Deferred Tax Assets	338,68.17		365,84.66	
Dererred Tax Liabilities	(118,53.71)	220,14.46	(139,84.61)	226,00.05
Current assets loans and advances				
Inventories	1321,76.91		1470,44.26	
Sundry debtors	522,82.85		489,26.97	
Cash and bank balances	35,503.19		69,804.80	
Other current assets	23,89.08		52,77.71	
Loan and advances	539,47.15		594,41.79	
	2762,99.18		3304,95.53	
Current liabilities and provisions				
Liabilities	(2959,42.98)		(2590,79.14)	
Provisions	(1158,86.86)		(1123,46.37)	
	(4118,29.84)		(3714,25.51)	
Net current assets		(1355,30.66)		(409,29.98)
		2362,56.67		3563,82.40

HINDUSTAN LEVER LIMITED

Profit and Loss account for the year ended 31st December, 2005

Figures in brackets represent deduction

	2005 *Rs. lakhs*	*2004* *Rs. lakhs*
INCOME		
Sales	**11060,54.62**	9926,94.64
Other income	**304,78.65**	318,83.38
Total	**11365,33.27**	10245,78.02
EXPENDITURE		
Operating exenses	**(9,617,21.50)**	(8489,57.90)
Depreciation	**(124,45.32)**	120,89.94
Interest	**(19,19.31)**	(129,98.43)
Total	**(9760,86.13)**	(8740,46.27)
PROFIT BEFORE TAXATION AND EXCEPTIONAL ITEMS	**1604,47.14**	1505,31.75
Taxation for the year –current tax	**(223,00.00)**	(266,00.00)
–deferred tax	**(41,00.00)**	(54,73.62)
–fringe benefit tax	**(30,00.00)**	—
Taxation adjustments of previous year (net)	**44,03.67**	14,69.52
PROFIT AFTER TAXATION AND BEFORE EXCEPTIONAL ITEMS	**1354,50.81**	1199,27.65
Exceptional items (net of tax)	**53,59.63**	(1,93.28)
NET PROFIT	**1408,10.44**	1197,34.37
Balance brough forward	**644,79.91**	818,60.74
Available for distubution	**2052,90.35**	2015,95.11
DIVIDENTS :		
On equity shares :		
Interim — Rs. 2.50 per share- declared on 30th July, 2005	**(550,31.09)**	(550,31.09)
Final — Rs. 2.50 per share - proposed	**(550,31.09)**	(550,31.09)
Tax on distributed profits [includes differential Rs.5,26.23 lakhs on final dividend for 2004]	**(159,62.46)**	145,53.02
Transfer to General Reserve	**(142,00.00)**	(125,00.00)
Balance Carried forward	**6,50,65.71**	644,79.91

Calculate accounting ratios and explain the financial performance of Hindustan Liver Ltd. based on these accounting ratios.

5. Consolidated Balance Sheet and Profit and Loss Account for the two years, 2005 and 2006 of Infosys are given beJow.

INFOSYS
Consolidated Balance Sheet as at

in Rs. Crore

	March 31,2006	*March 31,2005*
SOURCES OF FUNDS		
SHAREHOLDERS, FUNDS		
Share Capital	138	135
Reserves and surplus	6,828	5,090
	6,966	5,225
Minority Interest	68	—
Priference Shares Issued By subsidiary	—	94
	7,034	5,319
APPLICATION OF FUNDS		
FIXED ASSETS		
Original cost	2,983	2,287
Less: Accumulated depreciation and amortization	1,328	1,031
Net book value	1,655	1,256
Add: Capital work-in-progress	571	318
	2,226	1,574
INVESTMENTS	755	1,211
DEFERRED TAX ASSETS	65	45
CURRENT ASSETS, LOANS AND ADVANCES		
Sundry debtors	1,608	1,322
Cash and bank balances	3,429	1,576
Loans and advances	1,297	1,024
	6,334	3,922
Less: Current Liabilities and provisions		
Current liabilities	934	656
Provisios	1,412	777
NET CURRENT ASSETS	3,988	2,489
	7,034	5,319

INFOSYS

Consolidated Profit and Loss Acount for the year ended March 31, 2005 and 2006.

in Rs. crore except per share data

	March 31, 2006	*March 31, 2005*
Income from software services, products and business process management	9,521	7,130
Software development and business process management expenses	5,066	3,765
GROSS PROFIT	4,455	3,365
Selling and marketing expenses	600	461
General and administration expenses	764	569
	1,364	1,030
OPERATING PROFIT before interest, deprecition, amortization, minority interest and exeptional item	3,091	2,,335
Interest	—	—
Depreciation and amourtization	437	287
Operating profit bfore tax, minority interest and exceptional item	2,792	1,846
Other income, net	139	124
Provision for investments	1	—
Net Profit before tax, minorit6y interest and exceptional item	2,479	2,172
Provision for taxation	313	326
net Profit after tax and before minority interest and exceptional item	2,479	2,172
Income form sale of investment in yantra Corporation (net of taxes)	—	45
Net Profit after tax, exceptional item and before minority interst	2,479	1,891
Minority interest	21	—
Net Profit after tax, exceptional item and minority interest	2,458	1,891
Balance brought forward	1,415	71
Less: Residual dividend paid	—	2
Additional diveidend tax	—	2
	1,415	67
Amout avialable for Appropriation	3,873	1,958
Dividend		
Inte im	177	134
Final	234	176
Silver Jubilee special dividend	827	—
Total dividend	1,238	310
Dividend tax	174	42
Amout transferred to general reserve	242	191
Balance in profit and loss account	2,219	1,415
	3,873	1,958

Required: Compute liquidity, profitability, and financial position ratios and give your observations about finanacial health and earning patential of the company.